MW00811450

JOURNEY

WORLDS APART

NICK DERISO

TIME PASSAGES.

Published by Time Passages, LLC
4157 Mountain Road, #231
Lake Shore, MD 21122
www.timepassages.net

First paperback edition: December 2023.
ISBN, Hardcover (978-1-7343653-8-2)
ISBN, Paperback (978-1-7343653-9-9)
ISBN, Ebook (978-0-578-22140-3)
Library of Congress Control Number: 2023951096

Cover design by Todd Bates.
Cover illustration by Daniel Belchí Lorente.

WORLDS APART

Praise for Nick DeRiso

"Believers in Journey's entire journey should embrace Nick DeRiso's JOURNEY: WORLDS APART with open arms. This is a compelling deep dive into the rather complicated history of one of the most enduringly beloved bands in rock history."
  — *David Wild, former Rolling Stone writer and contributing editor*

"Journey was amazing in their resilience and it's hard to say enough about their chops: Steve Perry, he really has a talent that is so extreme, it's scary. Steve Smith is the world's baddest white boy on drums. Ross Valory, always there, always dependable—a fabulous bass player with the best sense of humor. Neal Schon, I'm telling you he is the master. For me, there's nobody who touches Neal. We had the best crew of road men and women ever! Everyone came together because of the determination of Herbie Herbert. Without Herbie, none of this would have ever happened. JOURNEY: WORLDS APART takes fans all the way back. It's as close to how it was then as you're ever going to read.
  — *Pat Morrow, former longtime Journey road manager and Nocturne CEO*

"From 'Don't Stop Believin'' to 'Separate Ways,' Journey unconsciously wrote the band's autobiography in their songs. Nick DeRiso's JOURNEY: WORLDS APART follows that long, strange 'journey' from the stage of Woodstock to Trump's Oval Office in almost granular detail, detailing a long-running battle of the band. A must-read for all Journey fans."
  — *Joel Selvin, former San Francisco Chronicle music writer*

For a band of its stature and impact, there's precious little literature out there about Journey. Nick DeRiso's JOURNEY: WORLDS APART fills that gap in a comprehensive, well, journey through the band's 50-year-plus career. Packed with up-to-date facts and, most importantly, context, WORLDS APART offers plenty of insight for fans both faithful and casual—going all the way back to its roots in Santana and steering us through the songs and albums, the personalities, the soap opera dynamics, and the determined wherewithal that have kept Journey riding through it all. There's much more to this band than "Don't Stop Believin'," and WORLDS APART gives us all of it.
  — *Gary Graff, longtime (not South) Detroit music critic and author of Alice Cooper at 75*

ACKNOWLEDGMENTS

For Leisha, who altered my life's course, and my children, whose own chapters are still being written. For my father, who taught me about perseverance, faith, and the importance of red wine. For the English teachers and newspaper editors who inspired me along the way, and the letter writers who most certainly did not. For the coworkers, fact-checkers, and proofreaders who played unseen but such critical roles of support. For Tommy, who first believed in stories like these, and Rob, who helped me live them. And for everyone in South Detroit, wherever you are.

EDITORIAL & DESIGN

Bill August..Editor / Proofreading
Rory Aronsky..Fact Checking / Proofreading
Daniel Belchí Lorente ....Cover Illustration
Todd Bates ....Design
Rik Forgo..Layout

HOW TO USE THIS BOOK

Time Passages books track a band's history one season at a time. The important moments in a band's origin story appear as an event. Dates are estimated using the best data available, and are nested within a specific season. These events are categorized to give readers a view of milestones for different band members that illustrate how their individual stories overlap and sometimes comingle. Informational graphics help illustrate important milestones in each band member's story, keeping pace with everything from singles releases to collaborations, touring partners, and televised appearances. Those informational graphics cover:

SEASONS

SUMMER 1969

Time Passages tracks the passage of time in the history of the band and its members by season (spring, summer, fall, and winter). The season header indicates the beginning of a new season and the stories that follow occur during that period. The dates used for the book's timeline is based on publication dates of the citations, and when that is not available a best guess estimation is used.

COLLABORATIONS

Identifies when members of the band participated with other artists in duets/group sessions, or provided studio support for other musicians. The intent is to show how band members contributed their talents to—and were sought out by—other artists.

Example:
▶ Aynsley Dunbar played drums on **Michael Chapman**'s album, *Rainmaker*.

[ ] END NOTES

Citations for the source material for stories are at the end of each article. Full listings of all citations can be found at the end of the book.

RELEASES

Releases are either singles or albums and follow the following format: (band, band members, title, and designation).

Examples:
▶ **Santana** (with Neal Schon, Gregg Rolie), *Caravanserai* (album)
▶ Journey, "Lovin', Touchin', Squeezin'" (single)

NUGGETS

Nuggets are small anecdotes, news bites, and other tidbits that inform about what's happening with the band and its members during a specified season. Information is gathered from newspaper and magazine articles, and online news sources and databases, with the nugget's source tagged at the end of each entry.

ON THE ROAD

Tracks who the band toured with or appeared onstage with for a given season. Tours and tour partners are highlighted, as are appearances with other artists for one-off shows for rock festivals and televised concerts. Sources include Setlist.fm, The Concert Database, and publications including *Rolling Stone*, *Creem*, *Circus*, *Billboard*, *Cashbox*, and *Record World*.

Example:
▶ Journey, with 3 Doors Down, Cheap Trick, Def Leppard, Gotthard, John Parr, Kansas, KISS, Motorhead, REO Speedwagon, Twisted Sister, Whitesnake

TABLE OF CONTENTS

CHAPTER 9: FORGET ME NOT

CHAPTER 10: SIGNS OF LIFE

CHAPTER 11: CITY OF HOPE

CHAPTER 12: THE WAY WE USED TO BE

DON'T STOP BELIEVIN':
JOURNEY CONJURES A MULTI-GENERATIONAL POP CULTURE PHENOMENON

It wasn't the biggest song of the year. In fact, Journey's "Don't Stop Believin'" finished at No. 72 on *Billboard* magazine's year-ending Hot 100 singles of 1982.

It wasn't even the biggest song from Journey's *Escape*, which spun off not one but two songs that finished higher on the charts than the No. 9 selling "Don't Stop Believin'": the No. 4 hit "Who's Cryin' Now" and their monster No. 2 ballad "Open Arms."

It didn't have a typical song structure, not referencing the title until 3:22 in, after three verses, two pre-choruses, and some abbreviated instrumental passages.

"Yeah, that was Steve Perry," songwriting keyboardist Jonathan Cain said. "I give him all the credit for that. He had this thing: 'Well, they're going to want to play this over and over again, so we're not going to wear that chorus out. It's too good, Jon.' So, it broke all the rules in a good way."

Critic **Deborah Frost** didn't even mention this song by name in a contemporary review for *Rolling Stone*, which awarded the *Escape* album just 2 out of 5 stars. "Don't Stop Believin'" is also set in a place—South Detroit—that doesn't actually exist.

"When I first heard it, it's a great tune," drummer Steve Smith admitted to interviewer **Matt Wardlaw**, "but I felt like there was a lot of great songs on that record."

None of that mattered, not to future *Glee* fans, not to future baseball fans, and not to future *Sopranos* fans. "The world chooses what it chooses," Perry later told the *Tampa Bay Times*, "and time does what it does." Smith could only describe this turn of events as "kind of inexplicable, but wonderful."

"Don't Stop Believin'" would "become a soundtrack of people's lives, and they bring their kids and say, 'This is what I listened to when I was a kid.'" Cain said. "All this stuff, it's pretty great. We're most proud of that."

But why? Perspective is ultimately hard-won, and it has no preset schedule, the Hot 100 notwithstanding.

"I think that the dust of time of an era has to settle before we can see the mountains that are left standing," original MTV VJ **Martha Quinn** said. "Like, if you look at **Modern English**'s "I Melt With You," that got to No. 78 on the charts, but now everybody knows that song. It's an '80s classic. This is one of my favorite categories—songs that didn't chart well but lasted a really long time. **AC/DC**'s "You Shook Me All Night Long" is another one; it got to No. 35. But these songs have somehow stood the test of time. Not all songs do, but these songs do."

In this instance, maybe it's because Journey is speaking to something bigger than ourselves, something worth waiting for. "It's about hope and will," Journey co-founder Neal Schon told ABC. "We wrote very positive songs. It was a brighter sound. Happier, upbeat, but still rock."

They weren't alone in that, of course. But there's something about this song's essential optimism that transcends its moment, something about its structure that never grows old.

"There's a self-help aspect of music, for people who need to turn to music to get through whatever they're dealing with, you know—a shitty marriage, a shitty job, an illness," longtime *Rolling Stone* writer and editor **David Wild** said. "I think this song offers strength and soul in a pop-rock song format. I think it's so grand and big and epic that it becomes an anthem that's not limited to one era, and it inspires people."

"Don't Stop Believin'" is most often associated with the finale of HBO's *The Sopranos*, but its revival traces back to the 1998 **Adam Sandler** comedy *The Wedding Singer*. Then **Charlize Theron** asked to use the song in her Oscar-winning 2003 turn in *Monster*.

Perry got in contact with the film's director, **Patty Jenkins**, after connecting with the featured scene. "That became the beginning of the resurgence of the song," he told *Kerrang*. Soon, Journey would find a home in TV series like *Laguna Beach: The Real Orange County*, *Family Guy*, *Scrubs*, and in other films including *Bedtime Stories* and *The Comebacks*.

"At the time, it was a big song," Schon told Wardlaw, but "there were a lot of big songs on the record and some were bigger than 'Don't Stop Believin'". So to have it resurge and become like this national anthem, it's really wild."

The Sopranos' series-ending diner scene from 2007 sparked a tidal wave of downloads, then "Don't Stop Believin'" became a principal theme for *Rock of Ages*, first on Broadway in 2009 and then in the 2012 film version starring **Tom Cruise**. "It has become a phenomena. Like an anthem or a hymn," Schon's fellow original member Ross Valory told *Hallowed Magazine*.

By 2021, Journey had the rare distinction of amassing one billion streams for a single song. "I don't know if you could have predicted it at that time," Quinn argued. "I don't know what the special sauce is, necessarily."

She added: "I know with Journey, people might point to it being the finale song in *The Sopranos*, but I feel like it wouldn't have been picked to be the finale song of *The Sopranos* if it wasn't already gaining momentum in our hearts and minds. That's why it came to the producers' attention. I feel like it was kind of a thundercloud in the distance that kept growing, and growing and growing."

Cain and Schon immediately approved usage of "Don't Stop Believin'" for HBO's mobster drama, but Perry held out. He wouldn't sign off until mere days before the finale aired, because he worried that the song was going to be used in some ironic way as a moment of gangland violence unfolded. Its elemental message of hope meant too much to him.

"So, I had to swear to not tell nobody, which I did, and they told me how the show ends," Perry told *GQ*. "But I didn't see it until the first time it aired, that Sunday night. I stood up and screamed."

Conflicted mobster Tony Soprano cues the song up on a jukebox before the episode—and the series—ends with a smash cut to black. Creator **David Chase** clearly built these scenes around "Don't Stop Believin'." As Perry sings "just a city boy," Tony's son arrives at the diner. His daughter parks the car underneath a lamppost when "streetlight people" follows.

"So they're really correlating the visuals to the moments of the song," Perry told the BBC. "If I hadn't given approval, they'd have been screwed!"

Emboldened, Perry approved a cast recording on *Glee* in 2009, and downloads of both the original song once again spiked—as did the cast version. "We were no longer an old band playing for old fans," former late-period Journey manager **John Baruck** told *Billboard*. "We had three generations at our shows."

A legacy moment was suddenly new again. "I think it's a song that gives permission to dream. It really does," Cain said. "It's a song that says, 'You're not stuck where you think you are.' That midnight train going anywhere, it gives people possibility—and new people are welcoming that song every decade."

By then, "Don't Stop Believin'" had already become a rally song for the Chicago White Sox's path to the 2005 World Series. Later, it accompanied the San Francisco Giants' 2010 postseason run. Perry himself led singalongs from the stands.

Journey never had a No. 1 song, but they finally had their defining moment.

The group's roots stretched back to Woodstock, as co-founder Gregg Rolie sang **Santana** to glory. Santana's road manager Herbie Herbert and their wunderkind guitar recruit Neal Schon completed Journey's embryonic nucleus, rising from the ashes of one of the 1960s' most meteoric bands as nothing more than a notion. Then Steve Perry and Jonathan Cain helped hurtle this new band to mega-stardom.

Schon may have been the only constant member, but the throughline with Journey had always been faith. "Don't Stop Believin'" wasn't just a song. It was proof of concept.

"Who wants to keep believing? That would be everybody, you know?" Cain added. "And I think it's a certain song in uncertain times. You have this certainty about that song, and it has this rhythm to it that's just very assuring and very sure of itself. From the beginning piano line, it speaks—and it speaks to hope. I think people are looking for hope."

WOODSTOCK

As Journey's star peaked in the mid-1980s, its name would become synonymous with power ballads and eviscerating guitar solos. But the band emerged as an offshoot of Santana's original lineup, which itself gained fame in Bethel, New York in the summer of 1969—the summer of Woodstock.

Journey's Foundation Forms Around Santana in New York

The Woodstock Music & Art Fair had not yet become a cultural signifier as future Journey co-founder Gregg Rolie took the stage with **Santana** on August 16, 1969. "At the time," Rolie said, "it was just another festival."

It was not, of course—not for a generation of rebellious youth, not for the rapidly changing rock genre, and certainly not for Santana. They claimed a prime time evening spot before even issuing an album thanks to some furious string-pulling from the legendary promoter **Bill Graham**. Working as the band's de facto manager on a handshake deal, Graham allowed his name to be used by Woodstock promoters while securing much more famous acts on the condition that Santana could play, too.

They arrived at 11 a.m. and would hit the stage at 8 p.m. Carlos felt like he had plenty of time to take some mescaline and then come down. He did not. "This guy came over," Santana remembered in **Marc Shapiro**'s *Back on Top*, "and said, 'Look, if you don't go on right now, you guys are not going to play.' "

They rushed onstage at about 2 p.m. and began a tribal communion with the Woodstock crowd that would hurtle Santana to collective superstardom. Carlos was still stoned and later admitted to remembering little of their performance, in particular early on, but it was simply unforgettable for everyone else.

"Carlos was a better guitar player then—way better," longtime San Francisco music critic **Joel Selvin** said. "Now, he's like this actor that has a couple of patented moves. So he cranks those out and drops them on top of whatever beat they're playing, and everybody goes 'ooooo.' But I'm telling you, Carlos in 1968 and 1969 was a different animal. He was searching, he was probing. He was trying stuff—failing and succeeding. The end product was just an incredibly open-hearted, exciting sound."

Santana's seven-song set featured two subsequent charting singles, including the Top 10 smash "Evil Ways," yet will always be defined by their performance-closing exploration of "Soul Sacrifice." "That song is just infectious, and I think that's the reason it connected with that generation and the generation that came

after," Rolie said. "It's become a classic; I hate to use that term, but it has. At the time, though, we were just trying to connect—and we did."

Every member of the band was credited in the composition, this relentless instrumental built outward to Carlos's boiling, angular bursts of guitar from a fearless rhythmic core: Rolie's chugging B-3 line encourages a hailstorm of percussive delights amid the acrobatic drumming of **Michael Shrieve**. "The rhythm is unbelievable," Rolie added. "That was all built on jamming, and that was the way we played. We made parts out of the things we jammed."

Carlos was finally emerging from his mescaline-induced haze, too. "By the time we got to 'Soul Sacrifice,' I had come back from a pretty intense journey," Santana told Shapiro. "Ultimately, I felt we had plugged in to a whole lot of hearts at Woodstock."

Everybody loaded out with a crew that would soon add future Journey manager **Herbie Herbert** as a roadie and production assistant.

"We flew in and we played, then stayed and saw **Sly Stone**—who was awesome," Rolie said, "but as we drove out, we started passing all of these people—500,000 people. That's when it dawned on me. If I had known what it was going to be, I might have been scared. At the time, we thought of it as just another gig. It turned out to be the mother of all of them." [2, 60, 139]

SUMMER 1969

NUGGETS
▶ **Aynsley Dunbar's Retaliation** was one of Blue Thumb Records' first new acts, sandwiched in between LPs from **Ike and Tina Turner** and **Albert Collins**. —*Record World*
▶ Aynsley Dunbar joins **John Mayall** as drummer for his well-received *Looking Back* LP. —*Cashbox*

COLLABORATIONS
▶ Aynsley Dunbar played drums on **Michael Chapman**'s album, *Rainmaker*.

Continued on Page 21

A TEENAGE GUITAR PRODIGY BECAME JOURNEY'S BACKBONE

Neal Schon found his greatest fame inserting compact solos into power-ballad hits, leaving him typically under recognized among important rock guitarists. But the self-taught former prodigy's canny blend of speed, precision, and soulfulness formed the foundation for every incarnation of Journey.

His vision and technique were so advanced that **Carlos Santana** asked him to join **Santana** while Schon was still in high school. "Neal is very distinctive when he plays his melodic stuff in Journey, but he can play anything and anybody," Santana and Journey bandmate Gregg Rolie said. "He's just a very gifted player in that fashion and has been since I first met him when he was 15 or 16 years old."

It typically comes down to feel for Schon, who has an innate sense of what to leave in and what to leave out.

"His chord knowledge is nothing short of absolute brilliance. He can't name them, which has always been so bizarre," Schon's **Hardline** bandmate **Johnny Gioeli** said. "We'd be like, 'What is that chord?' and he'd say, 'I don't know, man.' We'd laugh, but he can

just hear it—and play it. He's a brilliant guy. Besides his vast chord knowledge, it's melody over mind. I learned that from him. For Neal, it's about the melody of the song, not how intricate it should be."

Born on February 27, 1954 to **Matthew** and **Barbara Schon** on Oklahoma's Tinker Air Force Base, Neal lived in New Jersey for a time before landing in California, where he attended Aragon High School in San Mateo.

"His dad was a clarinet player in the jazz world and the symphonic world," future Journey tour manager **Pat Morrow** said. "When Neal grew up, he was first bassoon in the California State Orchestra, which is made up of all the high schools across California—the best players. The bassoon is fucking incredibly difficult to play. So, Neal grew up in that incredibly demanding discipline of the bassoon—and he never looked back. He graduated to the guitar, and his dad supported him all through it."

Soon, this precocious child of an accomplished musician and veteran singer was sitting in with anyone who would have him—including **Eric Clapton**. "His father was a music teacher, so he had some support for that that

Carlos Santana (left) and Neal Schon rehearse backstage in San Francisco before a show. Schon joined Santana near the end of 1970.

he wouldn't have had if his father was like my father," said veteran San Francisco music critic **Joel Selvin**, with a huge laugh.

Santana offered Schon the chance to follow his dream, and he dropped out of Aragon. "I think that Carlos, in his own right, is just like a monster. He's so open-minded and has always been so musical," Schon said. "He's still a teacher for me. Carlos just knows so much about music. I'm extremely blessed to even have done it, when I was 15 that many years ago in 1970."

Two albums followed, 1971's *Santana III* and 1972's *Caravanserai*, before Santana's lineup began to splinter. It was time for the mentee to move on. Schon had already made an impression on **Herbie Herbert**, Santana's deeply ambitious road manager.

Herbert proposed a new band with Schon and fellow ex-Santana member Gregg Rolie at its center. "Neal Schon, no matter what he achieves, no matter how much money he makes, no matter what goes down, he will always be the most underrated guitar player in history," the late Herbert told **Matthew Carty**.

Rolie would give way to others as Journey moved from its jam-band roots toward a sleeker, more pop-facing sound. Perry eventually departed; so did his replacement. Drummers and bassists came and went, as Journey built and rebuilt itself. The guy typically swinging the hammer on these renovation projects was Neal Schon: He's the one who found Arnel Pineda, Journey's longest-serving front man.

"There's a lot of cats that I know personally that won't be mentioned who just kick back and rest on their laurels," longtime Schon collaborator **Marco Mendoza** said. "Neal, it's in his DNA. He's gotta create, he's gotta play. One thing about Neal, he's a true musician—regardless of the success, and all that. He's constantly creating and reinventing."

Along the way, Schon somehow found time for side projects ranging from the somewhat esoteric (**Jan Hammer**) to the overtly familiar (Hardline), while still showing his ability to hurtle a song up the charts (**Bad English**).

"Neal's a brilliant guitar player ... and he loves to play. I love Neal, I do," said his Bad

English bandmate **John Waite**, while noting the natural tensions that exist. "You can't have a great singer in a rock band without a great guitar player. It's a relationship that's confrontational, and it's one that's extremely emotional. It's loud; it's like a musical argument—or at best, a musical conversation. Without the guitar player, the singer ain't much."

Music, quite simply, has been his life.

"Tina, his gorgeous first wife, she goes: 'Pat, he leaves his underwear on the dining room table and stands there playing the guitar—and he doesn't even pick up his dirty laundry," Morrow said. "She's complaining about him, and I'm thinking to myself, 'Yeah, but Tina, he can turn back the hem of the cloak of the gods when he plays.' The truth is, Neal was a motherfucker, man. He *is* a motherfucker."

At the same time, Schon held on fast to Journey's wheel. By the time they entered the Rock & Roll Hall of Fame in 2017, he was the lone co-founder to have appeared on every band project. His sound was holding everything together.

"Herbie built that band around Neal because he's a star on his own from a guitar standpoint," Perry told *GQ*. "There's nobody who plays like Neal Schon, to this day. I still miss his playing. I love his playing. We don't get along, but I love his playing. 'Cause he's brilliant."

Journey sold millions of records along the way, as Schon's sound came to encapsulate more than the emotional highs of **Cream**-era Clapton and the kind of **Jimi Hendrix**-inspired pyrotechnics that could bring down tall buildings. Schon also boasts the liquid fluidity of jazzman **Wes Montgomery**.

"I'll never forget, he did a BAMMYs award show up in San Francisco, and all the famous guitar players came out. **Richie Sambora** came out, and he was just wailing—and the crowd cheered," Gioeli said. "But then Neal came out and played one frickin' note—one blues note—and the crowd went frickin' ballistic. It was at that moment when I really learned melody over mind. It's the note you're playing and the way you play it. That guy can milk a note like a frickin' dairy farmer. It's just unbelievable, man. It's unbelievable." [4, 8, 11, 31, 37, 56, 60, 80, 337, 927]

> **Herbie built that band around Neal because he's a star on his own from a guitar standpoint. There's nobody who plays like Neal Schon, to this day. I still miss his playing.**
>
> —*Steve Perry*

Journey's Other Half Emerges With Frumious Bandersnatch

Despite the best efforts of some subsequently famous figures, **Frumious Bandersnatch**'s principal claim to wider fame was as a proving ground for other more notable groups.

Originally a college band dubbed **The All Night Flight** after a local overnight radio program, Frumious Bandersnatch produced a self-released three-song EP while appearing at some of the Bay Area's biggest venues. **Jack King** sang in every incarnation of the group between 1967 and 1969 before joining **Steve Miller**'s band with former Frumious Bandersnatch members **David Denny**, **Bobby Winkelman**, and Ross Valory. Fledgling Journey manager **Herbie Herbert** would eventually bring Valory and bandmate George Tickner into his new project.

They reached a high point in February 1967, opening for **Canned Heat** and the **Mothers of Invention** at the Fillmore Auditorium in San Francisco. "I was younger than those guys, however we all watched with envy as they went on to play the Fillmore at such a young age!" future Journey collaborator **Stevie "Keys" Roseman** said. "We would talk about those days, as we all grew up within several miles from each other. There was such great music out of the Bay Area during those times."

Tickner joined The All Night Flight in April 1967, when guitarist **Jimmy Fassio** received his draft notice. Bassist **Brian Hough** then suggested a name change, taking Frumious Bandersnatch from a character in **Lewis Carroll**'s *Jabberwocky*.

Not everybody was immediately on board. "I hated the name Frumious Bandersnatch and couldn't understand why we would ever change the name All Night Flight," guitarist David Denny said. "I told [Frumious manager] **Jim Nixon** and Brian Hough if they went ahead with that name, I quit—though I didn't because I loved playing in the band."

They abruptly split that November, however, after a thief broke into a waterfront warehouse they were using in Oakland and stole everyone's equipment—well, everyone but Tickner who had

Frumious Bandersnatch's Bobby Winkelman (left) and Ross Valory play at El Camino Park, Palo Alto, California on September 29, 1968.

taken his stuff home. The lineup briefly scattered, and Tickner began considering medical school.

Then Herbert, one of their fellow Diablo Valley College students, had an idea: Keep the cool name, but rebuild the lineup. King and Denny would remain, with the addition of Valory and the late **Jimmy Warner** on vocals and lead guitar. Warner had previously been a part of **The Goodtimers**, with Herbert as their manager, roadie, and sometime drummer. Herbert was promptly named road manager for the rebuilt group, and painted Frumious Bandersnatch over "The Goodtimers" on the side of his panel truck.

Singer Bobby Winkelman completed the new lineup in early 1968, and everyone moved into an unused space on an estate owned by Ross Valory's parents in Lafayette, about 20 minutes east of Oakland. It may have all seemed like a hippie dream, but King was still moved to write a prophetic song called "What is a Bandersnatch?" They were living hand to mouth, even after recording a trio of songs at Pacific High Studios.

For Herbert, it was a needed opportunity to learn what worked and what didn't. Unfortunately for Frumious Bandersnatch, the bad news often outweighed the good.

An initial 1,000 copies of their debut EP were pressed on the band's own Muggles Gramophone Works label, including a collector's-item run on purple vinyl. Locals quickly snatched them up, but Frumious Bandersnatch remained unsigned. These songs only belatedly saw wider release on a 1995 UK import album titled *Nuggets From the Golden State: The Berkeley EPs*. Three additional tracks, including the Valory co-written "45 Cents," eventually filtered out on other modern-era compilations.

By October 1968, Valory was gone. **Jack Notestein** took over, and they briefly signed with **Bill Graham**'s booking agency. This connected Herbert with his mentor, and quickly extended Herbert's knowledge base about the music business. A failed demo session followed at Golden State Recorders, however, and Warner walked out the door ahead of Notestein. Frumious Bandersnatch limped through a few dates as a trio before grinding to a halt in November 1969.

If nothing else, Herbert, Tickner, and Valory had gained invaluable experience along the way—and they had made important musical connections with Graham, with **Santana** on a variety of shared bills, and with one another. Valory returned for well-received Frumious Bandersnatch reunions in 1994, 2004, and, most memorably, in 2008 when the group finally recorded their first full-length album, *The Flight of the Frumious Bandersnatch*.

"The band has become such an underground legend and I'm happy that happened," said Denny, who has long since made peace with the band's offbeat moniker. "I don't think in all reality that it would have had the same mystique without the name." [41, 172, 175]

WINTER 1969–70

NUGGETS

▶ Gregg Rolie and **Mike Shrieve** join **Carlos Santana** as **Clive Davis**, president of Columbia Records, presents their first gold record for their LP *Santana* following a sellout at the Fillmore East. —*Record World*

▶ After two years in college, Steve Perry leaves Northern California and takes a part-time job as second engineer at Crystal Studios in Los Angeles. —*Hit Parader*

Ambitious Neal Schon Gets Noticed By Clapton, Santana

Gregg Rolie and **Michael Shrieve** discovered Neal Schon in 1970 after repairing to a small Palo Alto club called the Poppycock following another combative session for the **Santana** album that would become *Abraxas*. On stage was a teen guitarist with as much embryonic talent as he had ambition.

In fact, they were so impressed with Schon that they eventually engaged in an impromptu jam. Rolie and Shrieve decided to bring Schon into their recording sessions, but **Carlos Santana** was initially cool toward the youngster. Unperturbed, Schon happily tangled with **Eric Clapton**, another studio guest.

"This was just incredible," Schon told *Goldmine*'s **Peter Lindblad**, "and I was so shocked at the time I really think I just said,

'Hello' and 'Goodbye' to the guy." Unfortunately, Santana had once again ingested the wrong drug at the wrong time. "I came in and Eric and Neal Schon were jamming," Santana told **Marc Shapiro**. "I felt really bad because I wanted to play, but I had just taken LSD and I was just too out of it."

Schon was already playing with remarkable instinct—and almost constantly, to the detriment of his schoolwork. "You know what [manager] Herbie [Herbert] used to say? 'If brains was dynamite, he couldn't blow his nose,'" Journey tour manager **Pat Morrow** said, laughing. "But when he picks up that six-string lute and starts to blow, it is the most serious shit. The guy can play."

These jam sessions would punch Schon's ticket for fame. In the meantime, he was making a name for himself.

"I saw Neal sit in Monday night at Keystone Corner with **Elvin Bishop**'s band," longtime San Francisco Chronicle music critic **Joel Selvin** said. "He just blinded the place—just stepped up, and blinded it. This would have been in 1969, and the San Francisco scene was on. It was a thing, Monday nights at Keystone with Elvin, a blinking light on the scene—and here's Neal. He just electrified everybody. It was just right-in-your-face chops that you hadn't really heard before. That was the kid that sat in with **Derek and the Dominos**."

Schon joined them on November 19, 1970, at the Berkeley Community Theater, as Clapton toured in support of *Layla and Other Assorted Love Songs*. **Duane Allman** had served as a second studio guitarist, but Derek and the Dominos were appearing on tour without him. If he meshed, Schon might have played his way right into a superstar group.

"I used to pick up Neal from high school, and we were recording *Abraxas* at the same time. He wasn't going to high school; he was sitting in the quad playing guitar," Rolie said, with a laugh. "So, I brought him out while we were recording *Abraxas* and we jammed a lot at the studio. We did a lot of that, and I loved what he did at 15, 16 years old. He had a choice of either going with Eric Clapton and Derek and the Dominos or Santana at that point—because Eric had heard about him and seen him."

Schon said Clapton asked who he'd been listening to lately. "I told him: Him, and he didn't believe me," Schon told *Goldmine*, "so I picked up an acoustic guitar and I started playing note-for-note 'Crossroads' off the *Wheels of Fire* record. He was like, 'Wow!'" Schon said an invitation to follow Clapton back to England followed.

Derek and the Dominos cofounder **Bobby Whitlock** never thought adding Schon was a promising idea. "We weren't shopping for a guitar player. He just happened on the scene," Whitlock said. "He jammed with us and he said hello, and after that, he left. Eric said, 'What do you think of his playing?' and I said, 'Well, I think he's kinda busy.' It didn't fit what we were doing, you know?"

Whitlock also thought a leaner four-piece lineup provided a preferable showcase for Clapton, who was still trying to claim a solo voice after stints in the **Yardbirds**, **John Mayall's Bluesbreakers**, and **Cream**.

"Eric didn't need somebody to relieve him of guitar duties," Whitlock said. "He needed to be Eric Clapton, you know? That's what it was all about—him being a solo artist, and not really relying on anybody. Had we had Duane in the band, Duane would have been a huge crutch that Eric would have been happy to lean on. At that point in time in his life and in Eric's development, Neal would not have been a great aid. Like any other guitar player who would have been in that band, it just didn't work. It would have stopped the growth of Eric Clapton."

Then there was Schon's age: He did not even have his driver's license. Schon had to bum a ride to play with Clapton. "He was just a kid, and we certainly didn't need to be babysitting nobody," Whitlock added. "We were rock 'n' rollers, man. We were young men, and didn't need a little brother on the coattail—though we all loved his playing. A hell of a guitar player, he was."

When the band learned that Clapton was interested, they finally convinced Carlos to relent. "It was afterwards, is really what I gather," Selvin said, "because Derek and the Dominos and Santana hung out at Santana's rehears-

Continued on Page 26

UNAPOLOGETIC, INVENTIVE MANAGER ELEVATED JOURNEY

Founding Journey manager Walter "Herbie" Herbert was born on February 5, 1948, in Berkeley, California, and grew up in a middle-class East Bay neighborhood as something of a delinquent. He never really lost his sense of street-smart bravado.

"He speaks in a language that mixes Madison Avenue with the semi-literate backstage babble of the rock world," *San Francisco Chronicle* music critic **Joel Selvin** reported in 1982.

As a teen, Herbert was already road managing **Frumious Bandersnatch**, a Berkeley-based band that featured future Journey members George Tickner and Ross Valory. The legendary **Bill Graham** then hired Herbert to do crew work with **Santana**, where Herbert met Journey cornerstones Gregg Rolie and then Neal Schon.

He was slowly putting it all together—Journey, a business plan, the band's long-term strategy for success—and without any formal training. In Herbert's mind, he never needed it.

"There are no prerequisites to being in this business, educationally," he told Selvin as *Escape* was becoming the biggest-selling al-

bum ever issued by a San Francisco band. "Very few people understand radio, retail, the record company, the artist, and the role they all play and how it fits together."

But Herbert did. His vision brought the members of Journey together. His ground-floor sensibilities and bold business acumen made them superstars.

"He read '*How to Win Friends and Influence People*' by Dale Carnegie on LSD," Frumious Bandersnatch guitarist **David Denny** said. "I know that sounds far out, but in truth, he listened without interrupting people. He watched and learned until he knew exactly what and who he was dealing with, and how to achieve whatever was in front of him."

Herbert oversaw everything from voice lessons to lineup and producer changes, from business partnerships to the lighting and video screens. "He invented corporate sponsorship," Selvin said. "He had Budweiser paying him money just to put signage on stage."

When Journey's first three LPs underperformed, Herbert moved to hire a proper front man. He "fought for me to be in that band," Steve Perry told *GQ*. "We've had our problems too, but if it wasn't for Herbie, I would've had no chance to sing on that grand stage."

When neither *Infinity*, their first album with Perry, nor any of its singles got past No. 50, Herbert pioneered a novel approach: He contracted with so-called "foreground music" companies to get Journey's tracks played in retail outlets, mall common areas, and restaurants. Songs that had done little on the charts were suddenly everywhere.

Such was his vision that he mapped out Journey's discography by title, beginning with 1978's *Infinity*. The band followed this through until 1986's *Raised on Radio*, which Herbert had wanted to call *Freedom*. (Journey eventually released an LP with that title, after Herbert passed in 2021.) He managed everything in-house, from promotion and advertising to accounting—even trucking the equipment from show to show.

"He was the heart and soul of the whole thing, and he kept it going and kept it running back then," Gregg Rolie said. "He came up with so many fantastic ideas. We had our own trucks, we had our own semis—and then he would lease them out to other bands to pay for the trucks. That was brilliant. Most people go lease a truck from somebody else, but we got in the leasing business. Pretty smart."

His next-gen concepts for how shows were presented changed the industry. Their first live concert shoot, in 1977 at the Winterland in San Francisco, included a multi-camera setup. Herbert's production company was creating professional music videos for Journey years before the arrival of MTV. Next, the company turned its attention to improving the concert experience, bringing in a super projector and two enormous 25-by-50-foot screens.

"Once audiences get a glimpse of Journey's innovation," Selvin wrote in 1982, "no major rock bands will even consider working baseball parks without such a system." **The Who** came first, as they prepared for what the band then billed as a farewell tour. Suddenly, Herbert's company was also handling live video projection for everyone from **David Bowie** to **The Police**.

"He thought of rock 'n' roll as an arms race," Selvin said with a huge laugh. "And you know what? It is! In the end, I believe they made more money in the production end than they did in the music end."

Herbert bucked trends, eschewing print and radio advertising to focus on television and working directly with retail outlets. Ultimately, he would credit point-of-purchase sales for as much as half of Journey's sales at their early-1980s peak. He even set up a toll-free number where stores could request additional promo tools like cutouts of the band, banners, and streamers.

"That kind of progressive, long-term visionary kind of thing is missing from our business," Herbert confidently boasted to Selvin in 1980.

Herbert then took these new business principles out into the world. He also managed the **Steve Miller Band**, **Mr. Big**, and **Enuff Z'Nuff**, as well as a pair of Journey offshoot bands in **The Storm** (which featured Gregg Rolie, Ross Valory, and initially Steve Smith) and **Hardline** (Neal Schon and future Journey contributors Deen Castronovo and **Todd Jensen**). He co-managed **Europe** and **Roxette**.

Known for a sharp wit, Herbert could be as volatile as he was brilliant. He once threw a chair out of an office window during a disagreement with **Pat Travers**'s manager over tour billing. "I had to do that just to get the motherfucker's attention," Herbert told Selvin in 1978.

"Herbie could definitely be brutally honest, and he did not suffer fools gladly, but he was also the biggest supporter of his acts that you could possibly imagine," said **Ron Wikso**, second drummer for The Storm. "To hear Gregg and Ross talk about what he did for Journey, especially in the early days and also hear about some of his work with the original Santana band was really cool. He was a legendary guy in the business who is responsible for inventing and/or growing so many of the innovations that we now take for granted now at live shows—and I feel lucky to have worked with him."

Disagreements with Perry eventually led to his ouster as Journey's manager, but there remained one more twist in Herbert's tale. In retirement, he assumed a blues-band alter ego named **Sy Klopps**. "It was so much fun!" Herbert told the *Honolulu Star-Bulletin*. "If I'd known how much fun performing was, I'd have never gone into the business end of rock 'n' roll."

He released an album with the winking title *Walter Ego* before battling a "prolonged illness," according to assistant **Maria Hoppe**. Herbert died in October 2021 at age 73. "Herbie is an amazing part of this story," Selvin said, "and in many ways much more interesting than the musicians." [25, 56, 60, 71, 74, 80, 110, 114, 173, 375, 439, 440]

al hall after the Derek show. There were a lot of jam sessions, and I suspect a considerable amount of blow."

"At the end of the night, Clapton offered Neal a job," Selvin added. "That's when Santana kind of rethought the idea of having this kid hang out. He thought, 'Maybe he should join the band.'" [38, 60, 117, 375, 378, 379, 380, 927]

WINTER 1970–71

NUGGETS
▶ **Santana** has added another guitarist, Neal Schon, with the rest of the band remaining intact.
—*San Francisco Examiner*

COLLABORATIONS
▶ Ross Valory plays bass guitar on **Steve Miller**'s album, *Rock Love*.
▶ Gregg Rolie plays piano on **David Crosby**'s album, *If I Could Only Remember My Name*.

Santana Evolves As a Band, And Adopts Precocious Schon

Santana started out in a straightforward manner, before a heady mix of styles, races, and influences sent the band in a whole new direction.

"We named it Santana—well, actually **Santana Blues Band** at first, like a million blues bands named after one guy," Gregg Rolie said. "But his name printed really well, and it kind of covered what we were doing. Then the music changed, and we dropped the 'blues band.' The music became more ethereal and ethnic and different. Back then, the way we looked at it was, we weren't playing to a San Francisco crowd. We were playing internationally in our heads—because if we did that, we might be able to get across the street. I mean, really, 'Let's think as big as you can possibly think.' So we did."

Rolie eventually became certain that Neal Schon could add another key element: Unadulterated rock and roll. They already had a namesake guitarist, of course, but **Carlos Santana**'s approach would always be rooted in Latin and blues styles. "Carlos plays Carlos; he doesn't play anybody else," Rolie said. "He doesn't go anywhere else."

Carlos Santana (left) joins Ross Valory (center) and Neal Schon during Bill Graham's Day on the Green concert in Oakland, California, in September 1976. Carlos invited Schon to join Santana when he was just a teenager several years prior.

Meanwhile, Schon was an exciting if untamed talent. He would sometimes play too fast or simply too much—Schon certainly had when he sat in with **Derek and the Dominos**—but that fiery presence suited the rangy, eruptive sound that Santana had quickly established.

"He was pretty active on the fretboard; it was perfect for Santana," Dominos co-founder **Bobby Whitlock** said. "He was very talented, but it didn't gel with what we were doing. I think because he was young, he was playing all of that stuff. When you're young and you find out you can play, you tend to go all out, you know?"

Rolie's argument worked, and Santana installed Schon as the second guitarist in a lineup that now swelled into a blues-rocking conga-driven orchestra of seven. "I think the way Gregg probably presented it was, 'Look, we've got three drummers, and it adds something—and I think with the two guitars nobody could beat us,'" Santana drummer **Michael Shrieve** later told *Mojo*. "I think that was the approach, and I think it was very heady stuff for Neal to walk into as well."

Having supportive parents whose lives were also shaped by music helped. "I used to see Neal's mother Barbara at shows and at some point I asked her when he was 16 years old and had the opportunity to join either Santana or Derek and the Dominos with Eric Clapton, 'What was that like for your family?'" future Journey collaborator **Stevie "Keys" Roseman** said. "She was always very supportive of him and the answer was, 'We just let him choose where he wanted to go. We believed in him.'"

Santana was intrigued by what **Duane Allman** had brought to the Dominos' *Layla and Other Assorted Love Songs*, surmising that a second guitarist like Schon might take their music to similarly exciting new places. Others were less enthusiastic, including Carlos's friend and touring mate **Miles Davis**. "You don't need that little white motherfucker in there," Santana remembered Davis saying. "He actually came down hard on me," Santana told *Mojo*, "and I said, 'Well, fine, you don't hear it but I hear it, Miles.'"

Davis saw someone else playing his instrument as competition, but Santana—at least for now—welcomed another collaborative voice. "I went with what my intuition told me," Santana added, "and I still feel Neal is a phenomenal player."

The *San Francisco Chronicle* announced Schon's addition to the Santana lineup on February 21, 1971. He was a week shy of turning 17. "They took me under their wings," Schon later told *USA Today*. "They showed me the world. They showed me the ropes."

In time, Rolie's novel idea proved to be the right one. "I went to Carlos and asked, 'What do you think about having a second guitarist, having Neal join us'?" Rolie said. "And I was thinking the whole time, it's pretty hard to tell your guitar player that we need another guy. That's not going to float too good. 'What a great idea!' But that's exactly what happened, and those guys began learning off of each other. ... I thought it would work like that—and it did." [1, 38, 41, 51, 170, 375]

Santana Turns 'Black Magic Woman' Into a Top 5 Hit

Fleetwood Mac did not have much success with their 1968 single "Black Magic Woman," barely sneaking into the U.K. Top 40. But it made a massive impact on the drummer from **Santana**, who slipped a copy of the single to Gregg Rolie.

"**Mike Shrieve** turned me on to Fleetwood Mac when they were a blues band," Rolie said. "He knew I liked **Peter Green**, from when he was with **John Mayall's Bluesbreakers**. I thought to myself, 'I could really sing this.'"

He could. Rolie's career-making vocal would propel Santana's version of "Black Magic Woman" to No. 4 in the U.S. in January 1971. It also became a centerpiece for the band's million-selling *Abraxas* when paired with **Gábor Szabó**'s "Gypsy Queen," as Santana reached the top of *Billboard*'s album chart for the first time.

"Just a special song. Sometimes, a singer just connects with a song—and that was it," Rolie added. "The song had such a realism to it."

Still, Rolie spent months trying to convince the others to try "Black Magic Woman." "So, I brought it into the band, not the recording but the chord changes, and during rehearsals we would play it," Rolie later told *Glide*. "It took a year of talking people into doing this."

Santana was a stalwart fan of British blues and he eventually relented during a sound check in a parking lot in Fresno, California. "It's always been extremely inviting to hear blues really executed by English people," Santana told the BBC's *Guitar Greats*, "because they take the best of the black and the best of the white ... so all of a sudden, blues becomes like water and can take on any color."

He immediately began constructing his solo. "I remember saying, 'Hmm, I can bring a little bit of **Otis Rush** here and a little bit of **Wes Montgomery** here' – because I just think like that," Santana told *Rolling Stone*. "It's kind of like a chef, bring a little bit of oregano and jalapeños and garlic and onions."

Despite the long journey they'd taken to get there, the long-awaited session for "Black Magic Woman" was a breeze. "When it came time to record," Rolie said, "I sang it once in the studio—one of the few times I did that—and it was done."

Years later, Santana said that he still returned to the frisson of those early moments around the song as he prepared to solo on stage. "When I play 'Black Magic Woman,' I think of Otis Rush and Fresno in a parking lot," he told *Rolling Stone*, "and it gives me the same results."

But trouble was brewing within Santana, as Carlos took a more central role in decision making during the *Abraxas* era. These arguments over song selections were intensifying, just as the band was coming into its own commercially.

"We were too young to appreciate it the first time around," Santana told *Rolling Stone*. "I was so invested in my agenda. It was my, my, my, my, my, my. Also, nobody was equipped to handle the adulation."

When Carlos brought "Oye Como Va" and "Samba Pa Ti" to these sessions, he had to endure significant pushback about whether to include them. Santana would not budge. In fact, he threatened to quit.

The fissures in the band were widening. [2, 120, 177, 593, 887, 888]

SANTANA, SCHON CHEMISTRY YIELDS A VIBRANT SOUND

PATHWAY ALBUM
Gregg Rolie & Neal Schon

Santana III | Columbia Records
September 1971

Santana III should have been an unfocused dud, considering that it was recorded in the run up to their post-Fillmore finale meltdown.

Beyond the excesses of the day, the album was completed in a drawn-out process that involved discarding work done with early producer **Eddie Kramer** while trying to integrate Neal Schon into their core sound. There were scores of overdubs, as the two guitarists attempted to find their ways.

Yet returning to the studio, away from the stresses and temptations of the outside world, ended up reestablishing **Santana**'s fragile bond. There were still arguments—notably over the use of outside musicians, when the **Tower of Power** horn section sat in on "Everybody's Everything"—but they established common ground once more.

"We were still at a point where we could sit down in the studio and just talk about something and start playing it," **Carlos Santana** told **Marc Shapiro**. "One of us would say, 'Listen' and the others would listen."

That's very much how the opening "Batuka" happened, as they found inspiration from a **Leonard Bernstein** piece that the Los Angeles Philharmonic sent over while Santana was preparing for a joint appearance with the orchestra. The results, dominated by thunderous rhythms and twinned guitars, couldn't sound less like classical music—but it certainly sets the stage for the nearly unremitting frisson to follow.

Released in September 1971, *Santana III* touches on inviting Latino soul with "No One to Depend On" and "Everything's Coming Our Way," both of which inevitably became Top 40 *Billboard* hits. "Toussaint L'Ouverture," named after the principal leader of the Haitian Revolution, finds organist Gregg Rolie elbowing his way forward into a frenzied three-man solo front. "Taboo" is simply gorgeous. Santana also expands upon their instrumental brilliance with smart reworkings of **Gene Ammons**' "Jungle Strut" and **Tito Puente**'s "Para los Rumberos."

Throughout, Schon's soaring flurries and stomping wahs stand in thrilling contrast to Santana's patented blues cries and Chicano moans. On their best days, Schon and Santana were already almost telepathic. "As a kid, we hung out so much. ... We hung out every day," Schon said. "He and I just really click. Musically, there's nothing that we can't jump on top of and make it sound really good, really quickly."

Still, during moments like "Toussaint L'Ouverture,"

Drug Use, Musical Direction Splinters Santana's Core

Santana headlined closing night for the Fillmore West on July 4, 1971, taking the stage after midnight. But they said goodbye to more than **Bill Graham**'s legendary venue: The band's classic-era lineup would never appear together again.

Drug use had slowly overtaken most of Santana, in particular bassist **David Brown**. Everyone was increasingly distracted by the pleasures of the flesh offered out on the road.

"Several of them were real street people," longtime **Herbie Herbert** associate **Pat Morrow** said, "and they didn't know from anything. I mean, they were just thrust into that life without warning. It was an interesting, a very interesting sort of social experiment. You take these kids that are really street kids from the Mission, and all of a sudden, they're standing on stage at the Grammys and that kind of shit."

They sometimes had trouble getting back to the music. "What I wanted was the band to listen to me and rehearse more—that's what I wanted," **Carlos Santana** told *Mojo*.

"I said, 'We have dust collecting on the platinum albums and we don't rehearse and we start to suck, to my standard,'" Santana added. He ultimately blamed their rush to fame, citing "excess, drugs and not sleeping and not having the wisdom or the knowledge or the common sense to put things in perspective."

Some of their disinterest could also be chalked up to creative drift, as the others did not share Carlos and **Michael Shrieve**'s burgeoning interest in fusion. They encountered some bad luck too: **José "Chepito" Areas** suffered a brain aneurysm and was replaced by **Willie Bobo** and then **Coke Escovedo**.

Areas eventually returned, but Escovedo stayed on—and, for some bandmates, became an in-

something of a joust appeared to be emerging between Santana and Schon. As sessions continued, they reportedly kept redoing and redoing their parts in a bid to one up each other—to the point where engineer **Glen Kolotkin** later insisted that Schon actually recorded over his best Santana-era solo. Still, the newcomer clearly challenged and excited Santana, and Schon more than held his own.

"What a huge step and platform that was for him. It was a perfect fit," **Bobby Whitlock** of **Derek and the Dominos** said. "I've got nothing but positive things to say about Neal Schon. I remembered him throughout my own career, and watched him grow and develop from afar. It's good that it worked out the way it did."

Together, Carlos and Schon provide a brawny reminder that Santana's most important contribution to the wider Latin music legacy was in replacing traditional brass instruments with the guitar. "We were really quick in the studio. Everybody played live," Schon later told *Goldmine*, "and there were a few solos that were overdubbed – and I usually got 'em in one take. ... Great record; I love it to this day." Boasting a more approachable song cycle, this album also easily followed *Abraxas* to the top of the charts, but *Santana III* occasionally lacked its predecessor's darker complexity. That led some to unfairly overlook it at the time.

What no one knew was that this would stand as the classic-era lineup's final musical statement. Santana was moving into freer, more spiritual plac-

Santana's *Santana III* did not have the band's name anywhere on the cover, so CBS Records applied a round sticker with "Santana" on the LP's shrink wrap.

es, and not all of his bandmates were along for the ride. "I started to listen and began to realize that, as a musician, I wanted to do more than just crank up 'Evil Ways' and 'Black Magic Woman,'" Santana said in the BBC's *Guitar Greats*. "So, I wanted to see if we could fuse rock 'n' roll and jazz."

The transition, in fact, had already begun. Santana's era-closing performance at the Fillmore West, recorded the same day sessions for *Santana III* ended, included a lengthy examination of **Miles Davis**' "In a Silent Way." [4, 38, 120, 141, 379]

creasingly destabilizing presence. Then there was also Santana's simmering feud with Chepito's fellow percussionist **Michael Carabello**. At one point, when Carlos was haranguing Shrieve about the group, the drummer countered: "You can't make them do that. It's not your group." **Marc Shapiro** reported that Santana shot back: "Not yet."

They had just concluded sessions for *Santana III*, Neal Schon's debut with the group. Santana should have been riding a wave of fresh momentum. Instead, for largely unexplained reasons, Carlos decided Carabello had to go.

"It was less music, and much more personal," longtime *San Francisco Chronicle* music critic **Joel Selvin** said. "Carlos was becoming more important in his own mind, and less collaborative. The whole thing came to a head over him and Carabello having a beef."

Santana gave the others an ultimatum as they prepared for the next leg of touring on the East Coast: "I'm not going out unless he's out."

Woodstock began to feel very distant. Back then, "everybody was involved," Gregg Rolie said. "I go back and listen to it. I remember the arrangements and ideas, and how things came about from constant jamming." Now, songs were being stitched together with overdubs, and Carlos was suddenly acting as a kind of CEO.

Then, in a shocking turn of events, the others decided to keep Carabello and hit the road without the band's namesake. "Carlos demanded that they fire Carabello, and they refused—then they went off on tour without Carlos," Selvin marveled. "That was unthought of! Carlos is sitting back in Mill Valley going, 'What the fuck just happened to me?'"

The Boston show went off without a hitch, as Schon competently handled Santana's parts. Fans in Washington D.C. were less kind, reportedly shouting objections at the teen. Carabello offered to quit to save the band—and Areas and Brown split too. Carlos would return to a lineup now without its all-important percussion unit—and, on top of that, he would still have to face a seething Gregg Rolie.

"I'll play, but don't look at me," Rolie told Santana in an angry confrontation reported by Shapiro. "Don't talk to me." The group stumbled forward, eventually pulling short-lived percussionist **Mingo Lewis** out of the audience to fill the musical holes.

"From that point, Carlos exercised total control of the situation," Selvin said, "and you know Gregg Rolie did not appreciate this guy rolling over him. Gregg Rolie was a fully formed human being with a great deal of intellect. I don't think that was comfortable for him. It may have been more comfortable for people like Mingo Lewis, who were just happy to be in the fucking game."

Looking back, Herbert said this ugly end drew a straight line to his next big idea. They had somehow moved forward, if only briefly, without the percussionists and even without Carlos Santana. "In effect," Herbert told *Rolling Stone*, "you had Journey right there." [51, 60, 114, 140, 178, 179, 927]

Herbert Quits Santana, Forms Session Band with Schon, Rolie

There wasn't supposed to be a band called Journey. Instead, **Herbie Herbert**'s stated purpose was to bring together a group of talented local musicians who could be available for recording sessions being held in San Francisco. He dubbed them the **Golden Gate Rhythm Section**.

"It'll be something like **Muscle Shoals**, where there are a group of guys who would play with different people, as studio-session guys," Golden Gate Rhythm Section drummer Prairie Prince said. "That was the first concept."

Now playing a more central role in managing **Santana**, Herbert admitted in the *Music of the Night* documentary that he'd become "disenchanted musically, and I really was a rock 'n' roller more than I was a fusion-oriented, jazz-oriented player."

Santana was in the midst of an unhappy, and poorly selling, tour in support of *Caravanserai* that would never make it to a regularly held free New Year's Day gig at Diamond Head Crater in Hawaii. Herbert split with Carlos in late 1972, and quickly assembled a prototype Journey lineup for the Honolulu show featuring Neal Schon, Gregg Rolie, bassist **Pete Sears**, and drummer **Greg Errico**.

But first Herbert had to resign his post with the Santana organization. He dialed up **Bill Graham** and "said, 'I'm gonna call Gregg Rolie and Neal Schon, and put together a band.' I'd missed them so badly." Herbert told **Matthew Carty** the idea was to return to "something that rocks, instead of this fucking semi-fusion-jazz Latin bullshit thing."

Graham asked when he planned to do this, and Herbert said he replied, "As soon as I hang up, because I got a gig at the Crater five days from now."

They were billed simply **Sears Schon Errico**. Rolie, who by then was running a restaurant with his father in Seattle, was listed as a special guest. "The music was amazing, nothing at all like Journey," Sears told **Dmitry Epstein**. "Not that Journey wasn't good, but we got into some pretty out-on-the-edge instrumental jamming."

The setlist included a cover of **Jimi Hendrix**'s "Voodoo Chile (Slight Return)" and a set-closing update of "Black Magic Woman" with Rolie. "That was the closest we came to getting a lead singer," Sears added. He attempted to phone **Steve Winwood** to discuss joining, "but I never managed to get him on the line. There was no talk of any band called Journey yet."

Sears Schon Errico didn't last but the idea did, as Herbert began assembling a Bay Area-based **Wrecking Crew** of sorts. He connected first with Schon, who was then part of a very early version of the **Sly and the Family Stone** offshoot **Graham Central Station** with Errico. "You can be so important to rock 'n' roll," Herbert remembered telling Schon in the *Music of the Night* interview. "To be lost in the realm of R&B is inappropriate."

Schon agreed to join Herbert's new enterprise, then they contacted Rolie. "It was my concept; it was my idea," Herbert said in a 1980 special focusing on Journey by the Blue Jean Network. "I basically drafted or recruited each and every individual in the entire organization, musician by musician, starting with Neal Schon."

He reached out to Ross Valory and George Tickner, whom Herbert knew from **Frumious Bandersnatch**. The Golden Gate Rhythm Section lineup was rounded out by Prince, who was working with an unknown and struggling band called **The Tubes**. Herbert "was managing The Tubes, and he saw there were some problems there—but he really liked my drumming a lot," Prince said. "So he goes, 'Would you like to join in on this new band?' It wasn't really a band, just

a group of musicians that are going to record."

Initial practice sessions were hosted by Valory, who loved the Golden Gate Rhythm Section concept. "In the early '70s, many artists and bands came to San Francisco to develop their own sound with the San Francisco environment," Valory told *Hallowed Magazine*. "So we considered the idea to begin with of becoming a local rhythm section for recording with various artists."

Rolie left the food service industry, and never looked back. He proved to be a critical piece, the most veteran of the crew—and the only singer. "Herbie was trying to resurrect Gregg Rolie as a vocalist," former San Francisco music critic **Joel Selvin** said.

Something clicked along the way, however, and the Golden Gate Rhythm Section took on a life of its own. "So, we got together and rehearsed at Ross's place, and everybody immediately fell in love with each other," Prince said. "We thought, 'Wow, this is great.' Immediately, the chemistry was there. It was so much fun."

Valory could feel it, too. "The whole thing began very experimentally," he told the *Press Enterprise*, "but from the very beginning, I had no doubt Journey would be huge. I just knew it."

Sears Schon Errico had one more lasting impact on Journey: Sears took a moment at an unrelated recording session to introduce Schon to future drummer Aynsley Dunbar. Ironically, Dunbar would eventually leave after four Journey albums to join Sears in **Jefferson Starship**.

In the meantime, Journey hit the road. They had no other choice. Herbert had ended his management agreement with Santana in 1973, but Rolie was still contractually tied to the band's old label. Unfortunately, Columbia Records had just endured the failure of **West, Bruce and Laing**, made up of members of **Cream** and **Mountain**. Herbert said they were now wary of bringing in another supergroup.

"So in 1974, I decided to create a touring situation," Herbert told *Cashbox*, "as if the tours were supporting the release of new hit albums." He leveraged all of his old contacts, even earning the new group an opening spot for **Steely Dan**.

Continued on Page 32

"By the time the Columbia contract was finally signed," Herbert added, "we were already established as a band that could move tickets."

Jefferson Starship, an offshoot of **Jefferson Airplane**, ended up on Journey's path toward more pop-oriented sounds, and both Dunbar and Sears were gone by 1984.

"People became concerned about sales and airplay," Sears told Selvin. "We weren't that band. We were a hippie band. We weren't Journey." [30, 56, 60, 85, 117, 177, 236, 237, 375, 381, 382, 481]

FALL 1971

RELEASES
▶ **Santana** (with Neal Schon, Gregg Rolie), *Santana III* (album)
▶ **Santana** (with Neal Schon, Gregg Rolie), "Everybody's Everything" (single)

NUGGETS
▶ *Santana III* scored gold upon its release with two million advance orders. Santana is now three-for-three: three albums, three gold records. —*Cashbox*
▶ Aynsley Dunbar has been busy the last couple months. He joined **Shuggie Otis** on his Epic LP, *Freedom Flight*, and then played drums for **Frank Zappa** on his *200 Motels* album. —*Cashbox*

Santana Hits with 'Everything,' But Trouble Starts Bubbling

Santana's "Everybody's Everything" is a raucous party inside a 45, as Gregg Rolie tests the upper end of his vocal register amid a storm of percussive fun. In fact, the lyrics are mostly indecipherable. The assembled musicians just plug in and play.

It was the vibe of the era. "It was basically the chemistry between all the people together that made that sound," Neal Schon told the *Arizona Republic*. "The songs were pretty much secondary, I would say, to the actual playing."

"Everybody's Everything" became Santana's fourth career Top 20 *Billboard* hit, and the highest-charting song from *Santana III*. It was also, however, at the center of one of this session's biggest disagreements—this time, over the use of outside musicians. Suddenly, there was a small army involved. This kind of rising musical tide would have swept away a lesser player, but the **Tower of Power**'s funky sharp guest-starring horn section was simply no match for one of Neal Schon's most memorable early solos. "I actually played lead guitar on it," Schon told *Goldmine*, "and Carlos played rhythm guitar and bass."

Released in October 1971, the single belied everything that was happening behind the scenes, and everything that lay just ahead for Santana.

"There became some very different camps," Santana drummer **Michael Shrieve** later told *Mojo*. "Neal and Gregg were strongly relating—and there were problems with Carlos as well. Carlos was starting to move in his own direction."

Santana's muse would be reignited by Shrieve's collection of jazz records, though Carlos was admittedly slow to warm to the likes of **John Coltrane** and **Miles Davis**. "I thought jazz was phony, cocktail, suit-and-tie bullshit music," Santana told **Andy Gill**, "and I was into the gutbucket, cut-and-shoot thing, where there's no floor, just dirt, and you play shuffles and blues."

Shrieve convinced him to listen more closely, to really absorb these new musical ideas. "I discovered that jazz was a more intelligent, sophisticated way of articulating the blues, with European, sophisticated changes," Santana told Gill. This revelation would also shift his commercial fortunes: It would be a decade before they had another Top 20 hit, with "Winning."

"Carlos was trying to play jazz, and quite frankly, I can listen to it, but I'm not a jazz player. Nobody in the band was—including Carlos," Rolie said. "The stuff we were playing, it was like we were leaving back the audience we built. It's not what I would have done, so I left and Neal left—everybody left." [1, 51, 127, 180, 379]

FALL 1972

RELEASES
▶ **Santana** (with Neal Schon, Gregg Rolie), *Caravanserai* (album)

Santana Shifts Musical Gears; Fed Up, Rolie, Schon Decamp

In just three years, **Carlos Santana** had gone from unknown to platinum superstar to man without a band. He turned to God. And jazz.

The two things were inextricably linked in forging **Santana**'s new musical path. Ongoing success for *Santana III* and its singles gave him a window to take the first tentative steps. He started by collaborating with **Buddy Miles**, who rose to fame with **Jimi Hendrix**'s **Band of Gypsys**. They produced a surprise hit concert LP, but that was a stopgap measure and not a true way forward.

Santana's new LP, *Caravanserai* took shape around Santana's remaining partnership with **Michael Shrieve**, a friendly presence from the most recent band lineup who shared an interest in both fusion and religion. Carlos began assembling a more jazz-leaning core of musicians, but the sessions were tentative at first. Unlike some of his new collaborators, Santana did not read music. He was very much still feeling things out.

The final lineup of contributors makes clear why they chose the Persian title, which roughly translates into a roadside inn for travelers. Regular contributors included Santana band veterans like Shrieve, Gregg Rolie, Neal Schon, and percussionist **José "Chepito" Areas**. In all, however, more than a dozen people helped complete the album, which arrived in October 1972.

Santana made clear that Rolie and Schon's contributions were just workmanlike. The pair "already had their eyes to do Journey," he told **Marc Shapiro**, "and so they basically showed up, played their parts and split." Santana filled the musical space with turns by jazz guys like **Lenny White**, **Hadley Caliman**, and **Tom Harrell**, who helped Santana and Shrieve nurture their new vision.

"During the making of the fourth Santana record, they were really at odds with each other," **Herbie Herbert** said in 1984's *Music of the Night* documentary. "There were drug problems and all of the attendant problems of that era. They didn't really see eye to eye; they didn't work together in the studio."

Instead, the LP was dotted with contemplative open spaces and orchestral asides that very much reflected Santana's recent focus on meditation. "It wasn't even like a Santana album," Carlos later admitted to the *Las Vegas Sun*. "It was like career suicide, and I like career suicide once in a while. It can open up a lot of possibilities."

Columbia Records president **Clive Davis** got wind of things and was so concerned, he went to the studio to observe one of the mixing sessions. Davis had a paternal approach with Santana but did, in fact, deem *Caravanserai* "career suicide."

In *Carlos Santana: A Biography*, the guitarist remembered responding: "I know what you want but I can't give it to you, because I don't hear it." There would be a price to pay for that mentality in terms of sales, Santana conceded, "but I didn't care."

The results were too rock focused for jazz radio, and far too jazzy for rock radio. Loyal fans sent the album to No. 8 on the *Billboard* chart, but *Caravanserai* became the first Santana release not to earn double-platinum status. As Clive Davis predicted, the album had no hit singles.

Neal Schon loved "Song of the Wind," which featured a shared improvisation with Carlos, but it did not even chart. "I actually played the first solo on that," Schon told *Goldmine*. "You know, it's two chords, and we just improvised and played."

This new musical direction ended up bringing Carlos closer with Shrieve, though perhaps nobody else. "Gregg didn't like it, Neal didn't like it, the roadies didn't like it," Shrieve told *Mojo*. "The record company didn't like it, and so Carlos and I got really protective about it." Santana's destination was becoming all too clear: "By the third album, it was like a meteor disintegrating already," Carlos told *Q* magazine. "By the time we did *Caravanserai*, I had no band."

Rolie and Schon exited these sessions more certain they had made the right decision to leave. "Simply put, we played with passion and we broke up with passion," Rolie later told the *Lancaster Journal*. "Carlos and Shrieve wanted to take it one way. I did not want to do that." [51, 189, 190, 191, 194, 206, 236, 379]

SANTANA VET WAS JOURNEY'S FIRST VOICE, KEYBOARDIST

Gregg Rolie was a suburban kid who loved the British Invasion bands of the 1960s. At one point, he was in a Top 40 cover band called **William Penn and His Pals**, where he actually wore a ruffled shirt.

"It was kind of a takeoff on **Paul Revere and the Raiders**," Rolie said. "It was huge in the Bay Area. That was my first introduction to really playing for people in theaters."

Not exactly the makings of a Latin-rock band legend. But Rolie, more than all of that, was intuitive. **Herbie Herbert**, who served as a road manager for **Santana** and then manager of Journey, once described Rolie as "so smart that he's probably disqualified as a musician," longtime San Francisco music critic **Joel Selvin** said.

That's almost how it turned out, actually. "I was going to be an architect," Rolie told *Glide* magazine. "When I had the opportunity to start up Santana with Carlos, I jumped on it." Journey then rose out of the ashes of Santana's final classic-era lineup.

Rolie would be recognized by the Rock & Roll Hall of Fame as a rare two-time inductee, first with Santana and then with Journey. He'd leave Journey on a platinum-selling mountaintop, and they only got bigger. Those he collaborated with thereafter were gifted with hard-won knowledge from someone who started not one but two of rock's best-known groups.

"Journey has become this runaway freight train with no brakes," Rolie said as the group marked its 50th anniversary. "People come in and out, there have been all these changes, but Journey keeps going. It just keeps going and going. I'm proud to have been a part of building something like this that has reached millions of people and continues to do so. That's amazing to me."

Born on June 17, 1947 in Seattle, Rolie grew up in the Palo Alto area of California, and that's how he entered **Carlos Santana**'s orbit. A friend saw Carlos playing during a local talent show at **Bill Graham**'s Fillmore Auditorium and put the two together for a jam session. This being the 1960s, there was lots of noisy rock—and no small amount of weed. When the cops came to bust everything up, Santana was the first one to take off.

"All I saw was Carlos' back," Rolie told the *Mercury News*. "He was about 20 yards away, running for this field, because he was a street rat and he knew what was up." Rolie finally caught up to Santana, and they hid in a near-

by tomato patch until the police left. "And that was the beginning of all of it," Rolie added.

Originally dubbed the **Santana Blues Band**, the group always boasted a multi-racial lineup in the style of **Sly and the Family Stone**. Like the name implies, however, they originally had a much narrower focus. Then the rhythm section was replaced, as percussionists **Marcus Malone**, **Michael Carabello**, and **José "Chepito" Areas** joined. Bassist **David Brown** and drummer **Michael Shrieve** completed the makeover.

Santana had a different vibe now, pulsing with exciting Latin cadences amid the bluesy lines created by Carlos and Rolie. "The whole world changed right there," Rolie told *Glide*—yet he remained cautious. "I was going to give it five years, and if nothing happened then I'd go back to school."

Rolie felt his early tenure with the group had been its own kind of miracle anyway. "Being as the rest of us lived such different lives anyway and came from such different backgrounds," Rolie told *Mixdown*, "it was amazing that we got together in the first place."

Rolie did his best to guide the band through the first rush of fame, remaining the straightest in a group that had a few serious drug users. He also held the line when Carlos's musical focus began to wander. "The leader of that band, from Day 1, from Woodstock through—I mean all of it: Gregg Rolie," Herbert told **Matthew Carty**. "He ran that band."

Herbert found Rolie working in a restaurant when he decided to create a new group after Santana blew apart. Herbert knew just who could balance out the still-young Neal Schon's flinty ambitions with the appropriate amount of maturity and experience—and Rolie was happy to exit a difficult situation.

Rolie fronted Journey for three albums, then shared the spotlight with newcomer Steve Perry on a trio of subsequent multiplatinum studio projects. With his next band at an early pinnacle, the ever-practical Rolie exited off of fame's highway to start a family.

But he wasn't done with music: Rolie issued a series of solo albums, was part of **The Storm** with fellow Journey co-founder Ross Valory, and took part in some notable Santana-related reunions. He also completed a career circle by becoming one of the longest-serving members of **Ringo Starr's All-Starr Band**, a dream come true for an early **Beatles** fan. [25, 50, 51, 56, 60, 167, 177, 181, 182, 375, 375]

LOOK INTO THE FUTURE

Adrift from Santana, Neal Schon, Gregg Rolie, and Herbie Herbert began searching for a musical identity. Joining with musicians from Herbert's recent past, they would form a jam band that would quickly transform into a San Francisco favorite. Journey was born.

Golden Gate Rhythm Section Reborn as Jam Band—Journey

Neal Schon was bursting with new rock ideas after a stint playing R&B. Gregg Rolie could not have been more thrilled to put away his apron and oven mitts. Both of them were sparking with rhythm guitarist George Tickner, a fresh presence who locked in immediately with fellow **Frumious Bandersnatch** alum Ross Valory and drummer Prairie Prince.

"Neal and **Herbie Herbert** called me. I was in the restaurant business, and they saved my life," Rolie said. "Don't get in the restaurant business. You need at least 1,000% of capacity to make it work. Nobody eats in the same place every night. So anyway, that was difficult, but they called me up and said, 'We're starting a band.' I left Seattle and joined in on what they were doing."

Instead of backing visiting superstars, however, the Golden Gate Rhythm Section was suddenly creating their own music. "We started writing songs together," Prairie Prince said. "I contributed some stuff to those early tracks that ended up being on their first album."

They recorded still-unreleased demos at Wally Heider Studios in San Francisco, now known as Hyde Street Studios. "We had an engineer named **Stephen Jarvis** who also grew up with Ross and George and Herbie back in their high school days in the East Bay," Prince added. "So, he was an up-and-coming engineer, and he engineered the first demos that eventually became the record."

Rolie never believed that Herbert was trying to build a sessions band. "It was supposed to be designed for singers or players that came into San Francisco. We'd have a ready-made band that could play what they wanted," Rolie said. "But I think they lied—I think it was a band all the way," he added with a laugh. "And that's OK."

Now, they needed a new name. The group submitted their newly recorded demos to KSAN-FM, a local radio station, with the idea of airing them and then inviting listeners to submit postcards in a naming contest. The winner was to receive a lifetime pass to any future concert.

Things did not go as planned. Instead, they drew such fan-suggested—and obviously quite unusable—band names as Hippie-potamus and Rumpled Foreskin. Roadie **John Villanueva** fi-nally came up with the name Journey, during a legendary bull session with Herbert.

Their manager liked the name, Prince said, "because everybody was so taken with this soaring, powerful music. It felt like a journey to him, rather than just a rhythm section."

Problem: Villanueva could not claim the prize since he was an employee. They brainstormed a made-up winner's name instead, landing on **Toby Pratt**. "We lied and said that somebody listening to the radio had called in with it," Schon later told the *Tampa Bay Times*, "but actually it was somebody on the inside that was working with us."

Next problem: There was a real guy named Toby Pratt, so Rolie said they quickly put together some sort of prize package. Despite these mishaps, Journey finally had a name—and the makings of a debut album.

"Gregg Rolie is the voice of 'Black Magic Woman' in Santana," future tour manager **Pat Morrow** said, "and Neal is this wunderkind guitarist. These guys are, like, poised on the brink of success. Neal is writing these tunes like 'Of a Lifetime,' and Gregg is still great, you know—an incredibly successful, romantic singer and rock star."

By March 1973, Herbert had also created Nightmare Productions, Inc., codifying the business side of things. [30, 83, 85, 174, 181, 236, 238, 330, 375, 375, 927]

SPRING–FALL 1973

NUGGETS
▶ Rhythm guitarist George Tickner will be joining **Merl Saunders** and **Jerry Garcia** at their show at the Ontario Motor Speedway. Tickner is replacing **Tom Fogerty**, who is working on his own LP.
—*Record World*

COLLABORATIONS
▶ **Rod Stewart** cuts a track with **The Aynsley Dunbar Retaliation**, "Stone Crazy," that is now being released on the *History of British Blues, Volume One*, on Sire Records.

COLLABORATIONS (cont.)

▶ Aynsley Dunbar played drums on **David Bowie**'s album, *Pinups*.
▶ Aynsley Dunbar played drums on "Berlin," "Men of Good Fortune," "The Bed," and "Sad Song" on **Lou Reed**'s album, *Berlin*.
▶ Aynsley Dunbar played drums on **Flo & Eddie**'s album, *Flo & Eddie*.

ON THE ROAD

▶ **Journey**, with Herbie Hancock, and Santana.

Lightning-Fast Start, But Band Loses Prince to The Tubes

Journey's first official concert, ironically enough, was opening for **Carlos Santana** on December 31, 1973, at **Bill Graham**'s 6,500-seat Winterland Ballroom in San Francisco. They arrived with a clutch of winding originals that would make up the bulk of Journey's first album.

"Nobody had heard of the band, but immediately they were taken," Prairie Prince said. "You could hear it from the audience. We got a great response—just because it was so powerful, you know? It was not something that people had really heard before. Gregg Rolie was the vocalist, obviously, but a lot of it was just intense instrumental stuff—mostly with Neal just wailing away."

That was the blueprint, Rolie argued. "The way I look at the early Journey stuff is, if we played that now, we'd be out with **Phish** or the [**Dave] Matthews Band**," he said. "We were a great jam band."

Prince, however, found himself stuck between two worlds—Journey and **The Tubes**. "I hadn't really decided which way I was gonna go," he said. "The Tubes had another drummer at that point, and he was very sick with cancer—and he was only 21."

Herbie Herbert's adeptness at scheduling huge shows was carrying everyone along. "The New Year's Eve night was introduced by Bill Graham's partner **Jerry Pompili**, and he says: 'This is a new band that's going to start off the new year, 1974,'" Prince added. "Then we ripped through everything that we knew to that point. I think we had an hour in the opening slot for **Santana**, which I thought was pretty amazing."

Tickets for this debut show were $6.50 in advance, and $7.50 at the door. They performed five of the seven rangy originals that would appear on 1975's *Journey*, including "In the Morning Day," "Kohoutek," "In My Lonely Feeling / Conversations," and "Topaz." Journey also wildly reimagined **The Beatles**' "It's All Too Much," which they would officially record in 1976 for *Look Into the Future*.

This was heady stuff at the time. "The first edition of **Mahavishnu Orchestra** lived from 1971-73; the fusion version of **Return to Forever** had just started in '73, which was the same year that Journey started," future Journey drummer Steve Smith said. "I think Journey was ahead of the curve in those years because fusion was just happening then, so for a rock band to incorporate that approach into their music was daring and innovative."

Journey was set to appear at Herbert's annual Diamond Head Crater event the next day on January 1, 1974, but Prince had to make a stop first. The Tubes actually played one New Year's Eve 1973 concert as well, in Santa Cruz—an hour and a half away from where he had just played at the Winterland Ballroom.

"So as soon as I finished the opening slot with Journey, I rushed to The Tubes's New Year's Eve show, which didn't start until 10 or 11," Prince said. "I did that show, rushed back after that, went to sleep for a couple hours, and then got on the plane and flew to Hawaii that next morning, really early, with all the guys from Journey."

Prince had to make a decision. He played the Hawaii date with Journey but ultimately chose to remain with The Tubes, a band that grew out of his youth back in Arizona. He said he told Herbert: "I love these guys in Journey. I think it's the most astonishing, wonderful music, but I have to be dedicated to my brothers in The Tubes."

The band's other drummer, **Bob McIntosh**, succumbed to cancer before The Tubes recorded their first album. The group dedicated "Golden Boy," from their 1977 LP *Now*, in his honor.

Meanwhile, Journey was starting over with someone new, and they only had a matter of weeks before their next huge show. [2, 9, 30, 331, 335]

As the Dunbar Era Begins, Journey Signs with Columbia

Journey did not settle on a replacement for Prairie Prince until just four days before Aynsley Dunbar's scheduled debut at San Francisco's Great American Music Hall.

That gave the former **Frank Zappa** drummer precious little time to get up to speed on a setlist which played out as "sort of a **Mahavishnu Orchestra** thing at that point," *San Francisco Chronicle* music critic **Joel Selvin** said. Still, Dunbar heard something he liked in these free-form song structures.

"It was the arrangements and dynamics of Journey that got me hooked into it," Dunbar told the *Albuquerque Journal*. "I was tired of playing rock 'n' roll and straight-forward, no-thinking music. ... It took a lot of looking to find a band that could interest me."

Dunbar's first concert with Journey was on Saturday, February 2, Selvin confirmed. In a concert review published the following Monday, February 4, 1974, he was particularly taken by Journey's version of "Kohoutek"—calling it a "crushing instrumental tribute to the 'comet of the century.'"

Journey also played "Topaz," which would later appear on their debut album, and an update of "It's All Too Much" by **The Beatles** that Selvin praised as "ultra-heavy" in his review. "No new band appearing in San Francisco in the past 12 months (at least) has been such an obvious smash," he added.

They were fortunate to have clicked so easily with Dunbar: **Herbie Herbert** arranged for a number of record label executives to be on hand at the Great American Music Hall. Journey ended up signing with Columbia, extending a relationship that Selvin reported was already in place through Rolie's continuing contract from the **Santana** days. That was not the only way Rolie and Neal Schon's former bandmate loomed over the proceedings.

"The band was so obscure to the people down at the newspaper office," Selvin said, "that they demonstrated [his review of Dunbar's first Journey show] with a mugshot of Carlos." Santana did not perform that night. [60, 63, 94]

SPRING–SUMMER 1974

NUGGETS

▶ **Lou Bramy** and ex-Santana production manager **Walter Herbert** have formed Spreadeagle Productions, which will manage a new San Francisco group called Journey. The band is made up of former **Santana** members Gregg Rolie and Neal Schon, George Tickner (previously of **Merl Saunders** and **Jerry Garcia**), Ross Valory (previously of **Steve Miller**) and Aynsley Dunbar (**The Mothers**, **Lou Reed**, **John Mayall**). The band's name was picked via contest promotion on local radio station KSAN, and the winner received a lifetime pass to all the band's personal appearances around the world. —*Cashbox*

COLLABORATIONS

▶ Aynsley Dunbar plays drums on **Herbie Mann**'s album, *London Underground*.
▶ Neal Schon plays guitar on **José Areas**'s album, *José 'Chepito' Areas*.
▶ Aynsley Dunbar plays drums on **Mick Ronson**'s album, *Slaughter on 10th Avenue*.

ON THE ROAD

▶ **Journey**, with Aerosmith, Brian Auger's Oblivion Express, Bachman-Turner Overdrive, Black Oak Arkansas, Climax Blues Band, Cold Blood, Eagles, Harvey Mandel, Jo Jo Gunne, Mahavishnu Orchestra, Nova, Soft Machine, Stoneground, and The Tubes.

Perry Auditions for Tower of Power, Tours with Privilege

Steve Perry was still dreaming of stardom when he briefly joined the horns-driven Edmonton, Canada-based band **Privilege** in the mid-1970s. **Herbie Herbert** said Perry also auditioned for **Tower of Power** before taking over from Robert Fleischman as Journey's front man.

Continued on Page 43

DUNBAR BROUGHT RESOLUTE POWER TO RHYTHM SECTION

Aynsley Dunbar actually started with violin lessons, but he quickly switched instruments: "It didn't go over to enough people, but I saw that drums did when I was about 11 1/2," he later told the Associated Press. "What I saw in drums was power, being able to powerhouse a band."

Dunbar methodically learned, beginning with only a snare, then adding a bass drum and hi-hat. He installed a small tom next, then cymbals. "If I'd had the whole drum kit, it might have been too much all at one time to understand," Dunbar told *Modern Drummer*. "By just having the snare drum first, I spent more time practicing the basics."

Born on January 10, 1946, in Liverpool, England, Dunbar left school at 15 to focus on music. He dabbled in the then-hip Merseybeat genre, but at one point was reduced to playing swing music with a bunch of married guys in a local group called the **Merseysippi Jazz Band**. Better musical opportunities beckoned in London.

Dunbar soon caught the attention of **John Mayall** and then **Jeff Beck**, before he formed his own late-1960s era group, **The Aynsley Dunbar Retaliation**. Offers to join the **Jimmy Page**-era **Yardbirds** and **Jimi Hendrix**'s band followed, but Dunbar left for the United States and an eight-LP stint with **Frank Zappa**. He also became an in-demand studio presence, appearing on **Lou Reed**'s *Berlin*, and **David Bowie**'s *Pinups* and *Diamond Dogs*, among others.

Along the way, Dunbar developed a hard-won sensibility about his craft: Drummers should play with both great sensitivity and great freedom. "A lot of American drummers have the feel but they have no feeling," Dunbar told *BAM* magazine. "They've got no idea how to adjust and play behind a soloist."

His split with Bowie was telling, as it followed an attempt to get Dunbar nailed down with a long-term contract. When he declined, Dunbar told *Modern Drummer* that Bowie's management said: "'Well, if that's the case, I guess we don't need you in our organization.' I said, 'That's OK with me. Bye.'"

Dunbar could be no less mercurial after heading to San Francisco, where he would connect with Journey for a four-album stint that rose from humble jam band origins to 1978's multiplatinum *Infinity*. "We called him the Queen of England," said **Pat Morrow**, who first came on board as a drum tech. "He was

such a fucking pain in the ass, but I was able to tame him and work with him."

One of Morrow's regular duties, he said, was procuring libations for a traditional English drink. "He would take a quart bottle of ginger ale and a quart bottle of whiskey, drink half the ginger ale and fill it back up with Scotch," Morrow added. "He carried his plastic soda bottle around all day."

At first, Dunbar served their purposes as a "fusion/progressive rock band based upon a lot of soloing ... kind of like **Santana** but no percussion," Gregg Rolie told *Glide* magazine. Dunbar's strength, Rolie added, was that "he could really help drive it to get it high."

Success came with a price for the ever-inventive Dunbar as Journey streamlined their approach with the arrival of Steve Perry: "They wanted me to play note for note behind them, and I wouldn't do it," Dunbar told *Modern Drummer*. "So, they put up with it for about 4 1/2 years before they told me to get out."

Even after he joined Journey, Dunbar continued as a first-call sideman: His second album with Bowie sideman **Mick Ronson** arrived just months before Journey's debut in 1975, as did the first of two LPs with longtime **Neil Young** collaborator **Nils Lofgren**.

Sessions for Lofgren would unfold in the more open atmosphere that Dunbar preferred, as Lofgren and bassist **Wornell Jones** arrived with only rough song sketches.

"The theme was to play and sing live, getting a raw, emotional take early on," Lofgren added. "So while Wornell and I had prepared, Aynsley came in having never heard a note. ... This way, when we actually counted off a take, we all got inspired by a super fresh sound with the three of us reacting with interplay that was brand new to us."

That was not the direction Journey was suddenly headed. Besides, Perry had expressed reservations about Dunbar even before taking over as front man. "He was afraid of Aynsley Dunbar not having a groove, being too white a British drummer with very minimal exposure to soul or R&B and not strong on the backbeat," Herbert later told *Melodic Rock*.

Dunbar closed the door on Journey as easily as he had with Bowie, shifting over for **Jefferson Starship**'s next three LPs. He would also play with **Whitesnake**, **Ronnie Montrose**, **UFO**, and **Keith Emerson**. [33, 44, 82, 147, 177, 334, 376, 927]

TOURING-WEARY GUITARIST DEPARTED JOURNEY EARLY

Largely forgotten today, second Journey guitarist George Tickner was brutally dismissed as an "inconsequential cog who made a quick exit" by an Independent Press Service writer in the early 1980s. In truth, he was anything but unimportant.

Tickner co-founded **Frumious Bandersnatch**, the Berkeley-based group that gave future Journey manager **Herbie Herbert** important early experience in guiding bands. The same unsigned group later featured Journey bandmate Ross Valory, and Frumious Bandersnatch's split with Tickner played a key role in Valory's subsequent exit.

They would go on to share membership in the local band **Faun** before joining Journey. "I wasn't bored with Frumious, but I had other

PROFILE: GEORGE TICKNER

musical things I wanted to do," Valory later told **Bruno Ceriotti**. "I was sort of chasing after George Tickner and his music, for which I had a great affinity."

Tickner was born on September 8, 1946, in Syracuse, New York, a country away from the East Bay suburbs in Contra Costa County where Frumious Bandersnatch would play a foundational role in Journey's story. Tickner quickly built up his own musical pedigree, having sat in with Bay Area favorites **Jerry Garcia** and **Merl Saunders**.

He then became one of the first people Herbert connected with Neal Schon after they decided to start Journey. In the beginning, Tickner played a key role in the songwriting process, even if only in the form of roughly hewn chord changes with goofy titles like "Sketches of Pacheco," **Joel Selvin** later remembered.

"I met George in high school. I can remember sitting in his parents' house in Lafayette listening to George play guitar," Frumious Bandersnatch bandmate **David Denny** said. "He was so confident, and his rhythms were majestic! I knew even way back then he had something special in his guitar playing, and it didn't surprise me that he and Neal Schon wrote some of Journey's first amazing instrumental music together."

Tickner's approach was new and exciting for bandmates who had gotten used to **Santana**'s creative process. "He came up with chordings I have never heard," Rolie told Selvin for Journey's *Time*[3] box set liner notes. "He had these massive hands, and he would de-tune his strings and come up with these voicings that nobody else could."

Even early on, Tickner tended to play a steady, sometimes unnoticed role on stage, focusing on rhythm guitar duties while Schon followed his restless solo muse. Selvin's first report on Journey, published after a February 1974 show at the Great American Music Hall in San Francisco, mentions Tickner's "rock-solid grounding"—but nothing else.

Studio work revealed deeper complexities. Subsequent collaborator **Stevie "Keys" Roseman** described Tickner as "one of the most distinctive guitar players, and the opposite of Neal. Not often flashy—slow hand, if you will. However, you certainly knew who was playing."

Tickner would earn writing or co-writing credits on three of the seven songs from Journey's 1975 debut, but he was growing unhappy. "I didn't like the touring, the traveling, the pace," Tickner told *Billboard*'s **Tom Vickers**. "I saw it was turning me into something I didn't like."

His discomfort on stage was painfully obvious to Tickner's bandmates, long before he finally came off the road to attend medical school in 1975. "George loved the studio but didn't care for huge live venues, which made him nervous," Denny added, "so I'm not surprised he left Journey in its early days."

Tickner's absence created more musical space, in particular for Schon. "With George there was a tenseness," Rolie told Vickers, while praising the "more loose and relaxed" shows that followed. "He wasn't really into it. He likes writing, but onstage he didn't really enjoy himself."

By then, Tickner had collaborated on two more songs from Journey's 1976 follow-up *Look Into the Future*—including the titanic closer, "I'm Gonna Leave You." He would also co-write the instrumental "Nickel and Dime" from 1977's *Next*. "I get along with them very well," Tickner told Vickers. "There's no animosity."

He later created a recording studio with Valory called The Hive. They were also part of the short-lived instrumental trio **VTR** with Roseman. VTR's 2005 album, *Cinema*, included guest appearances by Neal Schon, Steve Smith, and Prairie Prince. But once again, Tickner's tendency toward shyness reared its head.

"Writing, recording, and generally hanging out with those guys during the VTR sessions were both challenging and some of the finest and most creative times in all of our careers," Roseman said. "By that time, George had become somewhat reclusive and would become more so as time went on. George could be quite difficult, but the trade-off was his playing."

This history made it all the more astonishing when Tickner made an unannounced appearance with past and present members in 2005 to celebrate Journey's new star on the Hollywood Walk of Fame. He then retreated out of the public eye once again, before passing away in 2023. [41, 63, 81, 84, 169, 172, 175]

Privilege had just released a single, simply titled "Rock and Roll," which the *Star-Phoenix*'s **Ned Powers** said had "vast potential." It was part of *Enjoy*, the 1974 LP recorded at producer **Gary Paxton**'s studio in Bakersfield, California.

Perry ran into them during that trip out west, when Privilege opened for **Ike and Tina Turner** at P.J.'s in Los Angeles. "We developed a nice friendship," Privilege leader **Andy Krawchuk** told **Graham Hicks** of the *Edmonton Sun*. "Unfortunately, I had to cut it short as we had a gig at the legendary Pussycat A Go Go in Las Vegas."

Perry was asked about joining when Privilege returned to Canada. Krawchuk thought Perry's honeyed vocal style might blend nicely with their gruff vocalist **Randy Broadhead** to form a **Righteous Brothers**-style combination. Perry came out for a cross-country Canadian tour.

They seemed to click. A show listing from the *Star-Phoenix* in Saskatoon from August 9, 1974, praised Privilege for "digging deeper into the rhythm and blues routine, with the spark coming from two vocalists." The listing described Perry as a "high-note specialist."

"He sang with us across Canada," Krawchuk said, "but it was getting cold and he really had a problem with winter, California boy that he was. By the time we got to Montreal, he'd had enough of our weather."

Outside of a period where he fronted his own **Alien Project** group for about six months in 1977, Perry went back to a distinctly rural life. He had incurred so much debt from various demo sessions that he was forced to chip in on carpentry projects at his stepfather's turkey farm.

Then Perry passed a reel-to-reel tape to Herbert at the Kabuki in San Francisco. "The problem was I didn't have a reel-to-reel player," Herbert told *Classic Rock Revisited*. "It just sat in my office and my buddies who I grew up with, Tower of Power, were looking for a singer."

Herbert supplied the tape, and Tower of Power liked what they heard. The audition went well, too. "I said, 'Why didn't you put him in the band?'" Herbert remembered. "They said, 'He was white. We wanted a black guy.'"

Herbert eventually staged his own successful audition. Perry would later appear with the Tower of Power horns on a guest-packed 1978 *King Biscuit Flower Hour* performance that doubled as Steve Smith's debut with Journey. [376, 409, 547, 548, 550, 551]

FALL '74 – WINTER '75-76

RELEASES
▶ **Journey**, *Journey* (album)
▶ **Journey**, "To Play Some Music" (single)
▶ **Jonathan Cain**, "'Till It's Time To Say Goodbye" (single)

NUGGETS
▶ Journey, the much-talked-about Bay Area group that includes ex-**Santana** members Gregg Rolie, Neal Schon and Aynsley Dunbar are just finishing their anxiously awaited debut LP. —*Cashbox*
▶ The new October label is an extremely impressive one. "'Till It's Time to Say Goodbye," a self-penned offering from newcomer Jonathan Cain, offers a strong, clean production that frames his soulful vocal performance; he sounds capable of sitting in on any gig with **Chicago** right now. —*Cashbox*
▶ The industry buzz on Journey grows as the band gets a full-page story on their new album, *Look Into the Future*, and their progress. —*Rolling Stone*.

ON THE ROAD
▶ **Journey**, with Aerosmith, Angel, Blue Öyster Cult, Companion, David LaFlamme, Frankie Miller Band, Hot Tuna, Humble Pie, Ian Hunter and Mick Ronson, Iron Butterfly, Moby Grape, Montrose, Nightshift, Pablo Cruise, Quicksilver Messenger Service, Redwing, Robin Trower, Sammy Hagar, Santana, UFO, Uriah Heep, Window, and Y&T.

Journey Releases Debut Single, 'To Play Some Music'

Gregg Rolie takes center stage for "To Play Some Music," the first—and only—single from Journey's self-titled debut.

His gurgling organ powers the track's beginning, his warmly inviting voice carries a song he co-wrote with Neal Schon, and his smart switch to synth sends "To Play Some Music" into an orbit that Schon rockets right past: His guitar solo is as short as it is acrobatic.

Released a couple of months after its parent album, "To Play Some Music," earned notable praise from *Cashbox*: "From its opening organ riffs clean through to its rocking solo parts, Journey explodes with a solid, tightly produced disc that'll have 'em movin' from Detroit to L.A. Should be a formidable entry for the former Santana folks. Gregg and Neal have got it together. It cooks."

Unfortunately, "To Play Some Music" would appear on exactly zero charts. Journey nevertheless continued to live up to its theme: They were going to play some music, wherever and whenever possible. **Herbie Herbert** made sure of that.

"That was all very deliberate, and Herbie was quite specific about it," San Francisco music writer **Joel Selvin** said. "The first part of the plan was to get the band up in front of as many bodies as you can. So, it was constant touring. Any fucking bill they could get on, they were on."

The nights may have been fun ("we're only sorry that we have to end the show," Rolie sings on "To Play Some Music"), but the days were often grueling. "We'd drive 13 hours—no hotel, jump out of the car and jump on stage," Schon later told *Billboard*.

Journey would be in one vehicle, with the crew in the other. "We just got out there and flogged it. We worked hard at it," Rolie said. "We started with rental cars, and prying [drummer] Aynsley [Dunbar]'s hands off the wheel. 'We're here, we made it!' Then there was the Winnebago tour, where he had to push the damn thing in because it failed. That was with **Heart** in Spokane, I'll never forget that. 'We're big now!' Here we are pushing the damn thing in."

For the time being, reliable transportation and chart success would have to wait. "Some hard dues were paid in the first three years of Journey," Schon told the *Arizona Republic*.

Herbert, as always, stayed focused on the bigger picture: Journey was building the kind of area-based fandom that would have completely eluded a studio creation like the **Golden Gate Rhythm Section**.

"We decided that the music that we were making was better than, and too important to just to be given away as sidemen for other people's projects," Herbert said in 1984's *Music of the*

Night documentary. But he also knew there was still "a lot of room to grow—especially in the area of composing and songwriting, singing and harmonizing, and performing and entertaining."

Meanwhile, Rolie and Schon left that Winnebago in the state of Washington—for good. "Neal and I of course flew back. 'I don't want to get back on that thing.'" Rolie said. "I asked Herbie later, 'Did it break down again?' He goes 'Yes,'" the two-time hall of famer added, laughing. [240, 324, 326, 327, 328, 329, 375, 383, 384]

SPRING–SUMMER 1976

RELEASES
▶ **Journey**, "She Makes Me Feel Alright" (single)

NUGGETS
▶ Journey, **Santana** played to 40,000 as part of **Bill Graham**'s Day on the Green in a day themed as "The San Francisco Sound." **Jefferson Starship** headlined, and **Pete Frampton**, **Tower of Power**, **Steve Miller**, and **Boz Scaggs** were also part of the show.
—*Billboard*

COLLABORATIONS
▶ Aynsley Dunbar plays drums on "Incidentally...It's Over," "Share A Little," and "Can't Get Closer (WCGC)" on **Nils Lofgren**'s album, *Cry Tough*.
▶ Aynsley Dunba plays drums on **Sammy Hagar**'s album, *Nine on a Ten Scale*.

ON THE ROAD
▶ **Journey**, with Baby, Jeff Beck, Black Oak Arkansas, Dr. Feelgood, The Electric Company, Electric Light Orchestra, Elvin Bishop, Golden Earring, Natural Gas, Nils Lofgren, Ted Nugent, Robert Palmer, Quicksilver Messenger Service, Rare Earth, REO Speedwagon, Rush, Todd Rundgren, Santana, Sons of Champlin, Boz Scaggs, Starcastle, Tower of Power, Thin Lizzy, Wet Willie, and Wishbone Ash.

Schon's Friendship with Jan Hammer Starts at Sound Check

A chance meeting on a Texas stage in July 1976 led to one of Neal Schon's most enduring musical partnerships outside of Journey.

The pre-Steve Perry edition of Journey had shared a bill with **Jan Hammer** and **Jeff Beck** during one of promoter **Bill Graham**'s massive multi-act Day on the Green concerts, held one month earlier at the Oakland Coliseum. Then they hit the road for a national tour.

"In the afternoon, for the sound check, Jeff couldn't make it," Hammer said. "He was tied up somewhere. We needed to check Jeff's guitar, so it was all ready for the night."

Standing side stage was one of Hammer's biggest fans from his days in the original **Mahavishnu Orchestra**. "I never missed one of those concerts if it was somewhere close by or I could fly to go to see that," Schon later told **Kaj Roth**. "It completely messed me up. It was like a spiritual experience to see those guys and listen to them."

"So Neal said, 'I'll play,'" Hammer said. He handed Schon a guitar Beck would play later in the evening. "I got on the drum kit, and we started playing and we really hit it off."

Talk, of course, turned to studio work—but their busy tandem careers kept the duo apart for years.

"Neal is such a spark. He begins playing, and things start happening right away," Hammer added. "After that, we talked off and on about doing something, but it didn't happen again until the [1981 **Schon and Hammer**] album *Untold Passion*."

Schon and Hammer later reunited for 1982's *Here to Stay*. Hammer then served as an occasional guest performer on Schon's solo projects, appearing on "Fifty Six" and "Tumbleweeds" from 2012's *The Calling*, and then "Schon & Hammer Now," "NS Vortex," and "Talk to Me" from 2015's *Vortex*.

"I loved the fact that he played like a wicked guitar player," Schon told *GQ*, "and was always curious what I'd sound like playing with him." [55, 80, 183]

Continued on Page 50

Long-Jam Debut Makes Splash, But Few Waves

Journey arrived at CBS Studios in San Francisco in November 1974 with a pedigree from **Santana** and a legacy of rangy musical heroics. So naturally, the label paired the band with **Roy Halee**, a pipe-smoking, overly meticulous eccentric who was best known for work alongside the acoustic singer-songwriting duo **Simon and Garfunkel**. The results were mostly ignored.

"Halee was just nuts," longtime San Francisco music critic **Joel Selvin** said. "I remember him stalling the session for like four hours while he waited for the right microphone to be delivered. He was a really fussbudget old-time engineer, and these guys were raring-to-go young guys that could have ripped a new one in any tape he put up on the console."

Despite his attention to such subtleties, Halee did not seem to really grasp how to record a full-on rock band. Journey arrived in April 1975 with a sound that sometimes felt too muted. Still, he had an admitted passion for the group. In fact, he would claim some responsibility for their deal with Columbia Records.

"I actually signed them!" Halee told *Mix*. "I thought that band was unbelievable! Neal Schon really knocked my socks off. What a player! And Aynsley Dunbar was a fantastic drummer, of course."

At one point, the album was to be named *Charge of the Light Brigade*, after a later-discarded demo. (Journey played "Charge of the Light Brigade" at their New Year's Eve 1973 debut concert, but the song quickly disappeared from their setlists.) Instead, they opted for a self-titled LP that sought to distinguish Journey from their Latin-spiced roots in **Santana**.

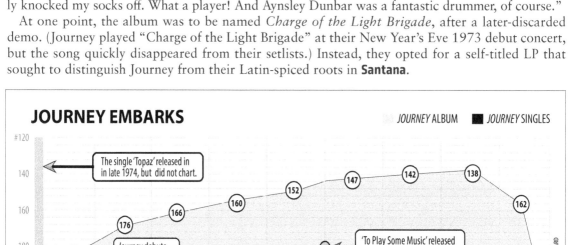

JOURNEY EMBARKS

JOURNEY ALBUM ■ JOURNEY SINGLES

The single 'Topaz' released in in late 1974, but did not chart.

Journey debuts first week in May

'To Play Some Music' released in June, but did not chart.

SOURCE: BILLBOARD

MAY 1975   JUNE 1975

Journey's first album didn't reach the top of the charts as the band had hoped. Instead, it hung out at the bottom half of the *Billboard* 200 for most of May 1975. Its low trajectory wasn't uncommon. Their brand of long-jam rock was better suited for the nascent FM movement. The LP did get a minor boost when *Rolling Stone* gave it a positive review in early June, helping it peak at *Billboard*'s #138. *Cashbox* and *Record World*, the other two publications tracking album sales, pegged the debut's high marks at #124 and #177, respectively. It wasn't an awe-inspiring launch, but Columbia Records had patience since their deep Santana roots were so profitable. But those suits were still watching closely.

TOP CHARTING WEEK: *BILLBOARD*—*June 21, 1975*

1. Elton John, *Captain Fantastic and The Brown Dirt Cowboy*
2. Paul McCartney and Wings, *Venus and Mars*
3. Earth, Wind & Fire, *That's the Way of the World*
4. The Who, *Tommy / Original Soundtrack Recording*
5. Alice Cooper, *Welcome to My Nightmare*
6. The Doobie Brothers, *Stampede*
7. Bachman-Turner Overdrive, *Four Wheel Drive*
8. Chicago, *VIII*
9. The Beach Boys, *Spirit of America*
138. JOURNEY, *JOURNEY*

The group's plug-in-and-go mentality was emphasized in the liner notes, which helpfully added: "We suggest that you play this record at the highest possible volume in order to fully appreciate the sound of Journey."

The notes should have added that fans would need to find a comfy spot too: Most of the songs stretched past the five-minute mark, including the explorative instrumentals "Kohoutek" and "Topaz." (A notable exception was the upbeat, far more accessible "To Play Some Music," which came in at a trim single-length time of 3:19.)

"Originally, the band was very self-indulgent," manager **Herbie Herbert** explained to *Rolling Stone*. He pointedly complained about Journey's initial reliance on "a lot of long solo excursions created specifically to set up Neal Schon for his guitar statements."

That throwback concept may have defined Journey, but it did not necessarily limit the band. "Of a Lifetime" blended fusion with the spacey **Pink Floyd**-ish flights of fancy. "Topaz" made the clearest musical references to Gregg Rolie and Schon's time with Santana, despite being a solo composition from the soon-to-exit George Tickner.

Schon was very much in his element. "Those are my roots, where I came from—blues fusion, and a bit of jazz," he said.

Tickner and Schon worked themselves into an interlocking frenzy to "In My Feeling / Conversations," before "Mystery Mountain" brought things to a suitably towering conclusion. Ross Valory's poet wife, Diane, added a lyrical assist to the Journey finale, three years before playing a key role in the Steve Perry-era breakout single "Wheel in the Sky."

"They didn't have the vocalist [Perry] yet," Halee told *Mix*, "but they could really play, and their material was good, and they had this craziness and drive I thought was really magnetic."

Though clearly a mismatch, Halee made a smart choice when he recommended that Schon double his first-take solo on the nearly seven-minute-long opener "Of a Lifetime." Schon immediately nailed the repeat performance,

EXPLORERS IN A FAR-OFF WORLD?

Journey's first album cover was designed by the late veteran art director **Nancy Donald** with photographs by **Steve Silverstein**. Donald had lots of experience in album design by the winter of 1974, almost all of it developing album packages for Columbia Records, including **Paul Revere & The Raiders**, **Barbra Streisand**, **Johnny Mathis**, **Freddie Prinze**, and **Percy Faith**. Donald would later earn a Grammy nomination for **Boz Scaggs**'s *Silk Degrees* album package. But Journey's debut cover was far different than anything she had done before. The front cover evoked a spacey feel with the band floating aimlessly like a quintet of Major Toms. The back cover (inset) was based on a Silverstein aerial shot that Donald superimposed below a towering mountain range. If the intent was to show the band as explorers of a far-off world, she succeeded. The band was less moved. When asked to reflect on the album cover's artistic meaning, drummer Aynsley Dunbar dismissively quipped he had no idea what it was about.

Columbia Records seriously attempted to pitch their new band to the masses. The label ran full-page ads in *Cashbox*, *Record World*, and *Billboard* to raise attention, and there was at least a glimmer of success. Journey's debut album was reviewed well in the trade press, and *Rolling Stone* gave it a solid review—not insignificant for a fledgling band. The promotional ads were built off the spacey album design concocted by art director **Nancy Donald** and projected the band above some distant planet. Other ads, like the one above published in *Cashbox*, continued the far-off world theme. The promotional effort was strong, but the results were poor. Journey's album stayed on the charts for nine short weeks, and it never cracked the *Billboard* Top 100 LPs. The album sales were important to Columbia because there was no singles activity on the album replete with long jams. The format was unfriendly to AM radio and the album did not have a single that charted.

stunning Halee. "His jaw was on the floor," Schon told Selvin for the *Time³* box set liner notes.

On stage, the songs stretched out even further. "'Of a Lifetime,' man. They would bring the house down," tour manager **Pat Morrow** said. "No singer, no single, no bubblegum—but the playing, Neal's playing. I mean, he would do solos on 'Of a Lifetime' that are still some of the most memorable shit I ever heard—and I heard a lot. I heard a lot of acts."

This more wide-open early approach might have found a wider audience, Rolie argued, in the throwback jam-band era still to come. "It was based on jams, real eclectic—very different," Rolie said. "That's still really valid today. It's almost like, 'What, are we ahead of our time'? You know, in a way—yeah. And that's kind of what was going on: It just didn't catch at that time."

More than half a decade past Woodstock, however, rock was becoming more compact and polished. "The first album was this distillation of all the hip and cool music shit that they'd been listening to, and that they were impressed by," Selvin said. "Plus, they also were under the impression that the Santana thing that was going on before *Caravanserai* was something to be comped on, right? They were still thinking that that was kind of hip."

Instead, *Journey* disappeared without a trace. Its best showing, in fact, was a paltry No. 72 in Japan. "The thinking was, it would be instantly successful," Selvin added. "Honestly, you had Roy Halee producing the fucking thing—and it just went thud."

Herbert would eventually take more direct aim at Journey's penchant for extended instrumental passages. "Our first album sold about 100,000—to our cult, our peers: the musical community of America," he told *Rolling Stone*. "And if we wanted to rise above that, we had to decide that we were willing to apply ourselves."

When Journey reconvened at CBS Studios in August 1975 after touring through the summer, they were understandably ready to move on. They had been performing this material since New Year's Eve 1973—when Prairie Prince was still in the band. "The songs didn't change at all, Aynsley just had a little different take on them," Prince said. "They were pretty much the arrangements I had made. He's just a different style player than I am."

Schon admitted that they had simply been living with these tracks for too long. "It was hot material when we started with it in the early stages," he told *Billboard*, "but after playing it for over a year, we got pretty sick of it." [12, 30, 60, 63, 83, 169, 219, 375, 375, 386, 927]

Cincinnati Enquirer
March 29, 1975

Journey music is not screaming, loud, and metallic rock and roll. But it is, unmistakably, rock and roll, firmly rooted in rock basics with no attempt to bring in other motifs. The music is all new, composed by group members, extremely creative and inventive beyond what you normally hear from a new group. The music is definitely ... complex, building throughout the album to a series of climaxes then falling, then building again. Each instrument, played by a genuine five-star pro, is spotlighted in turn. The instrumentals are the album's chief delight. The band is tight—extremely so—and thoroughly competent. The vocals aren't the best ever laid down, but you hardly even notice the short-comings. Watch for Journey soon at the top of the heap.

— *Jim Knippenberg*

The Pittsburgh Press
April 6, 1975

Something good very well could be coming in the group called Journey, if the album of the same name is any indication of their skill. The personnel is highly experienced (keyboard man and vocalist Gregg Rolie and guitarist Neal Schon from Santana, drummer Aynsley Dunbar from just about everywhere) and are adept. Several songs have above average appeal: "To Play Some Music" (commercial rock) and the instrumentals (Rolie is no great shakes as lead singer) "Kohoutek" and "Topaz," particularly the latter with its shimmering delicacy yielding to flux-fledged boogie. There's no glaringly bad aspect to the disc, save perhaps that the music of "Mystery Mountain" never really gets going and is a poor match to the lyrics.

— *Pete Bishop*

Rolling Stone
June 5, 1975

Journey is the third and best group to grow out of the original **Santana**. Unlike **Azteca** and **Malo**, it's not merely a spinoff. Keyboardist and singer Gregg Rolie and lead guitarist Neal Schon—both formerly with Santana—have come up with a more energetic and less contemplative music than **Carlos Santana** has been making lately. The rhythm section is led by Aynsley Dunbar's complex and experienced drumming, while producer **Roy Halee** has contributed to the group's original sound by placing Rolie's piano within the rhythm section and leaving Schon's guitar as lead instrument. His sensitive mix prevents the lackluster vocals from intruding on the band's instrumental strength. "To Play Some Music" is the album's most commercial cut. A strong beginning.

— *Cynthia Bowman*

Steve Smith Joins Jean-Luc Ponty for First Major Tour

Jean-Luc Ponty began a tour in October 1976 with a new drummer who was well versed in jazz—but not, Steve Smith admitted, in the jazz-rock violinist's particular style.

"Before Ponty, I was still mainly involved with playing big-band jazz and the jazz influenced by **Miles Davis** and **John Coltrane** from the 1960s," Smith said. "That was my focus, as an up-and-coming drummer. I hadn't really played fusion yet."

Instead, Journey's future drummer toured for a couple of summers with **Franklin "Lin" Biviano**, a veteran trumpeter who had played with oldguard figures like **Maynard Ferguson** and **Buddy Rich**. Smith had also sat in with clarinetist **Buddy DeFranco**. None of these performances was going to be confused with bands like the muscular, genre-bending **Weather Report**.

Still, the 22-year-old Berklee College of Music student clicked with Ponty, while also discovering that he had an inborn knack for jazz that incorporated more contemporary musical concepts.

"When I played with Jean-Luc Ponty, fusion playing came to me very naturally—just as it came to the first generation of fusion drummers like **Tony Williams**, **Billy Cobham**, **Lenny White**, and **Alphonse Mouzon**," Smith added. "They were jazz drummers who started playing bigger kits with more of a rock and funk approach to jazz. It came very naturally to me, and I really enjoyed playing on the big drums in a powerhouse kind of setting."

These shows were obviously on a different scale than Journey, but that does not mean they were without inherent pressure. Jean-Luc Ponty was in the midst of establishing himself as a leading jazz-rock figure, after working with **Frank Zappa** and **Elton John**, then joining **John McLaughlin**'s **Mahavishnu Orchestra**. Ponty had released the well-regarded *Aurora* earlier in 1976, and *Imaginary Voyage* would follow in November. He was building toward consecutive Top 40 hits with 1977's *Enigmatic Ocean* and 1978's *Cosmic Messenger*.

Growing ever more confident, Smith joined Ponty for the *Enigmatic Ocean* sessions. He also left behind his small original Gretsch kit after Ponty asked him to get a double bass drum set like the one used by Cobham, a fellow Mahavishnu alum.

"That Ponty gig was a big transition for me and that was the doorway into being a rock drummer," Smith told *Modern Drummer*, "because once I got the double bass drum set I really started operating at a different dynamic—playing loud, playing hard, which then led me to eventually playing with **Ronnie Montrose**."

It's actually a path that mirrored so many of the genre's earlier greats, Smith argued.

"Most interviews you read with guys like **Charlie Watts**, **Ginger Baker**, or **John Bonham**, they say they were listening to jazz drummers," Smith said. "It just so happens that they grew up in a culture, and a time, when they—and their peers, guys like **Jack Bruce**, **Jimmy Page**, and **Eric Clapton**—were playing the music of the youth culture."

So, leaping from Jean-Luc Ponty to Montrose to Journey, as Smith soon would, made its own kind of sense.

"Early rock was very close to jazz and blues and in those days, there was a tremendous freedom in the music that no longer exists," Smith added. "So, I wouldn't say they were rock drummers who incorporated jazz. I think they were jazz-inspired drummers who wrote the book on how to play rock. They are now regarded as the early generation of rock drummers." [3, 245]

Turbulent Mid-Air Media Mixer Promotes Look Into the Future

Columbia Records was still dreaming up innovative ways to promote Journey, even as label executives grew worried about disappointing album sales. At least one of them was high-flying, indeed.

The label ushered members of Journey, a group of rock media representatives, and CBS employees onto a DC-9 for a quick 3 a.m. spin after the March 30, 1976 show at Atlanta's Electric Ballroom.

Described by *Cashbox* as "Journey's Night Flight," the chartered plane took off from the airport about an hour after Journey's last curtain call, *Billboard* reported. Unfortunately, the weather wasn't cooperating. Journey's plane flew directly into "black and choppy skies."

The flight finally smoothed out as the DC-9 reached the South Carolina coast, according to *Billboard*: "When the seatbelt signs went out, members of Journey mingled with the other guests amid stewardesses hustling drinks and food to the passengers."

Journey manager **Herbie Herbert**'s role in this is unclear, but a jet-fueled joyride perfectly aligned with his offbeat promotional acumen. On the other hand, his charges could hardly have cared less about that side of the business.

Neal Schon once loudly complained in the lobby after a live radio interview. "He goes, 'Hey, man, how come we gotta do this shit?'" tour manager **Pat Morrow** remembered. "I go, 'Is making you a multi-millionaire a prepossessing enough reason?' I could tell, the thing that bothered him the most was he didn't know what prepossessing meant."

Cashbox reported that Columbia's regional director and regional marketing manager were among those on board the DC-9, along with Schon, Gregg Rolie, and Aynsley Dunbar. Journey returned to a "rain-slicked Atlanta runway at 5 a.m.," *Billboard* added, noting CBS had gone to "new heights in promotion."

The national tour for *Look Into the Future* was underway. [386, 534, 536, 542, 927]

Journey Plays Its First Concert As True Headliners

Journey logged dozens and dozens of tour stops before achieving one critical milestone: They finally played their first headlining show on June 2, 1976, at the Santa Monica Civic Auditorium in California.

This early capstone belied Journey's very humble beginnings. "So, I'm walking around the gigs in flip-flops and a pair of shorts and a T-shirt, 45 grand in cash in my briefcase," said **Pat Morrow**, who'd now become their tour manager. "We're doing everything in cash. We've got no money. We put the rental cars and the hotels on Herbie's mom's credit card."

They were still often better received on the road than on the charts, as *Look Into the Future* reached a *Billboard* peak of only No. 100. In a *Record World* review of a summer 1976 show, **Harvey Kubernik** said "I'm Gonna

Leave You," the closing track from *Look Into the Future*, "immediately seized the audience." "Midnight Dreamer" also "earned the group a standing ovation halfway through the evening's performance."

After **Thin Lizzy** opened, Neal Schon offered typically "fluid string work, filled with spacy passages," Kubernik added. That helped spark three encores following Journey's main set, with their cover of **The Beatles**' "It's All Too Much" as a highlight.

Not everyone was as kind as Kubernik. In its April 3, 1976 issue, *Billboard* magazine included a scathing report from a March concert where Journey opened for the **Electric Light Orchestra** at the Beacon Theatre in New York City.

Nancy Erlich said Journey earned a good response from the crowd and gave Aynsley Dunbar's performance a nod, "but this relentless, unmelodic style of music was tedious even in 1968, when it was at least fashionable." All Journey needed now, she concluded, "is a songwriter."

Ironically, Columbia Records had placed an advertisement promoting *Look Into the Future* on the first page of the same edition of *Billboard*.

Journey would go on to play a string of dates with **Santana**, beginning with **Bill Graham**'s San Francisco band-themed Day on the Green on June 5 before 40,000 people. Journey then opened Santana's six-week Amigos tour of Europe later in 1976. But Santa Monica still loomed large, as Journey steadily climbed toward the top of concert posters. [295, 533, 539, 545, 927]

Roy Thomas Baker Signs Exclusive Deal with Columbia

Roy Thomas Baker signed an exclusive contract with Columbia Records in late 1976 that would eventually bring him into Journey's orbit. He would shepherd the band to its first platinum-selling albums, applying a stacked-vocal approach from his time with **Queen** that transformed Journey's sound.

Record World reported the deal in January 1977, noting Baker was already slated to work

Continued on Page 54

JOURNEY CO-FOUNDER NAVIGATED TWO BAND TOURS

Ross Valory's future in music was mapped out through a group of friends in Lafayette, California, who would collaborate with him every step of the way to induction into the Rock & Roll Hall of Fame.

Bandmates from his high school would form **Frumious Bandersnatch**, before several of them moved on to the **Steve Miller Band**. **Herbie Herbert** and George Tickner both worked with Frumious before helping to form the nucleus of Journey with Valory. In fact, Valory's relationship with Herbert actually went back further than Frumious Bandersnatch. He was a member of the **Mystics**, a late-1960s-era Contra Costa County band that signed on for Herbert's very first managing gig.

This made Valory a kind of living history for the area, and a key source for director **Ramona Diaz** when she filmed the band-focused documentary *Don't Stop Believin': Everyman's Journey*. "He was my go-to person. He's like the institutional memory of Journey," Diaz told *Film Courage*. "He's seen all the ups and the downs."

The ups included helping drive Journey toward multiplatinum success, as well as stints with **Todd Rundgren** and **Michael Bolton**, with the downs defined by being fired by Journey not once but twice—in 1985 and again in 2020. (He was briefly replaced both times by Randy Jackson, who earlier guested on "After the Fall" from 1983's *Frontiers*.) In the meantime, the ever-loyal Valory would return to those same old friends, creating a series of typically intriguing side projects.

"Ross is someone I admire immensely," Frumious Bandersnatch bandmate **David Denny** said. "Ross was always positive, and since I've known him been joyous and fun to be around."

This impish sense of humor defined Valory as much as his self-taught bass playing. He took time out at the Rock Hall to admonish an auto-adjusting microphone for not rising to the proper height. "Good morning," Valory memorably said during Journey's first turn on the *Midnight Special* in April 1978. "Welcome to the Midnight Pretzel—Special! This is our first time as ghosts—hosts—on the show." Journey's U.K.-based publicist **Joe O'Neil** would later describe Valory as "definitely, 'Oops! Wrong planet.'"

Born on February 2, 1949 in San Francisco, Valory was a multi-instrumentalist, but he had actually never played a bass guitar when future Frumious Bandersnatch bandmate **Jimmy Warner** asked him to join a high school group called **The Goodtimers**. Warner instructed him to "get your mom to go down to Jimmy Webb's Music," Valory told *Bass Musician*. "Get her to rent a bass and an amplifier for you, and I'll show you all the parts. Then ... we'll make change and have fun."

He taught himself the instrument, and by the time he thought to get proper lessons, Valory had already developed a unique personal style based on using the bottom four strings of a five-bass string set. He had also emerged as the ultimate team player. "Bass is important, but not as a feature instrument," Valory later told *Billboard*. "It's there as a subconscious, a stomach-moving pulse."

Valory's parents encouraged his passion for music, allowing Frumious Bandersnatch to live on the family compound early on. He would practice bass "for hours and hours," Denny said. "He was developing an original style with his fingers, allowing him to play amazing riffs which consequently got him standing ovations when he and [drummer] **Jack King** would take solos together at the Fillmore during our sets as Frumious Bandersnatch."

Valory would go on to play in **The Storm** with Journey bandmates Gregg Rolie and Steve Smith, in **The VU** with Prairie Prince, and in **VTR** with George Tickner and Journey collaborator **Stevie "Keys" Roseman**, another neighborhood friend. He was part of Herbert's **Sy Klopps Blues Band** between stints with Journey. He also rejoined Frumious for their long-awaited full-length debut, 2008's *The Flight of the Frumious Bandersnatch*, while continuing to work on various individual projects with his old pals.

"Ross and I have been lifetime friends and he has helped me over the years by playing on some of my personal albums," Denny said. "Working with him is always great. He adds so much to any music he's involved with."

In Journey, others would sometimes sketch out the bass parts. Steve Perry first auditioned "Lights" for the band while playing bass, Jonathan Cain created a first draft for Valory on "Who's Crying Now," and Schon developed the bass line for "Stone in Love."

But nobody sounded quite like Valory. "There's a difference," he told the *Times-Picayune*, "between who wrote the part, and who owns it. I own it." [47, 175, 175, 196, 201, 210, 244]

on the third solo album from **Mott the Hoople**'s **Ian Hunter**. Journey's Baker-produced *Infinity* arrived a year later, followed by *Evolution* in March 1979.

Their relationship with Baker quickly soured. Steve Perry described him as an aloof presence who got more credit than he deserved, often at the expense of his trusted engineer **Geoff Workman**. "Roy comes in," Perry told *Hit Parader*, "has a piece of cheese and says, 'I love it' or 'I don't' and he leaves."

Manager **Herbie Herbert**'s issue was Baker's one-size-fits-all studio technique. "I'm not a fan of Roy Thomas Baker," Herbert told author **Neil Daniels**. "He had done those Queen records, and I didn't like producers that seemed to put their mark on bands ... marking off their territory."

Rolling Stone magazine later described him as a "megalomaniac" in a review for 1980's *Departure*, their first after splitting with Baker. His "meddling," writer **John Swenson** added, "isn't missed."

Still, fans snapped up some three million copies of both *Infinity* and *Evolution* in the U.S. alone. Baker also helped Journey make their first-ever trip to the Top 20 with "Lovin', Touchin', Squeezin'" in the summer of 1979.

With those initial milestones achieved, Journey began its drive on the long road to lasting fame. [537, 538, 541, 543]

Struggling with Singles, Band Tries Again with 'Spaceman'

Journey's final pre-Steve Perry single represented an intentional, if still haphazard, move toward the mainstream.

Released on February 28, 1977, "Spaceman" clocks in at a relatively brisk four minutes, while boasting approachable music and an easily understood narrative. Those are notable qualities from a band that was still filling out LPs with expansive songs like "Nickel and Dime," which originally included three sections.

Journey smartly lopped off the third part, getting "Nickel and Dime" to a more manageable four minutes. (The leftover parts had time signatures of five and 10, inspiring the name.) But Aynsley Dunbar had recently switched to double bass drums, giving everything a deep and heavy feel. Columbia Records made Journey replace Ross Valory's raucous, **Mahavishnu**-esque "Cookie Duster" with something more commercial.

This was all before **Herbie Herbert** began the search for a front man. "I've always wondered why there weren't more voices happening, but it's a growth curve," Steve Perry later told the *Messenger-Press*. "They were definitely an instrumental progressive band slowly but surely coming around to a wider spectrum."

On the far other end of that spectrum was "Spaceman," which might be the original line-up's most pop-leaning song. They obviously had high hopes for the track, slotting it first on *Next* and then issuing it as the album's lone single. Unfortunately, "Spaceman" failed to chart anywhere, joining a string of such failures like "She Makes Me (Feel Alright)," "On a Saturday Nite," and "To Play Some Music."

Still, the single boasted "a really good melody, with lyrics by Aynsley Dunbar," Gregg Rolie said. "That was one of his first attempts at writing lyrics." Dunbar ended up with songwriting credits on five of the eight songs on the *Next* album.

Unlike so much else on *Next*, and before, "Spaceman" was a remarkably restrained song with themes of stark alienation and sadness. By the end of the album, however, Journey had reverted to the less focused, grinding rock of "Karma." [2, 116]

FALL–WINTER 1976–77

RELEASES
▶ **Journey**, Next (album)
▶ **Journey**, "Spaceman" (single)

NUGGETS
▶ Journey joins **Santana** on a six-week European tour as an opening act. —*Cashbox*
▶ Future Journey collaborator **Narada Michael Walden**, formerly of the **Mahavishnu Orchestra**, signs an exclusive long-term recording deal with Atlantic Records. —*Record World*

NUGGETS (cont.)

▶ **Queen** producer **Roy Thomas Baker** signs an exclusive deal with Columbia Records to produce the label's bands, including **Starcastle** and **Journey**.
—*Record World*

▶ **Jean-Luc Ponty** gave a well-received performance in an odd location for a master jazz musician—Nashville. Nonetheless, his acoustic and electric violin duets were mesmerizing. [Future Journey drummer] **Steve Smith** and ex-**Mahavishnu Orchestra** bassist **Ralphe Armstrong** were strong compliments. —*Cashbox*

ON THE ROAD

▶ **Journey**, with The Alpha Band, Artful Dodger, Black Sabbath, Eric Burdon, Cheap Trick, Coconut, the Earl Flick Band, Electric Light Orchestra, Heartsfield, Kansas, Lynyrd Skynyrd, Mystery, Pentwater, Santana, Steve Hillage, Stoneground, Target, The Jim Hearn Band, and Y&T.

Perry's Alien Project Ends As Bassist Dies in Tragedy

Steve Perry was on the cusp of signing a deal with his band **Alien Project** in 1977 after their demo tape caught the attention of Columbia label executive **Don Ellis**. Then disaster struck their bass player **Richard Michaels**.

"Unfortunately, he got killed in a car accident on the Fourth of July," Perry later told *Rockline*. Alien Project was set to ink their contract the following week. "When you're starting out in this business, that's what you look for—to get a record deal," Perry added, "and it just shocked me."

Perry was so devastated that he considered quitting the music business. He had grown close to Michaels, whom Perry has described as "a wonderful singer, a wonderful bass player, and a great guy." Perry was not sure he could refashion the special chemistry they had created together on a demo tape highlighted by the track "If You Need Me, Call Me."

Following Michaels's crash, Ellis sent Alien Project's tape to Journey manager **Herbie Herbert** without telling Perry, and that song convinced Herbert he had found a replacement for the short-tenured Robert Fleischman. "It came on," Herbert told *Rolling Stone*. "The first words: 'If you need me, call me.' Not even 15 seconds, and I'm on Mars!"

First, they had to separate from the singer Journey already had. "I went, 'We got a heavy job to do. We gotta get rid of Fleischman, and then we gotta get this guy,'" Herbert added.

Herbert reached out to Ellis, who called Perry to offer his condolences—then mentioned the opportunity with Journey.

"The record company said that they liked what I was doing and told me that Journey were looking for a new vocalist," Perry told *Sounds*. "From then on, things happened very quickly."

Journey would be a multiplatinum act in less than a year. "I was just intrigued by how he really changed the sound of Journey," said influential classic-rock radio executive **John Gorman**. "Prior to Steve Perry, it was a different band. It didn't do well for radio. They were developing their own sound away from **Santana**, but they hadn't found that hook yet. That didn't happen until Perry came on. He completed the sound of the band."

It had all started nonchalantly enough. "We just asked him to come up and hang around while we finished our tour that year," Ross Valory told *Jam Magazine*. "Just to cruise on the road with us on a casual basis, just to see what it was like."

It did not take long for Perry to notice who formed the band's foundational partnership: "I think there is a very tight allegiance between Neal and Herbie that will never go," he told *Song Hits*. "They are like brothers." Still, Perry soon discovered a long-ago connection: Schon had once given Perry a ride from the Kabuki Theater in 1972, though Schon had no idea Perry sang. The duo soon began writing songs together.

Schon was quickly warming to a vocalist—and Herbert was enthusiastically describing

Continued on Page 63

Journey Holds Fast to Long-Jam Roots for *Future*

One album into their career, and Journey was already at a crossroads.

"We had built quite a following being one of the original jam bands in San Francisco," Neal Schon told *Goldmine*. "You know, people really enjoyed seeing us live. We weren't selling any records, but we were selling lots of tickets."

That was not exactly what label execs at Columbia were expecting when Journey rose from the ashes of **Santana**. **Herbie Herbert** leaped into action, providing sensitivity training while also lining up a vocal instructor named **Bianca Thornton** to sharpen their skills.

"With each album, prior to Steve Perry, the group became much more song-oriented and vocal-oriented," Herbert said in the *Music of the Night* documentary. "Initially, the first album [was] just Gregg Rolie singing. By the second record, there was a lot of harmony activity."

Herbert was saying the right things, and everybody certainly seemed game: "There's a lot of talent involved in this band. We're ready to try anything," Gregg Rolie told *The Evening Sun* back then. "Yeah," Schon replied, "There are endless possibilities. We're just finding out what they are."

To be honest, so was everyone else.

"Instead of heavy metal, Journey's sound can best be described as heavy space," *Billboard* reviewer **Tom Vickers** wrote in 1976. "Shedding some Latin influences in favor of rock, the group updates the psychedelic openness of the late Sixties **Beatles**, **Dead** and **Airplane** with their own brand of space rock."

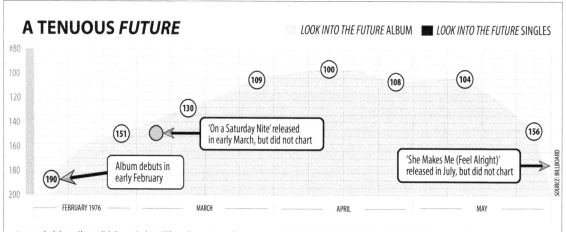

A TENUOUS *FUTURE*

LOOK INTO THE FUTURE ALBUM ■ *LOOK INTO THE FUTURE* SINGLES

'On a Saturday Nite' released in early March, but did not chart

Album debuts in early February

'She Makes Me (Feel Alright)' released in July, but did not chart

SOURCE: BILLBOARD

FEBRUARY 1976 — MARCH — APRIL — MAY

Journey's debut album didn't crack the *Billboard* Top 100 and managed just a short nine-week stay in the *Billboard* 200. With *Look Into the Future*, the band gave it another try and doubled down on the long jams their fans loved. Every song was between four and eight minutes, save for two. "On a Saturday Nite," with a 3:59 run time, was the most commercial song but did not chart. "She Makes Me (Feel Alright)" clocked in at 3:12 but didn't chart either. Although the LP managed to secure a longer stay on the charts—15 weeks—the formula was not working. It still sold to faithful fans, but there were too few of them. AM radio ignored it. FM radio briefly embraced it, but not enough to generate sales. Columbia Records was growing impatient.

Sources: Billboard, Cashbox, Record World

TOP CHARTING WEEK: *BILLBOARD—April 10, 1976*

1. Peter Frampton, *Frampton Comes Alive!*
2. Eagles, *Their Greatest Hits (1971-1975)*
3. Carole King, *Thoroughbred*
4. Bob Dylan, *Desire*
5. Bad Company, *Run With the Pack*
6. Queen, *A Night at the Opera*
7. Gary Wright, *The Dream Weaver*
8. Johnnie Taylor, *Eargasm*
9. David Bowie, *Station to Station*
100. **JOURNEY, *LOOK INTO THE FUTURE***

Look Into the Future arrived in January 1976 with the perfect title, as Journey attempted to retain this progressive feel even as the band moved toward a new song-focused industry standard. "We decided we'd taken that kind of music as far as we could," Gregg Rolie told *Rolling Stone*'s **Ben Fong-Torres**.

The changes just were not as dramatic as needed. Instead, Journey tried to get there by cheating with clever sequencing.

Side One of *Look Into the Future* was home to slightly more radio-friendly fare like "On a Saturday Nite," "Anyway," and their cover of the **George Harrison**-penned "It's All Too Much." Longer tracks like "I'm Gonna Leave You" (which lasted more than seven minutes) and the multi-section title song (their second-longest ever, at 8:13) found a place on Side Two.

The lead single, "On a Saturday Nite," certainly represented a confident move toward a mainstream classic-rock sound. "You're On Your Own" employed the slow-fast approach that would dominate rock a decade and a half later, while "Anyway" found Rolie at his most covetous. Nothing from **The Beatles**' sometimes-lightweight psychedelic period had ever sounded so tough and propulsive as Journey's update of "It's All Too Much."

They were planting seeds of future success—even if initially it would not be their own. Herbert spent years telling anyone who would listen that **Kansas** swiped the idea for "Carry on Wayward Son" from Journey's "I'm Gonna Leave You."

Anyone who'd seen them in concert, however, rightly assumed Journey would quickly begin unwinding these discreet moments. That's who they really were at the time.

"There is no promise that Journey will keep to the tight, rhythmic, tastefully restrained sound on stage," a *Berkeley Gazette* reviewer mused in 1976. "Most likely they will fall into prolonged guitar solos and deteriorate into crashing racket. However, their new album packs a mean punch, and Journey is obviously heading in the right direction."

In the meantime, any progress made in syncing with prevailing sounds had begun to feel too incremental for Columbia Records. "Midnight Dream" could have fit on contemporary album-oriented radio playlists, but it was still more than five minutes long. Rolie built on that accessibility with "She Makes Me (Feel Alright)," but then Schon's metallic outbursts willfully nudged the song back toward hard rock.

"Yes, it was vocal, but it was more improvi-

Austin American-Statesman
February 20, 1976

The Columbia Records information sheet on Journey describes the band's music as "heavy space." What a concept! Deep philosophical questions must follow such a statement. What's heavier than space? Heavy garbage? Light universe? Supernova rock? Just how heavy is space? Fortunately, for Journey, space isn't that heavy. Certainly the band performs hard rock, but the music is controlled and only occasionally becomes absurd. All four band members have reputable past associations. Guitarist Neal Schon and vocalist-organist Gregg Rolie are **Santana** exes. Bassist Ross Valory played with the **Steve Miller Band**, drummer Aynsley Dunbar worked with **Frank Zappa** and **David Bowie**. It would be difficult for four such musicians to miss and *Look Into the Future* is a sharp second effort.

— Kelly Hodge

The Berkley Gazette
February 20, 1976

Journey's debut album a year ago was a journey in the wrong direction. The only thing they accomplished was breaking the sound barrier while standing still. The album was sacrificed to spacey, sometimes brilliant, but always loud, drawn-out guitar solos. On their second stab at success, *Look Into the Future*, they come a lot closer. The first side is by far the strongest with four powerhouse tunes, led by "On a Saturday Nite." There is no promise that Journey will keep to the tight, rhythmic, tastefully restrained sound on stage. Most likely they will fall into prolonged guitar solos and deteriorate into crashing racket. However, their new album packs a mean punch, and Journey is obviously heading in the right direction this time.

— Evan Hosie

Rapid City (S.D.) Journal
March 14, 1976

Some of the steaming energy of early Santana is reborn with the emergence of Journey, whose founding members Gregg Rolie and Neal Schon played with Santana in the great *Abraxas* days. Journey plays mostly straight-ahead, four-man rock, forsaking the Latin percussions of Santana. For those who may have picked up the group's first album, *Journey*, last year, *Look Into the Future* continues on the same path. What I find most likable about Journey is a tendency to slip into the speedy freneticism of groups like REO Speedwagon. Thus far Journey has broken no new ground, but when they stick to the soaring guitar-dominated rock that they do so well, it nicely fills the void left when Carlos Santana went the Mahavishnu Orchestra route.

— Ron Kroese

Journey—the best of the West.
(Not to mention the East, South and North.)

They began their tour in California and released their album in January. And the musical phenomenon that is Journey hasn't slowed down since.

Journey's taken its biting and gutsy brand of rock on the road, coast to coast—breaking club attendance records and setting off standing, dancing ovations every place they've played. Journey's new album, "Look Into the Future," is one of the most heavily-played records on the FM air. And they just keep getting hotter and better and tighter and bigger.

Journey. There's no end in sight.

Journey. "Look Into the Future." Now playing somewhere nearby.

On Columbia Records and Tapes.

Journey decided to dump the curious, spacey theme of their first album design and went with a more mystical feel for their second, *Look Into the Future*. Journey manager **Herbie Herbert**'s then-partner in Spreadeagle Productions, **Lou Bramy**, was credited with the design concept. It featured a crystal ball in the foreground and the four members of Journey spaced in the corners of a long room. The back cover duplicated the look, but replaced band members with glowing silhouettes, as though they had been teleported to another place and time. The inner sleeve had photographs of the band in similar rooms as the cover illustrations. Co-lumbia Records, which went all in with the marketing and advertising on the band's first LP's spacey concept, opted to simply publish a photo of the band (above) with a thumbnail of the album superimposed into Aynsley Dunbar's hands, presumably so that the record-buying public would know what the album looked like. The promotional ads, like every Journey album release before Sony's acquisition of Columbia Records, included a full-page ad for the band in all the major trade publications, including *Billboard*, *Cashbox*, and *Record World*.

sational, more of a jam band, representing sort of the flavor of the San Francisco scene at the time," Ross Valory admitted to *Bass Musician*.

Unfortunately, that scene was proving to be far too local. *Look Into the Future* fared a total of 38 spots better than *Journey* on *Billboard*'s album chart, yet only reached a paltry No. 100.

The cover was conceptualized by early Herbert associate **Louis "Lou" Bramy**, with artwork by **Rick Narin** and photography by **Ethan Russell**. Even Journey couldn't explain its meaning when prompted.

"Don't ask us," Aynsley Dunbar told *Circus*. "With all those album covers, they made Journey look like we were supposed to be the Journies from outer space," Schon added.

Still, in all its extraterrestrial weirdness, the artwork from *Look Into the Future* seemed to tell the truest story of what was inside. "In a sense I think we were like a mini **Mahavishnu** that was more rock 'n' roll, progressive. Definitely progressive fusion rock," Schon told *The Austin Chronicle*. "We were experimenting a lot, but it was very progressive."

They'd eventually widen their gaze. A new era would dawn, and new fans would soon arrive. But a funny thing happened as Steve Perry's subsequent pop-leaning tenure came and went: Rolie successfully carried this sound forward, long after leaving Journey in 1980—and a younger generation's ears received it differently.

His stripped-down version of the title track from *Look Into the Future* emerged as a highlight of Rolie's two-night appearance with guitarist **Alan Haynes** in 2012 at New York City's famed Iridium. Rolie later included the song on an album recorded during the shows, then rearranged "Look Into the Future" to create a new studio version for 2019's *Sonic Ranch*.

Other early favorites like "Kohoutek," "I'm Gonna Leave You," and "Mystery Mountain" became part of Rolie-sung turns with **Journey Through Time** and were subsequently featured on the offshoot band's self-titled 2023 LP. "Of a Lifetime" also provided a signature moment when Rolie came out for an encore in Austin during Journey's 50th anniversary tour.

"We blew up the Internet afterwards," Rolie said. "There was one person who wrote, 'Should I know this song, "Of a Lifetime"? It was awesome.' If you thought Journey started in 1977 when Steve Perry arrived? Well, no, then you wouldn't know." [84, 109, 201, 236, 242, 333, 368, 375, 395, 479, 913]

Cars pull in to park outside the Starwood in West Hollywood, California, on January 24, 1976, where Journey was opening a four-night engagement. The *Los Angeles Times* gave the band solid marks that opening night, though it did ding the group's proclivity for 10-minute instrumentals. The band did earn praise for its choice of including **The Beatles**' "It's All Too Much" in its set.

Longtime Journey tour manager Pat Morrow (right) with roadie John Villanueva (who was credited with naming Journey).

MORROW SCALED JOURNEY LADDER TO LEAD NOCTURNE

Pat **Morrow**'s winding path from music shop employee, to Aynsley Dunbar's drum tech, to Journey road manager, to a founding partner with an industry-leading production firm, began with getting jilted.

"My childhood sweetheart had actually run off with my best friend—and he was a snake to do it," Morrow said. "But he did it and I never have recovered from it."

The New Yorker said his life began to fall apart. "I was starting to drink and get fucked up," he admitted. "Like, I couldn't get myself together in any way."

Then **John Draper**, an old college buddy, called Morrow with a timely job offer. "He's working for Studio Instrument Rentals in San Francisco," Morrow said. "Turns out they do everything for everybody in terms of equipment rentals. So regularly coming through their doors is **The Tubes** and **Santana**, **Azteca**, and **Malo**."

Morrow just had to find a way to get there. "So, my dad—bless him—lends me his Texaco credit card, and he gives me leeway to use it across the country. I've got a '69 Ford pickup with three on the column, and I put everything I own in the fucking bed of the truck. My buddy, who's a carpenter, builds me a little cover for the back of the bed, and I go out west with nothing but a pickup full of bullshit."

At first, Morrow crashed with Draper at Project Artaud, a hippie commune. "I get there on a Sunday, and Monday morning, I'm working at the store," Morrow said. "That was my first day in rock 'n' roll, and I did 46 years before I wasn't working in rock 'n' roll anymore and I retired."

Morrow was at Studio Instrument Rentals when **Herbie Herbert** walked in and changed everything. "Upstairs, they're building a new studio for The Tubes," Morrow said. "Herbie is the guy in charge of putting that together and helping The Tubes out—and he's managing the newly born Journey with Gregg Rolie and Neal Schon."

Soon, Morrow had become part of Herbert's nascent operation. "I go from working in the warehouse as a schlepper and a van driver to becoming the drum roadie for Aynsley Dunbar," Morrow said.

"The only guy that could handle him—this is a true story—was me," Morrow added. "Because I would just deal with him like, 'Hey, you know what? Go fuck yourself. You pull your pants on one leg at a time, like every-fucking-body else, and you can kiss my ass.' But instead of reacting with anger and a temper—he had a bad temper—Aynsley is, like, amazed."

Herbert was impressed with how he handled the Dunbar situation, and quickly promoted Morrow: "My role expanded from a year after tour managing in '74-'75 into kind of the production manager and the leader of a two-man crew that included **Kenny Mednick** doing lights and **Tom Brown** doing the stage and me tour managing, ultimately. I mean, I just gradually took over all the duties."

There was a reason **Herbie Herbert** once called Morrow "my best right hand." As Journey's fixer, he handled everything from travel to security to accounting. Soon, he'd take over Nocturne, Journey's tour production subsidiary. Herbert may have had the big ideas, but Morrow was often the person making them into reality.

Herbert had begun by trying to cut deals for lights, sounds, and trucking, but found Journey could build out their own operations for less. Then they started leasing everything out to other bands. As Journey made the leap to larger venues, Nocturne moved into video production—and that quickly became the company's principal focus.

Morrow had a natural interest in this side of the business as a former student of photography and film at Ohio's Antioch College. Soon, **The Who**, **The Police**, **Judas Priest**, **David Bowie**, and others were under contract.

Yet Morrow remained steadfastly in the shadows. He took a cue from his father, **Hugh Morrow**, the longtime chief of staff for New York governor and U.S. vice president **Nelson Rockefeller**.

"One of the things that I always noticed was my dad kept a very low profile," Morrow said, "and I basically did, too. I mean, I was well known in the business to the other players, promoters and artists and stuff—but I always took a back seat to Herbie."

He also never cared about the money, and Morrow reminded Herbert of that in one of their last conversations before he died in 2021. Morrow said, "All I remember is how much we laughed and the funny, funny, wonderful, funny shit we got to do—and it's true," Morrow said. "I mean, it's like running away to the circus."

Still, there was one iron-clad rule while out on the road: Cocaine was off limits. "Everybody knew if you're wired, you're fired," Morrow said. "We were a pot band, you know. We were reefer and beer. That was Journey. We never even had whiskey after Aynsley."

Morrow continued in this role until the early 1980s, when he said a disagreement with Perry led to his shift to Nocturne. "Herbie was very sweet to me," Morrow said. "He moved me sideways, increased my salary and put me in charge of the production company—but from the office of Journey."

Steve Clark, The Babys' tour manager, initially took over. Then, in an appropriate twist, **Benny Collins** later succeeded him after serving as drum tech for Steve Smith.

Morrow branched out into band management after Herbert's retirement in the early 1990s, first with **Steve Miller**. He remained with Nocturne until the turn of the 2000s, while also working with **Night Ranger**, **Tower of Power**, and **Huey Lewis**, among others. His relationship with Journey had ended when Herbert's did.

"You know, Herbie retired and got pushed out by Perry, and the band went on to be managed by **Irving [Azoff]** and others—and, you know, it all fell apart from then on for me," Morrow said. "I stopped having an interest in the band in about '95, '96. It just wasn't my band anymore. But, you know, whether it's romance or business, things don't last."

Morrow's old pal, John Draper, worked in Journey's video department before also becoming a tour manager, overseeing dates with **Madonna**, **Michael Jackson**, and others. "He was responsible for turning my life around and getting me out of New York," Morrow added. "If I'd stayed in New York, I'd probably be down in the Bowery drinking right now." [894, 927, 930, 931, 932, 934, 935]

CAIN ARRIVES WITH DEBUT LP, *WINDY CITY BREAKDOWN*

PATHWAY ALBUM
Jonathan Cain

Windy City Breakdown
Bearsville Records
April 1977

The good news for future Journey member Jonathan Cain: Legendary manager and talent scout **Albert Grossman** caught a performance of the **Jonathan Cain Band** at a bar and signed them to Bearsville Records in 1976.

Turns out, he shared Cain's Chicago hometown, and had even gone to the same school, Roosevelt University.

The bad news? Grossman wanted the Los Angeles-based Cain to record this debut album at his label's in-house studio in upstate New York.

"I said, 'Why can't we just do it here? It would be so much easier,'" Cain remembered in a talk with journalist **Randy Patterson**. "We had several studios we could have done it at" closer to home. Grossman insisted, and as Cain said in the documentary *A Better Man: The Faith Journey of Jonathan Cain:* "Everything that could have went wrong kinda went wrong."

The New York sessions got underway in the heat of summer, but Cain said the conditions were less than ideal. The air conditioning was out, they kept running out of tape, then the tape machines would break, he lamented. Then the unremitting summer rains made the rehearsal rooms too steamy for any work to get done. Cain was also certain the place was haunted.

He and the others started slipping away to New York City to party. "After feeling stuck in the wilderness for days," Cain wrote in his autobiography, *Don't Stop Believin',* "we all began to go a little nuts."

Windy City Breakdown ended up having a lot more in common with yacht rock than anything Cain did during his subsequent tenures in **The Babys** or Journey. He sensed Grossman's growing disapproval and asked him to come to the Chateau Marmont in West Hollywood for a meeting.

"First he got me stoned—good and high—and then he told me that he didn't like my record and he wasn't going to put it out," Cain told Patterson. Frustrated and angry, Cain stormed out, contacted his lawyer and they forced *Windy City Breakdown* onto store shelves in April 1977.

The album tanked, and Bearsville Records dropped Cain. Criticism came from all sides. Cain told *Creem* that he ran into **Foghat** manager **Tony Outeda**, and Outeda openly wondered whether Cain should have handed vocal duties over to a bandmate who had a higher voice. Cain pushed back, hard: "I say, 'The guy with the high voice ain't got the balls to sing. I'm the fuckin' singer.'"

Cain's bravado would not last. He made another pass at solo stardom, recording a demo with **Steve Lukather** of **Toto**, **James Taylor** bassist **Leland Sklar**, and future Journey touring drummer **Mike Baird** at Studio 55. But Cain got no further label interest, temporarily ending what had already been a five-year quest for stardom in Los Angeles.

"I got a day job selling stereos," Cain said in the *A Better Man* documentary. Then English singer-songwriter **Robbie Patton** contacted Cain about co-writing some songs. Patton had also heard that The Babys were auditioning new keyboard players. Cain would not be selling hi-fi equipment much longer. [54, 234, 246, 247]

Perry as a blend of **Jefferson Starship**'s **Marty Balin** and singer-songwriter **Jesse Colin Young**. "When I first heard his tape," Herbert told San Francisco music writer **Joel Selvin** back then, "I went through the roof—and it's an 18-foot ceiling." [47, 67, 80, 109, 149, 209, 248, 386, 410, 552]

SPRING–SUMMER 1977

RELEASES
▶ **Jonathan Cain**, *Windy City Breakdown* (album)

NUGGETS
▶ Journey's "Spaceman" makes it to the playlists in Chicago and St. Louis, but two months later, it's not getting airplay anywhere else. —*Cashbox*
▶ Reflecting back on why he replaced Aynsley Dunbar in **John Mayall**'s band, **Mick Fleetwood** said that Dunbar, while a great drummer, was getting too complicated for the music that Mayall was doing. —*Record World*
▶ Fresh off producing **Dusty Springfield**'s comeback album at L.A.'s Cherokee Studios, veteran producer **Roy Thomas Baker** will be helping Journey produce and engineer their upcoming LP, *Infinity*. Baker's recent deal with Columbia brings some economy and affordability, and the decision to bring the famed producer to the studio is driven by veteran Columbia exec **Mike Dilbeck**. —*Billboard*

ON THE ROAD
▶ **Journey**, with .38 Special, Atlanta Rhythm Section, Boston, Captain Beyond, the Charlie Daniels Band, Electric Light Orchestra, Emerson, Lake & Palmer, Hard Tommy, Judas Priest, Nils Lofgren, Lynyrd Skynyrd, John Miles, Manfred Mann's Earth Band, Ted Nugent, Pousette-Dart Band, REO Speedwagon, Southside Johnny & The Asbury Jukes, Starcastle, Styx, Edgar Winter, the Womack Brothers, and Gary Wright.

Ponty Brings Smith Into Studio For Innovative *Enigmatic Ocean*

Steve Smith's recording career predated his debut on Journey's 1979 album, *Evolution*. It even predated his time playing rock music.

Instead, Smith came off the road with fusion violinist **Jean-Luc Ponty** to complete a jazz-leaning record with sweeping prog-rock pretensions. Issued on September 1, 1977, *Enigmatic Ocean* opens with an overture and two short pieces before giving way to not one but two lengthy multipart suites.

"I wanted to connect in a way that wasn't evident and it wasn't easy at first," Ponty later told arts writer **Danny Coleman**, "but little by little it changed. So, that was my goal."

Four records into his tenure with Atlantic Records, fans had gotten a handle on Ponty's unique vision. They made *Enigmatic Ocean* a landmark LP, as Ponty soared into the *Billboard* Top 40. For Smith, this was a landmark for another reason.

"Because it's the first album that I ever recorded!" said Smith, then in his seventh semester at Berklee. "I had done a little bit of recording when I was coming up in Boston, but it was the first time I was ever in the studio playing on a complete album."

They began by charting everything out. "Jean-Luc had us learn new music, as all good musicians did back then, by writing charts," Smith added. "There were no computer demos in those days. He wrote very good charts for all of us and left room for us to interpret his music."

There were also no overdubs, Smith added. "We played live in the studio and you hear our performances as they happened."

"The albums got a lot of success, even beyond my hopes," Ponty admitted to Coleman. "We got a chance to be picked up by progressive rock radio, jazz radio, different formats, and a lot of college and university radio."

Smith learned later that his association with Ponty would bring him to Journey's doorstep. Turns out, "they came to see Ponty when we played at the Aurora Ballroom in Cleveland," Smith said, though he admitted that "I hadn't really developed a rock style yet." Smith would start building toward that after joining **Ronnie Montrose**'s band. [3, 5, 249]

With Journey's third album, Columbia Records focused on building an identity for the band. The label had taken out elaborate full-page ads in the trade press for Journey's debut album and *Look Into the Future*, but band manager **Herbie Herbert** conceded that the bulk of their sales were coming from the band's fans, especially those who closely identified with their former groups—namely, **Santana**, the **Steve Miller Band**, and **Frank Zappa and The Mothers of Invention**. Advertising and promotions for *Next*, like the full-page ad above in *Billboard*, aimed to get radio stations identifying the band as more than just the parts of their previous groups. The hope was that deejays would help fans get on a first-name basis with the group. It worked to some degree as *Next* charted higher than either of the previous two albums, but long-jam albums were falling out of favor and Columbia gave Journey an ultimatum—write some hit singles or find another label. The band would address that ultimatum soon.

Success Elusive As Journey's Musical Path Shifts

Journey was already moving toward their platinum-selling future when *Next* arrived in February 1977, focusing on shorter tracks and a more varied vocal approach.

Too often, however, they still slipped back into old habits: "Jamming," Neal Schon admitted to **Ben Fong-Torres**, "was the easiest thing we could do."

The result was an occasionally unsorted album that attempted to pair atmospheric **Pink Floyd**-inspired songs like "Spaceman" with the romping **Deep Purple**-ish "Hustler." (The latter featured some of Aynsley Dunbar's most salacious lyrics: *"Screamin' women love me, just can't resist. ... So lock up your women, like you know you should."*)

The waking-dream quality of "Here We Are" sits uncomfortably beside edgy fusion asides like "Nickel and Dime." "I Would Find You" is the closest *Next* gets to their subsequent incarnation's soaring anthems, but none of it played like a hit single.

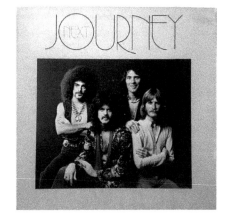

It wasn't for lack of trying: They were out on the road some nine months out of the year. "We had built this cult audience in quite a few places, because we had toured extensively for three years, and very hard," Schon told *Goldmine*.

The only problem? Journey's records were still bombing. *Next* reached Journey's highest chart position to date. As a sign of how poorly things were going, however, the LP only got to No. 85.

Rolie argued that *Next* was simply ahead of its time: "You know, a lot of metal players connected with that album," he said. "Songs like 'Hustler'—I wrote the music for that—had such a rough edge to it. They picked up on that stuff."

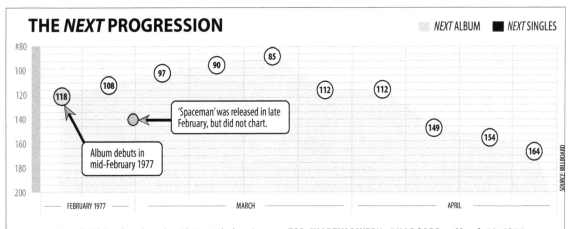

THE *NEXT* PROGRESSION　　　　　　　　▨ *NEXT* ALBUM　■ *NEXT* SINGLES

118　Album debuts in mid-February 1977

'Spaceman' was released in late February, but did not chart.

SOURCE: BILLBOARD

FEBRUARY 1977　　　　　MARCH　　　　　APRIL

Journey tinkered with its album formula with *Next*. The long jams that were so inspirational to concertgoers needed to translate to album sales, so with the new LP, so they began shifting to somewhat shorter, more commercial songs. Four-and-a-half-minute songs replaced the six-minute-plus songs, but the commercial viability was still missing. The album debuted on the *Billboard* 200 in mid-February at #118, and the band finally cracked the Top 100 albums in early March, but *Next* sputtered after that, peaking at #85 in mid-March. Progress was made—a positive sign for a band on its third album. But the execs at Columbia Records were nearly out of patience, and manager **Herbie Herbert** set out to adjust the formula yet again.
Sources: Billboard

TOP CHARTING WEEK: *BILLBOARD—March 19, 1977*

1. Barbra Streisand & Kris Kristofferson, *A Star is Born* (soundtrack)
2. Fleetwood Mac, *Rumours*
3. Pink Floyd, *Animals*
4. Eagles, *Hotel California*
5. Stevie Wonder, *Songs in the Key of Life*
6. The Steve Miller Band, *Fly Like an Eagle*
7. Boston, *Boston*
8. John Denver, *John Denver's Greatest Hits, Volume 2*
9. George Benson, *In Flight*
138. JOURNEY, *NEXT*

Yet **Herbie Herbert** once again thought he heard Journey's best ideas put to better use elsewhere: "Nickel and Dime," he argued in an interview with **Matthew Carty**, formed the musical basis for **Rush**'s "Tom Sawyer."

Schon said Columbia Records finally issued an ultimatum, instructing Journey to add a true front man or risk losing their deal. They'd had enough of the band's incrementalism—and Herbert wholeheartedly agreed. "By the third album," Herbert told *Rolling Stone*, "the group was vocally prepared to support a new musician who would have equal proficiency with the voice to Neal as a guitarist or Aynsley as a drummer."

He pointed specifically to their newly varied approach on *Next*, which found Schon singing "Karma" and "I Would Find You." "It was very vocally oriented," Herbert said in the *Music of the Night* documentary. "The stage was then perfectly set."

First, however, came some decidedly tough love. Herbert said they had to work on composing. "You guys are a bunch of zeros," he remembered telling Journey's original quartet in the *Rolling Stone* interview. They also had to work on their stage presence. "You don't wanna move a muscle," he added. "A few facial expressions and Neal in his little velvet suit. That was it." He

The wild, mystical spacey themes that drove Journey's first two album covers were ditched for a less elaborate approach for their third LP, simply titled *Next*. Art director **Bruce Steinberg** used a studio portrait of the band for the cover, which was more routine for a mid-1970s rock album, but it gave fans a better look at the band than their first album package. Steinberg's back cover (inset) offered a similar friendly shot of the quartet laughing on a hilltop field. The inner sleeve and liner notes included song lyrics. They thanked the recording studio, His Master's Wheels, in San Francisco, mastering engineer **Bruce Botnick** (with a nod to CBS exec **Mike Dilbeck**), and, among many others, their manager **Herbie Herbert**. But there was still one more novelty in the package: a winged triangle design printed on the sleeve's opposite side, which was attributed only to "Mansfield." The triangular illustration may have been the first attempt at a band logo.

bluntly informed them: "You can't sing."

Unfortunately, not everybody in Journey was ready for change. "Myself," Schon admitted to the *Arizona Republic*, "I was completely happy where we were." Future lead singer Steve Perry absolutely sensed that when he arrived. "I can't speak for them," Perry told *GQ*, "but I'm sure that if they could have been successful the way they originally set out to be, that would have been fine with them."

Schon also felt Journey had finally made headway opening for **Lynyrd Skynyrd** in 1976. "It was more a guitar-jamming audience and they just ate it up," Schon told the *Republic*. "They loved us. Everywhere we played with Skynyrd, we were commanding two, three encores."

Schon thought they were on the right track, despite Columbia Records' ominous misgivings. "I went, 'Wow, so it's just finding the right audience,'" Schon added, "and right about that time, the label came to us and said, 'If you don't get a new front man and write some radio-oriented songs ...'"

Journey tried out **Robert Fleischman** in the

The mysterious "Mansfield" artwork printed on the inside sleeve of the *Next* album may have been an attempt at a band logo before one existed. Feathers and wings eventually became part of many of the Journey artworks developed by Stanley Mouse and Alton Kelley starting with the *Infinity* LP.

summer of 1977, before hiring Perry. Then Lynyrd Skynyrd's tour plane went down on October 20, 1977. "How tragic for those guys. They were such great people, too," Schon told *The Austin Chronicle*. "Out of that, **Kevin Elson**, their sound mixer, we met him. He was one of the survivors on that plane."

Elson started doing live sound for Journey before coming on board as co-producer for 1980's *Departure*. He then produced or co-produced *Dream, After Dream, Captured, Escape, Frontiers,* and *Generations,* as well as the concert album *Escape & Frontiers Live in Japan*.

When Perry left the band for good in the late 1990s, Journey occasionally returned to some of their earliest songs—including "Hustler" from *Next*. By then, Jonathan Cain had taken over for Rolie, updating some of Dunbar's original lyrics.

"No offense to Aynsley, but I just wouldn't sing those," Cain told *Melodic Rock*. "Then I found out that Gregg had a big problem singing them. I said, 'Too bad I wasn't around.' I would have fixed them for him." [2, 56, 80, 109, 180, 236, 242, 913, 914, 915]

....

Record World
February 5, 1977

Journey's sound has grown in refinement with each new release, *Next* representing its third LP in as many years. A spacey, hard-rock quartet, an underlying good-time feeling stems from not taking the bizarre too seriously. "Hustler," "Here We Are," and "Next" express that sentiment.

San Francisco Examiner
February 13, 1977

The third album by the Bay Area hard rock champs, *Next* shows considerable progress from the group's first two efforts. Vocals have been emphasized, and shorter, more tightly arranged songs are substituted for the lengthy cuts that dominated the first two releases. Neal Schon still supplies the fiery guitar solos but also debuts credibly on this album as a lead vocalist.

— Andy Low

Tucson Citizen
February 15, 1977

With Journey's latest album, *Next*, the band's determination soars fast and unfettered on acid-tinged wings. The group continues looking a bit forward to an electronic future, with more songs full of synthesizer seedings that may be cultivated in upcoming productions. "I Would Find You," guitarist Neal Schon's only vocal, is an especially impressive meld of past and present, flavored by the future. The rest of the tracks, with keyboardist Gregg Rolie handling the words, are ever slightly more civilized— but scarcely enough to inhibit Schon's free-living guitar solos.

— Chuck Graham

A FRONT MAN CHANGED JOURNEY, BUT NOT STEVE PERRY

Herbie Herbert moved quickly to install a front man in Journey's lineup, tracking down a singer who had recently done a showcase for Columbia Records. Los Angeles–born Robert Fleischman did not have much of a resume yet, but he had a big voice in keeping with a new wave of bands like **Boston**, **Foreigner**, and **Styx** that would soon dominate the airwaves.

He was part of a larger shift in direction: "I went to the label and begged them not to drop the act," Herbert later told author **Neil Daniels**. He offered to "change to a pop formula, and we'll get a lead singer."

Then he latched onto Fleischman, who had a fan in the head of Columbia's A&R department. Fleischman took part in weeks of rehearsals held at Studio Instrumental Rentals, across the street from CBS Studios in San Francisco. He stayed with Gregg Rolie.

"In the beginning, it really worked out well," Fleischman later told *BAM Magazine*. "We really got on well, and there was a free flow of ideas." Turned out, Fleischman also had a flair for songwriting that would gird Journey's subsequent album.

"It's a whole new ballgame," Ross Valory told the somewhat circumspect San Francisco music writer **Joel Selvin** back then. With the addition of Fleischman, Selvin argued, "Journey now sounds like some British import model rock band, with the soaring glee club harmo-nies than the retooled version of early **Santana** the band started out as."

They hit the road together, playing a long string of dates with **Emerson, Lake & Palmer**. "We started writing some songs, and it started growing," Fleischman later told radio host **Sheldon Snow**. "There was a chemistry there."

So why did Fleischman only last in Journey from June through October 1977? He says he was under contract with **Barry Fey** and could not get management details worked out. Herbert and others say Fleischman began to struggle with his newfound fame.

"He got LSD right away—lead singer disease," Selvin said. "He started diva-ing around, and that just wasn't popular with that crowd. Believe it or not, given what happened to them later, they were pretty egalitarian. It was a very crew-heavy scene, with Herbie and [road manager] **Pat** [**Morrow**] having come up out of the ranks. The diva thing was just not acceptable."

Meanwhile, disgruntled fans of Journey's early jam-band sound were reportedly flipping off Fleischman from the front row. He has allowed that "there were problems. I toured with them for months, really exhausting work, wrote a lot of songs that I think really changed the musical direction of the band," he told *BAM*. "Unfortunately, I never got to record them."

Fleischman unknowingly came face to face with his replacement on July 10, 1977 at

Soldier Field. He was introduced to Steve Perry, who watched their performance from the side of the stage—but the crew lied about who Journey's next singer really was. "So, Fleischman had made himself sort of unpopular in the band in very short order," Selvin said, "then they showed up with someone they introduced as [Journey roadie] **Johnny Villanueva**'s Portuguese cousin."

Perry continued traveling with Journey, and in one remarkable moment, they even managed to sneak Perry on stage before a show in California.

"They told Robert Fleischman during sound check that he had a radio interview, which was bullshit," said **Josh Ramos**, guitarist on Fleischman's 2005 album *World in Your Eyes*. "They needed him gone so that they could bring Steve on."

Selvin added: "They maneuvered Fleischman out of the hall at Long Beach during sound check, then put Perry up for three songs. Herbie said it was over halfway through the first song." Ironically, one of the tracks Perry sang, in what amounted to an audition, was an unreleased song Fleischman co-wrote called "All For You."

Journey and Fleischman parted, while their relationship with Perry continued to grow. Herbert told **Ben Fong-Torres** that Fleischman "gave me some static about not getting enough of the spotlight" after a concert, "and I said, 'You're gone. Adios.'"

Later in August, Schon and Perry wrote "Patiently" in a hotel room—a lightning-bolt moment for Schon, who had been unsure about adding a front man.

"I remember the first night that Steve Perry came onstage with us, and we played a couple of the songs that we had written. The audience was like, 'I don't know about that,'" Schon told *Goldmine*. "It was so different that it really kind of threw them off course, you know."

Schon seemed to have started out in their camp, but then their collaboration blossomed.

"We sat down … and I had these chords for 'Patiently,' and he just started singing and writing lyrics," Schon added. They completed "Patiently" in 45 minutes. "Lights" came next, and Schon said the song happened even faster.

"It was just pretty much listening to him sing and me humming a few things, and organizing the chords, the arrangement, and adding a few sections," he told *Goldmine*. "That was that."

Perry was officially in the band by October. Meanwhile, an understandably embittered

Less than two years after being dropped by Journey, Robert Fleischman reappeared with a solo album, *Perfect Stranger*, released by Arista Records in 1979. Fleischman cultivated strong backing support for the album, including getting **Jimmy Iovine** to produce the record. Journey members Greg Rolie and Neal Schon provided keyboards and guitar work, and Fleetwood Mac bassist **John McVie** pitched in too. *Record World* gave his single, "All for You," a strong review and compared it favorably to **Boston**. But neither the single nor the LP caught on.

Fleischman saw 1978's *Infinity* arrive with three songs he had co-written. "Journey," Fleischman matter-of-factly told *BAM* a year later, "was a stepping stone."

He put out a largely ignored solo debut called *Perfect Stranger*, which included an update of "All For You." But Fleischman's heart did not seem to be in it, even back then.

"What I'd really like to do," Fleischman added, "is join another band. I'm really not comfortable carrying the whole thing on my shoulders. I kind of feel naked and exposed."

Fleischman did just that, collaborating in the mid-1980s with an ex-**KISS** guitarist in the **Vinnie Vincent Invasion**. Journey's version of "All For You," now simply titled "For You," was not officially released until *Time*[3] arrived in 1992. By then, Fleischman had also briefly been part of **Asia** during their embryonic stage.

Fleischman said Schon was initially very angry about his termination, a notion bolstered by the guitarist's appearance on *Perfect Stranger*. Herbert confirmed it years later: "When I put Steve Perry in the band, Neal Schon was not even on speaking terms with me, 'cause that guy hated [Perry] so much," Herbert told **Matthew Carty**. "He flat out didn't want him. I flat out knew he was the guy." [60, 66, 109, 145, 242, 257, 405, 466]

OPENED THE DOOR

Journey was evolving. After three unsuccessful albums, a commitment to musical change was required. Songs got shorter and a dynamic new singer arrived. Now they would have to learn to sing, play, record, and, most importantly, write together. The chemistry was there, and success was just around the corner.

WINTER 1977–78

RELEASES

▶ **Journey**, *Infinity* (album)

NUGGETS

▶ Journey has added Steve Perry on vocals, and the band is releasing a new LP entitled *Infinity*. It was produced by **Roy Thomas Baker**. —*Cashbox*

▶ Journey and **Sandy Welch** double up at the Old Waldorf in San Francisco. Journey has recently been augmented by the addition of lead vocalist Steve Perry, whose rounded tones are supplemented at times by the throatier vocals of keyboardist Gregg Rolie, who formerly carried the vocal load for the band. The group also teamed recently for the first time with **Queen**'s producer **Roy Thomas Baker**, who produced the just-released Columbia package *Infinity*. —*Billboard*

▶ Journey is introduced by **Wolfman Jack** and plays a three-song set on the NBC late-night show, *Midnight Special*. Ross Valory welcomes viewers, and gives way to Steve Perry who introduces the night's second performer, **Eddie Money**. —*NBC*

ON THE ROAD

▶ **Journey**, with Caldera, Eddie Money, Greg Kihn Band, Montrose, Sandy Welch, Santana, and Starwood.

Journey, Perry Start New Era At San Francisco's Old Waldorf

Journey briefly returned to its original four-man lineup after Robert Fleischman's departure. Then they brought out Steve Perry for an encore in early October 1977 that would permanently alter the band's trajectory.

"Dressed in all white, dark-haired Perry sang two tunes from an upcoming album, currently being recorded," longtime San Francisco music critic **Joel Selvin** wrote a couple of days later. "He appeared fully confident and poised, and sang with considerable power."

Neal Schon came to love the surprising soul influences that Perry brought to their sound. "Anybody that ever listens to Sam Cooke would go, 'Wow, that guy sounds like Steve Perry,' if they didn't know about him—but really it's the other way around," Schon told *Billboard*, "and God bless Steve for that."

Among the career-shifting tracks Journey played as part of this sold-out multi-evening stand at San Francisco's 600-seat Old Waldorf was one that Selvin incorrectly guessed was titled "The Lights of the City." But like Fleischman before him, Perry was not warmly greeted by fans waiting for Schon's latest flurry of notes.

Selvin praised Journey's ability to refine their approach in this intimate setting, as well as the band's growing confidence in using stacked vocals. Even then, however, Perry's arrival appeared to be career altering. Selvin noted that Perry might "add the long-missing X-factor."

He did, of course. "When you look at their history, going back to **Santana**, these are guys that really had chops," said well-known classic rock radio executive **John Gorman**. "I thought Journey on their own was a good band, but they were still kind of looking, you know? They were trying to find their way, post-Santana. Afterwards, when they found Perry, I mean that became one of the bands of the year, without a doubt."

Perry's appearance at the Old Waldorf culminated in a lengthy side-stage apprenticeship that doubled as an opportunity to get to know one another. At first, "I wasn't completely sold" Rolie admitted about Perry in an interview for Journey's *Time³* box set. "I don't think anybody was."

Then Perry borrowed Ross Valory's bass on August 13 and played a portion of the song that would become "Lights" while backstage at the Swing Auditorium in San Bernardino. As the reformulated group joined voices in harmony, Rolie said "it dawned on me right then that this could really be great." Five days later, Perry and Schon wrote their first song together.

Various sources, including the liner notes for *Time³*, place Perry's official debut date on October 28. But Selvin's original review appeared on October 3, 1977, followed by a student-written piece in the *Stanford Daily* on October 6. Most importantly, Journey's addition of a front man was the hook they needed. Going forward, the person holding the microphone, whether it was Steve Perry or not, would dominate headlines. "Everybody has to have this focus when they write about a band," Rolie said. "They have to have a focal point, always a focal point—so they can make the headline. They design what the band is by their headline. And then you go, 'Well, that's not quite true but OK, we're getting somewhere.' It happens all the time, and that's what happened with us."

Fleischman was sent packing, a switch he described as a backroom deal to curry favor. Columbia Records had obviously lost faith in Journey, but Fleischman argued there was also too much at stake with Perry. Label A&R rep **Michael Dilbeck** was funding Steve Perry's demos, Fleischman later told radio host **Sheldon Snow**. "He really wanted Steve to have a great band behind him. So, he kept bugging **Herbie [Herbert]** about Steve Perry."

Herbert countered that he had never gotten over hearing those demos, which Perry had recorded with his doomed pre-fame band **Alien Project**. In fact, Herbert said Journey's next singer was on his mind even while he was on the way to sign a deal with Fleischman. "I was crossing the Golden Gate Bridge," Herbert said in 1984's *Music of the Night* documentary, "and I thought about Steve Perry."

Whatever the reasoning, "they had to ease Fleischman out," Selvin said. "They were doing these benefits at the Old Waldorf for NORML, the National Organization for the Reform of Marijuana Laws—a cause dear to Herbie's heart. They bring Perry out for the encore. It was instantly obvious: 'Oh my God, this is the missing part. This should do it!'" [60, 169, 236, 242, 251, 252, 290, 375, 410, 410, 416]

Three Albums Later, Journey Finds an Iconic Band Image

Skeptics at Columbia wanted to hear Journey's new music first.

"When Journey's A&R man flew to CBS headquarters in New York City with the nearly completed track of 'Lights,' we all knew we had a star lead singer—finally!—and a hit track," said **Bob Sherwood**, the label's senior vice president in charge of promotion. "That's when their overall company treatment and support moved from successful AOR band to potential superstar status. This meant prioritizing all as-

Journey's signature look first appeared on the band's fourth album cover, *Infinity*. The artwork was developed by the renowned San Francisco duo of **Stanley Mouse** and **Alton Kelley**, who spent "a couple of months" on the cover while working on other projects. This signature look would endure over five decades.

pects of their career."

They dispatched in-house Columbia Records designer **Tommy Steele** to discuss cover ideas with **Herbie Herbert**, who had used a rotating group of artists to complete the sleeves on Journey's first LPs. The results ranged from flimsy (1975's *Journey*) and weird (1976's *Look Into the Future*) to rudimentary (1977's *Next*).

Herbert had since brought in the new team of **Alton Kelley** and **Stanley Mouse**, underground San Francisco artists who would update Journey's image for a new era. Ross Valory made the introductions. **Jim Welch** would soon come on board as Journey's art director.

Some combination of this trio shaped the art on a career-defining run of albums, beginning with Journey's most elaborate cover yet. *Infinity* featured the earth and moon set among multicolored wings, with a surrounding infinity symbol spelling out the band name.

"When this artwork came in, we were all blown away," Steele said. "I recall it being a rather large piece of art and was really impressed with the painterly craftsmanship."

Mouse said he and Kelley worked "maybe a couple of months" on the cover, which was defined by its Möbius Strip or sideways figure eight. He remembered getting paid "probably about $3,000. Nowadays, it would be like 10 times that amount."

Born Stanley George Miller in 1940 in Fresno, California, Mouse was the son of an artist who had worked on *Snow White and the Seven Dwarfs*. He grew up in Detroit, where this Disney connection led to a new grade school nickname. Soon, he would become well known for drawing mice too.

Kelley was a mechanic turned artist who crossed paths with Mouse when he brought in a broken-down 1965 Porsche after returning to California. They founded Mouse Studios in a converted firehouse in San Francisco where **Janis Joplin** had once rehearsed with **Big Brother and the Holding Company**.

An East Coast transplant, Kelley had a font of ideas. Mouse was a tireless creator. Hundreds of psychedelic-era rock posters would emerge from their South Haight workspace, including one featuring **The Grateful Dead**'s soon-to-be-iconic skull and roses.

"The first one we did for [them], we spelled their name wrong. We wrote great, like G-R-E-A-T," Mouse revealed, with a laugh. "Well, that's how they should have spelled their name!"

The connection provided a basis for Columbia Records' only reservation with Journey's new hire, though the issue was quickly resolved.

"We only hoped that Stanley's artwork wasn't too much affiliated stylistically with his work for The Grateful Dead," Steele said. "It turns out not to have been a factor as Journey had its separate fan base and *Infinity* sold three-times platinum—which was incredibly successful in those days and the best sales to date."

The back cover of *Infinity*, which pictured Journey amid a hearty laugh, was shot by L.A. rock photographer **Sam Emerson**. Steele said Herbert likely selected the image, which Steele then completed by repeating the Möbius Strip. "I merely had to compose that photo and get it retouched," he said, "with the complete Journey *Infinity* logo at the top."

In time, however, Steele began to have second thoughts about the photograph. "Seems like the back cover image was too playful in hindsight, more of an outtake," he said. "They might have been better served if they had picked a more

iconic rock group photo—but that's what was chosen and that's how it printed."

Welch had links with The Grateful Dead too. His ad agency was hired to work as art directors for promoter **Bill Graham**'s shows, including a career-turning double-headliner featuring **The Who** and the Dead. Welch later became The Grateful Dead's art and merchandising director.

Herbert, an inveterate Deadhead, was bound to enter their lives. "He asked me to help him realize his vision of developing the band's image and merchandising," Welch later told interviewer **Scott Sullivan**.

Kelley, Mouse, and Welch would continue to refine and sharpen Journey's image, both together and apart. Welch stayed the longest, working on band and solo projects like Steve Perry's *Street Talk* and Neal Schon's *Vortex* over the years. Kelley died in 2008, but Mouse remained a creative force through the 1990s for Journey and other projects. [420, 581, 582, 584, 585, 817, 928]

Tour Begins with Montrose, and a Refocused Steve Smith

Steve Smith was making a musical shift from jazz and fusion toward rock when Journey asked his new boss to serve as an opening act on their tour in support of *Infinity*. **Ronnie Montrose** would play after **Van Halen** during a string of concerts that began on January 20, 1978, the same day Journey's first album with Steve Perry arrived on store shelves.

Journey discovered a drummer who had transformed himself into a rock guy. Neal Schon came to love Smith's musicality, and the way "he thinks outside of the box," the guitarist told *Ultimate Classic Rock*'s **Matt Wardlaw**. "He thinks drums, [so] everything he plays, he's meant to play. There's not too much that happens by accident with that man on drums."

Ronnie Montrose was also transitioning to something new. He had discarded the more song-focused approach from when **Sammy Hagar** was fronting the **Montrose** band for music that pushed toward new frontiers.

"Ronnie Montrose had just put out a solo album called *Open Fire*, an instrumental record

Continued on Page 83

ROY THOMAS BAKER GUIDED JOURNEY'S *INFINITY* SOUND

Roy **Thomas Baker** first encountered the concept of layering sounds long before it became a standard studio trick. As a young staffer at Decca in the early 1960s, Baker learned on primitive four-track recording machines.

He later remembered meeting Gregg Rolie, Neal Schon, and Aynsley Dunbar during an embryonic stint at Trident, working with Dunbar on **Frank Zappa** sessions, and Rolie and Schon with **Santana**. By then, Baker had graduated to eight-track technology.

He began working with **Queen**, having sharpened his studio skills to the point where Baker knew to use Scotch 250 tape in winter and Ampex in the summer, because Scotch did not convey so much heat-related studio static. He helmed sessions for 1975's *A Night at the Opera* at multiple studios, with roadies running Queen's tapes from facility to facility to combine overdubs. Endless overdubs would actually end up wearing out the tape, but Queen seemed to intuitively understand that achieving their operatic goals required this painstaking process.

With his next group, though, Baker had to start over. "Journey didn't know enough about multitrack guitaring and vocals," he told *Recording Producer Engineer* magazine. At one point during his initial sessions

with the band, a *Minneapolis Star* reporter watched as Baker sat idly by for almost an hour of Ross Valory's off-key attempts at background vocals, content in the knowledge that he could fix it all simply by doubling or tripling the Journey bassist's voice.

"Roy has enabled us to pull off some ideas we really wanted to do, like multitracking vocals," new front man Steve Perry told the *Pittsburgh Press* back then. "It gives the appearance of being loud when it really isn't. It gives us the strength and width of when we're playing live."

Once again, Robert Fleischman said he played a key role, despite having only spent a matter of months with Journey prior to Perry's tenure. "Before I left, I introduced the band to Roy Thomas Baker, who was the producer of Queen," Fleischman told *Richmond Magazine*. "That's how they got Roy to produce their first big album, *Infinity*."

None of Journey's three pre-Perry albums had gotten any higher than No. 85. With Baker, 1978's *Infinity* went all the way to No. 21. "We did so many different things on that record that I'd never tried, or even thought about doing," Schon told the *San Francisco Examiner*. "I learned a lot from Roy."

Journey's follow-up to the ground-breaking *Infinity* was the three-times-platinum

Baker-produced smash *Evolution* in 1979, which spawned their breakthrough Top 20 hit, "Lovin', Touchin', Squeezin'." Nothing would ever be the same for the band.

Baker's initial goal was simply to match the dynamism of their live shows, but it was not the only one. "Secondly, the songs had to be more commercialized—i.e., no million-bar-long self-indulgent guitar solos, which bore everyone silly," he later told *Recording Producer Engineer*. "Things had to be more to the point, like nice big choruses of vocals and big guitars."

In this way, Baker set a template for every success that followed.

The *Infinity* sessions unfolded at **Elliott Mazer**'s comically dilapidated His Master's Wheels Studio in San Francisco. The place was infested with rats and fleas, and bad wiring ran through open doors. "If any trucks went past," Baker added, "you had to stop. One night, it was windy and the roof started flapping, so they put bricks on it."

The setting ended up exacerbating Baker's idiosyncrasies. He mic'ed up Schon's Marshall amp with a Fender Stratocaster for "Lights," then "had me set up in a closet and the amp was cranked to 10," Schon told *Vulture*. "The mic was sitting in the back of the very echoey room."

Baker had been an engineer at Decca, but receded from that role as time went on. **Mike Stone** eventually emerged as a key engineering partner on Queen's *A Night at the Opera*. Queen then took over production duties before officially sharing them again with Stone for 1977's *News of the World*. By then, Baker was shifting over to Journey, with **Geoff Workman** serving as his engineer for *Infinity* and *Evolution*.

Many of the same studio tricks that Baker used with Queen remained, from an armada of guitars to those familiar multilayered vocals. Baker "spent hours with Neal doing what we called 'violin guitars,'" Perry told *Classic Rock* magazine—meaning "root notes, holding stuff, harmonies, doubling, sustaining and providing a thick texture to it all."

In the end, however, successor **Kevin Elson** said he felt what Baker "did best was handling the vocals, since he brought out the

vocal lines very well. Steve has a lot of his own ideas, but Roy's contribution was to integrate the voice well with the band," Elson told *Modern Recording*.

Baker would carry these stacked recording concepts from Queen to Journey and then on to **The Cars**. Their debut single, "Good Times Roll," was recorded between *Infinity* and *Evolution* and features nearly 50 voices—but only on one line. Baker took The Cars' three principal singers, layered them four times to 12, and four times again to 48.

Then Journey began to grow weary of Baker's quirks, and his stubborn adherence to a signature sound. "You know, Roy was just very flamboyant," Schon later told *Goldmine*, with a laugh. "He always had this king's chair, and he wore this king's crown. You know, it was Monty Python-like, for real."

Workman took over producing duties as Baker exited before 1979's *Departure*, with assistance from Elson, their in-concert mixer. Stone and Elson would then helm Journey's commercial breakthrough on 1981's *Escape* and 1983's *Frontiers*.

"The band didn't care for the mastering on *Evolution* and some of the singles, so I re-edited "Lovin', Touchin', Squeezin'" and remastered it," Elson told *Modern Recording*. "I got a different sound that they were real happy with. When it came time to talk about producers, the band decided that they wanted myself and one other person to collaborate closely on getting the album together."

In keeping with Elson's history with the band, Journey almost immediately started sounding more "live" in the studio. And Baker, it seems, was ready to move on, too. The advent of punk had led him to a much stripped-down approach with The Cars, aside from the vocals.

"What Roy gave us was the opportunity to try different textures and ideas," Perry told *Classic Rock*, "but the foundational aspect of the songs and the arrangements were done. Roy really gave us a direction, and from there the band found itself." [114, 226, 242, 261, 360, 363, 366, 367, 403, 431, 432, 433, 434]

> **Roy has enabled us to pull off some ideas we really wanted to do, like multitracking vocals. It gives the appearance of being loud when it really isn't. It gives us the strength and width of when we're playing live.**
>
> —*Steve Perry*

Journey Finally Breaks Through with *Infinity*

Collaborations with Robert Fleischman provided a tailwind for Journey's fourth album. Songs written in a rush of creativity when Steve Perry joined helped complete *Infinity*.

Fleischman ended up with a trio of co-writing credits while four others sprang from newer collaborations between Perry and Schon, beginning with "Patiently." Rolie, on the other hand, took a definitive step back, only co-writing three songs—and singing lead on just one.

Still, he was excited about the new pathways opening up for this edition of Journey. "When Steve Perry entered the band, I welcomed it," Rolie said. "I was spread pretty thin, playing three or four keyboards, harmonica, and singing lead. I thought this would be good, and we started writing songs in a different way."

It was not easy. They struggled to finish *Infinity* in time to hit store shelves on January 20, 1978. There were problems with the producer, problems with the studio, and a particularly vexing problem with a fire extinguisher.

Seeking to redirect Journey toward the pop charts, **Herbie Herbert** brought in **Queen**'s eccentric collaborator **Roy Thomas Baker** to produce the sessions. (The band had handled those duties themselves since Journey's debut collaboration with **Roy Halee**.) Baker arrived to find His Master's Wheels Studio completely lacking.

The San Francisco haunt was "a dreadful place with an ex-Neve mobile unit rolled into one room of a warehouse, and the studio at the back in another warehouse," Baker said in **John Tobler**

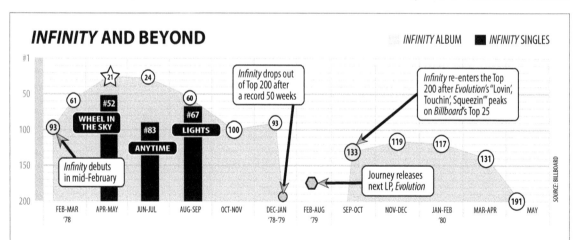

INFINITY AND BEYOND

INFINITY ALBUM ■ *INFINITY* SINGLES

Infinity drops out of Top 200 after a record 50 weeks

Infinity re-enters the Top 200 after *Evolution*'s "Lovin', Touchin', Squeezin'" peaks on *Billboard*'s Top 25

WHEEL IN THE SKY #52

ANYTIME #83

LIGHTS #67

Infinity debuts in mid-February

Journey releases next LP, *Evolution*

SOURCE: BILLBOARD

FEB-MAR '78 | APR-MAY | JUN-JUL | AUG-SEP | OCT-NOV | DEC-JAN '78-'79 | FEB-AUG '79 | SEP-OCT | NOV-DEC | JAN-FEB '80 | MAR-APR | MAY

The release of *Infinity* was a watershed moment for Journey. It was the band's first album to debut in the *Billboard* Top 100, and it remained there for 50 weeks, far longer than any other album they ever released. Additionally, the LP logged ten straight weeks in the *Billboard* Top 30—no small feat for a band that never had an album chart higher than #85. *Infinity*'s success was buoyed by three singles that scored high in AM and FM radio station playlists over the summer of 1978. "Wheel in the Sky" reached #52 on the *Billboard* charts, but "Lights" sold the Columbia execs on Journey's future. Journey now had the full backing of the label, which planned to invest heavily in its marketing and promotion. It would pay off.

Sources: Billboard

TOP CHARTING WEEK: *BILLBOARD*—May 6, 1978

1. Saturday Night Fever, *Original Motion Picture Soundtrack*
2. Wings, *London Town*
3. Eric Clapton, *Slowhand*
4. Kansas, *Point of Know Return*
5. Jefferson Starship, *Earth*
6. Billy Joel, *The Stranger*
7. George Benson, *Weekend in L.A.*
8. Jackson Browne, *Running on Empty*
9. Chuck Mangione, *Feels So Good*
21. JOURNEY, *INFINITY*

and **Stuart Grundy**'s *The Record Producers*. He bitterly complained about the insulation and windows: "Every time a big truck went past, you'd hear it—and obviously fire engines, as well." Ticks, fleas, and other vermin were also apparently a problem.

"You'd be trying to do some cable things in the studio, and rats would bite your fingers," Baker added. Their plight moved from annoying to ridiculous when Neal Schon was attempting a guitar overdub and a rat caused the equipment to malfunction. Everyone decided to have a drink. One drink turned into several, and by the time session work resumed, Baker said they were quite intoxicated.

Suddenly, a member of the crew poured a beer over Baker's head—then he picked up a fire extinguisher and sprayed everyone. He assumed it was a model filled with CO2; instead, Baker said the studio extinguisher was "one of the type that's filled with dust which you can't stop."

His Master's Wheels looked like a blizzard had passed overhead. A contemporary report confirmed that the recording equipment was nearly destroyed, with **Joel Selvin** memorably describing Baker's actions as "some kind of crazed pique." Selvin added that "a crew of 12 workers scrubbed the studio from stem to stern, leaving Baker with a gigantic cleaning bill to contemplate."

The tapes were somehow saved, and after hastily shifting sessions to Cherokee Studios in Los Angeles, Baker and Journey completed *Infinity* by the end of 1977. The LP then started spinning off seemingly ubiquitous singles, yet "Wheel in the Sky," "Anytime," and "Lights" never reached any higher than the first song's No. 52 finish on the *Cashbox* chart. Instead, *Infinity* doggedly made its way to three-times-platinum status on the strength of another relentless round of touring—and Herbert's flair for promoting the songs via non-conventional avenues like shopping mall PA systems.

Journey's album package included art from **Stanley Mouse** and **Alton Kelley** that gave the band its signature look and design that has become a mascot for the band. The album package included a straightforward studio photograph of the band that album designer **Tommy Steele** thought was "a bit too playful in hindsight ... more of an outtake."

"Infinity."
A significant new direction for Journey.

Journey has always been an exciting band. But there's been some changes lately that make the new album "Infinity" even more special, and the most important album of Journey's career.

Steve Perry has joined the band as lead singer, and the way his voice blends with the playing and singing of Greg Rolie, Neal Schon, Ross Valory, and Aynsley Dunbar is simply stunning.

All five members wrote songs for this album: there are ten cuts, and they're going to sound just as good on AM radio as Journey has always sounded on the FM dial.

And Roy Thomas Baker produced. Which means that Journey has the help of someone who's a veteran at taking bands in directions they've never traveled before.

"Infinity." The new album by the new Journey. On Columbia Records and Tapes.

JOURNEY
INFINITY
including:
Lights/Somethin' To Hide/Patiently
Feeling That Way Winds Of March

JC 34912

Produced by Roy Thomas Baker. Management: Herbie Herbert Nightmare, Inc. San Francisco

---

When Journey was close to wrapping production on *Infinity*, the band's A&R chief, **Mike Dilbeck**, flew to New York to give the increasingly impatient executives at Columbia Records a listen to the band's new sound and played a nearly-completed "Lights." "We all knew we had a lead singer—finally!—and a hit track," former Columbia Senior Vice President in charge of Promotion **Bob Sherwood** told *Time Passages*. "That's when the overall company treatment and support moved from successful AOR band to potential super-star status. This meant prioritizing all aspects of their career." Columbia followed through on that promise and embarked on a year-long promotional onslaught supporting *Infinity*. It started with full-page ads in the trade press, including one using cardboard cutouts of the band in an airplane, which piggybacked on a theme that the band used when they were promoting *Look Into the Future*. The stage was being set for Columbia to raise the band's profile higher than any other band of the late 1970s and early 1980s era.

It also helped that Journey's fourth album carried the best of what came before while adding smart new wrinkles, from Perry's delicate-then-soaring vocals to Baker's affinity for layered production techniques.

"We were a jam band early on and Perry came in, and we started designing songs," Rolie said. "I'd never really done that before, where the song came first. It was a song and then we'd elaborate. It became harmonies and it was an eye opener. It actually made me a better writer, because it opened my eyes to the fact that we could do this and continue that way."

"Winds of March," one of the Fleischman co-writes, sounded like a true meeting of two minds. Perry's honeyed croon defined its first two minutes, then Schon tore things to shreds over the remaining three.

"Open the Door" followed a similar path, as Perry took an early spotlight before Rolie helped lead everyone over a towering vocal bridge. Once again, a quickly elevating conclusion found Schon working among fewer binding conventions to create a torrential solo. "He's really phenomenal at layering," future Schon collaborator **Johnny Gioeli** said, "and hearing sounds within sounds."

In between, "Somethin' to Hide" serves as a power ballad signpost, years before Journey defined the genre with "Open Arms." Perry lets

out a final cry that is simply devastating.

Aynsley Dunbar rounded off Journey's swift transformation by employing a far lighter touch on this farewell recording with Journey, "I tried to play as simply as possible," Dunbar told *Rolling Stone* in 1978, comparing his approach to **Mick Fleetwood**. "And it certainly paid off, didn't it?"

Indeed, it did. Journey would score their first —but far from their last—multi-million-selling LP. *Infinity* rose to No. 21, while spending a mind-boggling 123 weeks on the *Billboard* album chart. "We toured for eight months out of the year and then we'd go in and record and then go do it again," Rolie told *Mixdown*. "When *Infinity* hit, and [Journey] became a platinum act, we finally built the sense of something."

Derek and the Dominos co-founder **Bobby Whitlock** was unsurprised that a now-grown Schon eventually reached millions of record buyers. "No—hell, no," Whitlock said, with a big laugh. "Not surprised at all."

Future Journey drummer **Deen Castronovo** was one of those buyers. "I grew up playing Journey songs," he later enthused to the *Lansing State Journal*. "I was 11 when I was learning drum parts off *Infinity*." [37, 38, 46, 52, 68, 105, 220, 340, 343, 344, 345, 346, 348, 350, 352, 354, 375, 375, 390]

Chicago Daily News
February 4, 1978

Infinity is Journey's third release, it might as well be their first, as the clarity of production and the addition of a first-rate lead singer Steve Perry have given the band a much stronger, song-based image. Journey now presents itself as a song band as opposed to a jamming unit. The difference is telling—the instrumentalists still shine, but now they work in a context that makes the package more enjoyable. Perry's vocals take that **Kansas-Queen** sound that essential step beyond the brand of sturdy derivative rock that characterized their first albums. Combined with the superlative drumming of Dunbar, and accentuated by the rich production of **Roy Thomas Baker** (of Queen fame), Journey has come up with an album that might well be the left-field hit of the winter.

— *Rich Warren*

The Berkeley Gazette
March 3, 1978

The new Journey LP is a stunner—their best record yet. With their new lead singer, Steve Perry, and ten tight tunes, this band is off to a fresh start. Because of their star-studded lineup, Gregg Rolie (keyboards, vocals) and Neal Schon (guitar, vocals)—both formerly of **Santana** and world-renowned drummer Aynsley Dunbar, everyone expected the moon from these boys, but all we got was an occasional falling star. One or two inspired tunes off each album weren't enough when the rest of the material was second-rate. *Infinity* is a cohesive, tightly controlled (no redundant guitar solos), highly melodic record. The single "Anytime" (great harmonies) is bulleting up the charts right now, and there should be another single hot on its heels. A great record, finally.

— *Evan Hossie*

Los Angeles Times
March 5, 1978

After three marginal heavy-metal albums that exhibited instrumental dexterity but little else, Journey has wisely expanded upon its previously modest pop intentions, developing a rich, melodic, vocally geared formula accentuated by a brilliant, muscular delivery. Newly acquiring a polished lead singer (Steve Perry) and a flamboyant, commercially oriented producer (**Roy Thomas Baker**), this quintet has concocted its most mature mainstream effort. On *Infinity*, Journey's compact arrangements still are overly shaped by ex-**Santana** members Gregg Rolie and Neal Schon's cosmic, psychedelic inclinations. However, the anguished and prophesizing overtones characterizing the group's earlier works have disappeared in favor of refined but dynamic execution plus simple, earnest lyrics.

— *Dale Kawashima*

The executives at Columbia Records were confirmed believers. Now putting the full force of its marketing and promotion arm behind Journey, full-page, full-color ads began appearing in the trade press—*Billboard* (inset), *Cashbox*, and *Record World*—and in *Rolling Stone*. Where the album cover for the band's previous LP was a simple group shot, the album package for *Infinity* was resplendent with bright colors and a creative illustration airbrushed by the masterful hands of San Francisco legends **Stanley Mouse** and **Alton Kelley**. It was a brand new Journey and the efforts by the band, its management and the label worked—*Infinity* became a multiplatinum album that set the stage for a decade as one of rock's most dependable hit makers and concert earners.

'WHEEL' ARRIVES AS JOURNEY'S FIRST CHARTING SINGLE

Journey's lead singer Robert Fleischman came and went in the blink of an eye, but he left something important behind: the band's first *Billboard* charting song.

"Wheel in the Sky" only got there after Fleischman helped shape a poem written by Ross Valory's wife into narrative form. Neal Schon created the melody out on the concert trail.

Journey was still racing from gig to gig in a cramped station wagon when road manager **Pat Morrow** said he wanted to pull over for a candy bar. Schon got out to stretch his legs, and offhandedly pulled an acoustic out of the back. He then combined those guitar lines with inspirational lines from **Diane Valory**. "It was like, 'wheels in motion,' or something like that," Schon told *Fuse*.

Schon handed these scraps over to Fleischman, who crafted it all into an actual song. Both would later lay claim to the song's title.

"I didn't care for the poem but there was a line in it, 'the wheels in my mind keep on turning,'" Fleischman told *Legendary Rock Interviews*, "so I changed it to 'wheel in the sky keeps on turning, don't know where I'll be tomorrow' and wrote the rest of the lyrics." Schon also remembered coming up with the title, telling *Fuse* that it represented "an infinity-type motion that goes on around the world."

Either way, making something of "Wheel in the Sky" represented a small triumph for Fleischman, whom Schon said "was a great songwriter, I thought—a great lyricist." But Fleischman never got to sing it in the studio. Instead, "Wheel in the Sky" became Steve Perry's first Journey single.

The track itself is notable for stretching almost 30 seconds before Perry begins singing. There is also a sizable twist, considering how heavy Journey's earlier music often was: Schon plays acoustic for roughly half of "Wheel in the Sky." They left aside a bridge Fleischman wanted placed before Schon's molten solo. This section has **Roy Thomas Baker**'s fingerprints all over it, as he builds texture on top of texture

with Perry's ethereal voice floating above it all.

Released in March 1978, "Wheel in the Sky" spent eight weeks on the *Billboard* chart, but only got to No. 57. "I saw a lot of potential in 'Wheel in the Sky,'" Valory told the *Fort Worth Star-Telegram* in 1979. "It got up there, but not quite far enough."

WHEEL IN THE SKY
By Neal Schon, Robert Fleishman, Diane Valory

HIGHEST CHARTING WEEK:
Cashbox, #52, May 27, 1978

ARTIST	SINGLE
1. Wings	With A Little Luck
2. Johnny Mathis	Too Much, Too Little, Too Late
3. J. Travolta & O. Newton John	You're the One That I Want
4. Andy Gibb	Shadow Dancing
5. Roberta Flack	The Closer I Get To You
6. Eddie Money	Baby Hold On
7. Chuck Mangione	Feels So Good
8. The Trammps	Disco Inferno
9. Atlanta Rhythm Section	Imaginary Lover
52. JOURNEY	**WHEEL IN THE SKY**

At the time, Journey was too busy touring to notice, as a staggering amount of work followed. The band played more than 170 cities in North America and Europe amid **Herbie Herbert**'s wall-to-wall marketing strategy involving posters, billboards, and radio promotions.

Perry was honestly just thrilled to see "Wheel in the Sky" inside a jukebox, a sign back then that any up-and-comer had finally made it. He found the single at a pizza place he was visiting with Schon in 1978, put two quarters in, and then sat back down to see the look on his bandmate's face when their music filled the dining area.

"The song starts, and he doesn't get it at first. All of sudden he looks at me and says, 'I love this song,'" Perry later told **John Stix**, "and we laughed." [97, 202, 226, 272, 347, 369, 370, 406]

inspired by **Jeff Beck**," Smith said. "That was in the air in those days, and Ronnie went in that direction, as well. He encouraged me to play in the rock/fusion style. That's what was appropriate for that music."

They clicked immediately, since *Open Fire* settled into the space between what Smith had been doing with **Jean-Luc Ponty** and what he would soon be doing with Journey. It's easy to see why it clicked with the fusion-leaning Schon too.

"Ronnie's sound was huge and his time was settled and consistent," Smith said. "I thought he played melodies with a lot of soul and feeling. I really learned a lot from Ronnie about constructing a strong set and presenting instrumental music in a way that communicated to a large audience. We had a ball playing together. In some songs, we played guitar and drum duets that stretched on and on. Offstage, he was fun and relaxed—but he was also a serious guy who was into psychology and philosophy."

Smith continued with Ronnie Montrose through September 1978, when Journey came calling. Bassist Ross Valory recognized soon-to-depart bandmate Aynsley Dunbar as the more accomplished drummer, but told *Rolling Stone* that Smith had a "better concept of the rock music we're playing."

Smith was adamant, however, that he would not have made a better choice from the beginning. After all, between 1973 and 1976, he was principally playing small-group and big-band jazz. He had not begun dabbling with fusion alongside Ponty, let alone rocked out with Montrose. He was, for the bulk of that era, actually a college kid at Berklee.

"Neal and I are the same age, but he was a child prodigy and I became a professional musician after many years of study and practice," Smith said. "I wouldn't have been ready for it first of all, and Aynsley Dunbar did a great job with that music." [3, 7, 9, 10, 109, 255, 386]

SPRING–SUMMER 1978

RELEASES
▶ Journey, "Anytime" (single)
▶ Journey, "Lights" (single)

NUGGETS
▶ Journey's road crew wheeled up to the Will Rogers Auditorium in Fort Worth with a $35,000 stage setup, constructed of tubular aluminum, chrome, and plexiglass to give the stage a seamless effect. The setup includes hydraulic risers and a rear projection screen. — *Fort Worth Star-Telegram*

▶ It's hard to believe that just six years ago Steve Perry was flying by the seat of his pants in L.A., while Neal Schon, Ross Valory, Gregg Rolie, and Aynsley Dunbar were eking out a living on the road in order to bankroll the next Journey album release. "I was starving in Los Angeles," says a shorter-haired, suede-and-denim clad Perry. "I was eating a lot of pork and beans, having no money for anything else. I went back to my home town with my gums bleeding. One dentist said I have some strange disease; that I ought to have all my teeth pulled out." A second dentist rescued Steve from that fate.
—*Circus*

ON THE ROAD
▶ **Journey**, with Aerosmith, Andy Gibb, Atlanta Rhythm Section, Eddie Money, Electric Light Orchestra, Foreigner, Heart, Marshall Tucker, Mitch Ryder, Nantucket, Pablo Cruise, Pat Travers Band, Patti Smith Group, Rick Derringer, Ronnie Montrose, Starcastle, Steve Miller Band, Ted Nugent, The Beach Boys, The Cars, The Doobie Brothers, The Rolling Stones, The Spinners, Thin Lizzy, Tom Petty and the Heartbreakers, Van Halen, and Wet Willie.

It Gets Really Weird After Traffic Accident in Detroit

"Oh, yeah," Steve Perry told *Crawdaddy* in 1979, "you get pretty crazy when you're out on the road awhile."

That was certainly the case when Journey stopped in Detroit on March 10, 1978, as part of the *Infinity* tour. They were still traveling from

Continued on Page 87

JOURNEY SECURES SUCCESS WITH R&B-INSPIRED PERRY

Heartbreak led Steve Perry to an interior place as a child, and that's where he discovered a love for music.

Born on January 22, 1949 in Hanford, California, Perry was the first American in this family of Portuguese immigrants. His father, **Raymond Pereira**—who would soon leave—was an aspiring baritone who owned a local radio station, while Perry's mother, **Mary Quaresma**, was a bookkeeper.

Perry was just 8 when his parents split, and he found himself devastated. "I became invisible, emotionally," Perry later told *The New York Times*, "and there were places I used to hide, to feel comfortable, to protect myself."

He would tuck himself away in the corner of the garage at his grandparents' home, where Mary subsequently moved. He listened incessantly to 45s and the radio, discovering **Sam Cooke** at 14 when a DJ cued up the hit single "Cupid." He found a lasting influence.

Mary eventually remarried **Marv Rottman** and the family moved to Lemoore, California. Her teenage son found a lasting sense of place, as Perry's songs would continually return to youthful themes of buoyed emotion and new freedom.

He later hinted at deeper-seated issues from his youth, beginning at the age of nine. "Things happened to me as a child that I still can't talk about—nothing to do with my parents, but things did happen," Perry told *The New Statesman*. "It happened to a lot of kids, as I find out."

Then he found his voice, joining the choir at College of the Sequoias in nearby Visalia. At that point, he aimed to follow Raymond into radio, but his desire to make music overwhelmed any attempt to continue that legacy.

"One of my needs to perform was the need to get myself heard," Perry added. "I'm not complaining—but there was nowhere to talk it out, so I got to sing it out instead."

In the meantime, Perry was absorbing an exciting blend of old and new influences. "Other than **Robert Plant**, there's no singer in rock that even came close to Steve Perry," later-era Journey bassist Randy Jackson told *Rolling Stone*. "The power, the range, the tone—he created his own style. He mixed a little Motown, a little **Everly Brothers**, a little **Zeppelin**."

There was more heartbreak to come, as Perry thought he had lost his best chance at a record deal after the bassist in his band **Alien Project** died in a car accident mere days before they signed.

But heartbreak had a way of spurring him to new creative heights: He helped Journey back to platinum sales with *Raised on Radio* in 1986, after his mother died. *Traces*, Perry's

long-awaited return to solo work, released in 2018, followed the cancer-related death of girlfriend **Kellie Nash**.

Beyond their love affair, Nash had also encouraged him to seek counseling for his childhood trauma. Perry began therapy in his 60s, before Nash's health took an awful turn. "A heart isn't really complete until it's completely broken and mine was completely broken after I lost her," Perry told NPR, but "from that came joy and songs and ideas."

He'd gotten into Journey through a combination of happenstance and pure determination, having first caught a ride with Neal Schon in 1972 after the guitarist sat in with **Azteca** at a San Francisco venue. It would be another five years before he got a chance to write with Schon, who had no idea Perry was a singer.

Then their label pressed for him to be the front man in Schon's band. "Journey had made a conscious decision, along with Columbia's—what's the correct word here?—request," Perry told *GQ* with a laugh, "that they become a little more song-oriented."

The 28-year-old Perry arrived, brimming with ambition. "Patiently," the first song he and Schon completed, "was really about the determination of me wanting to get next to those players," Perry said in an interview with *San Francisco Chronicle* music critic **Joel Selvin** for the career-spanning *Time³* box set.

The hard-playing Schon was initially skeptical but slowly bought into Perry's more directly emotional songs. "With Perry, the band finally has obtained a visual focus to its visceral music," Selvin wrote in 1978, while also praising Perry's songwriting contributions. "He is a poised and confident showman who knows both when to take the spotlight and when to relinquish it."

Perry and Schon scaled incredible heights together, combining with Gregg Rolie on a trio of triple-platinum LPs before elevating still further into diamond sales with a remade 1980s-era lineup featuring Jonathan Cain.

"I'm not taking anything away from Journey because they were super creative musically, and obviously later when they got Steve Perry, they had that commercial voice," original **Golden Gate Rhythm Section** drummer

Prairie Prince said. "Not to take anything from Gregg Rolie, but once they got Steve Perry, it was a whole different world. They had a formula, and they knew how to rock it—and I was proud of them for that."

At the height of Journey's success following 1981's *Escape*, Schon's relationship with Perry began to fracture. Solo albums, arguments over musical approach, long hiatuses, and hurtful accusations followed before Schon—and Journey—finally moved on without Perry.

His legend was already secure: "Steve Perry was my favorite," said Deen Castronovo, who would later take over some of Perry's parts with Journey and the **Journey Through Time** offshoot band. "So, for me to even sing a Perry song, I just try to do it justice, man. Steve is a god. To me, he's the greatest rock/R&B singer of my generation—bar none."

Perry's only departing request was that Journey go forward with a different name. When Schon refused, Perry extracted contractual concessions that could be described as punitive. Schon would have to pay dearly to get his band back.

Eager to be free, Schon agreed. But he later revealed that the deal was "forced upon us all to sign ... 10 minutes before we were to go on in Hawaii at a string of five sold-out shows," Schon said in a 2022 social media post. Journey was under extraordinary pressure, he added, as they'd already played the first two concerts. "Then our manager came to us, stating Steve Perry was not going to go on without us signing. Herbie claimed he didn't know what else to do, so he suggested we sign."

Schon described those signatures as having been obtained "under duress," since the band did not have "any time for any other legal to look at it." Still, with a new partnership agreement in hand, Journey could finally move on. What they couldn't do, however, was slip out of Perry's long shadow.

Journey's long-awaited induction into the Rock & Roll Hall of Fame was marred by questions about whether Perry would perform. He didn't. "We have," Perry told the Associated Press, "severely, emotionally gone our separate ways." [30, 69, 80, 131, 169, 253, 254, 363, 391, 408, 435, 642, 715, 833]

> **Once they got Steve Perry, it was a completely different world. They had a formula, and they knew how to rock it—and I was proud of them for that.**
>
> —*Prairie Prince*

show to show in a pair of limousines, building toward Journey's first-ever multiplatinum success with an LP that had only just arrived in January. Suddenly, traffic came to a standstill.

"Our driver slams into the car in front of us," Perry remembered. "Then the limo in back of us ran square into our limo. I was thrown into the backseat."

Luckily, everyone was OK—save for bouts of "heavy, heavy massive whiplash" that they had to battle with for the rest of the tour. The vehicles were nevertheless wrecked, and the sight of their crumpled frames sparked a hilariously destructive outburst from the band.

"We climbed out of the limos and we just started kicking them," Perry told *Crawdaddy*. "It was incredible!"

At this point, only two of the highway's five lanes were passable, creating a miles-long backup. "Cars are driving by real slow and here are these five guys kicking and leaping on two bashed-up limousines," Perry added. "People were flipping us off. We were flipping them off!"

Roadies with Journey's early-1980s opening act, **Greg Kihn**, later provided Perry with some karmic justice. Kihn said their prank involved "switching the names of the cities on his monitors—which embarrassed him on several occasions" as Perry misidentified where they were performing.

"Why? I don't know," Kihn told the *Tampa Bay Times*. "Maybe I was jealous. After all, Journey was the No. 1 band in America that year and what were we? Number 310?"

Still, it wouldn't be the last time Journey took part in some on-the-road shenanigans. That first tour together also found Perry and Gregg Rolie connecting 25 newly bought extension cords so that they could turn on a television and toss it down several floors into the hotel pool.

"It was a wonderful sight," Perry told *Crawdaddy*. "I'm telling you, man, it goes up in beautiful color. It explodes. It's great!" [414, 415]

Journey's European Debut Was a Quick, One-Night Stand

Journey's initial foray into Europe was not much more than a one-night stand.

They took the stage at the Pinkpop Festival on May 15, 1978, in the Burgemeester Damen Sportpark at Geleen in the Netherlands, after playing Folsom Field in Boulder, Colorado, just two nights before on May 13.

They'd play Arizona's Tucson Convention Center three days later, on May 18, 1978.

"It happened so fast that you didn't have time for jet lag," Gregg Rolie said, with a chuckle. "It's like it never happened. We went there; we came back. I was tired, but I didn't get that horrible feeling of being jet lagged."

It may have added up to a ridiculous number of frequent flyer miles, but the Pinkpop trek followed manager **Herbie Herbert**'s script perfectly. He tore through life with a ravenous appetite, taking Journey right along with him.

Still, for all of the attendant excitement surrounding their overseas debut, things did not go particularly well.

Rain from the day before meant that Pinkpop was a muddy mess, and now standing room only. A reviewer from the U.K.-based *Sounds* magazine lamented that the harried band "did not really live up to the promise displayed on their hot new *Infinity* album." *Sounds* took particular aim at Aynsley Dunbar, saying he "proved to be something of a disappointment on drums."

Meanwhile, Herbert was apparently horrified by the in-concert mix, according to Pinkpop. org. When local representatives from KRO Radio attempted to leave with tapes from the show, he reportedly scurried over to their car, flung open the door then raced away with the tapes. Someone from KRO was said to have found them in a heap inside a nearby garbage can.

Unfortunately, that was a harbinger. Journey would prove to be far more popular in Japan than they ever were in Europe.

Beginning with 1983's *Frontiers*, the band notched seven consecutive Top 20 albums in Japan—and just missed at No. 22 with *Freedom* in 2022. Meanwhile, they never cracked the Dutch Top 40, only had two career Top 20 albums in Germany and one Top 10 album in the U.K.

Still, at the time, they felt like they'd established an important new career beachhead. "Herbie made things happen that were amazing," Rolie added, "and it got us into Europe. That's where it started." [375, 485, 486, 492, 493, 494]

Journey.
The "Infinity" album achieves towering success.

Six months ago, Journey's fourth album, "Infinity," was released. We knew it was their best ever. But the long-lasting massive success at radio is surprising even us.

More than two-thirds of our AOR and Soft Rock tracking stations still include Journey on their playlists. Forty percent have "Feeling That Way" and "Anytime" s songs in heavy rotation.

And along with Journey's new sound came a new, younger, larger crowd of listeners. A generation that wants Journey to conquer AM radio, too. And has already given the band its first taste of gold.

"Infinity." Journey's destination is platinum.
On Columbia Records and Tapes.

Even though *Infinity* gave Journey its first gold and platinum albums, as well as its first charting singles, the band had not yet conquered AM radio, which was still at arms' length with the band. Manager Herbie Herbert and Columbia Records continued their promotional onslaught with more full-page ads geared to sway on-the-fence program directors. The first of this second round of full-page ads (above) was built around the image of an Air King compressor, which may have served as a metaphor for the pressure building around AM radio's acceptance of the band's success. Or perhaps it was just the sometimes-whimsical approach to marketing and advertising that Herbert applied to so many of his business dealings. Either way, the idea was that the band's label and management wanted those reluctant program directors to know that Journey fans were a younger, larger crowd of rock fans—and they needed to be heard on the then-required-for-success world of AM radio.

Queen's 'Bohemian Rhapsody' Leads to Journey's First Video

Queen once again served as a kind of precursor for later successes as Journey prepared to enter the world of music videos. This time, however, it had nothing to do with **Roy Thomas Baker**. Instead, late director **Bruce Gowers**'s groundbreaking work on the video for "Bohemian Rhapsody" led to an early collaboration with Journey.

Gowers would often describe the clip as "six minutes that changed my whole life." In its own way, "Bohemian Rhapsody" changed Journey too.

"It kind of stood the industry on its ear," said Gowers's former longtime partner **Paul Flattery**. "You can't say that 'Bohemian Rhapsody' was the beginning of music videos, but it was certainly the beginning of the music video industry—because once it happened, everybody suddenly awoke to the fact that you could treat these songs differently from just a representative performance or as karaoke, though that's a reference ahead of its time."

Journey contracted Gowers to direct a clip for "Lights," Journey's third single with new singer Steve Perry. The band invited Gowers back to shoot a trio of videos from 1979's *Evolution*, this time with Flattery as part of the team. They would create promotional films for "Lovin', Touchin', Squeezin'," "Lovin' You is Easy," and "Just the Same Way," but not before Journey's stickler of a manager had a word with Flattery about the earlier "Lights" video.

"I went to some *Billboard* conference, and **Herbie Herbert** was there," Flattery said. "He came up to me and he was blasting me for the Journey video which we had done—which I was not involved in. His big complaint involved Aynsley Dunbar, the drummer. His stomach stuck out in one of the shots. They were lined up, in kind of a profile thing that Bruce had done. It was like, '[Dunbar] complains to me about this every day'—because videos become a lasting legacy, if you will. All I could do is apologize."

Gowers quickly became an in-demand director because of his ability to deftly manage multiple camera assignments in an in-concert style setting, sometimes under brutal time constraints. He and his crew shot the *Evolution*

clips, for instance, at the Zellerbach Auditorium in Berkeley, California, just before **April Wine** took the stage for two more videos they'd complete with Journey's rig.

Flattery later reconnected with Perry following his solo debut, working on memorable videos for "Oh Sherrie," "Strung Out," and "Foolish Heart." [435, 436, 437]

FALL 1978

NUGGETS

▶ Steve Smith replaces Aynsley Dunbar as drummer for Journey. —*Cashbox*

▶ Journey makes the cover of *Cashbox* after their *Infinity* LP is certified platinum. The LP introduces fresh new emphasis on vocals with the addition of Steve Perry, and Steve Smith replacing Aynsley Dunbar on drums. —*Cashbox*

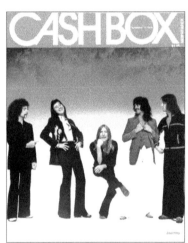

▶ Aynsley Dunbar was bounced from Journey because he was not deemed "a team player." —*Circus*

▶ Journey, this Bud's for you! The San Francisco band inked a merchandising agreement with Budweiser beer, which has supplied the band's fans with free posters and cigarette lighters handed out at concerts. Journey also cut a commercial—like a hard rock **Lou Rawls**—for the self-styled King of Beers. —*San Francisco Examiner*

Continued on Page 91

ALMOST CUT FROM THE LP, 'ANYTIME' FORGES A NEW PATH

Amid grinding sessions, Journey actually considered dropping *Infinity*'s second single altogether. They didn't like their performance and couldn't understand new producer **Roy Thomas Baker**'s vision for the song.

"When we recorded that, we did just the music, and we almost didn't finish it," Rolie said. "Remember, we came to this having been a jam band. When we finished the music, we listened to all of the tracks, and it didn't have the fire that we were used to."

Turns out, that was exactly what "Anytime" required. Baker, already justly famous for his layered productions with **Queen**, led them through a more measured take so that he'd have the proper foundation for a burst of vocal brilliance. It would, however, take time—lots of it—as Baker directed multiple voice sessions, taping them over and over until he'd made a sky-scraping construction.

"Anytime" was one of the songs where Baker overtly changed the band's musical pattern.

"The songs had to be more commercialized,"Baker told *Recording Engineer Producer Magazine* in 1979. "No more million-bar long, self-indulgent guitar solos, which bore everyone silly. Things had to be more to the point, like nice, big choruses of vocals and big guitars."

Meanwhile, Rolie said he and Neal Schon were moving from boredom to frustration, since they could not see past Baker's exacting studio work to a finished product. "We had never spent too much time doing all of the vocals," Rolie added.

Baker kept going, kept layering, and kept encouraging them to explore their voices as deeply as they'd always explored the guitar and keyboard. Finally, "Anytime"—and Journey's new direction—began to take shape. "They had exercised an instrumental satisfaction for three albums that they'll admit to," Steve Perry told the [Carthagena, Ohio] *Messenger-Press* in 1978, "and as they attained progressiveness instrumentally, they wanted to progress in vocals too."

Rolie started the song with a friend, and Neal Schon chipped with a line that recalled a favorite band from his youth with the **Beatles**-esque "Anytime that you want me."

The melody line sparked additional lyrics from since exiled-lead singer Robert Fleischman, who was fooling around at the piano inside Rolie's home. Perry's fresh vocal blend with Rolie did the rest.

ANYTIME
By Gregg Rolie, Roger Silver, Robert Fleishman, Neal Schon, Ross Valory

HIGHEST CHARTING WEEK:
Record World, #75, July 8, 1978

ARTIST	SINGLE
1. Andy Gibb	Shadow Dancing
2. Gerry Rafferty	Baker Street
3. The O'Jays	Use Ta Be My Girl
4. J. Travola & O. Newton-John	You're the One That I Want
5. Bonnie Tyler	It's a Heartache
6. Bob Seger & The Silver Bullet Band	Still the Same
7. Heatwave	The Groove Line
8. Meat Loaf	Two Out of Three Ain't Bad
9. ABBA	Take a Chance On Me
75. JOURNEY	**ANYTIME**

Weeks on Chart: 4
Billboard, #83, July 8, 1978

Released in June 1978, the highest-charting position for "Anytime" was No. 75 on *Record World*'s Singles chart, but the song could only reach No. 83 on the *Billboard* Hot 100 chart, and an even worse No. 101 on *Cashbox*'s list. But the single established an approach to voicing that would instantly redefine Journey. "When Steve Perry entered that band," Rolie later told *Mixdown*, "we started writing songs for singing first—not for the groove first and not for the solo work."

Saved from the cutting room floor, "Anytime" also became the first Rolie-sung song to chart since his **Santana** days. "As soon as the vocals were put in, the song came alive," Rolie said, laughing. "I'm glad we didn't can it!" [2, 50, 116, 349, 371, 431]

Infinity Tour Stokes Rivalries with Van Halen, Montrose

One of Journey's opening acts on the tour in support of *Infinity* would provide a key future member. The other was wreaking havoc—in more ways than one.

These concerts began with the up-and-coming **Van Halen** before giving way to **Ronnie Montrose**, who had Steve Smith in the drum chair. Journey closed out each night.

"There was a lot of 'guitar hero' energy on that tour and Ronnie wanted to get on stage and kick ass," Smith said. "We followed Van Halen, and we wanted to make it hard for Journey to follow us. There was friendly but fierce competition on that tour, with each group trying to outplay the other."

Numerous times, Steve Perry would later admit, Van Halen was the one doing the outplaying. "I am convinced that Journey became something we would not have become had we not spent time with Van Halen in 1978," he told *Rolling Stone*. "That band was so on fire and [guitarist] **Eddie Van Halen** was the driving, demonstrative force of that group."

Van Halen had just released their self-titled debut, giving fans the first taste of Eddie's groundbreaking new sound. They were hungry after emerging from time spent on the club circuit, and they were rowdy.

"It was a competitive guitar bill and ... at that time, Eddie was red hot," Neal Schon told *Ultimate Classic Rock*'s **Matt Wardlaw**. "But I was jamming hard, Ronnie was jamming hard. We were all jamming hard, you know?" He said he felt Journey held their own, "but I was glad I wasn't coming after Van Halen. That's all I can tell you."

As a freshman group, Van Halen had to make do with a poorly setup PA system, and short—or nonexistent—sound checks. Occasionally, they wouldn't even have catering. "They kept complaining about the monitor guy, that he

Continued on Page 93

Journey's first run at leading a major concert tour brought some new challenges to the band, including friendly rivalries with groups like **Montrose** and **Van Halen**, whose competitiveness pushed Journey to the edge every night.

Journey.
The "Infinity" tour covers more ground than ever.

Journey. The one rock band with "road work" built right into their name. In two years, over a million-and-a-half fans have seen their show. By summer's end, at least a million more will hear them on dates with the Rolling Stones, Bob Seger, Fleetwood Mac, and other top-flight bands.

Journey. One of rock's hardest-working bands, supported by one of the chart's hardest-worked albums.

"Infinity." Journey's destination is platinum.
On Columbia Records and Tapes.

JOURNEY TOUR: 7/12 Detroit, Mich. with Tom Petty. 7/13 Nashville, Tenn. with Foreigner. 7/15 Cleveland, Ohio with ELO. 7/16 Davenport, Iowa with Doobie Bros. 7/17 Wisc. with Van Halen. 7/18 Greenbay, Wisc. with Van Halen. 7/20 Tulsa, Okla. with Van Halen. 7/21 Jackson, Tenn. with Van Halen. 7/23 Louisville, Ky. with Ted Nugent. 7/27 Springfield, Mass. with Ted Nugent. 7/28 New Haven, Conn. with Ted Nugent. 7/29 Binghamton, N.Y. with Pat Travers. 7/30 Portland, Maine with Ted Nugent. 8/9 Pussa, Ohio with Pablo Cruise. 8/9 Cincinnati, Ohio with Jefferson Starship, Pablo Cruise. 8/17 Reno, Nev. 6/20 San Jose, Cal. 8/26 Anaheim, Cal. with ELO.

Produced by Roy Thomas Baker. Management: Herbie Herbert, Nightmare, Inc. San Francisco.

In successive weeks, Journey manager **Herbie Herbert**, along with the advertising and promotional arms of Columbia Records, prominently pushed Journey's latest album, *Infinity*, to the trade press to capture the hearts and minds of program directors across the country. The full-page ads published in *Record World*, *Cashbox*, and *Billboard* magazines were ripe with metaphors and allegories. Who would be so bold as to tout their up-and-coming band with a **Led Zeppelin**-like dirigible (above)? Herbie

Herbert would—and did—and apparently did not care about ruffling any feathers along the way. While the previous week's ad focused on getting the band on AM radio, the follow-up focused on Journey's well-exercised touring credentials. The ads touted Journey sharing the stage with A-list bands like **The Rolling Stones**, **Bob Seger**, and **Fleetwood Mac**. Also included was the band's entire summer touring schedule, which started in Detroit with **Tom Petty** and ended in Anaheim with **Electric Light Orchestra**.

was screwing them up tremendously," Gregg Rolie told *Mixdown*. A dozen or shows into the tour, Van Halen and their whole crew showed up with custom-made black shirts that said "Fuck Those Monitors" in red letters. "It was great," Rolie added. "It was so hilarious."

On stage for what Perry described to *Rolling Stone* as "eight weeks of 3,000-seater proscenium-stage gigs," Van Halen was limited to short 30-minute sets at the unpopular hour of 7:30 p.m., typically playing to half-full venues. Still, they were setting new land speed records.

"It's interesting to look at the elements that were present on that tour," Smith said. "I think Ronnie was under pressure to perform because the show featured some pretty amazing guitar playing. Eddie Van Halen had just arrived on the scene, and he was blowing everyone away with his virtuosity and new ideas on how to play the guitar.

"Neal Schon similarly came on the scene in the early '70s when both **[Eric] Clapton** and **Santana** asked him to join their bands—and Neal went with Santana at 16 years old," Smith added. "I think he blew people's minds in those days. Ronnie had also come on the scene with **Edgar Winter** in the early '70s and had blown some minds, too!"

Eventually, Van Halen took to swiping food—and then girls—from the headliner. They also reportedly blamed Journey for the damage after trashing the seventh floor of a Sheraton in Wisconsin. And then there was an infamous backstage food fight.

Former Van Halen manager **Noel Monk**'s 2017 memoir *Runnin' With the Devil* seemed to confirm a long-circulated story in which Perry burst into tears after being accidentally hit by a bowl of guacamole that Eddie heaved toward his front man, **David Lee Roth**. Perry's prized satin jacket with a Journey monogram was ruined.

"Wearing that, I felt like I was finally somebody," Perry told *Rolling Stone*. "The guacamole went on my left shoulder and my left arm. I looked down on it and I looked up at them and they sheepishly laughed like, 'Oh shit.'"

He said he left, "just pissed," but that no tears were shed. "No. There was no crying! I wouldn't cry over guacamole," Perry added, laughing. "It becomes folklore at some point. It becomes silly."

Schon missed Van Halen's earliest performances because his band's routine brought him on-site after the opening act was already off the stage.

"Journey stayed at their hotel until, like, maybe an hour before the gig, and then they would come to the venue," said **Josh Ramos**, who heard these stories directly from manager **Herbie Herbert** as a member of **The Storm**. "One day, Herbie goes there, and he wants to see the opening bands. He sees Van Halen and he goes, 'Holy shit.' Because Neal was a bad motherfucker back then; he was like the guy, and then all of a sudden, 'Who is this guy doing tapping and just crazy in his tone?' Herbie goes 'Neal, you've got to see this guitar player—and he was like, 'Yeah, yeah.'"

Finally, Herbert cajoled Schon into getting there in time to see Van Halen. Stunned, Schon did a deep dive into their music, hoping to figure out what the wunderkind guitarist was doing. "I'm trying to dissect it, which I was generally pretty good and able to do that with many records," Schon told *Guitar Connoisseur*. "Even with **Mahavishnu [Orchestra]**, I was like, I have no clue what this guy is doing. There's just no way you can do it on guitar."

Schon made a point of meeting Eddie Van Halen backstage, and they struck up a lifelong friendship. But that didn't mean Journey got to coast through the rest of the *Infinity* tour. Quite the opposite, in fact.

"They cleaned our clock plenty of times and woke us the fuck up pretty quick," Perry told Wardlaw. "They were so focused and so on fire that they were just relentless."

Perry says the Van Halen brothers' almost telepathic musical camaraderie also played a role in Aynsley Dunbar's looming exit. "In fact, because of the way Eddie and Alex [Van Halen] locked, eventually I convinced Neal that he needed to lock with his guitar [the same way]," Perry added. "In came Steve Smith." [10, 220, 258, 259, 260, 392, 393, 405]

As *Infinity* Tour Concludes, Aynsley Dunbar Exits Band

Journey concluded their tour in support of *Infinity* by returning on the undercard for a second time at Day on the Green. They'd even-

Continued on Page 95

JOURNEY'S SIGNATURE FRISCO SONG HAD AN L.A. ORIGIN

Steve Perry was trying to write an ode to Los Angeles but couldn't quite coax "Lights" into existence. Something just did not feel right about singing "When the lights go down in the city, and the sun shines on L.A."

So, he stuck the song in his back pocket. Then an opportunity to join Journey changed his life and changed the song.

Perry previewed "Lights" for the others in August 1977 in San Bernardino, during a period when he was on the road with Journey but not yet an official member. "It had a different feel to it when Steve first showed it to me," Neal Schon told *Vulture*. "It was more old-school blues."

These R&B-soaked influences would play a key role in Journey's swift change of musical direction. "I always looked at 'Lights' as being a song that could have been a soul song," classic rock radio stalwart **John Gorman** said. "That could have been a **Tyrone Davis** single. Anybody could have recorded that thing, and it would've been an R&B hit."

The second completed track of the Perry era fell in place within about 10 minutes when they returned to it while downstairs at Gregg Rolie's house in Mill Valley. This wasn't unusual during a period of dizzying creativity. "Our best songs came out of nowhere," Schon told *Fuse*, "and were finished very quickly."

Schon started by adding some **Curtis Mayfield**-influenced chordal rhythm playing to what Perry had begun. "He had the melody; he had the bass," Schon told *Vulture*. "I was like, 'What if we did this?'" Perry's new adopted hometown of San Francisco led to a crucial lyrical update—"L.A." became "the bay"—but Schon did something at least as pivotal: His rhythm-driven propulsion gave "Lights" an entirely different feel.

Once again, "Lights" didn't do much as a single, stalling at a surprising No. 68 on the *Billboard* Hot 100. Yet it continued to resonate for decades, finding a permanent home on Journey's setlist while soundtracking countless San Francisco-area sporting events. "The first stuff that we did together was some of our best," Schon later told the *Arizona Republic*, "because we went into it blindly."

The song's lasting popularity led to a No. 30 finish on *Billboard*'s adult contemporary chart for a live version of "Lights" released in conjunction with the *Time³* box set. *Infinity* just kept selling too. "Journey achieved the almost unprecedented feat of earning a platinum album for one million units sold," San Francisco music writer **Joel Selvin** marveled back then, "without the aid or benefit of a hit single."

LIGHTS
By Steve Perry, Neal Schon

HIGHEST CHARTING WEEK:
Record World, #63, September 16, 1978

ARTIST	SINGLE
1. Commodores	Three Times a Lady
2. A Taste of Honey	Boogie Oogie Oogie
3. Frankie Valli	Grease
4. Olivia Newton-John	Hopelessly Devoted to You
5. Exile	Kiss You All Over
6. Foreigner	Hot Blooded
7. The Rolling Stones	Miss You
8. John Travolta & Olivia Newton-John	Summer Nights
9. Andy Gibb	An Everlasting Love
63. JOURNEY	**LIGHTS**

Most importantly, "Lights" paved the way for a collaborative relationship that would take Perry and Schon to once-unimaginable heights.

"In addition to Neal Schon being one of the best guitar players on Earth since **Carlos Santana**," longtime *Rolling Stone* writer and editor **David Wild** said, "they had that duality of the lead singer and the guitar player—like [the Rolling Stones'] **Mick [Jagger]** and **Keith [Richards]** have it—as central figures in the band."

"Lights" also became the final Journey single to feature Aynsley Dunbar, who was having far more trouble accepting the band's repositioning as a radio-ready arena-rock group—in particular out on the road.

"They wanted to play everything exactly note for note according to the record," Dunbar told *BAM*. "I never wanted to do that, but I did it for the last album. It bored the shit out of me." [32, 44, 69, 180, 202, 261, 353, 410, 411]

tually become the first band to headline **Bill Graham**'s huge annual event four times, doing so in 1979-80 and 1982-83. Yet no appearance was more historically important than the show on September 2, 1978 at Oakland-Alameda County Coliseum, as their unhappy early drummer Aynsley Dunbar took a final bow.

"He did a very noble job I think, and a good job, of recording *Infinity* in a very simple style," Ross Valory told *Jam Magazine*. Everything changed, however, once they started touring the album. "All of the songs started getting real busy," Valory added. "Basically, he was bored with the new approach, and he was unwilling to hold to the parts."

Dunbar complained that Journey was "getting more formulated, note-for-note, every goddamn night. Everybody says, 'My god, that's a tight band.' It's tight because it doesn't do anything," he told *Rolling Stone*.

Over a four-album stint, Dunbar had helped transform a band that initially could not sell 200,000 records into one that sold millions. But he chafed at the concessions required to take the band into the mainstream, eventually separating himself from the rest of Journey. "He said that it was too simple, not adventurous enough," Neal Schon told *Sounds*.

This passion for the free-form approach of their earliest days wasn't contingent on its commercial appeal—or lack thereof. "You believe that financial success is gonna do it for you, but it never does," Dunbar told *BAM*. "All the financial success in the world can't touch your artistic feeling. Once that's destroyed, you can't really enjoy yourself."

Dunbar left for a turn-of-the-1980s tenure with **Jefferson Starship**, who at that point aimed to "play more rock and roll. They don't want to play so much MOR music, which, let's face it, is slightly boring," Dunbar added.

Journey had no such qualms. The next six albums without Dunbar sold an astonishing 25 million copies in the United States alone, beginning with *Infinity*'s three-times-platinum follow-up. "He had a very stiff, uncompromising attitude. It was like, 'Hey, I am who I am and this is the way I play,'" Perry told the Independent Press Service. "It was causing problems with the new music we were trying to get ready for *Evolution*."

It was left to **Herbie Herbert** to break the news. "The band was saying, 'Herbie, we can't go on with Aynsley anymore,'" Herbert told **Matthew Carty**, "and you've got to take care of it. You've got to fire him.'"

He'd already identified a possible replacement on stage with opening act **Ronnie Montrose**. "The drummer that he had, Steve Smith, was a monster," Herbert added. "We were watching him play with Ronnie Montrose every night, and we were like, 'There's our view of a replacement for Aynsley right there.'"

One more departure would follow in 1978: Journey's tour sponsorship by Budweiser brought charges of promoting teenage drinking. "I never thought of it that way," Herbert admitted to *Rolling Stone*. "When I was told that's what I was doing, I said, 'Well, when this agreement expires, I will not renew.'"

Dunbar's relationship with Journey would officially end, as it did with other future ex-members, after a flurry of legal activity. The drummer belatedly sued Journey in 1980, seeking back royalties. "Before the money came in, they squeezed me out," Dunbar told **Joel Selvin**. Both sides settled out of court. [44, 47, 56, 72, 81, 109, 125, 209, 386]

LADY LUCK

Three albums into the Steve Perry era had
Journey soaring. The band honed its musical
approach, and Columbia Records was convinced.
They were a tireless touring juggernaut, and
album sales fueled success never imagined.
But that success brought new tensions, and the
group was about to evolve yet again.

WINTER 1978-79

NUGGETS

▶ Journey is on national television on PBS *Best of Soundstage* where they perform "Feeling that Way," "Winds of March," "Lights" and "Wheel in the Sky."—*PBS*

▶ Ex-Journey drummer Aynsley Dunbar has stepped in to replace **Jefferson Starship**'s **Johnny Barbats**, who was seriously injured in an auto smash-up last November when he swerved to miss hitting a deer in the road. Like Barbats, Dunbar is a journeyman sessioneer with an impressive list of credits to his career—including stints with **David Bowie**, **Frank Zappa**, and **Jeff Beck**, among others. He'll tour and record with Starship until Barbats—currently recuperating at home in Comptshe, California—returns to the fold. —*Circus*

▶ *Head First* is the name of **The Babys'** forthcoming Chrysalis album. This first single opens with emotional piano playing by Jonathan Cain and matching singing by **John Waite**. The mood moves upbeat when the orchestration and drums kick in. This is Top 40 material.
—*Cashbox*

COLLABORATIONS

▶ Neal Schon plays guitar on "In Your Heart," on **Giants'** album, *Giants*.
▶ Gregg Rolie plays organ on **Giants'** album, *Giants*.

ON THE ROAD

▶ Blondie, REO Speedwagon, and Stoneground.

SuperJam 2 Becomes Smith's Debut Journey Performance

Steve Smith's debut with Journey did not occur in a crowded stadium, but instead on a crowded stage. Journey took part in one of the most unusual editions of the *King Biscuit Flower Hour* radio program, which typically included in-concert performances before throngs of fans. "SuperJam 2" was recorded on October 1, 1978 in the intimate Automatt Studio on Folsom Street in San Francisco, with a group of collaborators that also included **Tom Johnston** of **The Doobie Brothers**.

"I was at [Cleveland's] WMMS at the time and we ran *King Biscuit* on Sunday nights, and *King Biscuit* was always just snippets from different concerts—but they did an hour with Journey," longtime radio executive **John Gorman** said. "It was the only *King Biscuit* that wasn't a concert performance. It was live in the studio, right after Steve Perry joined the band, and the **Tower of Power** horns were also there."

Aynsley Dunbar had been gone only a matter of weeks, and Smith had never worked with any group with a proper vocalist. He'd been part of a series of high school and college bands, then backed up some established jazz guys. None of them sang. If someone took the mic, it was only a one-off from a full-time instrumentalist.

Yet these Automatt performances confirmed that Smith transitioned into Journey with a fluidity to match his playing. The stint with **Jean-Luc Ponty** had pulled Smith out of straight-ahead jazz into fusion, while a subsequent tenure with **Ronnie Montrose** stirred in more rock. Then **Montrose** supported Journey on their 1978 tour, and the next career door opened.

"During that tour, all the musicians hung out together and I got to know the guys in Journey, which eventually led to them asking me to join the band," Smith said. "Ronnie was supportive of that and knew that it was a good move for me. He could see that Journey had a strong future and that I was interested in taking the next step on my musical adventure, which was playing with a rock group that had vocals."

That familiarity helped quickly seal whatever fractures remained from the split with Dunbar. "We are a band now," Perry told *Billboard* in 1980, "whereas before there were four people going in one direction and one person going in another."

Journey hadn't yet begun sessions for *Evolution*, so Smith set about learning the band's older repertoire. It gave him a chance to dig deep into their initial, more improvisational music—and eventually to put his inimitable

Continued on Page 99

ROLIE-PERRY CO-VOCALS SHINE IN *EVOLUTION'S* LEADOFF

The first single from *Evolution* belied how much Gregg Rolie's outsized early influence was ebbing in Journey. He was once again front and center on "Just the Same Way," with Steve Perry adding jet fuel through counterpoint chorus and bridge vocals.

Record buyers, as before, stayed away in droves: "Just the Same Way" struggled to get into the Top 60 after its March 1979 release—much less the Top 40. That's no reflection, however, on the song itself as Journey once again deftly leveraged a gone-too-soon chemistry between Rolie and Perry. Built on a Rolie keyboard figure, "Just the Same Way" skillfully balanced Rolie's simmering sexuality with Perry's love struck optimism.

Unfortunately, they would only share the studio mic one more time before Rolie left. "I liked when we sang and traded off of each other," Rolie later told *Rock Cellar*. "I would have loved to have done more, but you get tired of hearing one voice. I know that I do."

Their contrasting vocals matched the contrasting narratives on "Just the Same Way," even as Rolie and Perry's differing musical backgrounds and influences took Journey into exciting new places in the studio. The band suddenly had an intrigue that it lacked early on, and a tension that would not exist again.

"That incarnation had a particular sense of groove that was very deep—a deep pocket and a settled feel," Smith said. "Gregg Rolie particularly added to that, because he was essentially a Hammond B-3 player coming out of a blues tradition and background and, of course, he was a mainstay in the original **Santana**. He brought a nice groove sense to the group."

Smith added that Perry "had a great sense of time and feel and he had the control to place his vocals exactly where he wanted them in relation to the groove. That is a rare quality. That particular incarnation of the band had a nice character that I really enjoyed."

The fact that Rolie's second and last charting song with Journey once again underperformed did not keep its parent album from streaking toward multimillion sales. Journey was already

out on tour promoting *Evolution*.

Ross Valory credited the album's success to that tireless roadwork, and the help of many friendly FM programmers. "What allowed the group to sell platinum albums without hit singles was the fact that we've been on the road

---

JUST THE SAME WAY
By Gregg Rolie, Neal Schon, Ross Valory

HIGHEST CHARTING WEEK:
Billboard, #58, May 19, 1979

ARTIST	SINGLE
1. Peaches & Herb	Reunited
2. Donna Summer	Hot Stuff
3. Village People	In the Navy
4. Suzi Quatro & Chris Norman	Stumblin' In
5. Wings	Goodnight Tonight
6. Bee Gees	Love You Inside Out
7. The Jacksons	Shake Your Body (Down to the Ground)
8. Cher	Take Me Home
9. Sister Sledge	He's the Greatest Dancer
52. JOURNEY	**JUST THE SAME WAY**

Weeks on Chart: 8
Cashbox, #63, May 12, 1979
Record World, #75, April 21, 1979
Sources: Billboard, Cashbox, Record World

---

for seven years," he later told the Blue Jean Network. "It's been done by other groups, but it is the unconventional way—and it's the long way."

Perry and Rolie recorded one more major vocal feature together, "Someday Soon," from 1980's *Departure*, before Rolie left for a solo career. Years later, Herbert still hadn't gotten over his exit.

"If you go and see his band play right now, he lets you know that he was a very big part of both Santana and Journey. A very big component, and really the leader, you know," Herbert told *Melodic Rock*. "It was devastating when he left Journey. I was fuckin' crushed." [3, 237, 262, 376]

stamp on it in concert. Journey's setlists would continue leaning in that direction until Gregg Rolie's 1980 departure.

"When I first started playing with Journey, the first two years approximately, we were still playing a fair amount of the original Journey material—instrumentals from the first three albums: *Journey*, *Look Into the Future*, and *Next*," Smith said. "Those were really a lot of fun to play. I loved that music."

Smith had been part of Ronnie Montrose's band for just a matter of months, but said there were no hard feelings. "I left Ronnie's group with his blessing," Smith said. "In fact, Ronnie and I worked together a few years later when he produced **Jeff Berlin**'s first album." *Champion*, which Smith enthusiastically described as a "fantastic jazz-fusion record," also featured guest turns by Neal Schon and **Rush** drummer **Neil Peart**.

"SuperJam 2" kicked off with "Feeling That Way" and "Anytime" before dusting off some of Perry's preferred R&B oldies from the likes of **Sam & Dave**, **The Impressions**, and, of course, **Sam Cooke.**

"I was listening because this was the 'new' Journey," Gorman said. "They'd just come out with the first Journey album with Steve Perry on it, and it really blew me away. He was so much like **Rod Stewart** in his early days, because he was really a white soul singer on those first solo albums, I felt the same way the first time I heard Journey on *King Biscuit*.

"It intrigued me—I mean, I remember it 40-something years later," Gorman added.

Journey would complete 1979's *Evolution* at Cherokee Studios before switching to the Automatt for 1980's *Departure*. The studio was also where sessions took place for LPs by Journey-related acts like **Santana**, **The Tubes**, Ronnie Montrose, **Narada Michael Walden**, and **Jefferson Starship**. **Blue Oyster Cult**, **Van Morrison**, and jazz legend **Herbie Hancock** also recorded there before its closure in 1984.

Legal issues kept "SuperJam 2" from appearing on store shelves, but bootlegs created from radio station copies proliferated. The only cut to earn official release was Journey's version of Cooke's "Good Times," which appeared on the *Time³* box set. [3, 10, 210, 409, 410]

SPRING 1979

RELEASES
▶ Journey, *Evolution* (album)
▶ Journey, "Just the Same Way" (single)
▶ **Robert Fleischman**, *Perfect Stranger* (album)

NUGGETS
▶ Former Journey singer **Robert Fleischman** unleashes his first solo album, *Perfect Stranger*, on Arista. **Jimmy Iovine** produced the LP, which may remind some listeners of **Boston**. —*PBS*

COLLABORATIONS
▶ Neal Schon plays guitar, and co-wrote the song "All for You" on **Robert Fleischman**'s album, *Perfect Stranger*.

ON THE ROAD
▶ AC/DC, Aerosmith, April Wine, Blackfoot, Brownsville Station, Cheap Trick, Cheech & Chong, Eddie Money, Fabulous Poodles, Graham Parker, Head East, Mahogany Rush, Mother's Finest, Pat Travers Band, REO Speedwagon, Steve Lukather, Ted Nugent, The Boomtown Rats, Outlaws, Toto, UFO, and Van Halen.

Journey's Success Shaded By Commercial Criticisms

As soon as Journey found real success, they felt the need to start justifying it.

"When we started out, the critics said we had no direction. Now, it's that we're openly commercial and should go back to what we were," Neal Schon complained to San Francisco music writer **Ben Fong-Torres**, who remembered one critic sneering that Journey's music was "for people who take Quaaludes."

That was hardly the last jab thrown at rock's most popular new punching bag. "It doesn't make me feel bad, actually. I swear," Steve Perry told *Creem*. "Everybody's got to hate something. If there's controversy, you're better off."

Continued on Page 104

Journey Advances a More Commercial Formula

Evolution was aptly named, as Journey set out to cultivate what had worked on their previous album.

In some cases, Journey was practicing addition by subtraction: Gone were Aynsley Dunbar, **Roy Thomas Baker**'s pancaked guitar overdubs, and His Master's Wheels' funky studio space. In other cases, they were more deliberate in building toward their superstar future with a tighter focus on Steve Perry, particularly on the song "Lovin', Touchin,' Squeezin'," and Neal Schon's early use of a Roland GR-500 guitar synthesizer.

"Knowing what *Infinity* did, we knew we could do that with *Evolution*," Ross Valory told *JAM Magazine* back then. "Because it was fairly similar, just a few new ideas in a slightly different approach in sound and mix."

"Sweet and Simple" followed the same soft/loud pattern established by *Infinity*'s "Winds of March" and "Opened the Door," concluding with a quickly ascending segment where Baker's famous multitracked vocals set the stage for Schon's patented pyro. "Just the Same Way" once again paired a dark and sensual turn on the mic from Gregg Rolie with a candied Steve Perry vocal—and the No. 58 *Billboard* single did a touch better than "Anytime" from *Infinity*, which could get no higher than No. 83. Perry even returned with a song paying tribute to Los Angeles, as "Lights" originally had—though "City of the Angels" was a far lesser song.

Journey also wisely decided to return to the space where they fled after *Infinity* got off to a decidedly uncertain start, sticking with Cherokee Studios in Los Angeles.

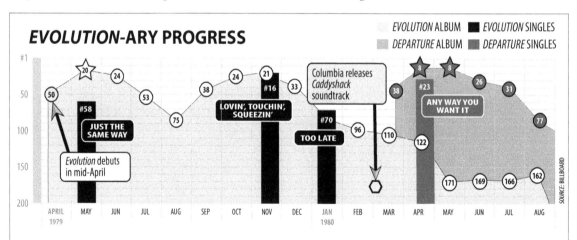

EVOLUTION-ARY PROGRESS

Journey's second album with Steve Perry as the band's front man was, indeed, evolutionary. *Evolution* debuted at #50 on the *Billboard* 200 in April 1979, the highest starting position of any of their previous works. Their previous LP, *Infinity*, did not have a single that cracked the Top 50, but *Evolution*'s "Lovin', Touchin', Squeezin'" climbed to #16 on the *Billboard* singles chart. And while they finally scored a Top 20 single, it was still just their first in eight tries. Their follow-up, "Too Late," another Perry-Schon collaboration, reverted back to their low-to-mid-charting singles that peaked at #70. But "Lovin', Touchin', Squeezin'" gave the band something they didn't have before: name recognition among the nation's radio program directors. They no longer had to fight as hard to get added to playlists. The next album, *Departure*, proved they had arrived.

TOP CHARTING WEEK: *BILLBOARD*—May 12, 1979

1. The Doobie Brothers, *Minute By Minute*
2. Peaches & Herb, *2Hot!*
3. Supertramp, *Breakfast in America*
4. Bad Company, *Desolation Angels*
5. Bee Gees, *Spirits Having Flown*
6. Blondie, *Parallel Lines*
7. Van Halen, *Van Halen II*
8. Sister Sledge, *We Are Family*
9. Village People, *Go West*
20. JOURNEY, *EVOLUTION*

Of course, not everything was as it had been—especially for Steve Smith, who was still adjusting to life with an ascending rock band. He'd always played a more supporting role before, drumming in service of someone else's ideas. With Journey, Smith would be a member in full.

"What was different for me was approaching the music from a compositional rather than an improvisational point of view," he said. "With Journey, I came up with drum parts that were a compositional part of the song, which was very different than what I did before."

That's to say nothing of the fact that these songs were anthemic, meant for thousands of riled-up rock and roll concertgoers to sing along with, rather than merely listened to by a handful of head-nodding hipsters in a pipe smoke-filled jazz den. Smith had ample space during Journey shows for a solo turn, but he was otherwise working within a more conventional 4/4 rock rhythm format, emphasizing the backbeats 2 and 4. Smith found the challenge invigorating.

"I had been playing a time-feel for jazz groups or fusion groups that didn't necessarily have a repetitive beat," Smith said. "With Journey, I had to focus my playing on the orchestration of the song and then stick to those parts. That was a change for me, and I found it interesting, as I had never done that before."

Evolution would not arrive on March 20, 1979 without a surprise or two. The low-charting "Too Late," a song of encouragement for a friend of Perry's who was battling drugs, showed Journey could construct a beautifully conveyed sentiment without attaching another scorching exit from Schon. "Do You Recall" felt like the exact midpoint between Journey's guitar-hero beginnings and Perry's penchant for light-filled reminiscence.

"Daydream" was simply a wonder, as the band somehow dived into meditative prog. Ironically, pitched battles took place before the track was finally completed. Baker sent Schon back to redo his solo, and he "must have played it 50 or 100 times and couldn't get it to come out the way I wanted," Schon told the *San Diego Union-Tribune*. "Finally, it came out. I just had to play it from the heart, because that's where the feeling comes from."

Then there was "Lovin', Touchin', Squeezin'," Journey's initial Top 20 single. They finally cracked the code, thrusting open the pop-chart floodgates for good. "The ultimate goal is not really the sales," Rolie cautioned in a contemporary talk with *Sounds*. "The sales are a measure of how many people are digging what you're doing."

As it turns out, there were now plenty of those people, as Journey also moved into the *Billboard* album chart's Top 20 for the first time. [3, 3, 48, 209, 227, 233, 351, 355, 356, 357, 361, 362, 363, 364]

The Boston Globe
April 26, 1979

Evolution may be Journey's strongest effort to date. The band's primary strength still lies in its instrumental virtuosity (particularly the soaring solos of lead guitarist Neal Schon), but its new song-oriented approach, which began on the *Infinity* LP, has also gelled. Lead vocalist Steve Perry, a fifth wheel during Journey's Orpheum concert last spring, now plays an important role. Most of the songs written or co-written by Perry are lyrically and melodically appealing, and his powerful vocals complement rather than compete with the other four instruments. Journey's rock 'n' roll may be grandiose and out of vogue, but for those willing to ignore the trends, *Evolution* should be an inspiring musical trip.

— Ernie Welch

The Shreveport Journal
June 15, 1979

Evolution has spawned some well-deserved hits for Journey, who has finally gotten their act together in their first consistently good album. "Just the Same Way" and particularly the pretty "City of Angels" are brightening up the airwaves, and there are several more songs on the album that would be a good bet for future hits. **Roy Thomas Baker**'s clean production showcases Neal Schon's guitar and Gregg Rolie's keyboards, which more than make up for Steve Perry's mediocre, sometimes off-key vocals. But best of all has to be a drummer named Steve Smith (no relation).

— Steve Smith

Los Angeles Times
June 24, 1979

On Journey's first few albums, the San Francisco-based group played an aggressive brand of hard rock, its thunderous instrumentals dominated by Neal Schon's lead guitar and Gregg Rolie's keyboards. But this album—the second with new lead singer Steve Perry—continues the band's move toward more commercial sounds of bands like **Toto** and **Foreigner**. Journey hasn't completely succumbed to the prefab slickness of those groups, however tempting the commercial rewards at the end of that path might be: *Evolution* strikes a fine balance between glossy pop songs and gritty rock. Such songs as "Sweet and Simple" and "Lady Luck" combine Perry's versatile high-pitched vocals and the band's instrumental intensity with admirable results.

— Steve Pond

SMITH BROUGHT JAZZ ROOTS TO BAND'S RHYTHM SECTION

Still trying to find his own voice, Steve Smith sat down on a drum stool previously occupied by a name-brand rock drummer. Aynsley Dunbar simply had not been won over by Journey's late-1970s commercial shift.

"He was just gritting his teeth and doing it," Neal Schon told *Kerrang!*. "He couldn't get the concept; he couldn't feel good doing it. He complained constantly."

In this sense, Smith's relative inexperience actually worked in his favor. He was a hard worker, a close study, and an open-hearted collaborator. All of that came in handy since Smith was also a jazz guy by pedigree, having studied at the Berklee School of Music before beginning his professional career with **Buddy DeFranco**'s big band at the age of 19. Smith wouldn't remain in one place for long, quickly moving into Journey's progressive-rock orbit by challenging himself through tenures with **Jean-Luc Ponty** and **Ronnie Montrose**.

"I was a 22-year-old college kid when I started with Jean-Luc," Smith said. "I did my first tours around the world with him and learned so much by having the opportunity to play with great players night after night." Smith was gathering the building blocks for a platinum-era run in Journey that he'd help define.

"The gig with Ronnie wasn't a straight rock gig," Smith added. "It was instrumental rock in a similar direction to **Jeff Beck**: Instrumental, virtuosic rock. It was the perfect gig for me, and the way I see it in retrospect, the perfect bridge that prepared me for the type of drumming that I developed playing with Journey. Ronnie told me to 'go nuts,' meaning play my ass off and really fill up the space in the music."

Smith was constructing his own unique jazz-meets-rock playing style, song by song and show by show. That process would continue into his early sessions with Journey, where an attention to detail helped Smith quickly integrate into the close-knit group.

Born on August 21, 1954, outside Boston in Whitman, Massachusetts, Smith combined that sturdy work ethic with a focus on playing in service to the music. Those who succeeded him quickly learned how difficult that role could be.

"I think there are several factors. For one thing, he just absolutely loves it and eats, sleeps, and breathes drumming," said **Ron Wikso**, who replaced Smith as drummer in The Storm. "He's always practiced way more than most people, and he's been doing it for his entire life." Every Journey album featuring Smith would sell a million or more copies, as he willed his way into rock's upper echelons. Yet Smith admitted that something was missing—something that traced back to his earliest days in music.

"While I was touring with Journey, I definitely focused my attention on playing that music to the very best of my ability, but there was still a lot of music in me that I felt like I wanted to express—and Journey wasn't the place to do that," Smith said. "Journey had a particular sound and direction, I could play in that direction, and it was satisfying to a degree—but I also wanted to play jazz with jazz musicians. The act of improvising with like-minded musicians is something that is essential to my well-being."

Smith restarted his jazz career in the early 1980s, founding **Vital Information** as an outlet for his first passion. "Even though Journey had a very busy yearly schedule... there would be a week here or there where I'd get together with some of my old friends from high school and Berklee College of Music days and play some gigs around Boston," Smith added. "That's how Vital Information came together."

Smith struggled with balancing his rock and jazz impulses from the beginning, having had to choose between joining trumpeter **Freddie Hubbard**'s band or Montrose's new group back in the 1970s. In the end, he found a way to do both: Vital Information would release more than a dozen albums, through ever-shifting lineups and Smith's stints in and out of Journey.

Something deeply ironic happened along the way: "I've had some people say things to me like, 'That's great that you learned how to play jazz after being a rock drummer,' or some equally ridiculous statements," Smith said.

"Playing jazz is my orientation to playing music. Jazz has its own language and syntax, and it is close to impossible to learn if you don't grow up with it," he added. "Playing any form of music requires study and immersion to play it well. But as a jazz-oriented musician, it is not too difficult to learn to play the other branches of U.S. music like blues, gospel, country, funk, or rock. That's because jazz incorporates all of those roots and more." [3, 5, 7, 25, 49, 237, 336]

Still, he couldn't help but become defensive, as the music press lined up against Journey. "When that audience wanted an encore, and they would not let you leave, it was just so gratifying," Perry would tell *GQ*, long after leaving the group. "I didn't need anything else, as far as an opinion on the show."

There was a sense of hard-won reward for **Herbie Herbert**, the canny manager who had masterminded their success right down to the album titles. "The songs went from eight minutes on the first album to four minutes on the second," Herbert told **Joel Selvin**. By the time they got to *Infinity*, Journey was learning how to craft effective musical statements "without being redundant—without using your own formula over and over again."

"Anytime" could not crack the Top 80. "Lights" barely sneaked into the Top 70. "Wheel in the Sky" couldn't break the Top 50. But Journey was about to soar into the Top 20; they were about to claim their second consecutive multiplatinum certification in album sales.

In some respects, the band may have simply been pushed to this plateau. Schon and Gregg Rolie had not necessarily wanted to move toward pop. But Herbert had the ambition, and Perry had the voice—and that changed everything.

Then there were larger trends, as disco faded. What would fill that void? Columbia Records did not think it was going to be anything so clearly linked to the Woodstock generation. "So there was a scramble to do something to modify what we were doing," Herbert told *Melodic Rock*. "So I said we'll change it. We'll go commercial. I'll put in a lead singer."

Now Rolie and Schon were increasingly on board with making simpler, more direct statements of musical purpose. Ross Valory wasn't in an apologetic mood, either. "Anyone who performs in the recording industry and on most stages is already in the realm of commercial music," he told *Crawdaddy*. "So, there's no differentiation, except in terms of the number of people your audience is comprised of."

Journey ended up meeting the moment, joining other bands like **Boston**, **REO Speedwagon**, and **Foreigner** who coalesced into classic rock's second wave. But Herbert left nothing to chance, spending some $25,000 by 1980 on framed platinum and gold albums that worked as commemorative thank-you notes to radio station representatives and label salespeople.

"There's a brand new audience out there, a totally new generation," Perry told *Kerrang!*, noting that the eras of **Cream**, **Jimi Hendrix**, and even **Led Zeppelin** had drawn to a close—and that had made room for other voices. "I don't think what we're doing now is a cop-out," he argued. "I don't care what they say about you. You know who you are."

Besides, Schon admitted no fondness for their years (and years) of struggle. "We wanted to compete, and we took the steps that we thought were right to do so," he told *Sounds*. "We're not copping out, we're just trying to make money. Otherwise, you can't live."

Thus far, these moves had not translated into hit singles. But Journey was clearly moving in that direction, as songs and solos that were once wildly expansive came into more radio-ready focus. Perry's ardent, broadly approachable composing style had gone a long way toward completing the puzzle.

In the end, Valory admitted that he didn't understand the critics' whole line of questioning. "When you're the underdog... they call you artistic," he later told the *Atlanta Constitution*. "However, when you succeed, all of a sudden you're 'commercial.' It's a matter of semantics. To me, commercial means art which is sold for money." [47, 48, 49, 54, 75, 80, 95, 109, 376, 386, 414]

Herbert, Nightmare Get New Digs; Eye Truck, Lighting Biz

As Journey moved into platinum-selling status, the band's assorted business dealings were also becoming larger and more complex.

It was a vision that grew out of Journey's earliest moments, as Neal Schon and Gregg Rolie played in an ad hoc configuration at the Diamond Head Crater Festival in Hawaii. **Herbie Herbert** had "put them on stage in front of 80,000 people, and the light bulb went on," Herbert told **Matthew Carty**. "That was the first day of '73, and by March 22nd, we were incorporated as Nightmare Inc., and moving forward to create a band that was as yet unnamed."

From these humble beginnings, Nightmare had grown to include a new transportation wing, dubbed Night Moves, with three company-owned tractor-trailer rigs valued at $80,000. They were rented out to others when Journey was not on tour, most recently to **Pablo Cruise**. In late 1979, **ZZ Top** was set to contract with Night Moves.

Meanwhile, Night Lights managed Journey's custom-built computerized lightning system, dimmers, and trusses. The **Eagles** partnered with Night Lights when Journey came off the road. This subsidiary eventually coalesced into a groundbreaking multilevel production company called Nocturne.

"We had explosive growth because we did a really good job," Nocturne lighting designer **John Lobel** told *Projection Lights and Staging News*, "and in five or six years, we went from doing one band to doing lots of bands and big tours with **Michael Jackson**, **Peter Gabriel**, and **U2**."

It was all part of a larger strategy of self-containment that kept everything under Herbert's watchful eye. "I just wanted to manage with the same adeptness that Neal Schon played his guitar. With the same level of expertise that made it look easy, even though it is hugely difficult," Herbert later told interviewer **Lori Baldassi**.

Herbert didn't take a percentage of the band profits, like most managers. Instead, he and members of Journey were all 1/6th owners, splitting profits and costs equally. "The truth is you really love these people," Herbert added. "I really loved my clients deeply and only wanted the best for them and wanted to do it in the most honest way."

He also provided some timely financial advice. For instance, Nightmare and its associated subsidiaries were already renting an entire floor of a

Journey had more on their minds than music as the band began charting consistently in 1979 and 1980. Band manager **Herbie Herbert** expanded their management company, Nightmare Inc., into the tour trucking and show lighting businesses, moving Journey and other rock bands from show to show and managing the light shows at those concerts.

San Francisco office building. If they wanted to continue expanding into the 1980s, it would be elsewhere. That gave Herbert an idea: He convinced the band to buy their own space as an investment property. Journey's main offices would soon shift to a house in Marina Heights.

Herbert continued as a shareholder in Nightmare even after his early 1990s retirement from managing bands. Journey was also initially co-owner of Nocturne before Herbert and Schon bought the others out in the early 1980s. Herbert sold Nocturne in 2011 to Production Resource Group, which changed the name to PRG Nocturne.

"I had a lot of people say, 'Well, you did that thing with Journey, and you know you're pretty lucky,'" Herbert told *Melodic Rock*'s **Andrew McNeice**. "And I say, 'Lucky, man, the harder I worked, the luckier I got.'" [376, 812, 813, 814, 815, 894]

SUMMER 1979

RELEASES
▶ Journey, "Lovin', Touchin', Squeezin'" (single)

NUGGETS
▶ After two years and two platinum albums, Neal Schon says he wants the band to go beyond album success. He wants Journey to have some hit singles, but not contrived ones and says "We're going to abort Mr. **Roy Thomas Baker** [their producer for those two albums] for our next album and get a more natural sound."—*Corpus Christi Times*

Violence Flares Before Journey Plays the World Series of Rock

Journey's appearance at the World Series of Rock on July 28, 1979 at Cleveland Stadium went off without a hitch, as the band continued to consolidate around a new fan-friendly sound that made "Lovin', Touchin', Squeezin'" their first gold-selling smash. Unfortunately, chaos raged everywhere else.

Begun by a local promoter and album-rock

radio station WMMS-FM in 1974, the World Series of Rock brought together some of the genre's biggest names—and this date was no different: The up-and-coming Journey was part of an opening bill in support of **Aerosmith** and **Ted Nugent** that also included **AC/DC** and **Thin Lizzy**.

The station had booked Journey at just the right moment. "*Evolution*," as former WMMS operations manager **John Gorman** later told Cleveland's *Plain Dealer*, "would go on to cement them as superstars."

Seating for the event was on a first-come, first-served festival-style basis, so fans hoping for a prime spot began gathering outside the night before. They eventually swelled to a crowd of 80,000 to 85,000 throughout the downtown area, detective **James Mooty** told *The New York Times*.

Unfortunately, a spate of criminal activity followed, much of it blamed by local news outlets on area gang activity. *The Times* reported at least 25 robberies. The Associated Press confirmed overnight stabbings and shootings, including one that proved fatal. As many as 75 people were arrested, some related to rock-throwing incidents after police moved in during the pre-dawn hours.

At the time, Cleveland police chief **Ed Rossmen** confirmed that only minor incidents took place once doors opened at noon at the 75,000-seat facility. "Medically, this was a very routine concert, one of the best in recent years," **Dr. William Wilder**, director of stadium medical services, told the Associated Press. But another fatality was subsequently reported after a fan fell while attempting to climb a backstop, according to Gorman.

This edition of the World Series of Rock was both the **Scorpions**' first appearance in the U.S., and the last Aerosmith show with **Joe Perry** through 1984. They broke up after a backstage argument, bringing the troubled event to a close—but not before a strong performance by Journey.

"I remember, Journey just won the crowd over," Gorman said. "People remember Journey at the World Series of Rock probably better than most of the bands—because they were just highly entertaining. When you can take 80,000 people and put them in the palm of your hand, that's a pretty big accomplishment."

Only one more World Series of Rock show took place. Organizers made sure there was assigned seating. [285, 286, 287, 396, 410]

FALL 1979

RELEASES
▶ Journey, *In the Beginning* (album)

Jonathan Cain Debuts On The Babys' *Union Jacks*

The Babys seemed on the verge of disintegrating during the recording of 1978's *Head First*, which the group completed as a trio after a split with co-founder **Michael Corby**. "It wasn't one of those things that happens in two months," front man **John Waite** told *Creem*. "It built up and built up to the point where we couldn't play together."

But then "Every Time I Think of You" became a Top 15 hit, sending *Head First* to The Babys' highest-ever chart position. They were reborn, but still in need of musical reinforcements. That's when Jonathan Cain walked into the SIR rehearsal studio, where the band was holding auditions.

Little did The Babys know that Cain "already had a process and a system and a routine that worked," said their then-new bassist, **Ricky Phillips**.

Cain found out about the opening via songwriting partner **Robbie Patton** and spent some time learning their music—even transposing the string and bass parts from The Babys' breakthrough hit "Isn't It Time" onto the keyboard. Cain was not particularly optimistic since he had heard they were planning to audition some 40 others, but he and The Babys hit it off.

"He seemed to have the same sense of direction, but we didn't realize at the time how great of a writer he was," Babys drummer **Tony Brock** said. "He played all of the previous Babys stuff perfectly, and had the groove, which we required—and plus, he had a good voice for backups."

It helped that Cain was so prepared. But Waite said he was most impressed by the newcomer's

sense of determination. "He got on the keyboards and it was really rock 'n' roll. He was goin' for it," Waite told *Creem*. "He got the gig immediately, and we said, 'Pack your case.'"

For the stoic Cain, this day had been a long time coming, but he could already sense The Babys were more of a way station than the final destination. "At first glance, the band seemed to be on its way to really making it," Cain wrote in *Don't Stop Believin'*, noting their two previous No. 13 hit singles. Babys manager **Chip Rachlin** informed him early on, however, that they had racked up nearly a million dollars in debt to their record label, after Chrysalis funded sessions and tours while the group struggled to break through.

Cain's weekly pay would be only $250, though it was "more than I got at Cal Stereo!" he later joked.

"When I walked in, Jonathan had just been hired. Little did I know that Jonathan and I would become so close," said Phillips, who had been knocking around Salt Lake City with a band called **Nasty Habit** before trying his luck in L.A. "We were able to walk in—the two Yankees in a British band—and we had this sort of immediate bond."

The collaborative spirit they quickly forged reinvigorated The Babys on *Union Jacks*, then carried the trio of Cain, Phillips, and Waite into **Bad English** with Neal Schon only a decade later. Released on January 8, 1980, *Union Jacks* included four songs credited or co-credited to Cain and Waite, while Phillips and Waite collaborated on three tracks—including the ambitious multipart "Union Jack."

"The band was pretty serious, behind closed doors and working on the music," Phillips said. "John was really, really particular. When I first joined the band, John said, 'Listen, if you've got an idea at 2 or 3 in the morning, call me and I'll put the coffee on. Let's get to it.' So we wrote "Union Jack" under that same premise. He wanted to do almost a mini-rock opera, so I wrote almost 30 minutes' worth of music with John, combined with a lot of music I had written before.

"That was my experience with John," Phillips

Continued on Page 113

Alton Kelley (left) and Stanley Mouse.

MOUSE, KELLEY ILLUSTRATED JOURNEY'S SIGNATURE LOOK

Jimi **Hendrix**'s untimely demise in 1970 ended up having a direct impact on how Journey shaped its own image a decade later, beginning with 1980's *Departure*. The cover art again featured the symbol of infinity—or Möbius Strip—created for 1978's *Infinity*. This time, a flying scarab also appeared, and it became a defining element.

Originally conceived by San Francisco art legends **Alton Kelley** and **Stanley Mouse**, the insect is commonly known as a dung beetle, and would return on the covers of 1981's *Captured* and *Escape*, 1988's *Greatest Hits*, 1992's *Time³*, 2001's *Arrival*, 2005's *Generations*, 2011's *Eclipse* and *Greatest Hits 2*, and 2022's *Freedom*.

Journey connected with the beetle's vaunted place in Egyptian reincarnation mythology, which grew out of a misunderstanding about how they procreate by rolling dung into a ball that doubles as a brood chamber for their eggs. "So the Egyptians believed it was the same insect that kept reincarnating," Ross Valory told *The Record* in Stockton, California, "and reincarnation and regeneration are a big part of Journey."

Kelley had been collaborating with Mouse since the late 1960s, long before their time with Journey and the arrival of the band's art director, **Jim Welch**. Mouse's connection with Valory went back to posters for his pre-Journey band **Frumious Bandersnatch**.

Inspired by his father's flair with a paintbrush, Mouse had shown an early interest in art as a youngster in Detroit. He'd find new ways to shape calligraphy, and then started drawing cars and "hot rod monsters" on T-shirts and sweatshirts. Airbrush versions followed.

Mouse was still in school when the psychedelic era arrived, "and everything exploded into smithereens," he said. He dropped out, then "took a caravan to San Francisco. And going across the bridge, somebody said, 'How long are you going to stay here?' And I looked at San Francisco from the Golden Gate Bridge, and I said, 'Forever,'" Mouse remembered.

Then his car broke down. "I drove this new Porsche to San Francisco and something went wrong with the axle or something," Mouse said. "I heard Kelley was a motorcycle mechanic, and I thought maybe he might be able to fix the axle."

Turns out, Kelley couldn't. "He didn't have the right tool, but we became friends," Mouse said, "and we had a lot of similar interests in, you know, hot rods—and let's just say everything."

Kelley was later part of a loose concert promotion organization called the Family Dog, who lived together on Pine Street in San Francisco while putting on shows at the Fillmore Auditorium, the Avalon Ballroom, and elsewhere. Kelley hired Mouse to do some poster work, and their projects included the now iconic skull-and-roses poster for **The Grateful Dead**.

"He was a great layout guy. He had great ideas. A great idea man, and I had the hands from airbrush painting all these thousands and thousands of shirts," Mouse said with a laugh. "So, my hand was like an Olympic athlete."

Kelley and Mouse briefly drifted apart in the late 1960s before reuniting when Kelley was hired to do "some signage at Woodstock," Mouse said. "We ended up living in Boston for a while, and we worked for this company called Intermedia, and they got us a job doing the Jimi Hendrix album cover.

Mouse and Kelley finished the cover project, but Hendrix overdosed, and it was never published as intended. The scarab was filed away.

In one sense, its reappearance on the cover of Journey's *Departure* was happenstance. They were going over earlier examples when Ross Valory landed on some unused art. At the same time, however, Mouse felt the imagery was part of a natural progression: "It was always leading up to that because, you know, these things already looked like scarabs."

The Möbius Strip remained. "Because of the implications of Journey's name, we tried to use symbols of different forms of motion," Welch told *Billboard*. "The infinity sign is a perpetual motion symbol. We started with that and built from there."

The scarab artwork for *Departure* was based on a shared design, but this Journey LP would become the first where Kelley completed the work alone. Mouse said he remained intrigued by the insect, and he and Kelley continued the theme on future projects. *In the Beginning* offered still another adaptation. Mouse handled the artwork for this compilation of pre-Perry tracks from later in 1979, and felt "it's the prettiest of all of the covers."

At first, Mouse said he and Kelley dealt directly with Herbert. Later, Herbert "would talk to Jim Welch and Welch would talk to us," Mouse said. Welch contacted Mouse about creating the cover for 1981's *Captured*, after he'd started a family. "The Journey *Captured* [art] is my tribute to this great love affair and [our] child," Mouse said.

Kelley wasn't involved this time. "On Depar-

ture, that's Kelley showing that he could do stuff without me—that he also had a hand," Mouse said. "Kelley's hand got better, and my conceptual thing got better. We both learned from each other. And so, *Departure* was him saying, you know, I can do something great myself. And then, *Captured*? That's my retort."

When it returned for Journey's *Escape* cover, the scarab had transformed into a spaceship. "This kind of comes back to my automotive designs," Mouse said. "If I had stayed in Detroit, I'd probably have been a car designer for Ford or something. I was good at car design. So this is where, unconsciously, my drawing this beetle is like drawing a hot rod. It's a vehicle."

Mouse, Kelly, and Welch had helped create what **Herbie Herbert** called "our signature style. It was instantly recognizable," Herbert told **Matthew Carty**. The band's name was stylized on the cover of *Escape*, yet "there wasn't a soul that walked into a retail outlet that didn't know immediately that that was Journey."

Mouse also submitted sketches for *Frontiers*, offering a couple of ideas on a robot theme. Flames surround one of the robots. Once again, the Möbius Strip and scarab appeared, though in a much more subtle form: "There is a scarab. Its head is popping out of it. And there's an infinity symbol in the snake tongues," Mouse said. He also offered mockups for *Raised on Radio* and later completed a stylized cover for the career-spanning *Time*[3] box set that—appropriately enough—found the scarab setting down on a landing strip. Mouse moved on and Kelley died, but Welch would continue collaborating on album projects with Neal Schon, Gregg Rolie, Steve Smith and Journey for decades. A variant of the scarab also appeared on 1988's multiplatinum *Greatest Hits* compilation—illustrated by Kelley—and its 2011 sequel, which shifted the background colors.

Journey assigned others to create scarabs for albums like *Arrival*. "He's our mascot, and he represents mystical Egyptian things: fertility, growth, everlasting life," Jonathan Cain told Knight-Ridder Newspapers. "It's been very powerful for us and brought us a tremendous amount of success and fortune." [106, 264, 266, 418, 419, 420, 477, 816, 817, 890, 891, 892, 893, 928, 929]

Note: See Appendix, Mouse & Kelley Journey Projects, for designs, pencil sketches, and other concept art illustrations.

EVOLUTION
OF AN IDENTITY

Herbie Herbert wanted Journey to have a signature, and he achieved that goal. Much of that recognition was tied to the use of scarabs in the band's album designs. Toss in a little magic from **Stanley Mouse** and **Alton Kelley**, and some guidance from **Jim Welch**, and Journey became a brand. The evolution of the band's look, scarabs and all, traces from 1977 to 2022 (so far).

1977

NEXT

The **Mansfield** illustration from **Next** was the first to incorporate wings and feathers in the album design.

1978

INFINITY

Infinity was the first 'signature look' design for Journey. Illustrated by Stanley Mouse and Alton Kelley, with the album package by Tommy Steele.

1979

EVOLUTION

Evolution worked in all Journey's signature elements: the Möbius Strip, planets, and brilliantly colored wings. Designed by Mouse and Kelley.

1980

DEPARTURE

Alton Kelley developed **Departure** solo, and Mouse said a friendly rivalry formed with his former partner. Kelley, he said, proved he had an airbrush 'hand' too.

HENDRIX DESIGN

Power of Soul was Mouse and Kelley's original artwork for Jimi Hendrix's fourth album. Journey loved the winged scarab and it became a design fixture.

1979

IN THE BEGINNING

Mouse worked solo on Journey's first compilation LP, **In the Beginning**. It was similar to **Infinity** and **Evolution**, and Mouse thought it the 'prettiest' of all.

1981

CAPTURED

Mouse worked alone to complete **Captured** artwork in acrylic airbrush. Jim Welch was art director for the LP and said it was his favorite album design.

1981

ESCAPE

Arguably Journey's most iconic album cover, Mouse illustrated the cover alone. The scarab spaceship bursting out of the planet emulates an 'escape.'

1988

GREATEST HITS

Journey was in stasis when CBS released **Greatest Hits** . Kelley returned to do the artwork solo, and it was thematically similar to his last project, **Departure**.

1992

1996

1998

TIME*

Mouse illustrated mechanized scarabs on a distant planet for the box set's cover and inside booklet. It was his last-ever design for Journey. Art director Jim Welch was credited with the concept.

TRIAL BY FIRE

Elements of Journey's previous designs were subtly present in **Trial By Fire**, including the scarab on a vase. Nancy Donald and David Coleman were art directors.

GREATEST HITS LIVE

The scarab returned disguised as a throne for a queen with a pastel, feathered dress. The Möbius Strip also returned. David Coleman was art director, and Steve Adler was illustrator.

2008

2005

2002

2001

REVELATION

The scarab returned Phoenix-like with **Revelation**, and a design that was unique to Journey. Jeri Heiden was art director, and Sara Cummings was illustrator.

GENERATIONS

Hints of **Captured** were in the **Generations** cover with the scarab's wings. Richard Mace was art director, and Craig Howell was the illustrator.

RED 13

The original art for the EP Red 13 was a simple approach, with no scarab. But a later issue brought the mascot back. Lahni Baruck was art director.

ARRIVAL

After a long hiatus, Journey returned with **Arrival** and the scarab came with them. David Coleman was art director and Chris Moore illustrated.

2011

2022

ECLIPSE

The scarab as a spaceship image returned with **Eclipse** with a dramatic ember design. Welch was back as art director, and Gabor & Zoltan were credited with the illustration.

FREEDOM

The fiery colors of the original Mouse and Kelley's original **Infinity** design returned with the scarab's familiar two-orb illustration. The Möbius Strip was missing from the cover, but was present on the back cover along with a different scarab design that was reminescent of the Steve Miller Band logo that Welch designed. Welch was art director, but also handled the design and illustration for **Freedom**.

PERRY'S 'NA-NA' CUT IS JOURNEY'S FIRST TOP 20 SINGLE

Nothing would ever be the same after "Lovin', Touchin', Squeezin'" arrived in June 1979. The stuttering rhythms and joyous na-na conclusion found on Journey's first-ever Top 20 hit finally separated the band from its jam-band roots.

But "Lovin', Touchin', Squeezin'" also disturbed the band's delicate internal balance, since this Steve Perry-written song recalled a real-life heartbreak. He had really wept, and truly wanted to die.

Ironically, the sleekly approachable single emerged from a jam session. That allowed the others to make a series of meaningful contributions, including Rolie's delightfully **Nicky Hopkins**-esque turn at the piano. "Gregg Rolie instinctively drifted that way, and it took the song into a real honky-tonk, barroom rock and roll kind of atmosphere," Perry later told **John Stix**. "Brilliant, I'd say!"

Steve Smith offered an unusual 12/8 blues shuffle, with Perry initially filling in for Ross Valory. "The song developed as a jam started by Steve Perry playing the bass," Smith said. "When Journey worked on writing new songs, it was a collaborative effort. The band wrote collectively in a rehearsal room. The music would develop in a jam session-style situation.

"Most of Journey's music was developed collectively at first and then fine-tuned into songs," Smith added. "I learned a lot from that situation and continue to write like that to this day. It's an effective way to write because it makes the most of the creative collaboration of all of the musicians involved."

Still, in the end, this tale of love gone wrong felt like it was Perry's alone. Even Smith's cadence recalled "Nothing Can Change This Love" by **Sam Cooke**, a key Perry influence.

For Perry, completing "Lovin', Touchin', Squeezin'" amounted to "love justice," as he told **Joel Selvin** in the *Time³* box set liner notes. He had actually watched from a window as his soon-to-be ex got out of a Corvette and offered the driver a lingering kiss goodbye. In his song's retelling, however, the girl who cuckolded him ended up getting cheated on herself.

Its "Hey Jude"-like ending—which sounds like a schoolyard taunt—then washed all of that hurt away, while helping "Lovin', Touchin', Squeezin'" become an instant concert singalong. **Ben Fong-Torres** saw it firsthand during a show at the Palace of Fine Arts in San Francisco.

"The audience," he groused in a *Rolling Stone* report, "stood up and did the inane waving-the-arms-over-the-head bit while the band crooned 'na na na na-na' ad nauseum."

LOVIN', TOUCHIN', SQUEEZIN'
By Steve Perry

HIGHEST CHARTING WEEK:
Billboard, #16, November 3, 1979

ARTIST	SINGLE
1. Herb Alpert	Rise
2. Michael Jackson	Don't Stop 'Til You Get Enough
3. Donna Summer	Dim All the Lights
4. M	Pop Muzik
5. Robert John	Sad Eyes
6. Commodores	Sail On
7. Kenny Rogers	You Decorated My Life
8. Eagles	Heartache Tonight
9. Fleetwood Mac	Tusk
16. JOURNEY	**LOVIN', TOUCHIN', SQUEEZIN'**

Like so many of the best creative moments for Perry, this ending occurred to him unexpectedly. "One time on the road, the 'na nas' suddenly came out when I was playing the bass with Neal [Schon] backstage," Perry told Stix. "I just started singing the 'na nas.'"

For Journey, this song opened the pop-chart floodgates—while also marking the precise moment when Perry came into his own. Before "Lovin', Touchin', Squeezin'," the group's highest-charting song had been "Wheel in the Sky," which stopped at a weak No. 57 on the *Billboard* chart. Their first four pre-Perry singles had not charted at all. [5, 5, 48, 49, 109, 138, 169, 271, 375]

added, "but Cain had a great experience because Cain, just being a couple of years older, was much more mature about the way he approached writing and the way he handled himself within the band. I was just this crazy guy who'd been sleeping on couches when I hit Los Angeles and got lucky."

Cain played the same role in The Babys that he would with Journey, leading them to a more synth-based, 1980s-specific sound. "At that time, there was no real plan to change the [musical] direction," Brock said, "but when anybody leaves a band the feel and the magic changes. It wasn't a thought-out process. He looked great, he played great—and that's what we needed."

The band's leadoff single, "True Love True Confession," fizzled—but then "Back on My Feet Again" became a Top 40 hit. Unfortunately, it would be The Babys' last one. Buried in a mountain of debt, they split up after releasing Cain's second LP with the group, *On the Edge*.

"We were writing and inspiring each other for a while there," Phillips added, "and it was very strong. Unfortunately, The Babys didn't rise probably to our potential, but it was still a really great time." [26, 39, 128, 263]

ANY WAY
YOU WANT IT

Three albums into the Steve Perry era had
Journey soaring. The band had honed its musical
approach, and Columbia Records was convinced
they were real. They were a tireless touring
juggernaut, and album sales were fueling
success they dared not even imagine. But that
success brought palpable new tensions, and the
group was about to evolve yet again.

WINTER 1979-80

RELEASES
▶ Journey, "Too Late" (single)
▶ Journey, *Departure* (album)
▶ Journey, "Any Way You Want It"
(single)

NUGGETS

▶ **Journey Takes a Trip to the Top:** One of the most pleasant and surprising success stories in recent years is the ascendance of the San Francisco-based group Journey to super-stardom. Begun as a collection of stellar musicians in 1975, Ross Valory and Neal Schon have won "Bammie" awards for *BAM Magazine* as best bassist and guitarist of the year, respectively—the group has gone on to platinum success with the record *Evolution* currently number 44 in *Record World*'s Album chart, and they grace the cover too ...

—*Record World*

▶ **WHATEVER HAPPENED TO PEACE, LOVE AND UNDERSTANDING?** The **Jefferson Starship** will play at **Howie Klein**'s X's in San Francisco on New Year's Eve, but drummer Aynsley Dunbar will still be nursing a bruised face. It seems that Dunbar, **Eddie Money** and their ladies were checking out the venue two weeks ago when an X's patron began getting a little too familiar with the English-born drummer's date.

NUGGETS (cont.)
When Dunbar suggested that the chap should stop, he was answered with a broken glass across the face. Dunbar then proceeded to deck the blowhard with an uppercut. —*Cashbox*
▶ With the release of Journey's *In the Beginning* LP the band crosses a milestone of having three albums in the *Billboard* 200. Leading the way is *Evolution* (#74), followed by last year's release and suddenly resurgent *Infinity* (#117), and *In the Beginning*, the band's newest album in the chart (#182). —*Billboard*
▶ **Jefferson Starship**, who has lost **Grace Slick** and **Marty Balin** and replaced them with **Mickey Thomas** and Aynsley Dunbar, says that despite the lineup changes, the band still has plenty of life. —*Billboard*

Journey Begins *Departure* Tour With The Babys, Cain

As with Steve Smith, Journey found their replacement for Gregg Rolie on a shared concert bill. They kicked off the tour in support of *Departure* on March 28, 1980 in Oakland, California with **The Babys**—featuring Rolie's successor Jonathan Cain on keyboards—as the opening act.

Journey "didn't have to look too far," Ross Valory told *Kerrang!*. "It seems that the people who end up joining the group end up being around the group first." He described it all as "an expression of 'What Was Meant to Be.'"

Cain hit it off with his future bandmates over the course of more than 100 dates from North America and to Europe before concluding the tour in Japan. But it did not start that way. Journey initially would only let The Babys use a partial sound system for their early set, and Cain was too shy to join in their post-show jam sessions.

"Neal and Steve Smith and I liked to jam, and we would wherever we could," Babys bassist **Ricky Phillips** said. "If we had a day off, we'd go have drinks at a club and we'd get up and play a song or something. I always said to Jonathan, 'You should join us.' He'd say, 'Nah, I can't play all that fusion stuff.' I said, 'Dude, we don't just play fusion.'"

"They did like to take it outside; when they were sitting in with somebody, they would go pretty far out," Phillips added. "But I said, 'Jon, you could hang. You could definitely hang with these guys.' It's funny how they ended up calling him, because he started sitting in with us a little bit—and they went, 'Oh, this guy is good.'"

As everyone grew closer, Journey plugged in more of their sound system. Ironically enough, Cain did not arrive as a particular fan of Journey. "I liked a certain essence of them. Some of the things I hated," Cain explained to *Kerrang* at the time. "They seemed to ponce around a lot, you know. ... I was on tour and I'd think, I don't like the way [Steve Perry] is dressed. I don't like the way he's even acting, you know."

But Perry's nightly vocal brilliance won Cain over. "The first thing that hit you was the voice. I thought, 'My goodness, what a voice!'" Cain said. "And they had a lot of cool pieces. I liked the nod to soul, because Perry was very much still singing a **Sam Cooke** kind of thing. I liked the fusion of it. Back then, they had that prog-rock thing going on underneath it all. So it was a really interesting combination of styles."

Then came the tour's May 30, 1980 stop at Springfield, Illinois, where the bands made a bit of history.

"Both buses rarely travel together, but this night we did," Phillips said. "I decided to get a beer, and there was a little club with a little bandstand—just a small, little teeny-tiny place connected to this Holiday Inn. I went in there and I sat down, and Perry walks in. He comes over and sits down with me, and there's just nobody in there. The band had just taken a break, and I think there might have been one or two people at the most sitting at the bar across the room—and I'm not even kidding. So Steve says, 'Ricky, you know 'Mustang Sally,' right?"

Every bass player knows "Mustang Sally," Phillips added. What he didn't know was that Perry was a talented drummer as well.

"So he goes and gets behind the drums, without even asking the band. I get the bass and put it on—and we start playing 'Mustang Sally,'" Phillips said. "Everybody in there hears Steve Perry's voice. It was just the two of us. It was chilling. The band is back there at the bar, and they're holding their beer

up to their lips and it's not moving. They're frozen, and looking at us like, 'Is this happening?' About halfway through the song, **Anne Marie Leclerc**—the background vocalist with us in The Babys—and Neal [Schon] walk in—and Jonathan."

One by one, each of them joined as Perry and Cain made their first musical connection on a postage stamp-sized riser.

"Then Perry says, 'Let's go into "Midnight Hour,"'" Phillips remembered. "So we did 'Midnight Hour,' and it's the same thing—goosebumps. **Herbie Herbert** is on the road at that time, and he says: 'C'mon guys, we've gotta go.' So, everybody takes off their instruments and runs out the door to the buses. Later, I'm thinking, 'This other band is sitting there going, 'Are you shitting me?' Nobody will ever believe that this happened, right?"

Meanwhile, Rolie was losing steam after building two consecutive superstar bands. He took notice of what was going on, even as his plans to leave were still coalescing. "The Babys had toured with us on my last tour and I watched Jonathan and I figured he could fill the bill," Rolie later told *Mixdown*. "So I pointed Journey in that direction."

Those jam sessions helped Journey see the wisdom of Rolie's shocking suggestion. "Neal and I hit it off. We actually were pretty good buds in the end," Cain told the *San Bernardino County Sun*. "We would go out and jam in the local clubs together, and Neal and I especially would play a lot out and about."

For now, however, Cain was still a member of Journey's struggling support act. [26, 49, 185, 220, 234, 407]

SPRING 1980

RELEASES
▶ Journey, "Walks Like a Lady" (single)

NUGGETS
▶ Journey's *Departure* LP debuts at #32 in the *Billboard* 200 giving the band four albums among the top-selling 200 albums in the United States.
—*Billboard*

A BUSY DAY IN CHICAGO: Steve Perry provides play-by-play during a benefit softball game between Journey and host radio station WLUP at the Rosemont Horizon Stadium on a breezy Sunday, May 25, 1980. Gregg Rolie pitched and Neal Schon was the band's designated hitter. Journey won the game in a rout, 17-7. A few hours later Schon had dropped his bat, picked up his guitar, and joined **Buddy Guy** and **Junior "Messin' with the Kid" Wells** at the 400-seat Biddy Mulligan's club on Chicago's north side for a night of blues.

NUGGETS (cont.)

▶ There was near riot outside State Fair Arena in Oklahoma City for **The Babys**-Journey concert where 200 people without tickets tried to force their way into the sold-out show. Journey didn't disappoint fans as the group exploded from a trap door in their two-level stage to launch into a rousing version of "Where Were You" to start the show. —*The Daily Oklahoman*

▶ Members of Journey participate in a not-for-distribution video called *The New Avocado Review*, starring themselves. In one scene, drummer Steve Smith greets a Journey groupie (his real-life girlfriend **Susan Gurnack**) at his hotel, and she is very disappointed to learn he is not Steve Perry. Dozens of other spoofs on rock stars is the brainchild of Ross Valory as a send-up of **Frank Zappa**'s *200 Motels*. —*Circus*

Recording for Planned Live LP, *Captured*, Begins in Montreal

Journey played a pre-recorded version of the instrumental "Majestic" from 1979's *Evolution* on August 8, 1980 at the Forum in Montreal, then dove into muscular versions of "Where Were You," "Just the Same Way," and "Line of Fire." It was, in some ways, just another night out on the road—except tape was rolling.

Those four songs would provide the opening salvo for 1981's *Captured*, Journey's first live album. The band recorded "Lights" and "Stay Awhile" in October 1980 at Tokyo's Kōsei Nenkin Hall.

The balance of the LP, however, came from May 1980 concerts at Detroit's Cobo Arena. Those signature Detroit shows are often mistakenly placed in August. Contemporary reporting, however, confirms that the band was at Cobo for a string of concerts held several months before, while dates in the northeast were underway by August.

Steve Perry, an inveterate perfectionist, would later admit he was often miserable. "Honestly, I didn't like recording music live," he told **Joe Benson** on the *Ultimate Classic Rock Nights* radio program. "I was young, and it used to put a

sort of requirement on me vocally—a concern, let's call it that. Everything had to be perfect."

That pressure to produce studio-quality performances tended to drain some of the fun out of things for Perry, who preferred to directly feed off an audience's energy. "I sing in my car, in the shower, but I don't sing like I am when I'm in front of people," Perry admitted. He said he "wasn't on edge as much as I was concerned that it be perfect."

Captured, which also helped put Gregg Rolie's tenure with Journey into perspective, soared to No. 9 on the *Billboard* album chart while selling more than two million copies. *Escape*, their first LP without Rolie, would arrive just six months later—and go 10-times platinum.

"I felt very proud that I helped to build something that went to that extreme," Rolie told *Rolling Stone*. "I've always felt that way. Yeah, without me doing this, that might never have happened. But it's not about me."

Other highlights on *Captured* included the only recording of "Dixie Highway," and a bonus studio cut, "The Party's Over (Hopelessly in Love)." Journey dedicated the LP to **Bon Scott**, the **AC/DC** front man who died in February 1980, calling him a "friend from the highway," referring to AC/DC's time as the opening act for Journey the year before on the *Evolution* tour.

Perry said their time together made Journey a better headliner—but only after AC/DC "spanked us bad," as he told Benson in a separate interview. "I just said, 'This is unbelievable. What is this?' And then I had to follow this band? Go out there, sing 'Wheel in the Sky?' What am I doing? They're killing me here!" [292, 372, 923, 924, 925, 926]

Citing Desire for Family, Less Grinding Tours, Rolie Taps Out

Gregg Rolie was tired by the time Journey reached Tokyo, Japan on October 13, 1980.

They had slowly climbed from jam-band anonymity to multiplatinum heights, as the band's most recent trio of LPs each sold three million copies in the U.S. alone. (His farewell live project, 1981's *Captured*, would become Journey's second-consecutive Top 10 smash.) Still, it's easy to see how Rolie might have become burned out.

Journey was typically out on the road for more than half of each year, then would head right back into the studio. This grinding schedule produced a new album in each of Journey's first seven years as a band. This was in stark contrast to the group Rolie had previously co-led, as **Santana** enjoyed a meteoric rise linked with their appearance at Woodstock in August 1969.

So, Rolie was as experienced as he was jaded. He'd seen it all, as **Herbie Herbert** soon noticed. When Journey's manager asked if there was anything that impressed him, Rolie replied: "I'm really impressed that we built this band," he told **Roy Abrams**. "This was not a phenomenon. This was built."

Journey's 1980s-era platinum successes may get the most attention, but the band had sold more than 11 million records before scoring their first Top 10 hit with 1981's "Who's Crying Now," co-written by Rolie's replacement, Jonathan Cain. By 1980, Rolie figured it was time for a break.

"I think he made $800 grand that year, and he just decided, 'Hey, that's enough!'" **Joel Selvin** said, with a huge laugh.

Rolie was also quite aware of how music was changing as a new decade loomed. He had memorably described the work of **Elvis Costello** as nothing more than "trendy" in 1979, while making a point of clinging to his own old-school attire. "I'm one of the last ones to change

my pants from bellbottoms," Rolie told *Sounds*. "There's a lot of wear left in these."

Rolie picked out his successor, recommending Cain from Journey's opening act, then packed his bags to go home. "I left because I wanted to start a family," Rolie said. "I didn't touch an instrument for two years. I'd been on the road for 14 years, and built two bands. I had just had my fill of it, and I wanted to change my life. So, I made an effort to do so."

Cain brought along a bank of synthesizers and a knack for storytelling that created the foundation for power-ballad glory. Journey would keep getting bigger, but with only Neal Schon and Ross Valory remaining from their initial core lineup.

Not everybody from Journey's past was on board with the group's continuing transformation into pop stars. "Once Steve Perry came in, I didn't listen to them as much," **Carlos Santana** told *Musician*'s **J.D. Considine** back then. "I do like Neal Schon, but I don't like Neal Schon just in that environment."

Like Rolie, he understood the music industry's looming changes—MTV would premiere

Continued on Page 125

Ross Valory (below, far left), Gregg Rolie, Steve Perry, Herbie Herbert, Neal Schon, and Steve Smith pose for a group shot at the going-away party that Journey threw for Rolie after he departed the band in late 1980.

A JOURNEY BEYOND EVOLUTION.

"Evolution," Journey's last album, began a new cycle in the band's career.

Supported by endless airplay and constant touring, it became the second Journey album to voyage beyond platinum. And the first to give birth to a Top-40 smash, "Lovin', Touchin', Squeezin'." Now Journey evolves again. With

"Departure"—an album that sets a course for even greater heights. With songs like the power-packed new single, "Any Way You Want It." 1-11213

Add to that Journey's relentless commitment to touring (where their concerts constantly sell out), and "Departure" becomes the next step forward. For a band that's arrived at the very top.

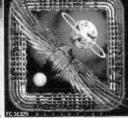

"DEPARTURE." A NEW JOURNEY BEGINS. ON COLUMBIA RECORDS AND TAPES.

Produced by Geoffrey Workman and Kevin Elson. Management: Herbie Herbert, Nightmare Inc., San Francisco.

Columbia Records was building on its advertising, marketing, and promotional approach for upstart Journey with the release of its sixth studio album, *Departure*. Regional promotional directors continued working the phones and stuffing the arms of program directors and deejays at radio stations with posters, tchotchkes, and a steady flow of tickets for them and their listeners to see the band live.

Meanwhile, the advertising wing of the label was dispensing with the more reserved approach they had taken with *Evolution*. *Infinity* had prompted multiple full-page ads in all the trade press—sometimes in consecutive weeks—but *Evolution* had garnered full-page ads in only *Cashbox* and *Record World* (and curiously none in industry heavyweight *Billboard*). But that changed with the release of *Departure*. Columbia returned to its full-page ad assault (above) in the three trades throughout March and watched as the album gave Journey's its highest-charting debut yet, and then nestled into the Top 10 of album sales in all three publication charts.

Departure was also the first Journey artwork delivered solely by **Alton Kelley**, who had amicably broken with former partner Stanley Mouse. Both artists would work separately on future Journey projects.

Departure Arrives with Fanfare, But Less Punch

Two multiplatinum albums into Steve Perry's tenure, Journey felt confident enough to move on from unorthodox producer **Roy Thomas Baker**. In truth, however, they did not go far.

Geoff Workman had been a Baker production assistant, while fellow co-producer **Kevin Elson** had been overseeing their concert sound. Workman was only listed as an engineer on *Evolution*, but he'd grown close with the band over the course of those sessions—and occasionally served as a de facto producer.

They also shifted from Los Angeles to the Automatt Recording Studios in Journey's hometown of San Francisco. Elson switched out the monitors, but otherwise the band used the studio as-is—a marked contrast after the endemic issues at His Master's Wheels in the *Infinity* era.

It was a time of consolidation as they gathered for the next steps in a path toward superstardom. And that's just where **Herbie Herbert** envisioned this project taking them. Never one to shy away from hyperbole, he dubbed *Departure* a "pivotal career masterpiece stepping stone" during a 1980 conversation with San Francisco music writer **Joel Selvin**.

"It will require a larger step than *Evolution* took from *Infinity*," Ross Valory acknowledged to *JAM Magazine*, characterizing those two LPs as "a logical progression. We didn't want to go too far beyond where we were at with *Infinity* in recording *Evolution* and lose [our] audience."

Released on March 23, 1980, *Departure* hurtled Journey to a new plateau as they made their first-ever trip into *Billboard*'s Top 10. Much of the pressure to get there fell on the shoulders of

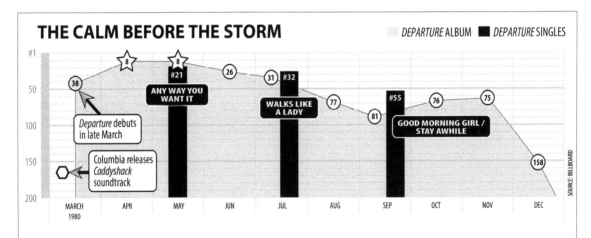

THE CALM BEFORE THE STORM

▨ *DEPARTURE* ALBUM ■ *DEPARTURE* SINGLES

Chart positions shown: 38, 8, 8, #21, 26, 31, #32, 77, 81, #55, 76, 75, 158

ANY WAY YOU WANT IT

WALKS LIKE A LADY

GOOD MORNING GIRL / STAY AWHILE

Departure debuts in late March

Columbia releases *Caddyshack* soundtrack

MARCH 1980 / APR / MAY / JUN / JUL / AUG / SEP / OCT / NOV / DEC

SOURCE: BILLBOARD

Expectations for *Departure* were sky high. *Infinity* and *Evolution* set the stage for what should have been a critical and commercial juggernaut for the band. Critics welcomed the album, but the responses weren't as positive. The effort was still potent. *Departure* was a major leap for Journey, as it was their first Top 10 album—a seminal event for any rock band. But where its predecessor LP, *Evolution*, showed remarkable staying power with 72 weeks on the charts, *Departure*'s stay was decidedly shorter—just 40 weeks. After its Top 25 leadoff single, "Any Way You Want It," the other releases were softer ballads that didn't get on-air traction. The band's momentum was somewhat slowed, but a band member change would come soon. Journey's next LP, *Escape*, would change the band forever. *Departure*, it would seem, was just the calm before the storm.

TOP CHARTING WEEK: *BILLBOARD*—May 3, 1980

1. Bob Seger & The Silver Bullet Band, *Against the Wind*
2. Pink Floyd, *The Wall*
3. Billy Joel, *Glass Houses*
4. Linda Ronstadt, *Mad Love*
5. The Brothers Johnson, *Light Up the Night*
6. Michael Jackson, *Off the Wall*
7. American Gigolo, *Original Motion Picture Soundtrack*
8. **JOURNEY, *DEPARTURE***
9. Van Halen, *Women and Children First*
10. Christopher Cross, *Christopher Cross*

Steve Perry, who wrote or co-wrote every song on *Departure,* save for Neal Schon's title track instrumental interlude.

"When he joined the group, he was a fine vocalist and a decent composer, but not much of an entertainer," Herbert told *Circus* in 1980. "Now he's grown and really earned his place at the forefront of this band." Herbert also spoke directly to how this evolution impacted band co-founders Gregg Rolie and Schon, saying "it shows how secure" they were to "let this new guy have the spotlight."

Perry would not have to share it much longer. Rolie added a delightfully greasy organ to "Walks Like a Lady," one of his favorite Perry-era Journey moments. But he only served as a principal vocalist on one song, "Someday Soon."

"I didn't want to quit singing, but it got diminished, there's no doubt," Rolie said. "I don't think Perry really liked me singing. 'I'm the singer.' Well, OK. But my answer to that is, you know, **The Beatles** did great with four singers. Four, right? Not one. There was a design to all of that: 'You've got to have a front man now,' and it was so they've got something to write about, and focus on. Now hopefully the front man in any band is going to rally behind the guys behind them that helped them be the front man. Bands are bands and they've got to live like that—and that's hard to do, especially when the press gets involved."

Departure would be presciently titled; Rolie left Journey after one more exhausting tour. In retrospect, he admitted that Perry's influence was already pulling the band away from him.

"We came from different styles and a totally different place," Rolie later told *Classic Rock Revisited.* "On the song 'I'm Crying,' I play organ the way that I would play it for myself and it just doesn't match his vocal very well." At the time, Rolie didn't hear it. "I thought it was great but now I don't," he added. "They just don't match up."

The same is not true for "Someday Soon," a perpetually optimistic moment featuring a vocal assist from Perry. "The thing is, that song was so difficult to write," Rolie said. "I ended up looking out the window, and the lyrics just wouldn't come. Finally, that's what popped into my head—someday soon."

Journey was clearly paying close attention to the bands they shared stages with, referencing **Thin Lizzy**'s vocal-and-guitar interplay on "Any

---

Billboard
March 8, 1980

The title here is somewhat deceiving as the quintet continues in the well trodden path it has traveled before. The group mixes blues-tinged hard rock with pop hooks and sensibilities into an often exciting and explosive brew. Neal Schon's guitarwork is still as fiery as ever (especially on the excellent "I'm Crying") and Steve Perry's expressive vocals are in fine shape. Unfortunately on the uptempo numbers, the band has a tendency to degenerate into repetitive boogie. However, the group sells well and the last LP had a top 20 single. Best cuts: "I'm Crying," "Stay Awhile," "Anyway You Want It," "Walks Like A Lady," "Someday Soon."

The Pittsburgh Press
March 30, 1980

With *Departure*, Journey has become San Francisco's answer to **Styx**, which isn't much of one. There's plenty of standard, above-average, heavy-duty fare, just progressive enough and just rocking enough to please their fans. Not much for newcomers though—no grabber like "Wheel in the Sky" and a general dearth of good material. The playing and performance are fine, especially from singer Steve Perry, who generally does a swell job, and guitarist Neal Schon. Without **Roy Thomas Baker** producing, however, *Departure* sounds a bit more amateurish than usual. When the quintet is on, it's worth hearing, especially on big rockers like "Any Way You Want It," "Where Were You," and "Line of Fire." Journey isn't on often enough to raise *Departure* above "adequate." While the music has bite, the grabber is sorely missed.

— *Pete Bishop*

Tulsa (Okla.) World
April 4, 1980

Journey's hard work has paid off. The San Francisco rock group has finally become a top concert and recording group. Its newest album, *Departure*, like its past efforts showcases the group's strengths—outstanding vocal harmonies, Steve Perry's wonderful lead vocals, and Neal Schon's flashy guitar work. But *Departure* is only slightly above average as a rock effort. Granted, there are some impressive numbers—the sassy "Walks Like a Lady," the opening fugue of "People and Places," Schon's awesome guitar work on "Precious Time" being the best. Other material, however, is too stiff and formal, and much too formulaic. Perhaps the best reason for Tulsans to invest in the album is the addition of Steve Smith as the group's drummer, a former music student at the University of Tulsa and a member of the **TU Jazz Ensemble**.

— *Vern Stefanic*

Way You Want It" to create their second-ever Top 40 hit. The outsized riffs on "Where Were You"—which immediately moved into the concert-opening slot—owe a debt to **AC/DC**.

"Walks Like a Lady" shot into the Top 40 next, before Journey's chart action finally cooled with "Good Morning Girl / Stay Awhile." This third single nevertheless showcased Perry's innate gifts as a singer, with the first segment unfolding as an impossibly gorgeous ballad, while the second explored his R&B roots.

Valory correctly guessed how experimental *Departure* could sometimes be, from Schon's rare vocal duet with Perry on "People and Places" to the sound effect from the 1965 R&B hit "Shotgun" by **Jr. Walker & The All Stars** that Perry places at the 2:09 mark on "Line of Fire." In the end, however, *Departure* lost its nerve with the concluding "Homemade Love," a by-the-numbers sludge-rocker that reverted to the worst impulses of their pre-Perry years.

But all of that work on "Someday Soon"

Jim Welch took a more pronounced role as art director for Journey's album designs. The band's image for *Departure* was illustrated by **Alton Kelley**, and was the first to use the scarab design. It was also the first Journey art since *Infinity* done without the illustrative talents of **Stanley Mouse**. The back cover featured vignette photos of each band member (inset), while the album sleeve employed a simple approach with a multicolored scarab with outstretched wings superimposed on a black background with album credits in white. The flip side kept the stark, simple approach with a **Peter Ogilvie** photo of the band on the roof of a high-rise building with the cityscape in the background.

eventually paid off. Years later, Rolie said the track became part of a university curriculum. "I remember Herbie calling me up and saying there was a college that wanted to use this song in their music department to show good songwriting. I said, 'Really?! Maybe I will finally get a degree of some sort,'" Rolie said with a laugh. [2, 71, 174, 209, 267, 375]

SINGLE: *ANY WAY YOU WANT IT*

CADDYSHACK TRACK ESTABLISHES BAND AS A HITMAKER

Steve Perry and Neal Schon were in Miami for a May opening date with **Thin Lizzy**, just days before the mayhem of World Series of Rock 1979, when they started a rhythm-scheme exercise based on the headliner's unique musical interplay. They had been knocked out by how the guitar and vocals went back and forth on front man **Phil Lynott**'s songs.

"I loved his ability and his phrasing," Perry told **John Stix** for *Open Arms: The Steve Perry Anthology*. "This guy is one of the more under-recognized geniuses of that era."

So, Perry sang, "she loves to laugh," and Schon responded with a riff. Perry sang, "she loves to sing," and Schon responded again. Then, "she does everything" led into another guitar riff—just like Thin Lizzy might have. "The riff kind of came to me from being around those guys," Schon told *Fuse*. "Any of their songs were kind of choppy, rhythm-wise like that."

They had the makings of "Any Way You Want It," a single that just missed the Top 20 after its release in February 1980 then gained new life that summer as part of a **Rodney Dangerfield** gag in the golf parody film *Caddyshack*. "It grew from there," Perry added. "Phil was a real poet; he was a frightening genius."

Perry and Schon played a rough sketch of this straightforward, frankly joyous new song for Journey in the back of the band bus. The simple guitar riff would go "all the way through the song," Schon told *Guitar World*, describing this as "another song where there's three chords to it, and that's it."

"It was pretty obvious it could be done real quick," an enthusiastic Gregg Rolie said in an interview with **Joel Selvin** for the *Time*[3] box set liner notes. They almost immediately hit a snag, however, when Rolie's chosen Mellotron began to malfunction. Co-producer **Geoff Workman** attempted to paper over the issue by doubling it with another recording of Rolie on his organ.

Selvin said the result, though originally unintended, "gave the song a kind of celestial ring" when paired with Journey's now-standard stacked vocals. Perry sang the chorus repeatedly, his inflections providing internal drama, with

Rolie sharing vocals in tightly focused bursts. "There is a vocal cluster in the chorus," Perry told Stix. "I was grateful to have Gregg Rolie there, who supported them and would come up with additional vocal clusters too." He always felt those clusters "give the chorus its sort of timeless quality."

ANY WAY YOU WANT IT
By Steve Perry, Neal Schon

HIGHEST CHARTING WEEK:
Cashbox, #21, May 10, 1980

ARTIST	SINGLE
1. Blondie	Call Me
2. Pink Floyd	Another Brick in the Wall (Part 2)
3. Air Supply	Lost in Love
4. Christoper Cross	Ride Like the Wind
5. Billy Preston & Syreeta	With You I'm Born Again
6. K. Rogers & K. Karnes	Don't Fall in Love With a Dreamer
7. Dr. Hook	Sexy Eyes
8. Bob Seger	Fire Lake
9. Billy Joel	You May Be Right
21. JOURNEY	**ANY WAY YOU WANT IT**

Decades later, Schon marveled that "Any Way You Want It" was still "our second most-downloaded song." But really, it seemed predetermined for heavy rotation at every local station. Journey was moving resolutely toward the middle of the road, long before the arrival of Jonathan Cain.

Joel Selvin compared this transformation to the role daytime soap operas play on television: "The band fills an obvious important programming need to a large segment of the audience that doesn't require great intellectual or deep emotional content," he opined not long after *Departure* was issued. "It is, in a sense, superficial gloss. But the shine is brilliant."

Dangerfield's character in *Caddyshack* clearly could not have cared less about what critics said, breaking out in a hilariously awkward dance as "Any Way You Want It" blared out of a golf bag radio. [60, 169, 202, 269, 281, 563]

within the year—so Santana had a theory. "Maybe that's why Gregg bailed out," Santana added. "Gregg is a musician. There are musicians, and there are entertainers. And the entertainers, I see 'em when I go to the circus."

Perry played a secondary role in Rolie's exit too. "No one got along too well with Steve," Rolie later told **Keith Langerman**, with a laugh. "I don't like to be pinpointed quite that way. But yeah, he made it an easier choice, that's for sure. It was time to go."

Rolie would become the rare person to earn induction into the Rock & Roll Hall of Fame twice, first with Santana and then with Journey. Still, Rolie said, "When I think about it now, the family that I have might be my best accomplishment." [1, 48, 60, 118, 211, 295]

SUMMER–FALL 1980

RELEASES
▶ Journey, "Good Morning Girl / Stay Awhile" (single)

NUGGETS
▶Former Journey drummer Aynsley Dunbar has sued the band's management arm, Nightmare Inc., in San Francisco Superior Court to recover lost publishing earnings. In turn, Nightmare countersued Dunbar. —*Record World*

COLLABORATIONS
▶ Neal Schon (guitar) and Steve Perry (backing vocals) on "Love or Money" on **Sammy Hagar**'s album, *Danger Zone*.

ON THE ROAD
▶ April Wine, Black Sabbath, Cheap Trick, Corbeau, Eddie Money, The Joe Perry Project, Judas Priest, Kenny Loggins, Leroux, Molly Hatchet, Pat Benatar, Russia, Sammy Hagar, Shooting Star, Sterling, The Babys, and The Doobie Brothers.

Festivals: Summer Blowout: Los Angeles; SuperJam: St. Louis

The Babys' final album, *On the Edge*, with future Journey keyboardist Jonathan Cain, was received warmly by the music trade press, but failed to find a sustained commercial following.

Babys Release *On the Edge*, Last LP with Jonathan Cain

The Babys' initial discography limped to a close with *On the Edge*, as financial issues, arguments over the group's direction, and continued struggles on the charts simply became too much to bear.

Jonathan Cain came away pleased with the LP, despite it all. "I think The Babys have probably been the most misunderstood band, and someday people are going to realize that we did make some good and serious attempts at making statements and musical concepts," he told *Kerrang!*, "and I'm proud that we went out on a high note."

Still, *On the Edge* stalled at No. 71 in the U.S. after its release on October 15, 1980, while the LP's lone single, "Turn and Walk Away"— co-written by the often-warring Cain and **John Waite**—stalled just outside the Top 40.

"We were really a great unit for a while," former Babys bassist **Ricky Phillips** said, "and then John Waite, he had strong ideas of who he wanted to be as a singer and where he wanted to go. Jonathan Cain was a very, very strong individual in his own right, and I think it was the first time [Waite] had had any pushback—not necessarily in a bad way, but in a creative way. So, it took a bit of a toll, and at a certain point,

Continued on Page 127

DREAM, AFTER DREAM

Journey spent a week in Japan after its last concert in 1980 to develop the music for the soundtrack to a Japanese fantasy film, *Dream, After Dream*. The album differed from the band's latest artistic designs composed by **Stanley Mouse** and **Alton Kelley**. The album package for the soundtrack included illustrations by **Koichi Kubodera** and art direction by film director **Kenzō Takada** and **Aki Morishita**, including an inside sleeve photograph by **Masatada Nagaki**.

ROLIE'S SWAN SONG WAS AN ETHEREAL FILM SOUNDTRACK

Gregg Rolie deserved a better musical send-off than *Departure*. It had been a multiplatinum smash, but by then the spotlight was firmly trained on Steve Perry.

Dream, After Dream would provide a more fitting farewell. Journey stayed a little more than a week after the shows in Japan to complete this import-only soundtrack album, featuring Rolie's last studio work with the band he co-founded with Neal Schon.

Rolie was a force again in this mostly instrumental setting, co-writing four of the LP's nine songs. He said the whole concept was guided by Schon, who first heard about the opportunity during a discussion with CBS/Sony vice president **Hiroshi Kanai** during the Japanese tour.

"He contacted or got contacted by the director from Japan who put that movie together—and so we're doing a soundtrack for a movie," Rolie said. "Schon's dad, who was a jazz orchestrator and real smart guy, helped with the arrangements. But it was really Neal who put that together."

Recorded in mid-October 1980 at Tokyo's Shinanomaki Studios, *Dream, After Dream* featured original music composed for a forgotten fantasy film titled *Yume, Yume No Ato* by fashion designer–turned–director **Kenzō Takada**.

Matthew Schon's contributions with orchestration, strings, and horns for this soundtrack were part of a series of collaborations with his son's band that included co-writing credits on "Winds of March" from

1978's *Infinity*, "Mother, Father" from 1981's *Escape* and "Livin' to Do" on 2001's *Arrival*. Matthew also did string arrangements for "It's Only Make Believe" on Rolie's 1985 self-titled solo debut.

Billboard reported in 1981 that the late Takada specifically asked CBS/Sony to "find a supergroup which would be willing to handle the soundtrack for his film." Thrilled when Journey signed on, Takada left the music "completely in the hands of the San Francisco group."

Herbie Herbert was overjoyed when he heard Takada was "looking for an American group that could do a **Pink Floyd**-type soundtrack," he told *Billboard*. He said Takada was reaching out to Kanai at the perfect moment for Journey.

The film was announced by *Billboard* in July 1980, following an introductory news conference held in June at the Imperial Hotel in Tokyo by distributor Toho-Towa. Filming began later that summer in Morocco, to be followed by a gala Paris premiere in early 1981.

Journey first met with Takada in Paris, Herbert told *Billboard*, "to watch rushes that had been shot in Morocco. They wrote the score later."

Rolie and Schon were in their jam band element again, but Perry contributed as well, co-writing five tracks including "Destiny," "Sandcastles," and "Little Girl"—the three songs featuring vocals.

"It was one of the easiest things we'd ever done, because it was just a series of moods and expressions," Perry told *Hit Parader*. "We did some crazy things with sound effects, but there are actual songs as well." He noted how well it all meshed with Takada's film, which Perry said had its "mysteries and fantasies" too. "It's really a good album."

"Little Girl" was the moment when *Dream, After Dream* melded Journey's still-battling impulses, as Perry's accessible way with the mic paired with the muscular prog of old. "It was the most Journey-esque number on the album," Rolie said in the liner notes for the band's career-spanning *Time³* box set. Instead, "Little Girl" became the 1982 B-side for Cain's co-written power-ballad smash "Open Arms," underscoring Journey's complete transformation. [375, 421, 865, 884, 885, 886, 940]

I could just see that John Waite was restless. Jonathan Cain was a taskmaster himself, and wanted just to get on about the business."

Stalwart Babys guitarist **Wally Stocker** and drummer **Tony Brock** had also begun to question the Cain-led shift toward synthesized pop.

"For Wally and I, that was not the direction that we wanted to go in," Brock said. "Wally and myself, the original members along with John Waite, we looked up to **Free** and **Bad Company** and [**Led**] **Zeppelin**. My drum sound was in between **John Bonham** and a **Simon Kirke** vibe. Wally was the **Paul Kossoff** of the band—and we were slowly getting pulled away from that.

"Of course, when Jonathan joined, it was pushing to the more commercial, more '80s sound," Brock added. "Wally and I didn't really enjoy it that much, although I'm not complaining. It was just a change in direction."

There had been three bona fide hits along the way, including two ("Isn't It Time" and "Every Time I Think of You") that reached No. 13, but it otherwise seemed like everything that could go wrong for The Babys eventually did. At one point, they had employed the same number of managers as they'd had albums.

The Babys ended up so indebted to their label that Waite's phone got disconnected during a session. The jokey band name wasn't helping: "If we'd been called the Adults, we would have sold more records," Cain told *Kerrang!*. "It's just the name—ah—sucks."

Then, to add insult to injury, they had to defend themselves in a lawsuit brought by a similarly named Texas-based group. Waite asked the members of **Baby** how much they would ask for in a settlement. "Know what they said?" he told *Melody Maker*. "Sixty thousand bucks. Shit, we haven't got that much."

When it all came crashing down, Brock had a sense of unfinished business. "Jonathan's influence is really strong," he said. "At the time, we saw nothing wrong with it. It was fresh. I would have liked to have carried on with where the old Babys started off and kept that direction—but it was not to be."

At least not immediately. Brock and Stocker eventually decided to reform The Babys, but Waite—who'd have his own chart-topping success as a solo artist and with **Bad English**—declined an offer to join. Cain was, of course, busy with Journey. So, they reformulated in 2013 around singer **John Bisaha**, then released a comeback record the following year titled *I'll Have Some of That!*.

Continued on Page 129

PERRY'S LOVE FOR BLUES SPAWNED 'WALKS LIKE A LADY'

Steve Perry brought the makings of "Walks Like a Lady" into the studio, having worked out its initial structure on bass. Then Journey's collaborative approach gave the song a new carnal heft.

Neal Schon plugged in and added a crisp one-take performance that clucks and calls. Perry dug deep, turning an otherwise routine set of come-hither lyrics that might have fallen flat in a pop setting into something far more sensuous.

Gregg Rolie had walked in while Steve Smith was fooling around on the Hammond B-3 and ended up employing some of Smith's licks. Smith's delicate brushwork allowed them all to shine.

Released as the second single from *Departure* on May 24, 1980, "Walks Like a Lady" could not match the chart performance of "Any Way You Want It." The song just missed the Top 30 on the *Billboard* chart and the Top 40 on *Cashbox*'s list. But that's unsurprising considering how different "Walks Like a Lady" was from its more pop-facing predecessor.

This was the closest a Perry-led incarnation of Journey ever got to blues—and he actually relished that. "You like to hear some blues?" Perry asked the crowd before playing "Walks Like a Lady" at Detroit's Cobo Hall in May 1980, then introduced Rolie and Schon. "We got two of the best blues players in the whole world here tonight. Two of the best!"

Perry made a similar inquiry during an August show at the Providence Civic Center in Rhode Island, drawing a confused response. "Anyone like to hear the blues once in a while?" he asked, according to a contemporary report by **Jim Sullivan** of *The Boston Globe*. He wrote that the crowd "weakly and confusedly" replied: "No!/Yeah!"

The fleet-fingered Schon certainly didn't see himself as a blues man: "There is blues in my playing, but for me it's more of a classical, symphonic blues experience," he later told *Billboard*. "It's knowing how to make a note cry when you want it to cry or sting when you want it to sting."

Still, when he stopped to draw in the rare

deep breath on "Walks Like a Lady," Schon recognized that he had gotten very, very close to blues. It just took playing "a real stripped-down, quiet, quiet blues thing, where the guitar's barely on." **ZZ Top**'s **Billy Gibbons**, who knows something about blues rock, picked up on it: Schon added that Gibbons said, "Man, I love the solo you did on that."

WALKS LIKE A LADY
By Steve Perry

HIGHEST CHARTING WEEK:
Billboard, #32, July 26, 1980

ARTIST	SINGLE
1. Billy Joel	It's Still Rock and Roll to Me
2. Paul McCartney & Wings	Coming Up (Live at Glasgow)
3. Elton John	Little Jeannie
4. The Spinners	Cupid/I've Loved You for a Long Time
5. The Manhattans	Shining Star
6. Robbie Dupree	Steal Away
7. Olivia Newton-John	Magic
8. Bette Midler	The Rose
9. Jermaine Jackson	Let's Get Serious
52. JOURNEY	**WALKS LIKE A LADY**

Weeks on Chart: 14
Cashbox, #41, July 26, 1980
Record World, #36, July 19, 1980
Sources: Billboard, Cashbox, Record World

Ross Valory's parts were again initially sketched in by someone else, and he followed along with Perry's outline during the sessions. Still, he added smart new touches out on the road, as heard on *Captured* and live clips from their stop at Osaka, Japan.

Late in his second tenure with the band, Valory would take over vocals on "Walks Like a Lady." He also sang the similarly rootsy "Gone Crazy" from 2005's *Generations*. "I just found a niche in the band's repertoire," Valory told the *Star News* back then, "as 'the blues guy.'" [3, 289, 290, 923, 924, 925]

Waite gave his blessing: "I love Tony, and I love Wally, and I wish them the best," Waite said. "I think they were meant to play together. That's what made The Babys work, to me, those two guys. Everything else was irrelevant. When Wally came to join the band, he was the last guy to join, and everything changed. I have giant respect for both of them, and I hope that they can take it where it needs to go."

For Brock, recording the more rock-focused *I'll Have Some of That!* felt like fulfilling a destiny once lost. "We just knew that we were one album short of making it over the top," Brock said. "We decided to reform The Babys, but John Waite still didn't want to do it after all of those years later. So we reformed it with a new singer. I got our sound back, and I'm proud of that—that we finally got back to our roots." [11, 11, 26, 39, 49, 129]

Cain's Missed Bus Ride Laid Foundation for Journey Role

Journey spent most of the *Departure* tour thinking about what came next, as Gregg Rolie positioned his exit. By the time they got to Japan for a concluding run of four shows, opening-act keyboardist Jonathan Cain had all but made his way into Journey.

"I had been eyeballing Jonathan for a while, because we were on tour with **The Babys** and I was watching Jon every night," Neal Schon later told *Billboard*. "I started hanging out with him. We had a lot in common musically."

His value was not just as a songwriting keyboardist. Cain also played guitar, a second element missing since George Tickner's long-ago departure. It was also a talent that had long eluded Rolie.

"I knew Neal wanted to have a rhythm guitar on some songs," Rolie told **Ray Shasho** for *Rock Star Chronicles*. "I can't play guitar for the life of me. These things hurt your fingers."

Cain's former Babys bandmate **Tony Brock** always joked that a missed bus also had something to do with cinching the deal.

"This is a true story: We were on the road with Journey, and the Journey bus was behind us—I don't know, I'd say a half an hour behind us, or so," Brock said. "The Babys pulled into a truck stop to get something to eat, and we all got out quickly because we were going to another show. Jonathan was in his bunk, but his curtains were closed. So we all got something to eat and came back on the bus, and the curtains were still closed. So, we—not knowing—went on the way down the highway."

Cain, however, had exited at some point while they were eating. Eventually, his bandmates discovered they had left him behind.

"We assumed he was still there," Brock merrily remembered. "We had to call the Journey bus and find out where they were. We told them to stop at the same truck stop to see if they could pick up our keyboard player. Fortunately, they found him—and Jonathan had a great time with Journey on the bus."

Brock added with a laugh: "I think that's how you get to join Journey!" [39, 277, 290]

STILL THEY RIDE

A decade after forming in San Francisco, Journey was on top of the rock world. Only two original members remained, but those new players were supercharging their success. The addition of another carried them even higher. Amid these victories came a desire to create outside the band, and chasing those dreams lit the fire of division.

WINTER 1980-81

RELEASES

▶ Journey, *Dream, After Dream* (import soundtrack)
▶ Journey, *Captured* (album)
▶ Journey, "The Party's Over (Hopelessly in Love)" (single)

NUGGETS

▶ Gregg Rolie, founding member of platinum Columbia act Journey, has left the band to pursue a solo career. Rolie's first post-Journey project will be production chores on the debut album by San Francisco band **4-1-5** —*Cashbox*
▶ Jonathan Cain, keyboardist for **The Babys**, has stepped in as Gregg Rolie's replacement in Journey. With leader **John Waite** still waylaid with a knee injury, Cain gone, a tour canceled and an LP slipping on the charts, The Babys have a lot to cry about… .
—*Cashbox*

Waite Injured in Onstage Accident; The Babys Split

The Babys were back on the road a month after Journey's *Departure* tour ended, hoping to prop up their LP, *On the Edge*. Then a freak injury put a period to their first era's story.

They were performing a December 9, 1980 concert in Cincinnati when an overexcited fan reached out for **John Waite**, who got tangled up while trying to break free. "He and I were at the front of the stage, and people started jumping up and they were trying to grab our feet," former Babys bassist **Ricky Phillips** said. "Someone grabbed his foot. As he pulled back and turned, his knee popped."

The Babys gamely "finished off the song we were doing and basically said goodnight," guitarist **Wally Stocker** later told the *Tribune Chronicle*. "Backstage, John was on the table, paramedics had been called and he was just screaming in pain."

This mishap would become a tipping point for a band nearly overwhelmed with other issues. Given time to reflect, Waite decided his Babys days were over. "That downtime was

not good for us," Phillips added, with a rueful chuckle. "It really led, probably, to the termination of the band."

The Babys tried to play the next night in Akron, Ohio. But Waite did not feel comfortable performing on crutches, so "the tour came to a blistering halt," Stocker added. "We were hoping at the time it was just a postponement and we could come back and fulfill those dates."

It never happened. Waite confirmed during an interview with *Creem* that he had "torn some cartilage." Phillips said he was pretty seriously hurt, and had to have knee surgery.

Suffering through the aftermath, Waite simply quit: "I mean, I quit completely and I bought a house with whatever money I had left from The Babys—which was almost zero," he told *Creem*. Waite decided to build upon his art-college background with a return to painting. He considered writing a novel. "I was absolutely fucking sick of the music business," he insisted.

The other Babys scattered. Brock and then Stocker joined **Rod Stewart**'s band; they played with **Air Supply** too. Brock sat in with **Elton John** and **Jimmy Barnes**, while Stocker was part of a re-formed **Humble Pie**. Waite eventually returned to music, scoring a No. 1 hit in the U.S. with 1984's "Missing You." By then, Cain was two albums into his tenure with The Babys' former touring mates in Journey.

"Journey had their eye on Jonathan at the start," Stocker told the *Tribune Chronicle*, "and there he was performing for them every night."

Journey road manager **Pat Morrow** connected with Cain a few months after The Babys split. "I got a call that summer saying that Gregg Rolie, the former keyboard player, was going to retire and that I had the job," Cain later told the *San Bernardino County Sun*. "That was that."

Cain was not exaggerating. Morrow did not ask Cain if he wanted to join. Instead, he said: "We decided you're our new keyboard player, how's it feel?" Cain recalled in the documentary *A Better Man: The Faith Journey of Jonathan Cain*. "I dropped the phone. 'Wait, wait. Say that again?'" Morrow confirmed the offer, and Cain asked when the band wanted him to audition. "There is no audition," Cain remembers Morrow saying. "You're in."

Continued on Page 133

JOURNEY PRODUCES NEW HIT WITH BAND IN TRANSITION

"After I left, it became more pop rock," departing Journey co-founder Gregg Rolie said. "It was a little heavier when I was in it."

That transformation is typically associated with Jonathan Cain's entry into the lineup, but it actually started with "The Party's Over (Hopelessly in Love)"—a studio song Journey tacked onto 1981's *Captured* before Cain became a member. Every element of the glossy new sound that would define Cain's debut on *Escape* was already in place.

"The Party's Over (Hopelessly in Love)" came together as Steve Perry ruminated on bass backstage at Cobo Hall in Detroit. In an interview with *Hit Parader* in 1981, Perry said he had heard Neal Schon's guitar line in his head, so he sang it to him. The tape was running anyway, as Journey recorded shows for the *Captured* LP, so they created a rough demo. All they had left to do was for Perry to complete an accompanying narrative, which he subsequently described as a "situation where a person is waiting for a phone call."

Journey returned to Fantasy Studios in Berkeley after the *Departure* tour to properly record the song. "The studio version sounds better," Perry added, "but not that different from what we started." Their friend, **Stevie "Keys" Roseman**, a Bay Area musician at work on another **Herbie Herbert**-helmed project in an adjacent space, handled the keyboard parts on the track.

"After the departure of Gregg Rolie, but before the permanent arrival of Jonathan Cain, they were trying to complete the otherwise live album and decided to throw in the studio cut 'The Party's Over,'" Roseman said. "Neal and I spent a little time around an acoustic piano and I learned the relatively simple chord progression quickly. That same day it was just myself, Perry, and Schon in the control room at Studio D, and after a couple of takes it all came together quite nicely."

Schon was already collaborating with Roseman on a doomed project over in Studio B. "I was there with a concept band called **A Thousand Lights**, which Herbie Herbert was hoping

would be the next big thing," Roseman added. "He was our advisor, and we had Ross Valory, Neal Schon, and George Tickner in tow. Unfortunately, too many drugs and large egos made any success elusive."

Instead, Roseman would help set Journey's 1980s-era musical path with "The Party's Over (Hopelessly in Love)," the band's fourth Top 40 *Billboard* hit. "It defined their sound for the next decade," Roseman observed. "None of us could have imagined what was going to occur over the next few years, and the huge success that the band would have."

THE PARTY'S OVER (HOPELESSLY IN LOVE)
By Steve Perry

HIGHEST CHARTING WEEK:
Billboard, #34, April 25, 1981

ARTIST	SINGLE
1. Hall & Oates	Kiss On My List
2. Sheena Easton	Morning Train (Nine to Five)
3. Grover Washington Jr.	Just the Two of Us
4. Juice Newton	Angel of the Morning
5. Blondie	Rapture
6. Steve Winwood	While You See a Chance
7. John Lennon	Woman
8. Styx	The Best of Times
9. The Police	Don't Stand So Close to Me
34. JOURNEY	**THE PARTY'S OVER**

Weeks on Chart: 14
Cashbox, #41, April 25, 1981
Record World, #41, April 25, 1981

A Thousand Lights disappeared without a flicker, though Roseman later joined **VTR** with Valory and Tickner. He still hopes to have the old "masters for A Thousand Lights baked so they can be released in some format," Roseman added. "Neal played a couple of unbelievable solos that still need to be heard. With three or four Journey members participating, I'm certain that it would garner much interest." [1, 41, 372, 421]

Cain arrived with an armload of ideas. "I know he wrote some songs that were on his first Journey record that would have been on our record," Phillips said. Among them was "Open Arms," which Waite had previously rejected. [26, 156, 185, 234, 294]

SPRING–SUMMER 1981

RELEASES
▶ Journey, *Escape* (album)
▶ Journey, "Who's Crying Now" (single)

NUGGETS
▶ Nurseries and kindergartens around the land are lamenting the latest news about **The Babys** that suggests that the group may be going the way of all flesh. Keyboardist Jonathan Cain recently left to join Journey, and now we hear that lead singer **John Waite** has left too. Waite will pursue a solo career with Chrysalis Records. —*Record World*
▶ For the record, and sorry, fellas: guitarist Neal Schon is recording an LP with **Jan Hammer**, but he is not "formerly" with Journey, as was reported here last week. He is still very much with the band. It is Gregg Rolie who left and was replaced by Jonathan Cain of **The Babys**. —*Billboard*
▶ For those who can't tell the players apart without a scorecard, both Neal Schon and Gregg Rolie are expected to don baseball uniforms when Journey and Nightmare Inc., management company for both, go up against KMEL-FM San Francisco's staffers in a game prior to the real thing when the A's play Chicago in Oakland on May 25. —*Billboard*
▶ Journey, which won top honors as best group in the recent Bay Area Music Awards and best male vocalist for Steve Perry, will be doing major outdoor dates this summer including the Mountain Aire Festival near San Francisco. —*Billboard*
▶ Jonathan Cain is making an immediate impact with his new band, Journey. Steve Perry said once Cain joined he had written or co-written half the new songs on the band's upcoming album, *Escape*. "We had twenty songs with Jon

NUGGETS (cont.)
in a month," said Neal Schon. "We want to get them all down and pick the best ones." —*Circus*
▶ Journey's "Open Arms" has been tapped for the highly anticipated animated film *Heavy Metal*, joining **Sammy Hagar**, **Black Sabbath**, **Cheap Trick**, **Stevie Nicks**, former **Eagle Don Felder**, **Steely Dan**'s **Donald Fagen**, **Devo**, **Blue Öyster Cult**, and **Nazareth**. The film will be released in August, and the soundtrack prior. —*Cashbox*

COLLABORATIONS
▶ Steve Smith plays drums on "Do You Miss That Feelin'" on **Marlon McClain**'s album, *Changes*.

ON THE ROAD
▶ 415, Aldo Nova, Billy Squier, Blue Öyster Cult, Hall & Oates, Point Blank, REO Speedwagon, Styx, Tensaw, and Triumph.

Cain Debuts with Journey as Band Readies for *Escape* Tour

Journey's next era unofficially began with an April 1981 performance at the Bammies, the San Francisco music awards show sponsored by *BAM* magazine. They then played six more preliminary dates in advance of the release of *Escape*, the first three of which began on June 7, 1981, in Ventura, California.

Jonathan Cain's former bandmates in **The Babys** were still coming to terms with the group's sudden implosion, but there were no hard feelings, according to bassist **Ricky Phillips**.

"I get a call from Jonathan Cain and he says, 'Listen, Journey is asking me to be the Gregg Rolie replacement. I need to talk to you about [Babys front man] **John [Waite]**; I need to talk to you about what's going on,'" Phillips remembered. "He said, 'I don't know if I can trust where John's at right now—whether he's into this or what's on his mind. He won't communicate with me.'"

Continued on Page 139

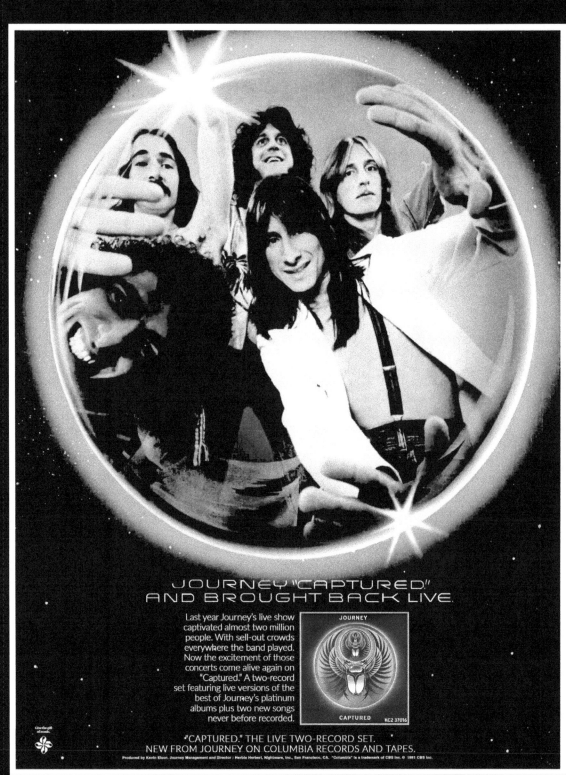

The design for *Captured* had two distinctive elements: the striking, innovative scarab beetle cover design illustrated by **Stanley Mouse**, and the **Jim Welch**-taken fish-eye lens photograph of the band on the back cover. Both images became—and remain—uniquely identifiable with Journey, The designs also proved effective in marketing and promotion, and Columbia used them to build a sales strategy around the strong imagery. Full-page ads appeared in the three main music industry weekly trade magazines—*Billboard*, *Cashbox*, and *Record World*—in early February. With hits like "Any Way You Want It," "Lights," and "Wheel in the Sky" already in rotation at a growing number of radio stations across the country, Journey singles were automatic adds for program directors. But *Captured* only had two new singles, and just one that was "radio ready"— "The Party's Over (Hopelessly in Love)." So with few new songs to pitch, the marketing and promotion revolved around connecting the band's legion of concertgoing fans with the live performances they had burnished their reputation on. The ads shouted "Journey Captured and Brought Back Live" (above, from *Cashbox*) to draw them back into the record stores, especially since a new studio record was still eight to 10 months away.

Live Album Runs Band's Platinum Streak to Four

Journey's first-ever live project extended their multiplatinum streak to four consecutive albums, while creating a capstone for Gregg Rolie's tenure.

"We had done all this groundwork," Neal Schon told *Billboard*. "We had *Infinity* that was hugely successful, *Evolution*, then *Departure*, then we came with *Captured*, a double live record from Detroit that just went ballistic for us and set the ground for what was to come next."

Released on January 30, 1981, *Captured* featured spirited versions of Journey's best-known songs and choice deep cuts spread out over two discs. Ross Valory was not surprised when fans pushed the project to No. 9 on the *Billboard* album chart.

"I would tend to think on the average, the stage performances are better than performances on the albums, soundwise and otherwise," Valory told *Hit Parader*. As time goes on, he added, "the song continues to grow and tends to become more unified and better performed."

Even with the album's expanded run time, several of Journey's typical in-concert offerings did not make the final cut, including "Of a Lifetime," "People and Places," "Opened the Door," and "Lovin' You Is Easy," among others. Those omissions did nothing to stop the album's momentum.

"The band had already exploded on tour, and the *Captured* record was exploding and the energy on that record was something you couldn't deny," Schon told *Goldmine*. "And so, I felt that at any point that whatever we came with, as long as there were good songs, it was going to be big."

In keeping, Journey made room for a pair of new tracks—one performed live (the romantic hitchhiking adventure "Dixie Highway") and the other in the studio ("The Party's Over (Hope-

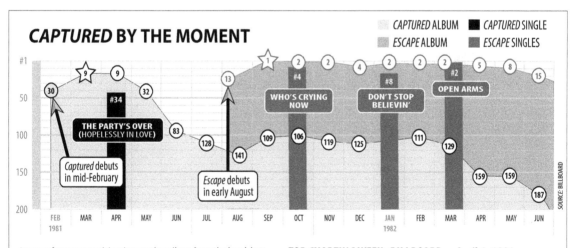

CAPTURED BY THE MOMENT

CAPTURED ALBUM · CAPTURED SINGLE · ESCAPE ALBUM · ESCAPE SINGLES

SOURCE: BILLBOARD

Journey fans were anticipating another album from the band, but there wasn't a lot of new material coming from the band soon. Heavy touring limited the amount of studio time to record new material, so the band and its management decided to release a double-disc live album to stem the tide until the new album was finished. They would use the live show they recorded in Detroit from the previous August. Steve Perry had written "The Party's Over (Hopelessly in Love)," which became the big single from the LP. Released in February, the double-LP set debuted at No. 30 and by the end of March it had risen to No. 9, just one spot lower than the high mark recorded by *Departure*. The album hovered in the *Billboard* Top 50 through May, but the album was just setting the table for what would become Journey's big breakthrough: *Escape*.

TOP CHARTING WEEK: *BILLBOARD—April 4, 1981*

1. Styx, *Paradise Theatre*
2. REO Speedwagon, *Hi Infidelity*
3. Rush, *Moving Pictures*
4. Steve Winwood, *Arc of a Diver*
5. John Lennon & Yoko Ono, *Double Fantasy*
6. Neil Diamond, *The Jazz Singer* (soundtrack)
7. The Police, *Zenyatta Mondatta*
8. Pat Benatar, *Crimes of Passion*
9. **JOURNEY, *CAPTURED***
10. Eric Clapton, *Another Ticket*

lessly in Love)," which previewed their sleek new 1980s sound.

Perry also had his gaze fixed firmly on the horizon: "We're looking at it with an optimism, that it's going to be fun, more fun than before," he told *Hit Parader*. "We're going to go out and do what we've always done."

The future would prove decidedly more exciting than that, as *Escape* took Journey to incredible new commercial heights. In the meantime, however, Gregg Rolie was leaving behind a band transformed. All eyes were on Steve Perry now. Rolie, who had four co-written favorites featured on *Captured*, credited the media for this turn of events.

"Everybody has to have this focus when they write about a band," Rolie said. "They have to have a focal point, always a focal point, so they can make the headline. They design what the band is by their headline. And then you go, 'Well, that's not quite true but OK, we're get-

ting somewhere.' It happens all the time, and that's what happened with us."

Rolie always said he'd simply wanted to get off the industry treadmill after co-founding two future Rock & Roll Hall of Fame bands. **Herbie Herbert** had a different theory.

"When they recorded the *Captured* record, he said, 'Man, this guy, Steve Perry, he's out of control. He's gonna fix this whether it's broke or not'," Herbert told **Matthew Carty**.

Jim Welch returned as art director, this time in control of the entire process. He brought back **Stanley Mouse** for the cover, and the result was another distinctive iteration of Journey's scarab beetle, following its premiere on 1980's *Departure*.

Welch told **Scott Sullivan** that *Captured* was his favorite Journey album cover, primarily because of its theme of a "band in action." He credited Mouse for the rendering, "so I didn't really design it, just had a part of the creative

Journey experienced some of their most creative and busy years between 1980 and 1982. During a break in the recording sessions for the upcoming *Escape* album at Fantasy Studios in Berkley, California (above), Neal Schon, Steve Smith, Steve Perry, and Ross Valory stepped outside to sign promotional artwork for their just-released *Captured* LP. Although it had just two new songs, the album shot into the *Billboard* album Top 10 and helped maintain the momentum the band had generated with *Infinity*, *Evolution*, and *Departure*.

process. ... The creative team made these happen. Each of us had input towards the end result."

Mouse would continue along the same narrative line with the art for *Escape*. "I did the [*Captured*] album in 1981, and it is a scarab that carries its eggs in a dung bowl," Mouse told *The Denver Post*. "It's the regeneration of life. *Escape* is the beetle breaking out of a planet, which was the dung ball he was pushing around."

Welch's biggest impact was elsewhere. Before, "the band did a lot of posed pictures," he told Sullivan. "Back then, they would send the cover art and photos to Columbia Records, and Columbia would do the package design."

He helped Journey realize something more interesting on *Captured*, beginning with a collage of inside images from out on the road. He also oversaw the back cover with its distinctive band photo, using airbrushing and a fish-eye lens. "Plus, from *Captured* on, I always did the mechanical package design, the film and the press proofs," Welch added. "This album was full of 'eye candy.'"

Journey dedicated *Captured* to **AC/DC** front man **Bon Scott**, who died unexpectedly as Journey was preparing to release *Departure*. They described him as "a friend from the highway," referencing AC/DC's earlier stint as an opening act for Journey.

Principal recording took place in May 1980, at Detroit's Cobo Arena inside Cobo Hall, with additional songs taken from shows in August at the Montreal Forum and in October at Kōsei Nenkin Hall in Tokyo. "We were over the top live at that point, playing stadiums," Schon told *Billboard*, and Journey was "rocking hard. There was a lot of energy on stage."

Yet, *Captured* would stand for nearly two decades as the only official document from Journey's shows. A gold-selling 1998 collection titled *Greatest Hits Live* finally collected songs recorded on stage in 1981 and 1983. Much later, Perry offered a clue as to why.

He actually had a deep dislike for performing while tape rolled, telling *Ultimate Classic Nights Radio* that he "wouldn't have almost as much fun as I could have if there was nobody watching except the audience." Perry openly blamed his perfectionism.

More archival material followed with 2005's *Live in Houston 1981: The Escape Tour*. By then, the Journey 2001 concert film with Steve Augeri had gone platinum. Later projects like 2009's *Live in Manila*, 2019's *Escape & Frontiers Live in Japan*, and 2022's *Live in Concert at Lollapalooza* offered their own updates from post-Perry iterations of the group. [242, 290, 375, 397, 398, 399, 421, 423, 880, 903, 917, 941]

··

The Berkeley Gazette
February 22, 1981

Journey's first live album features 13 of their most popular songs, along with two new tracks, one of which—"The Party's Over"—was recorded at Berkeley's Fantasy Studios. Journey is the most successful band out of the Bay Area in the last decade. In this two-disc set "Walks Like a Lady," "La Do Da," and "Dixie Highway" are over seven minutes long and suffer from being overextended. Neal Schon is an excellent rock guitarist, but is easily led down the road of the shrieking guitar solo. All in all, *Captured* does exactly what it hopes: it represents a live Journey concert complete with its many highs and occasional lows.

— *Robert Blades*

Oakland Tribune
February 27, 1981

Journey spent most of 1980 touring North America, Europe and Japan and their new concert LP, *Captured*, documents it. There's an abundance of energy, which captures the fun of Journey's shows. But these versions add nothing to the original studio cuts, so this album is just a souvenir for those who have seen Journey perform live. The tune selection will alienate long-time Journey fans who hoped the group would return to its earlier instrumental-based space-rock style. "Lovin', Touchin', Squeezin'," "Wheel in the Sky," and "Any Way You Want It" sound like routine performances, but side 3 gives the band room to work.

— *Larry Kelp*

Morristown (N.J.) Daily Record
March 22, 1981

Journey is business first, artistry second. Their first three albums emphasized their instrumental chops, but success didn't come until they simplified their repertoire and added Steve Perry. *Captured* summarizes the Perry era with every popular song they've written. But Journey's songwriting is lazy. "Wheel in the Sky" and "Any Way You Want It" show they can write a hook, but having thought of one, they give up the effort. The songs don't resolve themselves. They just repeat until exhaustion sets in. Despite the band's flattery of its audience (Perry thanks them for "letting them be on *YOUR* album") Journey's music is an insult to the very people who buy it.

— *Jim Bohen*

'CRYING' STARTS PERRY, CAIN'S WRITING PARTNERSHIP

Steve Perry was traveling north on Highway 99 from Los Angeles on his way to a writing session with new keyboardist Jonathan Cain when the beginnings of "Who's Crying Now" began to coalesce. All he had at that point, however, was "one love feeds the fire" on a mini-cassette player—and a chorus melody ending with the title.

Cain immediately connected with this scrap of song, as they worked out a B-section beginning with "only so many tears you can cry ...." Perry later told **John Stix** that he had never heard that particular combination of keyboard and solo voice before. "It wasn't Jon; it wasn't me—it was us," Perry added. "That was the beginning of our writing careers together."

This instant chemistry connected with a new generation of listeners: Released in July 1981 as the first single from *Escape*, the gold-selling "Who's Crying Now" became Journey's highest-charting single to date in both the U.S. (No. 3 on *Cashbox*, No. 4 on *Billboard*) and in the U.K. It remained so in England until the resurgence of "Don't Stop Believin'" decades later.

"Change has always been such a big part of our success," stalwart bassist Ross Valory later told the *Press Enterprise*. "Our success multiplied when we added Perry—and multiplied again when we added Jonathan."

Neal Schon, however, was once again struggling to fit into a new musical dynamic. He tried a more experimental solo approach that Cain and Perry felt did not work, but could not immediately come up with a replacement. Always an improvisational player, Schon felt like each successive idea was suddenly worse than the last.

"So the producers and the whole band were getting frustrated with me because I wasn't giving up," Schon told *Vulture*. "I probably did about, I don't know, 15 takes, and it was going nowhere slow."

Steve Smith had completed the music bed with an adroit cadence only heard during the choruses and as the song shifted toward the place where Schon's solo would eventually go. "Steve Smith was just awesome," Perry told Stix. "He was on it immediately. He knew what it needed to be."

But Schon was still stuck. Frustrated, he took a flowing, far more simple turn in the style of early mentor **Carlos Santana**. "I thought, 'Oh, this will shut them up,'" Schon told *Vulture*. "I went, 'There you go. That's what you want,' and they go, 'It's fucking perfect,'" he laughed. Perry, in fact, liked the solo so much he refused

WHO'S CRYING NOW
By Steve Perry, Neal Schon

HIGHEST CHARTING WEEK:
Cashbox, #3, October 3, 1981

ARTIST	SINGLE
1. Diana Ross & Lionel Richie	Endless Love
2. Christopher Cross	Arthur's Theme
3. JOURNEY	**WHO'S CRYING NOW**
4. Juice Newton	Queen of Hearts
5. Eddie Rabbitt	Step by Step
6. Sheena Easton	For Your Eyes Only
7. Stevie Nicks/Tom Petty	Stop Draggin' My Heart Around
8. Electric Light Orchestra	Hold On Tight
9. The Rolling Stones	Start Me Up
10. Hall & Oates	Private Eyes

to allow Journey's label to edit it out for single release. "I fought for that, because I knew no DJ would cut that song off with Neal's guitar wailing at the end of it," Perry later told *The New York Times*. "It was too brilliant."

The results definitively showed where Journey was headed, far away from their jam-band roots. That was fine with manager **Herbie Herbert**, who estimated in a contemporary interview with *Rolling Stone* that the group grossed more than $75 million in the 12 months following the summer 1981 arrival of *Escape*.

"Journey probably grossed more money in one year than the entire San Francisco music scene did in the five years between 1967 and 1972," he said while sitting in the conference room of a four-story local office building the band purchased in 1983. It all started, really, with "Who's Crying Now." [117, 124, 157, 227, 261, 273]

At this point in Waite's halting convalescence after the stage mishap in Cincinnati, Phillips says he was the only one getting return calls from their injured front man—and their communication was admittedly sporadic.

Cain told Phillips: "I don't want to pass something up that's right here, but I won't leave the band if we end this discussion thinking there's still a chance to do something good and move forward," Phillips remembered. "But I couldn't guarantee him a positive answer. I did have to say to Jonathan, 'You can't pass this up.' To pass that up at a time when we really don't know what we have would be foolish, and I'd have back you up on it. So, he made the move."

Bassist Ross Valory, who'd never been in an edition of Journey without Rolie, nevertheless said an easy familiarity had already set in before the new lineup hit the stage. "For our end of it, it was fairly smooth in acquiring Jonathan Cain in that he's even more versatile than Gregg," Valory told *Kerrang!*, "and in that he sounds like he's been with us for a while, at least that's the way it seems to me."

That's undoubtedly because Cain had spent so much time around Journey on The Babys' final tour. "I watched the set every night and I put myself up there in Gregg Rolie's shoes," Cain later told *Classic Rock Revisited*, estimating that he had caught as many as 40 of their sets. Cain said he would ask himself, "What would I play there? What would I want to say there? What do the fans want to hear right now?"

Escape would arrive in a little more than a month, so songs like "Stone in Love," "Dead or Alive," and "Lay It Down" were only just beginning to filter into the setlist. Otherwise, Journey was still very much relying on Rolie-era songs.

Still, the band's new alchemy was clear. "Jonathan's writing is more suited to Journey than it was The Babys, I believe," Cain's former bandmate **Tony Brock** said. "His songs came alive, even though he wrote fantastic stuff for us, because of Steve Perry's voice."

Neal Schon sensed a quickly building chemistry too. "I had been eyeballing Jonathan for a while because we were on tour with The Babys and I was watching Jon every night," he told *Billboard*. "I started hanging out with him, we had a lot in common musically."

Hall & Oates joined the bill less than a week later, as Journey and fellow opening act **Billy Squier** played three straight concerts during the Mountain Aire Music Festival at the Calaveras County Fairgrounds in Angels Camp, California. **John Oates** said he witnessed firsthand how Cain had transformed Journey.

"I feel Jonathan was the musical missing link to an already great band," Oates said. "They had the rhythm section, with guitar hero Neal Schon and the legendary voice of Steve Perry. The keyboard and composition talent of Cain put Journey over the top." [26, 34, 34, 39, 49, 290, 296]

FALL 1981

RELEASES
▶ Journey, "Don't Stop Believin'" (single)
▶ Schon & Hammer (with Neal Schon), *Untold Passion* (album)

NUGGETS
▶ At a press junket for *Escape*, rock journalist **Dave DiMartino** runs into Steve Perry and his girlfriend as they wait for the bus for an outdoor festival in Stockton, California, where they will be playing the next night. DiMartino notices a trophy sticking out of Perry's bag and wonders aloud what it is. "This is the 'prima award'" Perry laughingly boasts, which is given to the member of the band acting the most like a prima donna. "I got it last year," the singer said, and he's taking care of it this year too. *—Creem*
▶ *Creem* magazine corners new Journey keyboardist Jonathan Cain and asks how he feels about lead singer Steve Perry: "Steve has an instrument that God only gave so many people," Cain replies. "And God gave Steve a voice that rings like a bell. And inspires me. When I hear Steve sing, and sing words that I think about, and the melodies that we come up with...I get chills." *—Creem*

Continued on Page 143

CAIN PLODDED A TOUGH ROAD BEFORE JOINING JOURNEY

Journey was selling millions of records before Jonathan Cain joined. Then they started selling millions and millions and millions.

"I've said this often. If Jonathan Cain had not been my replacement," Gregg Rolie later told *Mixdown*, "and without his writing skills, I don't think they would have gone on to do half the things they did."

But Cain was no overnight success. Instead, he clawed his way to the top, inch by grueling inch, overcoming a life marked by childhood tragedy, devastating setbacks, and bad luck.

Born Leonard Friga to working-class Italian parents on February 26, 1950, Cain grew up in Chicago. He was playing accordion at age 8, piano at 12, and in several rock bands in high school. By then, he was also dealing with crushing guilt for having survived a catastrophic December 1958 fire at Our Lady of Angels when Cain was only in the third grade.

Mother Superior directed Cain's class outside, as the smell of smoke filled the first floor. Still, no fire alarm was sounding. "I thought, 'Where's everybody else? Where are the upperclassmen?'" he said in the film *A Better Man: The Faith Journey of Jonathan Cain*. They were trapped on the second floor, as the school became engulfed. "Now the windows were opening," Cain added. "Then kids start leaping out."

In all, 92 children and three nuns perished that day. Cain turned inward, finding some solace in song. "You know, I think if I hadn't had my school fire, I don't think I'd be the same guy—or have the same values," Cain said. "That was a shock for the eight-year-old mind, but then came music. My God, I'm sure glad I had music. I tell you what, I didn't have a lot of friends—but I had my music."

With the steadfast encouragement of his father, Cain attended the Chicago Conservatory of Music at Roosevelt University, using his talent at playing everything from polka to rock to fund his tuition. He eventually made his way west, like so many dreamers.

"My father saw [my sorrow] right away and led me straight to music," Cain said in a short documentary produced by White Chair Films in 2022. "He said, 'Son, you were saved for something greater, and that must be music.'"

Cain landed an early record deal, which led to a minor hit single with "Til It's Time to Say Goodbye" and a 1976 turn on **Dick Clark**'s *American Bandstand*. He initially recorded as Johnny Lee, before finding out that a country singer was already using that name. Cain fashioned the pseudonym that stuck after a clothier's sign he saw at a red light—**Michael Bain** on Sunset Boulevard toward Laurel Canyon.

The famous border radio rock DJ **Wolfman Jack** took an interest in Cain, but his debut album, *Windy City Breakdown*, went nowhere. "I got kind of sick of the music business for a while," Cain told the *San Bernardino County Sun*, "and I went and I sold stereos and I worked as a warehouseman, a forklift operator, and that kind of stuff."

Songwriting led him back to music, then to the doomed **Babys** and to Journey, with a stint in **Bad English** during a Journey hiatus.

Cain "was never the mensch that Gregg Rolie was—he was just the only replacement that was viable that we could find," **Herbie Herbert** told **Matthew Carty**. Ironically, Rolie was the one who suggested Cain to Journey's manager.

"I just said 'Gregg, how the fuck will I ever replace you? I want to shut this thing down.' ... I said, 'The fucking Babys stink!'" Herbert added with a laugh. "He's like, 'No, man, watch him again, watch him again. That keyboard player's got some talent.'"

By then, Cain had built a sensibility, one where real people's stories—their concerns, hopes, and dreams—drove his narratives. Cain also knew what made good songs tick.

"I think singers love him, including Steve Perry, because he gives them something that they can really turn a good melody over," Cain's former Babys and Bad English bandmate **Ricky Phillips** said. "Jonathan generally had some sort of melody idea himself—and then for them to be able to spin off Jonathan's ideas, I know it was satisfying for both [Babys and Bad English front man] **John Waite** and Steve Perry."

There would eventually be platinum successes, even if the critics never got on board. Of Bad English, *Musician*'s **J.D. Considine** simply said: "Grammar is the least of their problems."

Cain was unfazed. He credited his father, who'd once bolstered his flagging enthusiasm by saying: "Don't stop believin'." "When he saw I could sing any song on the radio and play boogie-woogie piano when I was four and was a ham, he got me lessons," Cain told the *Houston Press*, "and he supported me every step of the way."

Sweet though his songs may be, Cain developed a tough-minded sensibility borne out of some extremely tough times. Herbert said Cain played hardball after having already agreed to take over for Rolie, who was to receive a small portion of the revenue from both *Escape* and *Frontiers* as a severance package.

"I'm picking up Jon at the Oakland airport," Herbert told **Matthew Carty**, "the doors aren't even closed [and] he hands me a tape." The recording featured Cain's then-wife **Tané**. "Here's the deal," Herbert remembered Cain saying. "You manage her, you get her a label deal ... or take my keyboard out of the back, I'm out, I'm going right back to L.A, no Journey."

Herbert reluctantly agreed but said Cain's "comeuppance came very quick." Perry became annoyed by the praise being heaped on Cain during a premiere party for *Escape*. Herbert said Perry made so many dismissive comments to the group of media and radio personalities that Cain was reduced to tears.

"I said, 'Now, see what happens when you run into an even bigger asshole than yourself?'" Herbert remembered, while hinting that this kind of behavior had something to do with the exit of Cain's predecessor too.

As before, Cain steeled himself and kept going, whatever the backstage drama. "When you overcome tragedy, it makes you better in so many ways," Cain said. "It seems when that's when God shines, and he blesses us in the biggest ways. Something usually tragic has to happen and all of a sudden, change can turn into a miracle."

Cain hadn't always been so prone to discussing his faith, at least before his third marriage to televangelist **Paula White**. But Herbert—who admitted to KQED that he was a "borderline atheist"—said finding God had made him "a better Jon Cain."

White's role as **Donald Trump**'s spiritual advisor led to internal issues that spilled out into the public eye, ushering in an era of remarkable infighting even as Journey finally earned a spot in the Rock & Roll Hall of Fame. For now, that was well into the future.

Weaving in ideas from both Perry and Neal Schon, Journey issued their first, second, and third gold-selling Top 10 singles over just a few months in the early 1980s.

"Coming from an artistic side, everybody's got ideas and everybody thinks their idea is the best one," Phillips said, "but Jonathan unquestionably, undeniably had really good, solid ideas—especially for the time. The first Journey record—in fact, the first couple he did—definitely proved that." [26, 50, 53, 56, 185, 208, 234, 298, 400, 401, 407, 407, 903, 918]

NUGGETS (cont.)

▶ Journey makes the cover of *Record World* for the second time on September 5, 1981, and their eighth album, *Escape*, gives them their first ever #1 album.

—Record World

▶ Tossing TVs out of hotel windows is something of a rite of passage for most rock and roll bands, and such behavior wasn't beyond Journey either. Neal Schon was caught fondly remembering those times to *Kerrang!*'s **Sylvie Simmons** ... "Sometimes the urge still comes over you to pick one up and—I shouldn't say this" and cut off the chat before sheepishly disappearing toward the bar. *—Kerrang!*

▶ **Carlos Santana** joins Journey and his ex-bandmate Neal Schon onstage for a show encore at the Kōsei Nenkin Hall in Tokyo. It is the first time in eight years that Santana had played with his protégé. *—Billboard*

▶ Jonathan Cain is in Redwing Sound Studios producing wife **Tané Cain** along with engineer **Kirk Butler**. *—Record World*

ON THE ROAD

▶ George Thorogood, Greg Kihn Band, Loverboy, Michael Stanley Band, Point Blank, and The Rolling Stones.

Bad Match: Journey Detours To Open for The Rolling Stones

Journey was still in an uncertain career position, despite early success with the just-released *Escape*. Their musical approach had shifted enough that shows in support of what would become a juggernaut album were almost like a reintroduction.

So, playing a few opening dates with a legendary band like **The Rolling Stones** made some sense. Journey initially joined a bill with **George Thorogood and the Destroyers** for a pair of Stones concerts on September 25-26, 1981, at John F. Kennedy Stadium in Philadelphia that drew close to 182,000 fans nightly.

The initial reception could be charitably described as chilly. *Rolling Stone* said Journey struggled with "commanding this formidable structure," describing their first show as "abysmally muddy." The September 26 concert saw a marked improvement. Journey was "spirited and surprisingly effective," *Rolling Stone* added, and they "made audible points with the sizable hard-pop contingent in attendance."

Jonathan Cain disagreed with the whole idea. "I couldn't believe some of the assholes who were at that show," he told *Hit Parader*. "They were yelling that Steve Perry couldn't sing like [**Mick**] **Jagger**. I should hope not: Steve Perry's a trained vocalist. I'm not sure what Jagger is."

Herbie Herbert's former mentor **Bill Graham** was booking the support acts, which grew to include **ZZ Top**, **Prince**, **Santana**, **The J. Geils Band**, **The Go-Go's**, and **The Greg Kihn Band**, among others. The shows grossed millions, but Herbert became one of several opening-act managers who would question the individual impact of signing on for the tour.

"The dates will not result in any real growth for Journey in the marketplace," Herbert told *Record World* back then. He described their presence on the bill as a "personal favor" to Graham.

Journey then moved on for one more show with the Stones on September 27 at Rich Stadium in Buffalo, New York. Future *Rolling Stone* writer and editor **David Wild** had saved up his money to venture over from Cornell University—but his interest was entirely in the Stones.

Continued on Page 145

SCHON, HAMMER TEAM FOR IMPROV-INSPIRED 'PASSION'

Untold Passion held different promises for its protagonists. Neal Schon was clearly pining for more wide-open spaces where he did not have to shoehorn a solo into a preset number of bars. **Jan Hammer**, on the other hand, just wanted to rock.

"That was the reason why we even got together in the first place," Hammer said, "because of this combination of our minds and musical spirits. It's rock, but a very important part of it for us is improvisation."

They could not have emerged from any more diverse places before taking part in these loose sessions at Hammer's upstate New York home studio. Schon was fast approaching California-tanned superstardom, while Hammer was still building toward his own *Miami Vice* breakout after immigrating to the U.S. from Czechoslovakia just before the Warsaw Pact invasion of 1968.

The talented keyboardist's mother was a singer, and his dad was a doctor who had worked his way through school by playing music. Hammer initially seemed most interested in his father's main career before switching to his side hustle. His interest from the first had been in jazz, and early stateside stints with **Sarah Vaughan** and then the original **Mahavishnu Orchestra** followed.

By the late 1970s, however, Hammer was moving toward figures like **Jeff Beck**, putting him in Schon's orbit. "Jan's really a frustrated rock player, ya know?" Schon told *Creem*.

Still, Hammer struggled to find purchase with this new audience—principally, he argued, because label heads continued to view him through the lens of his early career choices. "They saw me as a jazz artist," he complained to the *Los Angeles Times*. "My audience was a complete rock audience, yet they saw me as jazz. I still can't believe it."

Collaborating with a hit-making guitar hero on *Untold Passion* had the potential to change all of that. Schon and Hammer got to work, recording very quickly as Schon had to fit in the sessions amid band obligations for Journey's blockbuster *Escape*. "We did it real fast," Schon told *Creem*. "We got together and wrote the material in the first three days. Then we laid it down and wrote lyrics to it afterwards."

Not surprisingly, the set's highlights are the instrumentals, notably the duo's funky entanglement on "The Ride" and the **Giorgio Moroder**-influenced title track. "When you

have a rock group like Journey, there's only room for Neal to play a little bit here or there—because those are songs with vocals," Hammer said. "We could feature much more of the instrumental fireworks—that's a good word for it."

But *Untold Passion* pulls its punches elsewhere, mixing in vocal showcases for Schon that ensure the LP misses achieving either one of its assumed goals. Whatever listeners thought of them, songs like "Hooked on Love" and "I'm Talking to You" are simply too conventional to provide Schon with any real break from the handcuffs of Journey's compact, radio-ready songs. At the same time, fused-out moments like "On the Beach" are undoubtedly familiar ground for a jazz-rooted figure like Jan Hammer.

Schon last handled principal vocal duties on 1977's *Next*, and unfortunately still had not developed an identifiable personal style. The duality of *Untold Passion* extended to the mic, where Schon sounded at times like an off-brand **Paul Rodgers**, and at others like a **Phil Lynott** impersonator.

Untold Passion got no higher than No. 115 after its release in November 1981, and Hammer again blamed the label. "They thought we were sowing our wild oats," he told the *Times*. "We created some good songs. I hate to see them go down the drain because the record company blew it."

In truth, however, the results were too jazzy for Journey fans, and too rooted in melodic rock for Hammer's long-term followers. [54, 300, 302]

He learned something about the Journey fan base's level of commitment, critics be damned.

"We probably got the shitty tickets that you would expect for a bunch of dumbass college kids sitting way up top," Wild said. "There was this very upstate New York couple sitting next to us and during Thorogood, they seemed unmoved. But during Journey, they stood and hugged and cried and sang along with every word—and no judgment, they seemed very happy."

As Journey ended their set, however, "the minute they put their lighters off from the encore, this couple packed up and left," Wild added. "As they packed up, I said, 'You know, The Rolling Stones are coming on, right?!' And they said, 'Yeah, no one can follow Journey.'"

As much as the group was starting over, Journey had already paid plenty of dues—and sold millions of records. Serving as a support act for The Rolling Stones also tended to feel a little retrograde because Journey had already opened for them a couple of times in the summer of 1978, toward the end of the main *Infinity* promotional cycle. "After that tour, Journey exploded in the markets they played," Herbert told *Record World*. "They helped us out, so we're returning the favor."

The Rolling Stones were entering a period of diminishing commercial returns as Journey soared toward their biggest career sales. "I think there was some concern about the market viability of the Stones," Herbert revealed. "They hadn't been in the market for three years, and [their early-1981 hits package] *Sucking in the Seventies* did terribly."

The Rolling Stones dug into their considerable archives to compile their next studio album, 1981's *Tattoo You*, while Journey continued gathering millions more fans like the ones Wild encountered in Buffalo. "It's very interesting to think about that now because at the time, that seemed utterly absurd to me," Wild admitted. "That seemed like the definition of insanity, leaving after Journey and before the Stones."

As a new millennium began to unfold, however, Journey songs like "Don't Stop Believin'" could still provide zeitgeist-shifting moments while The Rolling Stones' cultural currency seemed to fade. Wild's opinions changed too.

"I still love the Stones—absolutely love the Stones," Wild said. "But in this century, it's amazing how to a lot of young people, the Stones don't define endless cool like they did for me and for my generation—and probably for the one ahead of us and maybe the one after. For bands like Journey, because they've had these hits that are sort of coming out of reality shows or movies, they've been consistently rediscovered and re-embraced by different generations." [411, 484, 495, 544]

Schon's Side Gig Was Journey's Start Toward the Band's End

Journey completed six summer 1981 dates in Japan, then took a two-week break prior to playing a Toronto show in mid-August that officially kicked off the band's massive North American tour in support of *Escape*. Another seven-day pause followed before the hard-touring Journey reeled off more than 80 shows through the end of the year.

There was little room for a major outside project, but Neal Schon still found a way. He had never forgotten how he clicked musically with **Jan Hammer**, so Schon decided to look him up. The result was **Schon and Hammer**'s *Untold Passion*, a home-recorded album that was a little-noticed also-ran on the charts but changed Journey forever.

"It was during a time period when everybody had taken off for a vacation," Schon told *Creem* in 1982, "and since we could all do what we wanted to do during vacation, I chose to go to New York and see if I could get along with the guy."

The telescoped time frame did not impede Schon, who loved to work off the cuff. Unfortunately, the weather at Hammer's place was another story.

"It was happening pretty fast," Hammer said. "On the first day when Neal was coming over, there was a terrible ice storm. The car carrying Neal got stuck on the hill coming up to my house. He walked up the rest of the way, then he walked in and said, 'Hey, do you have a guitar here?'"

Hammer did, indeed—a Strat that **Jeff Beck**

Continued on Page 149

ESCAPE INTO A NEW JOURNEY

ESCAPE: JOURNEY'S LATEST BREAKTHROUGH.
FEATURING "WHO'S CRYING NOW."
ON COLUMBIA RECORDS AND TAPES.

Produced by Mike Stone for Mike Stone Enterprises, Ltd. and Kevin Elson.
Journey Management and Direction: Herbie Herbert, Nightmare, Inc.,
San Francisco, CA. "Columbia" is a trademark of CBS Inc. ® 1981 CBS Inc.

Journey's management gave the band a distinct advantage in marketing and promoting the group: the design team responsible for developing their image through art and illustrations was among the best in the business. The design team cultivated the use of their signature scarab, circular forms, the elements, and other aspects of nature in their album artwork, giving every album release a sense of style and grace uncommon in the rock universe. With its dynamic graphical use of guitars as spaceships, **Boston** (with art by **Paula Scher**) was Journey's only true peer in that realm of album art. The collective work of **Stanley Mouse**, **Alton Kelley**, and **Jim Welch** consistently gave the advertising division at Columbia Records a wealth of tools to employ in marketing the band over the previous four years. They enjoyed their greatest commercial design success when the band released its biggest album, *Escape*, in August 1981. Mouse's distinctive rendering of the scarab breaking out of the planet on the cover design was warmly embraced by the band and fans alike. The design was quickly retrofitted for use in promotional materials and ads and leaped off the pages of *Billboard* (above), *Cashbox*, and *Record World* just days after the album's official release. By that time, the image was already being emblazoned upon T-shirts and posters for fans worldwide, and it became one of the few rock images instantly recognizable within the music industry.

Journey Unleashes a Monster, Multiplatinum LP

Veteran *San Francisco Chronicle* music critic **Joel Selvin** was among the first people outside of the Journey camp to hear *Escape*.

"I went to the listening party at Fantasy Studio A—which was pretty fucking impressive at that time," he said. "It was this giant room with these huge ceilings. They brought us all in there, and they put on 'Don't Stop Believin'. 'Streetlight people' comes out and it didn't even get to the chorus and I'm going, 'Wow. This is gonna work.'"

It did. In fact, *Escape* would accomplish things no Journey album ever had, becoming their first chart-topper while selling an incredible 10 million copies in the U.S. alone—more than all of the band's earlier studio projects combined. Released on July 31, 1981, the LP also spun off a mind-boggling three straight Top 10 singles.

Manager **Herbie Herbert** would soon be merrily describing Journey to *Rolling Stone* as "the essence of the format of AOR radio," referring to the album-oriented rock format then dominating the FM airwaves.

Those with firsthand knowledge of the impact made by Journey's just-installed keyboardist were unsurprised by this meteoric rise. "Jonathan Cain brought in a more universally appealing songwriting approach," drummer Steve Smith said. "There was a special kind of magic with him in the band. We were able to write some very globally accepted hit tunes that were just fantastic."

Cain's former bandmates were not shocked, either. "It was more like, 'Yeah, I thought so. I knew it!'" ex-**The Babys** bassist **Ricky Phillips** said. "They already had a strong record behind them, or two, and then this one really pushed them over—they became superstars. Jonathan Cain got

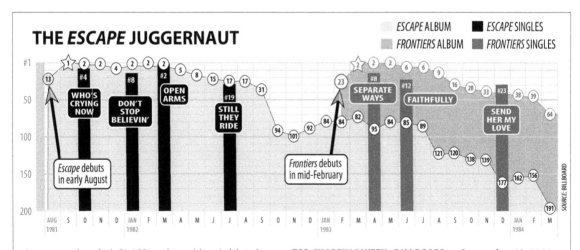

THE *ESCAPE* JUGGERNAUT

ESCAPE ALBUM ■ *ESCAPE* SINGLES
FRONTIERS ALBUM ■ *FRONTIERS* SINGLES

SOURCE: BILLBOARD

Escape was released July 31, 1981, and a week later it debuted on the *Billboard* 200 at #13, the first time a Journey album had ever debuted in the Top 15. It reached #1 for one week in September, displacing **Stevie Nicks**'s *Bella Donna*, but dropped out of the Top 3 the next week. It returned to #2 five weeks later, but could not overtake **The Rolling Stones**' *Tattoo You*, which kept *Escape* at #2 for four consecutive weeks. But the release of the singles "Don't Stop Believin'" and "Open Arms" brought a new surge in sales and catapulted *Escape* back into the Top 2, though it never reclaimed the #1 ranking. In those weeks Journey was held off by **Foreigner** (*4*), the **J. Geils Band** (*Freeze Frame*), and the **Go-Go's** (*Beauty and the Beat*). But few bands in that period could claim being in the Top 5 for 34 out of 35 of its first weeks on the chart.

TOP CHARTING WEEK: *BILLBOARD*—September 12, 1981

1. **JOURNEY, *ESCAPE***
2. Stevie Nicks, *Bella Donna*
3. Foreigner, *4*
4. Pat Benatar, *Precious Time*
5. Billy Squier, *Don't Say No*
6. Rickie Lee Jones, *Pirates*
7. Rick Springfield, *Working Class Dog*
8. The Rolling Stones, *Tattoo You*
9. Rick James, *Street Songs*
10. The Pretenders, *Pretenders II*

them there. Journey suddenly seemed to have so many songs that were good now. They just seemed to rise to the top."

Journey's newest member credited a fundamental change in how they approached the songs. "I thought it needed to be tied up in a lyrical way," Cain said. "Right away, I heard that they weren't singing to their fans. So, I watched it for a while and I thought, 'You know, if they sang a song for their fans, a song about their fans, they'd really connect'—because the fans love these guys. I knew that too.

"So when I came into the band, that was my observation," Cain added. "I said, 'Lyrically, you need to connect with these people that love you so much.' That was my message, and they took it to heart. Then we wrote *Escape*, which was all about the blue-collar guy who came to the Journey show, getting on that midnight train."

As the album sales stacked up, Journey shifted to larger and larger venues. "That was a game-changer for us," Smith told **Matt Wardlaw**, "because we went from playing 10,000-seat places to playing 60,000-seat stadium shows where we'd tour the whole summer." In some cases, Smith said they were playing two and three nights in individual cities.

Still, not everybody was on board—most notably *Rolling Stone*, which suddenly was longing for Journey's days as a starving, primarily instrumental act.

"*Escape* is less a testament to talent than the times," critic **Deborah Frost** sniffed. "Candy bars and the dollar aren't all that's shrinking these days. The latest victim of inflation is the value of a No. 1 album." In the end, she said "it's tough to fathom why either the band or its new LP is riding such a hot streak."

Longtime observers like Selvin would describe *Escape* as a revelation, though not always a positive one. "It was like a really sleek industrial design—a commercial product that had been industrially designed by a team of experts," Selvin said. "My ears were pleased; I could appreciate the sleek modernity of the whole thing. But as well designed as it is, God, it never really reached my heart—not like any number of more eccentric things ranging from the **Grateful Dead** to **NRBQ**."

Journey's ascension would be buffeted, time and time again, by those who questioned their radio-ready approach, their motives, even their manhood. Steve Augeri, then working in Brooklyn as a record store clerk, was not one of them.

Augeri placed *Escape* on the shop's turntable the day it came out—and was hooked. "I became a Journey fan," Steve Perry's future replacement later told Knight-Ridder Newspapers, "and for the duration of that record's chart life, I probably listened to it about three times a day." [3, 26, 60, 102, 121, 124, 297, 407]

Detroit Free Press
August 9, 1981

If you could scratch and sniff Journey's new album, it would reek of the aroma of freshly minted money. This is the band's most commercial effort to date. Side one of *Escape* is excellent, featuring three of the best ballads Journey ever recorded. "Who's Crying Now," "Still They Ride," and "Don't Stop Believin'" feature crystalline piano passages. Side two succumbs to exhibitionism. On "Lay It Down" Perry attempts to hit notes that aren't in his musical vocabulary, and the harmonies on "Mother, Father" have more layers than Prince Charlie and Lady Di's wedding cake. Despite a few flaws, *Escape* still contains some sterling rock performances.

— *Bruce Britt*

Pittsburgh Post-Gazette
August 13, 1981

"Who's Crying Now" is getting a lot of airplay from Journey's new album, *Escape*, and it sounds like "The Damage Is Done" from **Foreigner**'s first album. It also typifies the rest of the material on the album—each song sounds less distinctive and more like the work of another band. The sign of a strong group is that it can lose a member and bounce back. Journey hasn't recovered from losing Gregg Rolie, whose firm tenor provided a fresh counterpoint to Perry's sharper delivery. This is not the same band that recorded *Infinity* or *Departure*. Whatever is wrong may go back to Rolie's departure. Getting him back wouldn't hurt.

— *Gary Graff*

Los Angeles Times
November 24, 1981

Escape has been in the national Top 10 and songwriters Steve Perry, Neal Schon and Jonathan Cain seem to have been listening to a lot of critics' favorites. The theme-heavy LP recalls the wistful determination of **Jackson Browne**'s "Hold Out" in its "Don't Stop Believin'," the sensual nostalgia of **Bob Seger**'s "Night Moves" in its "Stone in Love." and you bump into the nights/streets/ idealism imagery of **Bruce Springsteen**. Even if the themes are more cliched than potent in Journey's hands, it's nice to see the band speaking in inspiring terms that invite the audience to think about potential and dreams rather than simply recycle macho tales of sex and drugs.

— *Robert Hilburn*

would play when he recorded there with Hammer. Within a matter of days, they had completed the in-house project with bassist **Colin Hodgkinson**.

"We wrote as we went along," Hammer added. "It wasn't any hard work. It was just a natural outflow between Colin Hodgkinson—I would call him a legendary bass player, because that's what he is—and Neal and I. All of the basic tracks were done with just the three of us."

Schon would later compare the results to **Jimi Hendrix**'s *Band of Gypsys*. "Jan sounds like **Buddy Miles** on drums and we're playing some burning rock 'n' roll," he told *Creem*. "There's some real good blues on it, too. Hard rock with blues."

Meanwhile, the PR push for Journey's *Escape* was still very much underway. "Who's Crying Now" had been on the charts for two months and was in the Top 5, and Columbia Records had just released "Don't Stop Believin'" when *Untold Passion* hit store shelves. "Open Arms" arrived months later. By that time, Schon's side project had peaked at No. 115, and set powerful forces in motion.

Perry said **Herbie Herbert** thought the Schon and Hammer record was a bad idea and remembered him trying to talk Schon out of it—to no avail. "I think the beginning of the end was when Neal started his solo career," Perry later told *GQ*'s **Alex Pappademas**. "Neal did a solo album, way before I was thinking about it."

At this point, Perry remained very protective of the group. "I was a real strong, gung-ho Journey person," Perry told the *Los Angeles Times*. "I wanted us all to stay together, and I was against anything that might pull us apart."

Unfortunately, *Untold Passion* seemed to have started that process. Schon and Hammer would return with *Here to Stay* in 1982, and soon Perry would be openly discussing how Journey was growing apart.

"I think the band is at a place where it needs to make some changes for itself," Perry told **Lisa Robinson** in 1984. "Some positive strength changes, I think." He said those changes were happening naturally, "because everybody has gone and done their separate projects."

He also correctly suggested that these solo LPs would ultimately "make a bit of a different group." [54, 78, 80, 183, 300, 301, 425]

WINTER 1981–82

RELEASES
▶ Journey, "Open Arms" (single)

NUGGETS
▶ At a December 12, 1981 Journey concert in San Francisco, lead singer Steve Perry brings up members of the 49ers football team who are in the audience and introduces them as "the next Super Bowl champions." His prediction comes true: the 49ers beat the Cincinnati Bengals in Super Bowl XVI. —*Songfacts*

▶ Journey opened the first three outdoor dates for **The Rolling Stones**, and the occasion wasn't lost on Jonathan Cain. "Just to have our paths cross like this is an honor. The Stones are a pinnacle of rock and roll. I'm in love with the new Stones album [*Tattoo You*], and I think there are kids who are just discovering the Rolling Stones for the first time. That's the exciting thing about rock and roll; if the youth remains in your music, then you are going to constantly attract new audiences." —*Circus*

▶ Journey has donated $70,000 to the "Save The Cable Cars Fund" in San Francisco. They raised the money at a December 2 benefit concert at the Cow Palace. Mayor **Diane Feinstein** accepted seven checks—$10,000 each from the band members, manager **Herbie Herbert** and promoter **Bill Graham**. The Fund needs a total of $10 million by September 1982 to save the San Francisco landmarks.—*Cashbox*

▶ **Carlos Santana** and Gregg Rolie have decided to kiss and make up. You'll recall Rollie and guitarist Neal Schon split off from **Santana** to form Journey, reportedly over differences in musical direction. Now Rolie is in the studio producing the next Santana album. —*Cashbox*

▶ In advance of four upcoming dates at The Forum in Los Angeles, Mayor **Tom Bradley** proclaimed November 22, 1981 as "Journey Day." —*Record World*

Continued on Page 152

CAIN'S SONG 'SCRAP' WAS A TRIBUTE TO FAITH, PATIENCE

The story of "Don't Stop Believin'" will always be about waiting. Waiting until the song revealed itself. Waiting for the right vocalist. Waiting for the chorus.

In one sense, Jonathan Cain had been carrying around what could only be described as a song scrap. This was, after all, simply a phrase—"don't stop believin'"—but a world of possibility could be found inside.

His father said it back in the 1970s, during "my down and out phase," Cain told *American Songwriter*. He had lost his record deal with Warner Bros., then his dog got hit by a car. Cain suddenly had a $1,000 bill from the veterinarian and was forced to ask his dad for a loan.

Cain admitted he had considered quitting the music business. He remembered saying: "Maybe I should give up on this thing, Dad, and come home to Chicago." Cain's father was steadfast in his support, encouraging him to stay true to his dream. "That's all I can say to you: Don't stop believin'."

Struck by their resonance, Cain wrote those words down in a notebook, five years before he joined Journey. He would not return to them until Journey had nearly completed 1981's *Escape*.

"Steve Perry asked me, 'Is there another idea around? We need one more song,'" Cain told *The Huffington Post*. Searching for inspiration at home one night, Cain came across the phrase—and immediately positioned himself at the Wurlitzer. He thought he had a chorus.

"A lot of times, things have to marinate when you're writing a song; it's a marinating process," he said in the documentary *A Better Man: The Faith Journey of Jonathan Cain*. "Just write it down. You'll know what it is later." Cain instinctively understood how to finish it, "because I had Steve Perry's voice in my head now."

Still, "Don't Stop Believin'" did not really define itself until he brought what he had to the others. Neal Schon developed the bass line, then created the music for a B-section that was later paired with "strangers, waitin' up and down the boulevard."

Schon also filled a critical early moment with some staccato lines that shaped the entire song. "It had the little guitar breakdown in the middle," Schon told *Ultimate Classic Rock*'s **Matt Wardlaw**. "I wanted to give a vision of a train going by or starting up and so that's where that came from."

Inspiration came from the classical music he listens to early each morning. "I don't get to rock and roll or blues until I get on my Harley later in the day," Schon told *Billboard*. "I hear that triplet that I do in the first solo before I get to the end solo in all kinds of symphonies."

DON'T STOP BELIEVIN'
By Jonathan Cain, Steve Perry, Neal Schon

HIGHEST CHARTING WEEK:
Billboard, #8, January 9, 1982

ARTIST	SINGLE
1. Olivia Newton-John	Physical
2. Foreigner	Waiting for a Girl Like You
3. Earth, Wind & Fire	Let's Groove
4. Hall & Oates	I Can't Go for That (No Can Do)
5. Rod Stewart	Young Turks
6. Commodores	Oh No
7. Diana Ross	Why Do Fools Fall in Love
8. JOURNEY	**DON'T STOP BELIEVIN'**
9. Quarterflash	Harden My Heart
10. Lindsey Buckingham	Trouble

Weeks on Chart: 15
Record World, #9, December 26, 1982
Cashbox, #8, December 26, 1982

They still needed lyrics for the verse. Cain kept going back to Schon's initial solo turn and was reminded of "Midnight Train to Georgia" by **Gladys Knight & the Pips**. He told *American Songwriter* that he asked Perry: "What about a midnight train going anywhere? And he's like, 'Yeah!'"

R&B would always serve as a touchstone for Perry, and longtime *Rolling Stone* editor **David**

Wild said it added a particular gravitas to his vocal turn on "Don't Stop Believin'."

"When I listen to it now, I hear soulfulness—which is always the problem with hard rock of any sort," Wild said. "I really don't like rock that doesn't have soul—and a lot of the production of music of that era and in FM rock, there's a lot of really well-played stuff that has no soul, I think. Steve Perry put his heart and soul into it."

Soon, Cain and Perry had created an entire world for a pair of star-crossed lovers. Returning to his era of disappointment in the 1970s, Cain described living above Sunset Boulevard in Laurel Canyon. This was where the couple would meet, among the restless rock stars, street hustlers, and always-aspiring actors.

"We saw the movie together," Cain told *American Songwriter*. "I think we wanted to write that song to say it's okay to dream … You're not stuck where you are."

Only they still had not reached that chorus—it was only initially referenced through Schon's guitar, creating a gripping tension. "Neal just came right out and played that melody before we sing it, which breaks all the rules," Cain added.

That riffed chorus, his phrase, would have to wait—and in the end, it would only be heard once. Cain pressed Perry on the decision, but he was adamant. "Steve Perry was the one that directed the way that went," Cain told *Classic Rock Revisited*. "He's the one who held off the chorus until the end."

He said this was what would bring listeners back, again and again. "It's not your usual verse, chorus, verse, chorus. It really is so cliché, what they considered a format for radio," Schon told *Vulture*. "The song never got to the fucking chorus until the end!"

One final element connected with Journey's most recent tour, as Perry recalled looking out over Detroit. "All of a sudden I'd see people walking out of the dark … and the term 'streetlight people' came to me," he told *The Telegraph*. "So Detroit was very much in my consciousness when we started writing."

He just needed another word to complete the lyrics. "I ran the phonetics of east, west, and north, but nothing sounded as good or emotionally true to me as South Detroit," Perry added. "The syntax just sounded right."

There is no South Detroit. Windsor, Canada is directly below, across the Detroit River. But Perry said he "fell in love with the line," so it stayed.

Schon developed the bass figure, but Ross Valory made it his own, doubling Cain's piano lines during the verses and soaring final chorus after muscling his way through the pre-chorus.

They finished recording, and Schon had a revelation. "I remember looking at everyone in the band and going, 'that's going to be a huge hit,'" Schon told Cox Newspapers. "Just because it doesn't have a number on it doesn't mean it isn't a bona fide hit in my mind."

Cain was the one who suggested its placement on *Escape*. "I said, 'Let's make it the first song on the album, because it sounds like it draws a listener in. Let's make it Track 1,'" he told *The Huffington Post*. "So that's how we sequenced the album."

This audience response to "Don't Stop Believin'," even back then, surprised Cain. "When we played that song at first, kids would push to the front of the stage and want to sing," he told the *Houston Press*. "What was it about that particular song?"

Perry was not sure, either. "I'm just amazed because we had a lot of great songs," he told NPR, "but that one I guess really touched a lot of people's hearts."

The wait was worth it. [53, 188, 234, 259, 261, 290, 296, 411, 483, 514, 867, 919]

I ran the phonetics of east, west, and north, but nothing sounded as good or emotionally true as South Detroit. The syntax just sounded right.

—Steve Perry

ON THE ROAD
▶ Greg Kihn Band, Loverboy, Red Rider

Journey Reinvents Tours with Amped Production, Technology

As Journey and Jonathan Cain got more comfortable with one another on the road, **Herbie Herbert** unveiled many of the audio and video advancements that would define the band's sound and visual presence.

"They developed a lot of technology, and they had a vision of what concerts could look like. It was into the future—far beyond what was there before," **Joel Selvin** said. "Maybe the parts and pieces were on the table, but nobody was thinking about putting them together."

Herbert's Nocturne Productions was now administering a trio of subsidiary companies that provided light and sound and a fleet of five semi-trucks to ship the equipment from show to show. A multi-instrument system would control things like trusses and dimming. Most importantly, on-stage video cameras projecting on huge screens brought the onstage action up close to even those tucked away in the cheap seats.

"I was there at the beginning of the tour when they didn't have it at Mountain Aire," Selvin said. "They weren't even featuring the songs from *Escape* yet. It was just Journey, with Jon Cain instead of Rolie. They brought the production in as they hit the stadiums."

Herbert and his team first became intrigued with the idea of projection while playing more intimate shows at Winterland. **Paul Becker**, who would eventually become Nocturne's video director, simulcast concerts at the venue's soundboard through a tiny black-and-white video machine.

"It was just for their own entertainment, along with running the soundboard. It was like a home unit that they could fuck around with," Selvin added. "It was fascinating to all of us, because it introduced an element into the concert mix that none of us had considered."

Selvin returned for Journey's December 10, 1981 stop in Oakland, California, a month after MTV filmed their performance at The Summit in Houston. Everything had changed.

Herbert executed a quick study to see if they could create a combination of technical advances that would transform live concerts, then put it into place in advance of the band's jump to larger venues.

"It was pioneering days, crossing the frontiers of live touring," longtime Nocturne CEO **Pat Morrow** said. "Really, one of the very first real stadium acts was Journey, and the rest followed. You know, a lot of people followed in our wake."

Loverboy, then opening for Journey, became the first outside band to ask Herbert about renting his new setup. **The Who** would be next. Herbert said **Bryan Adams** actually wrote a personal plea to Neal Schon.

"By the time they got to Oakland, I stood in the back of the stadium with Herbie and watched the whole thing—and it was just mind-boggling," Selvin said. "He had raised the bar so high with that kind of spectacle. Before that, the stadium was just a convenient way to get 50,000 people in to see a shitty rock show with a terrible sound system."

It was not all smooth sailing: Everything came to an abrupt halt during Japanese dates culminating at Yokohama in April 1982. Customs officials found a suspicious substance in Steve Perry's wardrobe case.

They gave Journey a pass, however, after the curious substance turned out to be a favorite tea that Perry always carried. The band's crew later sported custom-made T-shirts that read, "I Survived the Yokohama Tea Party." [56, 60, 73, 927]

SPRING–SUMMER 1982

RELEASES
▶ Journey, "Still They Ride" (single)

NUGGETS
▶ Journey's *Escape* wins best album at the annual Bammies in San Francisco. **Carlos Santana** wins best guitarist, Jonathan Cain wins best keyboardist, and former Journey percussionist Aynsley Dunbar wins best drummer. Meanwhile, Neal Schon and Jan Hammer win best debut album. —*Record World*

NUGGETS (cont.)

▶ **Pat Morrow** becomes a vice president for Journey's management crew, Nightmare Inc. and Nocturne, where he will be responsible for helping to manage Journey, newcomers **4-1-5**, ex-Journey keyboarder Gregg Rolie, and producer **Kevin Elson**. —*Cashbox*

▶ **IN THE TEXAS HEAT:** More than 65,000 people showed up for the Texxas World Music Festival (otherwise known as Jam V) on June 13, 1982. Journey headlined the event, and was joined by **Point Blank**, **Santana**, **Sammy Hagar**, and **Joan Jett** on a sweltering summer day in Dallas. The show had a variety of misfires. Plans for a show-ending jam with Hagar and Journey never materialized, and longtime Journey friend **Carlos Santana** refused to go on the stage with Journey unless he was specifically asked by a band member—any band member. But no one never asked. Part of that reluctance may have been because of how protective of the stage Journey had become. Their elaborate stage setup included a long, narrow catwalk that let the band get close to fans, but it was only erected for Journey's set. Hagar's guitar was stolen off stage during his set (he later recovered it and smashed it on stage), and Jett collapsed from heat exhaustion at the end of her hour-long set and was carried 500 yards to her backstage trailer. Fun times in the heat of Texas. —*Circus*

▶ Steve Perry was in the studio with **Kenny Loggins** and **Pat Benatar**'s **Neil Giraldo** working on a duet for Loggins' upcoming album. The surprising single, "Don't Fight It," is supposed to raise a little pop-rock hell.
—*Cashbox*

▶ Journey manager **Herbie Herbert** stretches his wings to also manage newcomer **Tané Cain** and her debut album. This included a full-page ad in *Cashbox*, *Billboard* and *Record World* in support of her single "Holdin' On." The LP was produced by **Keith Olsen** and husband, Journey keyboardist and songwriter, Jonathan Cain, who also wrote or co-write nearly every song on her LP. —*Record World*

COLLABORATIONS

▶ Gregg Rolie, producer on **Santana**'s single, "Oxun (Oshun)" and songwriter, arranger, and organist on Santana's album, *Shangó*.

▶ Jonathan Cain, songwriter, producer and backing vocals, and Neal Schon, guitar, on **Tané Cain**'s album, *Tané Cain*.

ON THE ROAD

▶ George Thorogood, Greg Kihn Band, The Rolling Stones

Cain, Journey's Machine Join To Push Tané Cain's Debut LP

Unsuspecting Journey fans might have wondered aloud why the former (and future) **Tané McClure**'s 1982 debut had all the markings of an official release.

Jonathan Cain co-wrote eight of its nine songs, and he sang the other one, "Almost Any Night." Neal Schon added guitar solos to three tracks, while **Herbie Herbert** and his close confidant **Pat Marrow** handled managerial duties. (Future *Raised on Radio*-era contributor **Michael Baird** was also featured on drums.)

Cain, Tané's husband at the time, secured this opportunity through some hard-knuckle negotiations, Herbert later told **Matthew Carty**. Cain had already agreed to take over for Gregg Rolie, Herbert said, when he demanded a separate record deal for his wife.

"You were committed on other terms and conditions, and you want to change the deal right now—and that is jive," Herbert answered. He said Cain replied: "Well, then call me jive."

Herbert said he was so incensed that he never even listened to her demo tape. Tané got a deal through RCA Victor, and her husband took over as co-producer on sessions for *Tané Cain*, along with **The Babys** collaborator **Keith Olsen**.

Tané was suitably impressed. "Just the physical feeling of singing and belting out a song that creates emotion—that alone was wonderful to me," Tané told interviewer **Johnny Caps**. "Just the

Continued on Page 159

JOURNEY RIDES CAIN, PERRY POWER BALLAD TO TOP FIVE

Jonathan Cain says Steve Perry confided something as they sat down to work on the second song they ever wrote together. Perry had been contemplating a solo project—just so he could record more ballads.

That's when Cain dragged over a 40-pound Wurlitzer to play his early sketch of "Open Arms." "We were just noodling around, and then he played this melody," Perry told **John Stix**.

Cain auditioned the song while still with **The Babys**, only to be sternly rebuffed by **John Waite**. Perry had a completely different reaction. "It started out as a wedding song for my first wedding, and I hadn't gotten around to writing the verses," Cain said. "I didn't know what they were but I knew I had a melody. Then when I played it for Perry, he just went, 'Oh, let's do this. I got this.' And we did and that was the beginning of our lyrical partnership."

Delicate to the point of fragility, the perfectly named "Open Arms" was like nothing Journey had attempted before. "I mean, [Steve Perry] sold every word. You just believe him," Cain said. "He had this amazing ability to get inside of a song and put the right emotion on it—and his read on 'Open Arms' is spectacular."

Journey "already had success," Cain later told *Classic Rock Revisited*. "*Infinity* was double platinum, *Evolution*, *Departure*, *Captured*—but we're thinking like **The Beatles**. 'What can we do next? Where can we take it?'"

"Open Arms" would take them all the way to the penultimate spot on the *Billboard* Hot 100. "It was No. 2 for a long time, and then it made the *Escape* album No. 1," Cain said. "It's been voted the top power ballad in all kinds of polls. A lot of people get married to it and proposed to it, and did other things in the backseat with it," he added with a laugh. "So, I'm proud of that one."

Waite wasn't the only one with reservations. "We quickly finished the song in an afternoon and brought it to the band, and they said 'What??'" Cain told the *Houston Press*. "But Perry had a conviction to go in a different direction."

In Cain, the frustrated balladeer in Perry had found a new ally. Perry found in Cain someone who spent a remarkable amount of time making sure that a small turn of phrase—notably, "wanting you near"—resonated just the right way.

"You know, he trusted me and I trusted him," Cain said. "He was fascinating to write with because he's such a technician. I'd never worked with a vocal perfectionist. I mean, he would memorize every line as we wrote it, then his voice—he'd put it in the register we wanted and deliver it how we wanted it. Steve rehearsed everything as we wrote it, so then when we got into the studio or rehearsal, he knew where it lived in his range. He was very specific about what words he wanted to say. I was kind of taken with it."

OPEN ARMS
By Steve Perry, Neal Schon, Jonathan Cain

HIGHEST CHARTING WEEK:
Record World, #1, March 6, 1982

ARTIST	SINGLE
1. **JOURNEY**	**OPEN ARMS**
2. The J. Geils Band	Centerfold
3. Buckner & Garcia	Pac-Man Fever
4. Joan Jett & The Blackhearts	I Love Rock 'n' Roll
5. Stevie Wonder	That Girl
6. Hall & Oates	I Can't Go for That (No Can Do)
7. Air Supply	Sweet Dreams
8. Diana Ross	Mirror, Mirror
9. Dan Fogelberg	Leader of the Band
10. The Oak Ridge Boys	Bobbie Sue

Billboard, #2 for six consecutive weeks, March-April 1982
Cashbox, #1 March 13, 1982

"Open Arms," not "Don't Stop Believin'," would become Journey's biggest single. Released on January 10, 1982, the track was kept from *Billboard*'s top spot for six consecutive weeks by **The J. Geils Band**'s "Centerfold" and then "I Love Rock 'n' Roll" by **Joan Jett and the Blackhearts**. "Open Arms" soared to No. 1 on the *Cashbox* and *Record World* charts, as Journey's radical remodel was complete. This sudden turn of events certainly was not lost on the two creative forces from Journey's earliest days.

"When Jonathan Cain joined the band," Gregg Rolie told *Rolling Stone*, "he came with some songs I couldn't write in a million days—and he did. And the band became successful because of it."

Neal Schon later admitted he had no idea how to meld his rock-first sensibilities with what he was hearing. "At the time, I didn't get it," he told *Fuse*. "That was the one that was like the black sheep to me off the whole record ... and I was scared to death of it, to tell you the truth."

But love songs came naturally to Cain in a way that they might not have for legacy members of the band. In fact, the first song he ever wrote—for an eighth-grade play, where a music teacher promised to leave a spot open—was about a classmate whom Cain had a crush on.

He would end up taking Journey a galaxy or more away from "Kohoutek." Critics like **Joel Selvin** pounced. "They went from an R&B sound to a pop sound. Gregg Rolie was a really soulful cat, an incredibly gifted and talented keyboard player—a very fine singer. Soulful, soulful," the *San Francisco Chronicle* critic added, before landing a quick jab.

"Jon Cain is a fucking weenie. He's never been cool. He's never been anything other than this namby-pamby puerile knucklehead,"

Selvin chuckled. "And that's what he brought to the band—that kind of weenie-ness that was just what they needed to get out of that San Francisco, hip, edgy, cool thing that Rolie represented. Now they could go mainstream and appeal to the youth of America."

Schon acquiesced to Cain and Perry, adding a strikingly reserved 15-second interlude at the 1:30 mark, but otherwise essentially backgrounding himself until the song's graceful conclusion. His comments, back then and during interviews from decades down the line, illustrated the difficult balance Schon was attempting to strike.

"I myself wanted even harder rock," Schon confessed to *Kerrang!*, "but I'm happy with the sound right now." Later, in his talk with *Fuse*, he admitted: "I was always concerned, like 'Is the rock there?' It was something different for me, and they both proved me wrong."

Journey's manager got on board too. "Even **Herbie [Herbert]** couldn't deny it," Cain said. "We heard it in the studio and it was like, 'OK, it's huge.'" [49, 53, 60, 181, 202, 274, 296, 407]

Power ballads existed long before Jonathan Cain (left) and Steve Perry joined Journey, but with songs like "Open Arms" and "Faithfully," the band refined the art form to platinum-selling heights that few other bands of that era ever experienced.

LIVE IN
HOUSTON

MTV was still just a fledgling network when it broadcast Journey's tour stop in Houston in November 1981. Journey was already a platinum-selling band, selling out tours across the country, but the high-profile concert airing brought new exposure to the group. The show introduced the group to many new fans, and Steve Perry's yellow leopard print T-shirt became iconic that night. Coupled with a solid new album release—*Escape*—the concert catapulted the band into a new echelon of rock acts and cemented their superstar status.

MTV'S SUMMIT BROADCAST CHANGED JOURNEY'S FUTURE

A stop on November 6, 1981 in Houston was more than Journey's second consecutive sold-out concert inside The Summit. This Friday show was their chance to leverage MTV, the newest form of music promotion.

"Journey was one of our earliest concerts, and we were hanging our hat on their credibility," former MTV VJ **Martha Quinn** said. "Like, 'Oh wow, Journey let us film their concert.' They were a very, very big band—so that was good for us."

The fledgling network transmitted this show to a worldwide cable audience, while the syndicated *King Biscuit Flower Hour* handled the FM radio simulcast. Members of Journey knew just how important this moment was, arriving with plenty of confidence.

"I can remember not even thinking about the cameras," Jonathan Cain told the *Houston Press*. "We were just clicking on all cylinders. ... The world was going to see what Journey had become."

"Who's Crying Now," the first single from *Escape*, had just peaked on the *Billboard* chart at No. 4 on October 3, and follow-up "Don't Stop Believin'" had only just begun moving up the Top 40.

"It was in that concert that Steve [Perry] said, 'Oh, I'd like to do a new song. Do you want to hear a new song?'—and that was 'Don't Stop Believin','" Quinn said. "It's funny to look back at it at that time. Like, 'Wow, that whole audience hadn't heard that song.' Unless you had the record, it was new to everybody."

Before MTV, **Herbie Herbert** had pushed their

latest single at various individual markets, first around their traditional home base on the West Coast and then—as Journey's commercial fortunes turned—nationwide.

"To break an act, you had to do it regionally," said **Paul Flattery**, a former writer for *Rolling Stone* who went on to produce a series of videos for Journey and Steve Perry. "So, the record label would strategize a campaign across America to break an act—or break a record. They might concentrate on an area in the Midwest, then they'd go here and there. That changed when MTV happened, because MTV became national radio, if you will."

Journey roared through eight of the 10 songs on *Escape* that night in Houston, rounding out the show with a few older favorites. "The concert still holds up for me," Cain told the *Houston Press*. "We were good."

For Perry, the Houston concert underscored how they were now completely inhabiting these songs. "When I heard 'Open Arms' I got choked up," he told *Melodic Rock*. He wasn't sure, years later, if he could get there again. "I had reached beyond the master recordings to what I knew it could be. For example, the lyric in the second verse 'wanting you near', that lyric is sung exactly the way I wanted it to be sung and I didn't know I hit it."

Along the way, Journey cemented their new superstardom, despite the fact that newer sounds were in ascension. At this point, MTV was still airing an intriguing blend of eras that left plenty of room for a former San Francisco jam band.

"New wave and synthpop were really coming into their own, and giving classic rock a run for its money," Quinn mused. "But ultimately, these were still bands that we still loved from the '70s. When MTV started in 1981, the '80s as we know it wasn't really happening yet. So, our first songs that we played on MTV were largely from the late '70s. We very much still had a rock 'n' roll frame of mind."

Cain was also solidifying his position in a band he would be part of for decades to come. As Journey's lineups shifted time and time again, he would end up as a member of the old guard—a situation that **Lawrence Gowan** of **Styx** compared with **Ron Wood**'s enduring role in **The Rolling Stones**.

"I saw the Rolling Stones and I had a good seat right up front where there is kind of a catwalk," said Gowan, who long ago replaced the legendary **Dennis DeYoung**. "So, **Keith Richards** walks by while they are playing 'Let's Spend the Night Together.' Then a few seconds later, **Mick Jagger**, he comes strutting by—and it's incredibly exciting, because you're looking at rock royalty here. And then suddenly, Ron Wood's right in front of me and it dawned on me then: Ron Wood is every bit as much a Rolling Stone as the two guys that just preceded him on this catwalk."

In time, Gowan argued that later-period additions can evolve from a newcomer into someone who "kind of embodies the whole thing." That was certainly the case by the time the Houston show formed the basis for Journey's first live concert project since 1980's *Captured*.

Journey featured songs from the Summit on 1998's gold-selling *Greatest Hits Live*, and then showcased them exclusively on 2005's *Live in Houston 1981: The Escape Tour* concert film. Perry, who served as co-producer for the movie, lamented the fact that there was no bonus material.

"MTV was three months old when we recorded this DVD. It was [a] baby in diapers—it had no idea what it was," Perry told *Melodic Rock*. "I tried to go back to MTV and see if they had other elements or extra footage lying around and they had nothing. ... All I had was the final cut because they had no idea what they were going to become."

Still, the long-departed Perry had to deal with the emotions associated with watching his former band at the peak of its powers. "I'd tuck my feelings back and not look at the screen till it passed," he said in a *Fan Asylum* Q&A. "I think in many ways, these performances are better than the masters."

Live in Houston 1981: The Escape Tour sold more than a million copies, a testament to the enduring interest in Journey's completely restructured sound.

"That incarnation had its own rhythmic concept. From my point of view, it was a little more driving and intense," Steve Smith said. "Things felt different because we were trying to fill up more space with our energy, so we tended to push harder in an effort to achieve that. The band in the early incarnation played smaller places, so comparatively, the playing was more intimate and relaxed."

One final detail stuck with Quinn, as a member of Journey added a special gravitas to the original broadcast: "The fact that Neal Schon was wearing an MTV T-shirt?" she marveled. "We were like, 'Oh my God!' That was the coolest thing ever." [3, 49, 53, 303, 412, 435, 920, 921]

ESCAPE'S FINAL HIT LOOKS BACKWARD TO PERRY'S ROOTS

Jonathan Cain and Neal Schon earned co-song-writing credits on the lonesome "Still They Ride," and Steve Smith showed off an accomplished dexterity. But the final charting single from *Escape*, released in May 1982, belonged in no small part to Steve Perry.

The song's main character, Jesse, never left the town of his youth, and still drives through its darkening streets looking for some connection. If you had found yourself in mid-century Hanford, California, you might have seen a young Steve Perry doing the same thing.

Perry has admitted that Jesse, this dreamer who refuses to give up on his youthful reverie, works as a metaphor for himself. Perry has long since left Hanford, but Hanford—where a plaque in his honor rests at Civic Park—has never left him.

"When cruising down Main Street at night," he later told **John Stix**, "if you caught the right timing, you could watch the traffic lights go green and the next block green in some kind of delayed rhythm."

Perry needed the right drummer to echo and amplify that indelible image—and found one in the quickly evolving Smith.

Softly murmuring at first, Smith urges this Top 20 single along when needed—and then pounds with sudden authority as "Still They Ride" builds toward an anthemic conclusion. "When he plays softly, he plays softly," an impressed Ross Valory later told the *Times-Picayune*. "When he plays loud, it's only to the limit of what sounds good."

Performances like this followed detailed conversations with Perry about time, tempo, and the spacing of his notes. "He made me very aware of those things," Smith told *Modern Drummer*, "because he needs them in order to do what he has to do."

Through this process, Smith's style was changing too. He had never played with such understated precision, and yet Smith was not giving away any power. "Usually, fusion drummers don't make good ballad or pop drummers, because they're too busy and they play too much," Smith's successor, **Mike Baird**, said in a separate

Modern Drummer interview, "but for that band, he curbed and added just enough of his own flair."

Schon made the kind of soaring contribution that "Open Arms" did not accommodate, while remaining careful not to distract from this song's melancholy core. Cain and Valory played in steady service of the moment too, as "Still They Ride" brought Perry—and so many others—back to their halcyon teenage years.

STILL THEY RIDE
By Steve Perry, Neal Schon, Jonathan Cain

HIGHEST CHARTING WEEK:
Billboard, #19, July 17, 1981

ARTIST	SINGLE
1. The Human League	Don't You Want Me
2. Toto	Rosanna
3. John Cougar	Hurt So Good
4. Survivor	Eye of the Tiger
5. Dazz Band	Let It Whip
6. Fleetwood Mac	Hold Me
7. Juice Newton	Love's Been a Little Bit Hard on Me
8. Soft Cell	Tainted Love
9. The Motels	Only the Lonely
19. JOURNEY	**STILL THEY RIDE**

"If you were caught in the right place in the wave of green," Perry said of those long-ago days on Hanford's streets, "you could cruise soulfully all the way through."

He would later inhabit a scene similar to Hanford in a clip accompanying 2018's Top 15 adult contemporary solo hit "We're Still Here," Perry's first scripted video in some 25 years.

Journey was not so lucky when they returned to rock with "Stone in Love," the last single from *Escape*. It charted in the United Kingdom, but never appeared on the main *Cashbox* or *Billboard* charts in the United States, yet still provided a reminder that Journey had not given themselves completely over to balladry. [137, 196, 261, 275, 283]

whole experience of being a singer was pretty exciting."

Despite his misgivings, Herbert mounted his typical full-court press: On August 21, 1982, *Billboard* reported album-release autograph parties in New York, Los Angeles, Atlanta, and Chicago, with a photograph of Tané signing a poster at another event in Dallas.

By Sept. 4, *Billboard* was listing her self-titled debut LP among the Top 5 for most added selections, two spots ahead of Steve Perry's new duet with **Kenny Loggins**, "Don't Fight It."

"The first thing you notice about Tané Cain is that she looks incredibly beautiful on the LP cover," noted a non-bylined 1982 item in *Billboard*'s Top Album Picks column. "Then you put it on and find out that she can sing just as well. And her songs are pretty good, too."

Billboard gave due credit to "husband/co-producer/songwriter" Jonathan Cain and Journey bandmate Neal Schon: "Together, they have put together a package with AOR credibility and AC accessibility on selected cuts." Tané was dubbed "an artist to watch."

The lead single, "Holdin' On," promptly appeared in the Top 40 on the *Billboard* Hot 100, reaching No. 37 in September 1982 behind a video that featured Jonathan Cain and some extras. But *Tané Cain* stalled at No. 121, notwithstanding her husband's best efforts. She was subsequently dropped by RCA.

The August 1982 edition of *Billboard* also included a display advertisement for the album noting the pronunciation of her first name in all caps: "TAWNEY." This was clearly a concern for McClure. Her only other notable releases included a phonetic spelling of McClure's first name.

"You Can't Do That" and "Burnin' in the Third Degree" from 1984's *The Terminator: Original Soundtrack* were credited to **Tahnee Cain** and **Tryanglz**. But this second high-profile opportunity likewise went nowhere. McClure's marriage to

Jonathan Cain soon ended, too.

They split following Journey's tour in support of *Frontiers*, the Journey LP that found Cain describing some of their challenges in the hit "Faithfully."

"The divorce proceedings lasted two and a half years, kicked me in the butt, and took more than a million dollars from me," Jonathan Cain admitted in his memoir.

"You know how karma works ... as you sow, so shall you reap," Herbert countered in his interview with Carty. "So he really harvested one there with Tané."

After that, Tané reverted to her maiden name and returned to acting. She'd made appearances as a child on her father **Doug McClure**'s 1960s-era TV show *The Virginian*, and this proved to be a much more natural fit. McClure appeared primarily in B-movies, but also scored notable roles as a singer in *Fear and Loathing in Las Vegas* and as Elle Woods's mother in the *Legally Blonde* films. [901, 903, 904, 905, 906, 907, 908, 909]

SEPARATE WAYS

After a rigorous multi-continent tour supporting
their most successful album ever, Journey was
perched atop the rock world. But Neal Schon
had a musician's wandering eye, and began
sowing some of those wild rocking oats outside
of the band. Others followed his lead, and the
separation that was supposed to be temporary
found a path to permanence.

FALL 1982

RELEASES
▶ Journey, "Stone in Love" (single, UK only)

NUGGETS
▶ Journey is holed-up in a Berkeley, California studio brewing up their next album with producers **Keith Olsen** and **Mike Stone**, but impatient fans will get to hear the band before that release. Journey is contributing two songs to the upcoming *Tron* soundtrack from Columbia Records. "We just kind of fell into it," said Journey keyboardist Jonathan Cain, who said that he, Neal Schon and Steve Perry watched the pre-release footage on a tour stop in Los Angeles. They liked it. *Tron* will be the first movie project for the band since *Heavy Metal* in 1981. —*Circus*
▶ Journey has become so successful on the West Coast that Los Angeles area fans bought 200,000 tickets to the group's concerts there in only 18 months. The Rose Bowl show alone was attended by 83,214 people. Such popularity may lead to an even higher living standard for Journey, whose members were paid a percentage of gross receipts at the Rose Bowl instead of the flat fee most performers get. One L.A. reporter calculated that under these circumstances lead singer Steve Perry makes $45,000 an hour on stage. Right now, Steve is working for considerably less; he and the band have booked a lot of hours at Fantasy Studios to make the next LP. —*Circus*

COLLABORATIONS
▶ Neal Schon, guitar solo on "My Time To Fly," "Crazy Eyes," and "Almost Any Night" on **Tané Cain**'s album, *Tané Cain*.
▶ Steve Perry, duet vocals, songwriter on "Don't Fight It," on **Kenny Loggins**'s album, *High Adventure*.
▶ Jonathan Cain, backing vocals, keyboards on "Remember the Heroes" on **Sammy Hagar**'s album, *Three Lock Box*.

Perry, Kenny Loggins Conspire To Raise Some Pop-Rock Hell

An offhand collaboration with Steve Perry ended up setting the stage for Kenny Loggins to become a first-call, 1980s-era soundtrack guy. He had scored a Top 10 hit with "I'm Alright" from 1980's *Caddyshack*, but then went silent for a couple of years.

That is, until Perry stopped by Loggins's place near Santa Barbara while Journey's *Escape* tour was on hiatus. Loggins admitted he was hoping to add a little rock grit to a resume of smooth pop and yacht rock. Perry was just looking to branch out.

Whatever their motivations, duets are "just something I love to do. I like to sing with other people," Loggins told the *Los Angeles Daily News*. "When it works, you end up with something that's bigger than the individuals."

They were certainly nothing new for Loggins, who rose to initial fame in a duo format with **Jim Messina**, then co-wrote songs with **Bob James**, **Jimmy Webb**, and **David Foster** on his first solo record. He went on to collaborate on **The Doobie Brothers**' 1979 single "What a Fool Believes," scored a No. 5 duet hit with **Stevie Nicks**, then returned to work with the Doobies' **Michael McDonald** for the No. 11 hit "This Is It."

"He had written some great music with Michael McDonald previous to this, and his own material was always stunning," Perry later told **John Stix**. "The time presented itself during a short break during a Journey tour."

They gathered in a music room at Loggins's house, with Loggins on guitar and Perry on bass. But nothing happened, at least at first. "I think he was trying to do what an artist often does when he knows what his album needs," Perry added, "which is to write in a certain needed direction. We are all guilty of that sometimes."

A frustrated Loggins took a break, while Perry continued absentmindedly playing bass. Then the line, "Don't fight it, don't fight it. It will only do you good" popped out of Perry's mouth. This was Perry's natural way of creating, rather than working on spec. He could never write a rainy day song when sunlight filled the room. It only worked in the moment.

Loggins wandered back in, "and I was doing that," Perry told Stix. "He sat down and grabbed the guitar and started playing along with me." Loggins suddenly realized all over again that his instincts had been correct.

"I like to collaborate," Loggins told the *Minneapolis Star and Tribune*. "It's a great way to grow quickly. You learn a lot about the craft of writing from the different ways that different people write."

They did not finish the song, which would reach the Top 20 after its August 1982 release, but they had made a terrific start. Perry went back on tour, leaving Loggins and producer **Bruce Botnick** to complete the track with co-writer **Dean Pitchford**.

Botnick then handed responsibility for the distinctive riff to **Pat Benatar**'s guitarist, **Neil Giraldo**, who Perry has called "one of the most naturally talented geniuses around." They left a space for Perry to sing, which he completed on the next tour break.

The results turned into "an experiment in pushing my limits to include rock," Loggins admitted in the liner notes to the 1997 compilation *Yesterday, Today, Tomorrow*. "To me, Steve Perry is one of the greatest rock singers of all time," Loggins told the *Los Angeles Daily News*, "and it is a joy to be singing with someone like him."

Pitchford went on to write the chart-topping title song from 1984's *Footloose* with Loggins, and Loggins's involvement with the soundtrack in turn helped Pitchford see his screenplay for the film transformed into a wide-release revenue-generating smash. Loggins then took "Danger Zone" from 1986's *Top Gun* to No. 2 on the *Billboard* Hot 100.

In the end, Pitchford was not the only big-screen connection for "Don't Fight It," which was nominated for Best Rock Performance at the 1983 Grammy Awards. A key sound effect came courtesy of Paramount Pictures.

"Don't tell anyone: The bullwhip is from the locker where they kept the *Indiana Jones* soundtrack sounds," Loggins later revealed to the *Tampa Bay Times*. "We snuck in there and we got the bullwhip and we sampled it." [91, 93, 269, 304, 305]

WINTER 1982-83

RELEASES

▶ Journey, *Frontiers* (album)
▶ Journey, "Separate Ways (Worlds Apart)" (single)

NUGGETS

▶ **Kenny Loggins** and Steve Perry are nominated for a Grammy for their duet, "Don't Fight It" on Loggins' LP, *High Adventure*. —*Cashbox*
▶ Journey's third source of revenue, after LPs and concerts, will be a pop-rock first. A home video game that takes its name from the *Escape* LP. Computer animation leads the simulated Journey-men past such "hazards" as groupies, photographers, and concert promoters before time and cash run out. —*Circus*

COLLABORATIONS

▶ Steve Perry, backing vocals and songwriter, on "Self Defense" and "Covered By Midnight," and Ross Valory, bass, on **Schon & Hammer**'s album, *Here To Stay*.

A Visit to a Terminally Ill Fan Gives Band a New Perspective

"Only the Young" has a very strange resume for a song that almost wasted away in the Journey vaults as an outtake. It became a surprise Top 10 smash for Journey, a bridge to rebuilding band camaraderie, and an inspiration to a dying teenager.

"It was actually written for the *Frontiers* record," Jonathan Cain told WCSX. Then discussions began—reportedly at the behest of Columbia A&R man **Michael Dilbeck**—about resequencing the album. "They wanted to put some other song in place of it." Cain lobbied for "Only the Young," but lost the vote—"and it just sat on the shelf there in the vaults."

Then the mother of **Kenny Sykaluk**, a terminally ill teen from Ohio, reached out in 1983 through the Make-a-Wish Foundation. He had been admitted to a cystic fibrosis clinic in Cleveland and hoped to one day meet his favorite band.

Journey was moved by the request and obliged, bringing along several items, including an autographed platinum album and a Walkman with a cassette recording of "Only the Young." Sykaluk would become the first person outside of the group's immediate circle to hear it.

"Slipping the headphones over Kenny's ears, we watched as the kid began to listen to our unreleased song," Cain said in his autobiography, *Don't Stop Believin'*. "While the tune played, Kenny looked up and his eyes got huge."

Written by Cain with Steve Perry and Neal Schon, "Only the Young" was suddenly transformed. So was Journey. "As soon as I stepped out of that hospital room, I lost it," Perry said in the liner notes to the *Time³* box set. "Nurses had to take me to a room by myself."

Sykaluk would die just hours later, with the Walkman still in his hand. Perry credited Cain with the key line, written "before we even knew about Kenny, about 'only the young can say they're free to fly away.'" With Sykaluk gone, the lyrics had taken on new emotional weight.

In the meantime, **Scandal** recorded "Only the Young" for their debut album. Journey's version remained unreleased until 1985, when it appeared on a movie soundtrack. Industry mogul "**David Geffen** somehow got a hold of it and called our manager and said, 'I have this movie, *Vision Quest*,'" Cain told WCSX. "And so we ended up taking it to New York to mix for *Vision Quest*."

By then, Perry had gone solo and there were questions about Journey's future. As "Only the Young" soared to No. 9, Sykaluk's spirit seemed to be guiding them back together. Months later, sessions began for 1986's *Raised on Radio*.

Syaluk's passing "changed my outlook on life," Schon said during Journey's episode of VH1's *Behind the Music*. "It makes you realize that the things you were making a big deal out of, maybe, were not so big."

"Only the Young" would open every concert on the subsequent *Raised on Radio* tour, then find a home as a bonus track on later reissues of *Frontiers*. It was certainly a winding path, but that made perfect sense for Cain.

"Each song has its place and purpose," Cain wrote in *Don't Stop Believin'*, "and 'Only the

Young' was meant to stay off *Frontiers* initially—simply because it belonged to Kenny." [317, 318, 319, 320, 442, 444]

Band Tensions Rise As Schon Works on Another Solo Project

Neal Schon's latest side project with **Jan Hammer**, 1982's *Here to Stay*, arrived just as Journey was gearing up to release *Frontiers*.

That might not have mattered if this second collaboration had not been far more conventional—with a glossy MTV-aired video to match—than their initial album, 1981's *Untold Passion*. Suddenly, Journey appeared on a collision course with its co-founding guitarist.

Hammer, for his part, was unapologetic. "I would like to reach the widest possible audience," he told *San Diego People Magazine*. "I've played music most of my life for musicians and for musician's friends. ... I want to play for common people." (Schon later described him as a "frustrated rock player," and it's a charge Hammer probably wouldn't deny.)

They never got to tour in support of *Here to Stay*, particularly after the project failed to crack the Top 100. Schon was already back in the studio with Journey, completing a follow-up to *Escape* that was set to arrive in February 1983.

Unfortunately, his bandmates felt a sense of betrayal. Solo albums, in Journey manager **Herbie Herbert**'s estimation, were the equivalent of cheating on your wife. It certainly appeared that way to Steve Perry.

"I think the beginning of the end was when Neal started his solo career," Perry told *GQ*. He had told Herbert he thought it was a bad idea, "that it would fracture the band on some level." But Herbert, who always thought of Schon as a son, refused to intervene.

Perry had been steadfast against working outside the group and expressed his displeasure, even after Schon released *Untold Passion* with Hammer. "I used to think solo albums would defuse the nucleus of the band," Perry told *Faces* in the run-up to his own solo debut. "I thought they would make the group seem scattered and not together."

Continued on Page 171

LEADOFF POWER ANTHEM CONTINUES PLATINUM STREAK

"Separate Ways (Worlds Apart)" was the lead single from *Frontiers*, a multi-week Top 10 smash in early 1983, and the perfect example of how Journey could mix in elements of R&B and blues without sacrificing modernity.

The song came together while they toured behind *Escape* and revolved around a backstage melody Steve Perry and Jonathan Cain developed on bass and keys, respectively. The lyrics would get some tweaks, but the band quickly began playing "Separate Ways" on stage—and Schon said there was a huge response.

"It doesn't matter where we put this song" in Journey's setlist, he later told *Guitar World*, "because it has always had a strong effect on the audience, all the way back to the first time we played it—before it was even recorded." Schon said fans had "an amazing reaction to it, without even knowing what it was."

Then came the video. Often the subject of derision, the clip became Journey's first choreographed project. Earlier videos were performance based, sometimes augmented with documentary-style backstage shots.

Perry argued against making more elaborate videos, but the industry was moving inexorably in this direction. "He'd always say, 'We're performers, we're entertainers, but we're not actors,'" Cain said in *I Want My MTV: The Uncensored Story of the Music Video Revolution*, "and we were not a very photogenic band."

It couldn't have gone worse in some critics' minds, as the choreography on the **Tom Buckholtz**-directed project asked Journey to play imaginary versions of their instruments during a video shoot at the Louisa Street Wharf in New Orleans.

"I had trepidation about playing the 'air' stuff," Cain told *Huffington Post*. "Really? We're going to 'air' perform? So, I was like, 'Oh, jeez, we're going to get killed. They're going to kill us.'"

He was right. The clip did not age well. A decade later, the results suffered merciless parody on MTV's *Beavis and Butt-Head*, where **Mike Judge**'s characters merrily agreed that the video "sucks." "We did it on a very inexpensive budget and didn't know what we were doing," Cain told the *Houston Press*. "Then *Beavis and Butthead* spent three years ripping it apart!"

Original VJ **Martha Quinn** disagreed with the criticisms then, and still does today.

"This is one of those third-rail topics: I always loved it. I thought it was fun; I thought it captured a really fun vibe," Quinn said. "If you went to a concert any day of the week, everybody was playing air guitar. It didn't seem weird to me."

SEPARATE WAYS (WORLDS APART)
By Jonathan Cain, Steve Perry

HIGHEST CHARTING WEEK:
Billboard, #8, March 19, 1983

ARTIST	SINGLE
1. Michael Jackson	Billie Jean
2. Bob Seger & The Silver Bullet Band	Shame on the Moon
3. Culture Club	Do You Really Want to Hurt Me
4. Duran Duran	Hungry Like the Wolf
5. The Pretenders	Back on the Chain Gang
6. Lionel Richie	You Are
7. Kenny Rogers & Sheena Easton	We've Got Tonight
8. JOURNEY	**SEPARATE WAYS (WORLDS APART)**
9. Hall & Oates	One on One
10. Styx	Mr. Roboto

Perry also brought along then-girlfriend **Sherrie Swafford**, which created another unneeded distraction when she became jealous of the featured models. "You're going to have a slut in your video?" Cain remembers Swafford asking Perry. "She had to be a not-good looking one," Schon added.

Manager **Herbie Herbert** finally convinced the band to go along with it all, Cain told the *Huffington Post*—mostly because they didn't have any other ideas. That left Perry to openly wonder if he'd have to write a song for Swafford to smooth things over. "And so he did," Cain told the *Post* with a laugh, years after "Oh Sherrie" became Perry's breakout solo hit.

"I know a lot of people may have said, 'Well,

Led Zeppelin wouldn't have done a video where they were playing air guitar,'" Quinn said. "Maybe that was too goofy, especially for a rock band when new wave was really coming up, and rock was trying to maintain its dominance and maybe its tough-guy dominance. I personally thought it was fantastic. I loved every second of it."

Cain takes it all in stride now, at one point admitting that the clip for "Separate Ways (Worlds Apart)" is "so bad, it's cool." Does he want fans to remember him just for playing air keyboard? "No," Cain told the *Houston Press*. "It's great if you were exposed to the band because of that video, but the song is bigger than that."

Journey was simply a victim of the age. "The air guitar and keyboards are cheesy as hell. I give it a 10 on the cringe scale," Schon told *Vulture*. "It's so silly, man. Journey was not a band that did well with videos that had storylines."

Divorced of these images, however, "Separate Ways (Worlds Apart)" can still take on powerful new meaning. In fact, trailer score composer **Bryce Miller** was so inspired that he asked Perry about using a snippet which focused more on his pained vocal in a 2022 trailer for the fourth season of Netflix's *Stranger Things*. Perry approved the clip, then contacted Miller directly to discuss creating a new extended version.

"Bryce had pulled that voice out and just surrounded it with different textures and different synths," Perry told *Rock Classics Radio* on Apple Music Hits, adding that he "lost his shit" while listening to the results. "It goes back to that optimism and sense of fun that people will return to, time and time again. People love that 'Separate Ways' video," Quinn said. "Rock aficionados may have said, 'Oh, that was cornball.' Well, ask people that are still doing send-ups today, down to every last camera angle. Those people love that video. That's something else you couldn't have predicted that would have stood the test of time—but it has. People love it." [53, 223, 261, 299, 303, 314, 315]

The Louisa Street Wharf was the location for the oft-derided video for Journey's "Separate Ways (World Apart)." The campy, low-budget video took on a life of its own, and fans are divided over how good—or how bad—it is that it actually became good as a parody of itself. The band did not care for it. Neal Schon called it "cringy," but 1980s legends like **Martha Quinn** loved it then and loves it now.

Frontiers represented a noticeable change in Journey's artistic approach to its albums. **Stanley Mouse** and **Alton Kelley**, the legendary illustrators who either together or apart had inked all the band's illustrations from *Infinity* through *Escape*, were not involved in the final *Frontiers* design. Mouse said he developed concept drawings for a robot figure that Journey's art director, **Jim Welch**, sought. But the final illustration for what became the album's alien head was credited to "Simon." The alien was dubbed "Elmo" by Journey.

Frontiers was the first album since *Infinity* that did not include the band's signature scarab emblem. The infinity symbol—a regular graphical

device—returned and was nested inside Elmo's mouthpiece. The design carried Journey's futuristic designs that fans were accustomed to. Welch said his vision for *Frontiers* was based on "tunnels" and the relativity of time and motion. "Light stays the same, but time bends," Welch told **Scot Sullivan**. "It was Einstein's theories for artist interpretation."

The design supplied Columbia Records with ample material to develop a promotional plan. Just six years removed from the release of *Star War*, the advertising team borrowed heavily from the film with the ads it ran in the trade press, using the film's iconic skewed perspective introductory text to describe the album (above, from *Cashbox*).

Journey Pulls Its Punch, But *Frontiers* Still Soars

The story of 1983's *Frontiers* is one of missed opportunities—and a widening chasm between Steve Perry and the other band members. There is no small amount of irony there, since the LP went six-times platinum on the way to a No. 2 finish in America, and remains Journey's best-charting album in the U.K.

"We started with back-to-back platinum records for *Escape* and *Frontiers*, with four Top 40 singles on each record," Jonathan Cain said. "Even with the incredible amount of touring we did, we were still able to able to crank out quality music. I wrote 'Faithfully' in about half an hour on a napkin. That was pretty supernatural."

But it could have been better.

Frontiers begins with a bang, as Journey unfurls the No. 8 hit "Separate Ways," the No. 12 favorite "Faithfully," and a pair of No. 23 singles in "After the Fall" and "Send Her My Love." Then the LP becomes more experimental, less structured. *Frontiers* quickly loses momentum.

There's a reason for that. The album was ready for pressing, with the track listing already confirmed, when Columbia A&R rep **Michael Dilbeck** recommended cutting "Only the Young" as well as "Ask the Lonely." "Back Talk" and "Troubled Child," interesting but less commercial songs, took their place.

On one level, this provided a welcome opportunity for the band members to stretch their creative muscles. "No one can say that songs like 'Back Talk' and 'Edge of the Blade' are reminiscent of things that appeared on *Escape*," Perry told *Hit Parader* back then. "We've got to keep chal-

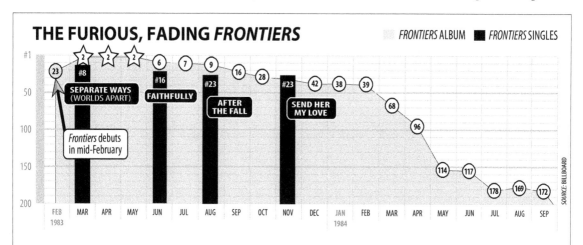

THE FURIOUS, FADING *FRONTIERS*

FRONTIERS ALBUM ■ *FRONTIERS* SINGLES

SEPARATE WAYS (WORLDS APART) #8

FAITHFULLY #16

AFTER THE FALL #23

SEND HER MY LOVE #23

Frontiers debuts in mid-February

SOURCE: BILLBOARD

Escape was a hard act to follow for Journey. The album spent 139 weeks on the *Billboard 200* before falling out in April 1984. *Frontiers* was released roughly a year and a half after *Escape*, and experienced a similar rocket-fast start, debuting at No. 23 (*Escape* debuted at No. 13). A week later *Frontiers* was in the Top 5 and would stay there for 35 weeks, alternately bouncing between No. 2 and No. 5, but never making it to No. 1. Like *Escape*, *Frontiers'* singles helped keep the album in the Top 10, but with slightly lower charting numbers. Roughly a year after its release, *Frontiers* began to fade, falling from a still-robust No. 39 in February 1984 to No. 68 in March. By September, it had fallen out of the Top 200, logging 85 weeks in the *Billboard* 200—an impressive run by most standards. But for Journey, *Escape's* standard of 139 weeks was tough to match.

TOP CHARTING WEEK: *BILLBOARD*—May 7, 1983

1. Michael Jackson, *Thriller*
2. **JOURNEY, *FRONTIERS***
3. Styx, *Kilroy Was Here*
4. Def Leppard, *Pyromania*
5. Men At Work, *Business as Usual*
6. Pink Floyd, *The Final Cut*
7. Lionel Richie, *Lionel Ritchie*
8. Hall & Oates, *H2O*
9. Duran Duran, *Rio*
10. Bob Seger & The Silver Bullet Band, *The Distance*

lenging ourselves to keep things interesting."

Steve Smith explained to *Hit Parader* separately that "the first side of this album is for the fans and the second side is for us. We wanted to test ourselves and see what we could do to build upon the music we'd done before."

Unfortunately, "Troubled Child" may be the weakest moment on *Frontiers*, and that was clear before "Only the Young" shot into the Top 10 after its later appearance on the *Vision Quest* soundtrack. "Back Talk" traces a return line to Journey's tougher free-form roots. The end result "was sort of a progressive record," Cain later told *Keyboard Magazine*. "Some of it failed, some of it was accepted. But I think the stuff that got accepted was the stuff that was really us."

The fun, loose "Only Solutions" could have also found a home on *Frontiers*, but instead ended up on the *Tron* soundtrack. ("If it sounds like something we made up on the spot in the studio," Neal Schon said in the liner notes for

Time[3], "that's because it is.") Cain's "Allies," another song that might have bolstered Side 2, appeared on **Heart**'s *Passionworks* album in 1983.

"Ask the Lonely" ended up on the soundtrack for *Two of a Kind*, the quickly forgotten film that reunited **John Travolta** and **Olivia Newton-John** of *Grease* fame. That meant few heard one of Cain's most direct references to the fire that consumed his school as an eight-year-old third grader: "As you search the ember, think what you've had—remember. Hang on, no don't let go now."

"Perhaps in a way, I was writing to the young boy scarred from that afternoon," Cain later wrote in his autobiography. "Visible signs couldn't be seen, like in some of my classmates, but they marred my insides."

Steve Smith admits that there were "a lot of very good songs to choose, and we did leave off two very good songs … but it was due to sequencing," he told *Las Vegas Weekly*. Back

Journey art director **Jim Welch** wanted a different approach than the standard band group shot for the *Frontiers* album package—he wanted the band to appear in motion, traveling through space and time. For the back cover (inset), he opted to have the band photographed while skydiving, then superimposed that image over the same type of blue circular time tunnel that appeared in the forehead of "Elmo," the nickname for the alien on the album's front cover.

then, he said, making "a strong statement musically" was "important to us in those years."

An expanded reissue of *Frontiers* arrived in 2006, including "Only the Young," "Ask the Lonely," "Only Solutions," and another outtake called "Liberty"—but by then, Perry had long since departed.

In one small way, the split actually traces back to the front cover art of this LP.

"I had this grand plan that I presented before the *Infinity* album," manager **Herbie Herbert** told **Matthew Carty**. "I said, 'Here's the title of all our albums—*Infinity, Evolution, Departure, Captured, Escape, Frontiers* and *Freedom*.'" Herbert had artwork in mind too. The plan was executed flawlessly, until they got to *Frontiers*—when Perry suddenly wanted a different image.

Perry got "that Elmo space guy," as Herbert dubbed him, but the switch represented a "real compromise from the quality of what our packaging had been."

Ross Valory was on board. "We're happy

about it," he told *Hit Parader*, "because the scarab thing was getting a little stale, and we feel this is a very different kind of album for Journey, so it's time for a different kind of cover."

Elmo unquestionably veered from what Herbert believed was an instantly recognizable, signature style. After that, Herbert said his relationship with Perry began to crumble. He described meetings that regularly degenerated into arguments with Perry and his attorney, as the others simply looked on—"like a tennis match."

Schon was starting to have his own issues with Perry, as well. He said he was doing a run-through on "Rubicon," the album's muscular finale, when Perry walked over and turned Schon's amplifiers down. "They want to hear the voice," Schon remembered Perry saying. "That was the start of it for me," he told the *New York Times*. [56, 150, 157, 169, 235, 297, 321, 407, 444, 445, 446, 447]

Edmonton Journal
February 3, 1983

A textbook case of the dangerous follow-up syndrome: how do you follow up a multi-million selling album that never probed or offended but was instead specially tailored to comfort the comfortable? The answer in *Frontiers*: repeat yourself. This is rock at its worst—a luxury item without a hint of necessity. The rockers ("Chain Reaction," "Edge of the Blade") carry MOR punch, "Separate Ways (Worlds Apart)" is a shot in the vein of "Don't Stop Believin'," but the songwriting rarely says anything that hasn't been stated equally well on billboards and bathroom walls. True-blue-forever-love and endless devotion (especially in "After the Fall" and "Faithfully") are superimposed on a comfortable, anesthetized bed of guitars and drums. *Frontiers* gets off the ground but the earth it scans is all previously mined territory.

— *Teresa Mazzitelli*

Detroit Free Press
February 20, 1983

Journey crams the word "love" into four of the five songs on Side 1. Whoop-de-do, right? Well, it probably set some kind of record, and it seems the only thing new for corporate rock's leading quintet—there's nothing fresh in this offering. Instead, the band holds forth at the same musical frontiers with a ten-song package that will do well with millions who bought the band's last release, *Escape*. The various music extremes have gotten more polar, and it's clear which songs are targeted for rock radio stations and which are aimed at adult contemporary and Top 40 formats. Anything guitarist Neal Schon contributes comes off hard and heavy, and Jonathan Cain and Steve Perry manage to pen one heavy one—"Separate Ways (Worlds Apart)," the album's first single, but most of the material written exclusively by the two leans to the soft side.

— *Gary Graff*

The Boston Globe
March 3, 1983

Journey tries to have it both ways on this album, tightening up their sound to shed their corporate rock image, but giving their fans more of what they already bought. The result is an uneasy compromise. The main departure is the title song, with a rhythmic, almost **Police**-like arrangement. It's Journey's most interesting piece of music since their early pre-commercial days, but gets sunk by its silly computer age lyrics. "Edge of the Blade" and "Chain Reaction" have promising opening riffs from Neal Schon, but both dissolve into predictable chorus hooks. The rest is typical Journey fare, with more of the grandiose love ballads that dominated their last few albums. The lyrics still get lost in greeting-card sentimentality. Credit the band for trying to diversify their sound, but not for succeeding.

— *Brett Milano*

'CORPORATE ROCK': CRITICS HANG A NEW LABEL ON BAND

By the time Journey released *Frontiers*, they were as much a company as a band. **Herbie Herbert** founded related subsidiaries to manage every aspect of their recording and touring operations. The vested members voted on major decisions board-room-style.

Then critics started using the label "corporate rock" as a cudgel against Journey.

Steve Perry pointed out that this was, in fact, standard procedure. Bands incorporate "in order to create a tax shelter and not leave penniless," he told *Rolling Stone*. "Everybody did that, but we got stuck with the label. Isn't that fascinating?"

Jonathan Cain felt it was personal. "That's jealousy. I think it's jealousy, because of the business aspect that Herbie had understood so well," he said.

Herbert was helping to rearrange the DNA of rock, bringing in business concepts to a culture that had essentially run on nothing more than sex, drugs, and a few power chords. The members of Journey were partners in these commercial entities, but they weren't equals. The vision, everyone openly admitted, was all Herbert's.

"Not many managers started out as road-ies, you know, and went through every phase of show business," Cain added. "Herbie had this extraordinary ability to start out as Neal Schon's roadie and end up with a PA company, then a lighting company. Then he has this vision of video, and brings video into rock. He was an extraordinary man."

He delved into the finest detail like a shaggy-haired walking spreadsheet. "We completely controlled everything vertically: album covers, the content, the songs. I sequenced each one of those records, and somehow fought to get the record covers the way they were, and I named all the albums," Herbert told *Melodic Rock*. "It's not an ego trip, it's marketing expertise. It's branding expertise."

It was all starting to sound more like Wall Street than Haight.

A rising group of younger rock acts tried to push back. "We were a reaction to all the pre-

tentiousness and cliches and all the bullshit," **Ramones** leader **Joey Ramone** argued in **Steven Blush**'s book *New York Rock*. "It was at the beginning of disco, the beginning of corporate rock—like Journey, **Foreigner**, all that shit."

Yet millions of record buyers, radio listeners, and concertgoers remained stubbornly immune to these criticisms. Classic rock station programmers like **John Gorman** viewed the disconnect with wonder.

"I really hate the fact that sometimes Journey gets lumped into that corporate rock label, you know, with all hooks in the right place," said Gorman, whose Cleveland station earned a platinum record from Columbia for its role in bringing Journey to wider notice. "I didn't look at Journey as just a solid band. There was a time with that band when they just clicked. I mean, it was a perfect team. It was like seeing a championship team when they were on stage."

Journey made no apologies for their rising industry acumen, though they never saw themselves as businessmen. The songs always meant more to them than products on a shelf. "I can't say it didn't bother me," Neal Schon told *Music Radar*. "Any time somebody takes a shot at you, no matter who it is, you take offense if you pay attention to it."

As decades passed, some of these same pundits began to see how they had treated the band unfairly. Time offered new perspectives.

"In that period between when I was like a young, asshole *Rolling Stone* writer trying to have whatever I perceived, rightly and wrongly, as credibility, I had a few experiences," said **David Wild**, who later wrote the liner notes to the platinum-selling 2001 hits package *The Essential Journey*. He realized, for instance, that their album image choices tended to make Journey seem more faceless.

"I think there is something about the name, which seems generic and new age," Wild said. "Like, did they ever have an album cover that had them on it? You know, the branding of it was like **Yes** in a different, earlier era. It was not a cult of personality; they weren't cool with the cool crowd, for a large part of their career. There are just some bands that are more the people's choice. But that being said, the longer I live, the more I respect people who were just simply great."

Journey's best-selling singles endured. Even songs that had not been huge hits found their place on movie soundtracks, TV shows, radio programs, and countless playlists. "The music that they played, it was as good as any of the pop music from the '60s," Gorman argued. "It was music that didn't have an expiration date. You know, whereas [**Toni Basil's** one-hit wonder] 'Mickey' did, 'Wheel in the Sky' didn't."

In the meantime, Schon said it helped to focus on their audiences more than their detractors. "I'd go out on stage and see packed arenas and stadiums," he told *Music Radar*, "and I'd just say, 'Hey, it doesn't matter. These people are here, and they love what we do, so that's what's important.'"

Genres rose and fell as time went on, even as a long-awaited critical evaluation led to Journey's induction into the Rock & Roll Hall of Fame.

"You know, music went to flannel rock, it went to grunge rock. Rock 'n' roll went through a lot of different phases," Cain said. "But calling Journey corporate rock was just ridiculous because we just played a lot of shows. We wrote music that was all over the map—so did **The Beatles**. So what, you know? The critics just loved to hate Journey for a while. But I knew it was gonna be a passing phase, because the songs were mightier than their pen." [376, 407, 410, 411, 449, 450, 451]

Perry said he warned Herbert, before *Here to Stay* arrived, that if Schon "does a second one, I'm probably going to end up doing one," Perry told *GQ*. For him, Schon's next LP with Hammer seemed to have tipped the scales forever. Steve Smith had been releasing jazz-focused side projects too.

"I thought they shouldn't do them but they went ahead and did them anyway," Perry told *Faces*. "I waited a long time, but I finally figured I might as well do one too. If they weren't worried about it, why should I?"

Journey toured behind *Frontiers* a few weeks after its release until September 1983. By the following April, Steve Perry's *Street Talk* was moving up the charts. [54, 80, 308, 309, 312, 313]

Atari Comes Calling, and Band Gives Nod for Video Game

Journey morphed into primitive digital images as the platinum-selling success of their first album with Jonathan Cain combined in early 1983 with a hot new video game trend. Data Age developed *Journey Escape* for the Atari 2600 console, allowing joystick-wielding fans to guide band members through a maze of obstacles on a trek to the Scarab Escape Vehicle. "America's hottest rock group is now a video game," the promotional material raved.

The opening sequence featured "Don't Stop Believin'" before players were beset by "Shifty-Eyed Promoters" (figures with giant heads wearing straw hats), "Love-Crazed Fans" (hearts with legs), and "Sneaky Photographers" (flashing lemons) along the way. Friendly roadies and a manager who looked something like the Kool-Aid Man provided help along the way.

"When you're the flavor of the month, things like that just seem to happen," Cain later told the *Lansing State Journal*. "People approach you for all kinds of things. Journey was hot, Atari was hot and everything worked out."

Journey Escape benefited from a $4.5-million ad blitz, according to a contemporary report from music critic **Joel Selvin**. An arcade version quickly followed. **Herbie Herbert** considered it another stroke of forward-thinking marketing genius: "These days," he told Selvin, "it's sex, drugs, rock 'n' roll and video games—and not necessarily in that order."

Most of Journey's members quickly jumped on board. The band was now reportedly adding a contract rider stipulating that video games be

Continued on Page 173

PERRY ELEVATED CAIN'S EMOTIONAL ODE TO SEPARATION

Journey was in the midst of a two-leg, 132-show tour in support of *Escape* in 1981, when Jonathan Cain was feeling disconnected. The extended time away from his wife **Tané**, whom Cain married in 1979, was putting additional pressure on an already-strained relationship.

"There were early signs that we would probably split apart," Cain told *American Songwriter*. "I knew I needed to do something that said, 'I love you, and whether or not you want to leave me, here it is.'"

Journey headed to Sarasota Springs, New York, and Cain began scribbling on a napkin. Above him was the looming moon, "and it looked like the midnight sun." Cain had the first line, but then sleep overtook him.

The next morning, Cain said the rest of "Faithfully" came to him in a rush. "Literally, in 30 minutes I had written that song," he told *Songfacts*. Cain worked out the musical part at Journey's next sound check. "I had the napkin in my pocket and I put it on the piano," he added. "I played through it and I thought, 'Man, this is good.'"

Steve Perry thought so too, though Neal Schon took some convincing—in particular, he said, because Cain's initial demo had more of an Americana feel. "It sounded like a beautiful country ballad," Schon told *Vulture*. "I couldn't quite imagine what it would sound like with us playing it."

They quickly put a more Journey-sounding spin on it, recording the finished track together—"It was crazy. There was no rehearsal," Schon told *Ultimate Classic Rock*'s **Matt Wardlaw**—then handed things over to Perry. He brought a previously unheard level of feeling to Cain's words.

"'Faithfully' is to die for. I mean, Jonathan Cain's lyrics are amazing, and Steve Perry gave it everything he had," former MTV VJ **Martha Quinn** said. "From the opening lines, he's just absolutely dripping with emotion. Every time you put the needle down, you can just feel it."

He got there in a moment of isolation. "Jonathan wanted to be in the studio and Steve refused," Schon told *Vulture*. "He said, 'No, you got to leave.'" Alone now, Perry found himself taking his vocals to uncharted places, amid these incredible moments of spontaneity.

The finished take was unlike any Perry ever tried. He credited that, in part, to the fact that Cain had written "Faithfully" in his own key.

"When I sang the word 'faithfully' at the very end," Perry told **John Stix**, "I reached for a note that was truly a cry out to my girlfriend at the time." Then there was the ending dance between Perry's "whoa whoa whoa" and Schon's guitar, which he conjured from thin air. "It's about the environment of the studio," Perry added. "You are able to watch certain tracks become bigger than life, right in front of your eyes."

With Perry's voice once again guiding the lyrics, "Faithfully" was another example of how Journey differed so much from **The Babys**. Cain had found a more willing partner for songs in the vein of "Open Arms" than former bandmate **John Waite** could ever be.

When Schon heard the finished take, he was stunned. "So coming back into the studio and hearing what Steve did," Schon told *Vulture*, "I was like, 'Oh my God! Amazing.'" [39, 261, 270, 303, 322, 323, 443]

FAITHFULLY
By Jonathan Cain

HIGHEST CHARTING WEEK:
Billboard, #12, June 25, 1983

	ARTIST	SINGLE
1.	Irene Cara	Flashdance...What a Feeling
2.	David Bowie	Let's Dance
3.	Culture Club	Time (Clock of the Heart)
4.	Men at Work	Overkill
5.	Lionel Richie	My Love
6.	Michael Jackson	Beat It
7.	Thomas Dolby	She Blinded Me with Science
8.	Naked Eyes	Always Something There to Remind Me
9.	Styx	Don't Let It End
12.	**JOURNEY**	**FAITHFULLY**

available backstage at their concerts. Steve Smith was even claiming to have set a world record on *Defender*, scoring 1.5 million points in 60 minutes, according to the *San Francisco Examiner*.

Unsurprisingly, they took *Journey Escape* on tour. "We put it in a road case," Smith confirmed to *Las Vegas Weekly*, "and we'd have it in the dressing room. And then I ended up with it!"

Unfortunately, Journey's game was a dud with consumers, and Data Age had filed for bankruptcy protection by May 1983. "Critics of the game contend the graphics were too simplistic, and the game not demanding enough given the general state of sophistication among video game enthusiasts," Selvin reported. "It was a lemon," added a local retailer.

Perry was never in favor of *Journey Escape*. "Everybody went against me on that issue—'cause I thought it was silly," he told *GQ*. Decades later, Perry was admittedly surprised to learn that a new generation of kids "think it's classic and wish they could find the arcade version, but I personally thought it was dumb."

One of those collectors wound up owning the band-played arcade game Smith had held onto for all those years. [76, 77, 80, 105, 316, 402]

Schon & Hammer's Second Try Was Consciously MTV-Ready

Neal Schon's first collaboration with **Jan Hammer** got no higher than No. 115 after eight weeks on the *Billboard* Top 200. Sights seemed to have been set a bit higher when they reunited a year later in 1982.

Here to Stay featured a more streamlined, MTV-ready approach—as seen in the video clip for "No More Lies," which went into light rotation on cable television. They collaborated with future **Styx** member **Glen Burtnik**, included a track ("Covered by Midnight") co-written with Steve Perry, and even attached a previously unfinished Journey song ("Self Defense") to the project.

In practice, Hammer said the sessions unfolded in much the same way as before. "We had a method of working together already down from the first album," Hammer remembered. "He came in and we did it even easier."

Still, he said, Columbia wasn't satisfied with the results. "It might not have been as wild as

the first record, but there was no conscious effort to make it sound more AOR or radio-chart accessible," Hammer argued. "The only difference was, at the end of the process we turned the music over to the label—and they said, 'We still need a key cut.'"

Schon admitted to **Kaj Roth** of *Melodic.Net* that disagreements marked this second collaboration. "At the time, I was playing a lot of commercially oriented music, so I felt like, 'If I'm gonna do this, I wanna do something that I'm not doing in the other camp,'" Schon said. "It was more of an artistic thing, and I wanted it to keep it like that."

Schon nevertheless knew how to create a hit single, and co-writer Burtnik was learning. (He'd later share composing credits on "Love at First Sight," Styx's most recent Top 40 song; and "Sometimes Love Just Ain't Enough," **Patty Smyth**'s No. 2 Hot 100 duet with **Don Henley**.) Burtnik and Schon got together with Hammer and emerged with a single.

"We went back and created 'No More Lies,' with that in mind—and it obviously worked out great," Hammer said. "As far as the rest of the album, there was hardly any difference from the way we worked on the first album."

Except for the Journey song. Even more than "No More Lies," "Self Defense" stood as the most obvious attempt to push Schon and Hammer into the mainstream.

"Self Defense" captures Journey's early-1980s

lineup (minus Jonathan Cain) at the peak of its increasingly rare hard-rock form, as Perry's background vocal elevates spectacularly over the guitar solo. Schon also delivers lead vocals, providing some tough interplay. Hammer's contribution was a small keyboard part.

"I knew the guys, and met them many times before," Hammer said, "but the 'Self Defense' track was something that they recorded and then ended up not using on an album. They sent me a multitrack to play a solo—and the funniest thing is, I don't think I can even hear myself playing on the final mix," he added, with a laugh. "I didn't have much to add to that. It was great to have a Journey track, but all I added was the solo."

A contemporary *Keyboard* magazine critic thought the resulting album "could easily bring a coliseum full of **Foreigner** fans to their feet." Meanwhile, the *Buffalo Evening News* said "No More Lies" "burns like a house afire." Unfortunately, none of it pushed *Here to Stay* up the charts—not the specially created single, not the Journey leftover.

Released in December 1982, the LP actually fared worse than *Untold Passion* on the *Billboard* charts and took longer to do it: Schon and Hammer's struggle to No. 122 unfolded over 12 weeks. They did not release anything together again until 2012's *The Calling*, a Schon solo project that had far more in common with *Untold Passion*.

"Jan wanted to have commercial success," Schon told Roth, "so that's why the second record sounds different. It's still all right, but I prefer the first record more." [183, 300, 306, 307]

SPRING 1983

RELEASES
▶ Journey, "Faithfully" (single)

NUGGETS
▶ Journey had its entire concert beaming to giant monitors on its own, private closed-circuit TV system. Fans saw the band running down the runway to the stage to open the show and

---

NUGGETS (cont.)
got close-up of them interacting with front-row ticket holders. They went off-script and performed "Don't Fight It," the hit single from **Kenny Loggins** and Journey's own Steve Perry.
—*The Lincoln (Nebraska) Star*

▶ As Journey began to tour, drummer Steve Smith stopped in Los Angeles to tend to business of his own: getting his solo **Vital Information** LP heard in the West Coast music capital. At his hotel with Smith were wife, **Susan**, and infant son, **Ian Matthew**. While Steve played a tape of the album for musician friend **Jeff Richman**, the baby studiously avoided a bowl of oatmeal his mother had prepared. "He just won't eat," the exasperated Susan said. "That's L.A. for you," replied Richman. "Everybody's on some kind of diet."
—*Circus*

Steve Smith Signs Solo Deal, Begins Parallel Jazz Career

Steve Smith was the drummer in one of the rock world's biggest bands, but jazz never stopped tugging at him.

"While I was touring with Journey, I definitely focused my attention on playing that music to the very best of my ability, but there was still a lot of music in me that I felt like I wanted to express—and Journey wasn't the place to do that," Smith said in a 2011 interview. "Journey had a particular sound and direction. I could play in that direction, and it was satisfying to a degree—but I also wanted to play jazz with jazz musicians. The act of improvising with like-minded musicians is something that is essential to my well-being."

He did not have to look far to find those like-minded individuals. In fact, Smith had been playing jazz with bassist **Tim Landers** and saxophonist **Dave Wilczewski** since the early 1970s. As Smith navigated through stints with **Jean-Luc Ponty**, **Al Di Meola**, **Ronnie Montrose**, and then Journey, he never let go of those musical bonds. Smith, Landers, and Wilczewski would get together every so often, writing songs and collaborating on stage with a diverse rotating group that included future **Genesis** sideman **Daryl Stuermer**.

By the time Smith decided to pursue a separate record deal in 1983, they had developed the core of a jazz band called **Vital Information**—and their own sound.

"Even though Journey had a very busy yearly schedule—we'd spend nine months on the road, be home for three months of writing and recording, and then we'd go right back out on the road again—there would be a week here or there where I'd get together with some of my old friends from high school and Berklee College of Music days and play some gigs around Boston," Smith said. "That's how Vital Information came together."

Smith then became the second member of Journey to go solo, following Neal Schon and setting a path for others. "The theory coming from Steve, and I kind of understood it, was that everybody'll go out and be able to express themselves musically in some other areas," Steve Perry told *GQ*, "and then when we reconvene, perhaps we will have discovered or found things that we can bring to the group to help the group evolve."

Journey attracted millions of new fans over the course of what was then a five-album tenure with Journey for Smith. Most had no idea about his past in jazz.

"It wasn't a departure at all," Smith argued. He suddenly found himself correcting fans he'd accumulated since joining Journey who misunderstood his career timeline by assuming Smith had only gotten into jazz later in life. Quite the opposite. Instead, he argued that "playing jazz is my orientation to playing music."

Vital Information, also featuring guitarists **Dean Brown** and **Mike Stern**, recorded their self-titled debut in January 1983 at a Rhode Island studio, then released it that summer. By September, as "Send Her My Love" became the fourth and final single from Journey's *Frontiers*, Smith was out on the road with his other band.

"In between Journey tours, we toured the USA with the Dutch guitarist **Eef Albers** replacing Mike Stern, who was on the road with both **Miles Davis** and **Jaco Pastorius**," Smith said. "In fact, we played some co-bills with Jaco's band on that tour. At the end of that tour, we record-ed *Orion*, our second album. After that, I just kept it going, always following my muse and trying new ideas."

In this way, Vital Information reinvigorated Smith, giving him a direct outlet for his own longer-form improvisational leanings while providing a spark during sessions with his main band.

"I had been continuing to play jazz throughout my time with Journey, but it was in clubs and under the radar when it came to the Journey fans," Smith said.

One naturally fed into another: "As a jazz-oriented musician, it is not too difficult to learn to play the other branches of U.S. music like blues, gospel, country, funk or rock. That's because jazz incorporates all of those roots and more."

The two jazz albums he recorded before splitting with Journey in 1985 opened the door for more than a dozen that followed. Smith came and went in Journey, including reunions in the 1990s and 2010s, but Vital Information endured.

What changed was the lineup around him, as Vital Information stretched into a fourth decade. Landers and Wilczewski departed, and Smith saw several talented collaborators come and go, including former **Santana** keyboardist **Tom Coster**. Along the way, Smith also started **Steve Smith and Buddy's Buddies**, in tribute to legendary drummer and bandleader **Buddy Rich**, and formed **Steve Smith's Jazz Legacy**. [3, 6, 80]

SUMMER 1983

RELEASES
▶ Journey, "After the Fall" (single)
▶ Vital Information, with Steve Smith, *Vital Information* (album)

NUGGETS
▶ NFL Films' **Steve Sabol** has filmed a Journey tour documentary, and segments of it have been interwoven into the band's concert experience, especially during cuts like "Faithfully," where the band is displayed on giant screens ten feet above their heads.
—*Circus*

Continued on Page 177

DID HEIGHT-OF-FAME SOLO ENDEAVORS DOOM JOURNEY?

The only problem with the well-oiled apparatus that **Herbie Herbert** had created to power Journey along was that it ground to a halt when the band did.

The **Hagar Schon Aaronson Shrieve** side project was largely managed in-house, but the return on investment was lesser by orders of magnitude. Now Steve Perry was in the studio to begin work on his debut studio project. Herbert was justifiably worried.

"Herbie argued against the solo albums," **Joel Selvin** said. "The machine behind the band at that point had taken over these giant headquarters on Columbus Avenue. It was a building which was five or six stories. They had hundreds of people working for them. They had trucking companies; they had graphic artists. Everything was done in-house, but without a touring operation, that can't be supported. Doesn't matter how many records you're selling."

Perry often tangled with Journey's manager, but in this instance, he was firmly on Herbert's side when it came to solo albums. "I thought they shouldn't do them, but they went ahead and did them anyway," Perry told the *Los Angeles Times*. "I waited a long time, but I finally figured I might as well do one too."

For Neal Schon, these outside LPs had effortlessly fallen into place. He simply released them, then rushed right back into the fold. But Perry said they formed the argument for making his own record: Schon had moved into MTV rotation with his second collaboration with **Jan Hammer**, and then definitively into their shared rock space with Hagar Schon Aaronson Shrieve.

"So in retrospect," Schon told *GQ* with a laugh, "maybe it wasn't the smartest thing I ever did, because he went, 'Well, Neal's doin' one. Why can't I do one?'"

Their hard-fought but often cloistered march to stardom had created a sense of restlessness. "They spent so much time together, those guys wanted to kick each other's asses," Herbert told Selvin in 1984, "and Steve Perry was definitely leading the march."

Perry copped to it in the *Raised on Radio* tour documentary: "I don't think that we were defined as to who we were individually or collectively, as a group. And we needed to break apart and touch the walls and find out what kind of a personal life you have left."

Even in 1984, not long after his solo debut arrived, Perry was clearly aware that *Street Talk* could prove to be deeply destabilizing. "It may be a little hard working with a band again and being part of that system where everybody

During Journey's heyday, Neal Schon (left) was working side projects with **Jan Hammer** and **Sammy Hagar**. Meanwhile, Steve Perry was developing his own solo album, and Steve Smith was launching his own side group, **Vital Information**.

has a big say in what happens," Perry told the *Times'* **Dennis Hunt**. "I'll have a different attitude with this experience under my belt."

Perry was pushing Herbert to give this debut the same sort of multifront marketing blitz given to recent band projects. "He had a gun to Journey's head," Herbert told **Matthew Carty**. "He said, 'Herbie, if you don't kick ass and perform for me on this solo record, there is never gonna be another Journey again.'"

"Running Alone," a deep cut from Side 2 of *Street Talk*, seemed to trace that road map to its logical conclusion. "Sometimes," Perry told *Song Hits* back then, "the reason you stay in a relationship, or a job, or a situation isn't because you love it. It's because you are afraid that you don't know what's out there and what's waiting for you."

Perry's time away would come at a critical moment—and not just because Journey lost its early 1980s commercial momentum. The band's other members were financially tied to Journey's business interests and couldn't rely on a splashy solo project to balance their personal ledgers.

"He held the economics over their heads," Herbert added. "By not touring in '84 and '85, he irreparably harmed financially Ross Valory and Jon Cain." He said Valory was forced into bankruptcy, and Cain narrowly escaped the same economic fate before Journey finally returned with 1986's *Raised on Radio*.

"What they did, and what principally Steve Perry did to break up the group, was absolutely fucking stupid," Nocturne CEO **Pat Morrow** said. "They turned their back on $100 million. If they'd have carried on into '84, '85, '86, five more years with Herbie at the helm and me running the production, we would have made a bloody fortune. There was no stopping us."

Instead, Selvin said Herbert's worst nightmare was suddenly coming true. "Perry does a solo record, and that stalls everything—and he's losing interest now," Selvin said. "Now there are personality problems; he's getting Lead Singer Disease. So, he doesn't want to do Journey anymore." [60, 78, 79, 80, 135, 242, 385, 474, 903, 927]

NUGGETS (cont.)

▶ Liberty recording star **Dottie West** stopped by Journey's recent *Frontiers* press conference in Los Angeles. West and Journey keyboardist Jonathan Cain met years ago at Nashville's Tree Publishing when Cain was a young, unknown songwriter. —*Cashbox*

▶ It's not official yet, but if Neal Schon has his way we might be seeing a Schon/**Eddie Van Halen** collaboration somewhere down the line. "Yea, it's true. Eddie ... and I would very much like to get together and get into the studio, if we can only get our schedules worked out." —*Circus*

▶ Neal Schon and Jonathan Cain take their turn as guest VJs on MTV's Guest VJs segment. —*Billboard*

▶ Neal Schon and Sammy Hagar are being secretive about the bass player for their new side band. **Denny Carmassi** *[Editor's Note: It was actually **Michael Shrieve**]* will handle the sticks. Speculation was that **The Who**'s **John Entwistle** might be rounding out the quartet. Neither Schon nor Entwistle would say "yes," but when Journey came to New York recently, Entwistle stayed at the same hotel, attended two Journey shows and "hung out with Neal," according to promotion man **Sandy Einstein**. —*Circus*

As *Frontiers* Tour Wound Down, Rochester Felt Like 'The End'

Journey's troubled concert on June 5, 1983 in Rochester, New York, was not the last stop on the *Frontiers* tour, which continued through September 6 in Hawaii. Still, it was the show **Herbie Herbert** later described as "the end of that fucking band."

It seemed like the sheer effort to get to this level had begun to pull at the seams of Journey. "We lived together when I first joined the band," Steve Perry told *GQ*, "and a lot of time spent together can chew on a friendship."

Journey would no longer serve as a working entity. "We weren't getting along on the road and *Frontiers* was no picnic," Jonathan Cain later told King Features Syndicate. "We knew we needed to get away and take a break."

Just two short years had passed since Neal Schon hailed Cain's arrival as a brand-new

Continued on Page 179

CAIN, PERRY COLLABORATE FOR BALLAD TO PAST LOVES

Steve Smith's forays into jazz had a direct impact on Journey's next single, "Send Her My Love." But the song's inspiration came from Jonathan Cain.

He was reminiscing about a teenage girlfriend backstage with a mutual acquaintance. "I looked at her and just said, 'Send her my love,'" Cain later told *Songfacts*. "I walked out, and it hit me: 'Wait a minute, that's a song!'" He immediately found Steve Perry, who sparked on the resonant turn of phrase. They had the beginnings of a song.

"Everybody you know, when they break up, they don't want to call each other," Perry told **John Stix**. Suddenly, people are speaking through intermediaries. "Friends will stop on the sidewalk and talk—then you walk away and say, 'Next time you see her, do me a favor and send her my love.'"

Cain said they finished the lyrics on the spot, which happened often during hectic road trips. Within hours they had a narrative, leaving it to the band to set about creating "one of the most cinematic songs I have had the pleasure of being involved with," Perry added.

At this point, Journey's sessions had a wide open, collaborative feel. They worked out songs together, with Smith regularly contributing ideas about rhythms and arrangements. He dove headlong into vintage vinyl for "Send Her My Love."

"The rhythm for that song was inspired by the **Joe Zawinul** composition 'In a Silent Way,' from the **Miles Davis** album *In a Silent Way*," Smith said. "The drummer on that was **Tony Williams** and he played quarter notes with a cross-stick on the snare drum—a very hypnotic groove. It was one of the first jazz-rock albums, and had a particular freshness because of the use of Fender Rhodes and an open modal playing style."

Schon achieved what Perry has described as a "huge, across-the-Grand Canyon dreamy feeling" on guitar by attaching a Lexicon 480L echo unit to his guitar rack. A recent heartbreak did the rest, Schon admitted. "I was really hurting inside," he told *Hit Parader*. "I had to wear sunglasses in the studio when we were listening to the playbacks, because I was sitting there crying."

All this lonesome anthem lacked was another signature turn from Perry. "Between the opening drum part, Neal's lick, and Jonathan's playing, everything is musically poised for me to come in," Perry told Stix. He nailed it, completing the last of four Top 40 hits from *Frontiers* as "Send Her My Love" went to No. 23 on the U.S. pop charts.

SEND HER MY LOVE
By Jonathan Cain, Steve Perry

HIGHEST CHARTING WEEK:
Billboard, #23, December 31, 1983

ARTIST	SINGLE
1. Lionel Richie	All Night Long (All Night)
2. Paul McCartney & Michael Jackson	Say Say Say
3. Billy Joel	Uptown Girl
4. Kenny Rogers & Dolly Parton	Islands in the Stream
5. Quiet Riot	Cum On Feel the Noize
6. Bonnie Tyler	Total Eclipse of the Heart
7. Pat Benatar	Love Is a Battlefield
8. The Fixx	One Thing Leads to Another
9. The Motels	Suddenly Last Summer
23. JOURNEY	**SEND HER MY LOVE**

Not bad for a song that was once nothing more than a deeply meaningful title. "I must admit," Perry told Stix, "that was perfect."

Journey did not release another new song until 1986, as Perry off-ramped with Schon and Smith in pursuit of solo projects. At that point, Smith was out of the lineup. In fact, he would not perform on another full-length project with the band until the mid-1990s, making Smith's sly polyrhythm on "Send Her My Love" one of his last classic-era contributions with Journey.

It had been a deeply personal one. The Miles Davis LP was one "I'd listened to and digested, and this is a great example of drawing upon your background to come up with ideas to inspire you how to play a particular song," Smith said. "With 'Send Her My Love,' that became an essential feel for the song—that quarter-note, cross-stick rhythm, and that comes straight from 'In a Silent Way.'" [5, 56, 135, 237, 274, 323, 407, 448]

start. "We feel like a real band now," he told *Kerrang!* in 1981. "There will be no more changes in [the] line-up."

Rochester, home to the aging Holleder Memorial Stadium, was part of a push into secondary markets that were important to Herbert. Journey would play huge venues in big cities, but also tucked-away places like Murfreesboro, Tennessee, and Pocatello, Idaho. The band's future, he always insisted, depended on their ability to build a fan base that was both wide and deep.

Still, some secondary markets were easier than others. Holleder had actually been in disuse, with dilapidated stands, poor parking options, and retrograde infrastructure. "I think I had to bring in power, rebuild half the wooden seats," Herbert later told **Matthew Carty**. "I just said, 'Let me spruce [the place] up for one last hurrah."

The promoters hoped to get around the parking issue by running sponsored buses between Holleder and Rochester's former War Memorial Auditorium, but that was it. They told Herbert they would not contribute to any other needed upgrade. He replied: "I don't give a shit; I got the money – I'll fix that place."

Journey had no trouble selling out the 20,000-seat Holleder, of course, and the show itself unfolded in a reliably professional way. But Herbert had spent an incredible amount of time, money, and energy to get the show off the ground, and the band members were still on a collision course.

An outbreak of pushing and shoving also marked the date as a crush of fans made a frantic bid to catch the next bus back to their parked cars afterward. Herbert had never felt so defeated.

"I mean, that was really the end," he told Carty. "That was the end of that fucking band, right then and there, that very day."

Journey did not just go on hiatus after the *Frontiers* tour. They barely spoke. It got to the point where Cain doubted they had a group anymore. "With that break came a certain amount of insecurity from our part," Cain said in the tour documentary for their 1986 comeback record *Raised on Radio*, "especially since we didn't really keep in touch as well as I'd liked to have kept in touch."

Perry, Schon, and Smith shifted their focus to solo work, but Cain and Ross Valory did not necessarily have the same options. In the meantime, an incredible run came to a grinding halt.

"I remember by the bicentennial, we were still driving across America in a little bobtail truck and then we come with this string of albums, *Infinity, Evolution, Departure, Captured*—the live album—then *Escape*," said longtime tour manager **Pat Morrow**. "Those five albums, you know, all go platinum and we're like the darlings of rock and roll. We're rolling."

Journey's subsequent concert film *Frontiers and Beyond* suddenly became particularly poignant. The movie builds toward this Rochester show, and the final bows at Holleder serve as the concluding scene.

"Everybody [was] onstage waving and singing, 'nah nah nah nah nah nah' [from "Lovin,' Touchin', Squeezin'" with opener] **Bryan Adams** and many, many people in the industry that you wouldn't know or recognize," Herbert told *Melodic Rock*. The action stops suddenly in a freeze frame, and the movie is over—both theatrically and, at least for a while, in real life.

Everything Herbert had built was dismantled and mothballed. "That stage alone cost $80,000," Cain told the *New York Times*. "It ended up in storage in Oakland. I think someone stole it."

By 1985, Holleder Memorial Stadium had been shuttered and torn down. [49, 56, 80, 113, 135, 157, 374, 927]

FALL–WINTER 1983

RELEASES
▶ Journey, "Send Her My Love" (single)

NUGGETS
▶ Neal Schon is helping his friends **Silver Condor** with their new LP, and **Waddy Wachtel** and **Rick Derringer** are joining in too. —*Billboard*
▶ The long-rumored collaboration between **Sammy Hagar** and Journey's Neal Schon will happen before year's end, Hagar says style of music...

NUGGETS

...has been a big question mark until now. "It'll be in the **Zeppelin**-**Rush** mold" Hagar explained after a show. "Not that we're deliberately trying to sound like those bands, but the material we've written so far has been in that general category—the power of Zeppelin and the melodic sense of Rush." Hagar says the album will be recorded live. —*Circus*

▶ Westwood One has a deal with Sammy Hagar and Neal Schon to record six of their Northern California concert dates this month for a 90- minute radio special to air in January. —*Billboard*

▶ **Olivia Newton-John** and **John Travolta** are trying to rekindle those *Grease* fireworks with the release of the motion picture *Two of a Kind*, but the movie is not doing well—the soundtrack, however, is having a moment, with Newton-John's "Twist of Fate" and Journey's "Ask the Lonely," getting immediately picked up by KAFM-Dallas and KBBK-Boise [Ed. Note: Stations had to play the album version of Journey's cut since it was not released as a single]. —*Billboard*

Supergroup? Schon, Hagar Join Forces for Short-Lived HSAS

It should have worked. Journey was a platinum band, just as **Santana** had been before. **Sammy Hagar** had also begun to claim his own place among million-selling acts. Yet a rock supergroup featuring Journey's Neal Schon, his former Santana bandmate **Michael Shrieve**, bassist **Kenny Aaronson**, and Hagar somehow sank without a trace.

Schon had hoped to work with Hagar since they began holding "magic" jam sessions in 1977 at the Winterland Auditorium in San Francisco. He also contributed to Hagar's 1980 album *Danger Zone*. Still, it took a few more years before the stars aligned for a standalone project.

The newly dubbed Hagar Schon Aaronson Shrieve (**HSAS**) finally gathered for a series of dates around San Francisco between November 9 and November 21, 1983. They chose the best tracks for the March 1984 release of their lone album and concert video, *Through the Fire*.

"The thing I really liked about the whole project was that so much got done in such a short amount of time," Shrieve told *Ultimate Classic Rock*'s **Matt Wardlaw**. "It was very intense, between recording the album and then doing a series of shows in the Bay Area and those being filmed, as well. It was like a month-long project."

Their first single was a curveball cover of "A Whiter Shade of Pale" by **Procol Harum**. "I just love that song," Hagar admitted to the *Chicago Tribune*. "That melody is so great that you could be singing about cat food, and it would sound like you're pouring your heart into it."

Still, fans clearly were expecting something else. The single stalled out at an embarrassing No. 94, and HSAS' *Through the Fire* failed to reach the Top 40. HSAS quickly drifted apart.

Some questioned their decision to schedule those high-profile concerts before releasing new music—and this group of critics eventually included Hagar. Others simply did not hear a single.

"I know you don't know the songs," Hagar told the crowd on HSAS' opening night, "but they all rock 'n' roll pretty good." Critic **Lee Sherman** later argued that Hagar was "accurately describing the pedestrian rock the band performed. ... Journey doesn't have to worry about losing its guitarist to this fledgling outfit."

Schon admitted that quickly writing the material and then recording it live was the only way to fit this long-hoped-for collaboration into their busy schedules. "When you're in the studio, obviously you work at things and try to get it sounding better, and we figured that nobody had the time to do that," Schon told Wardlaw.

Early on, Schon had mentioned a different rhythm section, including early Hagar collaborator **Denny Carmassi**, and **Tom Petersson** of **Cheap Trick**. Hagar might have been happier with the results if they'd remained. He specifically questioned why Schon brought in Shrieve. Calling him "a great rhythmical guy," Hagar argued in his autobiography *Red: My Uncensored Life in Rock* that Shrieve "wasn't a rock drummer at all—and we were a rock band."

HSAS also "cut the album live, which I thought was sort of adventurous," Hagar added. He and Schon scheduled days of promotional interviews, to no avail. "It might have been better if we'd gone into the recording studio, made the record and then done the shows."

Aaronson, who had originally come to Schon's attention while playing with Journey opening act **Billy Squier**, was disappointed that a proper tour never materialized. "The four of us should have played all around the country doing that record. But they didn't want to do it," he told Wardlaw. "They felt that they could sit back in their armchairs and sell records just by putting out a fricking video."

Trouble seemed to have been brewing from the beginning, as they struggled over who would receive top billing. "Everybody was saying that it should be Schon-Hagar, then they were saying it should be Hagar-Schon," Schon told the *Chicago Tribune*. They decided to flip a coin—and Schon lost.

Good thing: Hagar said he was going to demand top billing anyway. "If it was Journey,

that's one thing, because Journey's bigger than Sammy Hagar—there's no question about that," Hagar told the *Tribune*, "but Neal Schon on his own isn't."

HSAS would not be Schon's only star-crossed group with Hagar. They tried and failed to get **Planet Us** off the ground in 2002 before mounting a semi-reunion of HSAS for a couple of tracks on 2013's *Sammy Hagar & Friends*. Ex-**Van Halen** and Planet Us bassist **Michael Anthony** and **Chad Smith** of the **Red Hot Chili Peppers** took over for Aaronson and Shrieve.

Hagar later admitted to holding back a song that might have broken HSAS wide open—the Top 30 solo hit "I Can't Drive 55." He ended up recording it for his next album at Fantasy Studios in Berkeley, where Journey had most recently completed *Frontiers*. [89, 90, 148, 278, 441]

Continued on Page 189

Sammy Hagar and Neal Schon's side project produced a couple of memorable cuts that got into MTV's rotation. The LP's package (above) offered a simple design that played off the title, *Through the Fire*, with the band's moniker burning through the cover's background parchment paper. The inner sleeve showed photographs of the band on stage. But while it produced smoke, there wasn't much fire.

SWAFFORD BECAME PERRY'S FOCUS IN TOP 5 SOLO CUT

"'Oh Sherrie' is a perfect combination of all the moving parts working as they should—band, singer, production, melody, and lyrics," co-writer **Randy Goodrum** said. "It's a perfect record, in my opinion." Its beginnings, however, were anything but perfect.

"Oh Sherrie" started out as a demo with **Craig Krampf** on a drum pad and **Bill Cuomo** on keys. Perry was in the midst of a rough patch with then-girlfriend **Sherrie Swafford**, but struggled to convey his turbulent feelings.

Perry and Swafford remained "crazy in love," he later told the *Tampa Bay Times*, "and it was a very tough time because the band was peaking. … The truth is that it's hard to navigate a relationship when you're in the midst of such a ride."

She went to bed early one night, as Cuomo, Krampf, and Perry kept working. There were small musical breakthroughs along the way, as Cuomo added a distinctive turn at the beginning and end on the Chroma, an electric harpsichord-type instrument. Still, when he connected with Goodrum, all Perry had was a few loose phrases (including "hold on, hold on") and some placeholder humming.

Goodrum helped him match words to music, surprising Perry by instinctively echoing his sensibility and emotions. Goodrum had a unique approach that helped the process to completion. He had gotten a general idea of who the couple was and sensed a certain amount of drama in their relationship. So he focused on that as the song's main point, rather than immediately trying to craft a hook. Then he worked to fit his words into the places where Perry had only hummed.

Perry suggested an a cappella beginning, which he connected with the old **Four Tops** song "Bernadette." "I was a kid when I first heard **Levi Stubbs** scream it out by himself, and I never forgot it," Perry told **John Stix**. "I wanted the opening line —'should have been gone'—to have that same desperate reaching out."

Released in May 1984, "Oh Sherrie" roared to No. 3, but not before rhythm guitarist **Waddy Wachtel** led Perry back to rock for a moment. Wachtel noticed there was an open spot in the recording, so he asked engineer **Niko Bolas** what Perry was planning. "And he said, 'Yeah, Steve is thinking of a saxophone solo,'" Wachtel told *Guitar Player*. "To which I said, 'Oh, no, he's

not!'" Perry loved his off-the-cuff contribution, which followed the melody of the vocal while adding some exciting double-stops. "It was a rock song," Wachtel argued. "It needed a guitar solo. A saxophone? Are you joking?"

Perry connected with producer **Paul Flattery** after CBS video department executive **Debbie Norman** was impressed by his team's approach on a contemporary clip for **Earth, Wind & Fire** star **Philip Bailey**'s solo song "I Know." They added narrative content over the instrumental break, with a story he said was "completely lifted from **Harry Chapin**'s song 'Taxi,' where a taxi driver picks up a fare and it happens to be an ex-girlfriend who's now a very famous actress."

OH SHERRIE
By Steve Perry, Randy Goodrum, Bill Cuomo, Craig Krampf

HIGHEST CHARTING WEEK:
Billboard, #3, June 9, 1984

ARTIST	SINGLE
1. Cyndi Lauper	Time After Time
2. Deniece Williams	Let's Hear It for the Boy
3. STEVE PERRY	**OH SHERRIE**
4. Duran Duran	The Reflex
5. Night Ranger	Sister Christian
6. Huey Lewis and the News	The Heart of Rock & Roll
7. Lionel Richie	Hello
8. Irene Cara	Breakdance
9. Laura Branigan	Self Control
10. The Pointer Sisters	Jump (For My Love)

Contemplating his first-ever solo video in an age of rapidly spreading excess at MTV, Perry went the other way. "Steve didn't want the ordinary video," Flattery said. "He didn't want, you know, the girls and tights and the flashing lights and leather and all that kind of stuff. He wanted something a bit more classy, something that reflected his song."

Flattery's team suggested the story-within-in-a-story approach that showed Perry pushing back against a typically over-the-top shoot in order to film a more straightforward plea to Swafford. The rejected high-concept portion had an Egyptian motif, "but we couldn't find anywhere in L.A. to shoot it," Flattery said. "So we changed it from being an Egyptian motif to being a kind of Shakespearean one."

They decided to film at Los Angeles's architecturally appropriate Plaza Hotel, now known as The MacArthur, using stagehands and neighborhood folks as extras. "They actually fitted really well into those Shakespearean-type costumes," Flattery added. "I like to think of it as 'Richard III'—with Steve's hair."

The result became a longer-form video, with a potentially concerning two-minute intro. "The thing was, [director] **Jack [Cole]** was all about making what he called 'mini movies,'" Flattery said. "He was about making something that was not there in and of itself, just to sell the record. It was there to become a piece of entertainment they would want to watch. I don't recall the specifics, but nobody at the label at that time complained."

The "Oh Sherrie" video would not be complete, however, until they made one final tweak to the script.

"When we first cut the video, it didn't work—because, you know, you just saw Steve blowing up saying, 'I can't do this,'" Flattery said.

"So Jack pulled in an editor that was working in films, showed him all the stuff and the guy said, 'Look, it doesn't work because you have no sympathy for this guy. You just see him as a spoiled rock star.' What he did was, he re-edited the beginning to show multiple takes of Steve going through this kind of like ridiculous scenario—and then he finally blows up. That's what made it brilliant."

The clip ends with Perry escaping into the Los Angeles afternoon with Swafford in tow, as his overbearing director continues to plead for another take. She soon made a similar exit from public life, though Swafford's whirlwind brush with fame meant that reporters kept trying to make contact long after she split with Perry.

Swafford finally released a statement to **Marc Tyler Nobleman** in 2013, confirming that she had gone on to become an esthetician and yoga instructor. She said she never married and had no children. She cherished "my friends—including Steve—and my privacy," Swafford added. "It was so different for us! It was just love, nothing else!" [36, 272, 435, 453, 456, 457, 458, 460]

Steve Perry gazes into the eyes of former girlfriend and "Oh Sherrie" video costar **Sherrie Swafford** near the end of their music video in 1984. The concept video was built around Perry's reluctance toward the excess in music videos at the time.. The storyline was also used for a prequel video Perry filmed for "Strung Out."

IT'S GOT A RHYTHM ALL ITS OWN.

The first solo journey by
the lead singer of America's
premiere rock 'n' roll band
Steve Perry "Street Talk." FC 39334
Featuring the hit single,
"Oh Sherrie." 38 04391
On Columbia Records
and Cassettes.

Produced by Steve Perry.
Executive Producer Bruce Botnick.
Management Herbie Herbert.

Columbia ® are trademarks of CBS Inc. © 1984 CBS Inc.

John **Scarpati** was a wide-eyed photography student at the Art Center College of Design in Pasadena, California, in early 1984 when he started working with **Martha Davis** of **The Motels**. Davis introduced him to respected producer **Val Garay**, who was looking for a photographer to shoot an artist he was helping in the studio. An introduction was arranged, and Scarpati met Steve Perry, but it didn't dawn on him that it was *that* Steve Perry.

As he was driving home, "Lights" came on the radio, and in that shocking moment, he realized. When Perry flew into Los Angeles shortly after a photo session was arranged, Scarpati was told he would not have much time. If the shots turned out well, they said, he might get an image on the album's inner sleeve. Perry met him at his Highland Park studio, next to Frank's Camera, and they started the short session.

Scarpati pre-lit his studio's hallway and took 12 sheets of film using his 4x5 camera, including a variety of Perry—fedora in hand—leaning up against the wall. Later, when Perry reviewed the shots, he said he liked them and wanted to use one on the cover. Sure enough, Columbia Records approached him soon after and told him he got the cover photo—his first ever. That same photo then became the focal point for the album's promotional campaign; it was the centerpiece of displays in record stores across the country and on the pages of *Billboard* and *Cashbox* (above).

Gazing Backward, Perry Then Comes Full Circle

Steve Perry's first solo album has a complicated legacy. It was meant as a bold step away from Journey, but began with a notable callback. It marked his independence, but ended with a staged reunion.

Street Talk was released in April 1984 and featured major contributions from **Craig Krampf,** drummer in Perry's pre-Journey band **Alien Project**. Krampf played on "You Should Be Happy" and "Running Alone," while also earning co-writing credit on four of the album's 10 songs—including the singles "Oh Sherrie" and "Strung Out."

Sessions started loosely, Krampf told *Modern Drummer*. "At that time, in '81 or '82, he was just cutting to have fun. He said, 'I have the weekend free, and I'm coming to L.A., Krampf. Can you get a band together, a studio, and an engineer?'"

Perry, Krampf, and a few others began by tearing through an early version of "Strung Out." It was largely indistinguishable from the average Journey song in both construction and approach, but something more interesting happened when Perry moved deeper into these sessions.

The list of collaborators grew exponentially. One of them became a fulcrum for the whole project. Drummer **Andy Newmark** had told Perry, "If you ever do a solo album, you've got to get together with this writer named **Randy Goodrum**." They met over a four-day period, Goodrum told *Songfacts*, "and each day we wrote a totally different kind of song. And all four of them ended up on the record."

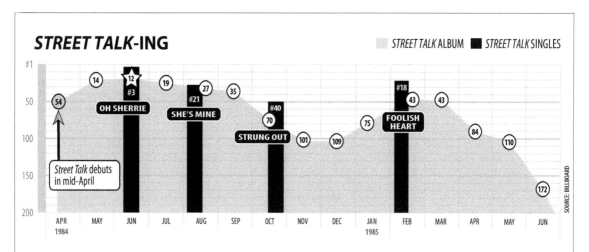

STREET TALK-ING

▨ *STREET TALK* ALBUM ■ *STREET TALK* SINGLES

SOURCE: BILLBOARD

When Steve Perry tested the solo artist waters, he instantly became the most successful Journey member to do so. *Street Talk* leaped into the *Billboard* Top 200 and began its campaign at No. 54 in early April 1984. A month later, the LP was in the Top 15 and album sales surged to keep the record in the Top 30 for three more months. Along the way, Perry scored a No. 3 hit with "Oh Sherrie" and a Top 25 single with "She's Mine." Then, nearly a year after his solo experiment neared the end—it fell out of the Top 100 in November 1984—Columbia released "Foolish Heart" and that single climb into the Top 20, carrying the album back into the Top 50. That surge kept *Street Talk* sales afloat for another four months before it finally fell out of the *Billboard* 200 in June 1985. Whispers began circulating that Perry's Journey days were over, but he was not quite finished yet.

TOP CHARTING WEEK: *BILLBOARD—June 9, 1984*

1. Footloose, *Original Motion Picture Soundtrack*
2. Lionel Richie, *Can't Slow Down*
3. Huey Lewis and the News, *Sports*
4. Cyndi Lauper, *She's So Unusual*
5. The Cars, *Heartbeat City*
6. Culture Club, *Colour By Numbers*
7. Scorpions, *Love at First Sting*
8. Michael Jackson, *Thriller*
9. Van Halen, *1984*
12. **STEVE PERRY, *STREET TALK***

Perry and Goodman's first attempt at collaboration was "Foolish Heart." They completed the music in two hours, and the lyric in another two hours. Then they "went to lunch," Perry told **John Stix**. "It was done. The version of the album is exactly what the demo was from our four-hour writing session."

It just took a while to get to that choice. They'd been set up in a writing room at Perry's house with a Fender Rhodes, a Linn drum machine, and a Teac four-track tape deck. Goodrum arrived with what he called "this little vamp idea," figuring it would give his new acquaintance a sense of his approach.

They developed a demo from that scrap of inspiration, then took their four-track recording to the studio. "We cut two or three tracks, and the tracks were really good, but they just didn't have the vibe of the demo," Goodrum told *Songfacts*. "And we were kicking ourselves because we knew there was something about that little demo."

The solution was to recreate their writing room vibe at Record One in Los Angeles. They brought in the same beat-up Rhodes and the same Linn with the same drum program, and tried again. Only then did the parts laid over by guitarist **Michael Landau**, bassist **Bob Glaub**, and the others begin to click into place.

"We just needed to have that little magic sort of whimsical dreamy loop that the Linn drum was doing, just sort of pulsate and create that vibe for 'Foolish Heart,'" Goodrum added. "That was a really good moment."

Journey's early 1980s commercial success swept fans along. "Oh Sherrie," Perry's ode to a soon-to-be ex, preceded *Street Talk* by a few weeks and quickly settled in at No. 3 on the *Billboard* singles chart. Casting its video provided one of the project's few speed bumps.

"Steve wanted to use his girlfriend, **Sherrie Swafford**," producer **Paul Flattery** said. "We were saying, 'Don't do it; don't do it—because there's going to come a time when you're not going to be together. Then your new girlfriend is not going to want to look at it, and you're not going to want to look at it.' This had happened to us so many times—but he ignored it."

On set, Perry's concluding interaction with Swafford may have provided some hint at what was to come: "The weird thing was at the very end, the first take we did, he goes: 'Hey, I kinda love you.' By take 6, it was 'I kinda like you,'" Flattery said with a laugh.

Perry took part in an inventive two-episode video treatment that linked with the clip for his subsequent single "Strung Out" to create one long narrative. "We were trying to make pieces of art as opposed to pieces of commerce," Flattery said. "And in those days, because it was the ascendancy of music videos, they were getting so much attention in and of themselves."

The obvious goal was to "build on the success of 'Oh Sherrie,' which was a huge, huge hit—and so we wanted to ride the coattails of that," Flattery said. "I don't know if anybody had ever done a sequel, let alone a prequel. What happened was, it gave MTV an incentive to play both together as a kind of a suite. So they would say, here's the new Steve Perry thing—and then of course, it would lead into his biggest hit, which wasn't a bad thing to do."

Flattery liked the results so much that his team returned to the two-part concept a year later with **Phil Collins**'s "Sussudio" and "One More Night." By then, "Strung Out" had followed "Oh Sherrie" into the Top 40.

Ironically, however, "Strung Out" had almost been scratched from the track listing. "The album was literally being mastered when somebody suggested pulling out 'Strung Out,'" Krampf told *Modern Drummer*. "It has that magic—that looseness—and it was a fun track."

Along the way, Perry more fully embraced his early passion for soul music on songs like "I Believe," "Go Away," "She's Mine," and "Captured by the Moment." "He is really a very, very interesting singer, because he has a strong R&B base," future Journey bassist Randy Jackson said in the tour documentary for *Raised on Radio*, "and to be in rock 'n' roll and have a strong R&B base like he does ... I mean, I would say he probably knows more about that music than I do."

Street Talk would become Landau's highest-profile collaboration with Perry, but by no means the last. "Steve Perry was always a very positive soul to be around, very funny and very humble—and obviously a very gifted singer," Landau said. Other ace session players making significant contributions included **Waddy Wachtel** and **Larrie Londin**, the latter of whom also joined Journey's rhythm section for the subsequent *Raised on Radio*.

Together, they created a solo debut that appeared to be racing toward an entirely new place. "Journey's stuff is very melodic and polished," Perry told the *Los Angeles Times* back then. "What I sing on my solo album is much more gutsy. The Journey sound doesn't allow me to do this kind of singing."

Perry dedicated *Street Talk* to **Richard Michaels**, the bassist who died just as Alien Project was on the cusp of signing a record deal. "This poor guy. His family was just distraught," Perry told *Rockline*. "I just thought I should do that for Richard because he worked so hard for so many years to be a bass player."

The album's title also had its roots in the old days. "*Street Talk* was going to be the first name of the group that was called The Alien Project," Perry added. "Since that never happened, I just decided to bring that to the present."

"She's Mine" just missed the Top 20, while "Foolish Heart" reached No. 18. Suddenly, *Street Talk* had become a double-platinum No. 12 smash. Emboldened, Perry settled on a huge change of pace for the final video, simply setting up to sing "Foolish Heart" on a spare soundstage near a piano.

Then **Tom Grubbs**, a free-spirited director of photography who later left the business to become a surf instructor, had a better idea: Why not slowly zoom in on Perry from the balcony, creating a powerful close-up, and then zoom back to conclude things?

This seemingly small production choice turned out to be outrageously expensive—sparking an internal dispute between Columbia's record executives and the label's still-new video department, according to a skeptical **Herbie Herbert**. "How can you charge a hundred grand, or whatever it was, for just a one-camera shoot from the balcony that swoops down on the stage and goes back?" Herbert asked *Billboard* magazine rhetorically.

> The goal was to build on 'Oh Sherrie,' which had been a huge, huge hit—and so we wanted to ride the coattails of that. I don't know if anybody had ever done a sequel [video], let alone a prequel. What happened was, it gave MTV an incentive to play both together as a kind of suite. So they would say, here's the new Steve Perry thing, and then, of course, it would lead to the biggest hit, which wasn't a bad thing to do.
>
> —*Paul Flattery*

Flattery countered that the equipment of the era simply could not accommodate that shot. "You didn't have a crane that could have the camera actually in the balcony and below the parapet, and then come up and go all the way down," he said.

"So, the solution was to build a fake balcony, which you could then strike as soon as the camera was clear of it," Flattery added. "Then you could get everything and everybody out of the way by the time you got down to the stage and the camera turned around. For something that looks so simple, that was a lot of hard work."

The final single from *Street Talk* arrived in November 1984, on the cusp of the year-end holiday season. Perry agreed to film an alternate ending for the "Foolish Heart" video where he joins his Journey bandmates in offering season's greetings to fans.

Street Talk had somehow brought Steve Perry full circle. They share a toast, then Perry announces the band is heading out to grab a bite to eat before their new recording session.

The point of the new shot, Perry told *GQ*, was "to just tell everybody that that particular phase of my career was now over and now I'm back to Journey." Perry added that "in my heart of hearts, I was never gonna leave Journey. I had no desire to."

The sentiment may have been real, but Flattery said the pressure to tack on a different ending came from above. "That was the record company, because the record company was being plagued with, 'Is Steve going to go back to Journey?'—and they didn't want to lose the cash cow that Journey was," he said. "So that was something that we shot to appease them."

Instead of art, Flattery argued, "that was pure greed." [36, 78, 80, 135, 248, 339, 435, 454, 455, 459]

ESTABLISHED HITMAKER HELPS PERRY FIND A NEW VOICE

Randy Goodrum already had a celebrated songwriting past before he unlocked Steve Perry's solo career.

Born in Hot Springs, Arkansas, Goodrum was a child prodigy, learning to play piano as a child. Living in a crossroads of the Deep South, he grew up around a diverse musical mix of rock, country, blues, R&B, and jazz—and Goodrum would end up dabbling in every one of those genres. He played in a local jazz trio that included future president **Bill Clinton** on sax before attending college, where a friend asked him to chip in on some songs for an original musical.

"I started coming up with some things," Goodrum later told *Songwriter Universe*. "The next thing I know, my friend became too busy, so I ended up writing the whole thing." Goodrum fell in love with the process, and graduated with a Bachelor of Music degree,

played in the U.S. Army band, then struck out for Los Angeles to see what fate had in store.

The answer: Not much.

Goodrum tried Nashville next, playing piano with **Roy Orbison** and **Jerry Reed** before he finally hit with "You Needed Me," a chart-topping 1978 song written for **Anne Murray**. **Michael Johnson** scored with Goodrum's "Bluer Than Blue" in 1978 too—and his songwriting career finally took flight. He had memorably contributed a pair of songs, "Love Lies" and "That's Why," on **Michael McDonald's** 1982 solo debut, when one of music's most well-traveled session and touring drummers had an idea.

"A mutual friend of ours, **Andy Newmark**, suggested to Steve that he contact me," said Goodrum, who eventually settled on the East Coast. "I think he mentioned some of my notable songs. Steve called me at my home in Connecticut and wondered if I'd be interested in writing with him for an upcoming solo project. I said, 'Of course, let's give it a try.'"

But that was only after Goodrum initially misunderstood who had called him. "I think it's the lead guitarist with **Aerosmith**," Goodrum told his daughter. "And she said, '**Joe Perry**?' and I said, 'No, Steve Perry,'" Goodrum told *Songwriter Universe*. His daughter ran to her bedroom, pulled down a Journey poster and raced back to the kitchen to show him the considerable difference. "I said, 'Ohhh,'" Goodrum admitted.

Still on the phone, Perry pitched Goodrum on the idea of working together on his first solo album, then asked when Goodrum would be back in Los Angeles. "Tomorrow," Goodrum replied. He didn't even have a plane ticket.

"I think he was a real fan of 'Bluer Than Blue' and 'You Needed Me,' and some stuff I'd done before that," Goodrum told *Songfacts*. "That whole album was a surprise, as if you were to walk down the street and see a $20 bill blow by." After quickly booking a red-eye flight back west, Goodrum decided he did not want to arrive at Perry's house empty-handed.

"When I got off the phone with Steve, I went to my piano and came up with the starting vamp and feel of 'Foolish

Heart,'" Goodrum said. "I figured that I should offer him what I do as a writer, rather than trying to knock off a Journey-ish song. It was a risk, as I thought that maybe Steve wouldn't be into it and we'd just have a cup of coffee—however, he loved it and it was our first co-write."

At this point, the typically fastidious Perry had gotten "more in the habit of digesting things and rearranging things and going back and working on the lyrics," Perry later told **John Stix**. Goodrum worked differently. They wrote the music for "Foolish Heart" over the first few hours, then Goodrum dove right into creating a companion narrative.

"He said, 'Let's skull out the lyric right now,'" Perry added. "I thought, 'Man, that's pretty rock 'n' roll—'skull out the lyric.' So we did." Hours later, "Foolish Heart" was complete—and a sturdy new songwriting partnership had been forged. "We started writing the tune at 11 a.m.," Goodrum said, "and finished a rough demo of it at 11 p.m."

It was the first song they wrote for what became *Street Talk*. Goodrum kept coming back, and the completed demos piled up. "I realized that Steve was looking for new ground musically," Goodrum said, "and we wrote for several days after 'Foolish Heart.' They were very adventurous songs, and luckily he recorded all of them on the project."

Perry's 10-track solo debut eventually included eight co-written with Goodrum. He would go on to win a Grammy for "So Soft, Your Goodbye," recorded by **Chet Atkins** and **Dire Straits'** **Mark Knopfler**, and compose hits like **Toto**'s "I'll Be Over You," **DeBarge**'s "Who's Holding Donna Now?", and **John Berry**'s "I Will, If You Will," among others. Songs Goodrum co-wrote with Perry also appeared on the 1985 USA for Africa charity compilation *We Are the World*, 1994's *For the Love of Strange Medicine*, and 2018's *Traces*.

"He's one of those friends and colleagues that when you call them up or vice versa, it's like you just talked to them 30 seconds ago, even though it might be three years," Goodrum said. "On those rare occasions that I'm in L.A. and he's got space, we usually always end up writing a song, or at least a part of one." [36, 274, 338, 339]

RELEASES

▶ HSAS (with Neal Schon), *Through the Fire* (album)
▶ HSAS (with Neal Schon), "Whiter Shade of Pale" (single)
▶ HSAS (with Neal Schon), "Missing You" (video single)
▶ Steve Perry, *Street Talk* (album)
▶ Steve Perry, "Oh Sherrie" (single)
▶ Steve Perry, "She's Mine" (single)
▶ Vital Information (with Steve Smith), *Vital Information* (album)

NUGGETS

▶ Is Steve Perry leaving Journey? The platinum success of his first solo LP, *Street Talk*, has him mulling it over. A spokesman for the singer said last month that Perry "hasn't made up his mind" whether to stay with the San Francisco-based megagroup, and sources close to the band say **Mickey Thomas** of **Jefferson Starship**, and **Brad Delp** of the in-limbo **Boston** have been mentioned as possible replacements. "Let's not be catty," says the group's manager, **Herbie Herbert**. "The economic incentive exists [for Perry to leave]. For him to make the same amount of money on a Journey record, we'd have to sell 7 to 8 million copies." Moreover, Herbert says, "Even other members of Journey have been calling me asking about these rumors." And? "I tell them to call Steve." — *Rolling Stone*
▶ Journey bassist Ross Valory and keyboardist Jonathan Cain win at the 7th Annual Bammies. —*Billboard*
▶ What if they formed a supergroup and nobody cared? Consider the case of **HSAS**, the four-way collaboration of **Sammy Hagar**, **Neal Schon**, **Kenny Aaronson**, and **Michael Shrieve**. Geffen Records hoped the union would yield another instant "supergroup" along the lines of **Asia**, whose debut album for Geffen logged nine weeks at No. 1 in 1982. HSAS' album didn't come close, peaking at number 42 in May. For a group's debut album to climb to number 42 isn't bad; it's just disappointing, because greater things were expected, owing to the Asia precedent and Hagar's solo star status. —*Billboard*

NUGGETS

▶ Awash in the success of Journey's *Frontiers* LP and his own solo project, *Street Talk*, Steve Perry says that he enjoys working in the studio and wants to guide others, including potentially producing the next **America** album. *[Ed. Note: He didn't produce, but he did provide backing vocals on "(Can't Fall Asleep to a) Lullaby.]* —Associated Press

▶ *Street Talk* is the debut solo effort from Journey front man Steve Perry, and the album has one Top 40 single with "Oh Sherrie." Parts of the LP recall the singer's home band, but it is a much more light and pop-oriented album, showing a varied and restrained musical palate. "Foolish Heart" is a beautiful ballad, while the dramatic "She's Mine" and "You Should Be Happy" show off Perry's hard-rocking side. Meanwhile, Journey's guitarist, Neal Schon, has watched his side band—**HSAS**—put a single into MTV's video rotation, a cover of **Procol Harum**'s "A Whiter Shade of Pale" with **Sammy Hagar** on vocals. —Cashbox

FALL 1984

RELEASES

▶ Steve Perry, "Foolish Heart" (single)

NUGGETS

▶ Neal Schon wrote a song called "I Can't Stop the Fire" for **Nick Nolte**'s upcoming black comedy film, *Teachers*. The soundtrack is being released by Capital Records, but Schon's problem was that Columbia Records would not give him permission to record it. Instead, the song was recorded by Bay Area rocker **Eric Martin**. —Billboard

▶ All the members of Journey came together to attend **John Waite**'s recent solo concert in the Bay Area. Things between Steve Perry and the rest of the band seem to be OK. —Circus

COLLABORATIONS

▶ Steve Perry, vocals on "Don't You Wanna Go To The Moon" on **Barnes & Barnes** album, *Amazing Adult Fantasy*.

▶ Steve Perry, backing vocals on "(Can't Fall Asleep to a) Lullaby," on **America**'s album, *Perspective*.

▶ Steve Smith, drums on "Heaven," on **Bryan Adams**'s album, *Reckless*.

Prince Asks for Journey's OK Before Releasing 'Purple Rain'

Prince had completed the title track for what would be his blockbuster breakthrough album, *Purple Rain*, when he realized it sounded familiar. He had his management team send a cassette of the song to Columbia Records, who then summoned Jonathan Cain to their Los Angeles offices.

Cain told *Billboard* that Prince got on a conference call with him and said: "I want to play something for you, and I want you to check it out. The chord changes are close to 'Faithfully,' and I don't want you to sue me."

Ironically, despite Prince's concern, evidence shows that he couldn't have directly plagiarized the song. He first tried out this progression during the sound check for a December 12, 1982 concert in Cincinnati, Ohio, according to *Prince and the 'Purple Rain' Era Studio Sessions*. "Faithfully" initially appeared on *Frontiers* months later in February 1983, and didn't debut on the *Billboard* singles chart until March 16.

Still, Neal Schon immediately heard the similarities. "I looked at it more like maybe he was influenced by the way I was playing guitar on that song," Schon told the *Star-Tribune*, "and the way the chords were descending." Cain heard a bit of "Faithfully" in the song's concluding "whoa whoas" too.

According to Steve Perry, that was manager **Bob Cavallo**'s main concern. He remembered Cavallo saying, "This is going to be the lead track of his movie, his first film, called 'Purple Rain,'" Perry told interviewer **Jill Riley**. "Would you listen to the end of it?"

Perry admitted it had the "same pocket. ...

If you listen to the outro, it's the same chords, the same tempo as the outro of 'Faithfully.' The only difference is, I'm screaming 'Faithfully' and he's singing 'Purple Rain.'"

But Cain, Perry and Schon "all talked about it and everybody said, 'Nah, it's the highest form of flattery. Let it go,'" Schon told *Billboard*.

Schon did, and later included his own update of "Purple Rain" on *Universe*, a 2020 solo album devoted to cover songs. "We loved him," Perry confirmed to Riley. "We were crazy about him. I was a fan, right from the get-go."

The admiration was mutual: Schon said he heard Prince wore out a copy of Journey's *Escape*, and Schon's *Santana IV* reunion record was one of six albums Prince purchased just days before his death.

Years later, Cain confirmed that Prince offered to make any requested changes to "Purple Rain." He said that was unneeded, and even refused a songwriting co-credit. "I told him I didn't see a huge problem and what he had was killer," Cain told *City Scene*. "I wouldn't ask him to do that. I left saying, 'Good luck, man. You got a hit.'"

The conference call ended as Prince gifted Cain with a cool perk. "He said, 'I'm coming to San Francisco, so I'll get you tickets,'" Cain told the *Star-Tribune*. While onstage that night, Prince noticed Cain in the front row at the Cow Palace and tossed him a keepsake.

"It's the same chords, but so what? Everybody gets inspired from somebody," Cain told the *Commercial Appeal*. "I got tickets to his show. I was way up front, and he threw a tambourine, and I caught it. Still have that tambourine." [205, 429, 430, 461, 462, 910, 911, 912]

I'LL BE ALRIGHT WITHOUT YOU

Eight albums into Journey's existence, Neal Schon was the lone original band member still standing. The huge success of *Frontiers* sustained the band's momentum, but follow-up solo projects dampened the flame. When they finally returned, their pop-rock magic was beginning to fade.

WINTER 1984–85

RELEASES
▶ Journey, "Only the Young" (single from the *Vision Quest* soundtrack)

NUGGETS
▶ Steve Perry will be joining with 45 other artists to record "We Are the World" on the *USA for Africa* benefit album. —*Cashbox*

▶ The *Vision Quest* soundtrack is a bit of a friends of Journey reunion. The band recorded the movie's theme song in "Only the Young," but also on the LP—distributed by Geffen Records, not Journey's label Columbia—are frequent collaborators **John Waite** ("Change") and **Sammy Hagar** ("I'll Fall in Love Again"). **Madonna**, **Don Henley** (backed by the **Go-Go's**), **Style Council**, and **Ronnie James Dio** join in too.—*Cashbox*

Perry, 45 Other A-Listers Lend Voices To 'We Are the World'

The constellation of stars gathered for "We Are the World" was such that even Steve Perry was humbled.

The charity single was recorded on January 28, 1985 by a hastily assembled supergroup that also included **Bruce Springsteen**, **Ray Charles**, **Tina Turner**, **Stevie Wonder**, **Bob Dylan**, **Hall & Oates**, and many others. The session was set on a date when many of them would already be in Los Angeles for the American Music Awards, being held the same night at the nearby Shrine Auditorium.

"We Are the World" had been composed by fellow participants **Michael Jackson** and **Lionel Richie**, with production duties handled by **Quincy Jones**. The song went on to sell more than 20 million copies, finding a place among the Top 10 in all-time sales.

Perry was just trying to get through the evening. Feeling a bit overwhelmed, he stole away to the catering room to gather himself. "There was all the lunch meats and the pineapples and so I'm eating lunch meat," Perry later told

Rock Classics Radio. "I look over, and there's **Bette Midler** and **Paul Simon**."

Everyone sat in silence for a moment, before Midler broke the ice: "It's a little overwhelming, isn't it?" Perry remembered Midler saying. His reply: "That's for sure."

This sense of surrealism continued, even while the session was underway. Perry happened to be in the control booth with Jones when Jackson recorded his vocal. He looked over at Jones and said, "Am I dreaming? Am I on drugs?"

When they all lined up in the studio, Perry found himself near his "Don't Fight It" collaborator **Kenny Loggins**. "It was pretty unbelievable," Loggins told the Palm Springs *Desert Sun.* "I had Bruce Springsteen on my left and Steve Perry on my right—two of the greatest singers in the world."

The session ultimately took some 12 hours, with plenty of stops and starts. Loggins said Springsteen's performance had a direct impact on how he approached things. "His voice came out as big as God—and hairier," Loggins remembered. "I thought, maybe I should get soft and not compete with it." Next came Steve Perry, who more than held his own. Daryl Hall followed.

"I always remember this story a friend of mine told me who was at the 'We Are the World' sessions," **Martha Quinn** said. "Daryl Hall was standing next to Steve, and Steve went into his solo—and Daryl was thinking to himself, 'Who's this guy?!' Obviously, he knew it was Steve Perry from Journey, but he didn't know the extent to which his vocals were so amazing. So, right then and there, Daryl Hall was like, 'Whoa, he's a force to be reckoned with.'"

"We Are the World" was collected on an album of the same name that featured nine additional songs, including "If Only For the Moment, Girl" by Perry. This hushed track was the product of a follow-up composing session with principal *Street Talk* co-writer **Randy Goodrum**.

"This song was written not long after the *Street Talk* record was released," Goodrum said. "Steve and I were looking for opportunities and space to write more of that 'new

Continued on Page 195

VALORY, SMITH FIRED AS JOURNEY BECOMES A POWER TRIO

Steve Perry was the driving force behind his solo debut, handpicking the songs, the players, the takes, and the mix. He was blunt about how a return to Journey would present new challenges.

"I know I like calling the shots," Perry told the *Los Angeles Times*, "in terms of the writing and producing and what the band plays."

Sessions for the album that would become 1986's *Raised on Radio* began with the lineup from *Escape* and *Frontiers* intact. But then Perry started calling the shots.

First, Jonathan Cain shifted to a more R&B-stoked compositional style to mimic the vibe of Perry's solo album. Then Perry took over the producer role, and decided the band needed a new rhythm section. Finally, Perry opted out of manager **Herbie Herbert**'s album-naming cycle, choosing a more personal title instead of *Freedom*.

"My original strategy was to keep the band intact, not to change anything," Perry told the *South Florida Sun-Sentinel* back then. But then "we ended up after three months with only a couple of keeper tracks. It was scary because we all saw the group in a different light."

The issue related to how these songs were initially composed. He and Cain had changed the early composing process, recording demos alone on a Mara Machines MCI 24-track recorder that Cain had found again years after he used it to complete "'Til It's Time to Say Goodbye"—the single that drew critical early attention from **Dick Clark**.

Perry and Cain would grow accustomed to using preset rhythm tracks. Once Journey shifted to the studio, Perry pushed for a session feel that more closely mimicked them. This atmosphere could not have been any further removed from the roundtable jam sessions Journey used to employ as initial song ideas were coalescing.

Eventually, everything ground to a halt. "When the record was half done, that's when they called me to say ... they wanted to get rid of Ross Valory and Steve Smith," Herbert later told **Neil Daniels**. "That was Steve Perry driving that. Of course, that was the stupidest fucking thing in the world."

Smith would only appear on three released tracks: "Positive Touch," "The Eyes of a Woman," and "Why Can't This Night Go On Forever." Valory, the band's co-founding bassist, was ab-

Journey bassist Ross Valory (left) was a founding member of Journey, and drummer Steve Smith joined the band in 1978, just as the band became commercially successful. They were both ousted in the fall of 1985.

sent for the first time ever on a Journey record.

"In my opinion, [Perry] became more interested in being a solo artist," Smith told *Modern Drummer*, "and enjoyed the feeling of writing songs with maybe one or two other people, rather than a whole group situation."

Perry's approach to production had not come out of nowhere. In the early days, before he caught on with Journey, he had worked as a tape operator at a Los Angeles studio. He had a hand in creating his own demos there.

But taking on producer duties for *Raised on Radio* soon turned into taking over. Journey "agreed to let him produce the records," Smith told **Joel Selvin**. "I actually thought he would be a great producer. Then he insisted on using whoever he wanted to play on the record."

Still, the band seemed to instinctively understand that the only path forward was in acquiescing to Perry. "The most direct, least complicated way to come back was with him," Valory told Selvin, "and do whatever it took to keep it going."

The meeting where Smith and Valory learned their fates did not go well, Perry said. "They had a meltdown," he told Selvin. "It was pride and integrity time."

Journey sacked the drummer and bassist as concessions, "to try to keep Steve [Perry] in the brotherhood," Cain said in his autobiography, Everyone had been unsure if he would ever return, so "we felt we had to pursue the music he wanted to make. I helped our band make the particular type of sound Steve wanted."

The results, however, "came at the expense of our two brothers."

They didn't look far for their studio replacements: Perry brought in the main rhythm section from *Street Talk*.

Larrie Londin replaced Smith on eight songs, while **Bob Glaub**—who played bass on all but two *Street Talk* compositions—appeared on the same cuts as Steve Smith. Randy Jackson returned on bass, reprising a role he played on Journey's "After the Fall" from *Frontiers*.

But they had wasted precious time. Recent recording budgets had been in the $75,000 range, according to Selvin. Journey spent half a million dollars on *Raised on Radio* and more than a year of painstaking recording.

The late Londin said he was never quite sure if Smith simply refused to play along with the click track because it insulted his years of experience, or if Smith simply could not. "I've heard both stories—but that's why they called me," Londin told *Tech Trek* in one of his last interviews. "I laid down the drum tracks and got my paycheck and that was the extent of my involvement."

That meant Journey had to find a new touring member. Jackson was a holdover for the subsequent live shows, but the proposed dates got pushed back three times while Perry tried to decide on another drummer. [59, 78, 100, 135, 283, 468, 469, 487, 488]

ground' music that was more uniquely Steve Perry."

"We Are the World" raised more than $63 million for humanitarian aid, while the triple-platinum album reached No. 1 in just two weeks. Perry's buoyant turn on the song was eventually among the most celebrated.

"I think it took a long time for all of us to look back and think, 'Oh my God, he was such an amazing singer,'" Quinn added. [36, 92, 299, 303, 467]

After Focusing on Family Life, Rolie Returns with Solo Album

Gregg Rolie had co-founded two bands that would ascend to the Rock & Roll Hall of Fame, selling millions of records while performing on signature stages. What he had never done before was construct his own record.

The breezy, surprisingly accessible *Gregg Rolie* arrived in 1985, after he had spent a few years focused on family life.

"I learned a lot, doing that first solo album," Rolie said. "Before, I had always relied on a band; I never had to design the whole thing. They were always a team effort, but when you go solo, it's totally different."

With **Santana** and Journey, there was a sense of shared responsibility. "Somebody would come in with a song, we'd play on it, you'd come up with your parts," Rolie told *Glide Magazine*, "and it's designed right there." Now, Rolie was suddenly in charge of things like hiring a bassist.

In spots, Rolie turned to old friends. Neal Schon takes a notable turn on "It's Only Make Believe." Their former Santana bandmate **Mike Carabello** earned co-writing credit on "Let Me Out," while **Carlos Santana** soloed on "Marianne." **Herbie Herbert** and **Pat Morrow** were still managing things on the business end, while **Jim Welch** oversaw art design.

Rolie also opened the door for new collaborators like future **Chicago** singer **Jason Scheff**, who added sweetened background vocals. **Starship** guitarist **Craig Chaquico** appeared on "Over and Over," while Chaquico's producer **Peter Wolf** played keyboards and arranged three tracks.

Wolf added a particularly modern touch to the record, very much in keeping with where Journey went musically after Rolie's departure. Still, none of it connected with the wider listening public, not even Rolie's early, more melancholic take on **Eddie Money**'s future No. 14 smash "I Wanna Go Back." "I did it first, and

Continued on Page 197

FRONTIERS LEFTOVER HITS TOP 10 AS *VISION QUEST* SINGLE

In an unlikely scenario, "Only the Young," in March 1985, became Journey's first Top 10 *Billboard* hit since "Separate Ways (Worlds Apart)" more than two years earlier.

The band had taken the recently completed song with them in 1983 to the bedside of **Kenny Sykaluk**, a terminally ill teen from Ohio, whose mother reached out to the band through the Make-a-Wish Foundation. The band played the song for Sykaluk in an emotional day, and he died the next day. Then the song sat unreleased for the next two years.

The band members had spent that period apart in every sense of the word, creating solo projects while barely speaking. "When the last *Frontiers* tour ended, we had a lot of internal problems," Neal Schon admitted in the *Raised on Radio* tour documentary. "So we decided to just take some time off, and just give it a breather."

This was no reunion: "Only the Young" languished in the vault after its last-minute scratch from the track listing for 1983's *Frontiers*. **Scandal** ended up releasing the song first as a track on their lone LP, 1984's *The Warrior*. At that point, "there was no Journey," Jonathan Cain told *Keyboard* magazine. "There wasn't going to be an album. There wasn't going to be another tour. The band was basically defunct."

Questions from fans and media followed them everywhere. "The members of Journey are vehemently denying reports that the group is splitting up," *Creem* reported in 1984. "Their management did, however, lay off 12 employees last month. None of them were Steve Perry, although he's the one most mentioned in the break-up tales."

Yet the smash-hit title track from *The Warrior* would push Scandal into the mainstream, not "Only the Young"—which seemed destined to remain a forgotten deep cut. That is, until it surfaced on the soundtrack for *Vision Quest* in 1985.

"Ask the Lonely," another song left off *Frontiers*, was also on a soundtrack. But it simply vanished as people stayed away from the 1983 feature film, *Two of a Kind,* in droves. "Only the Young" would make a much larger impression,

reaching No. 9 on the *Billboard* Hot 100.

A forgotten leftover was suddenly creating positive momentum again, even though "Only the Young" was simply a stopgap release. Part of it was the renewed attention from fans, but the suddenly ubiquitous old song also boasted a sense of determined romanticism that seemed to awaken something in Journey.

ONLY THE YOUNG
By Jonathan Cain, Neal Schon, Steve Perry

HIGHEST CHARTING WEEK:
Billboard, #9, March 25, 1985

ARTIST	SINGLE
1. REO Speedwagon	Can't Fight This Feeling
2. Madonna	Material Girl
3. Phil Collins	One More Night
4. Glenn Frey	The Heat Is On
5. Julian Lennon	Too Late for Goodbyes
6. Teena Marie	Lovergirl
7. Tina Turner	Private Dancer
8. Survivor	High on You
9. JOURNEY	**ONLY THE YOUNG**
10. Frankie Goes to Hollywood	Relax

"I really have to give credit to Jonathan Cain for coming up with the concept to write about … 'only the young can say they're free to fly away,' because there's a certain innocence that the youth have," Cain remembered Perry saying in his memoir, *Don't Stop Believin'*. "That's just a wonderful gift."

Cain called Perry, and Perry began contemplating another Journey album for the first time in a while. "You call it a breakup, call it some time apart," Perry mused in *Raised on Radio*. "Either way, it needed to get apart from itself— away from itself—and to see if it wanted to come back together."

Turns out, it did. Sessions for Journey's long-awaited comeback with 1986's *Raised on Radio* began in the fall of 1985. The band would open every show with "Only the Young" during the subsequent tour, their last with Perry. [135, 154, 463, 464]

he had a hit with it," Rolie said, matter of fact-ly. "That's the way it goes."

He continued tweaking, both in terms of song selection and musical approach, in the run-up to 1987's far-improved *Gringo*. "That was a new experience for me," Rolie admitted. "I got better on the second one."

Then Rolie says his label bosses suddenly lost their nerve, despite the fact that Santana and Schon also returned—or maybe because of that.

"They trade solos on a song called 'Fire at Night' that's still stunning," Rolie told journalist **Ray Shasho**. He said the song was starting to garner airplay in the Midwest when Columbia Records stopped promoting the album. He figured their reasoning was purely from a business aspect: "Why would they want to make me compete with Santana and Journey when they already had them?"

In the end, "I was lucky to get the jackets printed," he told Shasho, "but that's the record company, you know?" [2, 277, 465]

SUMMER 1985

RELEASES
▶ Gregg Rolie, *Gregg Rolie* (album)

NUGGETS
▶ Neal Schon joins heavy metal charity lineup for the famine in Africa, Hear 'n Aid. —*Cashbox*
▶ Journey's Steve Smith is working with Starboard Records' production of USA for Africa's "Children of the World," where "We Are the World" is performed by dozens of children and well-known performers like **Drew Barrymore**, bassist **Stanley Clarke** and **Earth, Wind & Fire**'s **Phillip Bailey**. —*Cashbox*

COLLABORATIONS
▶ Steve Perry, lead and backing vocals on "We Are The World" and "If Only For The Moment, Girl" on USA for Africa's album, *We Are the World*.
▶ Neal Schon, lead guitar on "It's Only Make Believe," on Gregg Rolie's album, *Gregg Rolie*.

Steve Smith Finally Hits #1 Backing Adams's 'Heaven'

For all the mountains climbed, Steve Smith never played on a No. 1 song with Journey.

The closest he ever came was "Open Arms," which sat at No. 2 on the *Billboard* Hot 100 for six weeks in 1982 behind **The J. Geils Band**'s "Centerfold" and **Joan Jett and the Blackhearts**' "I Love Rock 'n' Roll."

Then Bryan Adams phoned out of the blue.

He was opening for Journey in 1983 and had hit it off with Smith. "There were times when we hung on one of the band buses and watched people walking through the parking lot and coming into the arenas— which made for some incredible people-watching," Smith said. "I like to warm up before I get onstage. Most nights I would play along to Bryan's entire set underneath the stage. I had a practice pad and a drum throne. I would jam along to get myself ready to play with Journey. It was a fun way to warm up."

Adams was trying to finish a song called "Heaven" when sessions for the LP that would become 1984's chart-topping multiplatinum *Reckless* began to run long. Then, drummer **Mickey Curry** had to leave for a separate commitment with **Hall & Oates**.

"I was in my hotel room in New York City, and I got a call from Bryan," Smith said. "We were on the 1983 tour and it was a day off. Bryan asked me if I'd come down to the Power Station studio to record a song with him that he was working on for a movie soundtrack. I was excited to play on one of his songs, plus I wanted to experience the Power Station and work with his producer, **Bob Clearmountain**."

The film, 1983's *A Night in Heaven*, centered on the plight of male strippers. "The subject matter of the film wasn't really compelling— and I'm not dissing male strippers," Adams told the *New York Post*. So, Adams said, "Look, let's just forget what the film's about—let's just write a good song."

Unsurprisingly, *A Night in Heaven* bombed at the box office, sinking the soundtrack as well. "So for all intents and purposes, 'Heaven' was untainted. It was still a new, unheard song," Adams's co-writer **Jim Vallance** wrote on his official website.

Adams slipped the now-forgotten song into the track listing for *Reckless* and rode its power-ballad popularity to No. 1. "Heaven" also turned out to be one of Smith's easiest sessions. A kit was already set up, so he simply arrived—and started playing.

"By the time I got there, the band knew the song, and I took some time to listen to the track, learn the form, and then we started to record," Smith says. "I had developed some ballad chops playing with Journey, and I was able to easily adapt my concept. Bryan and Bob wanted the big toms fills and wide beat that I had used on Journey songs like 'Open Arms' and 'Faithfully.'"

He made one more contribution before returning to his hotel, and the ongoing *Frontiers* tour.

"After I came up with my approach, we got the song fairly quickly, if I remember correctly," Smith added. "Once we did get the track, they wanted me to play some more fills that they could possibly use, and I'm pretty sure one of those fills ended up on the fade near the end of the song."

Reckless arrived in November 1984, but Adams did not release "Heaven" as a single until April 1985—almost two years after he invited Smith over to complete the track. It topped the charts on June 22, 1985.

"It's a fantastic song with a powerhouse vocal, and I feel good that I got to make my own contribution," Smith concluded. "As big as some of the Journey hits were, we never had a No. 1. Bryan sent me a platinum album, which I still treasure." [470, 471, 472]

Wary of Losing Artistic Control, Journey Drops Music Videos

Following MTV's early-1980s debut, bands released music videos concurrently with their singles. That's how the record industry operated—until 1986, when Journey joined **Van Halen** in an attempt to return to the days when radio drove sales.

"You had MTV indoctrinating everyone with images," Steve Perry told *Kerrang!*. "Before the Internet, there was that; before YouTube, there was that."

Journey's "Be Good to Yourself" was no outlier. There had been no promotional clip for 1985's "Only the Young," and Journey likewise did not release a video for "Suzanne," which followed "Be Good to Yourself" in the summer of 1986.

Manager **Herbie Herbert** openly wondered why bands were now putting themselves "at the mercy of a video director" to conceptualize their work. Especially, he told *Billboard* magazine back then, when the result was only a "very short-lived, limited lifespan visual accompaniment."

One could easily connect these bad feelings to the fallout over Journey's widely mocked video for "Separate Ways (Worlds Apart)." But in truth, their stilted clip for "After the Fall" may have been even worse.

Frustration was understandably mounting for rock acts who came of age in the era before visuals meant so much. Still, nudging the paradigm back would not be easy.

"We all know that you shouldn't judge a musician or a song by appearances—but after the rise of music videos, we started doing just that," noted music historian **Ted Gioia** said. "Record labels grew obsessed with how their artists looked. I wonder whether less glamorous stars of earlier eras—**Janis Joplin**, **Chick Webb**, **Mildred Bailey**—would even get a chance under the new rules."

Back then, Perry said the focus on matched visuals "destroys the ability for you to absolutely take that song and make it your own," he told *Rockline*. "When you hear this song on the radio, you'll see the video in your mind."

These were the first tremors in what would become a seismic change at MTV, as the network eventually shifted from its original 24-hour music programming toward the modern-era slate of game shows and reality-based productions. The main venue for music videos by the time Journey released *Freedom* in 2022 was the Internet, which provided only a siloed, typically individual viewing experience.

"Sometimes you can't know, until a lot of time goes by, how amazing something was," original MTV VJ **Martha Quinn** said. "MTV is a perfect example. I think that we know MTV was blowing our minds and all that, but then *Remote Control* came along and all of the reality shows. That signaled the end of the golden era, if you will, of MTV. Over time, we started to appreciate that this was such lightning in a bottle. We were so lucky to have lived it. Sometimes it takes time to grasp that."

MTV may have been the best-known outlet for music videos, but they had already begun airing on USA Network's *Night Flight,* months before MTV debuted. Lesser programs like *Radio 1990* and the short-lived Cable Music Channel followed before VH1 launched in the mid-1980s. But MTV will always be synonymous with music videos, whether for good or ill.

"You can still hashtag #IWantMyMTVBack right now on Twitter, and you'll see a million tweets coming up," Quinn said. "Something that has a major cultural impact like that, partially because of its groundbreaking effect, it can't happen twice. You can't recreate the lightning bolt moment twice. So, we had it and we went with it, and it was a really good time."

Even in its absence, MTV's impact continues to reverberate—only now via the Internet. "We live with the consequences of this culture shift even today, long after MTV started to seem irrelevant to the music business," Gioia said. "What started on MTV survives on YouTube and TikTok." [113, 303, 394, 404, 452, 500, 628]

Prairie Prince Returns, But As *Radio*'s Graphic Designer

Prairie Prince's initial association with Journey yielded some signature introductory performances, while he retained a tandem membership in **The Tubes**. Then he contributed to demos that formed a foundation for Journey's first album.

Still, his principal interests were always in art and The Tubes, who shared a manager in **Herbie Herbert** back then. Given the choice, Prince gave way to Aynsley Dunbar.

"We had just moved up to San Francisco a few years before that," Prince said. "I was going to the Art Institute. All of my friends who eventually became The Tubes moved up there from Phoenix with me. We played around a little bit, and then we met Herbie. He'd started a management company."

At this point, The Tubes were still working on a handshake deal. "We didn't really sign any papers, but they took us on. We were called **The Beans** at that point," Prince said. "They started to manage us, and try to get us some jobs here and there."

The pressures of playing in two bands soon became overwhelming. Prince left as Journey's embryonic first lineup took shape, and The Tubes decided on signing with the management team of **Dan "Mort" Moriarty** and **Gary Peterson**.

Prince's association with Journey did not end there. Over the years, he returned to co-found an inventively designed shirt company called Mouthman with Ross Valory, and did solo sessions with Neal Schon.

The most memorable of Prince's Journey reunions, however, was as the co-art director of the album cover for the band's 1986's *Raised on Radio*. He and partner **Michael Cotten** finally broke the creative logjam surrounding Steve Perry's throwback art deco radio station concept.

"We were in upstate New York mixing the album, and we had some art concepts that Steven had come up with," Neal Schon told *Rockline,* but nobody could agree on how to move forward. "I suggested, 'Let Prairie take the artwork' with Michael Cotten," Schon said. "What they came back with was really great, and we were all really happy with it."

Prince got his master's degree in painting from the Art Institute in 1973, then formed a lifelong partnership with Cotten, a former Tubes keyboardist. Their work quickly expanded to include art pieces, set designs, and huge murals.

"Painting is my other profession," Prince told *Modern Drummer.* "I pretty much split my time between drumming and painting, set design, and all kinds of artwork production."

His most famous work was the enormous "Flying Records" mural on the exterior of Hollywood's A&M Records on La Brea Avenue. Unfortunately, after **Herb Alpert** and **Jerry Moss** sold A&M to Polygram in 1989, the image was painted over.

Prince later followed Journey successor Aynsley Dunbar into **Jefferson Starship**, with a tenure that lasted from 1992-2008. [30, 500, 507, 508, 509]

Continued on Page 201

CAIN DROPS 'PERRY-ISM' INTO BAND'S COMEBACK SONG

During a period of steep emotional distress, Steve Perry came up with a personal mantra: "Be good to yourself."

His long relationship with **Sherrie Swafford** was falling apart, even as his mother's health badly deteriorated. "That's a Perry-ism, something he'd always say," Jonathan Cain recalled in the liner notes for *Time*[3]. "I circled it in my notes."

A song with this empowering theme might have been the perfect platform to relaunch Journey, if they could ever finish it. Perry was shuttling back and forth to visit his ailing mom, and Cain—who had his own marital problems—was simply stuck.

Months went by. Eventually, Neal Schon helped them get the arrangement nailed down, earning a co-writing credit, but the lyrics were still unfinished. "Steve never had time," Cain added. "He'd just say, 'Work on it.'"

Inspiration finally struck on the day Journey was due to complete the song with engineer **Bob Clearmountain**, according to writer **Joel Selvin**. Cain was in the shower when it happened and raced back to the studio to share his idea without taking time to even dry his hair. That unlocked Perry's imagination too, and he nailed the vocal in less than an hour.

The result was a solid—and solidly selling—advance single that arrived weeks before Journey's long-delayed return to store shelves in April 1986 with *Raised on Radio*. "Be Good to Yourself" peaked in late May at No. 9, becoming just their second Top 10 *Billboard* hit since 1983's "Separate Ways (Worlds Apart)." The song also netted a Top 10 finish in *Cashbox*'s charts.

In a then-curious break with the established marketing approach of this era, Journey announced that there would be no accompanying video. Cain told King Features Syndicate that "we were physically and mentally exhausted from making the record and losing two band members in the process," Cain said. "Then we had personal problems to deal with in our own lives."

Journey likewise refused most interview requests as well as corporate sponsorship of the tour—a business arrangement they had helped popularize with an Anheuser-Busch partnership in the late 1970s.

"We don't want to be part of the hype machinery," Herbert told *Billboard*. "It's my feeling, and certainly the group's, that we'd like our music to speak for itself."

Journey debuted "Be Good to Yourself" on stage a few months later during the tour-opening August 1986 show at the Mountain Aire '86 II

BE GOOD TO YOURSELF
By Jonathan Cain, Steve Perry, Neal Schon

HIGHEST CHARTING WEEK:
Billboard, #9, May 31, 1986

ARTIST	SINGLE
1. Whitney Houston	Greatest Love of All
2. Madonna	Live to Tell
3. Patti LaBelle & Michael McDonald	On My Own
4. Orchestral Manoeuvres in the Dark	If You Leave
5. Nu Shooz	I Can't Wait
6. Mike + The Mechanics	All I Need Is a Miracle
7. Level 42	Something About You
8. Mr. Mister	Is It Love
9. JOURNEY	**BE GOOD TO YOURSELF**
10. Janet Jackson	What Have You Done for Me Lately

festival inside the Calaveras County Fairgrounds near Stockton, California. The concert and an accompanying documentary that followed would offer fans their first glimpse of the reconstituted touring lineup, featuring new drummer Mike Baird and the flamboyantly dressed bassist Randy Jackson.

Schon was more interested in Jackson's musical contributions than his sartorial choices. "He is totally bad," Schon enthused in the film. "This guy is probably one of the best bass players in the world."

Providing an olive branch, the documentary aired on MTV—and its footage was subsequently sourced to make a promotional clip for "Girl Can't Help It," the third single from *Raised on Radio*. Eventually, Journey also released a clip of their Mountain Aire performance of "Be Good to Yourself." [60, 113, 135, 169, 497, 498, 499]

SPRING–SUMMER 1986

RELEASES
▶ Journey, *Raised on Radio* (album)
▶ Journey, "Be Good To Yourself" (single)
▶ Journey, "Suzanne" (single)
▶ Journey, "Girl Can't Help It" (single)

NUGGETS
▶ **Sylvester Stallone** was amped about security as Journey's management planned a private affair for the release of their new LP, *Raised on Radio*, on April 30. CBS booked Stallone's Hard Rock Cafe in San Francisco for the album's launch party, but Sly reached out to Columbia to learn the exact security arrangements and whether there would be drugs there. There was definitely security there, but no word on the drugs. You guess.
—*San Francisco Examiner*
▶ **Huey Lewis** and **Mick Fleetwood** were among those who attended **B.B. King**'s recent concerts at San Francisco's Fairmont Hotel. Journey guitarist Neal Schon showed up last night and jammed into the wee hours with King during the second half of his extended set. —*Billboard*
▶ Claiming there aren't enough musicians involved in the making of guitars, Neal Schon has gone into business with pals **Rich Bandoni** and **John "Hawkeye" Griswold** to make some of his own. Actually, Schon will do the sales and marketing only— Jackson Guitars will manufacture them. But Schon designed and supervised the construction and "they are more than just products" developed by non-musicians, they are "truly instruments."
—*Cashbox*
▶ After postponing a series of summer U.S. dates, Journey hits the road in September. The band is rehearsing with bassist Randy Jackson, who hails from the Bay area and has worked with **Aretha Franklin**, **Whitney Houston**, and **Narada Michael Walden**, among others —*Billboard*

COLLABORATIONS
▶ Neal Schon, guitar, and Randy Jackson, bass, on **Joe Cocker**'s album, *Cocker*.
▶ Randy Jackson, bass, on "Night Train (Smooth Alligator)" on **Lionel Richie**'s album, *Dancing on the Ceiling*.
▶ Randy Jackson, bass, on "I Wanna Go Back" and "Endless Nights" on **Eddie Money**'s album, *Can't Hold Back*.

ON THE ROAD
▶ Andy Taylor, Device, Honeymoon Suite, Night Ranger, and The Outfield.

Unaware of the Looming End, Band Begins Perry's Final Tour

Steve Perry and Neal Schon had both released high-profile side projects during Journey's hiatus, but neither of them mounted a large-scale tour. As *Raised on Radio* neared completion, there must have been some sense of the grueling road ahead—particularly after the way Journey had flogged 1983's *Frontiers*.

They had done longer tours as recently as the *Escape* era, but Jonathan Cain told *Billboard* the *Frontiers* dates were more "dense," with "five or six shows a week." Schon guessed that they had "played more dates in one year than in the last two years before this," because the prior concerts were more "spread out."

Shows in support of *Raised on Radio* did not look all that much different, with 20 scheduled for October alone. They had to get road-ready, but first, they had to mend a fractured lineup.

Schon, Perry, and Jonathan Cain "wanted to do these songs but the band couldn't play them," Schon later told the *South Florida Sun-Sentinel*. "So we had to look and figure out where the weak link was. It turned out to be the rhythm section."

Principal *Raised on Radio* bassist Randy Jackson remained as Journey prepared to return to the stage on August 23, 1986 at California's Mountain Aire Music Festival II. Who would take over for Steve Smith remained an open question.

Continued on Page 207

J O U R N E Y

RAISED ON RADIO

**"RAISED ON RADIO." THE NEW ALBUM FROM JOURNEY.
FEATURING THE SINGLE, "BE GOOD TO YOURSELF."
ON COLUMBIA RECORDS, CHROME CASSETTES AND COMPACT DISCS.**

Produced by Steve Perry
Herbie Herbert Management, Inc.
Columbia. ● are trademarks of CBS Inc. © 1986 CBS Inc.

G rowing up, Steve Perry's parents owned KNGS, a commercial AM radio station in Hanford, California, which now operates under KIGS. Perry's deep affection for music and radio was rooted in those childhood memories. Perry's mother passed away before Journey finished recording their ninth studio album, *Raised on Radio*, and he successfully lobbied the band to have the album name and cover honor that memory.

The band considered several artists in early 1986 in search of the right concept, including veteran Journey illustrator **Stanley Mouse**, famed 1960s psychedelic rock artist **Victor Moscoso**, and former Journey drummer **Prairie Prince**, who was also a skilled artist. Prince said he was approached by someone in the band, "probably Ross or Neal and they asked if we could take this on, and we just sort of did."

When Prince and his partner, Tubes synth master **Michael Cotten**, started the project, the red "Raised on Radio" lightning-bolted, chrome-styled

logo was already completed by another artist. Perry, he said, wanted an illustration with an art deco style that hearkened back to the days of KNGS.

"The title was already done," Prince told *Time Passages*, "and then we worked the rest of the artwork around it." He and Cotten did the mountain background and the towers using pen and ink. Then they added the misty clouds with airbrush. The lightning bolts that connected the two towers in a Tesla coil fashion came next, and then the building's JRNY call sign.

"That was the first time I ever talked to Perry," Prince said, describing his meeting at a restaurant near Hanford. "He talked about how he grew up in the Central Valley and told us about the little radio station. He wanted the fog, and he wanted [the station] to have a lonesome feeling."

Prince said he and Cotten were proud of the final product. The Columbia team took the art and turned it into the *Billboard* ad [above] and the in-store displays, some of which he kept as mementos.

Style Changes, But Journey Still Rides to Top 10

Steve Perry lost more than his beloved mother when **Mary Quaresma** died in December 1985.

She had been his biggest supporter, buying him a special eighth-note necklace that he wore for good luck. Her marriage to **Raymond Pereira** led Perry to a lasting passion for radio: Perry's dad was co-owner of the former KNGS, which broadcast out of a distinctive art deco building located between Hanford and Visalia, California.

"She was dying during the writing and recording of that record, and in the middle of doing vocals, she died," Perry told *GQ*. "So I came home, took care of that, went back, finished the vocals, and … before I know it, we're on tour."

In the meantime, two bandmates, an agreed-upon album title, wives, and even the tapes themselves would all be lost.

"They went over to Sausalito to cut that record at the Record Plant, and Perry's mom is dying—and he's a complete mama's boy," San Francisco music writer **Joel Selvin** said. "He had a helicopter parked in the parking lot, and he was helicoptering to his mother's bedside from the sessions."

Just getting into the studio had required something that sounded an awful lot like couple's therapy. "We had to come to a crossroads where we just had to say, 'Okay, we need to look at our problems,'" Jonathan Cain told the *Chicago Tribune*. "Just like you need to do in a marriage, sit down and go through these things one by one."

Days turned into months as Cain tried to coax Perry back to his muse. As she lingered, Mary encouraged Perry to return to Journey—and he finally got back on track creatively. "She just didn't want to leave me here," Perry told Selvin back then. "It was her fleeting last strength of maternal love."

As they began to reconnect on stripped-down demos using a click track, Cain admitted that he repositioned his writing to accommodate the soul-leaning sounds of Perry's debut solo album. It was the first, but far from the last, concession required to coax Perry back for *Raised on Radio*.

Next, Perry engineered the ousting of Ross Valory and Steve Smith. "He quit the band, and to

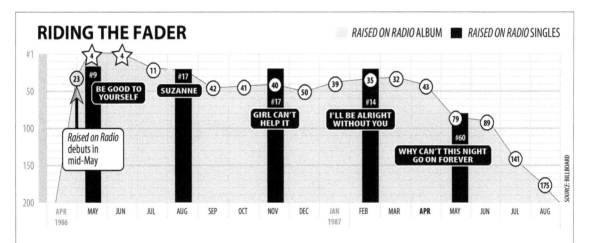

RIDING THE FADER

RAISED ON RADIO ALBUM ■ *RAISED ON RADIO* SINGLES

Raised on Radio debuts in mid-May

BE GOOD TO YOURSELF

SUZANNE

GIRL CAN'T HELP IT

I'LL BE ALRIGHT WITHOUT YOU

WHY CAN'T THIS NIGHT GO ON FOREVER

SOURCE: BILLBOARD

It was almost three years since Journey released an LP, but fans remembered them just fine when *Raised on Radio* was released in April 1986. "Be Good To Yourself" was the leadoff single, and it propelled the album into the Top 5 of the *Billboard* Hot 100. It parked for two months. *Radio* was an instant album hit on the *Billboard* 200, debuting at No. 23 (*Escape* debuted at No. 13, and *Frontiers* at No. 30). But Journey's chart longevity for albums was fading. *Escape* set a near-impossible bar to match. *Frontiers* could not maintain that same torrid record sales pace, and *Radio* fared even worse. Although a string of four Top 20 single hits kept the album in the Top 40 for a year, by the following summer it began its decline, and by August, it was out. The notion that 14 straight months in the Top 50 would be viewed negatively seems ridiculous, but Journey's previous achievements as sales juggernauts made it a reality.

TOP CHARTING WEEK: *BILLBOARD*—June 7, 1986

1. Whitney Houston, *Whitney Houston*
2. Van Halen, *5150*
3. Bob Seger, *Like a Rock*
4. **JOURNEY, *RAISED ON RADIO***
5. Patti LaBelle, *Winner in You*
6. Janet Jackson, *Control*
7. Prince, *Parade: Music from Under the Cherry Moon*
8. Pet Shop Boys, *Please*
9. Pretty in Pink, *Original Motion Picture Soundtrack*
10. The Outfield, *Play Deep*

get him to do another record, we agreed to his producing the record and that he could bring in anyone he wanted to play on it," Smith told *Modern Drummer*. "The band ceased being a band."

They informed **Herbie Herbert** during a hastily called meeting. He said he was livid. "Replace Smith and Valory? Over my dead body!" Herbert told **Matthew Carty**. "What the fuck—this is a group, this is a band! This isn't Steve Perry and his side band."

Herbert insisted that "these guys are going to be paid as if though they were here," adding that the decision to split with Valory and Smith "turned out to be a brutal mistake." Without them, Herbert said "it wasn't Journey. It was lame."

Now down to a nucleus of Perry, Cain, and Neal Schon, Journey essentially started over. "We brought in Randy Jackson on bass after trying for a couple months to cut the tracks," Perry told *Rolling Stone*. "We cut a lot with Randy Jackson and **Larrie Londin** and Jon and myself and Neal. We basically recut the record in ten days."

Freedom was slated to be the title of Journey's next album, according to Herbert's long-held naming convention. "Steve Perry, in order to go forward, insists now that he wants more authority and control," Herbert told Carty. "It was the *Freedom* record. [Perry decided] 'I don't want that title. I want to change it to *Raised on Radio*.'"

Refashioned cover art was created by early Journey member **Prairie Prince**. Perry's family radio station was depicted, with nary a scarab in sight. Perry attempted to tie it all together with a nostalgic title track that mentioned a string of early-rock favorites like **Chuck Berry** and **Buddy Holly**.

"Protracted negotiations take place," Selvin said. "[Perry] demands all kinds of things—like the firing of the drummer and the bass player—which nobody really had any problem with but him. He wanted to be named producer of the album. He wanted to be in control of naming the album. He wanted Journey to be his backup band—and he got his way, because he had the keys to the kingdom."

Schon also altered his sound to better match what Cain and Perry had begun, moving away from his typical army-of-guitars approach in order to focus on more tasteful single lines. He even tried something entirely different on

"I'll Be Alright Without You," though Schon has since discarded the song's unusual featured instrument.

"That guitar that I played on 'I'll Be Alright,' you would not believe what it is," Schon said. "It was one of those really ugly Roland 707 guitars that kind of looked like a weird synthesizer guitar." He might have gone with a Fender Stratocaster, then as now a Schon guitar of choice, but he was aiming for a new sound.

The Roland 707 featured a then-hip graphite body and neck. "It didn't vibrate—and that gave it a very even tone," Schon said. "So, I felt like it translated no matter where I was playing, up and down the neck on that one song."

The next stumbling block arrived in the form of the U.S. Organized Crime Drug Enforcement Task Forces, as the authorities tried to determine if Journey's studio had been purchased with illegal proceeds. "They confiscated our tapes and equipment for a couple hours, and we had to go in and straighten everything out with the feds," Cain told the *Chicago Tribune*. "But we got our tapes out, and it was cool."

Londin ultimately replaced Smith on all but three tracks, while Jackson and **Bob Glaub** took over Valory's role. They helped create some isolated moments when *Raised on Radio* sounded like typical 1980s-era Journey fare, including "Be Good to Yourself," "Girl Can't Help It," and "Why Can't This Night Go On Forever." Still, much of the rest of the LP did not.

Herbert wondered aloud if that was the goal all along after Perry called to complain when the No. 9 smash "Be Good to Yourself" became the project's lead single. Herbert said the song was chosen because it sounded like Journey. "That was the problem. It sounds too much like Journey," Herbert told *Melodic Rock*. "Well, too many of the other songs sound too much like a glorified Steve Perry solo record."

In some ways, *Raised on Radio* became an album about moving on—or at least trying. Certainly, that's true with "I'll Be Alright Without You." Cain later confirmed in the *Time*[3] interviews with Selvin that the song directly connected with everyone's recent trauma. "It's really the other half of 'Once You Love Somebody,'" the lovestruck ballad featured earlier in *Raised on Radio*.

There were more pronounced R&B influences, but also a softness associated with songwriting that did not initially include Schon's muscular touches: "If your cup of tea is **Mantovani** meets **Foreigner**—go for it," sniffed a reviewer for *Creem*.

Despite that, *Raised on Radio* reached No. 4 after its May 27, 1986 release, and ultimately logged some two million in sales. Journey added four more Top 20 singles to its resume, and "Why Can't This Night Go On Forever" became a mid-sized hit on adult-contemporary radio too.

In keeping with the theme, Journey decided against creating any videos for MTV. The album, after all, was not titled *Raised on Video*. "Be Good to Yourself" and "Suzanne" arrived without clips, and then live performances of "Girl Can't Help It" and "I'll Be Alright Without You" were released. "Why Can't This Night Go On Forever" was paired with a montage of tour images.

Randy Jackson was in rare fashion form during the concert recordings, particularly on "I'll Be Alright Without You" from Journey's November 18, 1986 appearance at the Omni in Atlanta. He sports a pink leather jacket with fringes while playing a matching pink polka-dotted bass. Meanwhile, Schon had already discarded the Roland 707, opting for a 1986 Schon Guitar by Jackson Guitars.

Schon admits he would not repeat his "I'll Be Alright Without You" studio experiment, even though the choice worked in the moment. "If I were to play it again," he said, "I would definitely play it on a Strat—or some of my new Paul Reeds, the NS-15s, or the bigger semi-hollow bodies. Those sound good, with really warm, like Strat-y tones—but with a little bit bigger body."

"I'll Be Alright Without You" crept three spots higher than the No. 17 finishes for "Suzanne" and "Girl Can't Help It," becoming Journey's penultimate Top 20 hit before 1996's No. 12 comeback single, "When You Love a Woman."

By then, Valory and Smith had been welcomed back. In the meantime, Selvin said Journey's original bassist was never far away during the *Raised on Radio* era: "Ross Valory went to every session, every day, and sat out in the game room playing pinball," Selvin said, "even though he never put a note on that record." [60, 80, 100, 215, 283, 291, 376, 501, 502, 903]

Detroit Free Press
April 27, 1986

This year's version of Journey is a far cry from the improvisational rock band it became when Steve Perry joined in 1978. Trimmed to a trio, the remaining members (Perry, guitarist Neal Schon, and keyboardist Jonathan Cain) have resolved themselves into a pop band that can reach back and pull out some rock licks (as on the first single, "Be Good To Yourself," and the title track), an approach similar to that taken by **Stevie Nicks**, **Phil Collins** and **Starship**. Thus, *Raised on Radio* is slick, accessible and full of potential hits. There are mid-tempo grooves and dance rhythms, attempts at white-bread funk and a few moody, slow songs like "Happy To Give" and "The Eyes of a Woman." There are shortcomings—primarily in the lyrics—but ultimately, the new focus of creative intent makes *Raised on Radio* the best record Journey has produced in years.

— *Gary Graff*

Los Angeles Times
April 27, 1986

The first Journey album since 1983's multiplatinum *Frontiers* is safe as milk—nothing on it cuts even skin-deep. The writing, playing, and production are predictably slick and contemporary, but also predictably empty. From the opening "Girl Can't Help It" (not the **Little Richard** classic) through the closing "Why Can't This Night Go On Forever," there is nary a lick nor lyric that could possibly be construed as a challenge to either listener or performer. Everything sounds calculated solely for airplay and sales. Artistic growth? Forget it! The only journey these guys seem interested in is to the bank. Steve Perry, Neal Schon, and Jonathan Cain may have been raised on these radio chestnuts, but judging by their music, they never really listened to what they said.

— *Steve Hochman*

Billboard
May 10, 1986

Journey, the heroes of the heartland's arena circuit, are now essentially a trio with the departure of bassist Ross Valory and drummer Steve Smith, leaving guitarist Neal Schon as the group's lone original member. But rotating personnel hasn't changed the group's signature sound one bit, now closely associated with the vocals of Steve Perry. Always tailor-made for album radio, the band plays its strong suit for all it's worth here, and virtually all tracks are ideal for the rock and pop formats. Best bets: "Girl Can't Help It," "Suzanne," "I'll Be Alright With You," and the first single, "Be Good To Yourself."

SESSION VETERAN'S PRESENCE GREW BEYOND THE STUDIO

Randy Jackson was born on June 23, 1956 in Baton Rouge, Louisiana. He knew he wanted to play bass before he entered high school.

Credit for Jackson's early interest in music goes to his brother, who played drums in a local garage band. Jackson noticed all the attention surrounding their performances.

"In the neighborhood where I grew up," Jackson told *Bass Player*, "we had what were known as block parties, with a local band in the neighborhood practicing on the front porch of one of the band members' homes. People would gather around."

Long before he became a TV talent show star, he was figuring out the contours of bass on a Kingston and then a Sears model. Jackson's taste ranged from rock to jazz to R&B. He even played an old-fashioned upright in high school.

"I just fell in love with the bass," Jackson added. His first teacher was the late **Sammy Thornton**, "a brilliant guy from Baton Rouge, and he was very old-school—very **James Jamerson** and **Chuck Rainey**," Jackson added. "I got good beginnings, at a great time, from a master."

His entrance into music would be half a world away from rock. "Randy was a jazz-fusion bass player who had come up with **Billy Cobham**," said Steve Smith, who worked with Jackson on some early-1980s **Tom Coster Band** projects before the bassist connected with Journey. "Now people know him as a judge on *American Idol*."

Jackson also played on a trio of pre-Journey records with **Jean-Luc Ponty** and sat in with R&B legend **Frankie Beverly**'s **Maze**. His dreams were coming true.

"I really wanted to be kind of a session guy, a musician and everything, play on lots of records and hang out," Jackson told *Creem*. "Later on, that transformed into 'I want to be a star.'"

He would be, though far away from a concert's lighted stage. Jackson became best known as *American Idol*'s longest-serving judge. He later served as executive producer on *America's Best Dance Crew* and bandleader for a revival of *Name That Tune*.

Despite all of that, Jackson still had a complete command of his instrument. "Randy is a monster bass player with unbelievable feel," said Neal Schon collaborator **Igor Len**, who toured with Jackson in the 2010s.

Jackson only released one album, *Randy Jackson's Music Club, Vol. 1* from 2008. Instead, his most notable musical contributions were often behind the scenes—including appearances on albums by **Bruce Springsteen**, **Aretha Franklin**, **Toto**'s **Steve Lukather**, and **Richard Marx**, among many others. Jackson followed his turn on "After the Fall," a Top 25 hit from Journey's *Frontiers*, with appearances on eight songs from *Raised on Radio*—seven on bass and one as a backing vocalist ("Positive Touch.")

He then assumed bass duties on the Journey tour that followed, cementing his relationship with Schon. Jackson also collaborated with Steve Perry on *Against the Wall*, a shelved late-1980s solo project. He then worked with Schon on 1989's *Late Nite* LP, and reunited with him for dates in support of Schon's *Vortex* in 2015.

"Randy was a surprising choice for me, because of his public profile and how busy he is," said Len, a key creative force on *Vortex*. "Again, his bond with Neal was so strong that he agreed as far as I know without any reservations."

Once Jackson secured the bass position for the *Vortex* tour, Len decided to help the newcomer with preparations. It was a telling moment.

"I didn't know him personally, so I decided to send him charts for each song just to speed up the learning time after the first day of rehearsals," Len said. "I emailed him a bunch of PDF charts, and got no reply." At the next rehearsal, Len asked Jackson if he had received them. "Randy replied, 'I don't need no charts'—and then he played perfectly," Len added with a laugh.

Decades after *Raised on Radio*, Jackson made a tantalizing revelation during a 2011 fan Q&A for *American Idol*: He said he still ran into Steve Perry from time to time—and they had discussed a possible Journey reunion. During his most recent visit, Jackson said he told Perry: "If you do it, I'll do it."

Turns out, Jackson did not have to wait long for that impossible dream to come true. He ended up working with Journey again on 2022's *Freedom*, appearing on 14 of its 15 tracks. Jackson passed on participating in the subsequent tour, citing back problems. But his passion for the band's music—and their story of resilience—was undiminished.

"Journey has been through so many iterations but is still ticking and doing well, continuing to evolve and be creative," Jackson told the *San Francisco Chronicle*. "This is one of those bands that reinvents itself all the time." [3, 40, 130, 135, 155, 216, 473, 496]

"Finding a drummer for the tour got really fucked up," San Francisco music writer **Joel Selvin** said, "because there was an album released and tour dates—and no drummer."

The drawn-out process went to excruciating lengths, dragging on for months. Journey auditioned and auditioned and auditioned. "Every famous, expensive drummer in the world was flown into Berkeley to try out," Selvin said. "I remember **Omar Hakim** was there, he was **Sting**'s drummer. They'd flown him in from London. Nobody was good enough for Perry—nobody."

Josh Ramos was working with the Schon guitar company, and often found himself on hand as the auditions dragged on. He said he understood why Perry was having so much trouble finding a suitable replacement.

"There's something about Steve Smith that really reflects the artist that he is," Ramos said, "because he can play jazz with **Vital Information** and he can still do Journey's huge stadium ballads, with all that room and space. He just knows where to put those big fills."

Multifaceted drummer Mike Baird estimated that Journey may have heard from as many as 70 drummers. "It had become an unbelievable scene," he told *Modern Drummer*. "**Chad Wackerman** has it. No, Omar Hakim has it. No, Mike Baird has it."

Ramos, who later worked with Steve Smith, Gregg Rolie, and Ross Valory in **The Storm**, knew of just the right person: **Atma Anur**, whose career included work with **Joe Satriani**, **Richie Kotzen**, and **Gregg Allman**, among others.

Anur landed a last-second audition, and Ramos came away thinking Perry was impressed. "I'm sitting there on the couch right in front of the studio watching them, and they start playing," Ramos said. "Atma was just fucking right in the pocket, man. Right after that, Steve Perry comes up to me. He goes, 'Josh, I'll have your baby any day. Thank you so much for finding him finally!' I said, 'You're welcome, Steve.'"

But Anur never heard back. "To this day," Ramos added, "I still don't know what happened."

Journey ended up with a familiar candidate. "Finally, they took this guy Mike Baird at the last moment," Selvin said. "That was a total hijacking of the band by Perry."

Baird said Journey wavered until the end. Schon wanted "an unbelievable fusionist," while Perry was looking for an "unbelievable R&B drummer," Baird told *Modern Drummer*. Meanwhile, Cain wanted a "pop drum-machine timekeeper. Sorry, it doesn't exist."

Continued on Page 209

R&B, TECH INFLUENCES DRIVE ANOTHER TOP 20 SINGLE

As a long-term relationship with **Sherrie Swafford** slowly disintegrated, Steve Perry did what Steve Perry does: Get lost in the reverie of imagination and youth.

"Suzanne," the second consecutive Top 20 hit from *Raised on Radio*, seemed to pay tribute to a long-ago crush, who had since become a movie star, and Perry's main character is tormented every time he sees her onscreen.

Echoes of **Harry Chapin**'s "Taxi" were apparent in the narrative, a concept that producer **Paul Flattery** also used in a **Philip Bailey** video before securing the job shooting Perry's first solo clips. But "Suzanne" could not be any different sonically from Chapin's 1972 Top 25 hit. And, of course, there would be no accompanying video.

Instead, Perry and Cain continued delving into R&B and electronics, with Schon sidelined from the songwriting process. The liner notes went so far as to list Cain as a "programmer" on "Suzanne," in a nod to the initial work done on his Oberheim DMX drum machine before he and Perry brought in **Larrie Londin** to mimic the part.

"The technology in music was changing, and with the help of my drum machine and sequencer, I wrote some demos that had a good groove," Cain said in his autobiography. Songs like "Suzanne," he added, would emerge with "a Motown feel to them—sweet soul with a backbeat." He favorably compared them to **Hall & Oates**.

Perry said he was proud of these changes, because "I thought that we needed to grow." He told *Melodic Rock* that he could envision Journey continuing along this musical throughline, "but I had a feeling that people kinda wanted us to stay in a certain genre and not move that far."

His feeling proved correct: "Suzanne" got no higher than No. 17, and questions began to swirl about the logic of avoiding MTV. Others wondered if Perry and Cain were simply moving too far away from Journey's rock roots.

Raised on Radio would become a double-platinum hit, but that nevertheless represented their weakest sales since before Perry arrived.

He admitted to *Billboard* that he thought "the album may have gotten hurt a bit because we didn't do the standard thing and release videos."

Still, Perry hailed the album's "exploration of grooves and changes and vocal styles and harmonies and choruses that were different from anything that came before," he told *Melodic Rock*. For him, those differences made it worth the gamble.

SUZANNE
By Steve Perry, Jonathan Cain

HIGHEST CHARTING WEEK:
Billboard, #17, August 16, 1986

ARTIST	SINGLE
1. Madonna	Papa Don't Preach
2. Peter Cetera	Glory of Love
3. Belinda Carlisle	Mad About You
4. Steve Winwood	Higher Love
5. Jermaine Stewart	We Don't Have to Take Our Clothes Off
6. Bananarama	Venus
7. Lionel Richie	Dancing on the Ceiling
8. Timex Social Club	Rumors
9. Berlin	Take My Breath Away
17. JOURNEY	**SUZANNE**

Weeks on Chart: 13
Cashbox, #20, August 2, 1986

The question of the main character's identity remained. Fans pressed Schon on the subject in a 1995 chat on CompuServe, suggesting that she might actually have been actress **Suzanne Somers**. He demurred: "I didn't write the song. It wasn't about anybody in high school that I knew!"

So the mystery would remain, but with some additional context. In a separate online Q&A session, Perry suggested that perhaps "Suzanne" was an entirely fictional character. "It was a fantasy encounter with a film star who also had a vocal artist career," Perry offered. "Real or not, she's real in the track." [490, 503, 504, 505, 506]

Randy Jackson (center) said outrageous outfits were required in the mid-1980s and Journey did not disappoint, with Neal Schon (left) and Jonathan Cain helping to lead the charge.

Baird finally convinced them only after becoming enraged. He said he told himself, "I'm going to go back in there, and I'm going to shove this beat so far up these assholes' butts that they're going to choke to death."

Their next lineup was set. Manager **Herbie Herbert** came away unimpressed and demanded Valory and Smith be paid even while absent. Herbert told **Matthew Carty** that "it wasn't Journey. It was lame."

In the accompanying tour documentary, Perry admitted that "basically, it is a brand-new band with brand-new positives and brand-new negatives. It's just like anything else." Still, Perry headed to Mountain Aire in a hopeful place: "Live is where the band lives," he said in the film which chronicled their first show. "It really does live live."

Journey got underway again, but Cain said a sense of unfinished business followed them. He described Jackson and Baird as "strangers to our Journey family" in his memoir. "The decision to move on without Ross Valory and Steve Smith would be one of those mistakes I regretted the most when it came to the band I joined in 1980." [56, 60, 100, 135, 137, 155, 405, 475, 489, 502]

FALL 1986

NUGGETS
▶ Call it strange karma, but while Journey was closing the first of its show at New Jersey's Meadowlands Arena with a rocking version of "Don't Stop Believin'," the New York Mets began rallying against the Boston Red Sox in the memorable sixth game of the World Series. Though the San Francisco rockers had played a great set, the post-concert backstage scene was more focused on the ramblings of NBC-TV's **Vin Scully** than the rocking onstage. —*Billboard*

Continued on Page 211

'GIRL' SCORES ANOTHER TOP 20 HIT, RETURN TO VIDEOS

With concerts underway, **Herbie Herbert**'s high-energy promotional machine had come alive again. And, suddenly, there was a change of heart about music videos.

Journey was unwilling to submit to a scripted production, but after three consecutive singles with no video, the band agreed to release a live performance. They paired "Girl Can't Help It" with footage pulled from the *Raised on Radio* documentary shot during Journey's tour-opening appearance at the Mountain Aire Music Festival II.

TV viewers finally got to see what the reconstituted Journey looked like. "We hadn't been out in a long time," Jonathan Cain told the *Chicago Tribune*, "and we thought it would be good to get it all down on film."

They had practiced tirelessly to get to that point. "I had about two weeks to learn 25 tunes," new touring drummer Mike Baird told *Creem*. The band rehearsed in a warehouse outfitted with a concert-sized PA system and stacks of Marshall amps—but no air conditioning. "You couldn't sit in the room and listen, it was so loud," Baird added.

They ran through the setlist, in order, at least twice a day. "Rehearsing for the tour, our energy and confidence grew," Cain told the *Tribune*, "and then we were ready to face a camera and say, 'Hey, we're back.'"

Journey's new drummer ended up breaking so many sticks, however, that ProMark developed a prototype model exclusively for Baird, who estimated it may have saved him half a million dollars out on the road. The band's studio recording of "Girl Can't Help It" did not call for such a heavy-handed approach. In fact, it was born of a deft sense of compromise.

Steve Perry had wrested control of Journey as their reunion project unfolded, taking over producing duties, switching out bandmates, and pushing their sound toward his own influences.

Cain and Perry attempted to find middle ground again by focusing on music they both loved, as "Girl Can't Help It" connected directly back to **Dionne Warwick** and **The Spinners**' "Then Came You." But unlike the Motown-in-flected "Suzanne," which only had songwriting credits for Perry and Cain, Neal Schon's influence permeates the third single from *Raised on Radio*.

"Girl Can't Help It" became the LP's second consecutive No. 17 hit while circling back to their classic approach: rock music with an undercurrent of R&B. It was also a powerful reminder of Perry's versatility. "He's just a great singer," newly installed bassist Randy Jackson said in the *Raised on Radio* tour documentary.

GIRL CAN'T HELP IT
By Jonathan Cain, Steve Perry, Neal Schon

HIGHEST CHARTING WEEK:
Billboard, #17, November 17, 1986

ARTIST	SINGLE
1. Cyndi Lauper	True Colors
2. Tina Turner	Typical Male
3. Boston	Amanda
4. Robert Palmer	I Didn't Mean to Turn You On
5. Janet Jackson	When I Think of You
6. The Human League	Human
7. Don Johnson	Heartbeat
8. Madonna	True Blue
9. Lisa Lisa & Cult Jam with Full Force	All Cried Out
17. JOURNEY	**GIRL CAN'T HELP IT**

"There's nothing that he can't sing."

Still, Jackson's presence on stage, and in the video for "Girl Can't Help It," created a new vibe. Jackson had a flair for the dramatic—both in his style of play and dress. "I love to be entertained when I go to the show—not only musically but theatrically, the whole thing," Jackson told Creem. "Entertain me. I came to be entertained."

Jackson's rhythm section partner certainly did his part in the clip, playing drums on "Girl Can't Help It" with relentless, muscular focus. That was good enough for Schon. "Michael Baird, he's a great guy—he's definitely got the big lead foot," Schon said in the tour documentary. "Him and Randy together, it's magic." [135, 491, 510, 511]

NUGGETS

▶ Radio International, in New York, plans to have its Thanksgiving special with Journey ready to air on the holiday. *Raised On Radio* is a two-hour program hosted by band members Jonathan Cain, Steve Perry, and Neal Schon. In the program they celebrate Thanksgiving with America as they would at home. The music they grew up with will be featured as the group reminisces about being home for the holidays. —*Billboard*

ON THE ROAD

▶ Glass Tiger, Honeymoon Suite, and The Outfield.

WINTER 1986–87

Perry Closes Out His Journey Concert Career in Anchorage

On the surface, Journey's tour for *Raised on Radio* was an eye-popping success. They were typically selling out arenas, coliseums, and civic centers with a mix of favorites old and new, along with key Steve Perry cuts like "Oh Sherrie" and "Strung Out."

Randy Jackson's exciting sense of style seemed to have rubbed off on the others, as Jonathan Cain brought out his own effervescent, neon-splashed clothes. "I was wearing crazy outfits," Jackson later admitted to *Entertainment Tonight*. "You know, you had to at the time."

Meanwhile, Neal Schon was completely in his element again, finally stretching out onstage around "Wheel in the Sky." "I found out once I didn't have it for three and a half years, it was a big part of my life," Schon said in the *Raised on Radio* documentary.

But something was clearly wrong with Perry as the calendar flipped from 1986 to 1987. "I remember by the end of that tour," Perry told *GQ* with a pause, "feeling musically toasty, feeling emotionally toasty, feeling vocally toasty."

Looking back, Perry said he had not given himself the appropriate time to grieve his mother. "She had a very intense relationship with him," longtime Journey road manager **Pat Morrow** confirmed. "When she died, we're sitting in folding chairs at the gravesite, and he jumps up and runs over to the coffin as it's about to be lowered down. And he hugs the coffin, going: 'I love you, mama. I love you, mama. I love you, mama.' She was everything to him."

The tour's end came sooner than anyone could have imagined. Perry called everything to a sudden halt after the February 1, 1987 show at Sullivan Sports Arena in Anchorage, Alaska. "I'm hearing that we're gonna be off for maybe a couple months, three months, six months, whatever," Schon told *GQ*, "but it turned out to be close to eight to ten years."

They had played dozens of concerts in support of *Raised on Radio*, and manager **Herbie Herbert** had hoped to line up still more. Now, a weighty sense of finality hung over everything. Cain said he stayed as long as he could in the Anchorage Sheraton lounge, signing anything handed to him by fans.

"I knew something was over," Cain wrote in his autobiography, "that this particular season was coming to an end." This would ultimately be "our last official concert ever with the front man who had sung his heart out since 1977."

The strain was beginning to show in Perry's performances. At that point, he had been on the road with Journey for most of a decade, initially with few creature comforts. Perry did everything he could to save his voice. He would avoid talking to anyone from the time the concerts ended until the next day at sound check, usually held around 4 p.m.

"Back then, I had a real bad rap in the industry for being inaccessible to the press and promotional people but it was a choice I made," Perry said in a *Fan Asylum* Q&A. "Being inaccessible was the price I paid to have a voice to use when I really needed it."

Early on, Journey lived on the bus, with Herbert renting a day room so the band could shower. There often would not be enough towels to go around, Perry recalled, so they had to share. Journey did not start getting their own hotel rooms—with dry towels—until after *Escape* shot to No. 1.

Plenty had happened since they began work on *Raised on Radio*, but this accumulated history was also weighing on Perry. "Frankly," Schon told *The New York Times*, "I don't know how he lasted as long as he did without feeling burned out. He was so good, doing things that nobody else could do."

By October 1986, Perry had asked Herbert to stop booking dates. In the interview with *GQ*, he remembered saying: "I just don't want to stay out here and keep doing this. Can't we stop?" Anchorage was the last of their previously scheduled shows.

"In less than a year," Cain lamented in his memoir, "my band would be over, my marriage would disintegrate—and, worst of all, my father would pass away."

Columbia Records tried to keep interest piqued in *Raised on Radio* by releasing the "Faithfully" knockoff "Why Can't This Night Go On Forever" in April 1987, but Perry and Cain's ballad could get no higher than No. 60.

Perry would never tour with Journey again.

"It was like this orbit that you were in and you got to come through the Earth's atmosphere and you got to burn up on the way," Perry told NPR. "And there was no other way except to burn up a little bit on the way in."

The odd part for Schon, he later told *GQ*, was that Journey "actually never even quit. ... It was just sort of left at a hiatus. And it was all based around Steve giving us a call and saying 'Okay, I'm fine now, I'm ready to go'. And it just didn't happen." [27, 80, 134, 135, 456, 512, 513, 514, 927]

SPRING–SUMMER 1987

RELEASES
▶ Journey, "Why Can't This Night Go On Forever" (single)
▶ Vital Information (with Steve Smith), *Global Beat* (album)
▶ Gregg Rolie, *Gringo* (album)

NUGGETS
▶ CBS TV, Columbia Records and rock band Journey collaborated to produce a new Journey music special, *Raised on*

NUGGETS (cont.)
Radio: A Rockumentary. **Michael Collins** directs the one-hour special that includes interviews with Steve Perry, Neal Schon and Jonathan Cain. It's the debut network television production for CBS Records, and it was a first for the band too. There are whispers that MTV covets the special, though no deals have been made, and home video is still under consideration. —*Cashbox*

As Perry Steps Aside, Side Gigs Fill Void for Other Journey-men

When Steve Perry went home, everyone else in the Journey camp scattered to fill the creative void with outside projects.

"I just had to jump out and get a life," Perry told the *Orlando Sentinel*. "I knew who Steve Perry was, the guy who toured and sang the songs, but I didn't know who I was anymore."

Acts like **Michael Bolton, Europe**, and **Jimmy Barnes** were the beneficiaries.

A hitmaker elsewhere, Barnes had never gotten higher than No. 109 on the *Billboard* album chart—with 1985's *For the Working Class Man*. Jonathan Cain co-produced, wrote a song, and played on that project, then returned for Barnes's 1987 follow-up, *Freight Train Heart*, with a bunch of friends.

"Jimmy Barnes is huge in Australia, the No. 1 male singer there still," Cain's former **Babys** bandmate **Tony Brock** said of the former **Cold Chisel** front man. "Jonathan got me into sessions in San Francisco, where Neal Schon, Randy Jackson and myself played on the album. We even all wrote a song together, 'Too Much Ain't Enough Love.'"

Trial by Fire producer **Kevin Shirley** heard something he loved—though he was not familiar with Journey back then. "I knew Neal Schon and Jonathan Cain worked with Jimmy Barnes, strangely enough, on the *Freight Train Heart* album," Shirley told *Music Radar*. "I had immense respect for them because I loved the work that they did on that."

Escape and *Frontiers* co-producer **Mike Stone** engineered *Freight Train Heart* too. But the LP only crept up a few more spots than *For the*

A group shot at the 1988 Bammies award ceremony in San Francisco spotlighted some of the collaborative relationships Neal Schon and Jonathan Cain cultivated. Both worked with **Sammy Hagar** and **Michael Bolton** to produce singles that went to *Billboard*'s Top 20. (Top row: **Robert Berry**, **Carl Palmer**, **Keith Emerson**, and Neal Schon; Bottom row: Jonathan Cain, **Eddie Money**, Hagar, **John Fogerty**, and Bolton).

Working Class Man in America, stalling at No. 104. By then, Cain had moved on.

Elsewhere, **Herbie Herbert** had already begun managing other bands, including **Europe**. He brought **Kevin Elson** along to produce 1986's *The Final Countdown*, which produced Europe's Top 10 hit title track. Herbert went on to work with **Mr. Big** and **Roxette**, both of whom also had sizeable hits.

With **Vital Information**, Steve Smith put out *Global Beat* in 1986 and *Fiafiaga* in 1988, while also sitting in with **Steps Ahead**, **Frank Gambale**, **Tony MacAlpine**, and **Dweezil Zappa**, among others. Ross Valory would later play bass on **Todd Rundgren**'s *2nd Wind*.

Brock's association with Barnes continued. "I got a chance to co-produce with Jimmy Barnes after that," he said. "Every album was No. 1 in Australia for months and months, and that was due to Jonathan bringing me in to play drums on *Freight Train Heart*. That was wonderful."

Cain, Schon, Jackson, and Mike Baird also collaborated with Michael Bolton on 1987's *The Hunger*, at one point sparking rumors that Bolton might replace Perry in a rebuilt Jour-

ney lineup. "We thought about it for a second," Schon later confirmed with *Classic Rock*. "Michael definitely had pipes—he was pretty bionic when I worked with him."

But Schon and Bolton did not always get along during the sessions, especially when he asked Schon to redo the solo on an update of **Otis Redding**'s "(Sittin' On) the Dock of the Bay" "about 200 times." Dismissing the idea of Bolton joining Journey, Schon concluded: "I didn't feel that we would get too far, that's all I can tell you."

Schon's 200 overdubs did not go unrewarded: "Dock of the Bay" reached No. 11. Then Cain inadvertently reset their career course when he bumped into former Babys front man **John Waite**.

"He calls me from New York, and says, 'You're never going to believe who I had dinner with last night,'" their old bandmate **Ricky Phillips** said. "I went, 'Oh man, are you kidding me? Are we going there?'"

Cain, Phillips, and Waite agreed to a loose jam session to feel things out. Three quarters of **Bad English** dropped into place. [26, 39, 224, 515, 516]

"GREATEST HITS"
15 JOURNEYS TO THE TOP.

Over an hour of non-stop music
from America's premier rock and roll band.

It's the ultimate Journey. Featuring 15 smash songs including
"Who's Crying Now," "Don't Stop Believin'" and "Open Arms"
plus "Only The Young" and "Ask The Lonely" —
two hit songs never before available on any Journey album.

JOURNEY. PLATINUM-BOUND FOR THE 7TH TIME.
"JOURNEY'S GREATEST HITS." OC 44493
ON COLUMBIA CASSETTES, COMPACT DISCS AND RECORDS.

"Columbia," [?] are trademarks of CBS Inc. © 1988 CBS Records Inc.

By 1988, Journey was essentially defunct. So what does a record company do when its bellwether rock band has broken up? They release a greatest hits album, with quality unused songs from the band's archives. That kind of material is usually scarce, but Columbia Records and Journey's still-active management had some songs up their sleeves.

The album cover and the marketing materials that would be built around the album presented a different problem. Since *Infinity*, art director Jim Welch had guided the album design packages for Journey's albums. **Stanley Mouse** and **Alton Kelley** tag-teamed through the Journey's LP releases from *Infinity* through *Escape*, and then the band began trying other artists and concepts.

Columbia likely indulged Journey's desire to push the envelope with the album packages and cover designs because the band more than made up for those expenses with album and singles sales. But a "greatest hits"

package was still an unknown, so there would be no elaborate packaging. Eventually the band would release a more comprehensive "hits" box set package with Time³.

Welch was not involved with the design of the album package—his name did not appear in the credits—but the band's management still looked into their recent past to find an illustrator. Alton Kelley returned to design the cover art, and the scarab became front and center again. The colors were reminiscent of *Infinity*, the first album cover he and Mouse designed in 1977. With the exception of an artistic rendering of the band's name on the inside sleeve, Greatest Hits was bereft of art or photographs.

If Columbia's intent was a low-cost, threadbare design, it achieved its goal. Still, the cover art was beautiful and was used for all the standard promotional material, including in-store displays and trade publications like *Billboard* (above). Journey was gone, but they were not forgotten.

'HITS' LANDS BIG, AND IS REBORN OVER AND OVER

Herbie Herbert never thought Journey should go on hiatus, despite the struggles they had trying to complete *Raised on Radio* with Steve Perry.

"When he left this profession, I would venture to say he was the foremost vocal stylist in the world," Herbert told the *Tampa Bay Times*. "At this point, I think it's their civic duty to get back together."

That did not happen, of course—but the outsized success of their 1988 *Greatest Hits* album proved the point. When Herbert spoke to the *Times* in 1991, the LP was racing past three million units sold. It kept selling, becoming certified 10-times platinum in 1999, then 15-times platinum in 2008.

Included were a pair of Top 5 hits, four Top 10 hits, and three Top 20 hits—along with lower-charting must-have favorites like "Lights," "Any Way You Want It," "Send Her My Love," and "Wheel in the Sky." "At the time, we threw that *Greatest Hits* together," Perry told *Billboard*, "because it was kind of like a given." As *Greatest Hits* became one of the Top 30 albums in the history of *Billboard* recordkeeping, its success inevitably spawned a sequel. Perry came on board as curator for 2011's *Greatest Hits 2*. The album tanked, barely cracking the Top 100, but Perry said he nevertheless discovered a deeper appreciation for what Journey accomplished.

Greatest Hits began its chart run in December 1988, with a February 1989 peak at No. 10, then fell off the charts in October 1990. A 2006 reissue added "When You Love a Woman," Journey's 1996 No. 12 reunion smash—just before *Greatest Hits* returned to the charts again.

The LP became only the third to spend 700 weeks on the chart, following only **Pink Floyd**'s *The Dark Side of the Moon* and **Bob Marley and the Wailers**' *Legend*. *Greatest Hits* continued to showcase songs that once ruled the airwaves—and still had a deep resonance decades later. "I forgot how good they were! The stereo separation. The echoes. The snare drum sounds," Perry told the *Tampa Bay Times*. "Neal's guitar is stupidly amazing, and completely still to this day underrated in my opinion." [456, 517, 518, 520, 521, 522, 523, 524]

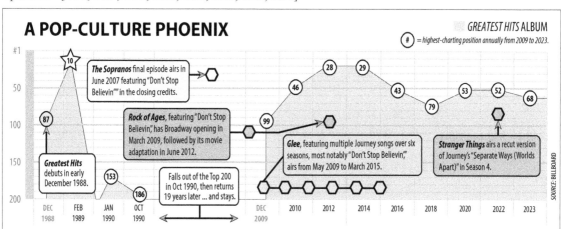

A POP-CULTURE PHOENIX

GREATEST HITS ALBUM

(#) = highest-charting position annually from 2009 to 2023.

The Sopranos final episode airs in June 2007 featuring "Don't Stop Believin'" in the closing credits.

Rock of Ages, featuring "Don't Stop Believin'," has Broadway opening in March 2009, followed by its movie adaptation in June 2012.

Greatest Hits debuts in early December 1988.

Falls out of the Top 200 in Oct 1990, then returns 19 years later ... and stays.

Glee, featuring multiple Journey songs over six seasons, most notably "Don't Stop Believin'," airs from May 2009 to March 2015.

Stranger Things airs a recut version of Journey's "Separate Ways (Worlds Apart)" in Season 4.

SOURCE: BILLBOARD

By winter of 1988, Journey was over. With no new material on the horizon, Columbia Records released an obligatory hits compilation album. Fans ate up the release, pushing it into the Top 10. It managed to stay in the *Billboard* 200 album chart for almost two years, and then disappeared for twenty years. In the summer of 2007, "Don't Stop Believin'" was the song picked to close out the final episode of the popular HBO series, *The Sopranos*. Two years later, the song was featured prominently in the Broadway musical *Rock of Ages* and its movie adaptation. Soon after, the song, along with a few other Journey hits, turned up repeatedly in episodes of *Glee*. And just like that, a forty-year-old compilation album became a consistent resident of the *Billboard* 200, surpassing all other albums for longevity except **Bob Marley and the Wailers** *Legend*.

TOP CHARTING WEEK: *BILLBOARD—February 11, 1989*

1. Guns N' Roses, *Appetite for Destruction*
2. Bobby Brown, *Don't Be Cruel*
3. Traveling Wilburys, *Traveling Wilburys*
4. Guns N' Roses, *G N' R Lies*
5. Poison, *Open Up and Say... Ahh!*
6. Edie Brickell & New Bohemians, *Shooting Rubber Bands at the Stars*
7. Def Leppard, *Hysteria*
8. Bon Jovi, *New Jersey*
9. Anita Baker, *Giving You the Best That I Got*
10. **JOURNEY, *GREATEST HITS***

Bad English

FORGET ME NOT

Journey was over. After a shortened *Raised on Radio* tour, Steve Perry opted out. Left with a sense of finality, the rest of the band looked for other creative outlets. Jonathan Cain and Neal Schon found Bad English. Ross Valory and Steve Smith rediscovered Gregg Rolie, and they formed The Storm. And Perry went into seclusion.

WINTER 1988–89

NUGGETS

▶ Congrats to ex-**Santana** and Journey guitarist Neal Schon and his wife, Beth, on the Aug. 15 birth of a son, **Miles Joseph**. —*Billboard*

▶ Comedian **Sam Kinison** is rounding up a bunch of his rock and roll pals to record the classic 1960's hit, "Wild Thing," that will be featured on his upcoming album. Among the rockers in the Sept. 13 shoot at a Hollywood studio were **Billy Idol**, **Steven Tyler** and **Joe Perry**, **Slash** and **Steve Adler** of **Guns N' Roses**, **John Waite**, Jonathan Cain, **Motley Crue** drummer **Tommy Lee**, **Richie Sambora**, **Whitesnake** bassist **Rudy Sarzo**, and all five members of **Ratt**. But who took the "Wild Thing" lead role in the **Marty Callner**-directed clip? None other than Kinison's good pal **Jessica Hahn**. Should be a riot!

—*Cashbox*

Disinterest at Sony, 'Stuck' Perry, Lead to Shelved Solo LP

Some 10 years separated the release of Steve Perry's first and second solo albums.

"I was riding my Harley a lot, all throughout the San Joaquin Valley," Perry told *GQ*. "I mean, back roads, where there's no cars, where there's nothing but coyotes. Just lettin' the wind kinda blow through me."

But there were roadblocks. Perry actually prepared an interim LP for release, titled *Against the Wall*, then shelved it.

"Melody," which sings like a woman's name but is really about recapturing a passion for music, was one of the lost treasures of these sessions—and another key collaboration with **Randy Goodrum**, who had played such a critical role on *Street Talk*.

By then, Goodrum had moved from Nashville to Los Angeles, opening the door for more regular songwriting sessions with Perry. Goodrum said he had the early makings of a song, and Perry began vocally answering the music. "It was one of those musical duets between voice and piano," Perry told **John Stix**. "I

always thought that should have been a single."

Decades later, Goodrum also gave special praise to the title tune as "a great song, track, vocal performance." So, he still did not understand why *Against the Wall* never saw the light of day. "Beats me," Goodrum said. "It's a head-scratcher for me."

Perry originally began work on these tracks before diverting into Journey's *Raised on Radio*, and then attempted to complete the album in the late 1980s. Those who were familiar with Perry's approach to the work may have suspected an age-old stumbling block: His tendency to bog down in perfectionism.

Producer **Kevin Elson**, who initially came on board in the *Departure* era, later told *Billboard* that dealing with that issue was one of his most important early tasks. It nearly sank *Raised on Radio*.

But the truth is, Perry's perspective had changed. He did not connect with those songs and sounds anymore. Even if he had, after Sony acquired Columbia Records in September 1989, Perry said the company's new management was lukewarm about the project.

The once-prolific Perry was stuck. As the silence unspooled, even former collaborators wondered what was keeping him from returning to music. Eventually, Perry himself seemed to have lost track of the passing years.

"I saw him one time and I said to him, 'How is the second album coming?' He says, 'Oh, it'll be soon. It'll be soon,'" said **Paul Flattery**, who produced videos for Journey and Perry's first solo project. "I said, 'You've been saying that for 10 years.'" Perry briefly pushed back on that timeline. "I said, 'Since we did those videos, I've gotten married, I've got two children.' I laid it out how long it had been—and he was, like, shocked."

Perry's *Street Talk* follow-up, *For the Love of Strange Medicine*, belatedly arrived in 1994, and then songs from *Against the Wall* slowly began to trickle out.

He released the first two ("Melody" and "It Won't Be You") with "Missing You" as part of the expanded second single from *For the Love of Strange Medicine*. Six more tracks were part of Perry's 1998 solo compilation *Greatest Hits + Five Unreleased*, including "When You're in Love (For the First Time)," the title track, "Forever Right or Wrong (Love's Like a River)," "Summer of Luv," "Once in a Lifetime, Girl," and "What Was."

Eight years later, Perry included the rest ("Can't Stop," "Friends of Mine," and a new take on the old **Alien Project** demo "If You Need Me, Call Me") on an expanded reissue of *Strange Medicine*. [36, 80, 274, 435, 477]

Cain, Waite, Schon Join Forces; Form New Band, Bad English

The prospect of reuniting with **John Waite** in a new band had Jonathan Cain thinking about the differences between his former **Babys** band-mate and Steve Perry.

With Perry, "you've got the boy next door who's shy and hasn't fallen in love yet," Cain said. "He's still looking for the girl. Then you have John Waite, who's Vampire Lestat. He has a harem, you know." Then Waite quotes the old Babys' song, "Midnight Rendezvous": "'That dress you're wearing is way past your knees'—come on!"

Cain reconnected with fellow Babys alum **Ricky Phillips** at the wedding of Cain's brother, Mugs. "He pulled me aside and said, 'We're about ready to announce that Journey is separating,'" Phillips said. "'We're going to split up the band, and I want to have something ready soon after that happens. Are you in?' I said, 'Let's do it. Are you kidding? I'd love to.'"

The Babys had been apart for most of the 1980s, but Cain and Phillips remained in contact. "Jonathan and I never stopped being friends," Phillips added. "That's the difference between the rest of the guys in The Babys, and Jonathan and I."

The same was not true about Waite, who had gone on to chart-topping solo success with 1984's "Missing You." Cain and Phillips wanted to feel things out before deciding. Everyone arranged for a loose jam to see if any magic remained. At this point, Neal Schon had not entered the conversation—but labels were already sniffing around.

"My manager wanted to see me make a hit record. She walked me into Epic, and she knew [A&R man] **Don Grierson**. She said: 'Here he is. John Waite, "Missing You." You want him?'" Waite remembered. "Don said: 'Yeah.'" But

Epic wanted to pair him with outside songwriters. Waite disagreed and decided that forming another group might help him create a united front.

"We had this great meeting, and then I went back and Don said: 'I'm going to find you some great songs to sing,'" Waite said. "And I went: 'Yeah, Don, but actually I've written a few of those myself.' I'm a writer, I think, before I'm a singer. But he was adamant. So, I put a band together which turned into **Bad English** so I wouldn't have to face Don by myself. I wanted to be on Epic, so I thought: 'Why don't I do a band?' Nobody expects that."

Cain mentioned the possibility of Schon joining the core lineup. He joined the rehearsals and "all of a sudden, it started sounding real good," Phillips enthused. "There was a mesh, a blend. It was the sound we were reaching for, immediately."

Schon had arrived with a personal admiration for Waite. "He's very much a poet-singer, the way he talks and sings really conveys a story," Schon told **Michael Cavacini**. "I always loved him in The Babys. I loved his solo material. Great solo records."

Still, Schon initially declined to join the group. This was the first time he had been out of a band since he was a teenager, and said he wanted to explore this newfound freedom. Schon's first solo album, *Late Nite*, would arrive in April 1989.

Cain, Phillips, and Waite began jam sessions with guitarist **Andy Timmons**, but that didn't last long. "All of a sudden, the door bursts open—and it's Neal," Phillips said. "He shows up at the rehearsal hall, and I was shocked. Jonathan must have known, though I never really asked him—but it all happened so fast at that point. The look on Andy's face, I'll never forget—because he knew exactly what was about to happen."

Bad English was almost a band. "Now we're in a situation with Neal," Phillips added. "We've got bass, we've got keyboards and guitar and really good vocals." But they still needed a drummer. Some 30 auditions later, they settled on Deen Castronovo—sparking a musical partnership with Schon that would last, off and on, for decades.

Cain began a quick transition back to the

style of writing Waite preferred. "It's just this whole different actor; he's another character—and I stay true to those characters," Cain said. The songs that appeared on their self-titled debut often boasted far different themes than anything released by Journey, despite featuring Cain, Schon, and their future collaborator Castronovo.

Along the way, Schon and Waite connected on a deeper level. "Him and I had great chemistry," Schon told Cavacini, "and, of course, Jonathan and him had built-in chemistry from their days together in The Babys. ... There was a lot of history in the band."

But that history did not always work in Bad English's favor. Small cracks formed from the first, and eventually widened to the point that the group crumbled.

During early writing sessions, Cain and Waite were working together while Schon and Phillips collaborated separately. "We had tapes with three, four, five song ideas," Phillips said, "and we were stoked—because we were on fire. We were writing some really good stuff, and we wanted to hear what they were doing."

They sent their songs to Cain and Waite, then waited a couple of weeks. Finally, Phillips "called up there, and said: 'What'd you think of what we sent up?' I'm the one that's on the phone, and Jonathan said: 'Oh, that's right, you sent something up here, didn't you?' I had to put my hand over the phone because I thought, 'If Neal hears that, he's gonna be pissed.' I got off the phone, and I just had a sinking feeling in my stomach."

There was already a "sort of a conquer-and-divide thing" happening, Phillips said, "and I don't know if it was intentional or just a work ethic thing. That sort of problem had been there, even in The Babys' days. So, I thought, 'Here we are again. We'll see what happens.'" [17, 26, 385, 407]

Schon, Old Friends Release His Debut Solo LP, *Late Nite*

Neal Schon thought he was in line to play guitar on **Mick Jagger**'s 1988 tour of Japan, the first by any member of **The Rolling Stones**. Instead, he ended up getting a jump start on his own career.

Schon told the Journey Force fan club that he "went to New York, and had a great time rehearsing with them for two days. Maybe politics got involved with it." Or maybe it was money. Either way, **Joe Satriani** ended up in Asia with Jagger.

"There was no problem with my playing—they liked the way I sounded," Schon added. "I think they got Satriani for much less than they would have paid for me."

The unexpected downtime led to *Late Nite*, Schon's solo debut. It also helped smooth over the bad feelings associated with how everything ended with Jagger. "I never even got a telephone call back," Schon told Journey Force. "I thought it was pretty unprofessional, but that's fine because I just ended up starting my own record anyway."

Compared to his diminished presence on *Raised on Radio*, Schon offers an utter torrent of musical ideas on *Late Nite*. In the end, even Schon admitted that *Late Nite* sounded a bit scattered.

"I listened to some of the stuff a while ago,"

Continued on Page 221

SPRING 1989

RELEASES
▶ Neal Schon, *Late Night* (album)

CASTRONOVO TAKES LONG PATH TO BAD ENGLISH, JOURNEY

Deen Castronovo was rescued from obscurity in his early 20s and thrust into the spotlight with a pair of platinum-selling bands in **Bad English** and then Journey.

He almost lost it all in an avalanche of addiction and bad behavior. "I'm just grateful to be alive," Castronovo said. "I've been through hell. My poor wife's been through hell, my family, my kids."

A stint in rehab helped Castronovo turn the corner. So did refocusing on his faith. "Life is good. You wake up in the morning, you don't have a hangover. I actually got money in my wallet. Like, 'Oh, good. I didn't spend it on stupid shit!'" Castronovo added, laughing.

Born August 17, 1964 in Westminster, California, Castronovo began his musical life in metal bands before running into Neal Schon. That led to stints in Bad English, then **Hardline**, and finally Journey, as Schon mentored Castronovo in the way Gregg Rolie once did with the wunderkind guitarist. Other than stints with the **Black Sabbath** family of bands (including both **Ozzy Osbourne** and **Geezer Butler**'s **GZR**), Castronovo's early professional life intertwined with Schon's.

Still, the transition from the **John Waite**-fronted Bad English to Journey in the post-Perry era was seamless, and not just because of Castronovo's longtime connection with Schon. "John's a soul singer—and that's what he had in common with Steve," Jonathan Cain said. "Both of those guys were very much pocket singers; they had to have that solid drum."

Castronovo joined Journey following Steve Smith's second departure in 1998, making his Journey album debut on 2001's *Arrival*. It was a particularly perilous time, as the group attempted to move on without Steve Perry.

"Thank God for Deen Castronovo," manager **Herbie Herbert** told **Matthew Carty**. "[He] was discovered by our old lighting designer when he was working out in Portland with this speed metal group called the **Wild Dogs**. The guy was the greatest speed metal drummer in history."

Castronovo later began displaying a surprising versatility as a singer, taking over lead vocals on "A Better Life" and "Never Too Late" from 2005's *Generations*. Castronovo also started singing on stage, providing a key backstop for Perry's successors—and then as a foil to Rolie with Schon's **Journey Through Time** splinter group.

In this way, Castronovo became an increasingly indispensable latter-era cog in the Journey combine. "Learning the subtleties and the nuances of Steve Smith's style of play —you know, it's not easy," Herbert told Carty.

"And he really is a big part of the vocals on tour. He's a much, much bigger part of the vocals than you realize."

Then Castronovo fell apart, just as he took on a concurrent gig as a full-fledged front man with **Revolution Saints**. He was arrested in June 2015 in connection with a drug-fueled domestic assault. Castronovo was later indicted on charges of rape, sexual abuse, and assault. His conviction led to a probation sentence, but not before Journey replaced him with **Omar Hakim** for their already-scheduled summer tour, which included the band's first-ever orchestral concert at the Hollywood Bowl.

In retrospect, Castronovo said he very much needed the break. "I had to take some time off and, pardon my language, get my shit together," he said. "I was a mess, and it was horrible what happened. But today, I'm doing great, clean and sober, working hard, doing what I need to do—and I put God first, family second. My job is third, where before it was all the other way around. 'I want to be a rocker, I want to play music and I want to party,' and everything was on the back burner."

Castronovo's road back was long. He did not return to the Journey lineup until 2021. Revolution Saints had jumpstarted again in 2017, followed by Castronovo's reunion with his Hardline bandmate **Johnny Gioeli** on 2018's Gioeli–Castronovo album *Set the World on Fire*.

"It was like immediate, absolutely immediate pickup from where we left off," Gioeli said. "I walked in and said, 'Jesus Christ, you got ugly as hell!' and we just started laughing. The jokes just flowed, like we never stopped. It was a great reunion."

Castronovo had already taken part in Schon's throwback Journey Through Time concerts before resuming his long-held spot at drums with the main band.

"I've really got a huge appreciation now, obviously, for family. I mean, that's the most important thing," Castronovo said. "I was so wrapped up in drugs and alcohol; family was way down the line. That was heartbreaking. But here I am today, and family is most important, and my job is great. I love what I do with Journey and I love what I do with Revolution Saints, but the beautiful thing is what I learned the most, being in treatment, is that if it all went away, you know what? I'm still all right." [14, 37, 56, 230, 407, 408]

he later told *Melodic Rock*. "It is pretty funny to go back and listen to that again. It is kind of like all over the map, musically."

Late Nite provided some closure by bringing Schon back together with a string of bandmates from Journey, including Jonathan Cain, Gregg Rolie, Randy Jackson, and Steve Smith. Future Journey member Deen Castronovo and touring drummer **Omar Hakim** also made important contributions.

Schon's principal collaborator, however, was Bob Marlette, who initially connected with Schon as part of a proposed **Santana** reunion that never took off. He also played a significant role in Rolie's 1987 solo album, *Gringo*, which included writing songs and contributing guitar and keyboards to three of its first four tracks. Marlette, Jackson, Hakim, and Schon comprised the core group on *Late Nite*.

While sessions for Schon's solo album continued, **Michael Bolton** planned a tour to support *The Hunger*, which featured contributions from Cain, Schon, and the *Raised on Radio* touring rhythm section of Jackson and Mike Baird. Schon stayed home to focus on promoting *Late Nite*.

In fact, he was hoping to score a key solo opening slot. "I'd like to go out and open for **Pink Floyd**, **Phil Collins**, **Genesis** or someone like that, because [*Late Nite*] is a more musical kind of trip. More instrumental," Schon said in the Q&A with Journey Force.

Solo tours would have to wait. In the meantime, however, Marlette would go on to become a key collaborator with **The Storm**, which featured Schon's Journey bandmates Rolie, Ross Valory, and Smith—including seven of the 12 songs on both their self-titled 1991 debut and 1995's *Eye of the Storm*. [525, 526, 527]

SUMMER 1989

RELEASES
▶ **Bad English** (with Neal Schon, Jonathan Cain), *Bad English* (album)

Bad English Lands Its Drummer After Seventeen Long Auditions

Members of the newly formed **Bad English** would play pool in the studio when not at work on their platinum-selling 1989 debut. Joking criticism that Jonathan Cain leveled after a poor shot by John Waite gave them a name.

Newcomer Deen Castronovo was dealing with a higher level of scrutiny. While the others shared

Continued on Page 223

BAD ENGLISH DELIVERS SCHON, CAIN AN ELUSIVE #1 SINGLE

With Journey stalled out, the wisdom of joining **Bad English** was obvious to Jonathan Cain. "For me, [rock music] is like a muscle," he told the *Lansing State Journal*. "You use it or you lose it. I didn't want to lose it."

Then A&R executive **Don Grierson** suggested Bad English use an outside writer for their debut LP's big ballad. Waite had to convince the others to give "When I See You Smile" a try, and not everyone was convinced.

"I voted no on it," bassist **Ricky Phillips** said, "and John said, 'Ricky, you've gotta support me on this. I'll make this a No. 1 song.' I swear to God, that's exactly what he said to me—and that's what he did. I didn't care. He said, 'I've had a No. 1 song. You don't know how that changes your career. A No. 1 song is huge.' And I still didn't care."

It was a frankly surprising conversation, considering the lineup featured an all-star amalgam of hit composers. Waite himself was a credentialed songwriter who was already known for his rugged individualism. But he argued on behalf of "When I See You Smile" as a favor to Grierson, who had been so instrumental in getting the band signed.

"Don was very generous, he was very kind," Waite said. "He'd come to the studio and make lots of suggestions. He was just the nicest guy. So, at the end of the record, he found this one song from **Diane Warren**, and I said to the lads: 'You know, without Don, we wouldn't be here. Let's cut this song as a way of saying thank you. If it works, great. If it doesn't, we won't put it on the record.'"

"When I See You Smile" obviously worked, but not everyone was happy about it. "I love Diane Warren. She's one of my favorite people; she's a brilliant talent," Phillips said, "but we were a rock fucking band. I didn't think we needed that."

To the surprise of no one, Neal Schon also wanted to push into grittier sounds. "I felt some of the strongest points of the first record were the

John Waite and Neal Schon of Bad English play at the Alpine Valley Music Theatre in East Troy, Wisconsin, in May 1990.

bluesy rock songs like 'Rocking Horse,' and stuff like that," Schon told **Michael Cavacini**. "I told John, 'That's the direction. This is what we have to do to gain a way bigger audience.'"

Except "When I See You Smile" sold more than a million copies on its way to the top of the *Billboard* Hot 100, becoming Bad English's signature song. "We cut it, and everybody knew it was a No. 1. It was like, well, doesn't that beat all?" Waite said, laughing. "It was our thank you to Don Grierson." [17, 26, 105, 217, 385]

cross-connections with Journey and **The Babys**, Castronovo arrived as an unknown. A stint with the Oregon-based **Wild Dogs** heavy metal band brought him into Schon's orbit through their mutual friend **Tony MacAlpine**—but Castronovo still had to pass the audition.

"Deen came in, blew my mind—and blew Neal's mind," Bad English bassist **Ricky Phillips** said. "But Jonathan was like, 'I don't know. He's trying to sing, and he's really edgy and really on top of the beat.' He sent him home. He sent Deen packing."

Cain remembered John Waite quickly losing patience with Castronovo's timing problems as well. "John wanted to 86 him," Cain said. "We had rehearsals and John said, 'This guy is all over the map.'"

An extended audition process followed, but Bad English could not connect with anybody else.

"So, Neal and I went to Waite and said, 'Let's get that kid back here. Let's work with him, let him know why he was sent packing and see what happens,'" Phillips added. "We had a little talk with him, we said: 'Lay it back.' He came from a really heavy-handed musical background—very, very aggressive trio-type stuff."

Cain played a bigger role in mentoring Castronovo than the others knew. "He couldn't keep a really good tempo," Cain said, "so I got him a click track with all the tempos and said, 'This is your friend.' You know, the click track made him a better drummer."

Cain and Castronovo kept it between themselves. "It was a secret click that I gave him, a little box that nobody saw," Cain said. "You know, 'Don't show this to anybody.' It had a little light that flashed, so you didn't hear it. I said, 'Watch the light, Deen. Stay with the light'—and he got the gig." [26, 407]

SPRING 1990

Rolie, Ex-Journey-men Gather for a Slow-Evolving Squall

Herbie Herbert was certain he could create another legendary band around Gregg Rolie.

He told Gannett News Service in May 1992 that Rolie's "success is not by accident. ... He's just a franchise-level player. It's like having **Joe**

Montana: You can build a team around him."

That's just what Herbert did, as Rolie anchored a new group called **The Storm** with ex-Journey bandmates Ross Valory and Steve Smith. The lineup also included Neal Schon-influenced guitarist **Josh Ramos** and vocalist **Kevin Chalfant**, a Steve Perry soundalike.

What to call the group presented its own challenges. "It was the most difficult and grueling experience, to try and get a name," Rolie told **Gary James**. "It took us longer to do that than to record all the songs and write 'em."

As the dilemma dragged on, they considered and then discarded The Storm. "You could come up with something that was different, that nobody had," Rolie added, "but the reason why is because nobody wanted it."

Then "it finally started raining in California," Rolie told James, and Chalfant's son suggested "The Storm." Chalfant called Rolie with "the perfect name. I said, 'Kevin, we crossed that off two months ago." But it stuck.

Ramos worked with Valory and Chalfant in a short-lived *Raised on Radio*-era group called **The VU**, which also featured Prairie Prince. Ramos still had dreams of rock stardom but ended up back at work on a horse ranch in Petaluma, California.

"I'd be going out every morning, saying 'God, please Lord, just please give me my chance'— because you know, all my friends were getting signed and I'm like, 'Man, when is it going to happen for me?'" he said. "I would just keep having the faith and so one day, Kevin calls me up. He goes, 'Hey, listen, I'm working with Gregg Rolie. You want to come over and do some guitars on these demos?'"

There were plenty of reasons for trepidation. For starters, The VU had come and gone unnoticed. Then, as Valory later admitted, "There's a hurdle, a stigma in which you have members of Journey in a band that isn't Journey and it doesn't ring the same way. It doesn't have the influence or the backing of the industry."

The Storm would not have that problem, at least not at first. They quickly signed a record deal with the just-established Interscope Records. Co-founder **Beau Hill** wanted to add a

Continued on Page 226

IS

JOHN WAITE

NEAL SCHON

JONATHAN CAIN

RICKY PHILLIPS

DEEN CASTRONOVO

Journey. The Babys. John Waite. Separately they sold over 33,000,000 albums. Together they've created Bad English.
A new band with a past perfect, present tense and future intense. Watch them do their damage.
Bad English. A band powerful enough to rock the rules.

"Bad English." The debut album featuring the first single and video, "Forget Me Not."

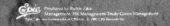
Produced by Richie Zito.
Management: HK Management Trudy Green Management
Epic, and are trademarks of CBS Inc. © 1989 CBS Records Inc.

As the 1980s came to a close, Journey had gone into a deep hibernation, and Jonathan Cain joined up with his former **Babys** bandmate **John Waite** to form **Bad English**. Neal Schon soon joined him, and the band took on managers **Trudy Green** and **Howard Kaufman**. As they prepared to roll out their debut album, they employed veteran album package designer **Hugh Syme**, who led the design work for every **Rush** album and many others, including **Whitesnake**, **Aerosmith**, and **Sammy Hagar**.

While Journey's album package designs were often built around the band's mascot scarab and futuristic spacey designs, Syme took Bad English down a more subtle path, electing to put the band's picture on the cover against a stark red textured background with Syme's weathered logo treatment displaying the band's name. "Trudy elected to have the band on the cover," Syme told *Time Passages*, adding that Green had a purpose in putting the band's faces on the cover rather than an illustrative vision that Syme had built his reputation on.

"In this instance, she wanted to make sure people saw that this was The Babys and Journey. And immediately, I knew that was good, and then I came up with the weathered lettering and treatment for the cover so it would have shelf appeal in the stores. It wasn't lavish like [Rush's] *Moving Pictures* or *Permanent Waves*. Sometimes, covers don't need to be complex or indulgent to be really good rock covers that depict a band. Less is often more."

Journey-Babys Mashup Rides Album Into Top 25

Journey and Bad English shared an inherent tension that must have seemed familiar—but this time, it was not only between harder-edged rock and soaring balladry. **John Waite** was leading the band into deeper emotional themes, when all Epic Records—and many of their fans—wanted was a big hit to rally around.

"The Journey audience wanted Journey, and **The Babys** audience wanted The Babys," Waite lamented. "But 'Forget Me Not' was based on the **Anne Rice** books. 'Ghost in Your Heart' was written, really, about some kind of unrequited suicidal love. There were darker themes—and you could see the audience wanting to just sing along. That was too sophisticated."

Waite solved the issue by turning to ace songwriter **Diane Warren**, who wrote "Don't Lose Any Sleep" for his 1987 solo album *Rover's Return*, after composing No. 1 hits for **Chicago** and **Starship**.

She provided "When I See You Smile," and Bad English joined Warren's other clients at the top of the charts. "It really is a celebration of the obvious things," Waite admitted to *Spin*, "but we get on great and it's just fun and apparently people like us because we're selling tons of records."

Before people could like them, they had to resolve naming the band. Graphic artist **Hugh Syme** dutifully began work on their album cover, but he had questions. Not with Bad English, but with what they were initially called.

"The original name of Bad English—I don't know if it's publicly denoted—was a particularly Germanic-sounding project called **Volte Wolf**, which sounded a tad Third Reich for my taste," Syme said. "I didn't know what it had to do with anything. It didn't scare me, but I felt concerned. It just felt odd."

He did some early sketches, including "a really nice graphic of a wolf with copper inks and black. It was gonna be a little bit Germanic and a little bit severe looking. But, you know, I didn't quite know where this was going except to speak up and say, 'I'm not sure I love the name.' And I was at a point in my career where it was not my nature to bite my tongue anyway, so I said so."

They went back to the drawing board—or, more particularly, a pool table—and came up with Bad English.

Their lead single, "Forget Me Not," only got to No. 45, but the third single, "Price of Love," rode momentum created by "When I See You Smile" all the way to No. 5 on the *Billboard* singles chart. "Possession" just missed the Top 20, while "Heaven Is a 4 Letter Word" settled at No. 66 on the Hot 100, and "Best of What I Got" missed entirely.

All of it had the hair-sprayed sheen of the late 1980s era. Epic paired the band with **Richie Zito**, who had just produced **Cheap Trick**'s chart-topping hit "The Flame." But those who dug more deeply into the lyrics discovered that Bad English was working with a more complex color palette.

"'Forget Me Not' was very much a dominant, sexual 'I will be your keeper'-type male," said Cain, who co-wrote all but two songs on *Bad English*. "That was about possession, with all of the sexual innuendos that John loves to deliver. 'Ready When You Are,' all these fun, fun songs, 'Best of What I Got'—they were sexual and hot. He needed that to be John Waite."

Those themes were easy to miss, even on Waite's solo smash "Missing You." "It's still that male, macho kind of lyric—very, very English, you know?" Cain added. "Sort of sexy, but I'm in charge. ... So, you stay true to that."

Deen Castronovo continued to mesh with the others, even displaying a previously unknown flair as a background singer. "We had no idea that he had this insane voice," Bad English bassist **Ricky Phillips** said. "No idea."

Cain had a clue, though, and brought Castronovo into the band's vocal mix. "I asked him to sing backgrounds because I knew he was singing," Cain said. "We got on the mic together for the 'Best of What I Got' session and I said, 'Oh, boy, this is powerful.'"

Elsewhere, familiar issues quickly began to bubble up again—in particular between Cain and Waite. Schon was also pushing the band to go in a bluesier direction, which Waite resisted.

"I loved Bad English," former Babys drummer **Tony Brock** said. "I thought that was really cool. But the people involved, Neal Schon and John Waite and Jonathan—they're all very strong-headed. I just couldn't see it lasting very long—which it didn't." [11, 26, 39, 217, 407, 916]

new rock band to the label's roster, so Herbert slipped him The Storm's demo tape.

Ramos quickly put away the farm tools but escaping charges of copying Schon was not as easy—even at the demo stage. "Gregg said, 'Wow, man, you sound like Neal'—and I go, 'Well, you know, he was my favorite guitar player.' I have other people that I listened to and I'm not all Neal, but I respect him. I had been following him ever since I was 14 years old."

The Storm completed a self-titled 1991 debut album, then saw their power ballad "I've Got a Lot to Learn About Love" rise to the Top 30. But the first signs of trouble for this band came before they ever mounted a tour: Steve Smith backed out.

"He goes, 'Well, you know, I don't really want to do that. I'm concentrating more on **Vital Information**; I want to be a jazz drummer,'" Ramos said. "But then I'm like, 'God, really? I get a chance to go out and tour with three members of Journey. Now we're not going to do it?'"

They ended up hitting the road with **Ron Wikso**, a friend who stayed on for The Storm's next LP. "Ron's a great drummer too—he's not Steve Smith, but he's pretty good—and he had the tour experience," Ramos added. "You know, he was on tour with **Cher** on big stages. I told Herbie and Gregg about him, and eventually, he got the gig."

Next, Herbert lined up a choice opening slot with **Bryan Adams**, who was supporting his four-times platinum *Waking Up the Neighbors* album. "He goes, 'There's a possibility that you guys can go on tour with Bryan Adams—and I'm like, 'What? Really?'" Ramos said. "He goes, 'Yep, we did Bryan Adams a favor back in 1983, where we had him open up for Journey. Now, he's basically repaying the favor.'"

Out on the road, the band's members were being comparing to Journey legends. "I would hear people in the audience going 'I didn't know Steve Perry joined The Storm' or whatever just looking at Kevin Chalfant," Herbert told *Melodic Rock* with a laugh. He admitted there was "enough of a similarity in resemblance and a great voice." The Storm would face far taller obstacles in a changing musical landscape. For now, however, they remained on the concert trail—later taking an opening gig with **Peter**

Frampton. Ironically, his headlining sets consistently suffered sudden downpours.

"As soon as The Storm was off stage, it would start raining," Valory told the *Birmingham Post-Herald*. Frampton stopped by the dressing room one night, Valory remembered, and said, "You've got a great band, but is there any chance you could change the name?" [61, 105, 112, 376, 405, 529, 530]

FALL 1991

RELEASES
▶ **The Storm** (with Ross Valory, Steve Smith, Gregg Rolie), *The Storm* (album)
▶ **Bad English** (with Jonathan Cain, Neal Schon), *Backlash* (album)
▶ **Vital Information** (with Steve Smith), *Vitalive!* (album)

Journey Gathers for a One-Off Bill Graham Tribute Set

Neal Schon and Jonathan Cain joined Steve Perry again on November 3, 1991 for a star-studded concert in honor of **Bill Graham**. The legendary promoter and live music venue owner had died in a helicopter crash on October 25.

After this performance, Perry would never play with Journey again.

Appearing as part of an event called the "Bill Graham Memorial: Laughter, Love & Music," Journey's slimmed-down trio shared the stage with other legacy California acts like **Santana**, **Jackson Browne**, **Crosby, Stills, Nash & Young**, and **The Grateful Dead**. Journey's three-song setlist at San Francisco's Golden Gate Park included "Faithfully" and "Lights," but it had been a little more than four years since they abruptly halted the *Raised on Radio* tour. Much had changed.

According to **Herbie Herbert**, changes in Perry's vocals forced Schon and Cain to significantly alter Journey's old songs. Meanwhile, Perry had forgotten the words—and asked Herbert for a lyric sheet.

"I got the words together and Perry still struggled to sing them down two whole keys from the original," Herbert told **Matthew Carty**.

He said Perry was hoping "people won't hear that these songs are being sung much lower than their original counterparts."

Despite these difficulties, Perry's presence made perfect sense. Journey had, of course, played their debut concert for Graham on the final day of 1973 at Winterland. Perry arrived some five years later, but his connection with Graham predated that by more than a decade.

"I was about 14 or 15 and my band, which was a group called **The Sullies**, had participated in a battle of the bands at [the] Frog Jumping Jubilee at a county fair. And one of the prizes for winning this competition was that you got to play the Fillmore," Perry told *Kerrang!*.

"Years later, I brought my youthful Fillmore Bill Graham moment up to Bill Graham when Journey was headlining the Day on the Green in Oakland," Perry said in a *Journey Asylum* fan club Q&A. "I don't think he really remembered that young kid … but I certainly will never forget it."

Still in high school, Perry went to the Fillmore with his mother and stepfather to be on a bill with **The Steve Miller Blues Band**, **Boz Scaggs**, and **Janis Joplin**. "It was amazing to play in that kind of environment," Perry told *Kerrang!*. "That's where it kind of started for me."

Graham protégé Herbert later hired him for a decade-long stint in Journey before Perry initially walked away. He eventually acknowledged the changes in his vocals.

"Singers live on the edge of being powerful, being strong, and not degrading their voice, and it's the most difficult edge to walk," Perry told *GQ*. "You feel like you're on a high wire all the time."

Back at the Bill Graham tribute in Golden Gate Park, ousted bassist Ross Valory stood by the soundboard—"still hurt and angry," according to the original *Time³* liner notes submitted by **Joel Selvin** to Columbia Records. The passage, which Selvin said Perry deleted before the label released the box set, also described how Schon "scrambled to transpose the many chord changes in his head" after they "lowered the key one entire octave."

Obviously, nobody knew this would be the last time Perry sang with Cain and Schon, whatever their difficulties in getting the performance off the ground. Yet what happened next

already felt vastly different from Journey's previous 1980s-era hiatus.

Back then, Cain was still confident enough in Journey's future to joke about the proliferation of solo projects from Perry, Schon, and Steve Smith. "The two Steves are thinking about opening up a kosher deli in Fresno," Cain quipped in an interview with *Hit Parader*. "Perry's convinced that sour pickles will strengthen his singing voice." [56, 60, 80, 544, 553, 554]

Bad English Releases New LP, But Disputes Force Breakup

Bad English followed in **The Babys**' footsteps in more ways than one. The lineup once again featured **John Waite**, Jonathan Cain, and **Ricky Phillips**—and they once again collapsed in a heap of personality conflict.

The worst of it, however, was that Phillips felt their second (and final) album, *Backlash*, pointed to bigger things. Bad English's inherent tensions were making the music more interesting.

"If forced to make a choice, I'd probably say the second Bad English record is the best of the two—even though it didn't have the No. 1 hit on it," Phillips said. "You could feel a little bit of angst within the band. You could feel that in the music, and it gave it an edge. It was a little less poppy. It seemed to be more like, we had a sound now."

Continued on Page 230

V eteran rock album designer **Hugh Syme** wasn't sure what confluence of events conspired to elevate him as art director for *both* post-Journey rock album projects—**Bad English** and **The Storm**—but he took the coincidental work in tride. The album package he engineered for The Storm was innovative in approach, and planned and executed in a way that would ikely not be attempted in today's Photoshop-driven art world.

Syme was contracted by **Jimmy Iovine**, the CEO of The Storm's abel, Interscope Records, and he met briefly with Gregg Rolie and he band. He then started work with **John Scarpati**, who, in another Journey-esque coincidence, also took the photographs for Steve Perry's *Street Talk*. Recalling the inspiration for The Storm's lesign, Syme said he "just wanted a Magritte-like man with a

black suit with an umbrella in a storm." Syme said the project required building a low-frame pool about 18 feet wide that wa filled with water and sandbagged in Scarpati's expansive studio which was previously a sturdy old brewery.

The man with the umbrella was standing in the water, and retouching was done by Syme on a $750 dye-transfer print to obscure the black vinyl used as a liner to merge the horizon with the sky. The frame was filled to about 10 inches deep. The sky was captured in camera as a huge 20-foot-wide painted backdrop courtesy of MGM Studios. The back cover continued the album's "storm" theme, depicting a sunken Volkswagen Beetle (inset) which Syme incorporated using the first version of Photoshop, then new and little-known image editing tool.

Rap, Grunge Mute Rolie's Journey-ish Reunion

The Storm was a redemption project for Ross Valory after Journey unceremoniously dumped him prior to *Raised on Radio*. It was a return to rock for Steve Smith, and a return to bands for Gregg Rolie.

"Playing with Steve and Ross again, it was like riding a bicycle," Rolie said. "Steve Smith is a great drummer, and Ross is Ross."

It was also a coming-out party for **Kevin Chalfant** and **Josh Ramos**, who shared more than a few respective qualities with Steve Perry and Neal Schon. Valory immediately connected with the others in the studio as they worked on a self-titled debut that arrived in September 1991.

His time away had been admittedly unhappy. "I've tried to think of other things I might want to do, but even if I did do them, I'd still want to be doing this," Valory told interviewer **Gary James**. "And I couldn't think of a better bunch of guys to be out there with than the people I'm working with right now."

For a while, they seemed to have met the moment. Perry had effectively disappeared, leaving a Journey-shaped hole in the musical landscape. The Storm appeared ready to fill the gap.

Songs like "Show Me the Way" recalled the fission of 1979's *Evolution* and 1980's *Departure*, when Smith first worked with Rolie and Valory. "I've Got a Lot to Learn About Love" had the same balladic arc as the best of their next era. "Still Loving You" brought in some of the dark yearnings of Journey's earliest Rolie-sung songs.

"Kevin Chalfant, The Storm's lead singer, and Gregg Rolie have gotten the idea to put passion and romance back into rock," Valory said in an AOL chat in 1993. "A lot of the music today has gotten really hard and really tough."

That eventually became The Storm's un-

doing. The era's twin movements of rap and grunge, both far more confrontational, were stronger forces. In 1992, Interscope struck a deal to distribute Death Row Records, home of **Dr. Dre** and **Snoop Dogg**, and The Storm dissipated after one more album.

"We were just coming into grunge and rap music, and so everybody, all of the record companies, they're like a horse with blinders on—they can only see forward," Ramos said. "They don't understand, or maybe they do, but in Europe, you have musicians of all kinds standing side by side. They play all different kinds of things; there's an audience for everything. Here, it's like, well, this is the flavor of the month—or the flavor of the year."

American fans still seemed interested in The Storm's sound. "I've Got a Lot to Learn About Love" reached the Top 30 before Interscope's focus shifted, and the label lost interest in marketing the band. Or maybe The Storm's failure was just a question of timing.

"Had Interscope not changed their style away from that kind of music, it would have been a different story," Rolie said. "Two years earlier, and we'd be talking about something else. But that style of music went out the window, and so did we."

The Storm would stagger through another studio project, but by then Smith was long gone. Valory returned to Journey, while **Ron Wikso**, Smith's replacement, began a long stint in the **Gregg Rolie Band**. Chalfant and Ramos were left to fend for themselves.

"If we would have come out in 1987 when Journey had just released *Raised on Radio*, we would have had success—because back then we were considered like the new Journey," Ramos lamented. "We would have at least had, you know, four or five years of having CDs out and going out on tours—but we never got a chance to do that." [2, 61, 405, 438, 560]

Had Interscope not changed their style away from that kind of music, it would have been a different story. Two years earlier, and we'd be talking about something else. But that style of music went out the window, and so did we.

— Gregg Rolie

Arriving a little over two years after the platinum-selling Bad English, the lead single "Straight to Your Heart" just missed the Top 40 but Backlash could get no higher than No. 72. There was no blaming grunge, the punk-metal hybrid which doomed so many legacy acts like this one, as it was just beginning to explode into the mainstream.

Instead, it was the same old interpersonal issues. "I was sad to see it go, but there were personalities that made the band more difficult," Waite said, "and that's just the way it went, you know?"

They released a second single, "Time Stood Still," which found a home in the Top 20 in the Netherlands, but it was not enough to save Bad English.

"Unfortunately, Jonathan and John started fighting amongst themselves," Phillips said. "I can't remember where I was when I heard this, but I got the news that it was over. 'Jonathan and John Waite don't want to be in the same room together.' I was like, 'OK,'" he added with a chuckle. "I can't say that I didn't completely see this coming."

They had factionalized from the beginning, and ended up in the same place as The Babys once did. The only difference was how quickly everything fell apart this time with Cain and Waite.

"I always used to say he had a 'book of bastards' and once your name was in it, that's it," Cain told **Michael Cavacini**, laughing. "So, I'm in the book of bastards."

Cain would ultimately place the blame on their decision to record the **Diane Warren**-penned "When I See You Smile," which he has since described as the "kiss of death." But there were money problems, label problems, management problems, and arguments over publishing and song direction.

"There was something about Bad English. I wish the guys could have stuck it out, because we were going places," Phillips argued. "There was nothing we couldn't do—but you know, personalities. People can get their feelings hurt. It ended up tearing at the fiber and then, boom, the next thing you know, everybody's moving on."

Ever the individualist, Waite held himself separate from the others. Despite Bad English's quick ride to success, some part of him was always going to be a solo artist. "I think I was the odd man out," Waite said. "An old girlfriend of mine once told me backstage at a Bad English concert: I was the guy that didn't fit—and I was glad," he added with a laugh. "I'm still glad."

Phillips subsequently did session work, appearing on **Jimmy Page**'s **Coverdale/Page** collaboration with **David Coverdale**, and on tour with **Ronnie Montrose**. He then began a lengthy tenure with **Styx**.

"Finally, a lot of the things I wished would have happened in my past with both Neal and Jonathan have come true. I'm experiencing a kind of 'reaping what you sow' in this band," Phillips said. "It's a hard-working band. They take it very seriously—and they've made a lot of mistakes, too. They've learned from theirs, whereas I didn't have the fortune of being able to work out the kinks with those bands and those guys."

In time, that helped Phillips get over the sense of unfinished business that surrounded both The Babys and Bad English.

"It was a shame, because John and I had just written 'Time Stood Still,' and it was opening up a new thing that was a little bit bigger," Phillips added. "There were a couple of other songs on the record that were quite good." [11, 26, 531, 532]

SPRING 1992

RELEASES
▶ **The Storm** (with Ross Valory, Steve Smith, Gregg Rolie), "Show Me the Way" (single)
▶ **Hardline** (with Neal Schon, Deen Castronovo), *Double Eclipse* (album)
▶ **Hardline** (with Neal Schon, Deen Castronovo), "Takin' Me Down" (single)

Rolie, The Storm Find Success With New Single, Adams's Tour

Everything was coming together at just the right time for **The Storm**. Opening shows with **Bryan Adams** began in March 1992, just as the band's debut single finished a chart run that peaked in the *Billboard* Top 30. That added a new dimension to The Storm's first show at the Shoemaker Center in Cincinnati, Ohio. They were not some anonymous support act.

"So usually you have like maybe 300, 400, 500 people in the audience for the opener, because everybody wants to see the main headliner—but we had, like, thousands of people," **Josh Ramos** said. "I peek through the curtain and I'm like, 'Holy shit.' At that moment, I just said, 'Josh, this is what you've been working for your whole life. This is why you sat in your bedroom with records and you homed in on your instrument—because this was your dream.'"

Some critics still sniffed at their throwback approach: The "band is only slightly more than a '70s throwback quintet," according to a concert report in *Variety*. The reviewer also accused The Storm of "serving up a tasteless brew of watered-down new songs and reheated old ones from their respective former bands."

Fans obviously felt differently. Released in October 1991, "I've Got a Lot to Learn About Love" spent 20 weeks on the *Billboard* charts, topping out at No. 26 on the Hot 100 in early 1992—and an impressive No. 6 on the mainstream rock radio charts.

Gregg Rolie was not that surprised. "There is a whole audience of people that I think have been forgotten," he told Gannett News Service back then. "I don't think you turn a certain age, and all of a sudden you like **Lawrence Welk**."

It all conspired to create the biggest highlight of Ramos's young career. Looking for moral support on opening night, he says he sought out bandmate Ross Valory. "Ross was there with a shot of tequila for me—because he always did a shot," Ramos said. "I go, 'Yep, I fucking need this,' and I drank it. But when we get on stage, I was still nervous."

Then Ramos said he heard his guitar ring out over the crowd. "I was like, 'Fucking yes. This is me now,'" he remembered, "and from that moment on, I was not afraid anymore. I was not nervous. I just loved it from that moment on. But I'll always remember that, that time right there that I was proud of myself actually for the dream that I had dreamed. Finally, it was realized—but as fast as it came, it also went."

Buffeted by shifting currents in the wider music scene, The Storm's early momentum evaporated. Suddenly, their label was more interested in hip-hop, grunge, and alternative rock.

"I think we sold about 400,000 albums and we went out on a tour with Bryan Adams and did some on our own," Rolie later told *Mixdown*. "But then the record company, which was Interscope, right at the pinnacle of our success, changed the type of record label they were going to be."

"Show Me the Way," the second single from The Storm's self-titled debut, missed the Hot 100 entirely, while also failing to crack the Top 20 on the mainstream rock charts. [112, 220, 405, 546]

Schon Moves Into New Project, Hardline, As Bad English Ends

Neal Schon was on to his next project before **Bad English** officially ended, and it all started around the family stovetop.

Dubbed **Hardline**, the group's founding lineup included brothers **Joey** and **Johnny Gioeli**, **Todd Jensen**, and fellow Bad English alum Deen Castronovo.

"It was a struggling local Hollywood band," Johnny Gioeli said. "We were breaking records in every single venue; we were selling out in 20 minutes. But we never got a record deal—which was largely because we didn't have the right songs. I realize that now."

He ran into Schon at a friend's party, and down the line Schon ended up marrying Gioeli's sister. The initial connection was purely as family members.

"We never looked to Neal for any help in music, ever," Gioeli said. "We got together on holidays, and we didn't even talk about music. Then my brother and I were playing some music in our kitchen, and it was Christmastime. Neal heard a song called 'Face the Night' that we were working on—and he ran into the kitchen. He said, 'Let me see the guitar!' That's when it all started."

"Face the Night" did not see daylight until 2002's *Hardline II*, when the band finally regrouped after Schon's return to Journey. But a musical spark was lit.

"We asked Neal, 'Are you interested in producing?' We never even thought about having Neal in the group. We were a bunch of long-haired guys—and to us back then, he was old," Gioeli said with a laugh. "Now, we're the damned old guys."

In typical fashion, however, Schon was ready to go all in. Bad English bassist **Ricky Phillips** said Schon initially approached him about coming on board, but he was in no hurry to jump back into another band situation. Schon said, "'Hey, Ricky, I think you're really going to like this band. It's right up your alley'— and he ended up being right," Phillips said. "I thought, 'It's a good record—but it wasn't Bad English.'"

Ironically, Gioeli said the fledgling group initially turned Schon down. "Neal was so in love with this music, and so passionate about this relationship. We all got along so well—we still do. So, he said he wanted to be in the band, and I said 'No.' He said, 'What!? I'm Neal Schon, man. You don't want me in the band?' I'm like, 'No, we have a different vision for this thing.' But eventually, we caved and it was a good move to cave—and that's how Hardline was born."

In keeping with the band's origins in the family kitchen, their debut album began in a decidedly lo-fi setting before switching to A&M Studios in Hollywood.

"Even though Neal was obviously already a famous guy, he was as humble and down to earth as he could be," Gioeli said. "We literally recorded in my at-the-time girlfriend's apartment. We had a little eight-track-to-cassette recorder, and Neal was right there."

Gioeli was impressed by this deep commitment to the music: "Working with him was always hard, in respect of getting the work done. He was definitely not the traditional partying rock guy. When we started on a song, it just plagued us until we were finished. It's all we thought about."

Schon, it seemed, had arrived with something of a chip on his shoulder after years with Journey and then Bad English.

"He wanted to prove himself as a real rock guitar player—not as a Top 40 pop-hit guy," Gioeli said. "You know, sometimes it doesn't matter how much you own, how much you have. It's what you want to accomplish, and to fulfill those visions for what you can do. For Neal in that time period, that was it. Every-

body saw him as a pop-guitar player, and he was like, 'No, man. I want to frickin' kick ass.' It was humble, it was awesome—and I think that record today still stands as a classic rock album."

Their debut album, *Double Eclipse*, produced two Top 40 hits on the mainstream rock charts: the original "Takin' Me Down" and a cover of **Danny Spanos**'s "Hot Cherie." Then rock music took a dramatic turn, and Hardline simply stalled out.

"It's too bad, 'cause I think that record could have done very well, but right after it was released, **Nirvana** was a hit," Schon told interviewer **Kaj Roth**. "Then it was just nothing but grunge on the radio."

Schon departed, opting to work for a time with **Paul Rodgers** before returning to solo work and then Journey. Hardline did not release its next LP for a decade.

"If I could have changed anything, going back into the past, I would have been more aware of how special that band was," Gioeli added. "I wish I was more aware of how powerful the band was at that time. It was just like, 'This is a good fucking band,' and where are we going next to play? That was it. I really didn't have a chance to appreciate it."

When Gioeli finally put Hardline back together, The Storm's **Josh Ramos** became Schon's belated replacement when timing issues prevented guitarist **Joey Tafolla** from participating.

"Joey, I think he said, 'Well, you know, I'm gonna need like five weeks [in the studio] to do the solos," Ramos said. "And I think Johnny said, 'No, man, we don't have five weeks.' So, they called me."

By then, Castronovo and Jensen had both left to join **Ozzy Osbourne**'s tour. Ramos would go on to collaborate with Gioeli on 2009's *Leaving the End Open* and 2016's *Human Nature*.

Gioeli then reconnected with Castronovo on 2018's *Set the World on Fire*. "It was like immediate, absolutely immediate pickup from where we left off," Gioeli said. "I walked in and said, 'Jesus Christ, you got ugly as hell!' and we just started laughing. The jokes just flowed, like we never stopped. It was a great reunion." [26, 37, 183, 405]

WINTER–SPRING 1993

RELEASES

▶ **Journey**, "Lights" (single, reissue)
▶ **Just-If-I** (with Neal Schon), *Just-If-I* (album)

NUGGETS

▶ There are two versions of the re-issued, re-packaged "Lights" single taken from Journey's upcoming *Time³* box set. There's a live version (produced by **Kevin Elson**) from the *Captured* album and the studio version (produced by **Roy Thomas Baker**) from the *Infinity* LP. It's nice to hear Steve Perry's ample chops again having not heard them for some time, but still, no one will ever be able to tell me he wasn't trying to sound like **Sam Cooke** all along.
—*Cashbox*

Herbie Herbert Launches Alter Ego Blues Band, Sy Klopps

Herbie Herbert was becoming understandably restless as Journey remained in dry dock. Then he had a life-changing personal loss.

"In my mind, the most incredible thing Herbie has done relates to the time his mother died," former Journey lawyer **Glen Miskel** said in **Jim McCarthy**'s *Voices of Latin Rock*. "This pushed him in the direction of playing guitar."

Herbert had a deep resume of experience in the business, working his way up from roadie, to manager, to owner and operator of huge entertainment production companies. Being inside the spotlight hadn't occurred to him.

"I never thought of myself as ever, ever becoming a musician," he told the *San Francisco Chronicle*. "I thought, 'I sure wish I could play the blues because I really have the blues.'"

As usual, Herbert gave himself entirely to this new side hustle. "He started playing. The next thing, he was playing guitar and singing," Miskel added. "Then he was gigging. Soon after, he was out opening for major bands as the **Sy Klopps Blues Band**."

Herbert chalked it up to divine inspiration.

"[Heretofore], I couldn't make a note ring out. Then, all of a sudden, I could play the minute I picked it up," he told the *Chronicle*. "I don't know where it comes from or how it got there, and I'm not going to question it."

To his great surprise, Herbert found he loved performing. "It's something I should have been doing the whole time," Herbert told the *Vallejo Times-Herald*. "I just had a ball."

He initially hid behind the band name, pretending there was a separate person named Sy Klopps. "In my cold, analytical view, I would not be involved with an artist like that or believe he has an economically viable future," Herbert said of his doppelganger.

He also shifted management responsibilities to trusted confidant **Pat Morrow**. "I don't stay on top of any business aspect of Sy Klopps at all," Herbert told the *Chronicle*. "I'm clueless—the dumb artist." Meanwhile, he carved out space in his corporate offices to build a new studio.

Herbert ended up releasing a trio of Sy Klopps albums. Among them was 1993's memorably titled *Walter Ego*, which featured contributions from Gregg Rolie, Neal Schon, Prairie Prince, and Ross Valory.

Schon "wanted an excuse to fuck around with a bunch of effects pedals and other gear," San Francisco music legend **Bill Kreutzmann** wrote in *Deal: My Three Decades of Drumming, Dreams, and Drugs with the Grateful Dead*, while Herbert "just wanted to be in a band, period, I think."

Sy Klopps played San Francisco's legendary Fillmore Auditorium a total of 14 times, longtime assistant and family spokesperson **Maria Hoppe** later told the *Chronicle*. One of their most memorable shows featured **Steve Miller**, which surfaced on the 1995 video, *Live at the Fillmore*.

Later, Herbert and Sy Klopps guitarist **Ralph Woodson** formed a side band with Kreutzmann called the **Trichromes**. They "got on a tour bus, went for six weeks with [Kreutzmann's **Grateful Dead** bandmates] **Bob Weir**'s **RatDog** and **Phil [Lesh] and Friends**," Herbert told *Melodic Rock*, "and I had the complete touring experience." Trichromes released the *Dice with the Universe* EP and a self-titled LP, both in 2002.

Continued on Page 235

MORE THAN A HITS COLLECTION, *TIME³* SUMS UP AN ERA

*T*ime³ felt like a platinum-selling good-bye. There was a sense of commemoration surrounding this career-spanning three-disc compilation's arrival in December 1992, six long years after *Raised on Radio*.

Then there was the fact that the two newest songs were demos completed especially for this set by Neal Schon and Jonathan Cain—without any participation from Steve Perry.

In the meantime, the collection featured all of the hits—and a heaping helping of deep cuts. Fans finally got to hear "Cookie Duster," the **Mahavishnu Orchestra**-inspired Ross Valory song that Columbia Records pulled off the *Next* album at the very last moment. "For You" provided **Robert Fleischman**'s official Journey debut. Gregg Rolie's "Velvet Curtain" was another *Next*-era scrap that only found its way onto *Infinity* after Steve Perry reworked it into "Feeling That Way."

"It's a massive overview of the humble beginnings of Journey," Cain told the New York Times News Service. "This box set is testament to a band that started out as a fusion-rock band from the streets to become a great rock 'n' roll band."

Of historic interest was Journey's previously unreleased cover of **Sam Cooke**'s "Good Times," from the *1978 King Biscuit Flower Hour* performance where Steve Smith made his debut. At that point, Perry was not yet publicly owning up to Cooke's huge impact on his vocal style.

Video producer **Paul Flattery** brought it up backstage when overseeing a Journey shoot in 1979 at University of California, Berkeley's Zellerbach Auditorium. He remembered Perry saying: "You know that; I know that—but they don't know that," Perry added, gesturing toward the crowd. "Let's keep it that way."

If there were any lingering questions about Cooke's influence on Perry, this update of "Good Times" puts them to rest. Still, Flattery says Perry's approach was his own.

"Steve is certainly one of the most distinctive vocalists in rock music," Flattery added. "Somebody once said, 'The art of creativity is disguising one's sources,' but I don't know that he disguised it. He just knew that most of the fans wouldn't have known of Sam Cooke. That was just a part of his style. He was a fantastic vocalist. There's no doubt about it."

Time³ also underscored just how creative the *Frontiers* era had been, with two more extras:

"Liberty" and **The Babys**-style "All That Really Matters," the latter featuring a rare Cain vocal.

Still, these previously unheard items were overshadowed by the sheer implications of "With a Tear" and "Into Your Arms," two bonus tracks that emerged from the *Raised on Radio* sessions. Schon and Cain held finishing sessions in 1992, but were forced to release them as instrumentals since there was no vocalist.

Perry loomed over the *Time³* box set in other ways. According to **Joel Selvin**, his accompanying liner notes were heavily edited by Journey's long-departed front man.

Manager **Herbie Herbert** "praised them to the skies—a 'heart punch,' he called it," Selvin said. "Perry calls up real friendly, like we're old pals, and he says, 'I can't wait to proofread your work.' That's what he called it, 'proofreading.'"

When Perry returned the notes, entire sections had been excised, Selvin said. [60, 169, 435, 640]

Herbert ended up breaking some huge news at San Francisco's Biscuits and Blues Club before Sy Klopps went dormant. MTV reported that he casually informed a crowd in late September 1995 that Valory was not on stage because he had reunited with Steve Perry, Schon, Jonathan Cain, and an as-yet-unnamed drummer for a new Journey project. [376, 574, 575, 576, 577, 578, 579, 580]

FALL 1993

NUGGETS

▶ Former Journey members Neal Schon, Gregg Rolie, and Ross Valory join up with the likes of **David Denny**, **Bobby Scott**, **Kee Marcello**, **Prairie Prince**, and **Norton Buffalo** under the pseudonym **The Legendary Sy Klopps Band**, and its album, *Walter Ego*.
—*Billboard*

Journey's Anniversary Event Draws Perry's Replacement

Members of Journey reunited in October 1993 to honor **Herbie Herbert**, celebrating the 30th anniversary of the group's founding. Steve Perry did not show up.

Gregg Rolie, Neal Schon, Aynsley Dunbar, Ross Valory, Steve Smith, and Jonathan Cain gathered at Bimbo's 365 Club in San Francisco, joined by an all-star cast of attendees including **Steve Miller**, **Gregg Allman**, **Buddy Guy**, **Moby Grape**, **Joe Satriani**, **Robert Plant**, and others.

Rolie took his customary role at the mic for live versions of "I'm Gonna Leave You" and "Of a Lifetime" before a special guest vocalist took the stage. "I didn't know who would perform," Herbert told *Classic Rock Revisited*. "**Moby Grape** came and performed and all these bands that I was friendly with, and Journey performed with **Kevin Chalfant**. I was shocked."

Chalfant had an earlier loose association with Cain as a member of the turn-of-the-1980s AOR group **707**, who came closest to wider fame with the Cain co-written "Mega Force" in 1982. Chalfant then co-wrote "Who You Gonna Believe" for **Cher**'s 1991 album *Love Hurts*, not long after she hired **Ron**

Wikso as tour drummer. Chalfant and Wikso were later bandmates in the Herbert-managed **The Storm** with Gregg Rolie.

Chalfant traded vocals with Rolie on "Just the Same Way," then took over for "Don't Stop Believin'" and "Separate Ways." By then, Cain had assumed his customary spot at the keyboard and Dunbar had traded spots with Steve Smith.

Once the surprise wore off, Herbert admitted the switch to stronger-voiced Chalfant made sense. He had been horrified by Perry's vocal issues at the massive tribute concert for **Bill Graham**. "Steve gave it everything he had," Cain argued in *Don't Stop Believin'*, "but his voice had dropped a whole step."

Chalfant acquitted himself well enough that he said momentum began to build for a long-awaited Journey reunion. "In the days following, Gregg, Neal, Jonathan and I started writing songs," Chalfant told the *Illinois Entertainer*. "I guess the idea was, 'Hey, Kevin could do this, so why don't we just do this with Kevin?' That was the plan, but that plan changed."

The popular theory was always that Chalfant lost the job when Steve Perry re-entered the picture. But Cain said Journey had not seriously considered Chalfant for front man duties before reuniting with Perry for *Trial by Fire*—or after Perry's final departure.

"We looked at him for a second," Cain told **Michael Cavacini**, but "we never talked about Chalfant or anybody. We just walked away from it realizing that we had come to an impasse."

When Journey returned, it was with **Steve Augeri** instead of Chalfant. Herbert thought Chalfant may have lost out because of something that happened during his time with Cain in 707.

"There is some kind of baggage there," Herbert told *Classic Rock Revisited*. "With Jon Cain, baggage is his middle name. That was a mistake, though. They really should have followed through with that."

Chalfant would later mount a tour dubbed "Kevin Chalfant's Journey Experience," with promotional material stating that he'd briefly replaced Perry in the 1993 Thunder Road benefit "by request of the band's late manager **Herbie Herbert**." That's not how Herbert remembered it: "I didn't pick the bands or book it," Herbert confirmed to *Melodic Rock*.

"Some Things Are Better Left Unsaid," a song Chalfant collaborated on with Schon and Rolie during their early-1990s writing sessions, finally found a home on the 2010 album *Burning Bright*, the most recent album from his group **Two Fires**, which also featured former Storm bandmate **Josh Ramos**. [376, 547, 555, 556, 557, 558, 559]

SUMMER 1994

RELEASES
▶ **Steve Perry**, "You Better Wait" (single)
▶ **Steve Perry**, *For the Love of Strange Medicine* (album)

Perry Offers Cautionary Tale In *Medicine*'s Leadoff Single

Journey lambasted the eccentric **Roy Thomas Baker** when he exited after 1979's *Evolution*, but his fingerprints were still on everything that followed.

Steve Perry's Top 30 solo hit "You Better Wait" arrived on June 28, 1994, more than 15 years after Journey's first Baker-produced single "Lights." Yet a very Baker-esque opening wash of wordless multitracked vocals shepherded in his new band.

"There's maybe as many as 20 Steves in there," Perry told *Raw* magazine. "It just sounds so creamy, doesn't it?"

This cautionary tale of a song spoke to the way youthful dreams can go wrong. Perry said he directed "You Better Wait" specifically at those who come to Los Angeles chasing fame, only to find themselves sidetracked by its excesses. "Because you can see people flipping across their dreams into problems," he told **John Stix** for *Open Arms: The Steve Perry Anthology*, "and losing sight of what they came here for."

That too suggested the Baker era, when Perry matured from uncredentialed newcomer to platinum-selling star. Once "You Better Wait" got underway, however, Perry moved confidently away from most Journey-isms.

It was no small surprise. Perry was not exact-ly promising a modern-era remodel. "Timeless music doesn't follow any trends," he told the *Orlando Sentinel* in a contemporary interview. "It stays true unto itself and isn't afraid to do that." Perry added he was unwilling to "chase after the flavor of the month because by the time you get there, it's changed."

He did not sound like someone ready to try something new. But a nervy, surprisingly episodic formulation unfolded. Perry tried out growling low-end vocals amid a nuclear-test-range riff. Guitarist **Lincoln Brewster** then paused for the requisite heart-squeezing solo, but "You Better Wait" otherwise swerved from guardrail to guardrail.

The result feels like the first—and the last—real attempt by Steve Perry to move past being Steve Perry. No small amount of credit goes to his newly minted backing group. They were fully vested through the creative process, echoing Journey's approach in their classic era without retracing it all step by step. That trust belied their decidedly light resumes.

Keyboardist **Paul Taylor** was previously with **Winger**, but Brewster was a new discovery of former Journey bassist Randy Jackson. Drummer **Moyes Lucas Jr.** simply knocked on the door as Perry went through another endless audition cycle, similar to the slog Journey endured before the *Raised on Radio* tour.

Brewster, Lucas, and Taylor earned co-songwriting credits on "You Better Wait," along with **John Pierce**, **George Hawkins**, and Perry. "He said, 'This is a band. ... I don't want a bunch of studio musicians doing the record and then have to audition guys to go on the road,'" Lucas told *Modern Drummer*.

In the end, it may have taken every one of their contributions to finally complete things. Perry later admitted that he struggled to align all the moving parts on this song. "That evolved so many times," he told Stix.

He still needed to get "You Better Wait" onto the radio and store shelves. By then, Columbia Records was owned and controlled by Sony, and his new bosses wanted a more conservative lead single. "Sony didn't like it, just so you know," Perry told *Melodic Rock*. "It's too bad because it used to be a music company. Somewhere along the lines, it became something else."

His intuition proved correct. Perry followed

"You Better Wait" with a trio of songs that more closely followed his old playbook, and only one of them charted at all—"Missing You" at No. 74.

The rush of attention around his return had quickly dissipated, but "You Better Wait" was not to blame. For all its interior innovations, the single was still authentically Steve Perry. The sentiment, if not the structure, fits into his larger arc.

Then, for whatever reason, Perry lost his nerve. The album-opening "You Better Wait" proved to be a notable outlier rather than a new creative direction, both through the rest of *For the Love of Strange Medicine* and into his next career move—an unlikely reunion with Journey. [273, 505, 515, 564, 565]

FALL 1994

NUGGETS

▶ Steve Perry begins a 91-stop tour for his new album, *For Love of Strange Medicine*, with singer-songwriter **Sass Jordan** as the opener. —*Billboard*

▶ Randy Jackson is feeling the holiday spirit. He picks up the bass for **Mariah Carey** for a couple cuts on her new *Merry Christmas* album, "Christmas (Baby Please Come Home)" and "Santa Claus is Comin' To Town," and then joins **Kenny G** for "Silver Bells" on his *Miracles: The Holiday Album.* —*Spin*

Shaking Off the Dust, Perry Cues Up 91-City U.S. Tour

Steve Perry hadn't toured for more than seven years when he took the stage on October 21, 1994 in Milwaukee. Yet there were no jitters.

"In a lot of ways, it's similar to riding a bicycle. But this time around, it's different," Perry told the *Hartford Courant*. "It's more exciting and more fun for me personally."

Working with the same band who helped complete *For the Love of Strange Medicine* certainly helped ease the transition. So did being able to pull from a deep well of songs, both solo and with his former group.

There were setlist tweaks as the tour progressed, but he consistently opened with "Only

the Young" before turning to early show favorites like "Girl Can't Help It," "Lights," and "Foolish Heart." A warm sense of nostalgia enveloped it all.

"It's been so long," Perry declared to the audience during a tour stop in Salt Lake City. "Last time we were in a room together I believe I was in another band called Journey. Am I right?"

His fresh-faced onstage collaborators took on unflashy support roles, often simply mimicking the old parts without adding much. Critics inevitably pounced.

Perry's vocals were described as "clean, firm and soaring" after a concert at Stabler Arena in Bethlehem, Pennsylvania, but the backing group was simply excoriated. Guitarist **Lincoln Brewster**'s leads were "formulaic," drummer **Moyes Lucas**'s backbeats were "draggy," keyboardist **Paul Taylor** was mechanical, and bassist **Todd Jensen** was "basically a non-presence."

Lucas countered that Perry's touring band was never supposed to be the focus. "If you see someone like Steve Perry, the highlight of the show is Steve," Lucas told *Modern Drummer*. "If I come off stage and people are going, 'Wow, man, you stole the show,' I did something wrong."

A stinging review in *Variety* took aim at Perry for failing to move "beyond the simple themes and cloying delivery" from his time with Journey, even while admitting that it was "fine with the crowd."

Unbothered, Perry began to feel emboldened enough to segue into principal influence **Sam Cooke**'s "Cupid" at the end of "I'll Be Alright Without You." "I'm just trying to sneak my soul, R&B and gospel influences into what I do," he told *Raw* magazine, "so that nobody knows what's going on—but hopefully they'll like it all the same."

Still, the most memorable part of the night for a fan base in the mood to reminisce involved the return of a key look from his days in Journey.

"He was really like Mr. Show Business," longtime San Francisco music writer **Joel Selvin** said. "They lowered the old ringmaster's coat from the rafters at one point, and he played this game of 'should I put it on or not?' The crowd just went nuts for it."

Perry, it seemed, had regained his passion

Continued on Page 241

Perry Returns with Deeply Personal Second CD

Journey's first six albums came out annually through 1980. They only issued three studio LPs for the rest of the decade. Steve Perry's muse had ground to a shuddering halt by the time *Raised on Radio* hit store shelves in May 1986. Along the way, he attempted a solo follow-up to 1984's *Street Talk*, only to see it shelved.

"At that point, I had nothing in my heart to sing about anymore," Perry told *Billboard*. "I was sung out."

Emotionally spent, Journey's former front man said he was suffering from fatigue, job burnout, "and all sorts of other things happening in my personal life as the result of that 10-year burn.

"I had to get off the merry-go-round," he told his hometown paper, *The Hanford Sentinel*, in December 1994. "And there is no easy way to get off when everyone else is on it with you. But I really felt my life depended on it. I couldn't make anyone understand it at the time, and I don't know if I can make them understand it now."

That time away allowed Perry to come to some important realizations, and one of them was reflected in the title of his long-awaited sophomore solo LP, *For the Love of Strange Medicine*.

"More times than I'd care to mention, I have hinged my happiness on outside stuff—strange medicine," Perry said. "Whether it's gambling, or relationships, or a new car, or winning the lotto, whatever. It's all strange medicine because it only works so long."

The road back was winding, but Perry did not travel it alone—at least not after the initial demo stage. *For the Love of Strange Medicine* would become an intimate, broadly collaborative project.

Perry co-wrote "Donna Please" with **Stephen Bishop**, who scored a few soft rock hits at the turn of the 1980s. Also chipping in were studio aces **Michael Landau** on guitar ("Anyway") and **Mike Porcaro** on bass ("Young Hearts Forever," "I Am," the title track, "Donna Please," and "Listen to Your Heart").

Perry grew close to keyboardist **Paul Taylor**, guitarist **Lincoln Brewster**, and drummer **Moyes Lucas Jr.**, all of whom had a hand in principal composing and sessions. Taylor "had a sense of melodics in his chord changes that I had not heard before and I liked it a lot," Perry told *The Han-*

ford Sentinel. Brewster's playing had "heart."

The album took more than a year to complete, but Perry found his muse really opened up with the help of this all-new band, and occasional writing partner, **Tim Miner**.

For instance, "Listen to Your Heart" grew out of the first jam session that Perry, Brewster and Taylor had with Lucas. "A lot of the songs were conceived in a jam/rehearsal situation, which is the best," Perry said. "They weren't conceived in a room with a keyboard and then [made] big—they were born big."

"I love working in that situation," he continued. "You get to hear it, you get to feel it, you get to stand in front of it. And that's [where] the real follow-through, emotionally, comes from."

Perry had stumbled onto Miner's records, and "I thought he had an incredible, emotional voice," Perry told interviewer **John Stix**. "I also heard that he wrote a lot of his stuff. I wanted to write with him." Miner's vocal style also had an impact on the sessions: "Because I had such respect for his voice, I think it helped me pull something out of myself I wouldn't otherwise have," Perry added.

First, Perry had to convince Miner he was not an impostor. "I thought I was being pranked by one of my friends or family," Miner said. "They have pranked me before exactly like this, pretending to be someone amazing who wanted to work with me. After some random quizzing—and there was no specific question—he finally said, 'Tim, it's me.' That is what convinced me."

Brewster had a hand in connecting them by passing along Miner's self-titled 1992 album, issued on Motown. Miner remembered Perry saying: "The last song on the album is 'Forgive Me.' I either want to re-record that song or write something that feels like that."

The album's liner notes for *Tim Miner* included contact information for his manager. "That's how Steve found me," said Miner who would co-write and co-produce "Missing You," while also co-producing "Anyway."

Landau, a critical figure on *Street Talk*, helped to solidify Miner's budding creative bond with Perry. "I have produced hundreds of artists and songs and my go-to studio guitar player for decades has always been my friend Michael Landau," Miner said. "When Steve asked me, 'Who should we call'? I said Michael, not realizing he and Steve had worked together many, many times too."

Brewster played a key musical role in the No. 29 hit "You Better Wait," a layered lead single that showcased Perry's more oaken vocals. He now accepted changes that had taken place during those grueling years with Journey. "I'm more proud of my voice now than I was then," Perry told the *Orlando Sentinel*. "It's different. It's matured a bit."

"You Better Wait" was another example of how collaborative these sessions were, even very late in the process. "I remember that it started out differently than it ended up," Perry told his hometown newspaper. As he was mixing the song with **Niko Bolas**, "we got this idea ... to start with the 'Ahhhhs.' At the last minute ... we were able to pull that idea off."

Perry recorded "Missing You" with the **Dallas Symphony Orchestra** and the single version followed "You Better Wait" into the *Billboard* adult-contemporary Top 25. The commercial landscape had shifted considerably since Perry released *Street Talk*.

Even Columbia Records' marketing vice president was blunt about the obstacles. "There have been a lot of changes since the last Journey album," **Diarmuid Quinn** told *Billboard*. "Radio has changed. Journey used to be an automatic add, but it's not the same world."

Perry ended up scoring an unlikely gold-selling Top 20 hit album, but "Missing You" would be his last charting single until his long-awaited comeback with *Traces* in 2018.

In the meantime, "Missing You" provided Miner's most indelible memory from the era, though this moment took place far away from studios like Ocean Way Recording and the Record Plant, where *For the Love of Strange Medicine* was completed.

"We had just finished recording the orchestra

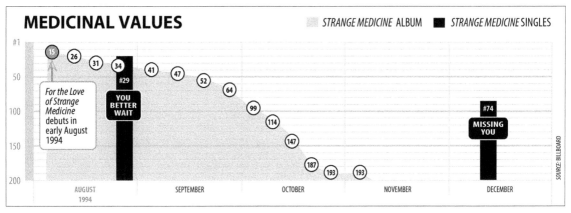

MEDICINAL VALUES

STRANGE MEDICINE ALBUM   STRANGE MEDICINE SINGLES

For the Love of Strange Medicine debuts in early August 1994

YOU BETTER WAIT — #29

MISSING YOU — #74

AUGUST 1994   SEPTEMBER   OCTOBER   NOVEMBER   DECEMBER

SOURCE: BILLBOARD

Steve Perry's long-awaited second solo album arrived with a bang in the summer of 1994, marking 10 years since he released *Street Talk*, his first multiplatinum album in 1984. Since then, he had gone through several iterations of his sophomore album. First named *Against the Wall*, it would evolve into *For the Love of Strange Medicine*. Along the way, he learned that things had changed at his longtime label. Columbia Records was acquired by Sony and was now Sony Music Entertainment. The music industry had changed a lot since then. Grunge and hip-hop had ascended and rock had declined. But *Strange Medicine* proved that Perry's fan base was loyal and eager to hear his work. Sony released *Strange Medicine* in early August 1994, and it debuted at No. 15 on the *Billboard* 200 chart—notable for Perry having been away for so long. The leadoff single, "You Better Wait," returned Perry to the Top 40, where it stayed for the month of August and into September. It would stay in *Billboard*'s Hot 100 for 15 weeks before finally falling out in late October. Sony released a second single, "Missing You," in November, which debuted at No. 87 and rose up to No. 74, but faded quickly. Even though "Missing You" got solid adult contemporary airplay, the single did not boost album sales. *Strange Medicine* would not re-enter the chart.

for 'Missing You' and Steve was staying in a near-by hotel that had a grand piano in the lobby with 50-foot ceilings and beautiful marble floors and walls," Miner said. "The acoustics were amazing! I sat down and just started playing 'Missing You' to hear it in that setting. He sat down next to me and began singing."

Miner said a crowd soon surrounded them: "It literally went from two people sitting at a piano to hundreds gathering around to listen to one of the greatest voices of all time."

Perry closed out the album by directly addressing his estrangement from Journey on "Anyway." Miner said the song emerged from "many casual conversations about his time with the band. Some were joyful and funny, and some were painful and hurtful."

Perry sang, "We believed in music. Brothers 'til the end. Nothin' stood between us. The fire burned within," but the track exuded regret. "We did believe in music 'til the bitter end," Perry told *Melodic Rock*, but communication kept breaking down.

"This is what the song is about," he said. "Just about every time somebody gets close to being able to talk about something that really needs to be talked about, it would get too emotionally close. And the best I could do was 'anyway, what was I saying?' You know what I mean? Everybody does this... 'Anyway, it's not important.'"

"We had that spark. We had that goalpost in our hearts, all of us," Perry added. He called "Anyway" his "homage to them, and I don't think any of the Journey members ever heard it, to be honest with you."

There was talk of a solo tour, and a denial that any reunion with Journey was in the cards. "I think they're pretty determined at this point to do what they want to do," Perry told the *Orlando Sentinel* back then, "and I think it's definitely without me."

The tour happened, and so did the reunion. *For the Love of Strange Medicine* peaked on the *Billboard* album chart in August 1994. By 1995, Perry had surprised Jonathan Cain with his first phone call in years, and Journey was suddenly rekindled. [24, 276, 515, 561, 562, 883]

New York Times
July 29, 1994

Let's not kid ourselves: The best of Journey was hands-down better than the best of **Duran Duran**; listening to Steve Perry's appealing husky vocals over Journey's sleek light-metal arrangements was one of the better guilty-pleasure/hope-nobody-sees-me thrills early '80s radio had. That is exactly why *For the Love of Strange Medicine*, Perry's first solo record since *Street Talk,* rarely stacks up to either that effort or Journey's best moments. Perry's voice is still a wonder, but he wastes too much time here on middle-of-the-road ballads. A couple, such as the gospelish "Somewhere There's Hope," are just fine, but too many sound too much the same. What was needed here were a few more sleek, strongly arranged pop rockers, such as "You Better Wait." On that song and a couple others, Perry's ability to ride atop the whipcrack production and sanded guitars would make any Journey fan sit up and take notice. It's too bad he holds himself back and goes for the pathos over and over.

— *Dave Ferman*

Knight-Ridder News Service
August 17, 1994

It's summer and you know it because Steve Perry's voice is on the radio. The former lead singer of '80s megarock band Journey brings back glorious, hood-thumpin' GTO rock with "You Better Wait," the single from his new album. "Wait," the first cut, is propelled by Perry's voice, whose strength and alluring whine makes it one of rock's most identifiable sounds. The song has bucket-like drums, a careening guitar solo and stunning background harmonies. As you listen, you drive a little faster, breathe a little deeper, feel capable of anything. None of the other songs on Perry's second solo effort has quite the same effect. "I Am" is a good example of how wrong things can go, with a cornball strings opening and one especially inane lyric, repeated: *"I'm lo-o-st in a world of emptiness."* Uh huh. Without classic tunes, Perry's voice acquires a cloying, peanut-but-ter-fudge-pie quality: At first rich and satisfying, it becomes less appealing with each bite, and impossible to finish.

— *Teresa Gubbins*

Miami Herald
August 17, 1994

If Steve Perry had been really clever, he would have included aspirin samples with his *For the Love of Strange Medicine* CD. It would have been the only original concept connected with this project, and anyone who has to listen to this overblown, truly wretched relic of bad '80s power pop from Journey's ex-lead singer is guaranteed a headache the size of Texas. It's not just that Perry is over-rated as a singer. Sure, he's got breath control and can bellow with the best of them; but more often than not he sings flat. Worse, his generic songs in the you-loved-me-once, why-don't-you-love-me-now vein sound more like rejects from the **Michael Bolton** catalog. This is Perry's second solo album. It'll please longtime fans to know Perry still sounds the same. But for the love of good music, all others must avoid *For the Love of Strange Medicine*.

— *Howard Cohen*

for touring. "I tell you it feels like we just left each other," Perry said in Salt Lake City. "I am grateful to be able to sing for you once again. You've always been the faithful ones."

Then Perry once again cut a tour short. *Billboard* magazine reported a "severe respiratory illness," and said Perry was prescribed bed rest. He ended up playing more than 50 shows, finishing in March 1995 back home in California.

Brewster, Lucas, and Taylor moved on to other projects. Still, the idea that all of this was leading to a reunion with Journey seemed utterly implausible—in particular for Jonathan Cain, following an incident at Perry's Warfield Theatre stop in San Francisco.

"I was turned away because my name wasn't on the list," Cain said in his memoir. He'd assumed **Herbie Herbert** was going to make sure there were passes at will call. "I did know one thing: I wasn't going to buy a ticket."

Taylor returned to work with **Alice Cooper** before touring with **Styx**'s **Tommy Shaw** and then reuniting with **Winger**. Lucas sat in with **Bruce Hornsby**, **Larry Carlton**, and **Solomon Burke**,

among others. Brewster made the most dramatic career change, exiting rock altogether to delve into faith-based music.

The initial transition wasn't easy. "It was a suit-and-tie church, and I had long hair and an earring," Brewster told *The Grand Rapids Press*. "It was like a bad '80s video." However, he said it was the right choice: "I wanted to give my life to something that has more of an eternal value," he later told the *Quad-City Times*.

Jensen, who had been a part of **Hardline** with Schon, worked with Alice Cooper before taking over for a returning Randy Jackson in Journey. By then, Perry was long gone. His willingness to delve so deeply into Journey's catalog on these dates also inadvertently played a role in the group's decision to move on after *Trial by Fire*.

"He was out doing a solo tour and he was playing Journey songs," Neal Schon told *Ultimate Classic Rock*'s **Matt Wardlaw**, "and so at that point, I went: 'There's no harm in Jon and I trying to re-form this band.'" [60, 564, 565, 566, 567, 568, 569, 570, 571, 572, 573, 589]

SIGNS OF LIFE

The breakup of Journey was never really official; it was just silently accepted. Steve Perry was mostly in isolation, peeking out briefly for a solo album. The rest of the band developed other projects. Then Columbia Records beckoned. Their nudge led to coffee, and suddenly a reunion was happening. It was nothing short of miraculous. It became short-lived.

SPRING–SUMMER 1995

RELEASES
▶ Neal Schon, *Beyond the Thunder* (album)
▶ Jonathan Cain, *Back to the Innocence* (album)

NUGGETS
▶ Jonathan Cain, the former keyboardist for **The Babys**, Journey, and **Bad English** will have music from his new Intersound Records solo album *Back to the Innocence* used in the May 22 closing episode of the TV mega-hit *Melrose Place*, which commands an audience of 25 to 35 million viewers each week. —*Billboard*

Schon's *Beyond the Thunder* Gives a Shout-Out to Perry

Neal Schon's first solo album in six years followed work with **Bad English** and **Hardline**. Ironically, the all-instrumental *Beyond the Thunder* also pointed to his next collaboration.

It was not only that Schon co-wrote all but two of the songs with Jonathan Cain, who also played keyboards and handled string arrangements on "Deep Forest." Or that Steve Smith returned to play on five tracks. Or that "Big Moon" so closely recalled Journey's melodic past by featuring the same guitar Schon used in the Top 15 1986 hit "I'll Be Alright Without You."

It was all the above, and more.

For Schon, *Beyond the Thunder* was a welcome return to open musical spaces that don't conform to any narrative. "It was harder to learn how to write for vocalists than doing the instrumental thing," Schon admitted to *Goldmine*, "because that's where I came from."

Cain's presence, however, provided its own steering winds. His lithe approach to songwriting gave the LP a gravitas not always present on Schon's typically fiery solo work—but it also seems to have kept Schon from getting untracked. In a manner befitting its title, *Beyond the Thunder* could be distractingly contemplative.

"This is the first record where I really concentrated to make sure it wasn't an overstatement," Schon said in the album's liner notes. "It's a whole lot easier for me to do those 20-minute fastball guitar solos."

Those were certainly scarce on *Beyond the Thunder*, as Schon seemed to have overcorrected. The LP included turns by **Chepito Areas** and **Michael Carabello**, Schon's former pre-Journey bandmates from **Santana** who provide some of the album's most animated exchanges. In the end, however, there were too few of them.

Thankfully, *Beyond the Thunder* is not remembered for its tendency toward a kind of smooth jazz journey. More memorable are Schon's liner notes, in which he also surprised many with a direct shout-out to Journey's long-estranged front man: "I think Steve Perry is going to like this record."

Their short-lived reunion for *Trial by Fire* would soon be underway. In the meantime, Schon said recording *Beyond the Thunder* had a grounding effect.

"I'm really excited about getting back together with Journey because I think the music we make will take on a whole new direction," Schon told *Musician* back then. "It's going to be more mature and experimental, too." [126, 242, 586]

Reunion Begins with Herbert Departing, Azoff Arriving

Herbie Herbert and Steve Perry had many disagreements over the years. How Journey ended up reuniting was one of them.

Columbia Records A&R executive **John Kalodner** played the matchmaking role with Jonathan Cain and Neal Schon, Perry told *Billboard*. He then met Cain at a coffee shop, admitting he was surprised his former bandmate's number hadn't changed.

"I said, 'Just listen man, before it's too late,'" Perry added. 'For reasons only God knows, there's a lot of people out there who love us, and I saw some of them not too long ago. Maybe it's time to try again.'"

Then they brought Schon into the conver-

Continued on Page 245

THE STORM RELEASES NEW ALBUM, BUT LABEL PULLS PLUG

Gregg Rolie had already led two bands to platinum-level success. His bandmates were confident he could navigate **The Storm** through whatever was ahead.

"Gregg got his degree at the University of CBS," Ross Valory told Gannett News Service back then. "It's kind of a profound change to have someone like that in the framework of the band."

As sessions for their second album got underway, The Storm was also adjusting to Steve Smith's replacement on drums. **Ron Wikso** had been with the band through the touring cycle, however, and felt he had a good handle on what was required.

"Needless to say, if you ask me, Steve is one of the most incredible monster drummers of all time," Wikso said. "I have to say that the idea of replacing him in The Storm was a little daunting, at first. Fortunately, the music was kind of in my wheelhouse, so to speak, and the rest of the guys were very cool and accepting of me when I joined the band."

Rolie got to work, eventually co-writing every song on an album that was to be titled *Eye of the Storm*. Unfortunately, they'd be confronted by a sea change in the industry. Flinty, harder-edged sounds like grunge and rap were moving to the fore.

Jimmy Iovine reacted accordingly. He'd co-founded Interscope as a rock label with **Beau Hill**, but recently signed a distribution deal to release songs by the likes of **Dr. Dre** and **Snoop Dogg**. "Right at the pinnacle of our success, [Interscope] changed the type of record label they were going to be," Rolie told *Mixdown*. "They changed their whole persona and that was the end of it."

Not long after The Storm completed sessions for this sophomore album, "Jimmy Iovine basically fired Beau Hill," **Josh Ramos** said, "and everything that Beau Hill had to do with was out the door." That included The Storm, whose debut LP had been produced by Hill.

"I was never a big fan of Interscope becoming the gangster rap capital of the universe," Hill later told *Noisecreep*, pinpointing The Storm as one of the bands that deserved better. "There is selling records and then there's selling your soul."

The Storm's former label offered one parting gift: "They said, 'You can take your album with you and try to get a deal somewhere else. You don't need to pay us,'" Ramos add-

ed. "Then they became this big rap label with **Suge Knight** and all that. It was, like, horrible, man, because Interscope was a great label, a new label—and, yeah, we had a chance."

That turn of events had a personal impact on Wikso. "Before it fell apart, we sat in [Storm manager] Herbie Herbert's office and listened to the whole record—and at that meeting, it was decided that one of the songs I'd co-writ-

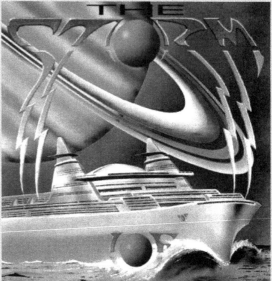

The Storm relied on the artistic talents of veteran designer **Hugh Syme** for their first self-titled album in 1991, but the group went back to familiar names for their second: **Alton Kelley** and **Jim Welch**. Some of the most iconic designs in Journey's history were developed by Kelley and **Stanley Mouse**, with Welch as art director. The Storm's design for *Eye of the Storm* employed classic Kelley artistic flairs, including the psychedelic letters emblazoned around a red orb (above, top) set against foreboding storm clouds, while the European release (bottom) featured a spacier design with a cruise ship plowing through the ocean.

ten, a song called 'Waiting for the World to Change,' was going to be the first single. I was, of course, elated at that."

It was the last of many missed opportunities for this star-crossed AOR group.

Ramos said one of their songs was considered by director **Ron Howard**'s hit 1991 film *Backdraft*. "But then all of a sudden, they wanted to change the words so that it would fit more to the movie, right?" Ramos said. "I mean, fuck, if I wrote the song, let's do anything to get The Storm out there—to get them, like, worldwide recognition. But Gregg said no, and we lost out on it."

Discussions to place "Call Me" from *Eye of the Storm* in a telephone commercial also fell through, Ramos said. The Storm couldn't survive without that kind of external help. Record labels and radio stations simply were no longer supporting albums like this one.

"There were a lot of people who would've liked to have heard it," Valory told **Mick Burgess**. "Unfortunately, the album was offered at a time when the industry really wasn't interested in that kind of music."

There were brief hints that Storm front man **Kevin Chalfant** might be brought into a reformulated Journey lineup including Rolie, Neal Schon, and Jonathan Cain. That concerned Herbert, who appreciated Chalfant's talent but felt "he was too much like [Steve] Perry," Herbert told **Matthew Carty**. "He would've been a problem child just like Perry was."

Members of The Storm had now scattered. Rolie sat in on a partial **Santana** reunion in **Abraxas Pool**, then re-established his solo career with Wikso in tow. Valory would go on to work with Herbert on the **Sy Klopps Blues Band**'s *Walter Ego* LP, before returning to Journey when they finally reunited with Perry in the mid-1990s.

By then it was clear to Valory why offshoot bands like The Storm struggled. "Unfortunately, we couldn't get arrested," Valory told **Mark Diggins**. "You're a member of Journey, but you're not Journey."

"Yeah, this was my whole dream for my whole life," Ramos said. "I just knew, 'Okay, this is what I want to put my heart into. This is what I'm going to do.' And to finally have it and then all of a sudden, it be taken from you because of whatever circumstances—grunge, rap? You know, it's like, 'God, really?'" [25, 112, 195, 220, 222, 405, 592, 793, 895, 903]

sation. But Perry did not want to work with Herbert again, Cain wrote in his autobiography. "He had a terrible animus toward Herbie," longtime *San Francisco Chronicle* music writer **Joel Selvin** confirmed. "Part of his negotiations were to minimize Herbie's influence over the band."

A conflicted Cain said it fell to him to let Herbert down easy. "I was torn between my loyalty to the man who took me from rags to riches," Cain said, "and an iconic singer and bandmate who made my songs famous."

Herbert, on the other hand, said Cain and Schon approached him first about re-forming—and he wanted nothing to do with Perry. Herbert said he chose retirement over managing a Perry-led lineup: "I'm not going to work with him again," he remembered saying. "I've had nearly 10 years of bliss not having to deal with that guy," he told writer **Neil Daniels**.

Either way, Journey chose to replace Herbert with **Irving Azoff**, an industry heavyweight who has worked with **Eagles**, **Steely Dan**, **Van Halen**, **Guns N' Roses** and others.

"There was something about him that gave me assurance that a lot of our business problems would be solved," Perry told **John Stix**, "and I'd be able to let go and just be a singer-songwriter with the band again." He felt Azoff would "take care of all the details, and it felt so good to know that."

Columbia Records wanted any reunion to feature everyone from their mega-platinum early-1980s era. Ross Valory quickly came on board, but Steve Smith needed convincing. A September 1995 rehearsal without Perry showed him that the musical connection remained. Perry joined them a day later, and everything fell into place.

Smith's return from the world of jazz provided a final piece for this musical puzzle, and it was deceptively important. "There are guys who maybe have a similar level of chops, and guys who play great in a few different styles of music," Smith's Storm-era replacement **Ron Wikso** said, "but in my opinion, at least, he has only a few peers when it comes to his overall musicality combined with his technique, knowledge, and experience."

Ironically, Smith came into the *Trial by Fire* era feeling like he was at a distinct disadvantage in those areas. He had played very intuitively the first time around and ended up getting sacked. "When I realized this reunion was inevitable, I decided to really do my homework on rock 'n' roll," Smith told *Modern Drummer* back then.

He also dug into mid-century blues, since it had been such an influence on Schon, and read a biography about **Sam Cooke** because he had meant so much to Perry. "I decided to approach the music from a completely different perspective, more from the roots of rock 'n' roll," Smith added.

That was just what others thought they had lost in the new arrangement with Azoff. Herbert was typically blunt in his assessment.

"I love Irving," Herbert told **Matthew Carty**. "He's who I'd want to replace me if you were gonna have a traditional, typical manager." Of course, no one could ever accuse Herbert of being traditional, having generously shared ownership shares and profits. He even arranged severance packages when band members left.

Azoff, however, is "not your partner," Herbert said he told Journey. "He makes a lot more money than you guys do." One of Herbert's staunchest supporters, Selvin argued the group had lost its soul. "They're just another Irving Azoff-managed band now," he said. "There's no 'band' in there anymore."

One way or another, however, Journey was re-forming. Perry admitted to *Billboard* that the reaction to their songs on his recent solo tour had an enormous impact. "Underneath it all, I was missing more and more being the singer of Journey than I ever thought I would," he said. [25, 60, 276, 587, 588, 590, 591, 922]

SUMMER 1996

RELEASES
▶ Journey, "When You Love A Woman" (single)

Heyday-Era Journey Gathers To Record Reunion Album

As with *Raised on Radio*, a period of trouble ended once Journey's creative engine rumbled to life. Jonathan Cain and Neal Schon just had to get Steve Perry into the room.

"The writing process was fairly easy and painless, like it always was between Steve, myself, and Jonathan," Schon said. "We got together and wrote the tunes, I believe, in a couple of weeks."

They brought in Ross Valory and Steve Smith later, once the demos had more defined shapes. Valory was more session-ready since he had been working in rock-based settings with **The VU**

and **The Storm**, while Smith had spent the interim focused on the jazz career he had relegated to the sidelines during his Journey years.

It took some time, but both had gotten over their ugly departures. "Along with the grief, there's also relief that happens simultaneously," Smith told *Modern Drummer*. "I started seeing it as: Now is the time to be a captain of my own ship, rather than a passenger on somebody else's."

Importantly, only two of the demos Cain, Perry, and Schon produced made use of synth bass or drum machines—thereby avoiding the musical logjams that happened with *Raised on Radio*. Valory and Smith readily filled those spaces.

When the band switched to the studio, recording sessions lasted from 11 a.m. to 5 p.m., five days a week—like a regular job. Most days, they would complete a song with verse, chorus, and bridge, with a melody and arrangement but not necessarily any lyrics.

Smith said Journey ended up with around 30 tracks in varying stages of completeness. They cut that pile down to 18 and completed them, then chose a final 16 for the record—including the hidden track "Baby I'm a Leavin' You" and the import-only "I Can See It in Your Eyes," which later appeared as a bonus track.

"It just kept coming," Schon told the *St. Louis Post-Dispatch*. "We had to stop and basically home in on some tracks because we could have kept on writing forever."

This was all before new producer **Kevin Shirley** put the band through relentless practice sessions, re-sharpening their skills until they were able to nail complete run-throughs.

Journey played these songs like they were on stage doing a set. The band completed most tracks in three takes or less. "It's Just the Rain" and the title track were initially fashioned with a drum loop, but Shirley insisted Smith follow along with the cadence during the recording sessions—rather than plugging in his performance later.

The resulting early-take performances yielded musical wrinkles both old and new. Schon got to indulge in some **Jimi Hendrix**-isms on "Castles Burning," which also recalled his early-era work with **Greg Errico**. Smith stirred in whispers of a hip-hop beat on "One More" and "Colors of the Spirit." Deep dives into the band's central influences also helped Smith connect in ways he could not before.

"Like when Steve would talk about this **Sam Cooke** tune or the feel of this Motown hit—back then, if he gave me a hint of what it was about, I could fake it," Smith told *Modern Drummer*. "But now I was coming at it more from having firsthand knowledge of what it was he was listening to."

Shirley had a musical background from performing with his band, **The Council**, and that enabled him to make smart suggestions about arrangements. He also insisted they attempt to fashion proper song endings, rather than relying on easier fades. This centering presence took pressure off the reuniting band members, who could focus on the music rather than any lingering frustrations.

Perry quickly realized something: "Individually, none of us made the magic as magically as we collectively make it together," he told the *Dispatch*. "All you had to do was put your guns down and get back together again." [283, 284, 590, 594]

FALL 1996

RELEASES
▶ Journey, *Trial By Fire* (album)
▶ Journey, "Message of Love" (single)

Band Turns To Vet Producer To Guide Long-Awaited Comeback

Columbia Records A&R executive **John Kalodner** handpicked producer **Kevin Shirley** to oversee Journey's comeback. Shirley came into *Trial by Fire* without any preconceived notions—and there was a reason for that.

"To be brutally honest," Shirley told *Music Radar*, "I had never even heard Journey until I started working with them. I didn't know a thing about them." A native of South Africa, Shirley worked in Australia before moving to the U.S. He had been busy doing engineering work with **Rush**, **Silverchair**, and the **Divinyls**.

Kalodner played "Separate Ways" for

Shirley, so he could familiarize himself with the reuniting lineup's musical approach. "I said, 'There's a lot of reverb on that,'" Shirley remembered, "and that was my only comment."

For Journey, *Trial By Fire* began a lengthy association with Shirley that lasted through a pair of Perry's successors. He oversaw their initial album with **Steve Augeri** (2001's *Arrival*), then **Arnel Pineda**'s first two albums (2008's *Revelation* and 2011's *Eclipse*).

"Kevin is really good with the band," Schon later told *Modern Guitars*. "He's a good peacekeeper for one! And he's very musical." Shirley also mixed 1998's *Greatest Hits Live*, which featured Journey concert recordings dating back to 1981.

Their relationship broke down during protracted sessions for *Eclipse*, and Schon and Cain ended up credited as co-producers on the record. Pineda re-sang many of the songs, while Schon switched out guitar parts. They moved string arrangements around too.

Schon said Shirley simply had scheduling issues. "I found the problem with Kevin, you know, is he is always so busy—he's all over the place. And it's hard to lock him down for enough time," Schon told *Melodic Rock*, with a laugh.

But Shirley alluded to problems within the band as they struggled to complete *Eclipse*. "There's people who want to be in a heavy rock band, and there's people who want to have hit ballads," he told *Music Radar*. "It's just a matter of who stamps their feet the loudest."

Journey ended up with **Narada Michael Walden** as co-producer on 2022's *Freedom*. Shirley went on to work with scores of other acts, including **Iron Maiden**, **Joe Bonamassa**, the **Thin Lizzy** offshoot band **Black Star Riders**, and **John Hiatt**, among others.

Kevin Elson was the only other producer Journey has worked with since *Trial by Fire*, returning for 2005's *Generations* after having collaborated on a series of projects during the band's turn-of-the-1980s heyday—a period that included *Departure*, *Dream, After Dream*, *Captured*, *Escape*, and *Frontiers*. [596, 597, 598]

Continued on Page 249

JOURNEY REKINDLES MAGIC AS 'WOMAN' FLIES TO TOP 15

Years ago, "Open Arms" had left Neal Schon dumbfounded. He simply did not know where—or even if—he fit in on this tender ballad penned by Steve Perry and Jonathan Cain.

"I was always the rocker in the band, and so I thought it was really soft," Schon told AXS TV. "When they brought it, I go, 'Are you guys kidding? This is like Mary Poppins.'"

Eventually, he played a part they loved, but Schon still had reservations. In fact, he dreaded debuting "Open Arms" in concert, fearing their audiences might think Journey had gone soft. "We played it the first time, and the audience went nuts," he added. "I turn to Steve afterwards and I go, 'I think they love that, man!' He looked at me like he wanted to take my head off."

Wisely, Schon never questioned Perry and Cain's instincts again. By the time they reconvened in the summer of 1996 to work on a lovelorn track called "When You Love a Woman," Schon had adapted so well that he earned a co-composing credit.

Meanwhile, Cain had been away from Perry for a long time, but something elemental remained: Perry's tendency toward longing rather than nose-to-nose passion, tender romance rather than sweaty sex. That was perfectly suited for the lead single from *Trial by Fire*.

"When we sat down to write 'When You Love a Woman,' he doesn't get the girl," Cain said. "She's waiting out there somewhere—and he's comfortable with being that guy."

As a trained musician, *Trial by Fire* producer **Kevin Shirley** had plenty of suggestions—and he placed a great amount of focus on this track. It had been nearly a decade since Journey had charted with an original song, and he sensed this one had hit single potential.

"The arrangements changed a million times on some songs, I can tell you that," an exasperated Schon said. "That got a little mind-boggling. Like a song like 'When You Love a Woman,' I remember that that arrangement changed about a hundred times. Around the 95th arrangement that came around, I'm like brainwashed. I don't know which one is which. But when we settled in, it was a very good arrangement."

Shirley had pushed Journey like never before in the run up to *Trial by Fire*, and "When You Love a Woman" showed how those preparations paid off. Shirley told *Mix* the band nailed the track in the first take—including Schon's solo.

"You'll hear the guitar starts when the solo kicks in—that's Neal," Shirley remembered. "He

WHEN YOU LOVE A WOMAN
By Steve Perry, Neal Schon, Jonathan Cain

HIGHEST CHARTING WEEK:
Billboard, #12, December 14, 1996

ARTIST	SINGLE
1. Toni Braxton	Un-Break My Heart
2. Blackstreet (featuring Dr. Dre)	No Diggity
3. Keith Sweat (featuring Athena Cage)	Nobody
4. En Vogue	Don't Let Go (Love)
5. Merril Bainbridge	Mouth
6. Celine Dion	It's All Coming Back to Me Now
7. Ginuwine	Pony
8. Barbra Streisand & Bryan Adams	I Finally Found Someone
9. New Edition	I'm Still In Love with You
12. JOURNEY	**WHEN YOU LOVE A WOMAN**

stops playing rhythm, plays his solo, then goes back to playing rhythm. That's the band playing. We later overdubbed an orchestra on it."

Schon was no longer against ballads like "When You Love a Woman." In time, however, he came to think better of how many were strung together on *Trial by Fire*, which too often unfolded at an atmospheric mid-tempo pace.

"When You Love a Woman" earned Journey its first-ever Grammy nomination, after the platinum-selling *Trial by Fire* rose to No. 3. Unfortunately, the degenerative hip problem that would derail a planned supporting tour and later end Perry's tenure in Journey had already become an issue.

Schon was eager to get out on the road, but Perry said, "Let's just get the video done." Perry told *GQ* he spent the entire time "packing my whole left side in ice between takes." [21, 80, 218, 221, 407, 427, 599, 600, 601

WINTER 1996-97

RELEASES
▶ Journey, "If He Should Break Your Heart" (Single)
▶ Journey, "Can't Tame the Lion" (Single)

NUGGETS
▶ **Studio D** in Sausalito, California, recorded music for the *Nash Bridges* Christmas episode. Musical director **George Michalski** assembled a band featuring Neal Schon and Ross Valory of Journey, **Carmine Appice** of **Vanilla Fudge** and **Rod Stewart**'s band, **E- Street** saxophonist **Clarence Clemmons**, and comedian **Cheech Marin** on vocals; **Joel Jaffe** engineered. —*Billboard*

COLLABORATIONS
▶ Neal Schon (guitar) and Gregg Rolie (vocals, keyboards) on **Abraxas Pool**'s album, *Abraxas Pool*.

Band Earns First Grammy Nom, But Summer Tour is Canceled

Journey received its first nod on January 7, 1997 when nominations for the 39th annual Grammy Awards were announced. "When You Love a Woman" was honored in the category of Best Pop Performance by a Duo or Group With Vocals.

It would have been a great selling point for an expansive reunion tour—and that's just what new manager **Irving Azoff** had planned.

"When Irving first met with us in the studio, he brought a brand-new briefcase that had more than $30 million worth of concert dates," Cain said in his autobiography.

But the brand-new briefcase lacked the one important component the band needed for the tour: Steve Perry.

He had slipped away to Hawaii in the summer of 1996 while on a short break before tour rehearsals began. "I went on a hike, one I had done many times before," Perry told *GQ*. "I

got to the top of this hill, and I was in trouble."

His left hip had been bothering him for some time, but this was different. Perry said the pain was too sharp and debilitating to be chalked up to the aging process. He saw a series of experts who confirmed a shocking diagnosis: Perry was suffering from a degenerative bone condition.

The recommendation, which Perry resisted, was hip replacement. "I believe it scared him," Cain added, "and his rebellious spirit didn't want to give in to what the doctors—and eventually the band—wanted."

Instead, Perry decided to explore alternative treatments first. Weeks turned into months, and his bandmates started getting restless. "They wanted me to make a decision on the surgery," Perry told *Rolling Stone*, "but I didn't feel it was a group decision."

"When You Love a Woman" did not win the Grammy, instead losing to "Free as a Bird" by **The Beatles** in February 1997. Journey has not been nominated since. "If it happens, it's a nice gesture and something to look at in memory of everything you've done and accomplished," Neal Schon told the Associated Press. "But you know what? I've got it in my heart."

By March, *Billboard* magazine had confirmed that there would be no summer tour, while Perry's "medical options are being researched."

"I think the tour was all set to happen," *Trial by Fire* producer **Kevin Shirley** told the *Observer*. "They had signed on to do the tour, and then everything fell apart. From what I understand, Irving took that plan and applied it to the **Eagles**."

The closest Journey got to another Grammy was in 2010, when a cover of "Don't Stop Believin'" by the cast of TV's *Glee* was nominated in the same Best Pop Performance by a Duo or Group With Vocals category.

Cain found himself actively rooting instead for **Train**'s eventual winner "Hey, Soul Sister." "It would have been strange to have the *Glee* version win a Grammy, when Journey doesn't have any," Cain told the *New York Post*. "I remember texting their singer **Pat Monahan** and saying, 'I'm praying for you, man!'" [80, 225, 428, 604, 605, 606, 607, 609]

Continued on Page 252

Reunion Album Finds Band's Fan Base Still Eager

Whatever critics thought of the music, *Trial by Fire* proved one thing: Even in the post-grunge era, there was still an audience for Journey.

A decade after their last album, Journey's reunion project became their fourth-consecutive Top 5 hit, selling a million copies in the United States alone. *Trial by Fire* also produced their 10th Top 15 single.

After so long together making music, fans could be forgiven for assuming it all came together with familiar ease. It most assuredly did not.

In fact, new producer **Kevin Shirley** put the newly reformed early-1980s lineup through a meticulous woodshedding regimen. By the time they headed into the studio, Journey was at cruising altitude. "When You Love a Woman" was done in a complete take, with only the orchestral backing added later—and that was the norm.

"The real challenge was, I don't think any of us were used to rehearsing as much as we did," Neal Schon said. "But it turned out to be a good thing. We rehearsed for a good six weeks. That's a long time. We basically rehearsed everything like we were going to play a brand-new record live, with no overdubs."

They essentially did, Shirley told *Mix*. Over and over and over. "It was a lot of work, but it was such a treat at the same time," he said. "The cool thing was when we got into the studio, they just played the songs." All Shirley really had to do was "just wait for magic to happen."

In this way, *Trial by Fire* did more than reinstate the lineup from 1981's *Escape* and 1983's

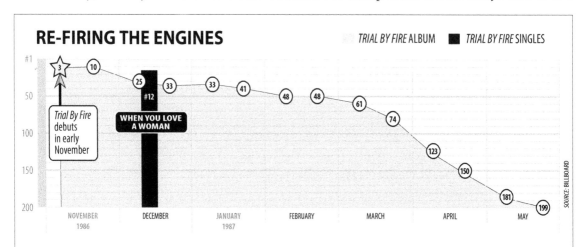

RE-FIRING THE ENGINES   *TRIAL BY FIRE* ALBUM ■ *TRIAL BY FIRE* SINGLES

Trial By Fire debuts in early November

WHEN YOU LOVE A WOMAN

#12

NOVEMBER 1986 — DECEMBER — JANUARY 1987 — FEBRUARY — MARCH — APRIL — MAY

SOURCE: BILLBOARD

The members of Journey might have been rightfully anxious about how they would be received by fans after a decade-long hiatus. But it was like they never left. *Trial By Fire* debuted at a remarkable No. 3 on the *Billboard* 200 chart, making it the highest-charting album debut in the band's history. It was helped a lot by the strength of the leadoff single. "When You Love a Woman" debuted at No. 17 on the *Billboard* singles chart and stayed in the Top 20 for 16 weeks—an amazing feat for a 24-year-old band in an incredibly competitive industry. The album stayed in the Top 50 through February, and three additional singles—"Message of Love," "Can't Tame the Lion," and "If He Should Break Your Heart"—charted well in the adult contemporary and mainstream rock charts, but but none cracked the *Billboard* Hot 100.

TOP CHARTING WEEK: *BILLBOARD*—*November 9, 1996*

1. Van Halen, *Best Of - Volume I*
2. Westside Connection, *Bow Down*
3. **JOURNEY, *TRIAL BY FIRE***
4. Celine Dion, *Falling Into You*
5. Counting Crows, *Recovering the Satellites*
6. Kenny G, *The Moment*
7. No Doubt, *Tragic Kingdom*
8. Alanis Morissette, *Jagged Little Pill*
9. Toni Braxton, *Secrets*
10. Keith Sweat, *Keith Sweat*

Frontiers. The album returned Journey to its original creative aesthetic, where songs emerged after long studio interactions. "There's something to be said about that," Schon added. "When you have the time to get everybody together like that and rehearse, you get very comfortable with the material, the arrangements."

Much had changed, but not Perry—or more specifically, the way his presence brought out such resonant things from Schon and Jonathan Cain. Cain said Perry originally only wanted to do a couple of shows. Once they gathered around a piano in the studio Cain built in Marin County, however, they suddenly had 14 songs—in just two weeks.

Released on October 22, 1996, *Trial by Fire* had its critics—both from within and without. But it nevertheless became something more than an unlikely comeback, instead casting everything that came before in a different light.

"Can I talk about Steve Perry for one second?" former MTV VJ **Martha Quinn** said. "In the '80s, it's another example of how the dust of time has to settle before we can accurately see what was going on. With Steve, it seems like: 'Oh, he's just another rock singer. That's what rock singers of our time sound like.' But Steve has probably emerged as the greatest arena-rock singer of all time. I don't think we knew that at the time."

To other ears, *Trial by Fire* sounded hopelessly out of sync, and a loose concept focused on spirituality did not really click. "It's hard to tell why other hapless '70s and '80s bands failed in comeback tries," one reviewer sniffed, "but Journey is here and with a vengeance, whether you wanted them or not."

Trial by Fire also cried out for more rock asides to balance its innate softness. "I tried to listen to it the other day again and I was like falling asleep," Schon later told **Kaj Roth**, with a laugh. "I take that one into my baby's room when she's getting tired."

Columbia Records was also taking a quieter approach since being acquired by Sony. Every Journey album had previously been greeted by full-page ads in *Billboard* or *Cashbox*. They were nonexistent for *Trial By Fire*.

In the end, however, this album finally gave Perry a chance to properly grieve for his mother. "'When I Think of You' is so pretty and tender," Cain said. "You know, we wrote it for Steve's mom, and I just think the melody is so good—and he sang it so well."

It's a song of remembrance, a song of good-byes. Perry would soon be saying his own, departing Journey for a final time. They were left to wonder what might have been. [21, 183, 218, 296, 303, 373, 407, 426]

Billboard
September 28, 1996

They're baaaack! The hotly touted Journey reunion disc *Trial By Fire* is previewed by a rock-edged power ballad that should have loyalists fondly reminiscing over such golden hits as "Open Arms." Steve Perry's voice is as acrobatic as ever, and Neal Schon's grand guitar riffing carries the album to an expectedly bombastic climax. If there's any quibble, it's that the band has largely ignored changes in musical trends. But the familiarity of this record has a warm, comforting feel that older audiences should find quite enticing.

— *Larry Flick*

San Francisco Examiner
October 20, 1996

Journey was the most successful band in the country when **Ronald Reagan** was president. Their formula was to create romantic fantasies driven by mid-tempo rhythms, lavish keyboards, smooth guitars, and polished production. *Trial By Fire* continues that tradition. "When You Love A Woman" has stormed the Top 40, and radio programmers are being flooded with requests for the tune from a now grown-up audience. Geffen Records' AOR guru **John Kalodner**, who resurrected **Aerosmith**, brought the band back together. *Trial By Fire* is the work of a band happy to hew to its AOR niche. By sticking to what it does best, the band could find itself comfortably returning to the limelight.

— *Steffan Chirazi*

Detroit Free Press
October 20, 1996

While fast-aging pundits 20 years ago heralded new underground punk as the only legitimate youth music, real American kids were buying 40 million Journey records. Now, with nary a patronizing nod to 1996 or the punk redux that fills the airwaves, Journey doles out its first studio album in a decade. This is unmistakably the Bay Area band that turned muscle car balladry into standard school-dance fare: thick, stratospheric harmonies, grand keyboards, reverbed drums, "baby forever" lyrics. The sound is dominated by guitarist Neal Schon's wiry blues riffs and Steve Perry's wailing vocals—albeit with a 47-year-old's grit. This album is an anachronism. If it scores it'll be on adult contemporary. But, hey— bombastic Journey beats a **Sex Pistols** cheez-reunion any sentimental '90s day.

— *Brian McCollum*

SPRING 1997

RELEASES
▶ Jonathan Cain, *Body Language* (album)
▶ Abraxas Pool (with Neal Schon, Gregg Rolie), *Abraxas Pool* (album)

Schon, Rolie Record with Santana Pals, Sans Carlos

Carlos Santana was notably absent when the rest of the surviving members of the early-1970s **Santana** band reunited as **Abraxas Pool**. The 1997 self-titled album they made in his absence grew out of a renewed sense of brotherhood.

"The creation of that music happened at a little cabin in California, and believe me, it was a cabin," Rolie said. "The sound went all over Marin County, though we never got a complaint. We wrote all of that stuff in 10 or 12 days. It was just pouring out of everybody."

A familiar sense of magic and wonder had filled the room. "This music has no barriers," Rolie told the *Los Angeles Times*. "You can't call it rock 'n' roll, you can't call it Latin, you can't call it jazz, you can't call it R&B, because it's all of the above."

Schon's most recent solo album, *Beyond the Thunder*, seemed to have opened the door for a Journey reunion. Then the tour fell apart. Those same sessions—which also featured former Santana bandmates **José "Chepito" Areas** and **Michael Carabello**—would also spark this collaboration.

They had provided notable sparks on *Beyond the Thunder*, which otherwise was "the type of stuff that comes out of me when I'm away from the road and away from rock 'n' roll for a while," Schon later admitted to **Gary James**. "You know, I've never made a record that was that mellow."

Abraxas Pool would be quite different. Schon "came over to my house and told me, 'I had forgotten how nice it was playing with percussion,'" Rolie told interviewer **Scott Sullivan**. "He then presented the idea of calling [**Michael**] **Shrieve**, Chepito, Carabello, and **Alphonso** [**Johnson**] to see what we should do."

Rolie phoned Shrieve first, and when he agreed, the newly minted Abraxas Pool began to pick up steam. Johnson, a late-1980s member of Santana, replaced the late **David Brown**. They approached Carlos Santana too, but he declined. "I don't think he relishes the fact that we're doing this," Rolie admitted to the *Times*.

Abraxas Pool would serve as an opportunity to reassert their own place in the band's considerable early legacy. "Carlos did not do that by himself. And I'd equally say that I didn't either," Rolie told *Rolling Stone*. "It was everybody."

The project also shined a welcome spotlight on a rhythm section that always gave Santana its eruptive propulsion. Timbale player Chepito Areas returned to the level of prominence he had enjoyed on albums like *Abraxas* and *Santana III*. "Back then, lots of bands were using click tracks or machines to make the time sound perfect on records, but we had Chepito," Schon told *Guitar Player*. "He sounded like a metronome with soul."

Areas wrote "Baila Mi Cha-Cha" and "Guajirona," and joined Carabello in co-writing "Ya Llego." The conga player also co-composed "Boom Ba Ya Ya" with Shrieve, who was credited on a total of five tracks.

It was sweet vindication for a drummer who had been lambasted in some corners for his presence in the more conventionally rock-oriented **Hagar Schon Aaronson Shrieve** supergroup. "I never felt like I was quite right in it, not that I did anything wrong whatsoever, but I'm not a heavy metal or rock drummer," Shrieve told *Ultimate Classic Rock*'s **Matt Wardlaw**. "I play lighter and rhythmically and more jazzy, and I can do funky stuff."

That certainly was the case here. As with the best Santana records, Abraxas Pool featured an intriguing mix of up-tempo instrumentals ("Boom Ba Ya Ya," "Baila Mi Cha-Cha," "Cruzin'") and desirous Rolie vocal features ("A Million Miles Away," "Waiting for You"). Rolie switched from Hammond B-3 to a Roland organ, giving everything a slightly lighter feel, while Schon made a lengthy guitar exploration on the pleasantly languid "Szabo."

"A Million Miles Away" was released as a single but gained no traction. "A great song," Rolie said, "and one of the few of mine that

I listen to regularly. I never do that." Their self-titled debut album likewise went nowhere, and Abraxas Pool became a one-off project.

In the end, for many fans, Abraxas Pool was indistinguishable from the 1971 tour when the Santana band briefly attempted to continue without their namesake guitar player. "That was a really good record," Shrieve later told *Rolling Stone*. "But if Carlos wasn't there, people didn't care." [2, 58, 168, 181, 211, 214, 441, 593, 602]

SUMMER 1997

RELEASES
▶ Gregg Rolie, *Rough Tracks* (album)

COLLABORATIONS
▶ Randy Jackson, bass, on **Billy Joel**'s single, "Hey Girl".
▶ Randy Jackson, bass, on **Kenny Loggins**'s album, *The Unimaginable Life*.

Schon Starts Decades-Long Collaboration with Igor Len

With no tour in the immediate offing, Neal Schon had gotten antsy. Steve Perry was clearly in pain, but he still would not commit to surgery. *Trial by Fire* had burned brightly, then quickly turned to ashes.

Schon dived into a partial **Santana** reunion with **Abraxas Pool**, and then returned to solo work. *Electric World* arrived on July 15, 1997, with a number of familiar names—including alumni from both Journey (Steve Smith) and Santana (**Alphonso Johnson, Walfredo Reyes Jr.,** and **Michael Carabello**).

The most intriguing collaborator during sessions held at Warehouse 7 in Oakland, California, turned out to be a newcomer. Keyboardist and programmer **Igor Len** would go on to become a longtime creative foil for Schon.

"*Electric World* created a template for all of this activity," Len said, "with a Latin feel and the presence of both Smith and early Santana member Michael Carabello."

It was not Journey. But then again, Schon's last turn in Journey had left a bad taste in his mouth. "So, that was very frustrating for all of us," Schon told interviewer **Michael Cavacini**, "because it had been so many years since we had been together. ... Then it was gone, that fast. And we had to decide at that point what we were gonna do."

Len admitted he was "clearly a no-name in this game," with a laugh. But a creative piece obviously snapped into place with Schon, as their collaborations stretched across the decades. It all started with *Electric World*, which featured five songs co-composed with the tech-savvy Len.

"This record was the first project I played with Neal and contributed as a writer," Len said. "I was introduced to Neal by one of our common friends, **John Hernandez**, as Neal was looking for a keyboard player. Along with keys, I brought the Roland DM-800 hard disk recording system to track the album. We also used Fostex ADAT machines because they were more dependable than Alesis ones."

Len's close creative relationship with Schon meant that he guided the others through some of their shared demos' twists and turns as *Electric World* came together in the studio. That did not always go over so well with veterans like bassist Alphonso Johnson, who had been a part of projects with **Weather Report, Phil Collins**, and **Chuck Mangione** before joining Santana in the late 1980s. He would later gig with **Steve Hackett** and **Bob Weir**.

"I could sense Alphonso's irritation when I was showing him bass lines in the tracks that I composed with Neal," Len said. "He didn't want to have any of that. There were some quite particular passages in the bass part that mattered to me, as they were supporting the harmony, turning it into an inversion of the chord. But I don't blame him—after all, who am I to show him anything, really? This was Alphonso Johnson."

Perhaps owing to Schon's relationship with the new-age-leaning label Higher Octave, *Electric World* reached the Top 10 on *Billboard*'s sub-chart devoted to the genre, even though it was nothing of the sort. Instead, this LP could be considered a milder, less interesting guest at a dinner party where Abraxas Pool might have dominated every conversation.

Len went on to work on several Schon solo projects including 2005's *I on U*, 2012's *The Calling*, and 2015's *Vortex*. Len also collaborated with Schon and Gregg Rolie on Santana's "Choo Choo," which appeared in 2016 on both *Santana IV* and *Live at the House of Blues Las Vegas*. [40, 385, 603]

WINTER 1997–98

RELEASES
▶ Jonathan Cain, *For A Lifetime* (album)

Santana Earns Spot in Rock Hall of Fame; Rolie Inducted

Tuxedo-clad patrons paid some $4,000 per pair of tickets on January 12, 1998 to the grand ballroom of the luxe Waldorf-Astoria in downtown Manhattan as **Santana** joined the Rock & Roll Hall of Fame. The celebration went off without a hitch, with no hint of the backstage drama that came before.

Baseball references provided a theme for the group. Upon becoming the first Latino inductee, **Carlos Santana** told the crowd: "It's a great honor. I almost feel like **Jackie Robinson** or something."

Percussionist **Michael Carabello** had already compared his fellow inductees to "the **Lou Gehrig**s and the **Babe Ruth**s" in an interview with **Joel Selvin** of the *San Francisco Chronicle*. "That's something that's here 'til, like, the end of the Earth," Carabello added. "Quite an honor."

The Hall of Fame chose to induct just six contributors from their first two albums, also including Gregg Rolie, **Michael Shrieve**, **David Brown**, and **José "Chepito" Areas**. Shrieve, who joined the lineup as a 19-year-old after an all-night jam session, said Santana "was like a street gang" back then, but "their weapon was music."

Later, things would get more complicated. Rolie and *Santana III*-era recruit Neal Schon split after 1972's jazz-turning *Caravanserai*, eventually forming Journey. That left only Areas and Shrieve from the classic era, and they

too were gone within a couple of years.

Future lineups shuffled to the point where members became facelessly interchangeable. Santana the band became associated solely with Santana the man, and his earliest contributors were typically overlooked, even by Santana. "Carlos actually wanted to be inducted by himself," Rolie said, "but it was truly a band, not just him. It only became his after the third album."

Former Santana stage manager **Herbie Herbert** said he also lobbied hard for Schon's inclusion, but Carlos blocked it. "If it was up to Carlos, he would have the original Santana band dismissed as nothing more than sidemen," Herbert told **Matthew Carty**, "… and nothing could be further from the truth."

Selvin was not surprised to hear about these behind-the-scenes machinations. "Carlos still is kind of an unchecked egomaniacal person—I guess they call them narcissists now," Selvin said. "He's just a phony, and if you keep that in mind with everything when you look at what Carlos does, it all makes sense."

Always levelheaded, Rolie considered skipping the whole thing.

"I got the call that I was going to get added to that and went, 'That's very cool, but I'm building a hot rod. Just send me whatever,'" Rolie told *Rolling Stone*. "I was building a '32 Ford." Then Rolie's drummer **Ron Wikso** called to intervene: "A lot of people get Grammy Awards and this and that, but the Rock & Roll Hall of Fame? It's here to stay."

Among the ceremony's most engaging moments was the Santana band's surprise onstage collaboration with **Peter Green** on "Black Magic Woman." Green was present as an inductee with his former band **Fleetwood Mac**, for whom he had originally written the breakout Santana hit. [1, 56, 60, 181, 611, 612, 613, 614]

SPRING 1998

NUGGETS
▶ JOURNEY'S END: Steve Perry has officially left Journey. "Journey was one of the more powerful, emotional parts of my life and I'm not ready to talk about it yet," said Perry, as he officially

NUGGETS (cont.)

announced the split on May 7 after weeks of speculation. However, Perry wanted people to know that the health issues that contributed to the parting were not life-threatening. Some reports speculated he was working on a solo album, but he said that is not true; however, his song from the *Quest for Camelot* soundtrack, prophetically titled "I Stand Alone," has just been released to adult contemporary radio.
— *Billboard*

Tensions Boil Over As Perry's Decision on Touring Emerges

Steve Perry felt his health issues were a private matter, so fans were left to wonder why Journey did not follow up a platinum comeback LP with a tour.

Neal Schon had been supportive—at first. Perry had said, "'Y'know, this is a personal issue, and I'm not gonna be pushed in a corner to get my hip fixed. When I'm ready, I'm ready,'" Schon told *GQ*. "And I said, 'I understand that.'"

Journey tried to get creative, suggesting that Perry return to the road using a stool. He refused. They mentioned simply going back into the studio to record a follow-up album. He refused.

As their silence unspooled, rumors inevitably followed. Many hinted that Perry was shying away from the road because of vocal concerns. "We sort of lost touch with the guy," Jonathan Cain told the *Huffington Post*. "It was almost two years that went by. A platinum record and we're not going to do anything?"

Former manager **Herbie Herbert** said he warned them that Perry would "get complete control of you and then if he has a little bit of a feeling of sympathy and compassion, he'll then tell you, 'Fuck you,'" Herbert told *Classic Rock Revisited*. "That's exactly what he did."

Herbert never believed Perry would tour behind *Trial by Fire*. He remembered telling the others, "I will eat shit ... you designate the time and place, if this motherfucker ever does one show with you," he added.

In the meantime, Journey lost Steve Smith. He had been an active member of the jazz community before their reunion, playing with **Steps Ahead** and his own band, **Vital Information**. "At the same time, I was doing drum clinics and had built a pretty varied career," Smith said. "When the *Trial by Fire* album came along, I had to take a two-year hiatus from all of that and become a Journey band member once again. It took over my life, 100 percent."

He got tired of waiting. "I made a decision that I wanted to focus on myself as an artist," Smith added. "I wanted to be in charge of my own musical destiny and development, playing mainly my own music as a bandleader, or working with musicians that I felt were exceptional."

Finally, Cain called Perry with an ultimatum. Journey had begun to audition other singers. "It's like you're standing at the altar, waiting," Cain told Knight-Ridder Newspapers.

Perry was stunned. "I said, 'You've tried out some singers?' And he said yes," Perry told *GQ*. "His exact words were ... 'We wanna know when you're going into surgery, because we want to tour.'"

Perry reiterated that his medical decisions were not up for a band vote, while making one critical request: "I said, 'Do what you need to do, but don't call it Journey'," Perry told *Rolling Stone*. "'If you fracture the stone, I don't know how I could come back to it.'"

But, as Schon pointedly told *Goldmine*, Perry "had already done it" by making Journey songs a cornerstone in setlists on his tour in support of *For the Love of Strange Medicine*. "So, at that point, Jon and I were the other two-thirds of the songwriting, and I said, 'Fuck this.'"

Herbert was watching all this unfold from a quiet perch in retirement, but he said he recognized the pattern. "So self-absorbed," Herbert told the *Times-Herald*. "He never considered others. And [people like Perry] are shocked when others don't consider them."

Schon remembered hearing **Steve Augeri**'s old band, **Tall Stories**, on the radio. "I was with a friend in my car and I pulled off the side and said, 'Does this sound like Journey or what?'"

Continued on Page 258

Steve Augeri (center) joined Journey as its new lead singer in 1998, but the addition required some legal maneuvering to appease former lead singer Steve Perry. L–R: Jonathan Cain, Ross Valory, Augeri, Neal Schon, and Deen Castronovo.

PERRY'S EXIT LEADS TO AN INCENTIVE-LADEN AGREEMENT

With Steve Augeri now on board, Journey did not want to cool their heels a moment longer. "They were frustrated," *San Francisco Chronicle* music critic **Joel Selvin** said. "They didn't have anything else to do."

Still, Steve Perry loomed large over everything—and not just because he had become the face of Journey over the preceding 20 years. If the band were to continue, they would have to agree to a severance package with some very expensive terms: Journey wasn't just paying to separate from Perry. They have also continued paying him ever since.

Perry said he immediately called his attorney following a contentious phone call in which Jonathan Cain revealed Journey was discussing replacements. "I said, 'Start the divorce,'" Perry told *GQ*. "And he said, 'What divorce?' And I said, '*The* divorce.'"

Perry would end up with percentages of their future albums, their live shows, and even any unspecific additional income. To begin with, Perry's share would be as high as a whopping 50 percent, according to court documents. Former manager **Herbie Herbert** said he had seen

it all coming, predicting early on that Perry would never tour behind *Trial by Fire*.

"I said, 'The only way that you guys are able to go forward now is to pay Steve Perry as if he were there'—which is what they're doing," Herbert told **Matthew Carty**.

Back then, it was difficult to imagine Journey with a new front man. Even Perry admitted to *The New York Times* that he and Neal Schon were like "salt and pepper, linked together forever, that voice and that guitar."

At the same time, having so much money erased from the top line of their revenue sheets made it that much more difficult to move on from Perry. "He shouldn't have done what he did," longtime Journey tour manager **Pat Morrow** said. "He owed them his life and instead, he turned around and fucked them all."

Journey had to pay a total of 50 percent of the net income due to Schon or Cain, whichever was higher, from the band's first two post-Perry albums. Perry was then to receive 25 percent of the same net income from their third studio project without him, and 12.5 percent from every Journey album that followed. All those figures were to be calculated after expenses.

Journey released a handful of albums and an EP since Perry's departure. The first two studio LPs and the EP featured Augeri; Arnel Pineda took over thereafter. Bands nowadays make their money on the road in the download and streaming age—so it's critical for them to maintain a robust touring schedule.

Once Journey returned, they knew the catalog would do the rest. "That's what determines it all: Do you have 8, 12, 13 songs that people want to hear on any given night?" former *Rolling Stone* editor **David Wild** said. "Journey, even without the guy who sang them, they can still play because great songs are worth their weight in platinum and gold forever."

But Perry also made a similar deal on revenue from Journey's concerts. He was to receive 50 percent of net income from Journey's first two tours after their split, 25 percent from the third tour, and then 12.5 percent from every subsequent tour.

"They have to go out there and work every day," Herbert told Carty, "and he gets a share of the benefits of their labor without having to be there."

Perry's attorney did not just negotiate a deal where he got a portion of "Schon or Cain's share, whichever is greater, of all revenues earned" from ticket sales, according to a 2020 court filing with the Superior Court of California. Perry also got part of "tour merchandise, tour sponsorship income and any tour support payments." Expenses could again be deducted, but they excluded "any salaries paid to Schon, Cain or any other member of the New Journey."

Perry's deal likewise entitles him to the same percentages of "miscellaneous income" not specifically covered by the album and touring agreements. In all cases, there was a floor on how little Journey could claim as net income.

"Notwithstanding anything contained in the foregoing," according to court documents, "in no event shall the Net Master Income be less than twenty percent (20%) of the total amount earned." At the same time, "Perry shall not be responsible for any losses in connection with the New Journey entity."

A jubilant Perry has admitted to prominently displaying documents confirming this deal. "I've got the fax on my wall, in my studio. May 8th, 1998, was the total release from all our contracts, and from Sony," Perry told *GQ*. Ironically, the soundtrack for the animated feature *Quest for Camelot* arrived the very same week, featuring two new solo songs from Perry—one of which he titled "I Stand Alone."

Journey had paid an unquestionably steep price, but the band felt they had to pay it in order to stave off the inevitable. **Lawrence Gowan**, who would later replace **Dennis DeYoung** in **Styx**, understood Journey's predicament all too well: "The first thing is that the band's life was extended, because of the huge step they took in changing members," Gowan said. "That is the reality of life that everyone in every band is going to face at some point: They have to figure out if this is the end."

In the years that followed, a non-disclosure clause ensured that terms of Perry's separation agreement were more rumored than known. Still, Schon would occasionally allude to the contract.

"We have a built-in deal with Steve which I can't really talk about," Schon later told interviewer **Michael Cavacini**, "but everybody benefits as long as we're still out there." Schon also once memorably grumbled to *GQ* that Perry "still gets paid like a motherfucker even though he shouldn't be. It's stuff like that I'm not allowed to talk about."

Turns out, Perry's golden parachute even covered how Journey's future album projects would be presented.

Sony was to affix "appropriate stickering indicating that there is a new lead singer and the name of that lead singer in a clear manner. If the first New Journey album sells less than one million (1,000,000) units, the second New Journey album shall include a similar sticker on its initial release." If the first record went platinum, "good faith" negotiations about a "similar sticker" on the second album would commence.

Journey's first two Pineda-led studio LPs reached the *Billboard* Top 20, but 2008's *Revelation* is the only post-Perry album to have gone platinum. *Freedom* could not get past No. 88 in 2022.

Meanwhile, Selvin indicated that Schon might not be able to come off the road, even if he wanted to, because Perry is not the only one making sizable cuts into his salary.

"I was at a party with Neal's accountant, who had probably had too much to drink," Selvin said. "He told me that Neal spent 50 minutes an hour working for his ex-wives—and this was some time ago." Schon later had to settle another lawsuit by ex-wife **Ava Fabian** before marrying **Michaele Salahi**. [56, 60, 80, 157, 411, 412, 616, 617, 618, 927]

Schon told *The (Moline, Ill.) Dispatch*. "'If we ever get back on the road, this guy can do it.'"

Soon, Augeri was on a flight from Brooklyn to California, and Perry was out. "That's kind of not a cool way of letting your singer go," Cain's ex-**Babys** bandmate **Tony Brock** argued.

Perry negotiated a lucrative exit package, and he never performed with Journey again—not even years later when they were inducted into the Rock & Roll Hall of Fame.

"Whatever happened when he was ill that time, I think he felt they violated the trust and defiled something about the spirit of Journey," longtime *Rolling Stone* writer and editor **David Wild** said. "You know, there are rock critics— maybe me back in the day—who would have really said, 'Come on, it's just a fucking corporate rock band.' But it wasn't for him, and it's not for these generations who can feel a song like 'Don't Stop Believin', and they believe it." [3, 39, 80, 106, 115, 225, 242, 411, 577, 606, 615, 639]

SUMMER 1998

NUGGETS

▶ Steve Augeri takes over on lead vocals for Journey with the band's new single, "Remember Me," co-written by Jonathan Cain, Neal Schon, and **Jack Blades**, of **Night Ranger** fame.
—*Billboard*

Brooklyn Bred: Native New Yorker Seizes Opportunity

Steve Perry's ugly departure even dented Neal Schon's familiar bravado.

Journey had scored a platinum hit with *Trial by Fire*, then followed that with 1998's gold-selling *Greatest Hits Live*. This convinced Schon "there was interest out there," he told *Deseret News*, but "everything was so centered around Steve Perry that I had my concerns."

Another Steve—Steve Augeri, from the Bensonhurst neighborhood of Brooklyn—convinced him otherwise. But Journey's potential replacement had already given up on his rock dreams when he got the call from Journey. At

first, he thought the call was a joke.

"I had a brother-in-law and best friend, Nicholas, that in addition to being my benefactor and patron through the lean years, was also a terrific prankster," Augeri said. "I wasn't about to be punked. By the second call and invitation, however, it started to sink in that this may actually be happening."

With his music career stalled, Augeri had turned to a skill set learned from his father, who trained him in the carpentry profession as a younger man. Augeri settled into work as a maintenance manager for New York City-area Gap stores.

Meanwhile, Journey was coming off years spent trying to coax Perry back. When it finally became clear that he was not going to return anytime soon, they began auditions, talking to **Geoff Tate** of **Queensryche** and **John West** of **Royal Hunt**.

Then Schon remembered hearing a song from Augeri's early-1990s band **Tall Stories** on the radio years before. To his ear, they had sounded like Journey—but more up-tempo. Schon tracked down Augeri through their mutual friend **Joe Cefalu**, a Bay Area musician who had known Augeri back in Brooklyn.

"I had retired for a year already when Joe called to say he heard through the grapevine that Steve had decided not to carry on any longer for one reason or another and that Journey was auditioning lead vocalists," Augeri said. "Coming from a lineage of underachievers, although flattered, I told Joe I thought the idea was crazy and that I was nowhere near in the league of Steve Perry."

Cefalu asked Augeri to put together a demo tape of songs anyway, with a promise to send them along to Schon. Augeri said he would, but never did. Instead, his friend "compiled a handful of songs from the Tall Stories album and that was that," Augeri said.

"It wasn't long after that I received a call from Jon and Neal individually," Augeri added. "I don't recall the sequence, but I can say the first call was met with silence, utter disbelief."

His resulting audition involved singing "Faithfully" for its composer, Jonathan Cain. "I said ... 'If you move me with this reading, then we'll talk,'" Cain told Thomson News

Service. "I was just flabbergasted with this guy. I just thought, 'This was meant to be.'"

They had talked about **Glenn Hughes** of **Deep Purple** fame, Schon later confirmed. One-time Journey fill-in **Kevin Chalfant** was also "considered at the time briefly," Ross Valory told interviewer **Mick Burgess**, "but we found Steve Augeri quite easily and he had all of the qualities that we needed and we quickly moved on with Steve."

Founding manager **Herbie Herbert** marveled over the missed opportunities. "They wasted, in truth, from the end of the *Frontiers* tour until they did their first shows with Augeri in '98 — that's 15 fuckin' years," Herbert told *Classic Rock Revisited*.

He had long recommended a clean break with Perry, but Journey wanted to wait. "They have infinite creative intelligence but when it comes to acquired knowledge, they couldn't be more," Herbert paused to consider it. "Ignorant is the word," he added. "They're just ignorant of the simplest stuff."

Augeri admitted plenty of early reservations about stepping in for a well-known commodity like Perry. In the end, he was correct about how difficult it would be.

Michael Des Barres had faced that kind of situation when he took over for **Robert Palmer** in **The Power Station** in 1985. "What is difficult is going into a family that already exists," Des Barres said. "It's about the personalities involved, more than the music. The music, you just belt it out."

Augeri did just that, eventually suffering disastrous results. But in the meantime, Journey released a new stand-alone single, "Remember Me," in June 1998 as part of the four-times-platinum *Armageddon* movie soundtrack.

Everyone's confidence soared. "We were looking for someone who could fill those shoes, but who had his own shoes as well," Valory told the *Quad-City Times*. "He doesn't sound exactly like Steve Perry. He's not—and we weren't looking for—a clone."

It was a different story out on the road. Journey was back to playing theaters and county fairs again on their just-launched comeback tour. They were starting over. Then the ceaseless Steve Perry questions began.

Herbert acknowledged Perry's "great, great talent," adding that nobody could compete "at his prime." But that was a long time ago. "You're comparing the current reality of Kevin Chalfant or the current reality of Steve Augeri to the memory of Steve Perry," Herbert told **Matthew Carty**. "And trust me, that memory is jaded, and dead-ass wrong."

As for the man himself, Perry was studiously avoiding it all. "Um, you know, I have such a hard time voicing any opinions with the new incarnation of the group," he told *Entertainment Weekly*. He treasured the old memories, but otherwise "really, it's none of my business." [56, 98, 103, 104, 151, 193, 222, 243, 527, 639, 698]

Jittery Augeri Navigates First Live Journey Performance

Journey took the stage on June 9, 1998, in San Rafael, California, for their first ticketed concert without Steve Perry in decades. In the run-up to the concert, they inevitably spent most of the time fielding questions about the band's former front man.

"Given Steve's condition, we waited a long time and we needed and wanted to move forward," Ross Valory told the *Spartanburg Herald-Journal*. "We decided we could continue without Steve." First, they would have to get through a jittery show at the tiny Marin Veterans' Memorial Auditorium. New front man Steve Augeri was so stressed out, it may as well have been Madison Square Garden.

"Before the show, there was a garbage receptacle," Augeri told *Rolling Stone*. "I stuck my head in there and relieved myself. I never had that happen to me before."

The concert at the 700-seat San Rafael venue served as a hometown warm-up before Journey headed to larger venues in Japan and the U.S.—but those were in the 1,500-capacity range. It was a big drop from the stadium shows of old.

"I give us about another year to a year and a half to get exactly back where we were," a hopeful Neal Schon told the Northeast Mississippi *Daily Journal*. "I really believe that's going to happen. Persistence wins every time."

Continued on Page 262

FIRST POST-PERRY SINGER WAS RESCUED FROM THE GAP

Steve Augeri felt like he'd had a good run. His band, **Tall Stories**, formed in 1988, signed with Epic Records, and released a self-titled debut in August 1991 that produced the rock chart hit "Wild on the Run."

Augeri then joined the latter-day lineup of **Tyketto**, which had earlier signed a label deal with Geffen. The band folded, however, after a studio album and live project.

"Growing up in Brooklyn, New York, in the '70s and being surrounded by multitudes of talented musicians for as long as I can remember, I had reached a level of success that was almost unthinkable," Augeri said. "Although it hadn't been an overnight success by any stretch of the imagination, nor did it come easy, it was still a level that would be considered pretty respectable and fortunate."

By then, Augeri was in his late 30s and had a family. Any larger dream would have to wait or end up going unfulfilled. He took a day job.

"After Tyketto's year-long run, however promising and pleasurable that was, it ended

and I spent a year working for the Gap stores as a maintenance manager—trading a microphone for a hammer and a Stratocaster for a screwdriver," Augeri said. "All the while, I was telling myself—or let's say, trying to convince myself—that I had a good run and that it was okay to walk away from a lifelong dream: 'Be responsible, be realistic, do the mature thing.'"

Augeri paused, then added: "But what's the fun in that?"

Born in 1959 in Bensonhurst, Augeri's love of music traced back to listening to R&B, soul, crooners, and country on the radio with his father. Then, like so many others of a certain age, he heard **The Beatles**.

"Ever since viewing the historical airing of The Beatles' debut performance on *The Ed Sullivan Show* here in the States," Augeri said, "myself and thousands of other kids were inspired to seek out or pick up and learn to play electric guitars, basses, and drums and have as much fun as they seemed to be having—to be a part of that new energy, to effect and engage people, an audience. I was swept up in that first British Invasion of the '60s. The seed was planted at the ripe old age of 5 years old. This is the path I want to follow."

There were a couple of other key moments. "Shortly thereafter, my Uncle Andy bought his son and I guitars from out of the now-defunct, but at the time very popular, Sears and Roebuck catalog," Augeri said. "From then on, my cousin Andrew Jr. and I would be in a band of one form or another for the next 15 years. But it wasn't until I reached the age of 15 that I made the conscious decision to seriously pursue music."

By then, a grammar school teacher had already cast Augeri in a fourth-grade musical. He was hooked. A career in music became a "dream of mine for as long as I can remember—however out of reach or unimaginable," Augeri said. "Music was encompassing, all consuming. It was an obsession. Now, how to get from point A to point B?"

He had played the 2001 Odyssey club, where the film *Saturday Night Fever* was partly set, when the venue held a "rock 'n' roll night" on Wednesdays—to Augeri's own estimated crowd of "about 10." He then continued his studies at the High School of Music & Art in New York City but returned home to start a band when the money ran out. His first real break was as a background vocalist for **Michael Schenker**, who gained acclaim with **UFO** and **Scorpions**. Augeri had also been a background vocalist with **Ted Nugent,** who at one point said: "Don't worry. Someday you'll be in front of that curtain."

Augeri then formed the early-1990s group Tall Stories before joining Tyketto. Journey was obviously on an entirely different plane. Even after taking over for Perry, however, not everything was as before.

He recalled then-Columbia A&R executive **John Kalodner** taking him to lunch and giving him some advice: "You got to think like a star, act like a star, be a star." Not long after, *The New York Times* reported that the door to Augeri's small backstage trailer swung open.

One of Journey's road managers informed him that there would be no dry cleaning at the next stop. "You want to do your own shirt again?" Augeri was asked. He quickly retrieved the Woolite and got to work.

With Steve Perry gone, the scale of everything had changed. At the same time, there were vicious reactions from Perry devotees among Journey's fans.

Augeri received much the same treatment that **Robert Fleischman** had when he earlier helped guide Journey from its jam band roots to a more song-focused approach. "When were on tour the first time," Fleischman told radio host **Sheldon Snow**, "I would come out and the first two rows would be flipping me the bird."

But then Perry stepped into the spotlight, and redefined Journey forever.

Augeri ended up recording two albums (2001's *Arrival* and 2005's *Generations*) as well as an EP (2002's *Red 13*). The Augeri-led Journey 2001 concert DVD was certified platinum. Otherwise, stiff headwinds only seemed to grow: *Arrival* stalled at No. 56, and *Generations* could get no higher than No. 170 on the *Billboard* album chart.

At the same time, Journey toured constantly between 1998 and 2006, and the strain eventually became too much for Augeri. Allegations of singing with a backing track had already begun to swirl when he abruptly left on July 4, 2006, after a show in Raleigh, North Carolina.

"I think the wear and tear of the road eventually took its toll on him and wore him down," Schon told *Billboard*. "Steve Perry was bionic to be able to do what he did for as many years as he did under our touring schedule."

Augeri had never gotten past those comparisons. He took some time off, healed his voice, then began putting his career back together—but with a far different proportionality.

Augeri returned to Tall Stories, which released 2009's *Skyscraper*. More than a dozen stand-alone singles trickled out with the **Steve Augeri Band** before 2022's *Seven Ways 'Til Sunday* arrived. It included previously unreleased co-writes with both Neal Schon and Jonathan Cain, which Augeri and his group updated for release. [151, 157, 257, 290, 624]

> **All the while, I was telling myself—or let's say, trying to convince myself—that I had a good run and that it was okay to walk away from a lifelong dream: Be responsible, be realistic, do the mature thing... But what's the fun in that?**
>
> — *Steve Augeri*

They certainly had a powerful new presence in the rhythm section, as Deen Castronovo also made his debut with Journey.

He replaced longtime drummer Steve Smith, who returned to his jazz career amid Journey's long layoff. "That was fine because I had my old friend Deen Castronovo sitting in the wings ready to go," Schon told *Melodic Rock*, "and he is just kicking some ass. He is more of a rock drummer."

Since his stints in **Bad English** and **Hardline** with Schon, Castronovo had appeared in far heavier musical settings. That included sessions for **Ozzy Osbourne**'s 1995 LP *Ozzmosis* and a portion of the subsequent tour. He also contributed to a trio of **Steve Vai** albums, as well as **Social Distortion**'s 1996 album *White Light, White Heat, White Trash*.

Castronovo nevertheless brought a long-term fan's contagious enthusiasm to every show. "It was an easy call adding him to the band since he grew up with Journey," Valory told the *Herald-Journal*. "It's amazing how well he knew the lyrics to all the songs."

In another sign of a changing of the guard, Journey's opening-night setlist featured several live debuts of songs from the *Trial by Fire* album, including "Can't Tame the Lion," "When You Love a Woman," "One More," and "Castles Burning."

Augeri was realistic about the rebuilding process ahead when discussing the San Rafael show. "We went out for a test drive," he told *Rolling Stone*. "That was a test drive. We went to Japan for a few shows. That was a test drive."

There would be many more potholes ahead, but joining Journey had undeniably bolstered Augeri's career. He did not need reminding.

"It's amazing when I think about how I've gotten a new lease on my musical life," Augeri told *The New York Times*. "'All I've ever wanted to do was to sing with a band in front of an audience.'"

Meanwhile, Schon had already begun pushing back against those who refused to let go of Steve Perry. "I do believe he wished the worst for us," Schon told the *Deseret News*. "But if he would have had that surgery, it would be him singing those songs again." [193, 527, 622, 623, 624, 626, 627]

Augeri's Debut Single Lands In *Armageddon* Soundtrack

Columbia Records A&R executive **John Kalodner** played a key role in Journey's transition to the Steve Augeri era—and not just in the expected area of song selection.

"I'll never forget the first time we met. He invited me to lunch at the Four Seasons on 57th in Midtown Manhattan. I showed up in full grunge wear," Augeri said. Kalodner had thoughts on how Augeri should conduct himself, his finances, and his style of dress.

"He advised me, in addition to keeping my eyes and ears open while working and writing with Neal and Jon, to save whatever money I might happen to make—rather than on fast cars and fast women," Augeri said. "And last but not least, to start dressing myself and start thinking of myself as a rock star."

Augeri felt like he had finally made it. "I walked out of the Four Seasons and that meeting floating 10 feet off the ground," he added. "I'll never forget John Kalodner's kindness and have always taken his advice to heart."

Kalodner also approved Journey's first single with Augeri. "Remember Me" arrived as the second song on *Armageddon: The Album*, a quadruple-platinum soundtrack released on June 23, 1998.

"'Remember Me' was one of 10 songs I recorded during a five-day audition when I was first flown out to Marin County to meet the band, as well as to see if we might click both musically and personally," Augeri said. "'Remember Me,' along with four other new songs, were then sent off to the label—to John Kalodner, to be specific. I can only guess that the powers that be approved enough to green light the band with myself going forward."

Written by Cain, Schon, and **Jack Blades** of **Night Ranger**, "Remember Me" was a utilitarian soundtrack deep cut. Even Cain knew they would have to make a bigger splash.

"There's a certain perception," Cain told the *San Francisco Weekly*, "and it's gonna take a hit record to change it. And that's what it's gonna take." At this late date, former Journey manager **Herbie Herbert** didn't like their chances.

"It'd be good if they had a record and had

some success," Herbert told *San Francisco Weekly*, "You know, you've got a much better shot at the lottery or your dick growing a foot, to be honest with you."

Still, its placement in a film that would eventually become the second highest-grossing of 1998 would kick off Steve Augeri's story in dramatic fashion—or so it seemed.

"'Remember Me' was added to the *Armageddon* soundtrack at the 11th hour, just under the wire," Augeri said. "It was a big win, a summer blockbuster movie with mega Hollywood stars. Then within the movie's context, the song is placed in a New York City Yellow Cab being demolished by a chunk of meteorite. It played for all of a nanosecond. Maybe someone or something was trying to tell us something, even before the train left the station." [151, 619, 620, 621]

WINTER–SUMMER 1999

RELEASES
▶ Steve Perry, *Greatest Hits + Five Unreleased* (album)
▶ Neal Schon, *Piranha Blues* (album)
▶ Steve Perry, "I Stand Alone" (single)

COLLABORATIONS
▶ Jonathan Cain (mixing), Ross Valory, (bass), and Prairie Prince (drums) on **Neal Schon**'s album, *Piranha Blues*.
▶ Neal Schon, lead guitar on **Fergie Frederiksen**'s album, *Equilibrium*.
▶ Steve Smith, drums on **Stef Burns**'s album, *Swamp Tea*.

Schon Reunites with Prairie Prince for *Piranha Blues*

Neal Schon returned to some of his deepest roots with his fourth solo album—and not just because *Piranha Blues* had such a rootsy vibe: The sessions found Schon reconnecting with his former **Golden Gate Rhythm Section** bandmate Prairie Prince.

Schon released *Piranha Blues* in July 1999, but MTV mentioned sessions as early as November 1997. "He was still trying to figure out how to make the Journey thing work," Prince said, "be-

cause after Steve Perry left, they had a few years there where they didn't really have a replacement. It was just this weird little time period."

That may account for Schon's turn toward the comfort of the blues—and of old friends. Jonathan Cain came on board as a mixer, while Schon brought in fellow Journey co-founder Ross Valory and then **Stevie "Keys" Roseman**, who had appeared on Journey's Top 40 1981 hit "The Party's Over (Hopelessly in Love)."

"Neal had this project *Piranha Blues* going," Roseman said, "and my lifelong friend Ross had recommended me to lay down some Hammond B-3 tracks. In typical Neal fashion, he said: 'Hey man, your name came up again and can you come by and listen to what we're doing?'"

Rounding out the *Piranha Blues* band lineup were harmonica player **Michael Peloquin** and singer **Richard Martin Ross**. Schon was particularly excited about the vocalist.

"He called me up and said, 'Hey man, I've got a bunch of new songs and this singer who was in **Bobby "Blue" Bland**'s band,'" said Prince, who also oversaw the inside album art. "I said, 'I would love to record with you. We can record at my studio over in Oakland.'"

Roseman described the setting as an artist's refuge where friends and collaborators drifted in and out—including "Prairie Prince and Steve Smith, even [early Journey member] George Tickner.

"We eventually moved my Hammond organ and Leslie speaker there so we could capture that very sought-after sound for *Piranha Blues*. I would sit for hours, just myself and Neal and all of his gear in the studio, learning the tracks. I was just amazed at how great a guitar player he was—and still is."

Prince was likewise impressed with Martin Ross's "super soulful, almost like **Paul Rodgers**-type voice. We tore it up, and I just really enjoyed that." He said a few informal performances followed, "and one was with **Eric Burdon and The Animals**—and Aynsley Dunbar was their drummer!"

Piranha Blues would not get wider exposure until 2010, during a run of concerts by the short-lived **Neal Schon Band**, which also featured Prairie Prince. [30, 41, 630, 631]

WINTER 2000-01

NUGGETS
▶ VH1's *Behind the Music* will air its special on Journey on Sunday, February 18. The band members will relive the chart-topping success they enjoyed in the '80s, as well as the challenges they faced in later years. — *Chicago Tribune*

VH1's *Behind the Music* Tackles Journey's Story; Tensions Grow

Journey's appearance on VH1's *Behind the Music* was set to air just weeks before the band's long-awaited comeback album hit store shelves. It should have provided a synergistic burst of interest.

Instead, the episode that premiered on February 18, 2001 focused on the now-departed Steve Perry, revealing stunning cracks in Journey's foundation. The current band lineup was largely ignored, while the depths of Perry's alienation were underlined again and again.

Nobody else in the band was buying it—particularly former manager **Herbie Herbert** and veteran journalist **Joel Selvin**, both of whom were interviewed for the program.

They claim Perry exerted complete editorial control over the episode, demanding edits and barring the others from making their own criticisms. "If you watch the documentary on VH1," Schon told *GQ*, "it's pretty much one-sided, with Perry, the way they edited that thing."

What started as a smart PR ploy ended up as something else entirely, because Journey had acquiesced once more in an effort to move on. "Now these guys got the bug to do this, and so powerful is that bug that they gave away the store," Herbert told **Matthew Carty**. "I mean, how they'll ever explain this to their children I can't imagine."

Promos for Journey's appearance on *Behind the Music* featured Perry's soon-to-be-infamous comment: "I never really felt like I was part of the band." Herbert said the original spot then cut to him as he said: "Yeah, that's like the Pope saying he never really felt Catholic."

After all, Journey had watched as Perry traveled separately during *Frontiers*-era tour dates

so girlfriend **Sherrie Swafford** could accompany him. They allowed Perry to shape *Raised on Radio* in his own image, to the point of firing two longtime members.

They came off the road abruptly at Perry's request and subsequently waited for years in the hopes that he would return—then waited years more while Perry mulled over his approach to a hip problem.

Herbert said Journey's *Behind the Music* commercial was pulled and the segment re-edited, with his comment about the Pope deleted. "Perry launched like an MX missile when he saw that," Herbert told Carty. "He went crazy."

Selvin, the longtime San Francisco music writer, found the final results both self-serving and rather boring. "Perry's one of the least interesting characters I've run across in my years here," Selvin said. "He's been a pain in the ass and a total phony."

Perry attempted to clarify his most infamous comment in a later conversation with *GQ*. "When we did the VH1 thing, I said there was quite some time where I never really felt part of the band." What he meant, Perry added, "was that there was a period of time where I always felt, from Neal, that I had to prove myself worthy…" Only later, "when it really took off, I think, did that question really get answered."

An expanded director's cut was eventually released, providing additional context. Still, a consistent focus on Perry and the presentation of their history through his personal lens continued to rankle his former bandmates.

"I'm glad that it came out, because it did so well … but it was definitely very candy-coated," Schon told the *Chicago Sun-Times*. Signed contracts meant that there were "certain things that we could not even talk about, and I was very frustrated about that."

Other complaints related to editing choices: Key insiders like road manager **Pat Morrow** sat for hours of interviews, but received no airtime. A discussion about the death of Perry's mother spooled out, while others who had endured similar heartache were ignored.

Much was also made of Perry's ignored request that Journey change names if they moved forward without him. "Don't crack the stone," Perry said he begged his bandmates. "Well, he did the same thing, way before we did!" Schon told *GQ*, referencing the most recent Perry solo tour with its Journey-dominated setlist.

Schon was also still hurt that "none of us were invited," he said. "Actually, Jonathan Cain tried to go down and go in and see him in San Francisco and they wouldn't let him in the building."

Steve Augeri's presence had not changed anything, as far as Schon was concerned: "To me, the stone was already cracked." [60, 80, 633, 634]

SPRING 2001

RELEASES
▶ Journey, *Arrival* (album)
▶ Journey, "All the Way" (single)
▶ Jonathan Cain, *Namaste* (album)

NUGGETS
▶ **ARTISTS VS. NAPSTER:** Journey's upcoming album got illegally released early courtesy of pirates using the file-sharing app Napster. It happened after the band had released the album in Japan in advance of its U.S. release. So the group went back into the studio and, with its own money, recorded two new tracks for the release in the States. "The old saying goes, 'You get lemons, you make lemonade,'" said Neal Schon. "We needed to have something different on this record that Napster didn't already have." But online feedback from fans suggested the pirated version was too ballad-heavy, so the three new cuts were rockers.
—*Billboard*

Tailored for *Billboard*'s Hot 100, 'All the Way' Falls Short

Journey made no secret of their desire to emulate the sound—and the successes—of the early 1980s on their first album without Steve Perry. They had gotten there in an organic way.

When Schon initially called about writing some new songs, "I thought: 'Well, we don't have a singer,'" Cain told the *Press-Enterprise*. But Schon replied: "My guitar is talking to me, and it's talking Journey."

That became a main impetus for hiring Steve Augeri, who shared an undeniable vocal likeness with their former front man. "If we had somebody who sounded different, then we wouldn't have called it Journey," Cain told the *Houston Press*. "It wouldn't have the same feeling."

So, their first album without Perry, and its only charting single, were always meant to recapture a bygone era—even with a pair of new faces. "All the Way" also found Deen Castronovo continuing to adjust in Journey's remade rhythm section alongside Ross Valory.

"I was in **Bad English** with Neal and Jonathan so I knew how good they were already," Castronovo told the *Press-Enterprise*, but not Valory. "To put it mildly, he's a monster bassist. Yeah, you could say I was a little intimidated."

Though it sometimes appeared Augeri had been hired simply to play the role of someone else, he was hardly a bit player in this scene: "All the Way" became one of six songs he co-wrote on *Arrival*. But he too understood his role as an understudy, gleaning all he could from established hitmakers.

"When you are surrounded by fine composers that make them sound like Rachmaninoff and Bach," Augeri told *Melodic Rock*, "… it elevates you and you only learn from them."

In the end, however, Schon had been right. Collaborating with Cain, Augeri, and **Taylor Rhodes**, they had written a ballad that very much felt like modern-era Journey. If this canny, orchestra-bolstered replica also felt like something far too expected, Augeri encouraged skeptical fans to dig deeper into *Arrival*.

"I think people will find that we're not afraid to take a few chances and we have grown a little bit," Augeri told Knight-Ridder Newspapers. "We didn't want to alienate the old Journey fans, so we sort of kept one foot out the door and one still in the room."

A determined Schon vowed to put Journey "right back where it was, and we are going to be relentless about it," he told the *News & Record*. "If you hammer and hammer at it and do not go away, all of a sudden everyone will be there."

It was more wishful thinking than anything. "All the Way" finished just outside the Top

Continued on Page 268

Band Reloads, But Napster Kills *Arrival* Sales

Journey was aware of the mountainous challenges ahead as they entered New York City's Avatar Studios without Steve Perry at the turn of the millennium.

"It was always something that we hadn't really addressed," Jonathan Cain told Thomson News Service. "We knew that with Steve, we could do it. Could we do it without Steve?"

They could. Journey just needed a new Steve.

The group had bolstered their belated return to the road with a singer who sounded like Perry too. Over the course of more than 120 shows in 1998-99, Steve Augeri turned out to be just the stage performer Schon thought he would be—years before Augeri ever joined Journey.

Schon had been riding around with a friend in the early 1990s when Augeri's former band, **Tall Stories**, came on the radio. "I felt like this guy really kicks my ass!" Schon told *Melodic Rock*. "It sounds like a rocked-out version of Journey—which is where I wanted to go."

Now Journey needed to prove itself to be a credible studio presence. *Arrival* was much more than that. Songs like "All the Way," which almost broke the Top 20 on *Billboard*'s adult-contemporary chart, showed that this new edition could uphold Journey's ballad brand. At the same time, "Higher Place" had a gutsy, prog-inflected vibe.

"It was a big deal for Neal and me to try to create that out of the ashes," Cain told *Classic Rock Revisited*. "Can we still be Journey without Steve in the room? I think we answered the question with that album."

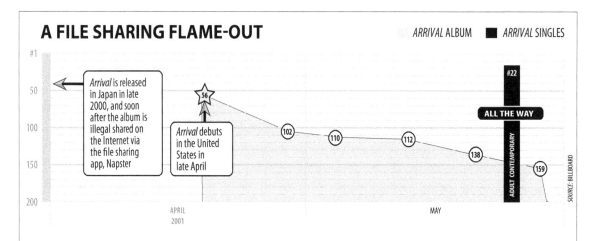

A FILE SHARING FLAME-OUT

ARRIVAL ALBUM   ARRIVAL SINGLES

Arrival is released in Japan in late 2000, and soon after the album is illegal shared on the Internet via the file sharing app, Napster

Arrival debuts in the United States in late April

#22
ALL THE WAY
ADULT CONTEMPORARY

56
102
110
112
138
159

APRIL 2001   MAY

SOURCE: BILLBOARD

It was an inauspicious start for the post-Steve Perry era, and new lead singer Steve Augeri deserved better. After spending months in the studio, Journey released *Arrival* in Japan. In the days before the Internet, this was a non-event. But things went awry when a Sony employee in Sweden released the entire album to the world on the controversial file sharing app, Napster. The result was the worst-charting Journey album since *Next*. The band went back into the studio and added a couple new tracks, but by then it didn't matter. *Arrival* was still being pulled down for free worldwide, and the new tracks were too. The album debuted at an anemic No. 56—a far cry from the No. 3 debut that *Trial By Fire* enjoyed. The single "All the Way" kept the album afloat for a few weeks, but by the end of May it was dead. Shortly after, Sony/Columbia dropped Journey.

TOP CHARTING WEEK: *BILLBOARD—March 3, 2001*

1. Now That's What I Call Music! 6, *Various Artists*
2. 2Pac, *Until the End of Time*
3. Ginuwine, *The Life*
4. Shaggy, *Hot Shot*
5. Bruce Springsteen & The E Street Band, *Live in New York City*
6. Dave Matthews Band, *Everyday*
7. Big Pun, *Endangered Species*
8. Limp Bizkit, *Chocolate Starfish and the Hot Dog Flavored Water*
9. Dido, *No Angel*
53. JOURNEY, *ARRIVAL*

"Signs of Life" represented the beginning of a new era, while "Livin' to Do" closed another one. Cain and Schon still had no idea if Perry would return when they began tentative work on "Signs of Life." Then "Livin' to Do" became Schon's final major collaboration with his father **Matt Schon**, who had made earlier contributions to 1978's "Winds of March" and 1981's "Mother, Father." The lyrics, completed with **Kim Tribble**, directly reference the elder Schon's struggle with terminal cancer.

"World Gone Wild" deftly recreated a "Separate Ways"-style groove, switching things up with an inspirational bridge. Elsewhere, an inventive call-and-response lifts the otherwise expected balladry of "Lifetime of Dreams."

New songwriting partner **Jack Blades** had four composer co-credits on "Higher Place," "World Gone Wild," "I Got a Reason," and "Kiss Me Softly." "I called him, and he just came in," Schon told **Michael Cavacini**. "If I work with him for half a day, we're always going to come up with a cool tune."

Despite the slings and arrows, Augeri proved to be more than a canny imitator. His work on "Loved by You" stayed modulated, as he sang with a much quieter certitude. He then unleashed a moment of controlled fury on "We Will Meet Again," as Deen Castronovo's inventive rhythm built toward a Roy Thomas Baker-esque crescendo.

With final mixing completed by returning *Trial by Fire* producer **Kevin Shirley**, Journey began preparing *Arrival* for release. Then the album got tangled up in a very time-specific issue.

Journey recorded *Arrival* during the Internet's quickly emerging song-swapping era, when trading songs instead of purchasing them initially became widespread. Journey's first album with Augeri leaked on the notorious file-sharing service Napster and suddenly began moving freely from hard drive to hard drive.

"Here we were, three months after being done with the project, and there [Napster] comes with the whole record," Schon told ABC. The band's label quickly tracked down the culprit, but the damage was done.

"Actually, we traced it down to someone in Europe within the company (Columbia Records), actually inside, had given it to a friend or something," Schon told **Allan Sculley** in a separate interview. "And the guy just burned a bunch of copies, and before you knew it, before even the Japanese version was out in Japan, it was out on Napster. It was pretty mind-boggling to me."

Premature release aside, fans pounced on the music, criticizing what they heard as the album's overreliance on ballads. Schon felt vindicated since he had made the same argument to Shirley and the band's A&R rep at Columbia, **John Kalodner**. Augeri took his share of lumps too.

Journey reshuffled the track sequence before setting a new U.S. release date in April 2001, adding "World Gone Wild" and "Nothin' Comes Close" from hastily called post-leak sessions. "What it finally boiled down to was, 'Look, we need to change up this record in order to have one over Napster and everyone who's got our record,'" Schon told ABC.

Ross Valory hailed the changes, saying the final sequencing reminded him of *Infinity*—Journey's first album with Perry. "But there's also so much new creative energy in the band right now," Valory told *The Press Enterprise*.

Arrival never recovered. Even with the two new songs, too many potential buyers had already downloaded MP3s of the album's tracks for free. Sales cratered and *Arrival* became Journey's first album not to at least go gold since 1977's underrated *Next*.

"A lot of bands have tried to put new stuff out," Cain's one-time bandmate **Tony Brock** lamented, "and it's hard, you know? They'd been riding off their old hits with Steve Perry."

Despite connections Valory saw with earlier LPs, "*Arrival* really just didn't arrive," he admitted to interviewer **Mick Burgess**. He openly wondered if their fans simply placed too much sentimental value on the older songs, but he had no clear answers. "I really don't know why it didn't do better 'cause there's some great material on there." [39, 98, 103, 115, 117, 222, 296, 385, 527, 632, 952]

Here we were, three months after being done with the project, and there [Napster] comes with the whole record.

— Neal Schon

20 on Billboard's adult-contemporary charts, while missing the main pop singles chart entirely. This was a disappointing sign of things to come: Journey never had another single charting on the Hot 100 after their final Perry-sung hit, "When You Love a Woman." [102, 117, 122, 625, 641]

SUMMER 2001

RELEASES
▶ Neal Schon, *Voice* (album)
▶ Gregg Rolie, *Roots* (album)

ON THE ROAD
▶ Bad Company, Billy Squier, Color, Joe Stark, John Waite, Night Ranger, Peter Frampton, and Styx

---

Rolie Rediscovers His Roots With Help from Old Friends

Santana's induction into the Rock & Roll Hall of Fame had Gregg Rolie thinking about a return to his old way of making music. But the title of the resulting album proved to be misleading for some.

Roots was not about returning to those specific sounds. It was more like the attitude.

"I didn't take into consideration the airwaves, radio, and who was going to get onto MTV and who wasn't, and all that kind of nonsense," Rolie told *Mixdown*.

He constructed the album the same way.

Rolie's former Journey bandmate Neal Schon took a notable guest turn, and ex-Storm drummer **Ron Wikso** played a critical role.

"Gregg and I became really good friends almost immediately after I joined **The Storm**," Wikso said. Their rehearsal studio was in Petaluma, California, near to where Rolie was living in Novato, about half an hour north of San Francisco. Wikso stayed at his house for weeks at a time.

They "just hit it off personally and we also really enjoyed playing together, so I think that was the foundation of it," Wikso added. "Gregg and I had stayed in touch fairly regularly in the years between when we stopped working with The Storm and when we first started working on the *Roots* CD."

Initially, their focus was not on recording an album. Rolie and Wikso were just hanging out, going to dinner, and playing golf. But Wikso regularly brought their conversations back around to creating new music. Then Rolie moved to Poway, California, near San Diego and closer to Wikso, and began writing again.

"Ron is really the one who got me out of my hammock," Rolie told *Goldmine*. "I tried to put him off at first, but he kept at me to do something and wouldn't let up."

Rolie's initial idea was to record an acoustic project, as heard on more elemental moments like "Domingo" and "Con Todo Mi Corazon." "It was going to be really low key," Rolie told *Classic Rock Revisited*. Performing on stage with Santana again changed his mind. "When I got back from that, I started writing all kinds of stuff, and I just let it fly."

Wikso started by cataloging his demos, which he recorded using the old ADAT tapes of the era. "So that was the first thing to sort out—getting his tracks into the computer and lining everything up," Wikso said. "You have to remember that this was 1999, so the technology was a lot different than it is now. Also, we weren't using recording engineers—it was just me and him."

Rolie eventually settled on an approach that was not quite Woodstock and definitely not what came afterward. "If you've heard the stuff we did together with The Storm, and you've heard the *Roots* or *Rain Dance* records we did together," Wikso said, "you'd know that musically, they're very different."

Roots boasts a rangy experimentalism that The Storm never achieved, but within settled, more mainstream constructions that Santana would not attempt until well after Rolie's departure. "I named it *Roots* and everybody thinks it is going back to my roots with Santana, which is fine," Rolie told *Classic Rock Revisited*. "It really is not that way at all."

Wikso replaced the automated drum tracks from Rolie's demos, then they brought in a core group of collaborators that included fellow Santana alum **Alphonso Johnson** on bass, guitarist **Dave Amato** of **REO Speedwagon**, and others.

Rolie sent those recordings to engineer **Tom Size**, who completed *Roots* at his Tomland studio, staging a mini-Santana reunion. **Michael**

Carabello and Schon ("Breakin' My Heart") both added parts, as did **José "Chepito" Areas**'s son, **Adrian**.

Despite those age-old connections, Rolie had finally found his signature solo sound. "I was just going to make it acoustic music and I had never done that," he admitted to *Mixdown*. "And then I opened the whole thing up." [25, 166, 174, 220]

SPRING 2002

Schon, Ex-HSAS Bandmate Hagar, Connect for Planet Us

Neal Schon was between Journey albums. **Sammy Hagar** was between groups. The stars seemed to have finally aligned again for the more visible half of **Hagar Schon Aaronson Shrieve**.

They built their next collaboration in 2002 around leftover songs from a second album by **Hardline** before Schon left the band. "I have a lot of material that I have written through the years that is on the heavier side," Schon told *Classic Rock Revisited* back then. "It has not found a home."

Schon brought along Journey's drummer and Hagar invited **Van Halen**'s bassist to complete a new band called **Planet Us**. He and Hagar considered adding another guitarist too. "One of the names I threw out was **Slash**," Schon added. "I had played with Slash before and I knew that we were compatible as two guitar players."

Then Slash missed their initial rehearsals alongside Deen Castronovo and **Michael Anthony**. "Finally, we recorded two songs without him," Hagar told *Melodic Rock*, "and it was so good that we were like, 'We don't really need anybody else because it was so good with Neal.'"

Planet Us got off to a fast start, completing "Vertigo" and "Peeping Through a Hole." "Sammy knew exactly what to do with it immediately," Schon told *Classic Rock Revisited*. "Him and I are very, very quick in the studio."

They debuted at the annual Bay Area Music Awards in April 2002, performing the two Planet Us originals. "We played in the Bay Area at the Bammies and just ripped the place apart," Schon told *Ultimate Classic Rock*'s **Matt Wardlaw**. "I'm telling you, it was like nothing I'd ever seen, and I've played live with a lot of different bands at the Bammies."

Schon, Castronovo, and Anthony also joined Hagar during solo concert encores on May 17 and 18 at the Hard Rock Hotel in Las Vegas. Meanwhile, MTV reported that "Vertigo" was pitched for Sony's contemporary *Spider-Man* film, but that did not happen. Neither did Planet Us.

Joe Satriani guested with the group in a March 12, 2003 appearance on the syndicated *Rockline* radio show, where Planet Us performed "Vertigo." "I kept on mentioning to Sammy about Joe Satriani ... and that I thought Joe would be great," Schon told *Ultimate Classic Rock*.

But Planet Us' initial explorations as a five-piece group went nowhere and the shooting star of this side project vanished. Hagar and Anthony rejoined Van Halen, and Satriani subsequently joined **Chickenfoot**, a post-Van Halen band featuring Hagar and Anthony. [441, 643, 644, 699]

SUMMER–FALL 2002

NUGGETS

▶ Fox Broadcasting is wheeling out a new multi-night *Star Search* lookalike show, *American Idol: Search for a Superstar*, airing on Tuesdays and Wednesdays. The premise is this: aspiring artists compete across the country to become a select few who will, if chosen, perform on Tuesdays then get mercilessly critiqued by a panel of musically inclined "judges." A takeoff of the popular British *Pop Idol*, the show's judges include British recording exec **Simon Cowell**, 1980s pop star **Paula Abdul** and recording studio maestro Randy Jackson (who also took a long turn as bassist for the pop-rock band Journey in the late 1980s). The season's winner gets a recording deal.
— *New York Daily News*

Continued on Page 271

COLUMBIA DROPS JOURNEY; BAND SELF-RELEASES NEW EP

Columbia Records had long ago insisted that Journey add a true front man, leading to the hiring of Steve Perry. So it was no surprise the label dropped the group not long after Perry's departure.

Journey chalked it up to larger trends in the music industry. The truth is, they had attempted to start over—but Perry's ghost still haunted them. *Arrival* became Journey's first album to miss the Top 20 since before he arrived. Everything was measured in this way.

"Losing the label was a shock to everyone in the organization, yet it was all the rage and rampant among the industry those days," front man Steve Augeri said. "The business was in flux more than usual, and we were swept up along with a host of other huge acts. If it were just us, we could take it personally—but it wasn't. Still, it hurt. It was a blow to everyone's ego."

The file-sharing fiasco was not the only reason the album's sales numbers were disastrous. Journey was struggling to connect with a long-standing fan base that was still holding out for Perry's return. *Arrival* stalled south of the Top 50.

"It's hard to say whether it was because of Napster or whether people were not interested in the new music," Valory told the *Toledo Blade*. "No one will ever know."

Neal Schon's typically positive spin hinted at what would happen next: "We are not signed to Sony anymore and it is really kind of cool," he told *Classic Rock Revisited*. "Now we get to do what we want to."

He decided to leverage Journey's newfound freedom with *Red 13*, an independently released EP created just for fans which broke most every one of Journey's modern-era rules along the way. "I wanted to put on our musical hats and get creative," Schon added. "Let's jump off the cliff and see if we can fly."

At the time, Schon compared the EP to the more experimental moments on 1983's *Frontiers*, but its heart and soul traced further back. *Red 13* recalled Journey's determinedly adventurous early period, in particular the expansive title song.

"There was no one from the major label breathing down our necks saying what we should be playing and not playing," Schon told the *Blade*. "We weren't thinking about radio at all."

Released on November 26, 2002, *Red 13* also

confirmed Augeri's place in this refashioned creative nucleus. He co-wrote three of four songs with Jonathan Cain and Schon. There were also additional contributions from several others—including **Geoff Tate**, the **Queensryche** front man whom Journey also considered as a successor to Perry.

The Tate co-written, **Pink Floyd**-esque "Walking Away From the Edge" was actually a holdover from the *Arrival* sessions and featured one of Augeri's first attempts at taking over for Perry. No longer working within Columbia Records' restrictive space, Journey was now confident enough to share these edgier new sounds.

"We had done *Arrival* and basically had done everything that the record company had really wanted us to do, and Neal just wanted to do something that he wanted to do—so we just kind of rocked," Jonathan Cain told interviewer **David Lee**, with a laugh.

Initially, Journey sold *Red 13* only through the band's website, but Schon said interest eventually built to the point that they felt it was worthwhile to issue an in-store version for the holiday season. It still failed to chart in America.

"The way I look at it is: Okay, I think there's very little radio left,'" Schon told *Ultimate Classic Rock*'s **Matt Wardlaw**. "So I feel like, why not? Why not stretch things out and make them a little more musical?"

Chastened, Journey did not issue another full-length album until 2005's *Generations*. [151, 184, 643, 645, 646, 647]

SPRING–WINTER 2003

ON THE ROAD

▶ .38 Special, Cheap Trick, Foreigner, Eddie Money, Not the Joneses, REO Speedwagon, Sammy Hagar, Styx, and Yes.

Festivals: Arrowfest 2003, The Woodlands, Texas

Steve Perry Becomes Friends With Filmmaker Patty Jenkins

For many, the cultural rebirth of "Don't Stop Believin'" will always start with its placement in the 2007 series finale of *The Sopranos*.

Not Steve Perry. He traces the genesis of this dizzying comeback to director **Patty Jenkins**'s film *Monster*.

The emotionally involving, tragic script finds **Charlize Theron** starring as real-life Florida prostitute **Aileen Wuornos** who was executed in 2002 after being convicted of killing seven clients. *Monster* premiered on December 24, 2003 to wide critical acclaim, with the Journey song featured in a dramatic early scene.

Suddenly, "Don't Stop Believin'" was current, not old. The first problem was that Jenkins had not secured the required permissions to use it. The second was that the production budget was spent. They had no money to pay Journey.

Theron, who would go on to win an Oscar for Best Actress in the film, wrote a personal plea to Perry.

"Basically, I was just shameless and begging like nobody's business," Theron told the *San Francisco Chronicle*, with a laugh. Luckily for all involved, Perry "really loved the film and said he saw what we were trying to do with the music," Theron told *American Songwriter*.

"It was the most beautiful adaptation of the song," Perry told *The Hollywood Reporter*, "and that kind of launched it with sporting events, the Chicago White Sox, *The Sopranos* …"

In fact, Perry was so engaged with the project that he began a long tradition of joining Jenkins during the post-production of her movies. With his music career on hold, there was plenty of time to indulge a secondary interest in film.

Perry pulled up a chair next to Jenkins and said, "Hey, I really love your movie. How can I help you?" Jenkins told *The New York Times*. "It was the beginning of one of the greatest friendships of my life."

The small-budget film suddenly had a surprising new ally. Theron specifically thanked Perry in a subsequent acceptance speech at the Golden Globes.

"Steve just really got into the story," she told the *Chronicle*. "He flew from San Francisco to L.A. and ended up spending two months with us. It was like we were in a band with Steve Perry!" [253, 687, 692, 693, 694, 695]

Schon's Planet Us Project Morphs Into Soul SirkUS

After leaving **Hardline** and watching **Planet Us** fall apart, Neal Schon was sitting on a growing pile of unreleased ideas. Then he met **Jeff Scott Soto** and **Marco Mendoza** in January 2004 at the National Association of Music Merchants convention in Los Angeles.

"We got along great, and he loved my versatility as a singer," Soto said, "which led to **Soul SirkUS**."

Deen Castronovo was held over from the Planet Us sessions but did not take part in the earliest writing sessions as Soto developed Schon's home recordings.

"Most were about eight to 10 minutes long, no real structure, just him playing parts over a drum loop that would repeat a verse idea like 16 bars over and over," Soto said. "I dissected each one, took sections I felt I could write strongly over, and cut and pasted them into four-to-five-minute songs. From there, I went to work and crafted melodies and lyrics, then demoed them to share with Neal."

Castronovo and a starstruck Mendoza subsequently joined to record the album that would become *World Play*—or the first version anyway. "I'm such a big fan," Mendoza said. "You can't be in this business, and not be a fan of

Continued on Page 273

Journey put their differences aside to receive a coveted star on the Hollywood Walk of Fame in December 2005. It was a multigenerational reunion that included (L-R) Jonathan Cain, George Tickner, Steve Perry, Aynsley Dunbar, Neal Schon, Robert Fleischman, Ross Valory, Steve Augeri, Steve Smith, and Deen Castronovo.

JOURNEY REUNITES FOR HOLLYWOOD WALK OF FAME HONOR

By January 2005, there had been some 2,274 previous Hollywood Walk of Fame ceremonies, each of them different in their own way. Journey would spend theirs doing something that had become quite familiar: waiting on Steve Perry.

Journey's fan club played a key role in securing this honor, submitting a presentation to the Hollywood Chamber of Commerce on the band's behalf. There was an administrative fee of $15,000 to construct the star, dig up the sidewalk, and put it in place. (By 2023, the cost was $75,000.)

The Chamber invited members of every generation of the long-running group and an impressive array of them accepted. Aynsley Dunbar and George Tickner from Journey's original incarnation rubbed elbows with next-era figures like Robert Fleischman and Steve Smith. The band's entire current lineup was there too, with Steve Augeri dressed in all white.

But as Neal Schon arrived, he still had not heard back from Perry. "I knew nothing about it, and nobody else knew [anything] about it," Schon told *Rolling Stone*.

Schon had gone so far as to plead for Perry to join them during a live interview one day earlier. A disc jockey on KLOS' *The Mark and Brian Show* asked, "'Is Steve gonna be there?' live on the radio," Schon added. "I said, 'You guys got

his number? Let's call him and invite him!'"

Schon said they never got through. Perry said he hung up on the DJs. "They wanted to be the ones that got me there! The kingmakers!" Perry told *Kerrang!*. "No, why don't you go fuck yourselves and leave me alone?"

Waiting was something of a theme with a Walk of Fame honor which had been too long coming, according to Schon. "I guess I would have been more slayed by it if it had happened about a century ago," he told *Guitar International*.

In fact, he sounded like he was almost trying to talk himself out of it: "Don't they have Disney characters on the Walk of Fame?" Schon asked the *San Francisco Weekly* back then. (They do.)

Meanwhile, Perry fretted over having "never met the singer, I'd never met the drummer," he told *GQ*. "And we do have some turbulence between us." Then Perry changed his mind.

"If I was going to go, it was going to be on my own terms," he told *Kerrang!*, confirming that he hired a private security firm to oversee the appearance. "I didn't even tell my attorney! I told no one."

Perry instantly became the focus of attention, seven years after severing ties with Journey. He told *GQ* that "it was really, really great to see everybody. At some point, in all our lives, we'd all contributed to that star on the ground."

He used time at the mic to pay tribute to their loyal fans. "You can have all the stuff that we knew it took, from management, with the crew and the best players, but without you, you don't got shit," Perry said from the podium. "This star really belongs to you."

Schon shared similar sentiments, praising "the fans that had showed up from all over the world. That was a much bigger deal than looking at the star in the sidewalk," he told *Guitar International*.

Perry said there was an immediate connection with his former bandmate. "He hugged me, I hugged him, and he said a few things in my ear—that are mine, I'm not gonna mention 'em," he told *GQ*.

During the ceremony, Perry said Schon kept glancing over. He said Schon's response was: "'What the fuck, y'know? I'm so glad you came. Wow.' It was a lift for me that I emotionally needed."

There would be a loose jam later that night at the House of Blues on the Sunset Strip where Fleischman rejoined the group. "Neal told me he wanted me to come up and sing 'Wheel in the Sky,' and later that night they introduced me and I went on stage to sing it," Fleischman told interviewer **John Parks**. Inspired by this return to performing, Fleischman formed a new band called **The Sky**.

Perry was conspicuously absent from the post-event festivities. Schon admitted he had not talked to him in years at that point. They would not speak again for longer still.

In the meantime, Perry admits that he visits the Hollywood Walk of Fame from time to time. He once found himself at a coffee shop right in front of Journey's star, just watching people go by. Soon, two younger fans asked a friend to take a photo.

"They laid down on each side of it and tried to pull sexy poses with the star," Perry told *GQ*. "And their friend was kind of hovering over them with a camera." Perry rushed out and joined the stunned trio. "They love the band enough to lay down on the sidewalk? In front of all these people walkin' around 'em and shit?" he added. "I thought, 'Okay. I'm layin' down, too.'" [80, 203, 452, 621, 635, 636, 637, 638]

Journey. Massive songs, and massive history."

There was a sense of musical discovery in the room, and the songs came together quickly.

"Without exaggerating, we got together on a Thursday, wrote some ideas and we went into the studio and did the rhythm tracks on a Friday," Mendoza said. "We got together again two weeks later, and we did the same thing.

"There was a lot of electricity and a lot of juices flowing around. Jeff Scott, I can't say enough about him and what he and Neal did together to complete the album."

By the time it was over, all but one of the old Planet Us ideas had been set aside. Soto had a hand in finishing some 12 songs, while completing one himself ("My Love, My Friend"). Schon (the title track) and Mendoza ("Abailar To' Mundo") both had individual songwriting credits as well. Schon and Hagar's "Peeping Through a Hole" re-emerged as simply "Peephole."

Schon noticed something special happening with this new rhythm section: "Deen and Marco just clicked as a bass player and drummer, in the early stages of that," said Schon, who would successfully pair them again later.

Soul SirkUS almost came to a sudden stop, however, when Castronovo got the flu and then bronchitis. "I was reading him, he was reading me," Mendoza said. "We're into the groove, the pocket—but Deen had some health issues, and couldn't go."

Soul SirkUS replaced Castronovo with a fusion and prog-influenced Australian drummer named **Virgil Donati**. His approach so impressed Schon that he had *World Play* reworked with Donati's drum tracks and added five more new songs.

"Working with Neal was easy as pie, we had a great deal of respect for one another musically and it really clicked organically," Soto said. "We got the incredible Virgil Donati, but I missed what we could have done with Deen, as well."

Soul SirkUS embarked on a short tour of the U.S. and Europe, before Schon returned to his day job. "Unfortunately, he got busy with Journey again right after—really busy," Mendoza said, "and that was the end of the project. There was talk about revisiting and getting together again in the future, but it never happened."

Still, this was the beginning of a lengthy period of collaboration between Schon and Mendoza. "From that point on—and this is really old school—he had me on the Rolodex," Mendoza said with a laugh. "There's a lot of mutual respect. I think he appreciated that—that I could pull it off, that I listened. I became one of the colors on his canvas, if you will." [14, 19, 31, 649]

Struggles Peak As Band's 12th Album Falls Flat

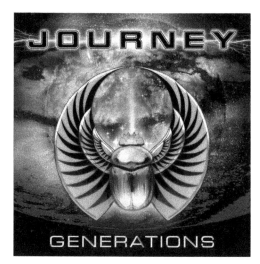

Journey was telegraphing a message when the egalitarian *Generations* arrived on August 29, 2005: Steve Augeri was not their long-term solution as front man.

How else to explain featuring everyone on vocals?

Augeri was a try-hard guy. Founding Journey manager **Herbie Herbert** recognized it from the first, favorably comparing him with Steve Perry and **Kevin Chalfant**. "Augeri's a much better guy than both of those guys, and is a much more solid citizen," Herbert told **Matthew Carty**. He's "maybe a little bit disadvantaged in the talent area, but if he's got more desire and more 'want to,' that makes up for it."

He'd been struggling on the road for a while, however, as a brutal touring schedule took its toll. Deen Castronovo increasingly filled the gap in concert as Augeri faltered in 2004. Castronovo only initially sang a couple of songs—"After the Fall" and "Mother, Father"—but then Augeri started taking off for as long as 45 minutes during these shows.

Soon, vocals on Journey's tour became a communal effort. *Generations* pushed Augeri aside forever.

Ironically, he'd arrived at these sessions on a creative high. At Jonathan Cain's suggestion, Augeri had gotten a new Apple computer which came preloaded with lots of new looping and recording tech. He quickly began fleshing out some ideas which excited and intrigued Schon.

Cain arrived later to complete *Generations* with some co-writing tweaks and additional songs. Augeri earned co-writing credits on five of the album's original 12 songs—including the solo compo-

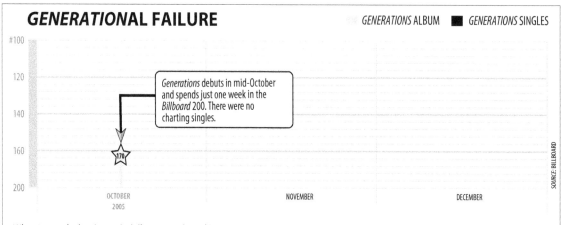

GENERATIONAL FAILURE

GENERATIONS ALBUM ■ *GENERATIONS* SINGLES

Generations debuts in mid-October and spends just one week in the *Billboard* 200. There were no charting singles.

SOURCE: BILLBOARD

When Journey's abortive *Arrival* album was released in 2001, it suffered when it was uploaded to the Internet via Napster before the band could officially release it. Sales suffered, and Sony/Columbia dropped the group. The band tried to respond by self-releasing its own EP a year later, *Red 13*, but it did not chart either. The post-Steve Perry era was not going well. With three years breaking in a new singer and time to develop new material, the band hoped *Generations* would flip the script. It didn't. Rather, it represented perhaps the worst release the band ever experienced. Even with the Napster debacle, *Arrival* debuted at No. 53, and still managed to stay on the charts for a month after that. *Generations* was on the charts for a single week, and had no charting singles. A change was required, and it would come soon.

TOP CHARTING WEEK: *BILLBOARD*—October 22, 2005

1. Ashlee Simpson, *I Am Me*
2. Rod Stewart, *Thanks for the Memory*
3. Martina McBride, *Timeless*
4. Nickelback, *All the Right Reasons*
5. Stevie Wonder, *A Time to Love*
6. Bun B, *Trill*
7. Depeche Mode, *Playing the Angel*
8. The Black Eyed Peas, *Monkey Business*
9. Alicia Keys, *Unplugged*
170. JOURNEY, *GENERATIONS*

sition, "Butterfly (She Flies Alone)."

The sessions that followed began as a homecoming. Journey returned to the Record Plant in Sausalito, California, where they had recorded 1986's *Raised on Radio*. They were also back with **Kevin Elson**, who served as producer on a series of turn-of-the-1980s triumphs.

All those older projects had featured a single voice. Augeri stepped aside as the others sang on about half a dozen songs for *Generations*, including their expanded editions.

Fans who had been to Journey's more recent shows were familiar with the approach. "This is a tradition that carries over from touring the last couple of years," Ross Valory told the *Star-News*, "where everyone was singing at least one song in the set."

But it all felt quite different inside an album's more intimate environment. Even standout Augeri moments like the **Glenn Hughes**-esque "Better Together" and the album-closing 9/11-themed "Beyond the Clouds" tended to get lost in the merry-go-round of other voices.

Nevertheless, Augeri says he understood the impulse to usher others forward. Even his studio showcases were suddenly taking extra effort.

"I remember Neal sending me back to the studio to re-record my vocal for 'Faith in the Heartland,'" Augeri said. "He felt I was just phoning it in, and you know what? He was right. At the time, I was singing with too much caution so as to not blow out my voice, which seemed to be more often than I care to remember."

Augeri had grown so uncertain about things that he had trouble engaging with the lyrics.

"It's one thing when you're out on the road night after night. You need to save some for the next town, the next show—especially if it's your third night in a row," Augeri said. "But in the studio, you've got to bare your soul, unbridle yourself, sing with reckless abandon—leave it all on the field, as they say. It was becoming increasingly more difficult to do that for me, physically as well as mentally."

Journey had no choice, even in Augeri's mind. "The obvious remedy was to spread the responsibilities around to everyone," he added, "and luckily and fortunately everyone was up to the task."

Castronovo provided the best guest turns. His quickly emerging talent as a lead singer was showcased on "A Better Life" and the **Jack Blades** co-written bonus track "Never Too Late."

This came as no surprise to Castronovo's former bandmate **Ricky Phillips**. "We didn't know he had that voice until the first **Bad English** record was done," said Phillips, who had asked Castronovo to track some backing vocals in his home studio. "I knew he had a nice voice, but I didn't know how good it was. I went back and said, 'You've got to hear this kid sing.' We started using Deen on everything, and now look where he is."

"Never Too Late" connected on a deeper level with Castronovo, a recovering alcoholic who teared up while they worked on the song. "It showed me where I was," he told *Melodic Rock*. Augeri willingly handed over lead vocal duties. "Steven came up and said, 'Man, that's yours.'"

Castronovo was highly critical of these performances, reminded again of Perry's towering impact after they shared in Journey's Hollywood Walk of Fame induction. "I was in freakin' shock," Castronovo told *The Morning Call*. "It was like, 'Oh my god, I got to meet Steve Perry.'"

Like everyone else, he'd been unsure if Perry would take part. "I was praying he would be there," Castronovo told *Melodic Rock*. "I don't have any right to be there—I don't have anything to do with that legacy, but he needed to be there."

Schon did a credible job on "In Self-Defense," updating an old **Schon & Hammer** track. But Valory ("Gone Crazy") and Cain ("Every Generation" and the bonus cut "Pride of the Family") were miscast on sessions where a healthy Augeri would have been the better choice.

Soon, Augeri would be gone. He never made it through the tour in support of *Generations*.

"It was our last record," Augeri said, "and I can say this without hesitation: For Neal, he absolutely had to keep moving forward. It was his lifeblood—especially when it came to creating music. Interesting music, not just drivel. It had to be top shelf. Jon too, of course. Nothing less than your best effort."

Journey had gone on without one Steve. Now, they had to go on without another. [26, 151, 158, 649, 663]

THE CHALLENGES OF FOLLOWING A LEGENDARY FRONT MAN

Steve Augeri was not the first person to take over for a legendary front man, and he certainly would not be the last. Still, his sudden exit begged a question or two.

Are soundalike successors simply doomed to fail? Is it better to have sung and lost your job, than to have never sung at all?

"The way I saw it, in my mind it was the equivalent of replacing any of the most famous singers in any of the most famous bands I'd been a fan of—pick one, anyone," Augeri said. "Now, insert this no-name unknown and watch the darts and arrows fly. Fly, they did—and for quite some time. But this was my shot, right?"

Singers face a brutal late-career reality: Their voices change, whether through overuse or because of aging—or both. At the same time, the economics of touring requires a certain number of shows to make these gargantuan undertakings worthwhile. The dates, and the days, add up.

As rock approached a new century, the longest-tenured vocalists were starting to slow down. What were their former bandmates to do? "So much of a band's identity is invested in the vocalist and in the vocal performances," San Francisco music writer **Joel Selvin** said. "So, if you have problems with the lead vocalist, you have to do something else."

Fans may pine for former vocalists, but that's no guarantee that their favorite bands can pull off their favorite songs anymore. Steve Perry remains a fixation "because he's the original, and because he was a great, great talent," **Herbie Herbert** told **Matthew Carty**. "What you're dealing with there is you're comparing the current reality of **Kevin Chalfant** or the current reality of Steve Augeri to the memory of Steve Perry. And trust me, that memory is jaded, and dead-ass wrong."

At the same time, there are enormous pressures involved for these new recruits. The songs can be both difficult to pull off and universally known, and it all happens before an often very skeptical fan base.

Lawrence Gowan had a typical response when contacted about succeeding **Dennis DeYoung** in **Styx**: "The main concern I had was, 'Well, wait, I gotta find out if I got the right vocal range,'" Gowan said. "So, we dusted off my *Grand Illusion* album and listened—and I realized, 'Oh, yeah, I can hit those notes.' That's the most critical thing going in, honestly: Can you hit those notes or not?"

Still, sounding the same is no guarantee of acceptance. Augeri was all too aware of that, but also felt like he could not pass up an opportunity like this one.

"No matter how dark things were going to get, no matter how much blowback Journey or I personally were going to be the target of, no matter how much criticism or grief the rest of the band was going to take, this was a once-in-a-lifetime opportunity," Augeri said. "It was my chance to prove I had the goods, if I had any place or reason to be making music at all—let alone with the caliber of a band as Journey. It was my life's goal, my life's dream. So, what can you do but put your best foot forward?"

Of course, many bands have seen their share of lineup changes, but the circumstances were not the same—nor were the successors. Instead, death was often a catalyst: **Brian Johnson** succeeded **Bon Scott** in **AC/DC**. **Johnny Van Zant** took over for his late brother **Ronnie** in **Lynyrd Skynyrd**. **Adam Lambert** became **Queen**'s longest-lasting replacement after **Freddie Mercury** died.

When members left on their own, bands were sometimes more apt to begin a new era rather than echo the one just ended—even at the risk of alienating long-standing fans.

"So much of this comes down to the audience's perception, you know?" Gowan said. "I remember when **Peter Gabriel** was suddenly not the lead singer in **Genesis**. I remember just thinking, 'Well, I'm finished with Genesis. That's over.' But had that not happened, would any of us have known how phenomenal—I mean, there are no words to describe how unbelievable **Phil Collins** was. Until then, I just knew he was the drummer, but to be a front man, entertainer—a phenomenal talent?"

During the era before **Jason Scheff** set a soundalike standard in place of **Peter Cetera** with **Chicago**, **The Moody Blues** made a dramatic musical turn as **Denny Laine** gave way to **Justin Hayward**. **David Coverdale** would take **Deep Purple** to places undreamt of by **Ian Gillan**. **The Doobie Brothers** also went through a seismic shift in the late 1970s.

"There was the **Tom Johnston**-to-**Michael McDonald** routine, where no one would mistake one with the other for a second," Selvin said. "That really worked out very well for The Doobie Brothers; it gave them a second ca-

reer. Same with AC/DC. They brought in Brian Johnson, and he wasn't a Bon Scott imitator at all. The band's sound was more important than the vocalist's sound."

Sammy Hagar did not even attempt to replicate **David Lee Roth**'s shtick in Van Halen. **Brian Howe** sounded nothing like **Bad Company**'s founding front man **Paul Rodgers**. **The Power Station** brought in the ambitious, more rock-focused **Michael Des Barres**, who could not have sounded—or looked—less like his sleekly debonair predecessor.

"**Robert Palmer**, I adored a decade before I did the gig," said Des Barres, while namechecking Palmer's early blues-rock work in **Vinegar Joe**. "In terms of joining the band, people would say, 'These are enormous shoes to fill'—and I said, 'I have big feet.' It's confidence, and confidence is not ego. It's just knowing that you can do what is required."

It's easier to build off that sense of self-assurance, however, when you're not trying to be someone else. Other bands gave singers like Gowan an opportunity Augeri never had, moving forward without a fixation on the past.

"They never asked me to sound like, act like, or in any way mimic Dennis DeYoung. I didn't even realize at the time that they hadn't asked me that," Gowan said. "You know, as YouTube began to come along and people's performances are on there more and more, I've seen people doing Styx impressions and it's like, 'Wow, he sounds way more like him than me.'"

That would never be the case with Journey, who had tied themselves so closely with Perry's approach at the mic. Soon, Neal Schon would join Gowan on YouTube, scrubbing through videos in an attempt to find his band's next singer.

Journey was hardly alone in looking for newer replacement parts so they could keep their well-oiled touring machine out on the road: **Lou Gramm**'s successor, **Kelly Hansen**, remained with Foreigner through their final tour. **Jon Davison** became **Yes**' long-term replacement for **Jon Anderson**.

They typically had far less chart success when creating new music, but that was not the point. These legacy bands were often simply trying to remain in the more lucrative live music space.

"The bands that continue to thrive, or even grow, after they replace a lead vocalist are rare. It's hard," Selvin argued, then laughingly added: "You've got to contend with Sammy Hagar singing 'Jump.'" [60, 151, 243, 412, 903]

CITY OF HOPE

The Steve Augeri era had ended abruptly and Journey was looking for a lead singer again. A new vocalist didn't have to be a Steve Perry clone, but good band chemistry was a prerequisite. Then, one day, Neal Schon stumbled on someone in the unlikeliest of places—a new frontman to lead them back to the land of gold and platinum.

SUMMER-FALL 2006

RELEASES
▶ Journey, *Generations* (album)

NUGGETS
▶ **OLD BANDS, NEW SINGERS:** There's a classic rock duel going on between two touring juggernauts this summer. Journey is touring with **Def Leppard** and has grossed more than $11 million in 18 shows (264, 301 in attendance with 82% capacity). Meanwhile, **Queen** and **Paul Rodgers** has grossed almost $13 million in 22 shows (166,716 in attendance with 62% capacity), giving the San Francisco rockers a slight statistical edge in the rock and roll world of old bands with new lead singers. **INXS** and **The Cars** are a distant third and fourth. —*Billboard*

ON THE ROAD
▶ Better Than Ezra, Blueground Undergrass, Def Leppard, Hot Apple Pie, Marcia Ball, Reneé Austin, Steve Riley & The Mamou Playboys, Terri Clark, The Charlie Daniels Band, Thousand Foot Krutch, and Watermelon Slim

Exhausted and Under Fire, Steve Augeri Bids Adieu

Steve Augeri had been handy as Journey willed itself back to life. "It was daunting," he told *The Daily News*. "I was an amateur being thrown into the deep end of a pool."

They toured relentlessly, reconnecting with fans one show—sometimes, one setlist—at a time. By 2006, they were playing huge festivals, and appearing on a hot ticket with **Def Leppard**.

It all happened amid an unremitting backlash. "The specter of Steve Perry is still there," Augeri told *The Monitor*, "and it will always be there."

Journey was up front about the fact that Perry was no longer fronting the band. The band billed shows as "Journey Featuring Steve Augeri," as had been contractually stipulated.

Yet powerful radio DJ **Don Imus** memorably offered to refund fans' money spent on tickets before a late-1990s performance at the Beacon Theatre in New York City. He told his listeners: "This isn't Journey."

"No Steve Perry, no Journey!" one fan exclaimed as Augeri arrived for Journey's Hollywood Walk of Fame induction in 2005. "He's a really nice man, but he's a fraud," she told the *San Francisco Weekly*.

Then Augeri started to wear down. His vocal issues were there all along, at first because of his inexperience, and at the end because Journey had been working so hard to win back fans.

Augeri overdid it on the first day of rehearsals for 2001's *Arrival*, just before worried label representatives were due to arrive. "I blew my voice out," Augeri told *Rolling Stone*. "For the first week or two, we were repairing the voice."

By the time Journey set out on the tour in support of *Generations*, Augeri was taking lengthy breaks during their shows. But the schedule never slowed, as the second straight year with more than 70 shows loomed. They were marathon performances too, sometimes three hours.

A string of European dates would precede Journey's return to the U.S. for shows with Def Leppard. The pressure, Augeri later admitted, was overwhelming. "If you go down, nobody makes a nickel. You go into the red," Augeri told *Rolling Stone*. "There's a bit of a psychological thing going on."

As Augeri audibly faltered, former manager **Herbie Herbert** said he wondered why Journey did not simply lower the song keys. At this pace, however, it might not have mattered. "You need recovery time," Herbert told *Melodic Rock*, "and you know what? As you get older, you need more and more of it."

Rumors about lip-syncing began percolating on message boards. Then a radio producer named **Svante Pettersson** openly questioned whether Augeri sang with a backing tape during Journey's June 9, 2006 appearance at the Swedish Rock Festival. That set off months of speculation, as one Journey fan launched a stand-alone site titled Escape to Tape that tracked instances where Augeri's vocals might have been augmented.

Internet sleuths claimed that Augeri was performing along to recordings from their earlier 2001 concert recording. By June 10, *Rolling Stone* had published a story with the headline: "Journey Vocalist Won't Stop Deceivin'."

Longtime Journey concert engineer **Kevin Elson** "got caught, I guess, up in Stockholm using a canned vocal off the hard drive," Herbert told author **Neil Daniels**. Augeri's live feed had been mistakenly sent to the radio booth. "They kept going, 'Wait, this guy can't sing. ... He's terrible.' Then they go out in the hall, and it sounds perfect."

The tour limped into Raleigh, North Carolina, on July 4, 2006, and Augeri was summarily replaced. Journey released a statement saying he would immediately leave to rest and recover from an "acute throat condition."

Band members continued to deny the lip-syncing allegations, and Augeri said he was barred from discussing it. "I can't answer that question," he told *Rolling Stone*. "I can't legally answer it."

That left Augeri to heal up and tinker with his vocal technique. When he finally returned to the stage, he strictly limited the number of solo shows he agreed to perform. Meanwhile, Journey briefly moved on with **Jeff Scott Soto** before settling into a lengthy era with **Arnel Pineda**. Journey then literally erased Perry's first replacement, re-recording the Augeri-sung songs "Faith in the Heartland" and "The Place in Your Heart" for 2008's *Revelation*.

Augeri said there were no hard feelings.

"I got one of those second chances. Some folks never get a first chance," he told *The Daily News*. "I made the best of it. I had a pretty good darn run." [102, 376, 621, 624, 650, 651, 652, 653, 654, 706, 794]

In A Bind, Journey Turns To Schon Protégé, Jeff Scott Soto

Journey was only eight shows into a celebrated 2006 U.S. tour with **Def Leppard** when Steve Augeri faltered on a Tuesday night in North Carolina. By Friday, his replacement was on stage.

There was no other choice. Journey had announced the first 34 dates, then added more in May. The band would now be on the road through a late November stop in Puerto Rico.

Jeff Scott Soto, Neal Schon's former **Soul SirkUS** bandmate, got the call to come help save the tour, and Soto was game. "Yeah, we just threw him out there to the wolves," Jonathan Cain told *Melodic Rock*.

Schon admitted to interviewer **Michael Cavacini** that with Journey "in the middle of a tour, Jeff was the only guy I could think of to come out and do it at a moment's notice."

Even leaving aside his association with two of Journey's current members in Soul SirkUS, Soto was not a complete novice. He provided vocals for a pair of mid-1980s studio projects by virtuoso guitarist **Yngwie Malmsteen**. Later, he dubbed the vocals of **Bobby Beers** (**Jason Flemyng**), lead singer for the fictional band **Steel Dragon**, in the 2001 film *Rock Star*, alongside **Zakk Wylde**, **Jeff Pilson**, and **Jason Bonham**.

Though it appeared as if Soto had mere days to prepare for his Journey debut, he actually had only a few hours.

"I was given the green light that I would be joining the tour, so I flew from L.A. to Virginia Beach on July 5, and met with the guys for a brief greeting," Soto said. "All day the next day I spent at the gym, walking around the city, basically on my own. On the morning of July 7, the day of my first show, I was presented the setlist for the first time. We discussed it on the bus ride over to sound check."

Warm-ups on the tour regularly rotated: One band had 90 minutes to sound check while the other got 10 before one concert, and then the schedule reversed for the next show.

"This day was theirs for the full 90 minutes, with a 10-minute line check for us. No one informed the Leps that we might need to swap to work in a new singer," Soto said with a laugh. "I got to do three songs with them and an hour later, I was in front of 22,000 people singing the full set. It was one of the most exciting moments of my life that I will never forget."

As far as Soto was concerned, however, everything led to this night in Bristow, Virginia. "My entire existence even before Yngwie was preparing me for Journey," Soto argued. "As a massive fan of this band, they were an insane influence on me as a singer and writer. That was prepping me to front my childhood favorite band."

That is certainly clear on the Perry-esque "Coming Home," a Soul SirkUS leftover Soto reworked for 2021's *The Duets Collection: Volume 1 with Deen Castronovo*. There were backstage moments during his first collaboration with Schon that pointed the way to this place as well.

"Even the fact that I would dabble with deep-cut Journey songs at Soul SirkUS rehearsals and sound check were my hint-hint, nudge-nudge moment to Neal," Soto said. "I knew this band's catalog inside and out, so much that I could be called at a moment's notice to stand onstage with them—which is exactly how it happened."

Soto sang "Wheel in the Sky" at the Nissan Pavilion, along with "Open Arms" and "I'll Be Alright Without You," among others. Doubters remained.

"There's still that segment of the population or even of the fans, as small as it is, and even in the industry ... it's like, this is Journey, but it's not Steve Perry," Ross Valory admitted to Utah's *Daily Herald*.

But Soto's bandmates did not view this as a stopgap measure. "It's a brand-new band," Schon told *Melodic Rock*. "The way management's looking at it now is this is a brand-new band. It's insane. I'm excited about the future now." [19, 99, 385, 656]

SPRING 2007

Journey Finds A New Singer on YouTube, But Not Arnel Pineda

Neal Schon often presents his discovery of **Arnel Pineda** as the result of a single deep dive into YouTube tribute singers. But Journey had been actively seeking to replace Jeff Scott Soto for months.

"I looked for a long time," Schon once admitted to *All Access Magazine*. "I found a couple of interesting guys."

The only qualification: Sound exactly like Steve Perry. "We could have gone in a completely different direction, but then why even call it Journey?" Schon told interviewer **Michael Cavacini**. "It's gotta sound like Journey, and Journey is a tenor voice."

Jonathan Cain's daughter thought she had found one in **Jeremey Hunsicker**, a sales rep

for a Virginia trucking company who fronted a Journey tribute act called **Frontiers**. YouTube videos confirmed his ability to carry the old material.

When Cain reached out in May 2006, Hunsicker initially assumed he wanted to discuss a legal matter relating to the cover band. Instead, they arranged to meet up at a Frontiers performance that weekend in Charlotte, North Carolina.

"He said, 'People think I'm crazy, but I'm getting Neal Schon and flying in to see your show,'" Hunsicker told *The Roanoke Times*.

Suitably impressed, Cain and Schon invited Hunsicker and his wife Sabrina to San Francisco in late June, not long after Journey officially let Soto go. Hunsicker said Soto reached out when he heard: "He e-mailed me: 'I hope they treat you better than me,'" Hunsicker told *The Times*.

They worked together for most of a month, emerging with the co-written song "Never Walk Away," which ended up as the opening track on 2008's *Revelation*. By then, Hunsicker was back at his desk at Saia LTL Freight in Roanoke, the proud father of a new son named Quinn.

"It was a crazy time," Hunsicker told *Houma Today*. "We were in the process of finalizing a deal when they changed their minds about me."

Hunsicker said Cain had called to make plans for a return visit later in the year to rehearse and record. There were discussions about a retainer. Hunsicker said he even got a voicemail from their management team that said, "Welcome to Journey."

Then Schon put the brakes on everything. "I became a prince and a pauper within a matter of hours," Hunsicker told interviewer **Ross Muir**.

Schon offered a curious explanation for changing his mind: "He was very good," Schon told *All Access*, "but he was a bit scary because he was almost too much like Perry."

Hunsicker said he only learned later that Schon had called him without telling the others. "Arnel was flown in in August," Hunsicker told *The Roanoke Times*, "and I never heard from Journey again."

Continued on Page 283

THE SOPRANOS TAP JOURNEY FOR ICONIC SERIES SENDOFF

As co-writers of "Don't Stop Believin'," Jonathan Cain, Steve Perry, and Neal Schon would have to sign off for its use in the finale of HBO's mob-themed hit show *The Sopranos*.

Cain and Schon were on board. Perry, however, was more circumspect. He worried that show creator **David Chase** might choose to mimic **Martin Scorsese**'s penchant for stylized violence by juxtaposing Journey's uplifting 1981 hit with a series-ending bloodbath.

"I didn't want to see a Scorsese moment where everyone gets whacked," Perry told *The Telegraph*. "Scorsese would do that."

Chase told interviewer **Marc Maron** that he brought the cast and crew in on the decision. He said, "Listen, I'm going to talk about three songs that I am thinking about for ending the show." They were **Al Green**'s "Love and Happiness," "Don't Stop Believin'," and another track Chase forgot.

Journey got the biggest reaction from everyone on set—and it was not positive. "They went, 'Oh, Jesus Christ, no. Don't do that! Ugh. Fuck,'" Chase added. He was undeterred because he felt like he knew the kind of musical choice mob boss Tony Soprano would make.

In the autobiography *Unrequited Infatua-*tions, cast member **Steven Van Zandt** remembered Chase saying: "'Tony is a classic rock guy. That's what he would have played.'"

Van Zandt, a longtime member of **Bruce Springsteen**'s **E Street Band**, was not sold either, though he had no particular issue with Journey. "They made terrific records, had one of the best singers in rock, and were huge."

Instead, he thought *The Sopranos* should uphold its reputation of featuring more obscure acts. "After ten years and seven seasons of the most amazing music ever used on a TV show, David wanted to use fucking Journey!" Van Zandt said.

Chase cared less about that than making a character-driven decision. "No matter what song we picked," Chase said in a Directors Guild of America Q&A, "I wanted it to be a song that would have been from Tony's high school years, or his youth."

Negotiations with Perry dragged on because the producers were wary of previewing a cliffhanger ending where Tony Soprano selects "Don't Stop Believin'" on a diner's jukebox before the scene famously cuts to black. What happens next remains an open question.

"Life is short," Chase said in the Q&A. "Either it ends here for Tony or some other time. But in spite of that, it's really worth it. So don't stop believing."

The crew shot multiple endings in order to keep the secret. "We all knew that we had agreed to the request to use the song in the last episode," Ross Valory told *Charlotte Magazine*. "We had no idea it would be the last song you heard."

Perry eventually agreed, though the conversation lasted until just days before the show aired on June 10, 2007. He signed off after Chase's office shared the gist of what happens on screen, but they did not reveal to Perry the episode's final plunge into darkness.

Already a fan of the show, Schon was struck by what unfolded—but not just because of the episode's quick-cut conclusion. The scene transported him to an earlier era with Journey—one long before "Don't Stop Believin'" became a multiplatinum Top 10 single.

Perry had once surprised Schon by playing "Wheel in the Sky" on a pizza parlor jukebox while on tour in 1978, before Journey had ever had a hit single.

"We were both jumping up and down," Schon told *Vulture*. "So I looked at that *Sopranos* scene with that memory in mind." He was unsure if Perry had shared the story with HBO, "but it was very similar to what actually happened with him and me. How beautiful is that?"

Deen Castronovo was the last to know. "Everybody else got to see it and I missed it," he told *The Morning Call*. "I don't know why, but I missed the damned thing. I had to go see it on reruns later on."

The Sopranos' much-anticipated series finale set a record at HBO, garnering 12 million viewers—and Journey was stuck on the couch with all of them.

The band had completed a well-attended string of shared dates with **Def Leppard**, then headed to Europe in March. A one-off show after a polo match followed in May in Leesburg, Virginia, but Journey had nothing else scheduled. This would become "the one year out of the last nine we didn't happen to be touring," Valory lamented to *Charlotte Magazine*. "It would have been nice to capitalize on it."

Instead, Journey did not return to the road until February 2008, with new front man **Arnel Pineda**. [261, 389, 482, 483, 663, 664, 665]

Without a clearer understanding of their reasoning, Hunsicker could only guess what happened. With a baby on the way, "I think that Neal said look, this is maybe not the best choice for Jeremey—nor the best choice for us," he told *The Times*.

Hunsicker continued with his Journey tribute band, watching as *Revelation* went platinum. [87, 88, 385, 659, 660]

Not Quite A Fit, Journey Parts With Soto After *Generations* Tour

Journey was still fronted by Jeff Scott Soto as *The Sopranos* went to black. Days later, they announced he had been fired.

Soto said he initially left without ever knowing why. "There are different versions, both what came from them and what I heard from those close to them."

Neal Schon and Jonathan Cain later described Soto as a stopgap figure, brought in only to finish out a string of concerts after Steve Augeri faltered.

"Jeff Scott Soto didn't have the legacy sound Journey was going for," Cain wrote in his memoir. He called Soto a "good singer" and thanked him for stepping in at a "crucial time," but said "we never considered him to be a permanent member."

Schon summed up this brief era with a rhetorical question to **Michael Cavacini**: "Did I think he was the right singer or the right personality for the band? I don't think anyone felt that he was."

Soto appeared to push back against those arguments with the Swedish band **W.E.T.** on their Journey-inspired self-titled 2009 debut. He admitted that he "intentionally added my Perry influence as if to show what my voice might have sounded like on new Journey songs. This is the closest to presenting this ideal to Journey fans. The ones who continued on with me hear and love it."

More W.E.T. projects followed, while Soto also released a string of solo albums and fronted his own eponymous band, **SOTO**, which he described as a "heavier version of what I do as a solo artist." Along the way, Soto has also worked with **Trans-Siberian Orchestra**, **Sons of Apollo**, former **Megadeth** bassist **David Ellefson**, **Whitesnake**'s **Joel Hoekstra**, and **Talisman**, which bid farewell in 2007 but has occasionally reunited.

Journey set the stage for much of it. "I loved every minute of the 11 months I got to sing and represent this band around the world," Soto said. "I get to say today with pride, 'I was the singer for Journey.'"

Meanwhile, Journey returned to an unhappy position much like the one immediately after *Trial by Fire*: They were associated with a hit project, but had no front man to sing the songs. "I couldn't take it," a frustrated Deen Castronovo told CBS. "I was goin' crazy."

Time spent with Soto had shown Schon precisely what the Journey lead singer gig required. "I believe his voice wasn't as high as what we needed," Schon told Cavacini. "We needed a high tenor to still sound like Journey."

Schon had not found him yet, but a once-homeless Manila bar singer named **Arnel Pineda** began appearing in amateur videos posted by Philippines-based **Noel Gomez** to the NDGOMEZ777 channel on YouTube. Pineda and **The Zoo** covered Aerosmith, Survivor, Led Zeppelin, Eagles—and, yes, Journey. He had no clue he would soon take center stage with the real Journey, succeeding Soto.

"In the end, it's their band, their decision, and as much as it would have been awesome to go the next stages, it didn't come to pass," Soto said. "It worked out for the best, anyway. Arnel has been tremendous with and for them in many ways, and pushed them forward more than I would have, I feel." [19, 160, 385, 657, 658, 667]

In the Market for a Singer, Schon Finds One—in Manila

Arnel Pineda had no idea Journey was reaching out to people they had found on YouTube. So, on June 28, 2007, when someone on the phone identified himself as Neal Schon, Pineda was understandably wary.

"I told him, 'I don't think you're Neal,'" an amused Pineda admitted to the *Marin Independent Journal*. "He was laughing his [behind] off. It took two minutes for him to convince me." That was only after Pineda asked for a face-to-face conversation via his webcam.

Schon had been scrolling through online videos for months when he came across Pineda singing with **The Zoo**. Despite the late hour, his first call was to Jonathan Cain. Schon insisted that he immediately log onto YouTube.

"I had a couple of glasses of wine in me. And I was like, 'You gotta be kiddin' me, Neal, right now?'" Cain told CBS. "Go!" Schon said, with a laugh. Cain said, "I went"—and he was likewise impressed with the diminutive Filipino's rendition of "Faithfully."

Even in a blurry clip from a tiny club, Pineda was a star in the making. "It was confined quarters but his singing was amazing," Schon told the *Pioneer Press*. "I told management and the band, 'I think this is the guy.' They thought I was crazy."

There were some complicated logistics to work out, but a connection had been made.

"You can tell within 10 bars of a song whether the drummer is on it and the guitarist is on it," said **Michael Des Barres**, who had earlier replaced **Robert Palmer** in **The Power Station**. "Same thing with a singer. They knew straight away that this guy was uncanny. So, the story is how the band responded to this guy's brilliance—not how the guy responded to Journey's brilliance. I think it's the other way 'round."

They had to get him to the United States. Schon told Journey's management about plans to audition Pineda. "They go, 'Oh, great. So where is he? L.A. or N.Y.?' And I said, 'Well, he's in Manila,'" Schon told *Guitar Connoisseur* magazine. "And people started laughing hysterically. Like, I'm crazy. You know?"

Immigration officers in Manila were similarly incredulous. "They went like, 'Really? Journey, as in Journey the band?'" Pineda told CBS. They actually asked him to sing "Wheel in the Sky," drawing curious looks from everyone else in the local office. "Anyway, it helped the paperwork come along," Schon added.

By August, Pineda was in a San Francisco workspace with the band. "It's not an easy feat to get someone from Manila over here in a flash," Schon told the *Pioneer Press*. "Three months was actually pretty fast."

Pineda did not look the part. He barely spoke the language. But he won the job. "It was crazy," Deen Castronovo told the *Deseret News*. "When he finally realized that we wanted him to audition and that it wasn't a joke, he did. And he blew us away."

Pineda became more confident in his performances, and Journey became more confident in their decision too. "I'm so happy that I found Arnel and things have worked out so well," Schon told KHON, "because we've helped him and his family have a new life."

Succeeding Perry would be easier after Steve Augeri. Pineda benefited from not having been the first, while also emerging in an era where replacing classic-era front men had become more common.

"Several bands have done it," said Cain's ex-bandmate **Tony Brock**, after **The Babys** reformed without founding singer **John Waite**. "Even **Foreigner** doesn't have the original singer, you know? Of course, Journey did it with a sound-alike to Steve Perry. Neal Schon and Jonathan Cain were such an important aspect of Journey that they could get away with it."

Still, Pineda had plenty of doubters—including some from inside the Journey family: "The guy can sing, he's great," *Raised on Radio*-era bassist Randy Jackson told *People*, "but no one … no one will ever be Steve Perry. He's one of the greatest singers to ever grace the microphone." [39, 132, 159, 160, 163, 229, 243, 661, 662, 667]

WINTER 2007-08

NUGGETS

▶ Journey has licensed its 1980 hit single "Any Way You Want It" to Activision for its smash video game *Guitar Hero 3*. Video games found classic rock in earnest in early 2006, when the company released its debut version of *Guitar Hero*. And after watching many classic rock bands added to the game's setlist for the first two years, Journey gave the OK to add the song to the growing library of game songs and watched it fly up the Activision's online leaderboard. Competitor game *Rock Band* would also add "Any Way" to its setlist, as well as "Don't Stop Believin'" in *Rock Band 4* in 2015. —*Billboard*

ON THE ROAD

▶ Calle 13, Chayanne, Earth, Wind & Fire, Nelly Furtado, and Peter Frampton.

Festivals, Viña del Mar International Song Festival: Viña Del Mar, Chile

Nervous Pineda Makes His Journey Debut in Chile

Journey's setlist on February 21, 2008, at Chile's Viña del Mar International Song Festival, was, as usual, one hit after another. They opened with "Separate Ways" and included "Lights," "Faithfully," and "Don't Stop Believin'" in the main set. The encore included "Any Way You Want It."

For the band's new front man, however, this was an entirely new experience. Arnel Pineda had gone from playing small venues in Manila to an unimaginably large platform after Neal Schon discovered him on YouTube.

Pineda also forever changed what had always been a quintessentially American group. "We've become a world band," Jonathan Cain told the *Marin Independent Journal*. "We're international now. We're not about one color."

The crowd at Quinta Vergara swelled to some 20,000 strong, while millions more were watching via a national television broadcast. Pineda was, quite simply, terrified. "I was trying to back out five minutes before," he told *Rolling Stone*. "I was like, 'Neal, I cannot do this. This is not built for me.'" He begged them for a return flight. "Like, 'Can I just go home and you know, just give me a ticket back to the Philippines'?" he later admitted to CBS.

Pineda would need more time to adjust to the scale of his new surroundings. "When we were waiting to go onstage that night," Ross Valory told *The Saginaw News*, "he told us he had no idea of what he was going to do."

Turns out, he would run around—a lot. This pinballing performance style expended some of his nervous energy, but it also began to take its toll on a suddenly breathless Pineda. "We can hear him but it was like a game of 'Where's Waldo?'" Valory added. "Instead of standing in front of the mic, he was running laps around the stage and the crowd was loving it."

Pineda had to learn to balance the impulse to race from left to right with the exacting requirements of replicating Steve Perry's approach at the mic. It was just the first lesson.

As a veteran front man of a local cover band, Pineda was familiar with the main song cycle's

Continued on Page 288

UNLIKELY PERFORMER ASCENDS AS JOURNEY'S FRONT MAN

Steve Augeri sang like Steve Perry. He also looked similar and conveniently shared Perry's first name.

Arnel Pineda was different in every way, save for his voice. "How could a simple guy like me sing for a band like Journey?" Pineda asked the *Philippine Daily Inquirer*. "It's very rare for an artist born and raised in the Philippines to penetrate the international market."

Born on September 5, 1967 in Manila, Pineda grew up in abject poverty. His parents, **Restituto Lising Pineda** and **Josefina Manansala Campaner**, were tailors, though they encouraged his interest in music. Josefina, in particular, pushed Arnel to enter youth singing contests.

When his father appeared with a tape measure, Pineda instinctively knew he was about to be fitted for yet another outfit for yet another singing competition. "No! No! No! No contest for me!" Pineda told CBS he'd respond, with a laugh. "I hated it because I'm so shy. I can only sing really loud when I'm beside my mother."

Then she died of heart disease when Pineda was just 13. Medical costs from her lengthy health issues left his family destitute, forcing Pineda's father to ask relatives to take in his younger siblings. Pineda left home to ease the financial burden, quitting school in order to work.

He eventually found himself with no place to live, sleeping in public parks or outside a friend's home. Pineda collected bottles or scrap metal to support his family. "I spent my teenage years on the streets," he told the *Mercury News*, "and it was no surprise that I never finished high school."

At 15, he met members of the local band **Ijos**. Though untutored, Pineda had been singing since he was just five. He quickly ascended to the front man position, and their friendly guitarist offered Pineda a small place to sleep under his stairs.

"Now, looking back, it was really hard, being hungry for days, asking your friends for food or your relatives for food," Pineda told the *Honolulu Star-Advertiser*. "It's not an easy thing."

Ijos evolved into **Amo**, and Pineda began covering his first Journey songs. The group memorably appeared in the Yamaha World Band Explosion Contest in 1988, broadening their fan base. They re-entered the same competition in 1990, this time under the name **Intensity Five**, and were runners-up.

Pineda released a solo album on Warner Bros. in 1999 before settling into a series of local cover band gigs with **The Zoo**, which featured his longtime collaborator, **Monet Cajipe**. *Zoology*, their debut album, appeared on MCA in 2007, just as Neal Schon discovered Pineda singing "Faithfully" on YouTube.

"After watching the videos over and over again, I had to walk away from the computer and let what I'd heard sink in," Schon told the *Green Bay Press-Gazette*. "I thought, 'He can't be that good.'"

Pineda's friend **Noel Gomez** played a key role in his ascent, uploading a series of Zoo videos under his NDGOMEZ777 handle and then acting as a liaison when Schon reached out. YouTube later permanently suspended Gomez's account over copyright infringement, but not before his channel had altered Pineda's career trajectory forever.

"So, then the really interesting part of it started—because he's a tiny Filipino dude," said **The Power Station**'s second vocalist, **Michael Des Barres**, who knows all about succeeding a legendary singer. "So, this is not the prototype of the iconic legend of a front man. Steve Perry was this sort of melancholy rock 'n' roll guy with terrific bangs. That conversation, I think, would have been hilarious—and, also, really difficult."

Pineda brushed it all aside. His first album with Journey, 2008's *Revelation*, went platinum. He fronted their last Top 10 adult-contemporary hit ("After All These Years") and their final Top 20 single on the same chart ("Where Did I Lose Your Love"). "Anything Is Possible" from 2011's Top 15 hit *Eclipse* just missed the AC Top 20.

By then, he had become a worldwide sensation. Director **Ramona Diaz**'s 2013 documentary,

> **When I went there and saw where he was living before he got in the band, I was just—the tears just rolled down, and I was like: 'This is an amazing story, for real.'**
>
> — *Neal Schon*

Don't Stop Believin': Everyman's Journey, traced Pineda's hardscrabble beginnings, concluding with a return Journey concert in Manila.

"When I went there and saw where he was living before he got in the band, I was just—the tears just rolled down," Schon told KHON, "and I was like: 'This is an amazing story, for real.'"

Yet it was always about the songs from before. That was clear when Pineda performed with Journey at their induction into the Rock & Roll Hall of Fame. He sang "Separate Ways," "Lights," and "Don't Stop Believin'," all from long ago and far away.

"They've been very lucky that when Steve Perry left, they had this backlog of hits," said **Tony Brock**, Jonathan Cain's former bandmate in **The Babys**. "If they could just get a singer in who could take over Steve Perry's vocals, they could still fill out arenas. That was their ace in the hole."

Ever humble, Pineda understood his role as the keeper of an earlier flame. He also never forgot his mother's sheltering presence, and the inspiration she provided. "I think it's her voice that carried me all through this pain that I've gone through," Pineda told CBS. "She taught me how to fight in the world. She was everything to me."

The fact that English was not Pineda's first language also seemed to have connected him more closely with Schon, who feels as if his instrument likewise transcends any native tongue. "It's like a universal language to me, something that anyone anywhere in the world could understand what I'm playing," Schon said in the 1986 *Raised on Radio* documentary.

At the same time, Pineda gets why some fans might still be frustrated with Perry's absence. He has since admitted that when he watches Journey videos, it's usually from their time with Perry.

Other classic rock bands are no different: "I mean, no offense to **Adam Lambert**. He's an amazing performer and he has an amazing voice, but I still watch the old [**Queen** videos] with **Freddie Mercury**."

So, when angry fans chant, "No Perry, No Journey"? Pineda says: "I understand it." [39, 107, 108, 135, 160, 197, 204, 243, 666]

lyrics. "Over and above the fact that Arnel knew all of the songs—because I didn't know any of the fucking songs—for him to walk in there knowing the songs, that's tremendous," said **Michael Des Barres**, who took over as front man for **The Power Station** prior to Live Aid in 1985. "So, dreams do come true, if you believe in them. He obviously did, from the very get-go."

Still, Pineda's first language was Tagalog, and English his second. He had been working on diction and phrasing with a specially assigned accent reduction coach. Pineda nevertheless started with his eyes largely downcast, without saying anything to the audience. He looked uncertain on the deeper cuts, including "Rubicon," "Ask the Lonely," and "Chain Reaction."

By the time he spoke extemporaneously, nearly 30 minutes in, Pineda had become assured enough to joke around a bit: "I am very, very blessed to be with Journey tonight," he said from onstage. "It's my first time. So, go easy on me, OK? Thank you."

Journey did. They did not perform any new songs, though by then Pineda had already completed work on the album that would become *Revelation* in the months after his original August 2006 audition.

Instead, this night was about building a bridge from Journey's storied past to Pineda's future. He seemed to intuitively understand where he appeared on that continuum. "I'm just happy enough to be in the band ... continuing their legacy that Mr. Perry has left behind," he told the *Honolulu Star-Advertiser*. "I know my place." [43, 107, 160, 163, 204, 243]

SPRING–SUMMER 2008

RELEASES
▶ Journey, *Revelation* (album)

NUGGETS
▶ A white-haired Jimmy Page got a backstage pass to see Journey perform at the Hammersmith Apollo in London. The former Zeppelin guitarist met with the band minutes before they took the stage in support of their new album, *Revelation. —Billboard*

NUGGETS (cont.)
▶ **WALMART TREATMENT:** The lesson for Journey: Don't stop believin', especially if you have Walmart on your side. The band's new album, *Revelation*, was released through Walmart, Sam's Club, and the band's website and it sold 105,000 copies in a week. The Walmart deal is another example of a veteran music act partnering with a retailer to reconnect with its fan base. "This is all new to me," said guitarist Neal Schon. "We finally found a way to get the word out there about our new music and that's been a problem in the past." The first-week sales were a 1,600 percent increase over their last album, *Generations*, in 2005.
—*Los Angeles Times*

ON THE ROAD
▶ 3 Doors Down, Cheap Trick, Def Leppard, Gotthard, John Parr, Kansas, KISS, Motörhead, REO Speedwagon, Twisted Sister, Whitesnake

Cain's 'After All These Years' Returns Journey to the Charts

Journey's "After All These Years" arrived in April 2008 as proof that Arnel Pineda could bear the weight of expectations surrounding another Jonathan Cain power ballad. It became the first Top 10 single for the band on *Billboard*'s adult-contemporary charts since 1996's "When You Love a Woman," making it clear that Pineda would be different from his immediate predecessors.

"He's wonderful, and he has this talent to cover and represent the sound and singing style that made the band famous," Ross Valory told *Charlotte Magazine*. "He makes it his own, though."

Journey constructed the rest of the song in the usual way, right down to Deen Castronovo's Steve Smith-inspired fills. What differentiates the track from Steve Perry's entire tenure is heard in the fine details of Pineda's performance.

"They have similar timbres," Cain told the Minneapolis *Star Tribune*. "But I think Arnel has a little edgier, smoky voice. A little more rock singer, if you will. Steve was a little more rhythm and blues."

For Perry's most diehard fans, Pineda was nothing more than a canny mimic. "It was hard in the beginning—with all the comparisons to Steve Perry," Pineda told the *Philippine Daily Inquirer*, "but like I've always said … I'm just trying to continue the legacy of the band."

This was not the only conundrum posed by the single's surprising success. "After All These Years" would have to find a place on setlists already weighed down with plenty of ballads.

Neal Schon straddled the fence, arguing for more rock songs while nodding toward their chart return. "That is very exciting for us because it's been a while since that's happened," he told *All Access Magazine*. Still, "we already have so many ballads we have to play and I don't want to put people to sleep."

He even floated the idea of creating a stricter schedule of songs for future albums, with eight rockers set against two ballads. "I think that's really more what we could use in our live performances," Schon added.

The issue resolved itself. Their final modern-day AC hits fell out of setlist rotation, and then Journey songs simply stopped charting. "After All These Years" would only appear on stage as an element of the solo instrumental medley performed by Jonathan Cain to introduce "Open Arms," with snippets of melodies from "When You Love a Woman" and "Patiently" also part of Cain's showcase moment.

"I always call it the seven-for-one solo," Cain told interviewer **Michael Cavacini**. "It just came out of us struggling with what ballad to play because we don't want to play a whole show of ballads." [197, 205, 389, 531, 660]

WINTER–SPRING 2009

NUGGETS

▶ **Cory Monteith** and **Lea Michele** take the lead singing "Don't Stop Believin'" at the end of the pilot episode of the Fox mega-hit high school musical show, *Glee*. The song would be sung in five more episodes during the show's six-year run. — *TV Guide*

NUGGETS

▶ Journey and **John Legend** headed up the Tailgate 2009 Show in the leadup to the Super Bowl XLIII game between the Pittsburgh Steelers and the Arizona Cardinals. **Bruce Springsteen** & **The E Street Band** handled the entertainment duties as the game's halftime show. —*United Press International*

Journey Plays Before 30,000 In Arnel Pineda's Phillipines

Arnel Pineda left Manila as a struggling bar singer with a big voice and bigger dreams. When he returned, many of those dreams had come true. He had emerged as the front man of Journey, and their first album together was streaking toward the million-selling plateau. Neither of Steve Perry's previous successors had come close to such heights.

"Without him, I don't think we'd still be out there," Jonathan Cain admitted to *Parade*. "He has such an innocence, a love, and passion for life and music."

Even as he hurtled to his own stardom, however, Pineda remained humble. "Anytime Steve Perry wants to walk in, I would be glad to step out," Pineda told the *Green Bay Press-Gazette*. "It's his right. It's his band."

In this case, Perry had not been the only obstacle standing between Pineda and acceptance. "Here's this Asian guy fronting for Journey—unheard of," Pineda documentary director **Ramona Diaz** told the *Salt Lake Tribune*. "It was just a shock. And, yeah, a lot of that was racism."

No such headwinds slowed him as the second leg of the tour behind *Revelation* began. Journey performed in Asia and Hawaii, including a celebrated stop on March 14, 2009 at the SM Mall of Asia Concert Grounds in the metro Manila suburb of Pasay.

Pineda was fully embraced, as some 30,000 of his countrymen finally got a chance to see the ever-energetic vocalist scamper from one end of the stage to the other—then nearly into their waiting arms from a perpendicular stage extension.

It had been that way from the very first. "I

Continued on Page 293

Pineda Era Revs Up with Walmart Fueled Surge

Journey had been writing in a desultory manner for some time, rendering them unprepared for the album Neal Schon wanted to make in 2008.

The group had two completed songs, begun as **Jeremey Hunsicker** briefly sat in during the previous summer. Arnel Pineda recorded over previous vocals for "Where Did I Lose My Love" and the Hunsicker co-written "Never Walk Away" during his subsequent audition rehearsals.

Meanwhile, Pineda was also preparing to navigate the difficult transition as Journey prepared for a huge tour. There would be differences of several orders of magnitude: "You have to play it differently when you use the big stage," Cain told the *Marin Independent Journal*. "It's different than playing a club in Manila. It's all just a process."

Then Journey's new manager, **Irving Azoff**, struck a deal with Walmart to carry a new album, originally envisioned as a re-recording of their greatest hits. There was talk of including a few new tracks, but nothing else.

"I was not keen on that," Schon told *Guitar Connoisseur*. "I thought, 'That sounds sacrilegious to me,' and as good as Arnel is and as much as I know he can do it, why would we want to do that?"

Azoff explained that this was the easiest path to getting a new record on store shelves, and they could avoid dealing with Journey's former label bosses at Sony. A set of cover songs was also another way to bolster their argument for Pineda as a flame keeper.

Still, new recordings of these ubiquitous hits would invite still more scrutiny—and those famil-

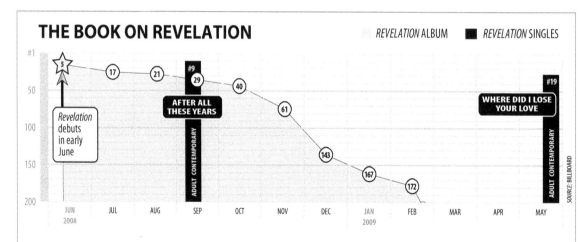

THE BOOK ON REVELATION

REVELATION ALBUM ■ *REVELATION* SINGLES

Revelation debuts in early June

AFTER ALL THESE YEARS — ADULT CONTEMPORARY

WHERE DID I LOSE YOUR LOVE — ADULT CONTEMPORARY — #19

SOURCE: BILLBOARD

JUN 2008 · JUL · AUG · SEP · OCT · NOV · DEC · JAN 2009 · FEB · MAR · APR · MAY

Classic rock bands in the late 2000s took to selling new albums exclusively through big box-ish retail stores. It worked wonders for **Eagles**, who just happened to share the same manager as Journey: **Irving Azoff**. So Azoff worked a distribution deal that sold Journey's new album, *Revelation*, only in Walmart and Sam's Club. The result? The highest-debuting Journey album since *Trial By Fire* in 1986, and the second-highest debut ever—even topping the band's bellwether albums, *Escape* and *Frontiers*. Making *Revelation* more accessible to Journey's fan base was crucial, and blending re-recordings of their hits with new material likely helped. But the new material was either not strong enough, relegated as new "oldies," or simply suffered from voluminous mainstream competition, because the new singles only registered on the adult contemporary charts.

TOP CHARTING WEEK: *BILLBOARD—June 21, 2008*

1. Disturbed, *Indestructible*
2. Various Artists, *Now 28*
3. Usher, *Here I Stand*
4. Weezer, *Weezer (The Red Album)*
5. **JOURNEY, *REVELATION***
6. Ashanti, *The Declaration*
7. Sex And The City, *Original Motion Picture Soundtrack*
8. Jewel, *Perfectly Clear*
9. 3 Doors Down, *3 Doors Down*
10. Chris Brown, *Exclusive*

iar sounds would not be easy to replicate.

Lawrence Gowan understood the unique challenge, having taken over for **Dennis DeYoung** both on stage and then in the studio as **Styx** re-recorded their own hits for 2011's *Regeneration: Volume I & II*. "When you're in front of a live audience, the beauty of that is you're in the moment," Gowan said. "You have the whole spirit of the night to embrace and to guide you as to what you do next. It's a very natural situation because it's in real-time."

Updating those same songs in the studio is a completely different experience. "Not just because your own interpretation of the song has to be incorporated into that," Gowan said, "but also the production, the engineering, the mixing. We are readdressing every single sound on the record to give it as authentic a rendition as possible. That is more difficult."

That was not Schon's principal concern. Instead, he simply wanted to add something to the agreed-upon rehash of the past. "I said, 'No, I don't want to do that; I want 11 or 12 new songs and 11 or 12 older songs,'" Schon told *The Daily Gazette*. "Then I think it's fine; people are definitely getting their money's worth."

The reasons for doing this were many. Bands like **Def Leppard** re-recorded their hits during a dispute with their label. **Foreigner** returned to 1984's chart-topping single "I Want to Know What Love Is" as a benefit for the Shriners Hospitals for Children.

Whatever the motivation, Gowan argued that these note-for-note covers could end up feeling meticulous and cold—like a science experiment rather than creating art. Journey's were no different.

"Although I've heard a lot of people praise what we did," Gowan said, "I found that was the more difficult thing to do because recording a song is a very unique moment. It's captured in time. So, it's really subjective as to whether people think we succeeded or not, but my vast preference is to make new music with the band."

In the end, the more pressing complication was that adding an equal number of originals to *Revelation* meant fast-tracking a second disc. "We didn't have a lot of preparation because we didn't plan on doing a full CD of new songs," Schon told *All Access Magazine*. Journey gathered in early 2008 at the Record Plant

in Sausalito, California, and began quickly assembling an album from what they had.

"Where Did I Lose Your Love" was a Steve Augeri-era leftover. They also did a quick cover of the Augeri-sung "Faith in the Heartland." The finished LP even included solo compositions like Cain's "After All These Years" and Schon's album-closing instrumental "The Journey (Revelation)." Hunsicker had been passed over as a front man but like **Robert Fleischman** before him, he would have a writing credit on Journey's next album.

Working with such speed brought out the best in Schon. With no time to second guess, the original songs on *Revelation* tempered any occasional tendency to play too much.

"One of the weird things is that Neal plays melodic lead guitar better than anyone else ever," producer **Kevin Shirley** told *The Observer*, "and yet he shies away from it because he wants to be flashy and histrionic and fast."

Meanwhile, Pineda was simply trying to keep up. At one point, they were feeding him a song a day. "There was a lot of pressure," he admitted in a separate interview with the *Marin Independent Journal*. "There were days I only slept two or three hours and I still had to learn the songs and record them."

The effort paid off: "Where Did I Lose Your Love" peaked at No. 19 on the *Billboard* adult-contemporary chart, following Journey's Top 10 finish for "After All These Years." *Revelation* became a No. 5 smash and reached platinum sales by December 2008, becoming Journey's first million-seller since Perry's return for *Trial by Fire*.

The *Los Angeles Times* reported that first-week sales of *Revelation* enjoyed a 1,600 percent increase over 2005's *Generations* with Augeri. "After me, they really exploded," Augeri admitted to *Rolling Stone*. "I think you could call me the buffer or the primer."

Journey stayed out on the road for two years, and Pineda's command of the new material improved on shared concert stages with **Heart** and **Cheap Trick**.

"A lot are checking him out for the first time. He'll have to earn their respect every night," Cain told the *Independent Journal*. "We went through that with Steve Augeri in 1998. It's 'Show me,' with their arms folded." [163, 212, 225, 388, 412, 624, 660, 668, 669, 670, 942]

NASH SPURRED WITHDRAWN PERRY TO RETURN TO MUSIC

Kellie Nash met Steve Perry by chance, and they spent less than two years together before she succumbed to cancer. He would never be the same again.

The Los Angeles–based psychiatrist initially caught Perry's eye when she appeared an extra in filmmaker **Patty Jenkins**'s segment of a Lifetime television anthology called *Five*, about women and breast cancer. Perry had befriended Jenkins years before and often sat in while she edited her movies.

Steve Perry and Kellie Nash at the premiere of the Lifetime film *Five* in 2011.

For this project, she cast real-life cancer patients as extras, including Nash. "The camera came across this girl sitting there laughing. I saw her smile," Perry said in a personal note on the *Fan Asylum* site. He asked Jenkins to rewind to the beginning. "As the camera again crossed Kellie's smile, I asked her to freeze right there."

Perry inquired about emailing Nash before Jenkins told him the awful news: "She said, 'Well, she was in remission, but it's come back, and now it's in her bones and in her lungs. And she's fighting for her life," Perry told NPR.

He emailed Nash anyway. "That was extremely unlike Steve, as he is just not that guy," Jenkins told *The New York Times*. "I have never seen him hit on, or even show interest in anyone before."

Their first conversation on the phone lasted nearly five hours. Their first date, in June 2011 at a local restaurant, only ended when the midnight hour loomed. "It was just an open book about every fear and every thought, every feeling," Perry told Yahoo. "She was just wonderful. And I couldn't stay away from her."

Over the years Perry had been part of serious relationships—most notably with **Sherrie Swafford**, inspiration for his solo hit "Oh Sherrie." But he'd never gotten serious about anyone—and he'd never married.

He said his parents' painful divorce served as a cautionary tale. "And I was around a band that went through several divorces in the course of our success," Perry told *The Guardian*. "I saw them lose half of everything multiple times."

This was different. Perry was leaving Nash's house after perhaps their fourth date when he was taken aback by his own rising emotions. He called her as he exited the freeway to turn around, asking Nash to meet him out front. "She went, 'What's the matter?'" Perry told Yahoo. "I said, 'Just meet me out front.'"

Things had only just begun, but Perry was already in love. Nash said she loved him too, "and when someone who has stage 4 cancer turns to you and says, 'I love you,' you're gonna feel it for the first time, which is what happened," Perry told CBS.

Nash brought up the specter of her illness. Perry told Yahoo he replied: "I look at it like a train with two tracks. Yes, the left track is you and I going through that [cancer battle] together, but the other track is just you and I."

At this point, Perry said he hadn't sung in years—not even in the shower. Nash changed that too. She asked him to sing one night as a way of making up after he'd made some small misstep.

"I said, 'Come on, you know I don't do that ...,'" Perry told the Associated Press. In a playful attempt to get past the moment, however, he asked Nash for her request. She picked "Open Arms." "I started singing it to her," Perry remembered. "And after I was done, she said 'OK.' So I was taken off the hook for it."

Nash's chemo treatments continued into the winter of 2011, as Perry continued to tumble head over heels. They began talking one another to sleep while in bed with the lights turned off.

Just before drifting off one night, Nash said: "Honey, this might take me. But it will never be able to touch our love," Perry told Yahoo. "It might get me, but it can't get our love."

Then Nash began experiencing debilitating headaches. An MRI confirmed that cancer had spread to her brain. She added radiation therapy to her regimen but then grew weary in December. After an emotional discussion with Perry, Nash decided to stop treatment.

January and February 2012 were some of their darkest moments together. But then Nash heard about a new treatment that was available in New York. "So we lived there for nine months and the drug kept her alive with a quality of life," Perry wrote on the *Fan Asylum* site. "We had the most magical summer of our lives together."

Along the way, Nash made an emotional appeal for Perry to recommit to his music career. He told the BBC she said: "I want you to promise me that if something was to ever happen to me that you would not go back into isolation."

Then in August, tests showed that the cancer had metastasized throughout her body. They tried another round of chemo before returning to California in November. Nash died at age 40 on December 14, 2012.

Perry was initially overcome with sadness. "I've lost my mother, my dad, and my grandparents who raised me. But this was the first time I ever grieved," he told Yahoo.

Two years later, Perry arrived at an **Eels** rehearsal, carrying his own microphone, fulfilling his promise to Nash. [253, 391, 687, 688, 691, 712, 715, 717, 877, 945]

remember like reaching for a solo," Neal Schon told *The Morning Call*, "and I get done with the solo and I open my eyes and I look around and I'm like, 'Where is he?'"

Journey released the nearly two-hour homecoming concert on DVD in October 2009. *Live in Manila* debuted at No. 1 on the *Billboard* video chart, as the *Revelation* tour finally drew to a close. After playing more than 140 concerts in 2008-2009, Journey would take a much-needed break in 2010. [108, 199, 671, 672]

SUMMER 2009

'Don't Stop Believin'' Becomes the Most-Downloaded Song

"Don't Stop Believin'" really did go on and on and on and on.

Journey's ageless power ballad reached one million downloads in August 2007, more than a quarter century after its release. "Don't Stop Believin'" then became the first catalog track to notch more than two million downloads, according to October 2008 SoundScan numbers.

This surge was powered in part by the song's placement on the cliffhanger finale of HBO's *The Sopranos* in June 2007. Sony reported that song downloads on iTunes rose 482 percent the following week. Demand at stores jumped around 100 percent at Target, Best Buy, and Borders.

Journey eventually boasted the top-selling track in iTunes history: "Don't Stop Believin'" topped the three-million download mark on the week of August 23, 2009, and then the four-million plateau in 2010. No other song released before 2000 had ever reached three million—much less four.

All this attention arrived despite an unusual construction that buried the chorus, and a character origin story set in an invented location. The song's eternal optimism just kept resonating with new listeners, not unlike Neal Schon's arpeggiated riff.

Gladys Knight and the Pips' "Midnight Train to Georgia" also provided a key image. "It's a magical place where a small-town girl and a city boy end up going on that midnight train to anywhere," Jonathan Cain later told the Minneapolis *Star Tribune*. "It's an imaginary fantastical place."

The same is true of "South Detroit," where one of the song's protagonists grew up. The Motor City is perched on the Detroit River, with Windsor, Ontario on the other side. "I tried north Detroit, I tried east and west and it didn't sing," as Perry recounted the story to the CBC, "but south Detroit sounded so beautiful." He only found out later that it is "actually Canada."

Canadians cheerfully went along with it, sending "Don't Stop Believin'" to No. 9 in their home country during its original chart run. Elsewhere, however, the continued popularity of "Don't Stop Believin'" rewrote chart history: The single peaked at an unimpressive No. 62 in the U.K. in 1981, only to surge to No. 19 on the week of November 7, 2009.

Journey remained atop the list of best-selling rock songs in digital history until early 2014, when **Imagine Dragons**' "Radioactive" pulled ahead. "Don't Stop Believin'" then became just the second track to earn one billion streams on Spotify in 2021.

Along the way, new generations continued to discover that its setting, in fact, does not exist. "It's the city of possibilities in your mind," Cain told *American Songwriter*. "That's what South Detroit is. So, leave it alone." [187, 188, 205, 673, 674, 675, 676, 677, 678]

WINTER 2010–11

Rolie Makes a Thoughtful Return With New EP, *Five Days*

Gregg Rolie's most recent album of new solo material was 2001's *Roots*. He'd been out of the spotlight since the 2009 live album *Rain Dance*. His return would be surprisingly intimate, and deeply insightful.

As a founding member of **Santana** and then Journey, Rolie appeared to audiences as a tiny speck playing keyboards in sold-out festivals and arenas. But he recorded 2011's *Five Days* EP live in his own living room, with his son, Sean, as producer. His whole approach was suddenly transformed.

"It was a little unnerving," Rolie observed. "I don't think I've ever done that. We always recorded the music first, and got that right, and then sang on top of it—and got that right. Doing it like this, if you make a mistake, you can't fix that. It was interesting to do."

Playing a piano his father had given him, Rolie offered a trio of new songs, re-examined two of his most memorable vocals from those seminal rock groups, and—in one of the more intriguing moments—took on the pre-war blues standard "Trouble in Mind."

Five Days would be self-released, decades after the end of his long association with Columbia Records. "The industry has kind of killed itself off. Especially labels, they've pretty much shot themselves in the foot," Rolie told interviewer **Paul Freeman**. "And so, it's a new approach."

The original "Love Doesn't Live Here Anymore" had the feel of a darkened cabaret, while "If I Went Home" found Rolie longing for the comforts of familiarity. The latter also boasted the EP's prettiest vocal.

Rolie always had the requisite melancholy menace to pull off "Trouble in Mind," but time had purpled his voice, making this version more effective. There was a gristly swagger to "Cool Little Mama," the third and final new song.

The focus for longtime fans, however, was a pair of songs he made famous with Santana and Journey. *Five Days* opens with "Black Magic Woman," which had become a career-making vocal with Santana. Rolie untangled the lyrics, replacing the torrid sexuality so familiar on 1970's *Abraxas* with something quieter and more uncertain.

Lyrics like "Don't turn your back on me, baby" suddenly had a previously unheard regret. Rolie also added a contemplative new turn on the piano, filling the blanks in the story. His playing ebbed and flowed, suggesting a fiery love affair's sped-up narrative. When his vocal returned, Rolie treated the song's final line like a meditation: "I can't leave you alone."

"Anytime" underwent its own very adult reimagining. The bravado of a young man who blithely accepted that his come-on would always work was now shaken by nagging doubts. Once a winking backdoor proposition, "anytime that you want me" began to sound like a lonely plea.

As with "Black Magic Woman," Rolie let "Anytime" spool out during the verses before rousing himself for the chorus. His reworked solo then emerged as a rollicking barrelhouse aside, like a moment of romantic frustration had shaken loose.

Lived experience transformed it all, but so did the interior setting. Rolie told *The Mercury News*: "My son's idea was, 'What are you going to do, build a bigger band? The way the music industry is, why not go the other way?'" [1, 167, 943, 944]

SUMMER–FALL 2011

NUGGETS

▶ Journey took a short break from their *Eclipse* tour to perform on NBC's *Today* show as part of the show's Morning Concert series. During the show, hosts **Matt Lauer** and **Ann Curry** gave the band the Nielsen Company SoundScan Award for "Don't Stop Believin'" being the best-selling classic rock track. —*Billboard*

▶ Billboard presents Journey with its Legends of Live Award, given annually to an entertainer for achievements in touring, concert promotion, and event production. Around since 2008, the award's previous recipients include **The Allman Brothers Band**, **Ozzy Osbourne**, and **Rush**. —*Billboard*

SPRING 2012

Don't Stop Believin' Documentary Premieres at Tribeca Festival

Arnel Pineda had to sing a Journey song to an immigration officer in Manila to prove he was actually traveling to the United States for an audition. News of this quickly spread through the larger Filipino community, eventually landing in the email inbox of documentary filmmaker **Ramona Diaz**.

A transplant from the Philippines living in Baltimore, Diaz called her Los Angeles-based manager and said, "Someone should be making this." She had no connections to the band, however, or funding in place. That led to an unusual agreement for Diaz to shoot for a single day, then edit the footage into a brief clip for the band to review.

"I was very familiar with Journey's music, 'cause who isn't?" Diaz told PBS. "Like I always say, you may think you don't know Journey but if you've been to a prom or a wedding in this country or elsewhere, you know Journey."

The group agreed to move forward with Diaz on the Pineda documentary *Don't Stop Believin': Everyman's Journey*, which pre-

miered April 19, 2012 at the Tribeca Film Festival. But she still had no funds. Production would stop and start as she paid off her credit card balances.

"I think they thought it would be a quick process," producer **Josh Green** told *Deadline*, "and at one point Arnel said, 'You're still here?'"

Diaz followed behind Journey's tour bus in her own car, staying in cheap hotels across town. She accepted other freelance work to help pay for the Journey film. "It was done with their cooperation and we had access to some of their music rights … but they didn't give money," Green added. "People mistakenly thought they were financing everything."

Don't Stop Believin' traced Pineda's meteoric first tour, from his daunting debut before millions of television viewers in Chile to the climactic return to Manila. There's a celebratory feel on stage, but Cain told Deen Castronovo behind the scenes that Journey would "have to re-educate" their fan base.

Journey was "playing to 1,500 people a night," Castronovo told *The Virginian-Pilot*, "and they were all arms-crossed, going, 'There's no way that this band is going to sound good without Steve Perry.'"

The film's most memorable scenes explored this darker undercurrent, far away from the spotlight, as Pineda dealt with the pressure, loneliness, and self-doubt associated with his new life.

"That first year he was not traveling with any entourage or assistant or family," Green told the *Milwaukee Journal Sentinel*. "He was in a brand new relationship in the band. And the camera became his conscience."

By the time the initial tour was over, Pineda had cemented his place in Journey. "If he leaves, we're not doing this anymore," Castronovo told the *Courier Post*. "We're not looking for another singer. We couldn't find anyone like Arnel again."

Don't Stop Believin': Everyman's Journey made it clear why. Pineda's shared Filipino heritage helped unlock his story, since Diaz could continue speaking with him when Pineda struggled in English. Among the first-time revelations in the documentary was Pineda's childhood homelessness.

Continued on Page 298

Schon Takes a Harder Path, But *Eclipse* Falls Flat

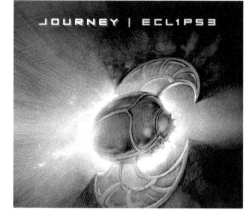

Neal Schon had been openly grousing about Journey's continued focus on earnest paeans to love. He felt they had banked so many from the Steve Perry era that there was no room for another in their setlists.

"I said, 'I don't understand the concept of continually coming with ballad-heavy records when we're not going to play any of them,'" Schon told *Ultimate Classic Rock*'s **Matt Wardlaw**.

And, frankly, Schon wanted to rock again.

The result was often an utter frenzy of guitars. "Neal said that we weren't going to do any ballads with *Eclipse*," Deen Castronovo told the *Courier-Post*. "He said Journey has enough ballads, and we made a really rocking Journey record."

Then Jonathan Cain showed up for these sessions with his usual clutch of heartfelt songs. Co-producer **Kevin Shirley** was caught in the middle. "It's not easy trying to make a record when there are opposing forces in the band," Shirley told *Music Radar*. "It's just a matter of who stamps their feet the loudest."

This time, Cain was out stomped. "I have to do what's in my gut and follow my own intuitions," Schon told Wardlaw. "I can't do what everybody else wants. That just would not be real, whether it's wrong or right. I have to do what's in my heart."

Schon and Shirley "locked horns a lot of this record," Schon admitted to *Music Radar*. "I fought with him, sure, but it was because I didn't want to do a typical Journey record." It was a matter, he added, of rebalancing their sound.

A TOTAL ECLIPSE

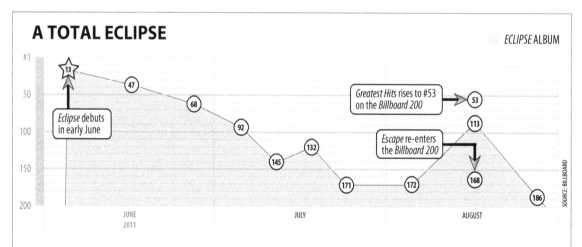

ECLIPSE ALBUM

Eclipse debuts in early June

Greatest Hits rises to #53 on the *Billboard 200* → 53

Escape re-enters the *Billboard 200*

SOURCE: BILLBOARD

There was a reason for optimism for *Eclipse*—especially since Journey's previous album, *Revelation*, enjoyed a four-month run in the Top 40. But despite a quick start, *Eclipse* lost momentum and fell from the charts. The absence of a hit single may have been the most significant problem—*Revelation* had two hit singles, but *Eclipse* did not have any charting singles. It did experience a minor surge up to #113 after the cast of the hit Fox TV show *Glee* earned a Grammy nomination for their performance "Don't Stop Believin'" in 2011. The soundtrack from that show was among the Top 10 albums, and it was likely no coincidence that both Journey's *Greatest Hits* and *Escape* had re-emerged in the *Billboard* 200 about that time. By the end of August it had dropped to No. 186, and it fell out of the Top 200 the week after.

TOP CHARTING WEEK: *BILLBOARD*—June 11, 2011

1. Lady Gaga, *Born This Way*
2. Brad Paisley, *This Is Country Music*
3. Adele, *21*
4. Various Artists, *Glee: The Music, Season Two, Volume 6*
5. Various Artists, *Maybach Music Group Presents: Self Made Vol. 1*
6. Various Artists, *NOW 38*
7. NKOTBSB, *NKOTBSB*
8. Foster The People, *Torches*
9. Jason Aldean, *My Kinda Party*
13. **JOURNEY, *ECLIPSE***

"Ever since Jonathan joined the band, he's tended to bring in the big ballads, and I bring the rock," Schon added. "What's different about this record is that I finally stood my ground."

Eclipse was strongest as it got going, opening with a stirring call for optimism on "City of Hope" that eventually deconstructs into an inferno of Neal Schon. Better still is "Edge of the Moment," with its foundation-rattling bottom end and wave after wave of crashing guitars. Schon had not played with that kind of furious abandon since the era of the spaceman afro.

"Very few people today realize that in the beginning Journey really was a hard rock band," Ross Valory told *Hallowed Magazine*. "Some people might get a bit surprised by the sound on the new album, but to me this is back to the roots."

Arnel Pineda finally seemed to be finding his own voice, after a period where Journey risked creative bankruptcy by re-recording old songs: "You can't go back to where you've been," he sang at one point. "Are you ready to try again?"

"I just want to be me with my voice and then I just want to relax and be able to share my own passion," Pineda told interviewer **Rob Herrera**, "but at the same time, still send the soul of Steve Perry out there."

Eclipse would reveal a loose theme of peace-seeking in a violent, fast-moving modern world, first enunciated in "City of Hope," and then expanded upon in "To Whom It May Concern." This level of inventiveness, unfortunately, proved unsustainable.

The LP eventually began to play a bit to expectation. "She's a Mystery" has the soft/loud dynamics that defined 1978's *Infinity*, while "Someone" comes off like an un-reheated leftover from 1981's *Escape*. "Anything is Possible" and "Ritual" recall Cain, Castronovo, and Schon's time in **Bad English**.

Still, there was no denying this album's tectonic strains. "Neal and Jon are like brothers that love each other, but Jon writes pop songs and Neal always wanted to be Van Halen," Shirley told *The Observer*. "There's no secret about that, even amongst them."

Released on May 24, 2011, *Eclipse* debuted at No. 13 as a Walmart exclusive, becoming Journey's second-straight U.S. Top 20 album release with Pineda. Cain initially toed the company line, describing the hard-rocking LP to the *Las Vegas Review-Journal* as "Journey with big combat boots on. And helmet and a rifle."

Unlike the platinum-selling *Revelation*, however, this album quickly tumbled back down the charts, selling only 100,000 copies. "*Eclipse* is a Catch-22. ... Occasionally, I'll hear a snide remark: 'Oh, they should've stuck to the formula,'" Schon told *Music Radar*, specifically mentioning "Don't Stop Believin'." "But that's the thing: We've already done that song."

Soon, it was Cain's turn to openly grouse: "We strayed from the formula. We strayed from classic Journey," Cain told interviewer **Michael Cavacini**. "It was really Neal's concept album. It was all guitars."

Schon later revealed that Shirley's compressed schedule forced the group to complete the album on their own. Portions of *Eclipse* were re-recorded, including some Pineda vocal retakes. Still, Schon pushed ahead. "We had big arguments on this record," he admitted to Wardlaw. "Regardless of whether I was right, wrong, indifferent, whatever, I just felt like I had to do it."

He said the songs found a new sense of purpose out on the road, but they would once again vanish from setlists as Journey returned to old favorites. *Eclipse* was typically shrugged off, if it was discussed at all, despite a laudable effort to update the rangy heavy fusion of Journey's earliest days.

This was not simply a throwback exercise. Schon was once again pulling and stretching his guitar muse as he had on Journey's first records, only now alongside a Steve Perry-sounding vocalist with a similar penchant for soaring expectancy. *Eclipse* could be, in its most successful moments, the best of both musical worlds—even if it clearly had no single.

Did that even matter anymore? Journey's last hit song was ages ago, and the industry itself had changed. "Radio is dead. Singles are dead," Valory told *Hallowed*. "There's no use in compromising it only to fit the singles concept, because there's no point in doing so anymore."

Instead, *Eclipse* boasted all the musical density and tough propulsion of 1977's underrated *Next*, with a dash of the approachable pop sensibilities that defined Journey's later hitmaking era. The experiment may not have completely succeeded, but at least they did not resort to photocopying the past again. [85, 221, 225, 231, 385, 558, 679, 680, 946]

"It could have been a five-minute film," Diaz told the *Journal Sentinel*, "but the camera loves Arnel, and I think he loves it back. Arnel with the big songs of Journey, the combination was really potent."

His rugged path to success mirrored the journey of *Don't Stop Believin'*, which was without a distributor even as it premiered at Tribeca. Cinedigm came on board the following summer. [162, 200, 231, 232, 681, 682]

Schon, Steve Smith Join Tribute to Ronnie Montrose

Neal Schon and Steve Smith said goodbye to a troubled legend on April 27, 2012 with Schon's former **Bad English** bandmate, **Ricky Phillips**, and a host of others.

Ronnie Montrose had died almost two months earlier amid a long battle with prostate cancer and depression. Suicide was confirmed as the cause days before the all-star gathering, which rocked the Regency Ballroom in San Francisco.

Smith toured with Montrose on a shared 1978 bill before joining Schon in Journey, while Phillips had been a touring and studio collaborator with Montrose in the early 2000s. *A Concert for Ronnie Montrose: A Celebration of His Life in Music* would give them a chance to push through their grief.

"Ronnie Montrose was a dear friend of mine—and Neal's," Phillips said. "We opened it up with 'Open Fire,' and 'Town Without Pity.' It was so much fun, just to pay homage and that tip of the hat with Neal—and to do something again with Neal."

The title track from 1978's *Open Fire* brought Smith back to a critical career point when he was considering a switch to rock following his 1976-77 tour with **Jean-Luc Ponty**. Smith nailed subsequent auditions with jazz great **Freddie Hubbard** and Montrose. He chose to roll with Montrose, who was about to launch dates in support of *Open Fire*.

"The way I saw it, my career was an adventure and I had options. Playing with Ronnie felt like a very interesting option," Smith said. "When I played with Jean-Luc, he had asked me to change from playing a small jazz kit to playing a double bass drum '**Billy Cobham**' kit—that was the way Ponty described it. I was enjoying playing the large kit and playing in a very aggressive high-energy fusion direction. If I took the gig with Ronnie, I could continue in that direction."

With Hubbard, "I would have gone back to the jazz kit and playing in clubs with acoustic pianos and acoustic bass, so the volume would have been much lower—which is closer to how I'm playing now!" Smith said with a laugh. "But for a 23-year-old kid, I wanted to see what rock 'n' roll was about. That seemed like a very interesting option, indeed!"

By the time Montrose's dates with Smith had concluded, he had become their top candidate to replace recently fired Journey drummer **Aynsley Dunbar**. Three separate tours in Journey would follow.

Remaining members of two Montrose-led bands also reunited at the tribute concert, including **Gamma** and his self-titled group. Schon's on-again, off-again collaborator and friend, **Sammy Hagar**, once again fronted the Montrose band with **Joe Satriani** taking Ronnie's role on guitar. **Marc Bonilla** joined the rest of Gamma, while **Denny Carmassi** served as drummer in both groups.

Others on hand included **Tesla**, **Alice Cooper**, **Eric Singer** of **KISS**, and **Eric Martin** of **Mr. Big**. A portion of the proceeds from the benefit show went to the Ronnie Montrose Fund for San Francisco Bay Area Musicians, administered through the Sweet Relief nonprofit foundation. [10, 26, 683, 684]

SUMMER 2012

NUGGETS

▶ Liberty Plaza is paying Journey $500,000 to play a private event near the Republican National Convention in Tampa on August 16. **Mitt Romney** and **Paul Ryan** allegedly paid for the gig, but their campaign denied it. Journey will be joined by **Kid Rock** and **Trace Adkins**. —*Forbes*

▶ Former Journey producer **Roy Thomas Baker** is suing Sony Entertainment for $1 million in damages for his work on 21 Journey songs. —*The Hollywood Reporter*

Rolie Begins Lengthy Run with Ringo Starr's All-Starr Band

Like many others, Gregg Rolie decided he wanted to be a musician after watching **The Beatles** on *The Ed Sullivan Show*. He would later lead Journey through a cover of **George Harrison**'s "It's All Too Much" on 1976's *Look Into the Future*.

But as with his **Santana**-era updates of **Peter Green**'s "Black Magic Woman" or **Tito Puente**'s "Oye Como Va," Rolie approached them through the lens of his own musical influences. He did not want to recreate these songs note for note.

"I've never played other people's music, sat in, and had to learn somebody else's music—unless I made it mine," Rolie said. "With 'Black Magic Woman,' we did it different from **Fleetwood Mac**. It's the same thing with 'Oye Como Va'—we did it the way we would do it. When Journey covered 'All Too Much,' we only built off part of it."

That mindset made for an uncomfortable personal moment when **Ringo Starr** invited Rolie to join the 12th edition of his long-running **All-Starr Band**. Rolie asked musical director **Mark Rivera** to send over the charts as soon as possible, and long hours of practice followed.

Rolie admitted he was still a bit overwhelmed when meeting Starr in person. "I look over and I can't believe I'm sitting here," Rolie said. "I literally can't believe this guy wants me, because without The Beatles, I was probably going to be an architect. When I got into music, I was like 15, 16, and I got bit by the bug like everybody else by those guys."

As they prepared to play, however, Rolie's heart sank. "Sitting in there, I thought this was gonna be the shortest gig I ever did in my life," he said. "Putting B3 on songs that never had a B3 on it, and trying to play piano. I'm not really a piano player; I play it, but I'm not a virtuoso of any kind on a piano."

Starr clearly disagreed, as Rolie became a staple of the All-Starr Band's longest-standing lineup. Rolie toured with Starr, **Steve Lukather** of **Toto**, **Richard Page** of **Mr. Mister**, and **Todd Rundgren** from 2012-2017.

"In the past, I've heard not everybody got along, or whatever," Lukather said. "You always run the risk of going: 'Well, this looks good on paper. Let's throw these guys in a room and see what happens.' You hope for the best, and musically, you go: 'OK, sure.' But do the personalities click? And we really did. It was very organic and natural."

Rolie was then part of two slightly reworked lineups with Starr in 2018-2019, before returning to solo work on 2019's *Sonic Ranch*. "I kept saying, 'Well, you know, I don't do this,'" Rolie admitted, "and seven years later, apparently, I do! I had a ball." [181, 375, 685]

FALL 2012

COLLABORATIONS
▶ Randy Jackson, bass, on **Don Felder**'s album, *Road to Forever*.
▶ Steve Smith, drums, on **Neal Schon**'s album, *The Calling*.

Schon, Smith Rediscover Early Journey Magic in *The Calling*

Neal Schon returned to Fantasy Studios in 2010 during sessions for *Eclipse*. But Journey could no longer replicate the rangier, deeply collaborative music-making approach of classic-era Berkeley recordings like *Escape* and *Frontiers*.

He would need Steve Smith for that.

Their reunion started as an opportunity for Smith to sit in on a few tracks, and precipitated a completely unexpected return to Journey.

"Neal and I have stayed in touch over the years, and we've always enjoyed playing together," Smith said back then. "Neal has been very busy with Journey for many years now and, when he had a recent break from their schedule, he gave me a call to see if I wanted to play on four tracks for a new instrumental solo album he was working on. I thought that sounded like a good idea, so I agreed to come to Fantasy Studios in the Bay Area and record for two days."

Schon arrived with a clutch of song scraps and his Line 6 looping machine. He left with his best solo album to date. "There was nothing planned at all. There were no songs, just a million riffs," Schon told *Premier Guitar*. "We

Continued on Page 301

SCHON MAKES AN UNLIKELY SANTANA REUNION A REALITY

Neal Schon always had a sense of unfinished business with **Santana**.

He had begun hanging around with the group as a teen during sessions for 1970's *Abraxas*, and only got to take part in the two albums that immediately followed. He left with fellow Journey co-founder Gregg Rolie only to see the Santana lineup turn into a merry-go-round.

Carlos Santana made no apologies. "It was time for them to do their own thing with Journey, and it was time for me to do my own thing," Santana told *Mojo*. "And whether they

After a persistent Neal Schon inspired a reunion of the *Santana III* band to record *Santana IV*, the surviving members jammed together at the House of Blues in Las Vegas in 2016.

liked it or not, I didn't fall off the cliff as soon as they left the band."

Santana certainly had later successes, not least of which was 1999's guest-laden multiplatinum *Supernatural* album. But it really became an idea, more than a band. "I like to feel Santana is an institution," Santana told *Rolling Stone*. "The players come and go, but a good team will always be there."

There would be partial get-togethers of the surviving early-1970s lineup: Rolie sat in with Carlos on 1982's *Shango*. **Michael Shrieve** joined Santana and Rolie for a celebrated 1988 reunion show in Fort Lauderdale, Florida. The closest they had gotten to a complete reunion was 1996's **Abraxas Pool**, which featured

Chepito Areas, **Michael Carabello**, Rolie, Schon, and Shrieve—but not Carlos.

By February 2013, Schon had begun openly lobbying to get everyone back together—and not just in the media. His attempts at persuasion were far more personal. Acting like a "guided missile," he simply hounded Carlos until he agreed.

"I couldn't shake him," Santana admitted to *Long Island Weekly*. "I'd go to the restaurant and he'd be there. I'd go to the shopping mall and he'd be there. And he was just so sweet, gracious and very persistent in a positive way."

Santana was impressed, since any reunion would return Schon to a two-guitar format—and a band-naming convention—that inevitably pulled away the spotlight. "I told him I was very honored and very grateful," Santana added, "because it was just so endearing the way he put ego or anything else aside. ... So, I said okay."

They called the others, and one by one, most of the *Santana III* lineup began to reconstitute itself. "We've all felt the same way. The timing of it, it's like the stars aligned," Rolie told the *Las Vegas Review-Journal*. "It's time for this to happen. It was time for this music to happen."

Santana, Rolie, Shrieve, and Carabello were joined in an updated lineup by modern-era band members **Benny Rietveld** and **Karl Perazzo** on bass and timbales, respectively. At one point, Santana confirmed that they were sorting through as many as 50 song ideas.

"We got together, and we rehearsed a few times," Schon said, "and we wrote some material. We managed to get into the studio and lay, like, nine or 10 ideas down. And—wow, we're off to a good start. That's all I can say. It's smoking. It sounds like the old band."

But Journey was still a going concern, as was the everyday edition of Santana. Years passed as they pieced together what would become *Santana IV*.

Schon co-wrote eight songs, and Rolie had a hand in nine—including the single "Anywhere You Want to Go," a solo composition. "From the very first day, it was like riding a bicycle; you never forget," Rolie told the *Review-Journal*.

"Shake It" began with a Schon riff, then evolved into something that reminded Carlos of **Fleetwood Mac**'s "That's Alright." Rolie credited Schon in the *Huffington Post* with playing "one of the best solos I think I've ever heard him do." "Shake It" ended up "being a little bit different," Rolie added, "but it has that roll of Santana. It's nothing but a groove on a heavy line."

They also welcomed contributions from newer member Perazzo, who helped out on five songs—including the rumbling opener "Yambu." Longtime Schon solo collaborator Igor Len earned a songwriting credit too.

In this loose atmosphere, Rietveld said to the *Review-Journal* that the revamped version of Santana operated "like a garage band from another planet." Most of the songs were completed in only a few takes. After recording "Fillmore East," Rolie told the *Huffington Post* that Carlos said: "Boy, it's a good thing somebody stopped us, or we'd still be playing this."

Despite the stop-and-start nature of the work, Santana was struck by how easily the remaining members of the band meshed after so long apart. "We still have the same intensity ... but we don't direct our intensity to tear each other apart anymore," Santana told *Long Island Weekly*. "We direct our intensity to validate each other and show how much we appreciate each other."

Time and time again, Santana gave credit to Neal Schon, who simply refused to take no for an answer. "Neal's heart convinced me," Santana told the *San Diego Union-Tribune*. In the end, Santana replied: "You're right, let's do something together, but with the original band."

At the same time, their surprising successes together—after so much controversy, and so many years—also had Carlos thinking about lingering issues within Schon's successor band: "I dream of Neal and I going to Fresno and talking to Steve Perry," Santana told Q104.3 FM. "If Santana can do *Santana IV* ... there's a chemistry between Neal and Steve Perry." [16, 40, 42, 127, 192, 689, 948, 949, 950]

just improvised and wrote it in the studio."

Schon doubled as bassist, drawing even closer to Smith. Keyboardist **Igor Len** helped round out the tracks. He also enjoyed a front-row seat as this creative partnership rekindled, then turned into an incandescent album-length project.

"I could feel that Neal and Steve were missing playing with each other, and I think it shows in how perfectly they blend together: Steve plays almost melodically, and Neal plays more rhythmically than I heard him before," Len said. "It was an amazing experience just to be there, and at times I was forgetting about the tracks in front of me on my Mac while listening to them."

They wrapped sessions for *The Calling* in less than a week. "I ended up playing the four songs in one day," Smith said, "so we started jamming because he didn't have any more tunes written yet. I ended up staying three more days and we finished 11 tracks in that time."

Released in October 2012, the results were notably controlled, as Smith provided sturdier frames for Schon's typically rousing notions. This firmer grasp allowed *The Calling* to reference various elements of Schon's creative arc—including Journey, previous solo work with **Schon & Hammer**, and **Santana**—without losing the plot.

"There's a looseness, but it's tight," Schon told *Music Radar*. "It's tight in that we didn't have songs when we walked in the studio, but when you hear the record, it's hard to believe that we didn't. It's complete."

Journey fans got a taste of both key ingredients of their classic Fantasy Studios-era formula with arena-rattling tracks like "Carnival Jazz" and "Back Smash," and the soaring pop balladry of "Six String Waltz" and "True Emotion."

Elsewhere, "Primal Surge" pushed harder, combining the typical Schon solo's familiar anthemic feel with this excitingly layered rhythm counterpoint. "Irish Field" reanimated the searching tone of Schon's work on *Abraxas Pool*, the underrated 1990s project featuring a series of **Santana** band alums—but with an overlay of emerald hues.

"Tumbleweeds" settled into a musky, propulsive groove that granted Schon a bold new freedom that Journey no longer could. "Fifty Six" traveled even deeper into the dark sense of mystery that surrounded Schon's time with Santana, but at a blinding pace more associated with 1970s jazz-rock.

Somewhere along the way, former collaborator Jan Hammer came to mind. Schon reached out and he agreed to add Moog sounds on both "Tumbleweeds" and "Fifty Six," completing another circle.

"I only do these guest shots if I really like the music. That's basically the criteria that I go by,"

Hammer said. "It was like riding a bicycle, really—except it was much more of a high-energy full-on, balls-to-the-wall rock record. When it comes to the amazing rhythm playing, the backing track that I was playing over made it so easy. I was so inspired by his energy."

The Calling ended with a surprising placidity, but even then, "Song of the Wind II" vastly improved upon the feather-light smooth jazz found on Schon's 2001 solo release, *Voice*.

Schon's collaboration with Smith was far from over. He would appear on Schon's 2015 solo album, *Vortex*, before returning to the drum chair with Journey in 2016. None of it would have happened without *The Calling*.

"Neal and I have an immediate chemistry, so we got right into a creative zone," Smith said. "We did the kind of jamming that we used to do with Journey, and then we experimented with moving the ideas around to create arrangements and finished songs. Igor Len was there to help flesh out the songs and, between the three of us, we just let the ideas come. We came up with the entire album in four days!" [8, 9, 40, 300, 603, 686]

WINTER 2012–13

Los Angeles Psychologist Kellie Nash Dies at 40

A Los Angeles doctor named **Kellie Nash** died on December 14, 2012 to little notice among Journey fans. But her final struggle, and the love they shared, helped guide Steve Perry back to his muse.

In the years after his blockbuster divorce from Journey, he had chosen a hermit-like existence in his childhood hometown of Hanford, California in the San Joaquin Valley. Perry would occasionally sketch out a rough song idea—including "Most of All" and "In the Rain"—but considered himself retired.

Then, director **Patty Jenkins** called to ask permission to use Journey's "Don't Stop Believin'" in the 2003 film *Monster*. Perry agreed, and the film proceeded to Oscar-winning critical acclaim. Newly relevant again, "Don't Stop Believin'" became associated with a string of pop culture moments—the World Series run

by the Chicago White Sox in 2005, the striking conclusion of HBO's *The Sopranos* in 2007, and the 2015 season of Fox's *Glee*, among others.

Less heralded, but more important, was the friendship that blossomed as Perry joined Jenkins during her film editing sessions. Jenkins turned him onto the music of **Eels**, with whom Perry would make a series of long-awaited live performances. She also connected him with Nash.

Perry could once again be found in the post-production bay as Jenkins completed work on a segment of *Five*, a multipart 2011 anthology for the Lifetime network that focused on living with breast cancer. He was struck by someone in "this scene where the camera is panning across this patio in a hospital meeting area. And I said, 'Patty, whoa. Stop. Who's that?'" Perry told *Yahoo Entertainment*.

The series featured plenty of big names, but Jenkins had specifically hired extras who would give everything the appropriate gravitas. "I surrounded them with people who are survivors, who are actively facing treatment," she told *Yahoo*.

Nash, a local psychologist, was one of them. Perry asked for her email address. He was clearly smitten, but Jenkins told the Associated Press she tried to warn him about the difficulties facing Nash: "You need to know one thing ... she's fighting for her life."

Nash's cancer had returned, metastasizing into a likely fatal Stage 4 diagnosis. "My head said, 'I don't know,'" Perry told *The New York Times*, "but my heart said, 'Send the email.'"

A deeply felt romance of less than two years followed, during which Nash drew out a promise from Perry to restart his career. [253, 687, 690, 691, 692, 693, 696]

SPRING–FALL 2013

NUGGETS

▶ Neal Schon is reportedly joining his old friend **Sammy Hagar** for his new album, *Sammy Hagar and Friends*, scheduled for release in September. **Michael Anthony**, **Taj Mahal**, and **Kid Rock** will be joining too.
—*Billboard*

NUGGETS (cont.)

▶ **FILM REVIEW:** Filmmaker **Ramona S. Diaz** releases a documentary called *Journey: Don't Stop Believin': Everyman's Journey*, an hour-plus feature that tells all of Journey's story, but emphasizes Arnel Pineda's amazing trip from obscure band singer in the Philippines to Neal Schon's YouTube discovery. The film culminates with Pineda's first tour as the band's front man. The payoff for everyone in this doc is the advent of a Filipino following for Journey, a new house for Pineda and his family, and a homecoming concert in Manila. Rated PG; in select theaters. —*Billboard*

Perry Reveals a Cancer Scare, And a Love Tragically Lost

Steve Perry retreated even further out of public life after a period where he occasionally appeared to lead sing-alongs of "Don't Stop Believin'" at baseball games.

Some tentative attempts to create new music followed, but he admitted to paralyzing worry. The successes of youth seemed to be stalking his muse: "Is it intimidating at some level to not want to disappoint people? Of course, it is," Perry told the *Tampa Bay Times*.

Perry had finally agreed to hip replacement surgery in 1998, almost two years after he was diagnosed with a degenerative disease. Yet there was much more to his extended absence: Perry had dealt with tragic loss—and then endured a cancer scare. He revealed both stories in a June 2013 post on the *Fan Asylum* website.

"Three weeks ago, a routine mole was taken off my face and the lab report came back melanoma skin cancer," Perry wrote. "I've had two surgeries in two weeks to remove all the cancer cells, and I've been told they think they got it all and no other treatments are required."

This setback followed the December 2012 death of his girlfriend **Kellie Nash**, who had been battling her own cancer during their relationship. "You want to know the truth? I've not said this to anybody yet: I believed our love would cure her cancer," Perry later told *The Guardian*. "I really did."

Perry was moved to discuss it all after a com-

forting chance meeting with former MTV VJ **Martha Quinn** at a street fair. "It was so great to see her and in a few short moments I told her most of this story," Perry wrote on the *Fan Asylum* site. "She asked if I'd take a picture with her and I said, 'If you don't mind my face scar.' She said, 'Not at all.'"

Much time had passed, but Quinn's regard for Perry's work with Journey had only deepened.

"At the time, we didn't appreciate how great he was," Quinn said. "It seemed like, 'Well, he's an arena rock vocalist. He's supposed to sound like that.' So, running into Steve that day, that's another one of those situations where I didn't think it was as big a deal as it turned out to be. I was just at the farmer's market, and I ran into him. I was like, 'Oh my gosh, I haven't seen you in so long.'"

For Perry, however, it was something far more meaningful. Nash's birthday was looming, the first since her death. "It was so great seeing Martha," Perry wrote. "I was a bit emotionally lost that day and seeing Martha got me grounded again."

Perry began a slow re-emergence. He made a surprise return to performing with the Los Angeles rock band **Eels**. Then the songs Perry had been so deliberate about would coalesce into his first album since the 1990s.

"We were just chit-chatting, and I didn't realize that impact that it would have—but I'm certainly glad to have played a positive role in his life," Quinn said. "I called it, 'MTV High.' We all went to the same high school, even if we didn't go at exactly the same time. So, Steve Perry didn't go to MTV High at the same time that **Simon Le Bon** did, but they all know each other—and those of us who are alumni, we all stick together." [303, 456, 687, 688]

THE WAY WE USED TO BE

Journey was back on the charts with Arnel Pineda as their new front man. A new feel-good era emerged as old band kinships were rekindled— and the rock and roll world finally recognized them for five decades of accomplishments. But as always, tensions arose to break the calm.

FALL 2013

Hagar, Schon Reconnect For Variant HSAS Album

Don Nix's blues-rocking "Going Down" had been part of countless **Sammy Hagar** setlists over the years. He had made it a concert staple with **Michael Anthony** and **Chad Smith** in **Chickenfoot**, as well as an offshoot bar band group with Anthony called **Los Tres Gusanos**.

All three returned for a new studio update of 2013's *Sammy Hagar & Friends*. The difference was Neal Schon, who completed what amounted to a reworked version of HSAS—**Hagar Schon Anthony Smith**.

Recorded live in the studio, "Going Down" started with a controlled—and quite expected—menace. Hagar's trusty Chickenfoot rhythm section provided a tight bottom end while he channeled the R&B roots that propelled the original HSAS through their low-charting early 1980s version of "Whiter Shade of Pale."

Then Schon arrived to rearrange the floorboards underneath them, employing a fleet, gritty approach that recalled his early days with **Santana** and Journey. "It's never been burned like that," Hagar observed during a video interview announcing the song.

Erasing decades of arena balladry with one solo, Schon helped the new HSAS draw a straight line back to ear-searing previous takes on this Nix classic by **Freddie King**, **Jeff Beck**, **John Lee Hooker**, and **John Mayall**, among many others.

As with so many of his best moments, Schon's solo was captured live. "He's one of those type of players [where] you roll the tape at all times," *Raised on Radio*-era drummer Mike Baird said in the 1986 touring documentary, "and you're gonna get somethin' that's really unique."

"Going Down" continued both Hagar's long musical association with Schon, and with Journey. Both **Aynsley Dunbar** and Ross Valory were considered when **Ronnie Montrose** was putting together a band to back Hagar in the 1970s. Hagar worked with Journey producer **Geoff Workman** on 1980's *Danger Zone* and co-wrote "Remember the Heroes" with Jonathan Cain for 1982's *Three Lock Box*.

Unfortunately, the subsequently aborted **Planet Us** project echoed the lost promise of his original HSAS collaborations with Schon. "HSAS was fine for me," Hagar told *Circus*, "but it was not what a lot of people hoped."

Fans wanted a tour back then, and so did their record label. But Hagar told them from the beginning that his schedule would not allow that. "All I wanted to do was get together [with] some friends and make a record," Hagar added. "That was absolutely to be the end of it."

Decades later, this is just what he would do, with "Going Down" and *Sammy Hagar & Friends*. "It was just two hours of playing and the rest of the time fucking around," Hagar told *Billboard*. "That band is so good that we got the first take on 'Going Down.'"

Sammy Hagar & Friends was released on September 24, 2013 and raced past *Through the Fire*, the 1984 low-charting lone release from an original lineup of HSAS that featured **Kenny Aaronson** and **Michael Shrieve**. Schon also appeared on a cover of **Depeche Mode**'s "Personal Jesus" as *Sammy Hagar & Friends* became Hagar's 11th LP to reach the Top 25. [135, 136, 480, 700]

SPRING 2014

Schon Revs Up Solo Engine In Berkeley Again for *So U*

Neal Schon's suddenly torrid solo pace produced his second album in as many years with *So U* on May 16, 2014. He had only managed two projects away from Journey in the entire previous decade: 2001's *Voice* and 2005's *I on U*.

He credited the wide-open atmosphere at Berkeley's Fantasy Studios, "where I made a lot of the biggest records I ever did with Journey," Schon said. "They treat me great over there; I feel like I am at home—and I've been pretty much living in there lately. There's been a lot of music coming out of me lately."

Schon decided to explore a different trio dynamic after creating *The Calling* with Steve Smith and **Igor Len**. *So U* brought him together again with Journey's Deen Castronovo and their former **Soul SirkUS** bandmate **Marco Mendoza**—but the trio explored a far different sound.

For Castronovo, it was another chance to

deepen a musical relationship that he compared to Schon's with mentor Gregg Rolie. "Gregg kind of plucked Neal from high school and took him in—that's kind of what Neal did with me in **Bad English**," Castronovo said. "I was playing with **Tony MacAlpine**, and he just kind of plucked me out."

After Bad English, Castronovo was part of **Hardline** with Schon, then worked with him during a short collaborative period with **Paul Rodgers**. Castronovo joined Journey after Smith's departure, then recorded Soul SirkUS' lone studio project with Schon.

"I'm 10 years younger than Neal. I think maybe Gregg's, like, seven or eight years older than him?" Castronovo added. "So, it's a very similar situation, you know, because Neal just grabbed me and everywhere he went, he took me with him. So I owe him a huge, huge, massive debt of gratitude. I really wouldn't have a career if it wasn't for Neal."

So U would allow Castronovo to step forward as a singer again, sharing the mic with Mendoza on a decidely rare Schon solo project with vocals. "Both of those guys, I felt, were worthy of being lead singers. They certainly sounded great together," Schon said. "We had done the Soul SirkUS album before. Deen and Marco just clicked as a bass player and drummer, in the early stages of that. So, we were looking to get back into that and sort of open it up musically, so it wasn't just all in a rock theme."

Jack Blades assisted with lyrics and contributed backing vocals, but Castronovo and Mendoza were so central to the creative process that they were given co-billing on the album. Other than "What You Want" and "On My Way," the balance of the tracks were completed in the moment.

"That was another project where he called and said, 'Can you be here in a few weeks? I'm going to be in the studio,'" Mendoza said. "It was completely on the fly. We got together for two days, and what you hear is the work that happened in those two days."

Blades then returned to the studio, where he and Schon worked on more lyrical ideas. The addition of these narratives inevitably led to comparisons with Journey—particularly on "Love Finds a Way." That song was constructed from parts that never coalesced during Journey sessions, including Schon's orchestration. "Love Finds a Way" emerged as "sort of a sister song to 'Troubled Child', off of *Frontiers*," Schon told *Guitar International*. "That song I had in my head for a long time. I thought it would be a Journey song, but it never ended up on a CD."

At the same time, however, *So U* was free to move further afield. For instance, "Exotica" found Schon "sort of tipping my hat to **Carlos Santana**," he told *Ultimate Classic Rock*'s **Matt Wardlaw**, "because it's sort of like a fusion-Latin rock thing. I definitely stretch out on that."

"Take a Ride" was built atop a leftover idea from Schon's time with Rodgers. "I just said to myself after I heard Marco's voice, 'Well, I think he's got a bluesy quality in his voice and he could hold this up,'" Schon told the *Huffington Post*.

Arriving while Journey continued a well-received tandem tour with **Steve Miller** and **Tower of Power**, *So U* would be quickly followed by another Schon solo album with Smith and Len. Work on the long-awaited reunion of the early 1970s lineup of Santana also continued.

Mendoza admitted he loved collaborating amid this whirlwind of activity, especially the free-flowing nature of the sessions. Still, he wondered if a bit more tinkering could have made *So U* an even better album.

"In retrospect, you think, 'Wow, it would have been cool to spend a little more time developing the songs and maybe taking it to another place.'" Mendoza said. "Not necessarily a better place, but maybe a better place where the results would have been different. That's the thing with Neal, though: He's always going to be on the move. I really respect that a lot." [12, 31, 408, 701, 702, 703]

SUMMER–FALL 2014

NUGGETS
▶ Journey guitarist Neal Schon filed a lawsuit against the city of San Francisco over a $240,000 fee to use a city landmark—the Palace of Fine Arts—for his wedding to *Real Housewives of D.C.* star **Michaele Salahi** in December 2013. —*Billboard*

NUGGETS

▶ Steve Perry returned to the stage twice in May when he took the mic for a couple Journey songs during two different **Eels** dates—the first in St. Paul, Minnesota, and then again the following week for four songs at the Lincoln Theater in Washington, D.C. He sang "Open Arms" and "Lovin', Touchin', Squeezin'" to a receptive crowd. — *Blabbermouth.net*

With an Eels Assist, Perry Returns to the Spotlight

Steve Perry was hanging out with director **Patty Jenkins** when he first heard **Eels**' *Daisies of the Galaxy* album. She said, "I'm curious if you've ever heard it," Perry told *Ultimate Classic Rock's* **Matt Wardlaw**. "I said, 'No, I actually haven't.'"

He dug deeper into their catalog, falling in love with the band's passion and its plainspoken approach. Jenkins eventually introduced Perry to bandleader **Mark Everett**, and Perry became a regular at their shows in 2003.

Ironically, Everett was no fan of Journey as a kid. "When I was young, living in Virginia," Everett told *The New York Times*, "Journey was always on the radio, and I wasn't into it."

Everett and Perry instead bonded over mallets and wickets. "He had a group of people he'd play croquet with in the back yard of his studio," Perry told the BBC. "They played for money and they were really good at it."

Then Perry started dropping by while Eels rehearsed—"uninvited and unannounced, but not unwelcome," according to the *Times*. Perhaps inevitably, Perry told the BBC that Eels members started pressing him to join in: "Well, are you going to sing a song with us?"

Perry finally relented, singing "Lights" at the urging of guitarist **Jeff Lyster**. It was "this great moment," Everett told *the Times*. "A guy who's become like **Howard Hughes**, and just walked away from it all 25 years ago, and he's finally doing it again."

Everett said he knew Perry was warming to the idea when he brought his own microphone to a rehearsal. Perry then sang with them as

Eels ran through "It's a Motherfucker" and "I'm Going to Stop Pretending That I Didn't Break Your Heart."

"I heard the song 'It's a Motherfucker,'" Perry told Wardlaw, "and I was taken aback by the songwriting simplicity of that." Somewhere deep down, it might have spoken to his pain over losing **Kellie Nash** too.

As they continued working together, a return to the stage began to take on the air of inevitability. Still, when Perry finally did, it was a complete surprise to everyone in Eels. He simply knocked on the door of their idling tour bus outside the Fitzgerald Theater on May 25, 2014 in St. Paul, Minnesota.

Inside, Eels ran through their usual set, then Everett introduced Perry for their first encore. "The interesting thing about this guy," Everett told the crowd that night, "is that he hasn't sung his songs for some 20, 25 years; he walked away from it because it didn't feel right."

They performed "It's a Motherfucker" that night before launching into "Open Arms" and "Lovin', Touchin" Squeezin'." But as Everett initially waved Perry on stage, nothing happened for a very long moment.

"I sat in the back and I waited—just to mess with him," Perry admitted to the BBC. "He's looking at me going, 'What's going on?'" Finally, Perry peeked out and said, "Now? Should I come out now?"

Perry admitted that he had no idea how he would be received, "because it was an indie crowd, a different generation, a different time," he told the BBC, "but the audience reacted like they knew me. So it was amazing."

It was also deeply unexpected. Perry had essentially turned into a ghost.

"In the intervening years, I tried to get him to perform on the Grammys a few times," said **David Wild**, who writes and produces the annual broadcast. "Obviously, there'd be nothing bigger than him singing 'Don't Stop Believin'' with somebody. I remember one time, I don't even know if we knew he had management. Like, we reached out through **David Pack** of **Ambrosia**, his friend. 'How do we get to this guy?'"

Somehow, Eels had.

Continued on Page 310

Marco Mendoza (left) and David Lowy of The Dead Daisies.

VERSATILITY DELIVERED MENDOZA INTO SCHON'S WORLD

Marco Mendoza's career certainly is not defined by his connection to Neal Schon. He has also collaborated with **Thin Lizzy**, **Ted Nugent**, **Black Sabbath**'s **Bill Ward**, and **Whitesnake**, among others.

Still, Mendoza kept circling back to Schon until he eventually came on board as a short-lived touring musician with Journey. Mendoza was part of **Soul SirkUS** in the early-to-mid 2000s, the **Neal Schon Band** in the 2010s, and Schon's 2014 album *So U*. He then appeared on Journey's 2022 *Live in Concert at Lollapalooza* LP, as well as a 2023 eponymous album from **Journey Through Time**, a Schon side project that brought in more of Journey's early material.

"I have never worked with someone so versatile as Marco," frequent collaborator Deen Castronovo told interviewer **Francijn Suermondt**. "He can sing anything, play anything—plus he has a heart of gold."

Mendoza shared a love for depthless hard-rock improvisation with Schon, and they both felt most at home when staying inveterately in the moment.

"When he's writing, he's moving so fast—and you better catch up to him, and stay on top of it," Mendoza said. "That's how he works. He's writing, and sometimes we're tracking at the same time. It's a trip. We're like a couple of kids. It reminds me of when you first started playing in a garage band. He's moving fast. He's got a huge vocabulary, just constantly moving."

The same could be said for Mendoza.

Born on May 3, 1963 in San Diego, California, Mendoza had a musical childhood. His mother was a singer, and his father played clarinet. When they divorced, Mendoza moved to Tijuana, Mexico, where he grew up with his grandmother. Inspiration arrived one Christmas morning in the form of **The Beatles**' 1969 album *Abbey Road*, and Mendoza asked to borrow his brother's guitar.

Mendoza's career appeared on track, but he almost derailed because of drug addiction and alcohol abuse. He has been sober since his late 20s, and that process opened the door for the gig playing bass on Ward's 1990 solo debut, *Ward One: Along the Way*. Mendoza ran into the longtime Black Sabbath drummer at an Alcoholics Anonymous meeting.

Mendoza then began a long association with **John Sykes** after the guitarist caught Mendoza at a local club in Studio City. Sykes invited him to join **Blue Murder** in the early 1990s. Mendoza collaborated with Sykes again in a reformed edition of Thin Lizzy between 1996 and 2007, continuing with the band in 2009 after Sykes departed. Later, he was in Sykes's solo band.

"Marco's just an amazing player," Sykes told *Melodic Rock*. "He's got a lot of heart and soul. He can play pretty much anything you want him to play."

Mendoza proved it by next connecting with **Whitesnake**'s **David Coverdale** for his *Into the Light* solo project, and worked with Whitesnake from 2003–2005—a period that produced 2006's *Live... In the Still of the Night*. In an echo of what Mendoza loved so much about working with Schon, he split from Whitesnake because he had other projects.

"He's a master musician. But he just can't sit still for two minutes," Coverdale told *Wisconsin Music*. "I love him very dearly and do sincerely wish him well. But I cannot conduct my life around somebody else's agenda."

By then, Mendoza had met Schon at the annual NAMM trade show. A few weeks later, he was sitting in with Soul SirkUS alongside Schon, Jeff Scott Soto, and Castronovo.

"As you can imagine, being surrounded by these cats, we just started jamming—and we clicked so well," Mendoza said. "It was meant to be. Right away, man, we got along. Neal was throwing stuff at me, and he really appreciated what I brought to the mix."

Schon liked Mendoza's taste and versatility. "I was in L.A. and saw him play at the Baked Potato with his trio," Schon said. "They did fusion-Latin jazz rock versions of, like, **Stevie Wonder** songs—and I was like, 'Wow. This guy can just sing his ass off, and play his ass off.'"

Mendoza joined **Black Star Riders** in 2012 before sitting in with Castronovo on Schon's *So U*. He also had a four-album stint with **The Dead Daisies**, beginning with 2015's *Revolución*, which included a live album in 2017.

Mendoza departed following 2018's *Burn It Down* and became part of Schon's **Journey Through Time** side project with Castronovo. A 2018 benefit show in San Francisco was followed by a few more dates, including Oakland, Phoenix, and Los Angeles. Schon reconnected with Gregg Rolie on some of Journey's most explorative songs—and they gave Mendoza a chance to marvel at the inventiveness of it all.

"These guys were ahead of their time," Mendoza said. "You look at the time frame, after the **Santana** thing when their music was being released—this was amazing. These guys were leaning on the prog side. With Gregg's voice and the B-3, I'm such a big fan of that sound. You get a little more inside the music, and you realize how far ahead they were musically."

When returning *Raised on Radio*-era bassist Randy Jackson could not join Journey's pending 2021 tour because of a back issue, Schon knew just who to call: "Marco Mendoza, a good friend of ours [who] plays great, he'll fill in for now," Jonathan Cain told ABC.

Mendoza dug further into the Journey discography. "To be readdressing those albums, it was a trip, man," Mendoza said. "One thing is true when you're a fan is that you're not really dissecting it or breaking it down. But when you get the call for something like this, you begin discovering all of these little jewels. You go, 'Wow! No wonder it sounded so good.' Ross [Valory], I have to give him a lot of credit. He and Aynsley [Dunbar] and then Steve Smith had such a strong bond, rhythm section-wise. There's some cool stuff happening here."

Still, Mendoza did not last long. He debuted on July 29, 2021 at the Byline Bank Aragon Ballroom in Chicago, and had been replaced by **Todd Jensen** by the time Journey began their Las Vegas residency on December 1. Jensen had previously been in **Hardline** with Schon and Castronovo.

Schon was initially nebulous about what happened, only stating that "it just wasn't gelling." Mendoza turned to solo dates, releasing the aptly named *New Direction* album in 2022. [14, 31, 718, 719, 720, 721, 722, 723, 724]

Inspired, Perry performed with them again on May 31, at the Lincoln Theatre in Washington, D.C., and on June 11 at The Orpheum in Los Angeles. "I missed it so much," he told *The New York Times*. "I couldn't believe it'd been so long."

Growing more comfortable, Perry added a meditative **Sam Cooke** update to the set for both subsequent appearances, placing "Only Sixteen" between "It's a Motherfucker" and "Open Arms."

He'd return to quickly coalescing album sessions, bolstered by the emotional honesty Everett brought to his songs. "He helped me get bold about taking some chances with songwriting," Perry told Wardlaw, "because he takes chances. He really does. He doesn't care, which is even more bold. And it's always great." [253, 411, 712, 713]

Journey Remains Silent in Studio As Outside Projects Proliferate

The members of Journey were entering a prolific period of recording—just not with Journey.

Neal Schon kicked off things by directing his firehose of ideas into solo projects, releasing 2012's *The Calling*, 2014's *So U*, and 2015's *Vortex*. Meanwhile, Journey had not issued an album since 2011's incendiary *Eclipse*, which enjoyed a commendable No. 13 *Billboard* debut, but quickly tumbled down the charts.

Journey produced annual new releases from their self-titled 1975 album through 1981's *Escape* and had only once gone more than five years without a new album. Now Journey faced surpassing the decade-long period of studio silence that followed their post-*Raised on Radio* split.

"We'll have to see what happens. I know that Arnel [Pineda] is definitely game for anything. He likes to rock," Schon said back then. "We'll have to see where Jonathan [Cain] is at. I definitely feel, for Journey, it's a different beast, you know?"

Pineda was feeling the same pull of history. "Personally, I'm still not satisfied," he told interviewer **Steve Prokopy**. "There are still a lot of things that we need to do to finally cement the deal that 'Hey, we've begun as something and gone to another thing,' you know?"

In the end, Pineda said the goal was to create a body of work that inspired fans to say, "Arnel was really able to contribute to Journey's legacy."

Of course, Steve Perry was dealing with his own creative drought, but he had recently returned to the stage with **Eels**. Hope for a Journey reunion of some sort inevitably followed, and that might have broken the creative logjam for Cain. He was still smarting over the meteoric disappointment of the guitar-heavy *Eclipse*, which he felt wrongly focused on only one element of Journey's established approach.

Cain lost an important songwriting partner in Perry, someone who understood his desire to speak from the heart. In the old days, his presence might have tipped the album in a different direction. "Perry had that pop sensibility. I followed his lead, he followed mine...and Neal added the rock edge to it," Cain told **Michael Cavacini**. "With Perry missing from the mix, do you ever get back to it? I don't know."

Perry's newest successor credibly inhabited the old songs, but Pineda was not a composer: Through two albums, he had just three co-writing credits—"What I Needed" on 2008's *Revelation*, then "She's a Mystery" and "To Whom It May Concern" from *Eclipse*.

Cain would soon begin a run of faith-focused albums with 2016's *What God Wants to Hear*, including six new albums through 2020. Deen Castronovo began fronting **Revolution Saints** in 2015 and they issued three albums over the same period. He also joined **Marco Mendoza** in **Dead Daisies** in 2016, remaining through two release cycles. There was even talk of a solo album from Pineda.

Schon admitted that his latest ideas might not really fit into a Journey record, anyway. "I think maybe it's more suited for my solo stuff — and to bring a bit of it into Journey, but only like in a live setting," he said. "I think that our records are just more about making songs, but then nobody's really all that jacked up about recording new songs in the band right now. I am, but I'm trying to get everybody else motivated."

As the stalemate continued, Cain offered a blunt assessment of Journey's recording prospects: He was not ready to return to the studio unless the others were prepared to "make classic Journey music," Cain told Cavacini. "If everybody is willing to make a legacy album like *Arrival*, I'm in. If you're not, I'm not." [13, 558, 705, 707]

SPRING-SUMMER 2015

Santana Announces Rolie Will Double-Bill on Journey Dates

A reunion of the early 1970s edition of **Santana** had been confirmed years ago, then the project lost momentum. Neal Schon and **Carlos Santana** released studio albums, while Gregg Rolie joined **Ringo Starr's All-Starr Band**.

But just when the prospect of a proper follow-up to 1971's *Santana III* seemed lost, Carlos announced some intriguing concert news: Rolie would rejoin Santana during four March 2015 shows in Mexico, including two that would be co-headlined by Journey.

Behind the scenes, *Santana IV*, their next album, was still proceeding, but only as schedules allowed. "We're doing *Santana IV* 'cause we stopped at *III*," Carlos told *Billboard*. "We went into the studio [and] we [did] some vocals. We are going to record some more."

Michael Carabello was already gone by the time 1972's more jazz-influenced *Caravanserai* arrived. Rolie and Schon were only part-time players on the record, then split not long afterward. **José "Chepito" Areas** and **Michael Shrieve** eventually departed as well.

"I think that everybody needed to grow in a different direction," Santana told *Long Island Weekly*, "and to experience different things for themselves."

The old magic remained despite time away and the scattered nature of the sessions. "It's definitely full circle, very exciting," Schon said. "Now, to come back to it again, and see it all coming together again, it's just going to be magical. Beautifully magical."

On 2014's *Corazón*, Santana reverted to the guest-packed approach that earlier hurtled *Supernatural* to multiplatinum sales—but never lost his enthusiasm for working with the classic lineup again. "To be in the same studio as Gregg Rolie, Michael Shrieve, and Michael Carabello... it's really incredible to make that circle complete," Santana told *Billboard*. [4, 42, 708, 709, 710, 711]

Perry Commences On-Again, Off-Again Sessions for *Traces*

Steve Perry had a new mindset in May 2015 as loose sessions began for his comeback album: He was determined to accept these songs, and himself, as they were.

"For me, it switched from perfection to emotional expression," Perry told *Forbes*. "It's a different Steve now." These expressions were often reminiscent, fragile, anguished: **Kellie Nash** had passed away two and half years ago.

"Whatever music showed up is where I said, 'Okay, I'm finishing that,'" Perry told *Ultimate Classic Rock*'s **Matt Wardlaw**. "Whatever my heart was painfully saying, 'Okay, then I'm finishing that.' Because if I'm not going to be honest and truthful to what shows up, then I'm full of shit!"

Perry knew Nash was terminally ill before they began dating but pressed ahead anyway. He had lost his mother and the grandparents who raised him. He had also "lost this career that I'd wanted so much, because I'd walked away from it," Perry told the *New Statesman*. Now, he risked losing someone else. "I justified it by telling myself, well, she's a PhD psychologist, maybe I need another shrink?"

As her health turned its final corner, however, she had asked him to make a promise. Nash saw something more for him in her absence: "She said, 'If something were to happen to me, promise me you won't go back into isolation, because that would make this all for naught,'" Perry told *The New York Times*, then began to cry.

Already threadbare from Journey's pitiless touring schedule, Perry's voice had continued to darken and fray. No one was a harsher critic. "My biggest problem is the singer that I'm working with," Perry told Wardlaw with a laugh. "It's probably the biggest problem I've got, is the love/hate relationship sometimes with my own vocal abilities or shortcomings."

He focused on writing instead. A reliably open-hearted composer, Perry aimed to go deeper. The sessions challenged him again and again. The goal was to put "even more of that vulnerability and emotional expression out there. And if you don't like it, then that's fine. If you do, that's great," Perry told *Forbes*. "The days of perfectionism don't hold water anymore."

He had been introduced to future *Traces* co-producer **Thom Flowers** through a mutual friend. "Steve was up for a Giants game and he loves studios, so he just wanted to stop by and say hello. I got to meet him then," he said. Perry mentioned working together, but the Santa Barbara-based Flowers was only "expecting to help him record some drums, and maybe help out with the studio a little bit. But we hit it off, and pretty quickly got some things together and he just said, 'What are you doing for the next few months?' And then we became great friends."

The first task, and it was no small one, was sorting through Perry's huge backlog of ideas. "It was daunting," Flowers admitted. "They were at various stages, you know. Some were really just rough sketches, and some were more fully fledged demos. I was just doing what I do, kind of picking the things that jumped out at me. We would get the demos together and that was one of the things he said: 'Well, you got this together in like 15 minutes, after I've been living with this thing for months!'"

Traces would not arrive for more than three years, as Perry pieced his muse back together. "When I sat by myself and started sketching ideas, I forgot that I had not gone into that place in a long time," Perry told Wardlaw. "And at first, it was a scary place to walk back into, like an old house you were raised in that you had not walked into since you were a kid."

He relied on Flowers, who brought perspective and fresh ears. "Sometimes, just having someone in the room while you're listening will make you hear it in a different way—even without any real feedback," Flowers said. "He had been working on it on his own for so long, I think it was important just having another person in the room to bounce ideas off."

Much had changed, but not his sense that an album was not worth releasing without a deeper context. "I don't need any money," Perry told CBS. "This is about the passion. But maybe it took a broken heart to get there, a completely broken heart."

Asked if his heart was still broken, Perry answered unequivocally: "Yes! Yes, it is still broken. But it's open. That's okay." [253, 714, 715, 716, 717, 858]

Journey Dismisses Castronovo After Domestic Violence Arrest

Deen Castronovo's year began far differently than it ended.

February 2015 saw the debut of **Revolution Saints**, a new side band with **Jack Blades** of **Night Ranger** and **Doug Aldrich** of **Whitesnake** meant to feature Castronovo as a vocalist. In April, he personally delivered a $10,000 donation to students at an Oregon high school after a fire swept through their music department.

By June, Castronovo was posing for a mug shot following a violent 24-day methamphetamine binge. He had slipped off the wagon after having a hip replacement and pins placed in his back. Castronovo needed pain meds to get through Journey's rigorous touring schedule. When they got back home, he descended into the darkest depths of his lifetime.

Police charged Castronovo with rape, sexual abuse, and unlawful use of a weapon. He entered rehab after his indictment as Journey scrambled to line up another drummer for their next set of tour dates. They secured a temporary replacement in **Omar Hakim**, who had appeared on a pair of Schon solo projects, 1989's *Late Nite* and 2005's *I On U*.

"It's a huge order for anyone to just come in if it wasn't Steve Smith, who played with us for years, or Deen, who'd been with us for two decades," Schon admitted to the *Regina Leader-Post*.

Then there was the compressed timeline. Castronovo was arrested on June 14 after police in Salem, Oregon responded to a call about a domestic disturbance. Hakim made his debut on June 20 at the Hollywood Bowl, where Journey was backed by the Hollywood Bowl Orchestra.

Hakim somehow guided them through the performance. "Omar plays with more intensity, not unlike Deen," Ross Valory told the *Times-Picayune*, "but he's got the musicality, the ears, and the technique in common with Steve Smith."

Castronovo was fired in August 2015, then sentenced in October 2015 to four years on probation. This would be his fifth rehab. He had already lost a marriage and had a previous stint in the Hazelden Springbrook treatment center in Newberg, Oregon.

Castronovo had also been arrested in 2012 under similar circumstances, after a neighbor reported a couple fighting across the street. He entered into a diversion agreement that required anger management classes and 80 hours of community service.

"Unfortunately the demons got the worst of him," Schon told *Billboard*, "but everything happens for a reason. It was truly time for him to work on himself and get himself straight."

Castronovo began drug and domestic violence counseling, facing hard truths while enrolled in a court-ordered 75-day inpatient treatment program. "Journey was my identity for so many damned years—and when it went away, it was hard," Castronovo said. "People would go, 'Oh, that's the drummer from Journey.' I'm like, 'No, I'm not the drummer of Journey anymore,' and it took me a while to get adjusted to that—because that was my identity."

He later enrolled in a voluntary 18-month post-treatment program that subjected patients to daily breathalyzer tests and random urinalysis, while **Revolution Saints** was also put on hold. They would not return until 2017's *Light in the Dark*, the same year he reunited with former **Hardline** bandmate **Johnny Gioeli** to release an album as **Gioeli-Castronovo**.

Castronovo attempted to fix his personal relationships and reorient his priorities: Going forward, there had to be more to his life than music.

"Probably the best thing that ever happened to me," he said, "was just to go, 'You know what? That is not who I am. That is what I do for a living. That's how I get the kids through college and make sure the grandbabies got all the Xboxes they need.'"

Castronovo would mention self-doubt tied to unspecified childhood trauma, but was careful to take responsibility for his own actions. He began openly admitting that he had been a verbally and physically abusive man. He said jail likely saved his life, and the second trip to Hazelden Springbrook changed him forever.

"Deen went through his tough personal time, which he's fully recovered from," Gioeli said. "He's just a great human. It's just great that he's recovered from all that shit in the past. We all have our peaks and our valleys."

Once the 2015 dates were complete, Hakim went back to a career that included celebrated work with **Sting**, **David Bowie**, **Weather Report**, and **Dire Straits**. Journey's drum throne was empty again—but not for long.

Schon had initially reached out to Steve Smith following Castronovo's arrest, but he was overseas on a European tour with his jazz band. Upon returning, Smith rejoined Journey for his third stint. [37, 196, 228, 408, 725, 726, 727, 728, 730]

SPRING-FALL 2016

RELEASES
▶ Santana (with Neal Schon, Gregg Rolie), *Santana IV* (album)
▶ Santana (with Neal Schon, Gregg Rolie) "Anywhere You Want To Go" (single)

ON THE ROAD
▶ Dave Mason, Santana, and The Doobie Brothers.

Schon's Solo Work with Smith Paves the Way for New Reunion

Vortex was constructed in much the same way as *The Calling*, even though Neal Schon had released another solo album in between.

He was back at Fantasy Studios in Berkeley with **Igor Len** and Steve Smith. **Jan Hammer** was also a special guest again on several songs, including their callback "Schon & Hammer Now."

The difference was, Schon had no governor this time. This was *The Calling* on steroids.

Len was looking forward to meeting Hammer, a personal hero. "I grew up on **Mahavishnu [Orchestra]** records, among many others, of course," Len said. "Years before, Neal actually said in an interview that I reminded him of Jan Hammer. I couldn't ask for a bigger compliment. I still remember the 'wow' feeling I had—and now Jan was coming to play? I was intimidated, I would not lie. Unfortunately, Jan was working remotely from his studio on the East Coast."

Released on June 22, 2015, *Vortex* arrived as Deen Castronovo's legal issues became common knowledge. As such, Schon's slow-boiling reunion with Carlos Santana may have been gar-

Continued on Page 315

SANTANA IV: A MASTERCLASS IN RECLAIMED STUDIO MAGIC

Carlos **Santana** might not admit it, but he was only the guitar player. Savvy label executives copped to it when they paired him with a series of guest stars to create 1999's second-act triumph *Supernatural*.

This collaborative spirit is also what animates *Santana IV*.

Gregg Rolie and Neal Schon brought out different complexities, decades after they left the lineup, while everyone scampered to keep up with **Michael Carabello** and **Michael Shrieve** as they showered these tracks with sensual and insistent rhythms. Carlos is transformed when confronted by his most important early foil in Rolie, while Schon cuts across **Santana**'s masterful liquidity with metallic counterpoints.

It was not a complete reunion, as classic-era bassist **David Brown** died in 2000. When the remaining early-era members reformed for 1997's **Abraxas Pool**, save for Santana himself, the bass player was **Alphonso Johnson**—a member of later-period Santana from 1985–1989. **José "Chepito" Areas** was not involved with *Santana IV* either, though Areas's son, Adrian, was in the **Gregg Rolie Band**.

Santana had continued with a series of other members, bringing bassist **Benny Rietveld** and percussionist **Karl Perazzo** along for these sessions. But the reformed band's focus was not on the past.

"There weren't many Woodstock stories, and I think that's because those stories have been told and related so often in popular media," Rietveld said. "They did much more reminiscing about the real stuff, about their first apartment together as a band, about players they started out with, high school, etc. Mostly, however, they were all focused on the task at hand, making the album. There was never a 'well, in the old days we would do this' attitude. It simply was all about, 'Let's make music here and now.'"

Every Hammond B-3 solo of Rolie's on the record was a first take. He knew intuitively where to fit it in because he well understood the infrastructure of Santana's unique guitar style. Rolie was there when it was built: "With Carlos, the best way to describe his playing is expressed by feelings," Rolie said. "Carlos has stuck to the roots of what he wants his guitar to sound like."

Santana IV may not have been the truly sequential heir to 1971's *Santana III*, which intro-

duced Schon while racing to the top of the U.S. charts. The lineup could never completely recapture the ardent sense of discovery of those first albums, or their boundless musical enthusiasm. Experience often makes it harder to replicate the loose intensity of youth. Still, the music exudes the joy they felt, as illustrated by the laughter that opened "Anywhere You Want to Go."

Santana was reliably inventive, though he seemed most inspired when presented with ideas among equals—rather than as the undisputed leader of an often rotating lineup.

"In all the times I've been in the studio with him, there's almost always one or two times where he'll come up with some really mad-sounding idea, and people will have these quizzical looks on their faces, and shrug and go, 'OK,'" Rietveld said. "Then the idea blossoms, takes shape, and suddenly the song or the piece has taken on a whole new purpose and direction, and it sounds spectacular.

"That's pretty much the same thing that happened with *Santana IV*," Rietveld added. "There were songs or song fragments that were brought in, and each piece was approached on its own terms. There was no blanket approach to all of it. I suspect that's probably how it was even from the first album, since it seems like such a natural process for Gregg, Neal, Mike, and Carabello."

They occasionally moved afield, as "Choo Choo" incorporated a house beat where they once might have chosen rumba or carnival rhythms. World music influences also girded "Come as You Are," but Santana always found their way home: "Leave Me Alone" reanimated their familiar "Oye Como Va" groove. The instrumental "Fillmore East" recalled their early days with manager **Bill Graham**, while "Sueños" echoed the suave atmospherics of 1972's *Caravanserai*—the last Santana LP to feature Rolie and Schon.

It was all held together by a chemistry only found as deep friendships are renewed—between Santana and Rolie, and between Rolie and Schon.

"We know a little bit more—well, [Neal] knows a lot more," Rolie said. "He can play just about anything. I know a little bit more about where I fit in and what I'm comfortable with and what I like hearing. I have been backing up guitar players all my life, where I lay a bed, as Carlos put it, while they play. That was my position, to fill up the room. So for me, it never changed. We play off each other because that's how we grew up. Same thing with Carlos: We grew up doing that."

In moments like the meditative "Blues Magic," everyone sounds like they are finishing each other's sentences. **The Isley Brothers' Ronald Isley** makes a pair of frankly carnal vocal asides on "Love Makes the World Go Round" and "Freedom in Your Mind," but by then, *Santana IV* sets itself apart from guest-packed recent albums like 2014's *Corazón*. They felt phoned in, while this album succeeded by sounding like everyone was in the room together.

But *Santana IV* was not recorded that way. Many of these songs were tracked separately, with audio files being shared instead of studio mics. Nevertheless, there was no denying the musical connection. "We really wanted to make it work for all of us and it did," Rolie told *Rolling Stone*. "It's what I would have done if I was directing things. I would have done *Santana IV* after *Santana III*."

If there is a criticism to be made, it might be that a few songs simply go on too long—as does *Santana IV* itself. For whatever reason, the same could not be said for their reunion tour. They never got past a few dates before Santana reverted to its current lineup.

"Management or Carlos pulled the plug on the whole thing," Rolie added. [1, 4, 18, 181, 375]

nering earlier headlines, but his renewed friendship with Steve Smith was more relevant.

"Steve and I definitely hook up on a different level these days," Schon said back then. "We're writing together. This stuff that we just recorded is on the ceiling, compared to *The Calling*—and I loved *The Calling*, musically. This record is just a bit more organic. You can tell it's built for playing live."

"El Matador," the album's advance single, framed the album's larger successes. Schon began in a place recalling the best parts of his early work on *Santana III*. There was a simply scalding intro before he launched the soaring locutions associated with his time in Journey. Smith offered an endlessly aggressive, fusion-focused bed of rhythm for the guitarist to continue building upon.

"The swinging part, the groove factor, having a nice swing feel—that is a universally accepted ingredient of what makes music groove," Smith said. "That was one of the things they liked about my playing."

Schon and Smith brilliantly tangled onward in this breathless fashion, with Schon burning while Smith bashed. That is, until the song's last third, when something utterly unexpected happened: Schon snatched up a Spanish guitar, for just a moment—and in that moment, "El Matador" finally exhaled, like a bull just before winding up for another snorting charge. They finished in a freefall of improvisation on the way back toward a recapitulation of the song's main figure.

All of it served to underscore the lingering symbiosis Schon and Smith still possessed from their time in Journey, but also how confining their time in that pop-hit machine really could be. This sounded, once again, like the kind of record they both always wanted to make.

As for the album's title? "That's the nickname that Carlos has recently given me," Schon said.

For Hammer, *Vortex* offered another opportunity to collaborate—but with everything turned up several notches.

"Basically, Neal has just loads and loads of very, very good tunes that are not quite finished," Hammer said. "They were just really burning; they were cooking rhythm tracks. So, he sends me things, and we talk on the phone. I'll say, 'Leave an opening here for me,' and that's basically how we've done it. That's much better than having to fly somewhere—which I hate," Hammer added, with a laugh.

Journey fired Deen Castronovo in August 2015. In November, Journey confirmed that Smith would replace him. Ross Valory seemed particularly enthused as they recreated the rhythm engine from all but one Journey album between 1979's *Evolution* and 1996's *Trial by Fire*.

This era also formed the heart of the setlists Journey played for decades. "He recorded 80 percent of the songs we're doing, so it's organic," Valory told the *Times-Picayune*. "It's back to the fundamentals of how the song was created, how we put our parts to it, how it was recorded."

Things were different with Arnel Pineda, who must have seemed like a newcomer to Smith. Pineda sensed that he was tentative at first, before they finally found musical common ground. "I could feel that he was trying to feel everything out and observe," Pineda told *Rolling Stone*. "When he got the good vibe again, we clicked." [3, 12, 32, 40, 196, 204]

Schon Reunites with Santana for Stirring House of Blues Gig

Neal Schon became **Carlos Santana**'s shadow as he worked to convince his initial mentor to reunite the early 1970s edition of **Santana**. That was little different from the way their relationship worked when Schon was still a starstruck teen.

"If he went to the store, I went to the store," Schon told the *Las Vegas Sun*. "He went down to the guitar shop; I was at the guitar shop."

Back then, this symbiosis helped shape 1971's *Santana III*, the first Santana album with significant contributions from Schon—and one of the last with Gregg Rolie. Fast forward some 45 years, and Schon's dogged persistence would lead to a celebrated March 21, 2016 reunion concert at the House of Blues in Las Vegas.

"I always thought it would be cool, and I was the one who pursued it—and, actually, I feel good about putting it all together," Schon said. "You know, I started running into Carlos a lot, here in the Bay Area. Everywhere I was, he was. We started talking a lot, and hanging out. And I just brought up the idea to him, and he slept on it for a good while. Then, all of a sudden, it was like: 'OK, we're going to do this.'"

The long-awaited *Santana IV* album was just weeks away as Santana took the stage with a lineup featuring Santana, Rolie, Schon, drummer **Michael Shrieve**, and percussionist **Michael Carabello** from *Santana III*. Carabello left after that album. Schon and Rolie departed following 1972's *Caravanserai*. Shrieve was gone after 1974's *Borboletta*. Bassist **Benny Rietveld** later succeeded the late **David Brown**, while percussionist **Karl Perazzo** took over for **José "Chepito" Areas**.

"So Neal started pursuing all of this and Carlos said he was almost pestering him, like, 'this is a great idea, we should do this' and Carlos finally said, 'Okay,'" Rolie told *Ultimate Classic Rock*'s **Matt Wardlaw**. "Getting back with these original guys and then having Benny, the bass player for Carlos and Karl Perazzo, the timbale player, it's a great band."

They opened the concert with "Soul Sacrifice," as Shrieve muscled through an updated version of the drum solo made immortal at Woodstock. "Looking at Carlos and seeing Gregg and Neal on the stage, and being next to Michael on the drums, it was fantastic," Carabello told *USA Today*. "It was like, at last, we were all in the same house again."

Rolie was showcased once more on "Evil Ways" before Carlos introduced Schon as "a person who's responsible for all this madness. He's the orchestrator of this insanity. He's my younger brother, and an incredible guitar player."

Later, Carlos made a direct reference to the bygone era of free love and psychedelia: "If you have any mescaline or LSD, this is a good time to take it," he told the crowd. But this was no nostalgia act. The reformulated lineup blended songs both old and new, as "Black Magic Woman" and "Oye Como Va" found a home alongside fresh material from *Santana IV*.

"I feel like they played as amazingly as they always did," Rietveld said, "but there's that extra spark when architects who have 100 percent respect and admiration for each other play together in the same room. Things just get levitated a bit more. What I saw was a constant recognition of genius, and enjoyment in their shared history. There were lots of smiles."

Santana was finally making good on a promise years in the making. "People say, 'Wow, it took them two years to do that?'" Rolie told the *Long Island Pulse*. "Well, that's not true; everybody was working. I was out with **Ringo Starr**, Neal Schon was out with Journey, and Santana was being Santana."

Ronald Isley from **The Isley Brothers** took a surprise turn during the encore, singing "Love Makes the World Go Round" and "Freedom in Your Mind"—a pair of new songs that would soon appear on *Santana IV*. Then Santana sent everyone home with the percussion-focused

"Toussaint L'Ouverture," before taking an emotional center stage bow.

"I gotta tell you, it was like riding a bicycle, getting back and playing with these guys," Rolie told Wardlaw. "Everybody's a better player and just more cognizant of what's going on and joyful to be doing it. It really was a lot of fun and it should be."

Rietveld initially had a two-year stint in Santana beginning in 1990, decades after the others departed, before returning in 1997. He experienced this reunion as both a trusted musical collaborator and unabashed longtime fan.

"I grew up playing and listening to those albums, so it felt really natural," Rietveld said. "And even in the course of the regular Santana performances, I'd constantly re-listen to the original bass lines to remind me of the original alchemy that went into it all, and to always rediscover things. So, finally playing them live with Gregg, Mike, and Neal was amazing—like stepping through time. The album covers I used to look at while listening to the music were suddenly springing to life, and I'm falling into the picture. It was amazing."

Santana would share the bill with Journey again on a trio of dates, beginning on April 13, 2016 at Madison Square Garden. *Santana IV* followed on April 15. "This is a dream come true for us," Carabello told *USA Today*. "The prophecy has been fulfilled. We are again, one." [4, 18, 170, 181, 732, 733, 734, 735]

WINTER 2016–17

Journey Joins a Strong Group of First-Time Noms to Rock Hall

Journey became eligible for the Rock & Roll Hall of Fame in 2000 but would not be nominated for another 16 years. Meanwhile, they watched as a series of their former opening acts were enshrined—including **Cheap Trick**, **Heart**, **Joan Jett**, and **Steve Miller**.

Of course, Journey had never been critical darlings. Music writer **Greil Marcus** memorably created the so-called "Journey Award" for worst album by a California band. "They made **Eddie Money** sound like **Muddy Waters**," he told *SF Weekly*. "It was the self-evident phoniness

in Steve Perry's voice—the oleaginous self-regard, the gooey smear of words, the horrible enunciation: It was the 'ci-tay' in 'Lights' that really made me want to kill."

Yet Journey nevertheless led 2016's fan voting from the beginning, despite appearing among a robust list of 19 nominees. The Rock Hall began offering this option in 2013, where the top five vote-getters make up a single "fan ballot" that is added to the pool of others. In every year so far, the fan's pick was later inducted—beginning with **Rush**, then **KISS**, **Stevie Ray Vaughan**, and **Chicago**.

This trend continued as Journey won the poll and was announced as part of the next Rock & Roll Hall of Fame class on December 20, 2016. Also included were **Yes**, **Electric Light Orchestra**, **Pearl Jam**, **Joan Baez**, and **Tupac Shakur**. Yes was the only act previously nominated.

"I guess it's better late than never, you know?" said Neal Schon, who remained confused about why Journey had to wait so long. "I really don't have a clue, but I just more or less kind of forgot about it. The main thing to me, the thing that means the most to me, has always been the same: It's the music, and the fans. The rest of it is all really nice to obtain and achieve, but the fans are really what it's all about. Making music is what they love, and what I love to do."

Journey's inductees would include Steve Perry, Schon, Gregg Rolie, Jonathan Cain, Aynsley Dunbar, Ross Valory, and Steve Smith—though *Billboard* initially reported that Dunbar had been overlooked. Perry's successors would not be inducted, nor was longtime former drummer Deen Castronovo.

Acts become eligible for induction 25 years after the release of their first record. The Rock Hall creates a list of nominees annually and sends ballots to a voting body of more than 1,000 artists, historians, and music industry figures. Journey's enshrinement was set for April 2017 at Barclays Center in Brooklyn.

"Of course, getting inducted into the Library of Congress with 'Don't Stop Believin'' and then into the Rock & Roll Hall of Fame, I pretty much never thought that would happen—but there it is," Cain said. "So, it's an honor. It's almost like being a Knight of the Round Table. You know, you get to represent your king and your country."

The question of whether Perry would perform

at the induction ceremony eventually dominated every conversation. But for now, members of Journey were simply taking it all in.

"I'm so grateful that our fans never gave up on us. I do feel we've had the credentials for quite some time," Schon said. "I'm very happy, and grateful, for such a long, great career—not only for myself, but Journey." [23, 407, 736, 737, 738, 739, 740, 741]

SPRING 2017

NUGGETS

▶ **JOURNEY'S TRUE BELIEVER:** Ahead of Journey's induction into the Rock and Roll Hall of Fame, manager **John Baruck** looked back nostalgically at how his boss, **Irving Azoff**, tasked him with rerouting the group's career following the exit of front man Steve Perry in 1998. "Irving had just made a deal with Walmart for Journey's *Greatest Hits*, and we had no lead singer." The fixer, Baruck said, was Internet sleuth Neal Schon who found Filipino karaoke singer Arnel Pineda on YouTube. When asked if there was a formula to getting a band like Journey into the Rock Hall, Baruck shrugged. "There is no formula," he said. "We worked for a long time with people that make those decisions: the voting membership and the fans. But it was also like, how can you *not* have a band as popular and successful as Journey in the Hall of Fame? The band is truly thrilled. I've got two tables of people coming and it's going to be a blast."
—*Billboard*

Will He or Won't He? Perry Once Again Keeps Everyone Guessing

Steve Perry remained enigmatic about his participation in Journey's Rock & Roll Hall of Fame induction, despite issuing an official statement the day after the honor was announced.

It was the portrait of brevity: "I am truly grateful that Journey is being inducted into the Rock & Roll Hall of Fame," he said—and nothing more.

Of course, Journey had waited on Perry before, and then waited again. There was the time when Perry wanted to go solo, and the time when he abruptly came off the road during the *Raised on Radio* tour and Journey went into a decade-long slumber. There was also the time when Journey made a huge comeback album, and then cooled their heels for almost two years waiting for him to decide on getting elective surgery. Then Perry showed up unannounced for their Hollywood Walk of Fame enshrinement.

A jubilant Neal Schon was taking it all in stride. "I don't have any hard feelings," he said. "You know, we've had our ups and downs, like all bands do—and sometimes it goes from member to member to member. So, I have nothing but a lot of gratitude and respect for everything we've done, and everyone that's been involved."

In the meantime, Schon reached out to Perry through his attorney, and via every available media source. The door was wide open. Current front man Arnel Pineda also confirmed he was more than willing to share the spotlight.

Months passed, as everyone waited for word from Perry—including organizers at the Rock Hall. "The band's welcomed him. The fans want it," marketing and communications vice president **Todd Mesek** told the *Cleveland Plain Dealer*. "He knows about it. We'll see."

Schon said he proudly held out until early bandmate Aynsley Dunbar was included among Journey's honorees. He said that Gregg Rolie was not initially on the list, either. But Perry's participation dominated fan conversations.

Perry later admitted to a pitched struggle with his own worries and expectations. On the one hand, he was concerned that "it had been so many years and the band's moved on," he told ABC. On the other, Perry did not want to upstage Pineda: "I love Arnel and I thought, y'know, out of respect for him and just where they'd gone, I thought I would just leave it alone."

Journey was set to be enshrined in the Rock Hall on April 7, 2017. As late as March 30, Jonathan Cain was still not entirely sure about Perry's plans. "As far as we know he's just going to accept the award and then skedaddle," Cain told the *Dayton Daily News*. "That's all I know, unless something changes."

In fact, Perry was listed as "TBD" on the official broadcast rundown for the ceremony—

not just for Journey's performance, but for the walk-up and acceptance speeches too. Once again, nobody knew what he planned to do.

"I definitely think that he will be there, as he should be," Schon said. "Musically speaking, I'd love to have him do a song with us – or two, or whatever. What would be even greater would be for him to do a song with Arnel too. I'm open to everything. I'm very open-minded to whatever happens, and any ideas that are brought forth." [21, 23, 749, 750, 751, 752, 876]

Cain Restarts His Solo Career From a New Vantage Point

Jonathan Cain had not released a solo project since 2006's *Where I Live* completed a two-album stint for the AAO Music label. In the meantime, he paid $280,000 for space to create Addiction Sound, a Nashville studio, in 2010, then married televangelist **Paula White** in 2015.

The rest of Cain's solo career would reflect

Continued on Page 324

Jonathan Cain restarted his dormant solo career when he opened his new Nashville studio, Addiction Sound. He then set out to help former (and future) Journey drummer Deen Castronovo get back in action.

JOURNEY BECOMES FIRST-BALLOT INDUCTEE TO ROCK HALL

Steve Perry took the stage with Journey as they were inducted into the Rock & Roll Hall of Fame on April 17, 2017 at Barclays Center in Brooklyn—but he did not sing with them.

Instead, he spoke last among a list of honorees that began with Neal Schon, then continued with Aynsley Dunbar, Gregg Rolie, Steve Smith, Ross Valory, and Jonathan Cain. "Are you fuckin' shittin' me? Any singer would give his ass for that shit!" Perry said, praising them on stage.

"I never seen a band like that in my life," he added, but "there was one instrument that was flying above the entire city of Los Angeles. That was the magic fingers of Neal Schon's guitar."

Cain later admitted he continued to hold out hope that Perry would join them for a song at Barclays Center. "We did a sound check rehearsal and I kept looking for him in the wings," Cain told the *Houston Press*, "but he declined to do it."

Instead, there were only a couple of shared moments backstage—and whatever the audience saw on stage. "I get a feeling there's a story in there somewhere that we'll just never know, or that Steve Perry chooses for whatever reason not to tell," Cleveland radio legend **John Gorman** said. "But Steve Perry is the kind of guy that when he says no, it means no."

Arnel Pineda finally got a chance to meet Perry in person. He had been pacing the halls in nervous anticipation when Perry finally stepped out of his dressing room backstage. "There was something endearing about the way he looked at me. He was meeting, like, a grandfather," Perry told SiriusXM, with a laugh.

They shared a huge hug in the busy hallway. "I had waited 35 years for that," Pineda told *Rolling Stone*. "It was dreamy. I couldn't believe I met him since he's very reclusive and he avoids people."

Perry then praised Pineda in his acceptance speech, something Smith described as a

Above: Jonathan Cain (far right) holds up the statuette for the Rock and Roll Hall of Fame's Award for Musical Excellence that Journey earned in 2017. Joining him, from left to right (above), are Aynsley Dunbar, Gregg Rolie, Steve Smith, Steve Perry, Neal Schon, and Ross Valory. Below: Valory (far left) and Gregg Rolie (right) play during the performance segment; Perry and Schon (center) thank attendees.

passing of the torch. "He acknowledged Arnel Pineda, which was really a beautiful moment," Smith told interviewer **Matt Wardlaw**.

Meanwhile, Schon found himself sneaking into Perry's dressing room, which he said "was locked down like Fort Knox." Still, "we had a good hang in there," Schon told *Vulture.* "I felt like I still knew this guy and we were still really great friends."

Though they had not spoken in so long, it seemed as if "not many years had gone by. I felt such a strong connection to him," Schon told the *Pioneer Press.* A photograph of the duo embracing on stage became the signature image from the night.

On the other hand, Rolie said he never had a direct conversation with Perry that night. "He does everything behind closed doors and I don't get it," Rolie told *Rolling Stone.* "I don't understand it and I don't care. I wouldn't do it that way."

After the speeches, Perry quickly excused

himself. He later described his reasoning in stark terms: "I'm not in the band," Perry told *The New York Times*. "It's Arnel's gig — singers have to stick together."

Journey performed "Separate Ways" with a current configuration that featured everyone from *Escape*, *Frontiers*, and *Trial by Fire*, save for Perry. Rolie and Dunbar took over for "Lights," which Schon dedicated to Perry, before the initial Pineda-fronted lineup returned for "Don't Stop Believin'."

"This is so long time coming, I thought it would never happen," Schon told the crowd in Brooklyn, then nodded to Journey's victory in the Rock Hall's fan voting. "This is all about you, the fans, and about the music we've made together."

Rolie echoed those sentiments: "Without music fans, this place is empty," he said. "This is really about all you guys, especially Journey fans tonight." [53, 181, 253, 261, 410, 662, 753, 754, 803]

how impactful this period had been.

He partnered with **David Kalmusky**, who engineered 2011's *Eclipse* for Journey, and former **Led Zeppelin** engineer **Chris Huston** to design the new recording facility, overseeing the construction in 2014 in Cain's adopted hometown.

He then began a return to consistent solo work there, shifting to faith songs for *What God Wants to Hear* alongside a studio group that featured surprise guest Deen Castronovo. "He's got God. He's on the road to recovery," Cain told *Billboard*. "I've been putting him to purpose and we've been playing and believing that he'll get restored and turn his life around."

Their musical connection was instantly renewed. Castronovo tracked more than a dozen songs with Cain over just two days—but only after altering his approach. Castronovo admitted his typical playing style was "very physical and very flashy and very showy," but this time he "went to a lighter stick," Castronovo told *Ultimate Classic Rock*'s **Matt Wardlaw**. "I played a smaller kit and the approach was just so effortless and so peaceful."

Kalmusky engineered *What God Wants to Hear*, as well as a series of Neal Schon solo albums between 2012-2015. He then helped Journey complete 2022's *Freedom*.

He had a musical background: his father **Kenny Kalmusky** had been in a 1950s-era group called **The Revols** with **Richard Manuel** before he joined **The Band**. Kenny later played bass with **Todd Rundgren**, among others, before his son David began an engineering career that also featured gigs with **Mötley Crüe**, **Joe Bonamassa**, **John Oates** of **Hall & Oates**, and **Keith Urban**.

"For me, the best and most critical thing is that David Kalmusky is the guy who's turning the knobs behind the console," Oates said. "He has a world-class collection of vintage gear and beyond his technical expertise, he is a well-rounded musician with great ears—and he's a badass guitar player as well."

Cain released *What God Wants to Hear* on October 21, 2016, followed by five more albums through 2020—and then *Arise* and *Christmas Is Love* in 2022. But he kept this new solo direction separate from his work with Neal Schon: "Journey's Journey," Cain told *CCM Magazine*. "It always has an identity. This music also has its identity and it has its truth." This burst of activity belied the complex relationship Cain always had with Christianity before meeting White.

When Steve Perry walked into early writing sessions for 1996's *Trial by Fire* carrying a Bible, they based the title track on Paul's First Epistle to the Corinthians. But Cain's faith had been badly shaken by a fire at his childhood school, and he proceeded to dabble in everything from the Baptist and Lutheran churches to Scientology.

His chance meeting with White on a Southwest Airlines flight finally led Cain deeper into religion. He joined her ministry, handling music at her City of Destiny church in Apopka, Florida.

"I continue to grow in lots of ways," Cain told *American Songwriter*. "I'm looking forward to seeing where God's going to take me next."

Meanwhile, Addiction Sound continued to expand. The facility space is home to the console from Studio B at the Record Plant in Sausalito, California, and an underground echo chamber meant to replicate the sound from Studio 2 at Abbey Road, among other gadgets.

"Addiction Studio appeals to me on many levels," said Oates, who has recorded a series of rootsier solo records there. "The large room is very well-designed acoustically and physically to cut live rhythm section tracks. The drums sound particularly good, and the sight lines are well thought out."

As Cain began to spend more time in Florida, however, he decided to sell. A music industry-related nonprofit foundation bought Addiction Sound in August 2022 for $4.2 million. Kalmusky was set to lease the space to fulfill remaining contractual obligations.

As for Journey, "They know I had a profound shift in my life," Cain told *CCM Magazine*. "I needed to change. I wasn't happy. They see me smile and they see me a different guy out there on stage." [34, 742, 743, 744, 745, 746, 747, 748, 809, 873, 874, 875]

SUMMER 2017

Rolie, Smith Pitch In to Complete Ronnie Montrose's Final Album

Bassist **Ricky Phillips** was not done honoring his old boss after taking part in 2012's *Concert for Ronnie Montrose: A Celebration of His Life in*

Music with Neal Schon and Steve Smith.

Ronnie Montrose had approached Phillips earlier in the year about completing a long-shelved duet project, and he intended to honor that commitment. "A month before Ronnie passed, he said, 'I listened back to the *10x10* record, and I want to finish it,'" Phillips said. "I was delighted and then a month later, he's gone."

Montrose originally had the idea of recording 10 tracks with 10 different vocalists back in 2003. Phillips gathered with Montrose and drummer **Eric Singer** over three days at **Doug Messenger**'s North Hollywood studio to lay down musical foundations for these guest turns.

Everything was carefully arranged in advance of the sessions, as Montrose took a few days to get all the equipment set. His attention to detail was such that he even agonized over the carpet. Then they tore through every song in a series of first takes.

"There was a certain chemistry going on between Ricky, Ronnie, and myself," Singer told interviewer **Mike Mettler**, "and it was captured the way they did those early Montrose records—live, and with no click tracks, none of that stuff."

Sammy Hagar, **Edgar Winter**, and others signed on, but the project began to lose momentum. Phillips was asked to take over bass duties with **Styx**, and Singer would soon return to **KISS**. Phillips initially attempted to continue working in both groups. "When I first joined Styx, I stayed with Ronnie, but it got to the point that I just couldn't do both," Phillips said. "It wasn't fair to Ronnie how little I was available."

Then Montrose's career went dormant for a couple of years after his prostate cancer diagnosis. *10x10* was shelved—until Phillips decided to take the lead in completing the album. "It had been sitting in the can forever—just waiting for him to finish it," Phillips said.

The process was painstakingly slow, as Phillips pieced together the songs in between commitments with Styx—including *The Mission*, their first new album in 12 years. He transferred all the old material from two-inch tape to digital, then began contacting people.

"I took it upon myself to get the tracks and take all of the people that Ronnie loved and admired and were his friends, and got them on

the record," Phillips said. "I finished writing the material that wasn't finished."

Gregg Rolie took over lead vocals for "I'm Not Lying." In an intriguing twist, Journey's short-lived 2000s-era front man Jeff Scott Soto sang backup on the track. Soto also added backing vocals on "Color Blind" and "Still Singin' With the Band." Elsewhere, **Glenn Hughes**, **Tommy Shaw**, and **Grand Funk Railroad** star **Mark Farner** were also featured vocalists, while **Steve Lukather**, **Rick Derringer**, **Marc Bonilla**, and **Def Leppard**'s **Phil Collen** added guitars.

"I was a huge, huge fan," Collen told *Guitar World*. "It may just take something like *10x10* to spur questions like, 'Well, who is this Ronnie Montrose guy?'" Bonilla added.

Phillips stepped away to help Styx complete *The Mission*, and it arrived the summer before *10x10* was issued on September 29, 2017.

After years of work, Phillips was thrilled with the results. He said *10x10* is "one of the few things that I listen to in my car. It's one of the few things that I've done that I play." [26, 768, 769]

Cain, Valory, Pineda Visit Trump White House; Band Feud Ensues

Neal Schon's relationship with Jonathan Cain was always defined by creative friction, as their contrasting approaches added a new complexity to Journey's songs.

"In the '80s when I first pulled in Jonathan Cain to take Gregg Rolie's place, we always butted heads pretty much musically," Schon said. "We came from opposite sides of the spectrum, and when we joined together, that's kind of what made the sound."

Over time, however, friction has a way of starting fires. One erupted when Cain, Ross Valory, and Arnel Pineda visited the White House on July 27, 2017, just before Journey's tour finale at New York's Classic East festival. The trio toured the briefing room, then posed for a photograph in the Oval Office with then-president **Donald Trump**.

Cain described Trump as merely an acquaintance, someone he met through his wife **Paula White**'s role as spiritual advisor to Trump. "He respects what I do," Cain told the *Minneapolis*

Continued on Page 328

Slow-Evolving *Traces* Returned Perry To His Muse

Steve Perry was nostalgic even when he was young. This gave his songs their magic and mystery and Perry-era Journey their sound of yearning, of seeking something unreachable.

Fans had to wonder, after so long away, what had become of him. Did Perry retain his essential sentimentality, and would that resonate in a modern age riven by online carping and social fragmentation? The risk with *Traces* was that Perry might try to contemporize an approach that had always seemed thankfully out of time.

Then the album arrived on October 5, 2018, and it quickly became clear that Steve Perry remained Steve Perry.

"There is a courtliness to him," said former *Rolling Stone* writer and editor **David Wild**. "Spending a day with Steve Perry, he exudes warmth. He exudes believing in what he's doing—and there's just a musicality, which makes it all the more shocking that he didn't do it for all these years. I thought it was kind of a minor miracle just to hear him again."

Wild became one of the first people outside of Perry's immediate circle who knew about *Traces*. He had written the liner notes for *The Essential Journey*, 2001's double-platinum smash compilation. Now, Perry asked Wild to help with the promotional cycle for his secret comeback album, including an on-camera Q&A.

Wild was working at Fox's *The Masked Singer,* but quickly decided to play hooky. "I just fucking went to be with Steve Perry," Wild said, "and it was one of the most delightful days of work you could ever imagine. What struck me when he did the record was like, 'Oh, yeah, the magic of him singing is 100% still there.'"

Former hitmaking writing partner Jonathan Cain could not have agreed more. "It's good to hear him singing again in the studio," Cain told interviewer **Michael Cavacini**. "He should be singing. That's what he was made to do."

Perry had guarded against the threat of modernity by keeping the prolonged sessions that produced *Traces* so intimate. His circle was small, there was initially no label, and the songs were discreetly involving. "No one had their foot on my neck saying, 'Are you done? Are you done?'" Perry told *The New Statesman*. "Fuck off."

He only rarely aspired to the outsized bravado of Journey's best-known period, instead trying to reconnect on a quieter, deeper level. He built on the power-ballad era's essential themes by personalizing them.

In this case, it was a love lost, one that was always destined to be lost. Girlfriend **Kellie Nash**'s remission had already ended when she first started dating Perry. This sense of borrowed time made every moment more resonant, and then it informed the songs.

"We can have mixed feelings and so can songs," Perry said in a Twitter Q&A with fans. "Sometimes, music can help me or others figure out our emotional complexities."

Released on October 5, 2018, *Traces* was vulnerable, confidential, meditative—particularly on ardent goodbyes like "Most of All." "Steve has a deep emotional well to draw from," co-writer **Randy Goodrum** said. "It's hard to write a song like that, but I like the challenge. I've always tried writing the songs other writers are afraid to, or simply don't want to go near."

At the same time, there were moments of sad serendipity. Perry wrote "In the Rain" prior to meeting Nash, but he kept it to himself—"because it's about such a profound loss," he told NPR. "I never played it for her because I didn't want to bring that energy into that struggle she was in to save her life." "Most of All," the song that sounds the most like a requiem for Nash, was also from before their time together.

"I grieved for two years—it was a whole new level of broken heart," Perry told *The Guardian*. "I worked through that and, the next thing I knew, I started writing music."

Perry scored a pair of Top 20 adult-contemporary hits from *Traces*, which became Perry's highest-charting solo album at No. 6. "No Erasin'" reached No. 18 while "We're Still Here" rose to No. 14. Both singles were about perseverance and lasting bonds.

"I think I was the first person to ask him about 'We're Still Here,' and I was taking that as, like, existential," Wild said. "Instead, it was him remembering how he went down to record something in Hollywood at one of the studios and all these young people and rock 'n' roll freaks were out, sort of crawling around—'streetlight people' as he once coined it. He was praising and connecting with them. There's still youth and still energy on the streets."

Nash had made Perry promise to resume his career should cancer take her life, or else he would have made their time together all for naught. He came back to those words—"all for naught," Perry told NPR. "There's got to be a purpose."

He found it on an album that Perry admitted helped him get in touch with "the honest emotion, the love of the music I've just made," Perry told *The New York Times*. But also, "all the neurosis that used to come with it, too. All the fears and joys."

His collaboration with **John 5**, "Sun Shines Grey," was surprising for more than one reason. The guitarist is known for his work with **Mötley Crüe** and **Rob Zombie**, performing hard rock a world away from Perry's R&B-inflected pop rock. "Sun Shines Grey" was also the closest *Traces* moved toward the stadium-filling heights of Perry's time with Journey, even if it failed to chart as the fourth and final single from *Traces*.

"We have a great time. He is the coolest dude and is such a great person," John 5 told WRIF. "Like if he wasn't Steve Perry and he's just like this regular dude, we'd [still] be great friends, because he's that cool."

Perry said "Sun Shines Gray" came together in a matter of minutes. Collaborating on the title provided a spark: Perry said the song wrote itself after John 5 connected the song's turbulent emotions with those days when the sun breaks through clouds of portent.

Perry described the results as "more emotionally available" during the Twitter Q&A with fans, specifically referencing the lyric: "We only give as much as we can show." "We're all so scared to give more of ourselves than we feel comfortable to do. That for me is a safe limit placed on one's self," Perry said.

Traces pushed hard against those boundaries, proving to be most powerful when Perry gave in to twilit reminiscence. Even his cover of **George Harrison**'s lonesome "I Need You" plunged the song to striking new depths. Perry said he sought out the blessing of **Olivia Harrison**, the former Beatles star's widow, before releasing the song.

They were connected through former **Tom Petty** drummer **Steve Ferrone**, a close friend of hers. Perry suddenly grew very nervous—"because when you're in the George Harrison environment, you just feel him there. And it's Olivia," Perry told Q104.3.

He said she listened to his update of "I Need You," then listened to it again. Halfway through the second time, Harrison stopped the recording. "George would have loved this version," Perry remembered Harrison saying. "And I'm telling you, I got the blessing."

Emotions were still running high during the final days of mixing, *Traces* co-producer **Thom Flowers** said.

"I remember the album was pretty close to being done and we actually had mixes kind of together, and we had people from the label over," Flowers said. "We were just letting people listen to it and just kind of standing in the background. I can't remember what song it was, but we were listening really loud—and it was really intense. I remember tearing up for the first time, because I knew the story. Steve walked up to me, and he was tearing up, too."

There was talk of a tour, and Perry even worked out new arrangements of the songs for onstage presentation with Flowers. "This has been amazing. Doing this has been cathartic for me," Perry told *The Guardian*. "I guess it's time to talk, it's time to be open."

Nothing ever came of those plans, however, leaving those long-ago performances with **Eels** as Perry's most recent concert appearance.

"We all know how many people are still out there, not really able to do it, and not looking good—and still, you know, showing up at a state fair," Wild said. "And maybe I'm wrong, but it could be his fear of ever being anything like that."

Wild marveled over the fact that Perry "thinks he can't sing, but we were filming him, I interviewed him, and then I watched him sing a bunch of the songs up to a mic in the studio. I'm not qualified to say that he hit every note exactly, but as a rock critic, he was fucking great. He was great then; he's great now." [36, 62, 253, 411, 688, 688, 712, 712, 715, 772, 858, 936, 937, 938, 939]

Star-Tribune. "I respect what he does. I'm a big fan of his golf courses. He saved golf, man."

Pineda came away with a sense of wonder. "It's not about who the president is," he told *Rolling Stone.* "It's the whole history of the White House. I was just amazed."

Schon, on the other hand, was outraged. He proceeded to flood social media channels with complaints, particularly after related news coverage misrepresented the visit as group sanctioned. NBC's story headline on the visit: "Journey, the Band, Poses for Pictures in the White House Press Briefing Room."

"I've discussed this many times with management and [counsel]," Schon wrote on Facebook the next day, "and they both agreed that there should never be anything to do with religious beliefs or politics with Journey."

He had complained about these issues before. "I feel very strongly about my beliefs [that] not one religion or politics should be involved in tarnishing the name brand Journey I've built," Schon tweeted on June 6, almost eight weeks earlier.

Of course, Journey had performed at the 2012 Republican National Convention in Tampa where **Mitt Romney** became the party's presidential nominee. Schon thought better of it, however, and turned down the RNC's next invitation in 2016.

"I'm not into taking any one side with politics," Schon told *The Tennessean.* "We're like a feel-good band. It's about hope, joy, love and good things in life."

Schon would soon take aim at Paula White, who was also on hand for the White House visit.

"I've stated how I felt about mixing religion and politics," Schon wrote in an Instagram update. "This is and has been an issue with myself[,] Mr. Cain and his now wife since he married." Schon later reposted a link to negative media coverage of White's ministry.

Former manager **Herbie Herbert** sounded appalled by Journey's very public dispute. "This is the mothership," Herbert told KQED. "Quit fucking around." But Cain remained initially silent.

Schon indicated, however, that much was unfolding behind closed doors. He claimed the others wanted to tour without him, and implied that he intended to put together his own offshoot group.

"I continue to grow and be completely creative and want to take the band Neal Schon's JRNY on an exciting new trip musically," he wrote on Instagram. Schon even briefly changed his Twitter handle to "Neal Schon's JRNY" before reverting to "Neal Schon Music."

Journey's feel-good induction into the Rock & Roll Hall of Fame back in April suddenly seemed like a lifetime ago. "I think [the band's enshrinement] has gone to everyone's head," Schon tweeted. "Not me."

Rather than basking in that historic achievement, the group was entering a turbulent new phase. Backroom machinations, open dissension, and legal action became commonplace, even amidst celebrations of Journey's 50th anniversary. [22, 204, 205, 208, 755, 756, 758, 760, 761, 762, 763, 765, 766, 767, 878]

WINTER 2017–18

Journey Announces New Tour, Saying Disagreements Are Over

In an astonishing twist, Journey's pitched off-cycle arguments would be followed by harmonious tours where everybody said the right things.

Asia co-founder **Carl Palmer** was struck by the way the warring factions in Journey interacted during their shared tour together in early 2017.

"Jonathan Cain and Neal Schon would pass each other in the corridor, and they would fist bump each other," Palmer told *Billboard,* "so you couldn't see any of that [animosity] at all." He didn't simply describe them as professional: Palmer said Journey was "probably the most professional band I've ever toured with."

Journey promised more of the same in January 2018 as they confirmed a long-rumored tour with **Def Leppard**. Schon credited Journey's shared musical history with smoothing things over: "It's like a healer," he said. "Music is the healer, you know? That's the thing that pulls people together."

Or they were just protecting a cash cow touring schedule. Either way, Journey would equally split headlining slots with Def Leppard on their first shared bill since 2006. Back then, Journey was attempting to move forward with temporary replacement Jeff Scott Soto.

Guitarist **Phil Collen** admitted in his auto-biography, *Adrenalized: Life, Def Leppard, and Beyond*, that they were unsure how this pairing would be received. That changed when the opening date at Camden, New Jersey sold out in 2006—with thousands more waiting to get in. "The tour was a raging success, and Journey was awesome," Collen said.

Schon's dispute with Cain went public in the spring of 2017 when he began a series of often-incendiary social media posts. Schon said Cain was bringing religion and politics uncomfortably close to the band, and worried about alienating any segment of their fan base. When Cain joined Ross Valory and Arnel Pineda at the White House to meet **Donald Trump**, they created a flashpoint.

All of it put the admittedly apolitical Pineda in a bind. "I try to stay away. It's like, 'Oh, the big boys are fighting,'" he told *Rolling Stone*. He was simply interested in the history of the place, marveling over the 1880s-era presidential desk. "I was just mesmerized by the table. I was like, 'Wow! This is truly 100 years old?'"

Cain described the current situation with Schon as a reset. Journey was moving on, he added, for the sake of the tour. By this point, Cain also felt their legacy was very much his own.

"Never in my wildest dreams did I think that I was going to be able to create this kind of lasting longevity when it comes to writing," Cain said. "I'm most proud of my songwriting and my relationship with Steve [Perry], and how we were able to craft these songs with Neal that mean so much to so many people. That's pretty overwhelming to think about."

Other far more serious issues loomed. By the time Journey's 50th year was over, Journey would sue its rhythm section, Perry would sue Journey, Schon would issue a cease-and-desist to Cain, and Cain would sue Schon, among other legal matters. Yet the tours kept happening.

"We've had some hard times," Schon said, "mainly because I think everybody is just going in different directions, away from everything we had done for many, many years. So, it was hard for me to understand. But the bottom line is, I respect all of the work that we've done to-gether as a band—and I respect our fans. I love our fans. So, it doesn't really matter if we don't see eye to eye any longer. When we get onstage, it's about the music, and it's about the fans." [22, 198, 204, 205, 407, 770]

Contestant Believin': Perry Makes Surprise Visit To *American Idol*

Gabby Barrett completed an emotional cover of "Don't Stop Believin'" on *American Idol* in front of former Journey front man Steve Perry.

She just didn't know it.

Perry was hidden in the audience for the May 20, 2018 episode, only standing up to reveal himself after Barrett completed the song. "It was the most amazing version I've ever heard," Perry told Barrett after they embraced. "Swear, it was beautiful, just beautiful. Thank you so much."

Barrett, then 18, described the experience as "insane. I'm actually surprised I knew who it was at first because he's older now," she told *People* magazine, "but I looked over and I knew his face."

Barrett's performance before the show's enthusiastic studio audience and judges **Luke Bryan**, **Katy Perry** and **Lionel Richie** was part of the two-night Season 16 finale. She also covered **Miranda Lambert**'s "Little Red Wagon" and sang an original called "Rivers Deep."

Then she held Perry's hand while Bryan praised her performance, hugging Perry once more before the program went to commercial. "I was like, 'Oh my gosh,'" she told *Variety*. "I had no idea he was coming, that was such an honor."

Perry had taken the time to meet with Barrett's proud parents, as well. "They love you," he told her, then pointed to the audience and the *American Idol* judges. "They love you! And they love you. And they love you."

She was competing against **Caleb Lee Hutchinson** and **Maddie Poppe**, but fell short. Even Barrett's No. 3 finish couldn't dim that shining moment with Perry.

"He said that my version was the best version that he ever heard. That's so crazy," Barrett told *People*. "My dad would always play Journey in the car and I remember watching him perform on the television."

Still marveling over Perry's surprise appearance, Barrett added: "Holy monkeys!"

Poppe was crowned champion, but Barrett didn't walk away empty-handed. She married fellow contestant **Cade Foehner**, who'd been eliminated during the Top 5 round. [882, 897, 898, 899]

SUMMER–FALL 2018

RELEASES
▶ Steve Perry, "No Erasin'" (single)
▶ Steve Perry, *Traces* (album)
▶ Steve Perry, "No More Cryin" (single)
▶ Steve Perry, "We're Still Here" (single)

High School Flashbacks Inspired Perry's Leadoff Single, 'No Erasin''

Steve Perry was born in Hanford, California, about 45 minutes south of Fresno in the San Joaquin Valley. He returned there after leaving Journey.

Perry's head was also back home as he composed the opening track for his long-awaited third solo album, 2018's *Traces*. "Everything I write comes back to high school. I know it sounds funny, but everything," Perry told *The New Statesman*. "Those moments are not to be tossed away."

"No Erasin'" once again transported Perry back to this bygone era, when dating meant parking by the farming community's numerous irrigation canals, then stealing a kiss. Memories came rushing in as he attended a class reunion, and Perry drew a creative line to his pending comeback.

In a literal sense, "No Erasin'" is about running into "someone you haven't seen in a long time in a location where you used to hang out and make out," Perry told radio host **Jim Brickman**, "but metaphorically, it's about the audiences that I've not seen in years."

That is one reason "No Erasin'" made the perfect reintroduction. Perry's best songs always commingled elements of memory with ageless themes of romance and longing, then democratized it all. Everyone is transformed into a small town girl or boy—and all of them, boy and girl

alike, inhabit the same lonely world.

The chance to escape often drives them, no different than Perry himself. "This is my big theory on Steve Perry: Beyond being a great vocalist, I think the secret and maybe why generations connect with him is he is an empath," former *Rolling Stone* writer and editor **David Wild** said.

The difference with "No Erasin'," and with Perry himself now, was that he had found the comfort of the past in his present tense. "It all comes from the emotions I grew into during my adolescence," Perry told *The New Statesman*, but "No Erasin'" is not trapped in the pages of the Lemoore High School yearbook. It's a full-circle song for a full-circle moment.

"No Erasin'" arrived as the lead single from *Traces* on August 14, 2018, with a roughed-in vocal that would have been relegated to the cutting room floor in another era. Perry's choice provided an initial preview of the brave intimacy that would define the LP.

"Well, it took," Perry told *Ultimate Classic Rock*'s **Matt Wardlaw** before pausing, "... a certain amount of risk on my heart's part to allow the rawness of that vocal to be enough for the song." In the past, he would have done another take, or 10. "But perfect doesn't mean more emotional," Perry added, "so this is a new area for me."

Traces' co-producer, **Thom Flowers**, found Perry to be exacting, but nothing like the rumored perfectionist of old. "I think a lot of artists and performers deal with that to varying degrees—especially those who have achieved a high level of skill and success," Flowers said. "I think it takes a bit of that to get that good, you know. It very well may have played a role in his decision to step away for a while, because it's exhausting, but I think he's also very self-aware and kind of in tune with himself and with music."

This album would be "more about connecting emotionally rather than being quote-unquote perfect," Flowers added. "He certainly has a high bar. I have seen that but like I said, he's very self-aware. There were points where we would be mixing or working on the song and he would go, 'You know what? The version we had two days ago was better.' The term he would use is, 'We've walked past it.' As with many artists, it certainly can be a struggle—but it also leads to some great work."

Whether running into an old flame or re-introducing yourself to an aging fan base, things had changed—but not everything. "Even though your lives are different, and you're in different places now, you still have that old connection," Perry told Brickman.

The protagonist from "No Erasin'," like Perry's voice, was older now and noticeably weathered. Maybe his best days are behind him—but what days they were. Perry had finally gotten a better grasp on the role his audience played in his career and personal arc. "Without them, I was not who I am," Perry told the *Tampa Bay Times*. "That needs to be said. They literally made me happen." [253, 411, 456, 715, 716, 771, 858]

WINTER 2018-19

Schon, Rolie's Splinter Project Reunites Journey Co-Founders

Neal Schon had long expressed a desire to return to Journey's past. He finally did with a benefit concert by a new splinter group on February 9, 2018 at The Independent in San Francisco.

Former principal collaborator Gregg Rolie joined him for a 30-song deep dive, with proceeds going to victims of fires that had ravaged the San Francisco region the previous October. Schon dubbed the group **Journey Through Time**.

"I started dabbling with the idea when we had some time off," Schon told *Relix* magazine. "I thought it would be fun to get together and dive into our older catalog, going all the way back to our first album."

The roots of this project trace back to the Steve Augeri era, when Journey briefly tried a chronological setlist. Schon and Rolie's *Santana IV* reunion likely provided another ruminative spark. Then there was the simmering tension between Schon and his current bandmates.

Journey Through Time rehearsed at the venerable Record Plant in Sausalito, California for about four days, mulling more than 50 songs along the way. For Rolie, there was once again an immediate sense of musical community with Schon.

"We play off each other because that's how we grew up," Rolie said. "Same thing with [formative bandmate] **Carlos** [**Santana**]: We grew up doing that. So when you start playing, you play off each other, and you're not quite sure what's gonna happen—and then it does. Getting back onstage with Neal was like riding a bicycle. 'You're gonna do that? Oh, that's a new one. Okay, well, let's do this.'"

A short tour followed more than a year later, with Journey Through Time returning on February 22, 2019 at the Jackson Rancheria Casino Resort in Jackson, California. Next was the Fox Theater in Oakland, but only after shifting "Just the Same Way" to the third spot in the slightly trimmed 25-song setlist.

"We went beyond just playing the greatest hits," Schon told interviewer **Michael Cavacini**. "We played deep cuts, and stuff off the records that some people have never heard before."

Set highlights included "Kohoutek" from Journey's 1975 debut album, "I'm Gonna Leave You" and Rolie's beloved title track from 1976's *Look Into the Future*, "People" and "Nickel and Dime" from 1977's *Next*, and "Daydream" from 1979's *Evolution*, among others.

Deen Castronovo, **Marco Mendoza**, **Marti Frederiksen**, and **Chris Collins** rounded out the Journey Through Time lineup. Mendoza said the challenge was remaining faithful to elements like Journey co-founder Ross Valory's familiar bass lines, while still trying to personalize the moment.

Mendoza admitted that "the recording situation is one thing, but then you take it on live and it takes another life of itself. I will adhere and try to stay as close as I can to the original parts, but then again put in my style. It's a constant thing in the back of your mind."

The brief tour continued March 1 at The Van Buren in Phoenix, with a final stop on March 2 at the Orpheum in Los Angeles. Journey's best-known songs were not ignored, as the shows closed out with "Any Way You Want It" and "Don't Stop Believin'," along with a cover of "Black Magic Woman." Rolie voiced a Top 5 hit version of the latter for **Santana** before Schon joined the group.

"We discovered that there wasn't anything we really couldn't play," Schon told Cavacini. "We dove into some Santana stuff because Gregg was there. It was wild. Really, really wild."

Schon once again reached out to Steve Perry on social media, this time about potentially taking part in these shows—but Perry had already dashed those hopes. Working with Schon in any capacity, he said, would stir up unnecessary expectations for a larger reunion.

"I left the band 31 fucking years ago," Perry reminded *Rolling Stone*. "You can still love someone, but not want to work with them." Besides, he added, "if they only love you because they want to work with you, that doesn't feel good to me."

Instead, Rolie shared the microphone with Castronovo on old duets like "Feeling That Way" and "Anytime." Castronovo also ably inhabited Perry's solo vocals, even while keeping expert time. Rolie came away with a new appreciation for Journey's former drummer.

"I think it's best put by a friend of my son's who saw Journey Through Time at The Independent in San Francisco—that was the first time we did it. He walks up to Deen and he goes, 'I'm convinced that you're only half human'—because he can do that," Rolie said, with a laugh. "I couldn't believe that he was singing the way he was singing and playing these complex things. It's amazing to me. He thinks 'What? Can't everybody do that?' 'No, no, not at all!'" [31, 375, 375, 606, 616, 784, 785, 786]

FALL 2019

NUGGETS
▶ It's an interesting time to be Jonathan Cain. Not only has he put out a book—a memoir called *Don't Stop Believin'* detailing his experiences as the keyboardist for rock band Journey, he's also released his third solo album called *The Songs You Leave Behind.*
—The Wichita Eagle

Rolie's Guest-Filled *Sonic Ranch* Makes Room for Neal Schon

Gregg Rolie had not released a new album for 18 years when *Sonic Ranch* arrived on October 11, 2019. But he had hardly been idle.

Rolie toured as a member of **Ringo Starr's All-Starr Band**, played some solo shows, recorded tracks with his All-Starr bandmate **Steve Lukather**, and assumed a cornerstone role for a **Santana** reunion album. Those earlier projects informed this one.

For instance, the lead single, "What About Love," was inspired by Starr's message of peace and love—and by the All-Starr Band's sound checks. "What about love?" Rolie rhetorically asked *Goldmine*. "Are you listening? This guy has been saying it for about 50 years."

Sessions stretched out over the years, with current and past collaborators making key contributions along the way. "We recorded all of the basic tracks, including the drum tracks for that record at a studio called Sonic Ranch," Rolie's drummer **Ron Wikso** said. "We recorded as a band. It was Gregg, me, and whichever bass player was playing on each particular song."

Then Rolie would call up one of his buddies. Lukather's contributions on "Give Me Tomorrow" and "They Want It All" were among the oldest, dating back to 2013 sessions held between tours with the All-Starr Band.

Rolie remained with **Ringo Starr** throughout this period. *Santana IV* arrived in 2016, followed by shows with the **Journey Through Time** spinoff group in 2018. "All this stuff took all my time and I couldn't finish what I started," Rolie told *Rolling Stone*. "And all those things took precedence."

Former Santana bandmate **Michael Shrieve** subbed for Wikso on "Only You," while Rolie's longtime guitarist **Alan Hayes** was featured on five tracks—including a gospel-tinged cover of the **Elvis Presley** favorite, "Don't Be Cruel."

Neal Schon flew in a solo for "Lift Me Up," once again illustrating how effortlessly these two musical voices intertwined—even when they were not recording together at the same time.

"Neal contributed his unique sound and style, which of course has been closely associated with a lot of the things he and Gregg have done together over many years—going all the way back to when they both played in Santana before they eventually formed Journey," Wikso said. "I think it's fair to say that they know how to complement each other very well, musically."

The bassist was **Alphonso Johnson**, an alum of both Santana and **Abraxas Pool**. He was joined by Rolie's longtime former bandmate **Michael Carabello** on "Breaking My Heart" and "That's The Way It Goes," both of which dated back to 2001's *Roots*. Schon originally played on "Breaking My Heart" too—but, curiously, not on the album's full-band update of the title track from Journey's 1976 release *Look Into the Future*.

Once the album was finally completed, Rolie enlisted his son **Sean Rolie** to help with a music video for "What About Love." Its jittery blend of candid backstage footage, performance clips from Journey Through Time, and open-road imagery served as a canny update of Rolie's image for a new era.

"It's different for me," Rolie told *Billboard*, with a laugh. "I sent it to my old Journey manager, **Herbie Herbert**, and he said, 'This is a great video. Did Sean help you with this?'" [25, 181, 778, 779, 780, 781]

SPRING 2020

Rinse and Repeat: Journey Fires Valory and Smith—Again

Journey fired the band's rhythm section in March 2020, in what they described as a squabble over control of the band name.

This was the second time they had split with Ross Valory and Steve Smith, who were both relieved of duty during early sessions for 1986's *Raised on Radio*. In the meantime, however, the dynamics had completely changed.

Back then, an ascendent Steve Perry spearheaded the change, taking over as producer following his debut solo album's success and then casting Journey's new music. He had since left, and Journey slowly reassembled their early 1980s lineup without him. Perry, replaced by Arnel Pineda, was still a shareholder in the band.

Then Neal Schon and Jonathan Cain said they began battling against an "ill-conceived corporate coup d'état" orchestrated by a pair of bandmates.

Valory and Smith were hoping to gain control of a related business entity that they believed owned the group's name, according to a suit filed on March 3 by the Miller Barondess law firm in the Superior Court of Contra Costa County,

California. Their alleged aim was to "hold the Journey name hostage and force Cain, Schon and Nightmare Productions to provide them with wind-fall payments for their retirement."

In truth, however, the rupture in Journey went far deeper. Valory and Smith had not acted alone. Nightmare Productions had been founded by Journey's original manager, **Herbie Herbert**, with a three-member board. As of early 2020, those positions were held by Cain, Schon, and Valory—with Cain as president and Schon as secretary. Perry, Herbert, and Smith were the other shareholders.

Journey's lawsuit contended that Valory and Smith wanted to expand the board to six members, install their own allies, and oust Schon and Cain. **Skip Miller**, who served as lead counsel for Schon and Cain, said they agonized over bringing this action against two bandmates who were "once considered their brothers." Still, Miller said their "devious and truculent behavior" left the band "reluctantly with no choice but to act decisively."

Valory and Smith's departure was confirmed in a letter, also dated March 3. "Like a marriage, we had a lot of years together," Cain told interviewer **Michael Cavacini**. "There were a lot of misunderstandings, and things happened. People move on."

Smith had been voted in as the new president of Nightmare Productions and Valory as secretary during a Nightmare Productions shareholder meeting held on February 13, in San Rafael, as confirmed by court filings. Journey's suit claimed Valory and Smith wanted to take on these roles so they could rewrite the licensing agreement for Journey's name, ensuring they would have access to future proceeds.

Lawyers for Journey argued the move would not have worked: Official documents indicated that Nightmare Productions did not directly control the Journey mark. Instead, Cain and Schon held these rights as part of an earlier exit agreement with Perry that allowed them to move on.

Perry also retained a vote in all the band's business matters, which complicated Journey's steadfast attempts to frame this as a failed corporate takeover by the rhythm section. Balloting at the February 2020 meeting of Nightmare's shareholders told a quite different story.

Valory and Herbert attended the meeting in

person. Cain, Perry, and Smith took part by phone, as did lawyers for both Perry and Schon. Attorney **Tom Jorstad**, a longtime Herbert confidant, was there as an in-person proxy for Smith and Perry.

Schon did not attend the meeting, while Cain abstained from voting. Only later did they team up to fire Journey's bassist and drummer, then file a $10 million lawsuit. "I've known these guys for a long time," Schon told *Rolling Stone*. "I didn't agree with the way they went about business."

However, the motion to expand the board to six members had been passed by Herbert, Perry, Smith, and Valory, as confirmed by Journey's own court filings. The same voters affirmed Smith as president and Valory as secretary of the board, with Cain again abstaining. Jorstad was later elected chief financial officer for Nightmare Productions.

Instead of absconding with the band name, as had been accused, the reconfigured board filed a dispute before the U.S. Trademark Office's trial and appeal board over Schon's attempt to register a similar mark for his new splinter group, **Journey Through Time**. This document was dated March 3, the same day Schon and Cain made their explosive legal claims concerning a so-called coup d'état.

A countersuit filed a month later by Valory also argued the board was protecting Journey from conduct that would injure the value of a trademark owned by Nightmare Productions.

Documents submitted to the U.S. Trademark Office described Schon's proposed Journey Through Time mark as "substantially and confusingly similar" to Journey's original. Approval of this trademark, Nightmare Productions lawyers added, would "cause consumer confusion, mistake and/or deceit."

The trademark dispute was filed by attorney **Daniel J. Schacht**, who was also in attendance at February's Nightmare Productions shareholder meeting. [62, 618, 787, 788, 789, 790, 795, 796]

Band's New Tour Lineup Debuts, But Jackson, Walden Drop Out

Journey's lineup disintegrated in March 2020 just before the COVID-19 pandemic began, nixing a planned tour with **The Pretenders**. They would not unveil a new lineup until May 23, when Journey shared a socially distanced performance of "Don't Stop Believin'" for a UNICEF fundraising event.

Narada Michael Walden became an official band member after collaborating with Schon on his recent solo project, *Universe*. Randy Jackson returned after appearances on *Frontiers* and *Raised on Radio*, then a subsequent tour. **Jason Derlatka** moved out from side stage, where he'd begun providing additional keyboards and background vocals in 2019. He had also sat in with **Journey Through Time** for an update of "Faithfully."

"It's been interesting, all the twists and turns it takes constantly," Neal Schon told the *San Francisco Chronicle*. "But it's kind of like that song, 'wheel in the sky keeps on turning,' you know. Journey keeps on turning."

A winking Jackson memorably promised to put away the pleather and the outsized hairdos from his last Journey tour, back in the neon-tinted 1980s. This lineup of Schon, Jonathan Cain, Arnel Pineda, Jackson, Walden, and Derlatka then appeared on the single "The Way We Used to Be," released on June 24, 2021. A cartoon video confirmed this new lineup.

As the quarantine era ended, however, Journey ballooned to a six-man lineup—and Jackson was no longer part of it.

Schon said he had not quite recovered from back surgery, even as the group's lucrative tour engine was grinding back to life with a pre-Lollapalooza show on July 29 at Chicago's Aragon Ballroom. So he turned to the bassist from Journey Through Time.

"I got called in at the last minute, and it was like running a marathon when you're not in shape," **Marco Mendoza** said. "We've had a little bit of history together. When he calls, I try to move some things around so that I can be available—because it's always a great experience. Before you know it, I'm in Chicago, and we're rehearsing all kinds of songs. Their catalog is so vast."

Schon also decided that Walden was not catching on fast enough. "We had been rehearsing for about five days, trying to learn about 30-35 songs," Schon told *Relix*. "And Narada was sounding great but I don't think he was familiar with the material."

Time was running short. Journey was left with one of two phone calls to make—Steve Smith or Deen Castronovo. "One is obvious but he's going to tell us to 'Go f yourself' because we just had a lawsuit with him." Schon added. "And I said, 'The other guy is Deen.'"

He turned to the drummer from Journey Through Time. "Deen is such a sponge," Schon told *Rolling Stone*. "He remembers stuff I wrote better than I do. ... He has a photographic memory on all Journey material."

The Aragon show was Castronovo's first in-concert performance with Journey since 2015. This double-drummer setup carried through to 2021's final stops in New York, where the group shared a Central Park stage with **Bruce Springsteen**, **Paul Simon**, and other big names, before playing on Long Island.

Walden is "another guy, like Smith, they're such iconic players and they have such an amazing gift," Castronovo told *Ultimate Classic Rock*'s **Matt Wardlaw**. "It was a lesson in humility. ... Narada is a badass, period."

Unfortunately, band members said Walden experienced a health scare. "We got through all the East Coast dates. And then Narada had a mild heart attack," Schon told *Rolling Stone*. "We got him home safely, and Deen continued to stay out with us."

It was a wake-up call for Walden, and Castronovo said Journey reluctantly split with their second drummer. "He's got new babies and stuff," Castronovo told Wardlaw. "He's like, 'You know, I need to be home.' I think that's kind of what happened. They both mutually agreed." [31, 133, 724, 786, 801, 802]

SUMMER 2020

Perry Returns with a Stripped-Down Version of *Traces*

Steve Perry had not made a complete concert appearance since 1995 during his *For the Love of Strange Medicine* tour.

He considered breaking this silence in 2018, after *Traces*. "It's always been on my mind," Perry admitted to *Rolling Stone* two years later. "My heart bleeds daily to be in front of people and to sing for them."

He even went as far as working up some new arrangements with *Traces* co-producer **Thom**

Flowers that were specifically designed for the stage. "We were toying with the idea of maybe a stripped-down kind of live situation, so we started playing around with the songs," Flowers confirmed.

Nevertheless, "we were aware during and after the making of *Traces* that there was a lot of stuff in there. I mean, a lot of it accumulated over versions of the demos and so part of the challenge of making that record was balancing that and pulling away what we could."

This proved difficult, however, because they had been living with the songs on *Traces* for so long. "Sometimes you get married to little parts," Flowers admitted. "That's an album, I think, that gets better on repeated listens—because there's so much there to uncover. You'll never hear it the same way twice."

Either way, these new arrangements certainly were not constructed for a massive world tour, Flowers added—"just maybe a couple of live shows." Perry's performances would have to match the quiet intimacy of the record. Unfortunately, no concert followed. "I don't think he was too keen on, you know, really touring," Flowers said. "That's a lot to ask for someone in their 70s, you know."

The Journey years had left their scars, sometimes quite literally. "I've got some physical injuries from touring," Perry told *Rolling Stone*. "It's a tough thing, touring." As a dedicated baseball fan, Perry's analogies inevitably returned to sports: "People's backs and necks start to go out. It's a young man's game, but I do miss it."

Still, as someone who was not the "type to phone it in," Flowers said Perry wanted to be able to "give 100% every night. I think he was well aware that a full tour might just be too much."

They were left with a detailed roadmap for *Traces (Alternative Versions & Sketches)*, which arrived on December 20, 2020. "Going back to just connecting emotionally, he saw right away that these songs still connected—in fact, possibly even better when they're just stripped down to the bare elements," Flowers said. "So, we did it more just as an experiment and a lot of them turned out great."

They hoped the reworked project would reveal more of its ardent emotions. "As a nod to a record that I believe in," Perry told *Ultimate Classic Rock*'s **Matt Wardlaw**, "I wanted people to hear the songs by themselves, just melody and lyrics stripped down—which is the ultimate [test] of the song, just the melody and lyrics."

At the same time, *Alternative Versions & Sketches* was meant to represent the end of this era. "The acoustic *Traces* is going to close the *Traces* chapter," Perry told *Rolling Stone*. "Then I'm opening up another chapter next year at some point."

After *Traces* arrived, Flowers noted that "there's still a lot of material just sitting there on hard drives that I would love to see the light of day. I don't know if they will." Instead, Perry's next chapter became *The Season*, his first-ever Christmas album.

Though dominated by familiar Yuletide fare, the performances shared a ruminative sensibility with the songs from *Traces*. Perry told the *Peoria Times* that he had recorded while picturing his younger self in front of the fireplace at his grandparents' house. "I never really want to hear too much rock at that point," he admitted. "I want to reflect on my youth, my childhood and my memories of my departed loved ones."

Again co-produced by Flowers, the tracks were completed at Perry's home studio with multi-instrumentalist **Dallas Kruse** and veteran drummer **Vinnie Colaiuta** from the *Traces* sessions. Perry released *The Season* on November 5, 2021, and it debuted at No. 6 on *Billboard*'s Top Album Sales chart, which tracks purchases rather than streams.

That almost matched the No. 4 peak of *Traces*, which had been Perry's first Top 10 in the 30-year history of the Top Album Sales chart. Still, no tour followed. Instead, Perry simply hosted an album playback of *The Season* on its release day via YouTube. [858, 859, 860, 861, 862, 863]

In a Legal Flurry, Journey Fires Azoff, Settles with Valory, Smith

Journey was in shambles before splitting with their rhythm section, as Neal Schon and Jonathan Cain had clashed publicly over politics and religion. Then a pitched fight to claim Journey as their own seemed to have realigned them once more.

"No one's stealing the brand," Schon told the *Cleveland Plain Dealer*. "Things took a turn, businesswise, that I didn't like, and that Jonathan didn't like and we decided not to go along with it."

In time, Schon said he pinpointed the cause of their issue. It was not **Paula White** or **Donald Trump**, or even Ross Valory and Steve Smith. It was **Irving Azoff**.

Steve Perry had insisted on a change in management before he would return for 1996's *Trial by Fire*, and Azoff came on board in hopes he could help Journey to the kind of comeback he engineered for **Eagles**. Journey would eventually return to platinum sales, in no small part because of Azoff's dealmaking skills with the likes of Walmart.

As time went on, however, Schon had become suspicious of those around him. He claimed his bandmates had discussed touring on their own—then he launched a preemptive splinter group.

Next, Schon charged Azoff with turning on him. "He said, 'Why don't you quit?' Schon told *Guitar Connoisseur*. "I said, 'I'm not quitting, man. I've been here forever. You just got here; why don't you quit?'"

When Azoff did not, Schon fired his firm. At that point, Azoff MSG Entertainment executive **John Baruck** had been connected with Journey for some 20 years. Still, Schon argued that removing the middleman actually helped ease tensions with Cain.

"We found out that there was a lot of miscommunication that I felt was coming from management," Schon told *Rolling Stone*. "The divide-and-conquer situation was going on."

Journey then brought in management firm Q Prime—but only long enough for the group to announce the resolution of their legal issues with Valory and Smith.

Out-of-court negotiations had finally ended this mortal threat to Journey. Q Prime issued a statement in April 2021 stating that everyone had "resolved their differences and reached an amicable settlement agreement."

Schon and Cain acknowledged the "valuable contributions" made by the rhythm section "to the music and the legacy of Journey." Valory and Smith wished their former bandmates "much success in the future."

Terms were never disclosed. Journey turned their focus to a summer tour set to start in May with **The Pretenders**.

"During the negotiations, I spoke with Steve and Ross," Cain told interviewer **Michael Cavacini**. "I don't have any ill will toward anybody. We're just happy to move forward and be Journey again."

Then Schon and Cain took over as Journey's co-managers. In a *Billboard* interview, Schon remembered telling Cain: "We don't need these guys, man. I swear to God, I'm mostly doing everything, anyway."

This arrangement allowed them to redirect the standard 15 percent fee back into their own pockets, though *Billboard* reported that Cain shared a portion of his 7.5% with Arnel Pineda.

For now, all this turbulence seemed to have somehow carried Cain and Schon to a better place. "There's still magic there," Schon told *Rolling Stone*. "He's still creating amazing music, even without me, but us together, we create something that really sounds like Journey." [62, 212, 787, 791, 792, 879]

Universe Helps Solidify Bond Between Schon, Walden

Neal Schon and **Narada Michael Walden** were both wunderkind players, and they moved in the same Bay Area music circles.

Walden was in his early 20s when he was asked to join the second incarnation of **John McLaughlin**'s **Mahavishnu Orchestra**—a Schon favorite. Schon had been asked to join **Santana** as a teen. By the mid-1980s, the Michigan-born Walden was operating Tarpan Studios in San Rafael, California, where Schon lives. They shared collaborators in **Jan Hammer** and Randy Jackson.

Then they started joining one another on stage. Journey had "opened up for Mahavishnu after Narada was in the band. And I'd seen him live," Schon told *Guitar Connoisseur*. "I played with him throughout the years, because we live in the same town. And we'd always end up jamming."

In some ways, their collaboration on *Universe* had the feeling of destiny. Still, when Schon approached Walden around 2017 about collaborating, he had no idea how firmly Walden would take hold of the reins.

"I figured he'd come back to me in a couple months and play me a couple tunes," Schon told interviewer **Michael Cavacini**. "Instead, he called me four days later and he had seven tunes written and I was like, 'What?'" These were not leftover songs, but all-new originals.

They recorded on and off for a couple of years, and Schon discovered that Walden worked in a deeply structured way that challenged him. "I usually go in blindly, with drums, and I just kind of create stuff on the spot," Schon told *Guitar Connoisseur*. "But this was very honed in because he comes from a song place."

Released on December 11, 2020, *Universe* kept placing Schon in unusual circumstances. Rather than sitting at the project's center, Schon only contributed a few interior song ideas. "I decided just to sit down and just be the student and let him produce me," Schon said.

Walden created nearly complete music beds for Schon to inhabit, playing drums, keyboards, and synth bass—and he had specific ideas about what the guitarist should do.

"He sang the melodies he wanted me to play on guitar," Schon told the *Star Tribune*. He said Walden required him to precisely emulate what was sung, in a process far different from Journey songs where vocals would be present.

"At first, I took his vocal melodies to be just a roadmap for me to veer off of and do my own thing," Schon told *Guitar Player*, "and I started doing that almost immediately." Walden quickly halted the sessions to ask: "Where's my melody?"

Once complete, Walden's synth-based arrangements were bolstered by an orchestra, giving the record a symphonic feel unique to Schon's discography. "The only way I can describe it," Schon told the Star Tribune, "it's me playing with an orchestra and an ass-kicking drummer and rhythm section."

Walden's originals were paired with updates of **The Beatles**' "Hey Jude," **Prince**'s "Purple Rain," **Stevie Wonder**'s "I Believe," and **Jimi Hendrix**'s "Voodoo Child." Schon also returned to "Lights." "It's very melodic, powerful and majestic … and it's probably one of the best sounding records I ever made," Schon told Cavacini.

They both came away with something.

"Doing *Universe*, I learned a lot about how to simplify things and stay really tuned in to the melody," Schon told *Guitar Player*.

Meanwhile, "in the making of that album, we became really close," Walden told *Marin*

Continued on Page 340

Gregg Rolie and Herbie Herbert.

JOURNEY'S FOUNDING MANAGER, HERBIE HERBERT, DIES

If Santana had never had a road manager named Walter James "Herbie" Herbert, Journey would not exist.

If Herbert had not created his next band around Neal Schon, Gregg Rolie might still be working in the restaurant industry—and Steve Perry would have remained a hopeless romantic stuck in a tiny farming community in California's San Joaquin Valley.

Herbert had not directly managed Journey in years when he died on October 25, 2021, but his keen vision, attention to detail, and forward-thinking promotional and business practices still formed the group's foundation.

"Clearly, I wanted to do exactly what we've done," Herbert told *Billboard*, as Journey became a diamond-selling juggernaut. His goal, quite simply, was "becoming the biggest American band that's ever been. And we've succeeded in doing that."

Herbert first thought of putting Schon and Rolie together and led the effort to bring in Perry. Then he revolutionized the concert industry using video, advanced sound, and synergistic production techniques.

"I used to sit in front of his desk. He'd have meetings with the band, and I'd listen to everything," Gregg Rolie said. "He would tell you, 'Here's the plan.' You might say, 'Well, I don't know—but I think you do, and so I'm in.' That's how it worked. He just had one idea after another. Herbie became the focal point."

At the same time, Herbert was inventing innovative approaches to marketing, such as point-of-purchase campaigns that allowed Journey to have success while sidestepping traditional outlets and critical reception alike. It took a few years, and a few albums, but things soon changed for a group that had once been nothing more than a locally popular jam band.

Recruiting Perry brought in a whole new demographic. "They weren't held in high regard. They sure the fuck weren't **The Police**," Herbert told *San Francisco Weekly*. "But if [guys] wanted to get laid, they'd better go to that show anyway—because all the girls were there."

By 1980, his Nightmare conglomerate included two publishing companies, a real estate investment partnership, and a merchandising company, according to *Billboard*. The company was owned in equal shares by everyone in the band and Herbert, who was essentially a sixth member. His successes were their successes.

Journey was also traveling with the most sophisticated production setup out on the road. Herbert's company eventually took over all of it, in a move that came down to dollars and cents. "We tried to do video with existing companies and we found out that they wanted an arm and a leg," co-founding Nocturne partner **Pat Morrow** told *Billboard*. So, they shifted to "attacking it as a production problem, and we found, as with the other things, that we could do it better ourselves for less."

Herbert added a lighting subsidiary to a portfolio of businesses that included a fleet of tractor-trailer trucks to carry Journey's equipment. Nocturne emerged as one of the live music industry's leading production companies.

"Herbie—an amazing man. He was the heart and soul of the whole thing, and he kept it going and kept it running back then," Rolie said. "He came up with so many fantastic ideas. We had our own semis when we finally got to a stage to have them—and then he would lease them out to other bands to pay for the trucks. That was brilliant. Most people go lease a truck from somebody else, but we got in the leasing business. Pretty smart."

Herbert became Journey's mentor, their biggest cheerleader, and their conscience: He took care of a succession of key contributors when they left or were fired, creating nest eggs for Rolie, then Ross Valory and Steve Smith.

On the other hand, Morrow told *Time Passages*, he always worked for peanuts—but that wasn't a concern for this inveterate hippie.

"I think a big key that nobody knew about was that Herbie was demanding and very precise and had to have things—everything—his way," he said. "But I chose over everyone else to be Herbie's guy. I was totally loyal and respectful and worked for nothing for 30 years. We had a great, great run together."

Along the way, Journey's members earned

He would tell you, 'Here's the plan.' You might say, 'Well, I don't know—but I think you do, and so I'm in.' That's how it worked. He just had one idea after another. Herbie became the focal point.

—*Gregg Rolie*

unimaginable wealth, but Herbert could not stop them from squandering these gifts—first by going on hiatus at the peak of their powers, then by selling off the band's many assets, then by tossing him aside before their long-awaited reunion, then by devolving into public bickering and legal actions. Later, he became a vocal, sometimes savage critic.

Beyond his underlying role in Journey, Herbert also managed a series of other hit acts before retiring in the early 1990s, including the **Steve Miller Band**, **Europe**, **Mr. Big**, and **The Storm**, a Journey offshoot band that included Rolie, Valory, and Steve Smith.

"To hear Gregg and Ross talk about what he did for Journey— especially in the early days—and also hear about some of his work with the original **Santana** band was really cool," said **Ron Wikso**, who replaced Smith in The Storm. "He was a legendary guy in the business who is responsible for inventing and/or growing so many of the innovations that we take for granted now at live shows, and I feel lucky to have worked with him."

In the autumn of his years, Herbert invited members of Journey back for a little fun, as a loose side band he called **Sy Klopps** expanded to include guest turns by Schon, Prairie Prince, Valory, and Rolie. He then quietly retired the band.

By the time it was over, Herbert had lived out a four-step career arc that he had cannily predicted years before. Stage 1, Herbert told interviewer **Lori Baldassi,** was: "Who in the fuck is Herbie Herbert?" Stage 2 was: "Get me Herbie Herbert—no one else will do."

Stage 3 followed, where Herbert suggested bands would say: "Find me a young, hungry Herbie Herbert who isn't so rich and successful and wants to do it all." Finally, there was Stage 4, in which everything comes full circle: "Who in the fuck is Herbie Herbert?"

Always a robust figure, Herbert had become frail and noticeably thinner in later years. Longtime assistant **Maria Hoppe** told the *San Francisco Chronicle* that he died after a "prolonged illness" at his home in Orinda, California. He was 73. [25, 375, 476, 477, 547, 574, 621, 818, 857, 927]

Removed from the band after a 2015 domestic violence arrest, a rehabilitated Deen Castronovo (above) was welcomed back into the Journey fold on New Year's Eve 2019.

Living. "And then ... he asked me if I'd like to join Journey. And I said, 'Yes, of course.'" [205, 212, 214, 280, 616, 782, 783]

Castronovo Returns in Spirited First Post-Pandemic Concert

Journey's July 29, 2021 concert at the Aragon Ballroom in Chicago marked the band's first live performance since New Year's Eve 2019. They were also introducing a new lineup before a Saturday appearance at Lollapalooza.

But the night was defined by the redemption of Deen Castronovo, who had been kicked out of the band after an ugly 2015 domestic violence arrest that nearly ended his career. Neal Schon's call to return could not have come at a more tragic—or opportune—time.

"Well, actually, I got the call on the 19th. My mom passed away on the [20th] of July 2021, and Neal called me the next morning—which was just, I mean, the universe," Castronovo recalled. "He said, 'We need you to come out and

help out for these shows,' and it was heavy. So there was a lot going on, and the stars aligned, Jesus aligned, God aligned, Buddha aligned. All of it just aligned and everything just worked and fit perfectly."

Castronovo had remained friends with Steve Smith, even though he would replace him twice in Journey. Castronovo never failed to mention that he had been "ripping off" Smith every night in concert.

At the same time, he had kept his time in Journey in perspective. At one point, Castronovo argued that his most important contribution had been purchasing all their albums and attending every Journey show held in his hometown of Portland, Oregon. He had helped them buy their "cars and their houses," Castronovo said to *Michigan Live*, but that was it.

Then Castronovo appeared on *What God Wants to Hear*, the faith-focused 2016 album that jump-started Jonathan Cain's solo career. After years away, a door seemed to have cracked open—even if it was ever so slightly.

"I knew he needed a gig, and I just called him out of the blue," Cain said. "I had plenty of Nashville studio guys that could play my Christian stuff, but I thought that it was a time to connect with him—and I was right. That sort of pulled him back into a confident place."

Fast-forward a few years, and the timing of a reunion with Journey may not have been ideal, but Castronovo understood the inherent risks of relapse for an ex-junkie dealing with such heartrending loss.

"When my father died, that was a tough one," Castronovo said. "I almost lost it on that one. Mom, as well. That was really tough. So Neal calling was like a blessing, a huge blessing from God. I was like, 'OK, I got to stay in this. My mom would be livid if I screwed up.' So I'm very, very grateful. It's a beautiful time."

Cain said he had a renewed belief in Castronovo because he had stuck with his program—and, at the same time, had shown deep contrition. "He repented. I think he felt like he had really created his own tragedy," Cain said. "When you're ready to recognize that you're in your own way, then you change. Until that happens, there's really no hope that anything different is going to take place."

Castronovo initially joined a two-man in-concert tandem with **Narada Michael Walden** before once again becoming Journey's sole drummer.

"The funny thing is, dude, I can't remember my name some days," Castronovo said. "I can't find my keys. Where's my phone? But the weirdest thing, we went into rehearsals the first time and I remembered every beginning, every middle part, and every ending. It's just those songs. It was the soundtrack to my teen years, all the way from the time I was 10 or 11 years old on. That was such a beautiful feeling. It was like I never left."

By then, Walden had already completed his parts on their subsequent album *Freedom*, but Castronovo returned in time to remind Journey fans of his versatility by providing lead vocals on "After Glow."

Castronovo would also soon begin reconstituting **Revolution Saints**, completing a fourth album titled *Eagle Flight* with a reworked lineup featuring **Whitesnake**'s **Joel Hoekstra** and **Foreigner**'s **Jeff Pilson**.

"Even though it was a rough time for me emotionally, I needed that," Castronovo said.

"I needed to just go, 'OK, mom's gone. Now I got to get in here,' because that would have been the time to blow it—to relapse." [37, 229, 230, 407, 408, 777]

WINTER 2021-22

Hardline's Todd Jensen Settles Journey's Rhythm Section

When Neal Schon was not in court or a lawyer's office, he was searching for the final person to complete Journey's lineup. The group began a month-long residency in Las Vegas on December 1, 2021 by introducing their third bassist in less than two years.

First, Schon said Randy Jackson was unable to tour as he recovered from back surgery, then he became unhappy with **Marco Mendoza**. "Marco is an excellent bass player, excellent singer, excellent guy—but it just wasn't gelling," Schon told *Rolling Stone*.

At this point, Mendoza had played in nearly a dozen concerts with Journey and the splinter group **Journey Through Time**, not to mention various other Schon-led projects. Suddenly, Schon said Mendoza was not providing enough space for his guitar.

Schon turned to a familiar face. "I suggested Todd Jensen at that point," he told *Rolling Stone*, and "Todd fits like a glove," to *USA Today*.

Jensen had been part of **Hardline**'s founding early 1990s lineup with Schon and Journey's newly reinstalled drummer Deen Castronovo. The same trio backed **Paul Rodgers** on tour dates that produced the live *The Hendrix Set* EP in 1993.

"Todd, I've known for so many years," Castronovo said. "I used to watch him play, dude, when I was a little kid. I was, like, 14. He was in a band called **Sequel**, and they would sneak me in, right? And Todd, to me, was Sequel. I'm sure everybody in the Portland music scene will tell you the same thing. I mean, Sequel was a band of four guys, but Todd was the guy. He was the badass in the band. I have such a long relationship with TJ. He's a brother for life."

More importantly, Jensen also served as Steve Perry's touring bassist for 1994-1995 dates with setlists that typically included 10 or more Journey songs. "And so I went, 'Well,

Continued on Page 344

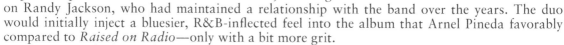

Pandemic Sequesters Journey's *Freedom* Plans

Freedom was fashioned like no other Journey album, even if the results returned to the mean.

"We had so much going on legally after the last tour, and then the pandemic hit," Neal Schon told *Relix*. "So I decided I had to start getting busy and started writing some music downstairs in the house." He was not thinking about constructing Journey songs. He was not even on guitar, but instead fooling around on a keyboard.

It all served to open up Schon's muse. These offbeat early ideas in turn sparked Jonathan Cain's imagination, and a discussion began in earnest about who would replace Ross Valory and Steve Smith.

Schon suggested **Narada Michael Walden**, who had just helped complete his *Universe* solo album. Next, he brought on Randy Jackson, who had maintained a relationship with the band over the years. The duo would initially inject a bluesier, R&B-inflected feel into the album that Arnel Pineda favorably compared to *Raised on Radio*—only with a bit more grit.

Journey now had a nucleus to build around, but pandemic-era precautions kept everybody at home. *Freedom* would be cobbled together remotely, save for Schon and Walden. They built the song bases, and the others added their parts later.

"It was a long distance record that was made in multiple studios and then brought togeth-

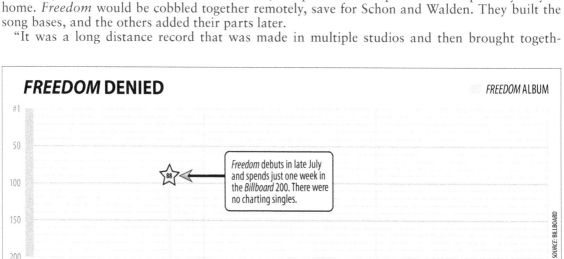

FREEDOM DENIED

FREEDOM ALBUM

Freedom debuts in late July and spends just one week in the *Billboard* 200. There were no charting singles.

SOURCE: BILLBOARD

It took Journey a long time to complete their follow-up album to *Eclipse*, about 11 years. That gap between albums is longer than many classic rock bands ever stayed together. The long period between albums did not seem to help. *Freedom* was released on July 8, 2022, and initially surged—it peaked on the *Billboard* 200 at No. 88 that very same day. But then the wheels fell off. By the following week it had vanished from the charts entirely. It was a stunning turn for a band used to charting success. The last time a Journey album performed so poorly was *Generations*, which also logged just one week on the *Billboard* 200, but at a more anemic No. 170.

TOP CHARTING WEEK: *BILLBOARD—July 23, 2022*

1. Bad Bunny, *Un Verano Sin Ti*
2. Brent Falyaz, *Wasteland*
3. aespa, *Girls: The 2nd Mini Album (EP)*
4. Harry Styles, *Harry's House*
5. Morgan Wallen, *Dangerous: The Double Album*
6. Drake, *Honestly, Nevermind*
7. Future, *I Never Liked You*
8. Lil Durk, *7220*
9. The Weeknd, *The Highlights*
88. JOURNEY, *FREEDOM*

er and mixed," Cain told interviewer **Michael Cavacini**. "We'd jump on the phone a lot to go over things." This unconventional approach was probably for the best, considering everything that had gone on between the band's principals.

Journey offered an early preview with "The Way We Used to Be," a surprisingly groove-focused single released more than a year before *Freedom* arrived on July 8, 2022. "The lyric has a sort of angst to it, and the question was 'can we ever get back?'" Cain told the *Cleveland Plain Dealer*. He was talking about the pandemic, but could just as easily been referring to his band.

For Schon, the early portion of these sessions recalled 1980s-era work with **Jan Hammer**. "He would play drums, I'd play live lead guitar ... and then we'd overdub bass and everything else after that," Schon told *Forbes*. "But it had that live feel because I'm playing live with the drums."

Jackson worked in Los Angeles while Cain called in from Florida. "It was a little bit challenging to make during the pandemic, but we did it," Jackson told *Bass Player* magazine. "It was wild at times, not being in the same room."

As the rest of the lyrics came together, Cain said a certain theme emerged: "The message of this new Journey music," he told Cavacini, "is to be grateful for what you've got." Echoes of Cain's everyman songs of old began to reverberate. The music traversed the same well-worn path.

By the time it was over, Cain admitted they were directly comparing these new songs—and even the sequencing—with *Escape*. "They're trying [to forge a new musical path]," Pineda told interviewer **Rob Herrera**, "but at the same time, they're trying to stay somehow in the tradition, in the legacy. It's a 50-50 thing."

Pineda's Zoom calls with Walden took place in the middle of the night since he was quarantined in the Philippines. Walden and Journey engineer **Jim Reitzel** then produced Pineda's vocals in real time.

"I share my computer, like mirroring," Pineda told *Rolling Stone*. "They can see what's happening in my laptop. It allows them to hack it for a moment and then they can hear it." Sessions had to be stopped at least once, however, when it began to rain so hard in Manila that the downpour was audible inside Pineda's home.

After all of the turbulence that preceded it,

change seemed to have done Journey some good. "There's a different strut to this record altogether," Schon told ABC. "[M]any people probably can imagine that ... replacing a whole rhythm section is gonna change the overall rhythm, feel in the band. And personally, I love it."

Deen Castronovo rejoined the touring lineup too late to contribute to the rhythm tracks on *Freedom*, but Journey still found a place for him to make a last-second contribution.

"We were finishing up the album. And the music to 'After Glow' came to me," Schon told *Rolling Stone*. "It's the last song I wrote on the album." He initially asked Castronovo to add background vocals in a remote session, then encouraged him to try the lead.

"I'd never heard the song and didn't know anything about it. But I went in there and we did a Zoom," Castronovo told *Ultimate Classic Rock*'s **Matt Wardlaw**. "I did it, and I was like, 'Oh, my gosh.'" His comeback was suddenly complete.

This wireless, stitched-together process allowed them to overcome the pandemic and lingering bad feelings to produce Journey's first album in more than a decade. "I feel like, for me, it goes back to maybe the *Infinity* era, when I first started writing with Steve Perry, to what we are now ... and what we're becoming," Schon told ABC.

Still, working remotely also dictated a return to the familiar. Their direction was set, it seemed, during the earliest overdubbing sessions.

Schon initially took Jackson's place simply to give the demos a more defined shape. "I'd lay down a bass part because it helped everything feel more glued together," Schon told *Vintage Guitar*. But then Jackson sometimes simply built off this rudimentary template rather than adding his own thoughts.

In this way, an album that seemed to have started out with a different intent made a soft landing into the expected. *Freedom* quickly diverged from its R&B-tinged beginnings.

Then there was its length. Likely because Journey had no outside producer, this conversation dragged on and on. At more than 73 minutes, *Freedom* was almost twice as long as Journey's earliest platinum-selling records—with no concurrent hit singles to serve as tentpoles. [62, 204, 279, 281, 312, 473, 724, 777, 786, 791, 820, 821, 841, 946, 947]

Todd knows the material,'" Schon told *Relix*.

"Steve liked his feel too," Schon added. "Steve, being a great singer, knows a lot about where the drums should sit, where the vocal's supposed to sit, where the bass is supposed to sit."

Jensen arrived with a portfolio that also included tour work with **Alice Cooper** and **David Lee Roth**, as well as an appearance on 1997's *Underground* by ex-*Rainbow* front man **Graham Bonnet**. Jensen also further strengthened his Journey credentials by taking part in one-time singer Jeff Scott Soto's guest-packed 2005 album *Cover 2 Cover*, which also featured Castronovo and Aynsley Dunbar.

"Todd is a really sound and reliable person and musician," Hardline front man **Johnny Gioeli** said. "That's why he was a great fit for Hardline, and that's why he's a great fit for Journey. He plays well, he's solid, and he sings great. He's a pro, so you can always count on him."

Mendoza would appear on Journey's *Live in Concert at Lollapalooza* album in late 2022 and then Journey Through Time's self-titled 2023 live album. But Schon immediately saw Jensen as potentially "being a permanent member," he told *Rolling Stone*.

He made no apologies for the recent merry-go-round in Journey's rhythm section. "As a person, I refuse to go backward, and I refuse to sit in neutral," Schon told *Billboard*. "Anybody is replaceable."

Still, it all led Hardline's Gioeli to develop a snarky nickname for the new lineup: "Journey-line," he said, laughing uproariously. "Journey-line, we call it." [37, 133, 290, 408, 724, 786, 797, 798, 799, 800]

SPRING–SUMMER 2022

RELEASES
▶ Journey, *Freedom* (album)

Stranger Things' Season 4 Drew 'Separate Ways' in a New Light

Volume 1 of the soundtrack from Season Four of *Stranger Things* arrived on May 27, 2022, months after its trailer sent Journey's "Separate Ways (Worlds Apart)" back up the charts. Sales surged an astounding 208 percent over the previous week, according to a report in *The Wrap*.

Composer **Bryce Miller** and the boutique music company Alloy Tracks collaborated on this short remix of the 1983 single, using artificial intelligence software to isolate Steve Perry's vocal. They then surrounded him with keyboards and orchestral elements to create a marketing clip that was shrouded in a ghostly new sense of foreboding.

"As soon as I can get rid of dated-sounding guitars and drums," Miller told *The New York Times*, "I can build a more contemporary production that is pulling from more pop music sounds."

Perry absolutely loved it.

Alloy Tracks founder **Troy MacCubbin** found out when he got a call from a number he did not recognize. "So I thought it was Netflix calling to talk about what we had done," MacCubbins told *Flood Magazine*.

The person on the other end of the line was deeply curious about how they had separated the vocal. "At the end of the conversation, before he hung up, I was like, 'Sorry, who am I talking with?'" MacCubbin told *Forbes*. "And he's like, 'It's Steve Perry from Journey!'"

Miller had already done similar so-called "trailerizations" for *House of Gucci* (**Blondie**'s "Heart of Glass"), *Wednesday* (**The Rolling Stones**' "Paint It, Black" and the "Addams Family Theme"), and *The Batman* (**Nirvana**'s "Something in the Way"), among others. He said he had always wanted to tackle "Separate Ways," and finally got the chance when the Trailer Park marketing group contacted him about *Stranger Things*.

The plot and tone fit perfectly. Still, it took Miller months to rework the short snippet. Perry got involved when Alloy Tracks began contacting the song's composers for approval.

Interest piqued, Perry had asked MacCubbin for Miller's number. "I called him up and said, 'Look, I have this idea—just for fun, let's see if we can extend it,'" Perry told *Flood Magazine*.

They got together, and Miller began combining clips from other remix attempts. Most artists who license songs simply sign off on their use and then cash the check, but Perry enjoyed taking a more hands-on approach. "He had some specific mixing notes," Miller told *Forbes*.

Within a day, they had a full song mockup to send to the *Stranger Things* team. Perry remembered sibling executive producers **Matt** and **Ross Duffer** quickly calling him back to say: "'We've got to have this on the record!'" Perry told Flood. "So now, all of a sudden, we're mastering it down for the soundtrack!"

"Separate Ways" ended up soundtracking a key moment during the eighth episode of Season Four, then rode the *Stranger Things* momentum to millions in YouTube views. "I really think that this is the next equivalent of a *Sopranos* moment for a whole new generation," Perry told *Flood Magazine*.

Perry vowed to continue their partnership, leading Miller to seemingly joke: "We're a band now." Turns out, Perry was not kidding. "As soon as we finished '*Stranger Things*,'" Miller told *The New York Times*, 'he's like, 'What are we doing next?'"

Their "trailerization" of "Any Way You Want It" for Hulu's *Welcome to Chippendales* debuted that October. [836, 837, 838, 839, 840]

Heeding Perry's Advice, Journey Moves to Protect Pineda's Voice

Steve Perry struggled as a singer to meet Journey's pitched demands. Steve Augeri likewise struggled. Then it was their successor's turn.

Arnel Pineda had gotten some desperately needed rest when the pandemic halted concerts, but worries remained. Journey's songs, written in youth, were once again fraying their front man's vocals.

"At that point in time in music, you kind of had to get in the outdo-the-next-kind-of-cat mode," Perry admitted to SiriusXM. "I just kept pushing myself for greater heights. I just really wanted to keep outdoing my own capabilities."

Couple these challenging keys and soaring choruses with the inevitable aging process, and the task grows harder every year. Eventually, the voice fails entirely. "It's just inevitable. It's going to happen," Augeri told *Rolling Stone*. "There's going to come a time where you can't do five shows in a row. It's not possible."

Vocal cords simply are not resilient enough to keep pace with these touring assignments, Los Angeles-based vocal coach **Ken Stacey** told

Ultimate Classic Rock. "The entire industry is built on the premise the artist is going to stay out there and work," he added. "The problem is that is not conducive to a healthy voice."

Knowing this, Perry stopped to give Pineda a small piece of advice when they were finally introduced before Journey was inducted into the Rock & Roll Hall of Fame. "He whispered something to me, through my assistant **Yul [Sessions]**, which I learned after the meeting," Pineda told the *Las Vegas Review-Journal*. "He said, 'Tell him to take care of his voice.'"

Journey only performed 15 shows in 2021, but Pineda still had noticeable problems—particularly at the iHeartRadio Music Festival. Rounding the corner on a record-smashing 15 years as Journey's front man, Pineda would appear in nearly 60 concerts in support of 2022's *Freedom*.

Deen Castronovo had returned to the line-up—and returned to subbing at key moments, just as he had with Augeri.

"Deen is just a monster drummer, and an amazing singer," Neal Schon said. "I've been pushing him for years—you know, 'you've gotta sing; you've gotta sing.' He's like our hidden weapon in Journey, still to this point. He sings a lot of high stuff live, and if Arnel goes down, if he gets sick—which is inevitable; it just happens—then we let Deen sing, and he does an amazing job."

But that was no long-term solution. Some sort of breakdown was seeming inevitable.

"Singers, and I can vouch for this obviously, we have our nights where shit is not working," former Schon collaborator **Johnny Gioeli** said. "You're not 100 percent, because you're fatigued or you have some stress. Everything affects the voice. Arnel can be great one night, and struggle on another. That's normal. That's normal for singing live."

They decided to hire a pro to work with Pineda. "He's been struggling, and we brought a vocal coach out who is fantastic," Deen Castronovo told interviewer **Matt Wardlaw**. "He came out and was coaching Arnel with how to deliver a little bit differently."

Randy Jackson recommended **Dave Stroud**, who had worked with contestants on multiple seasons of *American Idol*, as well as with **Justin Timberlake**, **Demi Lovato**, and **Michael Jackson**, among others.

The risk for those who sing too often, or use bad form, is a potentially career-ending injury. Pineda was doing both. "Singing is an athletic experience," Stroud told *Huffington Post*. "However, just like if I go to the gym a lot ... but I have poor form, I will do more damage the more time I spend at that activity."

As they worked through a new approach, Pineda offered a startling revelation: He had been having trouble hearing on stage for years.

"I think it was something that he didn't know if he had the liberty to say 'Hey, I need to fix this' or 'You guys need to try something different here,' either get a new soundman or whatever," Castronovo told Wardlaw.

Journey replaced their soundman during the 2022 shows, and Pineda's performances were suddenly transformed. "Arnel sounds very, very strong," Neal Schon told *Rolling Stone*. "He's back in there, I feel, like when we first got him." [14, 37, 624, 777, 787, 803, 804, 805, 806, 808]

FALL 2022

Court Filings, Public Bickering Erupt Before 50th Anniversary

Neal Schon and Jonathan Cain's decision to co-manage Journey finally smashed their relationship to pieces. The timing could not have been worse, as Journey prepared to celebrate their 50th anniversary.

They argued over a splinter group, and they argued over trademarks. They argued over a credit card. They argued over control, and they argued over their wives. It seemed they argued over everything.

These disputes usually all played out on Schon's social media channels rather than in the studio or on the band's bus. "Don't go to the fans about it," Cain pleaded in *Rolling Stone*. "If you had a problem with it, talk to me."

In so many cases, as *San Francisco Chronicle* music writer **Joel Selvin** contended, money woes drove all these issues. Yet Schon admitted to extravagant purchases as if Journey was still bathing in revenue from physical media sales rather than eking out a living with tour dates.

"The record industry changed so radically," former *Rolling Stone* writer and editor **David Wild** said. "Where these bands used to make fortunes off of their catalog in record sales, it became about the brand for merch and the brand, more importantly, for continuing to live tour. So, every band that you thought was going to stop touring 20 years ago, that's exactly when they all went back on the road."

Some, however, toured more than others. Then there was Journey, who toured incessantly, quickly wearing down Steve Augeri before Arnel Pineda came on board.

Late founding manager **Herbie Herbert** once estimated that Journey played more shows during Augeri's eight-year tenure alone than the band ever did with Steve Perry. "They need to get themselves into a financial position where they do not need to tour every year," he told *Classic Rock Revisited*, "but they can't seem to break away from that."

Schon blamed the costly exit agreement that was forcing Journey to pay Perry not to sing. *Billboard* estimated that Perry made about $400,000 from Journey's 2022 dates, some 35 years after his last tour with the group.

He said Perry's parting demands arrived as they were mounting the first tour without him, and Journey's legal team did not have time to look over the documents. "Herbie claimed he didn't know what else to do, so he suggested we sign," Schon posted on Instagram. "We did sign, but I will say under duress."

Yet Perry was merely the easiest target when it came to Journey's money woes.

Schon tried to address his financial situation by selling his publishing rights. That provided a quick infusion of cash, but he also missed out on associated royalties when Journey songs kept returning as streaming hits through synch licensing. (By 2019, the U.K.-based Hipgnosis investment firm had also bought out Cain, Herbert, Ross Valory, and Steve Smith.)

Schon then sold his guitars. He even turned his wedding to **Michaele Salahi** into a pay-per-view event. But he kept spending. Schon estimated that he purchased another 150 guitars during the quarantine era. "I kept buying, buying, buying, buying, and it became like a hobby," Schon told *People*. "It was like being hooked on something."

Billboard reported that Journey grossed

$31.9 million in 2022, nearly doubling their take in just five years. The band's nine-show 2019 residency in the Colosseum at Caesars Palace in Las Vegas alone grossed nearly $6 million, according to *Pollstar.*

As the 50th-anniversary tour continued, Deen Castronovo told *Ultimate Classic Rock* that professionalism was nonetheless carrying them along. Backstage, things looked much different: *Billboard* reported that Schon and Cain had hired off-duty officers to stand guard outside of their respective dressing rooms. Beyond the money, something much more had been lost.

Schon filed a lawsuit in October 2022 arguing that Cain had "improperly restricted" access to Journey's corporate credit card, which contained "millions in Journey funds." Cain responded in January 2023, describing Schon's spending as "completely out of control." Cain said Schon charged some $1 million in personal expenses, including $104,000 for jewelry and clothes in a single month in 2022.

Schon and Cain agreed to bring in outside management, hiring former tourmate **Def Leppard**'s **Mike Kobayashi** in December 2022. Kobayashi was gone by early 2023. Schon admitted that they had only tried Q Prime "for a second." Then Schon took over. He later confirmed that his wife was now the band's road manager, as Michaele continued to become more involved on the business side.

At the same time, Schon's attorney accused Cain's spouse, televangelist **Paula White**, of accessing Journey's bank accounts without Schon's consent. White's lawyer told the *New York Post* that Schon and Cain's respective 50 percent shares in Journey were being administered by personal trusts on the advice of Schon's attorney. Cain said he had made White a personal co-trustee separately upon their marriage, and agreed to remove her if that would keep the peace.

"Oh, they fucked it all up. It's the lesson of life: You don't fuck your friends and you don't worry about money," Nocturne CEO **Pat Morrow** said. "Money means nothing, man. We suffer the compromise of money because it's so fucking important to us. But it's wrong. It's not worth it." [60, 411, 422, 547, 792, 820, 842, 844, 845, 846, 847, 848, 851, 852, 853, 856, 890, 927]

Augeri Releases Debut Album with Assists from Schon, Cain

As with so many long-awaited debuts, Steve Augeri's *Seven Ways 'Til Sunday* included songs written over several years. Two of them tracked back to his time in Journey.

"It took a pandemic for me to get motivated," Augeri said, "for fear of them dying on the vine so to speak."

Augeri used the time away to heal, having blown out his voice trying to will Journey back after Steve Perry's exit. His path to recovery involved a new commitment to sing authentically, rather than trying to mimic Journey's long-departed front man. He had also noted their ongoing squabbles, pointedly admitting that he would not return even if asked.

Instead, Augeri focused on a self-titled band that included **Adam Holland**, **Craig Pullman**, and **Gerard Zappa**. They had all been members of **Valentine**, the AOR act with whom Augeri released a 1990 eponymous album on Giant/Reprise, prior to launching **Tall Stories**. Augeri produced *Seven Ways 'Til Sunday* at Hi-Hat Studio in New York City, with additional sessions in Atlanta, Nashville, and Georgia.

He advanced the album with the singles "If You Want" in February 2022 and then "Bated Breath" in July. At this point, the **Steve Augeri Band** had been around for a decade. Even so, "Desert Moon" and "Never Far From Home" were always going to be of the most interest to Journey fans.

The crunchy Neal Schon co-written "Desert Moon" had been sketched out in a private moment while they waited for the rest of the band to arrive for rehearsal on one of Augeri's last tours with Journey.

"I got behind [Journey drummer] Deen [Castronovo]'s kit and Neal and I jammed—and it was for the most part conceived in less than a couple of hours," Augeri said. "We gave it a whirl with the band either that afternoon or soon afterwards but it didn't seem to fit, not at the time anyway."

Still, Augeri said he "always thought 'Desert Moon' had potential, so I filed it away and when it came time to round out my album, I dusted it off and gave it a facelift. It was also the last track I sang before finally deciding to stop procrastinating and get on with releasing *Seven Ways 'Til Sunday.*"

Augeri was glad he did. "I think it adds the heavier element that balances things out and certainly represents my love for heavy music," he said. But the sessions presented a challenge.

"Truth be told, Neal's original guitar parts were more ethereal and frankly way more complicated than I could ever reproduce as a guitarist myself," Augeri said. "So, I had no choice but to rework pretty much most if not all of the guitars, except the chord progression."

Meanwhile, Augeri said the Jonathan Cain co-written "Never Far From Home" went back to around 2002. "I remember because the original refrain was 'times like these' and we all know how big a hit that was for the **Foo Fighters**," Augeri admitted. "I was a day late and a dollar short."

Cain "reworked the chorus with a great new melody and lyric," but the results were again "not quite fitting into the Journey mold—probably less so than 'Desert Moon,'" Augeri said. Instead, "'Never Far From Home' has sort of a Nashville twist to it, bringing me back to my father and uncle's influence on me and their love for country and western music—which is a phrase you don't hear much anymore."

After *Seven Ways 'Til Sunday* arrived, Augeri joined a 2023 package tour with **Bret Michaels** of **Poison**, **Night Ranger**, and others. But rather than playing his new songs, Augeri could once again be found returning to Steve Perry-era favorites like "Separate Ways (Worlds Apart)," "Don't Stop Believin'," "Faithfully," and "Any Way You Want It." [629, 810, 811]

WINTER 2022-23

Legal Woes Greet Band As Historic Tour Approaches

There was good news, bad news, and worse news as Journey prepared to launch their 50th anniversary North American tour in 2023.

They had finally settled a trademark dispute with Steve Perry. But a simmering argument over Jonathan Cain's relationship with **Donald Trump** had begun to heat up again—and Cain and Neal Schon's differences got more personal.

Schon credited his wife, Michaele, with discovering long-term issues with Journey's trademark. Schon and Cain then registered 20 of the band's song titles with the U.S. Patent and Trademark Office between February and May 2022 for use on various forms of merchandise. Perry would soon be visiting his lawyer's offices to craft a response.

In the meantime, Schon went to social media to explain how his legal partnerships with Perry and Cain worked, what had been trademarked and what had not, and other complicated legal issues involving things like licensing.

"People talk about the death of rock 'n' roll, and I've had to talk about it a fair amount," former *Rolling Stone* writer and editor **David Wild** said, "but we are definitely in this early end game of where a band is a brand, in many cases or in a number of cases, more than they are band. And I think that's what the arguments are over—you know, dividing the pie, and who owns the brand and who maintains the brand. When is the brand defunct? When is it not legitimate to call it something?"

Journey honored its concert commitments, but Cain and Schon kept to their sides of the stage for hits like "Faithfully." Cain told *Rolling Stone* that "it's kind of like if you have a fight with your wife. You live in the same house. You have to weather it and overcome it." Still, *Billboard* filed a damning report: "Another show: Check. Circus life: Check. Shared smiles: Absent."

Perry moved to cancel Cain and Schon's new trademarks in September 2022. His motion accused them of making "false and misleading" statements, arguing that they no longer had standing to claim trademarks after selling their publishing rights to Hipgnosis. His lawyers also said a long-standing licensing agreement required "unanimous agreement and consent" among the songwriters of any Journey song before it could be used commercially.

As this new issue wound through the court system, Cain arrived in November 2022 at Trump's Mar-a-Lago estate in Florida to perform a solo version of "Don't Stop Believin'." A cease-and-desist letter from Schon followed in December. The document described Cain's appearance as "extremely deleterious to the Journey brand," adding that "Journey is not, and should not be, political."

Cain fired back with a list of grievances in an official statement published by *USA Today*. "Neal and his wife recklessly spend Journey's money until there is none left for operating costs," Cain argued. "If anyone is destroying the Journey brand, it is Neal—and Neal alone."

Schon had likewise pushed back hard against Perry during the legal maneuvering over Journey's trademarks, calling his arguments "total crap." Perry's motion was rescinded in January 2023 without explanation—just weeks before Journey returned to the tour with special guest **Toto**.

Unfortunately, issues with band finances were far from settled. By February, Journey's longtime bank had cut ties with the group, according to *Billboard*, further complicating the management of day-to-day expenses.

Founding manager **Herbie Herbert** had once framed their growing dysfunction in historical terms, telling the San Francisco radio station KQED that Schon replaced Perry as a divisive force. "It's a tragedy," he added. "It's all rooted in financial issues, and it's too bad because it could be the undoing of what is a great business."

Unfortunately, Herbert was not around anymore to provide a voice of reason. Still, Journey might have found at least some common ground during his memorial services. There would be no full-scale band reunion, however, since Schon was absent.

Long-time *San Francisco Chronicle* music critic **Joel Selvin** spent part of his time at the event chatting with Steve Smith and his wife Diane. At one point, Selvin told them he had "gotten a text from Neal saying he wasn't going to be at the memorial, and I said I didn't understand why he thought I would care or why he thought we were friends. Diane says, 'Well, he hasn't sued you yet—and you're the only one,'" Selvin added, with a raucous laugh. [60, 411, 792, 795, 796, 834, 846, 849, 850, 851, 853, 854, 855, 856, 857]

Gregg Rolie Becomes Part of Journey Again—for One Night

Neal Schon understandably hoped to share the stage with Gregg Rolie as Journey launched its 50th anniversary tour.

They had started the band together after Rolie plucked him from obscurity to join **Santana**. "I was going to Aragon High School at the time," Schon told the *San Francisco Chronicle*. "Gregg would come by and pick me up around noon. I'd bring my guitar to school and I'd bolt."

They hid out in Belmont at an apartment belonging to Rolie's dad where there was a piano and a little guitar set up. Those loose jams started a career, back in an era of camaraderie that hardly seemed possible anymore with the band they would found next.

Rolie had more recently reunited with Schon in Santana, while establishing a lengthy tenure with **Ringo Starr's All-Starr Band**. "I mean, when I started playing in Santana, I knew a couple of chords and that's about it," Rolie said. "It was a matter of the attitude behind it and just growing with it. So to have done this twice, and then play with Ringo for seven years, which is almost longer than I did with Journey? I've had a great time."

But nothing came easy with Journey, not in this moment. Rolie would appear as part of their February 22, 2023 stop in his adopted hometown of Austin, Texas, but had to work hard to remain above the fray.

"I said this in the short bit I did before our set: Journey has become this runaway freight train with no brakes," Rolie said. "People come in and out, there have been all these changes, but Journey keeps going. It just keeps going and going. I'm proud to have been a part of building something like this that has reached millions of people... That's amazing to me."

Schon earlier announced what sounded like wider plans to welcome Rolie on stage for the *Freedom* Tour 2023. Dates were set to continue across 38 cities in North America, lasting through April in Palm Springs, California.

Then Schon and his wife Michaele both said Rolie's presence was vetoed by Jonathan Cain, who had long ago replaced Rolie in the lineup. Schon said he pushed back—hard.

"No one is going to dictate to me at this point what I can and cannot do in regards to Journey," Schon wrote on X, then known as Twitter. "It's my band and I'll own it as I should and make the right changes as needed." A follower asked Schon who he was referring to, and Schon responded: "Have a guess."

This was far from the first time Schon and Rolie had reunited—including solo projects, *Abraxas Pool* and *Santana IV*. Through it all, an inherent joy remained between the two old former Journey bandmates.

"I think the main thing is it just brings the smiles out of Neal and myself," Rolie said. "You know, if you write and record things like that, and then do them for years, it becomes inbred. You don't have to rehearse much, you just don't. You go back and say, 'What have I done?'—and then change it a bit, so that it's new but not too far off from the song. That's kind of what happened."

Nevertheless, their most recent collaboration in the splinter group **Journey Through Time** had also been the most controversial. One of original manager **Herbie Herbert**'s long-held criticisms may also have shed light on why Rolie's presence became an issue.

Cain was later tasked with singing Rolie's parts during Journey concerts, and Rolie "was such a strong vocalist," Herbert told interviewer **Matthew Carty**. "I mean, Jon Cain has struggled to sing as well as he sings today. Today he sings better than he has ever sung, and it's barely, barely adequate."

Schon got his way, and Rolie returned—but only for a single encore. "We have an extra special set tonight," Schon told the crowd at the Moody Center in Austin. "So, when we go offstage at the end of the show, don't leave."

Journey returned with Rolie to perform "Just the Same Way" from 1979's *Evolution*, "Of a Lifetime" from 1975's *Journey*, and "Feeling That Way" and "Anytime" from 1978's *Infinity*. They ended things by returning to Santana's inventive cover of "Black Magic Woman" with **Steve Lukather** from opening act **Toto**—and then Journey's "Any Way You Want It."

Lukather and Rolie had connected more deeply as bandmates in the All-Starr Band, performing "Black Magic Woman" night after night. "Luke and I did that with Ringo for seven years," Rolie said. "So it came up, and now two guitar players are getting to play off each other. It was a good evening. It was really good."

The reunion unfolded as organically as Rolie's in-concert interactions always had with Schon, despite what was going on backstage with the rest. "Neal and I talked about it and I said, 'What if we could go back 50 years and do 'Of a Lifetime'? It stunned people when we did it back then; it could do it again," Rolie said.

"And then, 'What about "Black Magic Woman'? … because you were in Santana with me for a couple of years, and we'll go back and do that song',' Rolie added. "I sang it then, which also was shocking to some Journey fans. 'I didn't know he was in Santana.' They didn't even know Neal was in Santana. History is a funny thing."

As engaging as this signature reunion was, Rolie said he loved an earlier performance much more. "Quite frankly, the sound check was it for me," Rolie said, "because I'm a one-take kind of guy. But then we went to play and it was stunning; the whole thing was just stunning." [375, 822, 823, 824, 825, 826]

SPRING–FALL 2023

NUGGETS

▶ The **Foo Fighters** had a surprise for fans at their Austin City Limits concert in October. **Dave Grohl** invited two-time rock hall of famer Gregg Rolie to play keyboards for "Oye Como Va." Rolie's family openly wondered if he would get asked to come onstage, and Rolie bet against it—and he lost.
—*UltimateClassicRock.com*

Schon Ships *Journey Through Time*, But There's a Problem

Before it became the subject of a deflating legal issue, **Journey Through Time**'s intimate February 2018 appearance at The Independent in San Francisco was many things to Gregg Rolie.

It gave him the chance to return to Journey's earliest era, when his collaborations with Neal Schon held sway. The chance to do some good, since the show benefited North Bay wildfire victims. The chance to work with Deen Castronovo, who sat in on drums while assuming the challenging job of singing in place of Steve Perry.

"I had a great time," Rolie told *Rolling Stone*. "First of all, I got to play with Deen and [bassist] **Marco [Mendoza]** along with Neal. I really connected to them. They are incredible players."

A live recording, simply titled *Journey*

Through Time, followed on May 19, 2023 on CD/DVD and Blu-ray formats from Frontiers Records. At last, fans could follow along as Rolie reignited Journey's rangy musical ambitions alongside Schon. At the same time, his duets with Castronovo harkened back to the balanced contrasts of Journey's first albums with Perry.

Castronovo sang these songs in their original keys too, without the use of an ear monitor. "Deen could always sing like that, but in **Hardline**, he was just a background singer," Castronovo's former bandmate **Johnny Gioeli** said. "It never fired a synapse in our head that, 'Hey, maybe Deen could cover a song.' It wasn't set up like that. True fact, though: The guy can sing. He's just immensely talented."

These songs dated back as far as Journey's self-titled debut, and more than one seemed to have been lost to history over the decades that followed. When Schon suggested that Journey Through Time return to "Daydream" from 1979's *Evolution*, Rolie did not even remember the song. "I went back and listened to it," he told *Rolling Stone*, "and went, 'Oh, I co-wrote it.'"

A short tour followed in 2019, but the Journey Through Time project seemed to have petered out when Schon confirmed this self-titled live project in March 2023, about a month after Rolie joined Journey onstage for a celebratory turn in Austin.

There was a problem: Rolie said Schon never got his permission to issue the recording.

Rolie's attorney, **Gary Stiffelman**, revealed in June that *Journey Through Time* had been "improperly released" in a letter about another matter to the Guitare en Scène Festival in Saint-Julien-en-Genevois, France. The correspondence from GSS Law in Tarzana, California, also said Rolie wanted to preserve the original show's fundraising intent.

"Mr. Rolie remains concerned that Mr. Schon is furthering the promotion of a Live Album and DVD Neal Schon released via Frontier[sic] records without obtaining appropriate licenses or permissions of the performing artists and songwriters/music publishing owners," Stiffelman wrote, "and without remuneration to the artists, or the intended beneficiary, a California wildfire victims relief fund, of the recorded 2018 event."

To this point, Neal Schon had been involved in legal matters with every major figure in Journey—except his original mentor, Gregg Rolie. Perhaps there was no other way for Journey's 50th year to go.

Unlike most of his fellow Journey songwriters, Rolie still controlled his own publishing. His signature would have been required before issuing more than a dozen of his co-written songs on *Journey Through Time*—including the first four.

Rolie also seemed to be keenly aware of how the *Journey Through Time* project had become a source of contention within the main band—and he wanted nothing to do with it. Rolie "intends to protect those works, the legacy and brand of 'Journey,' or his name and likeness from being used to harm or divide others," Stiffelman wrote.

The correspondence went on to reference the "already acrimonious and fractured relationship among Journey's remaining principals," while arguing that Journey has a "duty to their fans and legacy to unite and [not] further the band's division with acts of individual greed."

Stiffelman had initially gotten involved after Schon scheduled a similarly unauthorized Journey Through Time appearance at 2023's Guitare en Scène. Rolie said he had indicated to "Mr. Schon, Mrs. Schon, and all involved" in early June 2023 that he would not be appearing, in part over the "risk of deceiving fans."

Marketing materials, including at least one banner posted after Rolie contacted organizers, had "Journey" in a much larger font than "Through Time." Rolie told *The Wrap* that he had never confirmed his participation—"and still tickets were sold to good people under my good name, and under the name of Journey. That's not cool."

Rolie issued a cease-and-desist and the show was officially called off on June 23. Nevertheless, Stiffelman said Schon had reportedly been paid "at least $100,000" for the canceled appearance, while festivalgoers were stiffed. He added that Rolie had considered reaching out to "local counsel in France" if refunds were not granted. Meanwhile, Rolie told *The Wrap* that the issue with Frontiers Records was being dealt with "privately." [31, 37, 181, 616, 827, 830, 831, 832]

SORTING THE 'IT'S NOT JOURNEY WITHOUT STEVE PERRY' MENTALITY

Several networks had crammed into New York City's Times Square as excitement built on New Year's Eve.

Journey was to perform on *Dick Clark's New Year's Rockin' Eve*, prior to releasing 2022's *Freedom*—their fifth album without Steve Perry. Nearby, **Andy Cohen** was co-hosting CNN's *New Year's Eve Live* with **Anderson Cooper**.

Cohen came away decidedly unimpressed. "If it's not Steve Perry, it doesn't count!" he exclaimed to a cable broadcast audience. "You get it? It's not Journey!"

At that moment, Perry had not issued a single with Journey in more than 25 years, nor sung on stage with Neal Schon and Jonathan Cain in more than three decades. He had not toured with the band in 35 years.

Yet he still cast long shadows, even as Journey took part in one of pop culture's signature rites of passage.

A frustrated Schon said this endless fascination with Perry was simply exhausting. "I mean any time you change one person, it's not the same," he told *The Morning Call*. "It doesn't mean it's not good, though."

The long-tenured Arnel Pineda was nearing a notable milestone. He would soon serve as Journey's front man longer than all the others combined—including Perry. Along the way, Pineda's first LP with the band went platinum. He had sung on a Top 10 adult-contemporary hit single, a Top 20 AC hit, and another that just missed the Top 20.

Pineda also brought their legacy songs into a new century. "I've got to say, Arnel is so amazing because he does it every night and he's flawless," Deen Castronovo said. "He goes out there with both guns blazing, and I just watch him and I feel such appreciation. Like, man, how can you do that night after night after night and still sound great?"

Pineda's rags-to-riches life story inspired its own well-received documentary, while informing his interpretations of Journey's best-known songs.

"Who but Arnel should sing 'Don't Stop Believin',' with his story as a homeless boy in Manila?" Jonathan Cain said. "It shows the international appeal and the reach of that song. I mean, he heard that song thousands of miles away when he was a boy—and started learning it. We ended up taking a chance on a kid from far away, and he stepped up to the challenge. He's like a fine wine. He just keeps getting better."

Years turned into decades, and Perry never returned. For some, nothing else mattered. **Johnny Gioeli**, who had been bandmates with Schon, Castronovo, and **Todd Jensen** in the original incarnation of **Hardline**, said he remained conflicted. "Just like reforming Hardline: It's not Hardline," Gioeli said. "I'll be bluntly honest: Even though I have Hardline resurrected, it's not Hardline. I have the same feeling with Journey. It's great to hear those songs played again but to me, it's not Journey."

Perry had spent much of this time away in silence, finally releasing a solo album in 2018, nearly 25 years after his last. Then he began tinkering, releasing an acoustic version of his recently released third solo album, *Traces*, followed by a holiday record.

"I just think he's at a really good place in his life—and making music is only a small part of that," *Traces* co-producer **Thom Flowers** said. "He's really just making music because he enjoys it. There's no other real motive, other than just to go down in the studio and have some fun."

Perry did not mount a comeback tour, while consistently declining to sing with Journey again—even as they were inducted into the Rock & Roll Hall of Fame. His backstage meeting with Pineda at the event was described as a passing of the torch, but it felt more like a death knell.

"For all the sales and how many times they've played in a concert with or without him, I think something real cuts through—which is, like, this kid with a great voice who liked **Sam Cooke**, and who has some of that soul," former *Rolling Stone* writer and editor **David Wild** said. "There's something that happened in his relationship with Journey. Now we see, with all of these lawsuits, there's a lot of complicated feelings—but I don't think he could grin and fake anything. I think that's the only explanation for it."

Few expected that Perry could do justice to the old songs anyway. "I don't think he's hitting those notes anymore," former *San Francisco Chronicle* music writer **Joel Selvin** said, "and taking the keys down isn't really effective. You lower keys, and tremendous changes go on in the music. It doesn't have the same impact."

Schon, now the group's lone remaining original member, preferred to keep his eyes trained on the horizon. "Through time, I've replaced a lot of people," he told *The Indianapolis Star*. "A lot of them weren't easy to replace."

Still without Perry, Journey announced an extended 50th anniversary tour for 2024, again pairing up with **Toto**. Schon argued that "the majority of people, I believe, know the songs more than they know any of the musicians who are in the band."

Cohen begged to differ, and he was not alone. "It's not Journey!" he cried, looking directly into CNN's cameras. "No, that was not Journey. Steve Perry is Journey."

Pineda, like Steve Augeri before him, would never be forgiven for the original sin of not being Perry. It mattered little that his predecessor might not be able to sing the songs, even if Perry wanted to.

"The reason the songs translate around the world is, you feel it's not a joke or a contrivance for Steve Perry," Wild said. "Arnel is very good but you know, to be fair, he's a really good recreation of that soul. The soul of it carried to the Philippines. And you know, they're doing a good job of bringing that music onstage. Of course, it does not mean what it would mean to me if Steve Perry were in that band with Jonathan Cain. That'd be cool."

MOUSE & KELLEY

JOURNEY PROJECTS

Stanley Mouse and Mouse Studios, in cooperation with *Time Passages*, present a collection of illustrations, sketches, and conceptual drawings that Mouse and Alton Kelley developed specifically for Journey over the years. Although not a complete collection of art developed for the band, this selection offers readers a glimpse into the creative minds that helped build the visual identities of one of America's great rock bands.

All images reprinted with permission.
© Stanley Mouse & Mouse Studios.

Stanley Mouse and **Alton Kelley** were influential artists whose professional lives were deeply intertwined, impacting the counterculture and rock music scenes of the 1960s and beyond. Both born in 1940, Mouse in Fresno, California, and Kelley in Houlton, Maine, they found their way to the vibrant art and music scene in San Francisco during the early 1960s.

Their creative collaboration began when Mouse met Kelley while working on poster art for the Avalon Ballroom. Together, they created iconic poster art for bands like **The Grateful Dead**, **Big Brother and the Holding Company**, and **Jefferson Airplane**, becoming the in-house artists for the Avalon Ballroom and contributing to Family Dog Productions. Their distinctive style featured intricate lettering, bold colors, and psychedelic imagery, perfectly capturing the spirit of the counterculture movement.

In addition to poster art, Mouse and Kelley were well known for their album cover designs. They created memorable artwork for renowned bands such as The Grateful Dead, the **Steve Miller Band**, and Journey, helping shape the visual identity of these groups.

Their influence grew in 1967 when they, along with fellow artists **Rick Griffin** and **Victor Moscoso**, held the "Joint Show," showcasing their groundbreaking poster art. This exhibition solidified their status as key figures in the psychedelic art movement.

Although the 1960s ended, Mouse and Kelley's careers didn't. They continued to create art and contribute to the music scene through album covers and other projects, adapting to evolving artistic trends while retaining their unique style.

In the late 1970s, as Journey became more established in San Francisco's rock music scene, the band's bass player, Ross Valory, visited and saw the pair's design for the unreleased **Jimi Hendrix** album cover art, "Power of Soul."

Soon after, Journey had Mouse and Kelley working on Journey's upcoming album, *Infinity*. Released in late 1977, the beautifully intricate illustration featured an earth and moon set among multicolored wings and a surrounding infinity symbol spelling out the band name. Band manager **Herbie Herbert** believed the band had finally found a signature look. It was a huge step forward from the band's earlier cover designs.

For Journey's following album, 1979's *Evolution*, the artistic duo developed an intricate design that paid homage to their first design, *Infinity*, but incorporated a distinct color palette of green and blue hues. It would be the last project Mouse and Kelley teamed up on for Journey.

The band tapped Mouse to work solo on their next project—the artwork for their new greatest hits album, *In the Beginning*. That design closely followed the theme he and Kelley had developed for their first two projects with the band. Mouse considered the frisket-heavy blue and red design as the 'prettiest' of all Journey's album covers,

Journey worked with Kelley alone for their next studio album, *Departure*. The design featured a striking winged scarab in flight, symbolizing the band's ever-evolving music and journey through the music industry. The artwork mirrored the album's themes and the band's enormous growth.

Journey returned to Mouse for what became their biggest studio album ever, *Escape*. It was also easily the band's most recognizable cover. Adorned with their iconic scarab beetle bursting out of a planet, the illustration symbolized transformation and escape, aligning perfectly with the album's theme.

Later, Kelley would return to work with Journey on *Greatest Hits*, their second hits compilation, and Mouse would return to design the art for their *Time³* collection.

Kelley and Mouse, together and separately, demonstrated their ability to evolve their artistic style and adapt it to the ever-changing needs of Journey's signature look and visual identity.

POWER OF SOUL

ALTON KELLEY & STANLEY MOUSE

AIRBRUSH ON ACRYLIC BOARD

Jimi Hendrix commissioned Mouse and Kelley to develop a cover for his fourth album. Kelley and Mouse never worked directly with Hendrix during the creation of the unused cover image, though he and Mouse inadvertently met on an earlier occasion.

"Power of Soul" artwork was completed and ready for the cover, but Hendrix overdosed and died in September 1970; the album was not released. The artwork sat on a shelf for nearly a decade when Journey's Ross Valory visited Mouse and Kelley and saw the design. The illustrators had already worked on designs for Valory's previous band, Frumious Bandersnatch. Mouse and Kelley then began working on derivative concepts, and eventually the scarab became a fixture in nearly every Journey album design.

INFINITY & EVOLUTION

ALTON KELLEY & STANLEY MOUSE

AIRBRUSH ON ACRYLIC BOARD

Mouse and Kelley tag-teamed their way through the first two Journey albums. Their primary business, The Monster Company, was prolifically adding wings to T-shirts, posters, coffee mugs, decals, and more in a vast array of merchandizing in the 1970s and early 1980s. Journey's cover art for these albums reflected that trend. The designs for *Infinity* and *Evolution* were conceptually similar, incorporating brilliantly colored feathers with planets and moons, and Journey's newly ubiquitous Möbius Strip (the infinity symbol). Both designs required extensive frisket work, and those cutouts allowed for the airbrushed flourishes that gave the designs their signature appearance.

Evolution was the last Journey design Mouse and Kelley worked on together, though they would continue to work independently on

IN THE BEGINNING
STANLEY MOUSE

AIRBRUSH ON ACRYLIC BOARD

Mouse and Kelley parted amicably as partners in the early
1980s, but they continued to work with Journey separately.
Mouse was the first to do solo work for the band, creating
the frisket-heavy airbrushed cover for their first greatest hits
album, *In the Beginning*. Mouse said it was, in his opinion,
the prettiest of all the Journey covers.

DEPARTURE CONCEPT

STANLEY MOUSE

PENCIL SKETCH

Stanley Mouse worked up a cover concept for *Departure*
before the final project was given to Alton Kelley.

———

DEPARTURE

ALTON KELLEY

AIRBRUSH ON ACRYLIC BOARD

Journey chose Alton Kelley to design the cover for their fifth studio
album. It was significant for Kelley because up until this project,
he had been known primarily as an idea and layout guru, but not
necessarily an airbrush artist.

A DAY ON THE GREEN

STANLEY MOUSE

AIRBRUSH ON ACRYLIC BOARD

The design art that Mouse and Kelley developed for Journey wasn't restricted to album covers and sleeves. Posters were a key component of Mouse Studios' main work, so it aligned well when Journey was taking part in a major concert or benefit. Mouse developed the Day on the Green poster for the Bill Graham show at the Oakland Coliseum on July 27, 1980. It borrowed the soaring scarab that Alton Kelley designed for the *Departure* album. First prints of this poster are highly desired collectibles.

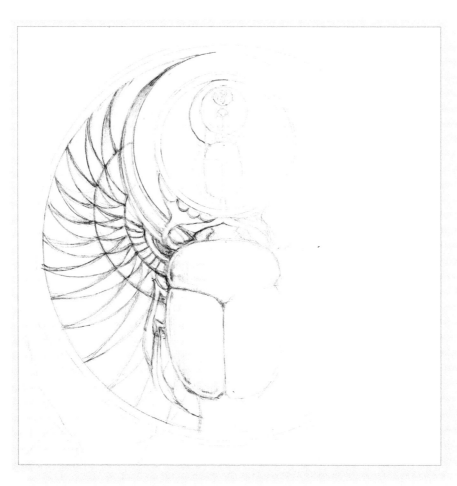

CAPTURED

STANLEY MOUSE

PENCIL SKETCH
AIRBRUSH ON ACRYLIC BOARD

One of Stanley Mouse's most intricate designs was the art for
Journey's double live album, *Captured*. There was a friendly rivalry
brewing between Mouse and his former partner, Alton Kelley.

The top sketch shows the original concept sketch for
the *Captured* design, and the two images below are the
final products, both finished using acrylic airbrush. Mouse said it
was dedicated to his wife and newborn child.

ESCAPE
STANLEY MOUSE

AIRBRUSH ON ACRYLIC BOARD

Perhaps the most recognizable illustration in the Journey canon,
Mouse switched gears on the scarab concept by turning the beetle
into a spaceship bursting out of a planet. Even today, it still appears
on T-shirts at concert venues, music stores, and retail outlets.

FRONTIERS ROBOT

STANLEY MOUSE

PENCIL SKETCHES

Sometimes Journey would solicit concept art for their upcoming albums from a variety of artists. Before Journey decided on the *Frontiers* art with the now-familiar blue Elmo alien, Stanley Mouse developed concept art for the band's consideration.

Mouse began his "robot" concept with a sketch drawing (opposite page, top) that kept the futuristic feel of Journey's earlier projects, including the scarab spaceship (below the robot's helmet), planets and orbs (in his hands and chest plate), the Möbius Strip (infinity symbol beneath the platform), and the feathered wings behind the robot that was borrowed from the *Captured* illustration. The second illustration incorporated the same elements, but placed the robot in a spacecraft's driver's seat rather than a throne.

FRONTIERS ROBOT
STANLEY MOUSE

AIRBRUSH ON ACRYLIC BOARD

A final concept rendering of Mouse's robot
was passed over by Journey, but many of the band's
symbols were incorporated into the design, including
the scarab spaceship from *Escape* (around the robot's
head), the Möbius Strip, and planets and orbs.

RAISED ON RADIO CONCEPTS

STANLEY MOUSE

CHALK ON BOARD

Mouse developed a few concepts for *Raised on Radio* that the band did not select as the final art. The design needed to incorporate images of old radio stations, towers, and possibly utilize a call sign of JRNY somewhere in the design. Mouse's second design (bottom left) added the call sign to the tower.

GREATEST HITS

ALTON KELLEY

———

Journey was in stasis in 1988 when Columbia Records released their *Greatest Hits* album. Alton Kelley was recruited to illustrate the cover for what would become a multiplatinum album. Kelley incorporated a colorful design and integrated the band's signature winged scarab along with two glowing orbs, but the Möbius Strip was missing.

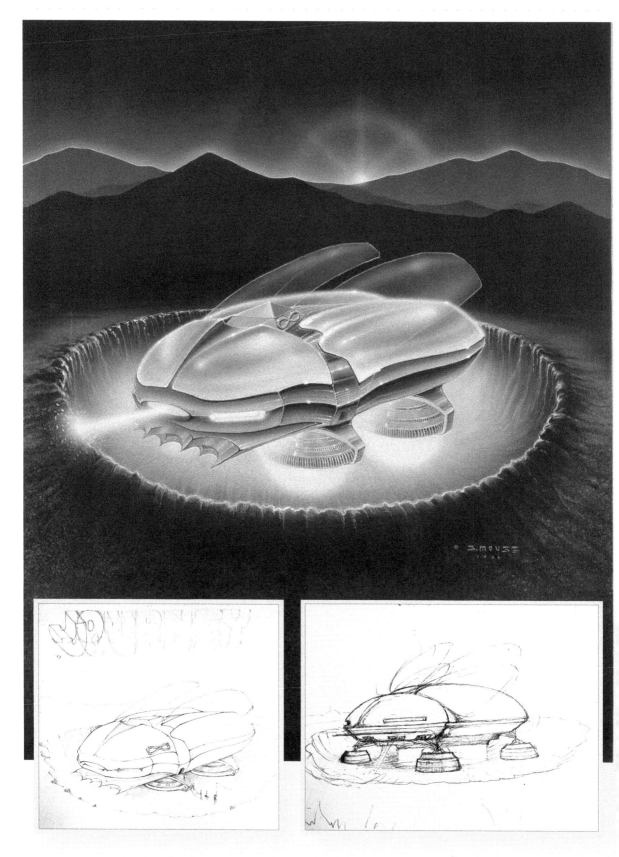

TIME³

STANLEY MOUSE

PENCIL SKETCHES
&
ACRYLIC ON BOARD

Journey released their *Greatest Hits* album in 1988, and it instantly became a Top 10 album. By 1992, expansive box sets had become popular—**Led Zeppelin**, **Crosby, Stills & Nash**, and **Aerosmith** all had recent successful box sets. Journey followed suit, reaching out to Stanley Mouse to develop theirs. His illustrations were designed around sketches of a scarab lander nestled inside a crater on another world (opposite page, bottom left). A refined version of that lander adorned the cover of the inside booklet, and a scarab vehicle with a drill cracking the surface of that world became the cover illustration.

MISCELLANEOUS DESIGNS

STANLEY MOUSE

PENCIL SKETCHES

Stanley Mouse developed many designs for Journey over the years. Some were ideas that were just drawn spontaneously, including various logo ideas (below), the scarab volcano design (opposite page, top) and the Journey "Encounter" illustration, an elaborate cover design that wasn't tied to any specific album project.

INDEX

BIBLIOGRAPHY

[1] DeRiso, N. (Mar. 20, 2011). Gregg Rolie, of Santana and Journey: Something Else! Interview, Something Else!.

[2] DeRiso, N. (Mar. 20, 2011). Gregg Rolie Discusses Santana, Journey and His Solo Career: Gimme Five, Something Else!

[3] DeRiso, N. (Jul. 10, 2011). Steve Smith, of Journey and Vital Information: Something Else! Interview, Something Else!.

[4] DeRiso, N. (Apr. 8, 2014). Neal Schon sparked the long-awaited Santana reunion: 'It's just going to be magical', Something Else!

[5] DeRiso, N. (Jul. 10, 2011). Gimme Five: Steve Smith on songs with Journey, Jean-Luc Ponty, Vital Information, Something Else!

[6] DeRiso, N. (May 9, 2012). Steve Smith celebrates 30 years of Vital Information: 'Always discovering new directions', Something Else!

[7] DeRiso, N. (Nov. 21, 2012). 'Not only a mentor, but a friend': Former collaborators remember late guitar hero Ronnie Montrose, Something Else!

[8] DeRiso, N. (Oct. 15, 2012). 'The kind of jamming we used to do': Neal Schon releases sizzling new video for title track of 'The Calling', Something Else!

[9] DeRiso, N. (Mar. 1, 2012). Journey bandmates Steve Smith and Neal Schon reunite, find 'an immediate chemistry', Something Else!.

[10] DeRiso, N. (Apr. 20, 2012). 'Ronnie's sound was huge': Steve Smith preps for Friday's all-star tribute concert to Montrose, Something Else!

[11] DeRiso, N. (Jul. 20, 2013). John Waite on 'Live: All Access,' the Babys, Bad English and going happily solo: Something Else! Interview, Something Else!

[12] DeRiso, N. (May 25, 2014). 'Just a bit more organic': After Journey tour, Neal Schon plans another solo project, Something Else!.

[13] DeRiso, N. (Apr. 25, 2014). 'We'll have to see': Busy Neal Schon unsure when Journey will return to the studio, Something Else!.

[14] DeRiso, N. (Jun. 15, 2014). 'He's like our hidden weapon': Neal Schon on the overlooked vocal talent of Journey's Deen Castronovo, Something Else!.

[15] DeRiso, N. (Jul. 15, 2014). Gimme Five: Neal Schon, Gregg Rolie + Steve Smith on Journey's 'Send Her My Love,' 'Anytime,' 'I'll Be Alright,' others, Something Else!.

[16] DeRiso, N. (Mar. 15, 2015). Partial Santana reunion gets under way early: 'We're off to a good start', Something Else!.

[17] DeRiso, N. (Jul. 20, 2013). John Waite on "Missing You," "Mr. Wonderful," "When I See You Smile" + others: Gimme Five, Something Else!

[18] DeRiso, N. (Jan. 22, 2022). Santana bassist Benny Rietveld: 2022 Interview, Time Passages.

[19] DeRiso, N. (Feb. 8, 2022). Former Journey frontman Jeff Scott Soto: 2022 Interview, Time Passages.

[20] DeRiso, N. (Oct. 15, 2016). How Journey Powered Up for Resurgent 'Trial by Fire,' Then Disintegrated, Something Else!.

[21] DeRiso, N. (Oct. 15, 2016). How Journey Powered Up for Resurgent 'Trial by Fire,' Then Disintegrated, Ultimate Classic Rock.

[22] DeRiso, N. (Jan. 19, 2018). Neal Schon Says Journey Are Ready to Move on After 'Hard Times', Ultimate Classic Rock.

[23] DeRiso, N. (Dec. 20, 2016). Journey's Neal Schon on Hall of Fame Reunion With Steve Perry: 'I'm Open to Everything', Ultimate Classic Rock.

[24] Miner, T. (Mar. 15, 2022). Tim Miner: Steve Perry Interview, Time Passages.

[25] Wikso, R. (Mar. 11, 2022). Ron Wikso: Gregg Rolie / Steve Smith interview, Time Passages.

[26] Phillips, R. (Feb. 28, 2022). Former Babys / Bad English bassist Ricky Phillips: 2022 Interview, Time Passages.

[27] Cain, J. (2018). Don't Stop Believin': The Man, the Band and the Song That Inspired Generations, pp. 18-19, Grand Rapids, United States: Zondervan.

[28] Cain, J. (2018). Don't Stop Believin': The Man, the Band and the Song That Inspired Generations, pp. 46-47, Grand. Rapids, United States: Zondervan.

[29] Cain, J. (2018). Don't Stop Believin': The Man, the Band and the Song That Inspired Generations, p. 81, Grand Rapids, United States: Vondervan.

[30] Prince, P. (Feb. 10, 2022). Former Journey drummer Prairie Prince: 2022 Interview, Time Passages.

[31] Mendoza, M. (Feb. 10, 2022). Journey Through Time bassist Marco Mendoza: 2022 Interview, Time Passages.

[32] Hamer, J. (Mar. 18, 2022). Jan Hammer: 2022 Interview, Time Passages.

[33] Lofgren, N. (Mar. 21, 2022). Nils Lofgren: 2022 Interview, Time Passages.

[34] Oates, J. (Mar. 20, 2022). John Oates: 2022 Interview, Time Passages.

[35] DeRiso, N. (Mar. 31, 2022). Michael Landau: Steve Perry Quote, Time Passages.

[36] Goodrum, R. (Apr. 7, 2022). Steve Perry Songwriting Collaborator Randy Goodrum: 2022 Interview, Time Passages.

[37] Gioeli, J. (Mar. 16, 2022). Neal Schon / Deen Castronovo collaborator Johnny Gioeli: 2022 Interview, Time Passages.

[38] Whitlock, B. (Mar. 30, 2022). Derek and the Dominos Cofounder Bobby Whitlock: 2022 Interview, Time Passages.

[39] Brock, T. (Apr. 7, 2022). Babys Drummer Tony Brock: 2022 Interview, Time Passages.

[40] DeRiso, N. (Apr. 18, 2022). Neal Schon collaborator Igor Len: 2022 Interview, Time Passages.

[41] DeRiso, N. (May 1, 2022). Journey collaborator Steve 'Keys' Roseman: 2022 Interview, Time Passages.

[42] Gil de Rubio, D. (Apr. 12, 2016). "Santana Reunites and it Feels So Good: Classic Lineup Comes Together for 'Santana IV',", Long Island Weekly.

[43] White, S. (Jun. 19, 2014). "Fans Don't Stop Believin' As Journey Makes Its Way to Mount Pleasant," The Saginaw News.

[44] Klein, H. (Feb. 16, 1979). "Let There Be Drums!" BAM.

[45] Herbert, H. (Jun. 1, 1978). No Longer an Uphill Road, Rolling Stone.

[46] Dunbar, A. (Jun. 1, 1978). "Journey: No Longer an Uphill Road," Rolling Stone.

[47] Barton, G. (Mar. 24, 1979). "Journey: Hold the (Balls on the) Line," Sounds.

[48] Robertson, S. (Aug. 4, 1979). "Journey: Do You Sincerely Want to Be Liked?" Sounds.

[49] Simmons, S. (Oct. 1, 1981). "Journey to the Centre of the AoRth," Kerrang!.

[50] Matera, J. (Mar. 1, 2002). "Gregg Rolie's Musical Journey," Mixdown.

[51] DiMartino, D. (Feb. 1, 2003). "Santana: In Search of Space," Mojo.

[52] Tobler, J. (Jan. 1, 1982). "The Record Producers," BBC Books.

[53] Ruggiero, B. (May 1, 2018). "Journey's Jonathan Cain: Still Believin' In Music and Other Higher Powers," Houston Press.

[54] DeMartino, D. (Sep. 1, 1982). "Journey as a Way of Life," Creem.

[55] DeRiso, N. (Mar. 22, 2022). Jan Hammer: 2022 Interview, Time Passages.

[56] Carty, M. (Jan. 1, 2001). "Castles Burning: The Herbie Herbert Interview," ESC4P3.com.

[57] Golland, D. (Jan. 8, 2003). "Jrnydv.Com's Exclusive Interview with Robert Fleischman," Journey Zone.

[58] Sullivan, S. (Mar. 1, 1997). An Interview With Abraxas Pool, Storm WWW Page.

[59] Fox, J.B. (Oct. 1, 1991). "Larrie Londin's Last Interview," Tech Trek.

[60] DeRiso, N. (May 12, 2022). San Francisco Chronicle Music Critic Joel Selvin: 2022 Interview, Time Passages.

[61] James, G. (Sep. 1, 1991). "Gregg Rolie and Ross Valory Interview: The Storm," Famous Interviews.

[62] Cavacini, M. (Jul. 23, 2021). Jonathan Cain On New Music, Journey, Steve Perry & The Lord, michaelcavacini.com.

[63] Selvin, J. (Feb. 4, 1974). "Journey's Smashing Blastoff," San Francisco Chronicle.

[64] Selvin, J. (Mar. 16, 1975). "Tubbs, Fourth Power Vocalist," San Francisco Chronicle.

[65] Hartlaub, P. (Jul. 28, 2021). "The Ultimate Journey San Francisco Timeline," San Francisco Chronicle.

[66] Selvin, J. (Jun. 5, 1977). "Journey is on a Brand New Trip," San Francisco Chronicle.

[67] Selvin, J. (Sep. 11, 1977). "The Tube Show at Art Sake," San Francisco Examiner.

[68] Selvin, J. (Oct. 30, 1977). "The Night the Studio Burned," San Francisco Examiner.

[69] Selvin, J. (Oct. 29, 1978). "Rock Journey Into Stardom," San Francisco Examiner.

[70] Selvin, J. (Jul. 1, 1979). "Brief Pit Stop for Journey," San Francisco Examiner.

[71] Selvin, J. (Mar. 2, 1980). "Datebook: Journey," San Francisco Examiner.
[72] Selvin, J. (Jun. 15, 1980). "Lively Arts: Aynsley Dunbar," San Francisco Examiner.
[73] Selvin, J. (May 2, 1982). "Lively Arts: Journey," San Francisco Examiner.
[74, 75] Selvin, J. (Jun. 20, 1982). "Journey to the Top: The Man Behind it All," San Francisco Chronicle.
[76] Selvin, J. (Nov. 7, 1982). "Rock Hits Video Games," San Francisco Chronicle.
[77] Selvin, J. (May 29, 1983). "The Game it Out, Concert's On," San Francisco Chronicle.
[78] Hunt, D. (May 13, 1984). "Journey's Perry Takes a Step on His Own," Los Angeles Times.
[79] Selvin, J. (Nov. 11, 1984). "Journey Bands Together for the Big Studio Trek," San Francisco Chronicle.
[80] Pappademas, A. (May 29, 2008). "Foolish, Foolish Throat: A Q&A with Steve Perry," GQ.
[81] Rhyner, M. (Jul. 14, 1983). "Journey Reaches Desired Destination," Independent Press Service.
[82] Campbell, M. (May 21, 1978). "Journey's Trip Has Been Backwards," Associated Press.
[83, 84] Vickers, T. (Jan. 24, 1976). "Journey's Long Road: From Santana to Space Rock," Billboard.
[85] Kallmalm, C. (May 11, 2011). "The Complete Story of Journey," Hallowed Magazine.
[86] Angelloz, T. (Feb. 26, 2009). "Tribute Band's Frontman Describes His Amazing Journey," Houma Today.
[87] Muir, R. (Feb. 1, 2012). "Conversation with Jeremey Frederick Hunsicker," Fabrications.
[88] Angelloz, T. (Feb. 27, 2009). "Tribute Band's Frontman Describes His Amazing Journey," Houma Today.
[89] DeKnock, J. (Jun. 10, 1984). "Hagar and Schon: When Two Top Rockers Join Forces," Chicago Tribune.
[90] Sherman, L. (Nov. 18, 1983). "Supergroups Makes Debut," Santa Cruz Sentinel.
[91] Britt, B. (Oct. 17, 1988). "Movies Are a Means to an End for Loggins," Los Angeles Daily News.
[92] Fessier, B. (Oct. 20, 1989). "Kenny Loggins: On His Own," Palm Springs Daily Sun.
[93] Bream, J. (Jan. 21, 1983). "Loggins Evolves in Music Adventure," Minneapolis Star and Tribune.
[94] Andrews, C. (May 20, 1976). "Rock's Best-Known Unknown," Albuquerque Journal.
[95] King, B. (Mar. 16, 1983). "Journey Moves Into the Video Age," Atlanta Constitution.
[96] Monitor, L. (Jun. 15, 2001). "Still Journey-Ing On," Birmingham Post-Herald.
[97] Kaye, R. (Jun. 20, 1979). "Journey Bassist Valory Earned His Way to the Top," Fort Worth Star-Telegram.
[98] LaBua, J. (Nov. 19, 1998). "Band Finally Makes Journey to Quad-Cities," Quad-City Times.
[99] Fox, D. (Jul. 27, 2001). "Journey Blows Through Utah on 'Arrival' Tour," The Daily Herald.
[100] Selvin, J. (Jun. 8, 1986). "Journey May Be Year's Rock Comeback Story," San Francisco Examiner.
[101] Condran, E. (Jun. 27, 2019). "Augeri on Journey to 4thfest," Cedar Rapids Gazette.
[102] Stout, A.K. (Jul. 9, 2001). "Replacement Vocalist Steve Augeri's Journey is Complete," Knight-Ridder Newspapers.
[103] Lowry, T. (Jun. 11, 1999). "Enthusiastic Fans Help Journey Keep Its Edge," Thomson News Service.
[104] Paiva, D. (Oct. 22, 2004). "Journey Rescues Vocalist from the Gap," Honolulu Advertiser.
[105] Hughes, M. (Sep. 2, 1999). "Journey Has Existed in Many Forms," Lansing State Journal.
[106] Rios, V. (Dec. 10, 1998). "Even with a New Singer, The Song Remains the Same," Knight-Ridder Newspapers.
[107] Goldstein, S. (Dec. 7, 2012). "Steady Journey," Honolulu Star-Advertiser.
[108] Liberatore, P. (Jan. 10, 2008). "New Singer's Journey Starts on YouTube," Green Bay Press-Gazette.
[109] Fong-Torres, B. (Jul. 13, 1980). "Manager Puts Journey on Road to Success," Rolling Stone.
[110] Burlingame, B. (Oct. 15, 1998). "Retired Roadie Sings the Blues," Honolulu Star-Bulletin.
[111] Tucker, K. (May 4, 1986). "Journey Goes Its Own Way: No Interviews or Videos," Philadelphia Inquirer.
[112] Albee, C.H. (May 6, 1992). "Rolie Back with a Storm," Gannett News Service.
[113] Everett, T. (Feb. 15, 1987). "Journey Hits Road to Back Hit Album," King Features Syndicate.
[114] Swenson, J. (May 27, 1978). "Journey: It's Been a Long One," Rolling Stone.
[115] Leary, S. (Nov. 22, 1998). "New Journey Leads Band to Q-C," Moline Dispatch.
[116] Wosahla, S. (Apr. 27, 1978). "In the Groove: Journey," Messenger-Press.
[117] Press-Enterprise. (Sep. 20, 2002). "It's Been an Eventful Trip for Classic Rock Group Journey."
[118] Considine, J. (Oct. 1, 1981). "Hard Pop, Suburban Rock," Musician.
[119] Gill, A. (Mar. 1, 1995). "Santana: 'Santana'," Mojo.
[120] Tobler, J. (Jan. 1, 1983). "The Guitar Greats," BBC Books.
[121] Frost, D. (Oct. 29, 1981). "Journey: 'Escape'," Rolling Stone.
[122] Ruggiero, B. (May 24, 2001). "Party on, Dude: Rock Package Tours," Houston Press.
[123] Bell, M. (Dec. 28, 1974). "Santana: Latin Limbo Dancing Over Hot Coals," NME.
[124] Goldberg, M. (Oct. 13, 1983). "San Francisco Rocks Again," Rolling Stone.
[125] Goldberg, M. (Jul. 7, 1983). "Take the Money and Run," Rolling Stone.
[126] Trakin, R. (Jun. 30, 1994). "Is There Life After Rock Guitar Godhead?" Musician.
[127] Gill, A. (Sep. 1, 1999). "Carlos Santana: Interview," Mojo.
[128] Goldstein, T. (Sep. 1, 1979). "The Babys' Playground Politics," Creem.
[129] Doherty, H. (May 19, 1979). "The Babys: Bringing Up Babys," Melody Maker.
[130] Vaziri, A. (Jul. 28, 2021). "How Journey Survived Another Lineup Change," San Francisco Chronicle.
[131] Rolling Stone. (Dec. 3, 2010). "100 Greatest Singers of All Time."
[132] Alexander, B. (Jan. 25, 2008). "Randy Jackson Weighs in on New Journey Singer," People.
[133] Seemayer, Z. (Feb. 18, 2021). "Randy Jackson on Giving Advice to Simon Cowell," Entertainment Tonight.
[134] Atad, C. (Jan. 19, 2021). "Paula Abdul and Randy Jackson Talk About Their 40-Year Friendship," Entertainment Tonight.
[135] Columbia Records. (Apr. 1, 1986). "Raised on Radio: 1986 Tour Documentary."
[136] Graff, G. (Sep. 3, 2013). "Sammy Hagar, 'Bad on Fords and Chevrolets'," Billboard.
[137] Flans, R. (Aug. 1, 1987). "Journey's Mike Baird," Modern Drummer.
[138] DeRiso, N. (Oct. 3, 2014). "Journey's First Top 20 Hit Was Released 35 Years Ago," Something Else!
[139] Shapiro, M. (2000). Back on Top, pp. 86-87, New York City, United States: St. Martin's Press.
[140] Shapiro, M. (2000). Back on Top, p. 114, New York City, United States: St. Martin's Press.
[141] Shapiro, M. (2000). Back on Top, p. 120, New York City, United States: St. Martin's Press.
[142] Shapiro, M. (2000). Back on Top, p. 124, New York City, United States: St. Martin's Press.
[143] Shapiro, M. (2000). Back on Top, p. 128, New York City, United States: St. Martin Press.
[144] Shapiro, M. (2000). Back on Top, p. 129, New York City, United States: St. Martin's Press.
[145] Seay, D. (Jul. 20, 1979). "Robert Fleischman: From Journeyman to Perfect Stranger," BAM Magazine.
[146] Mattingly, R. (May 1, 1982). "Aynsley Dunbar: Modern Drummer Interview," Modern Drummer.
[147] Mattingly, R. (May 1, 1982). "Aynsley Dunbar: Modern Drummer Interview," Modern Drummer.
[148] Secher, A. (Jun. 1, 1983). "Journey: Adventures in Frontierland," Hit Parader.
[149] Sutton, R. (Oct. 1, 1984). "Street Talkin' With Steve Perry," Song Hits.
[150] Greenwald, T. (Nov. 1, 1986). "Jonathan Cain: The Long and Winding Journey," Keyboard Magazine.
[151] DeRiso, N. (Jun. 11, 2022). Former Journey Frontman Steve Augeri: 2022 Interview, Time Passages.
[152] Fernbacher, J. (Jun. 1, 1983). "Meltdown, Anyone?" Creem.

[153] Stern, C. (Sep. 1, 1983). "Microphones Don't Get No Respect," Creem.
[154] Creem. (Dec. 1, 1984). "Rock 'n' Roll News: December 1984."
[155] Ciofi, B. (Sep. 1, 1987). "The Journey of Randy Jackson," Creem.
[156] Kordosh, J. (Feb. 1, 1985). "John Waite, For Me," Creem.
[157] Wise, M. (Aug. 17, 2003). "Faithfully, A Look Back in Wonder," The New York Times.
[158] Singer, K. (Nov. 10, 2005). "Hold on to That Feelin': Journey Still Plays Fan Faves," The Star News.
[159] KHON. (Feb. 23, 2017). "Journey Band Members Reflect on Special Connection to Hawaii."
[160] Blackstone, J. (Jun. 1, 2008). "A Journey Back," CBS.
[161] The Courier Mail. (Dec. 22, 2012). "Journey's Search for New Frontman Didn't Stop Their Music."
[162] Levy, P. (Sep. 26, 2012). "Documentary Chronicles Unknown Singer's Rise Into Journey," Milwaukee Journal Sentinel.
[163] Liberatore, P. (Jan. 11, 2008). "YouTube Tape Lands Filipino a Dream Gig as New Journey Singer," Marin Independent Journal.
[164] Pierce, S. (Sep. 30, 2013). "Cinderella Tale of Journey's Filipino Lead Singer is Fascinating," St. Louis Tribune.
[165] Brooks, B. (Mar. 7, 2013). "Specialty Preview: 'Don't Stop Believin': Everyman's Journey'," Deadline.
[166] Goldmine Magazine. (Mar. 23, 2008). "Veteran Santana, Journey Keyboardist Gregg Rolie Hits the Road Again."
[167] Freeman, P. (Jun. 22, 2011). "Gregg Rolie: His Musical Journey Continues," The Mercury News.
[168] Seigal, B. (May 30, 1995). "If Santana's Roots Can Be Found, Abraxas Says it Knows Where," Los Angeles Times.
[169] Journey, N. (1992). Album Credits/Liner Notes: Time3.
[170] Alexander, B. (Mar. 21, 2016). "Original Santana Band Reborn in Las Vegas," USA Today.
[171] BrunoCeriottiWeebly.com, Ceriotti, B. (Dec. 28, 2019). Frumious Bandersnatch: Day-by-Day Diary, Retrieved from http://brunoceriotti.weebly.com/frumious-bandersnatch.html.
[172] Ceriotti, B. (Dec. 28, 2018). "Frumious Bandersnatch: Day-By-Day Diary," Bruno Ceriotti Weebly.
[173] Whiting, S. (Oct. 26, 2021). "Herbie Herbert, Co-Creator of Journey and Manager of Santana, Dies at Home in Orinda at 73," San Francisco Chronicle.
[174] Wright, J. (Jun. 1, 2003). "Gregg Rolie Interview: Classic Rock Revisited," Classic Rock Revisited.
[175] DeRiso, N. (Jun. 23, 2022). Frumious Bandersnatch Guitarist David Denny, Time Passages.
[176] Shapiro, M. (2000). Back on Top, pp. 106-107, New York City, United States: St. Martin's Press.
[177] Derrough, L.M. (Apr. 14, 2017). "Newest Rock and Roll Hall of Fame Inductee Gregg Rolie Talks Past and Present," Glide Magazine.
[178] Shapiro, M. (2000). Back on Top, p. 125, New York City, United States: St. Martin's Press.
[179] Shapiro, M. (2000). Back on Top, p. 126, New York City, United States: St. Martin's Press.
[180] Masley, E. (May 9, 2016). "Interview: Neal Schon on Journey, Santana, Steve Perry and More," Arizona Republic.
[181] Greene, A. (Nov. 21, 2019). "Gregg Rolie Looks Back on His Days with Santana, Journey, And Ringo Starr," Rolling Stone.
[182] Varga, G. (Jun. 18, 2012). "Gregg Rolie: From Santana to Ringo, Via Poway," San Diego Union-Tribune.
[183] Roth, K. (Mar. 1, 2003). "Neal Schon Melodic.Net Interview," Melodic.net.
[184] Lee, D. (Jun. 11, 2003). "Jonathan Cain Interview with Electric-Basement.Com," Electric Basement.
[185] Mills, M.J. (Oct. 3, 2003). "Interview with Jonathan Cain," San Bernardino County Sun.
[186] Schwartz, M. (Jun. 13, 2007). "'Sopranos' Finale Has Perry 'Believin' In Chase," Entertainment Weekly.
[187] CBC. (Jul. 20, 2009). "Journey Song Cements Status as Cultural Touchstone."
[188] Uitti, J. (Dec. 15, 2021). "Behind the Song Lyrics: 'Don't Stop Believin'' By Journey," American Songwriter.
[189] Katsilometes, J. (Nov. 9, 2014). "Santana's Journey Might Well Include Journey," Las Vegas Sun.
[190] Ferguson, J. (Jun. 14, 2012). "Gregg Rolie 'Thrilled' To Join the All Starrs," LNP.
[191] Shapiro, M. (2000). Back on Top, p. 136, New York City, United States: St. Martin's Press.
[192] Goldberg, M. (Feb. 21, 1980). "Carlos Santana's Journey Toward Perfection," Rolling Stone.
[193] Iwasaki, S. (Aug. 6, 1999). "Journey on Road to Top with Hot New Singer," Deseret News.
[194] Sinclair, D. (Oct. 1, 1990). "Santana: Beam Me Up!" Q magazine.
[195] Diggins, M. (Feb. 9, 2013). "The Rockpit," Interview: Ross Valory – Journey.
[196] Spera, K. (Jun. 8, 2017). "Never-Ending Journey: Bassist Ross Valory and Bandmates Plan to Keep Playing the Hits," The Times-Picayune.
[197] Policarpio, A. (May 20, 2013). "Arnel Pineda: Journey to Go on a Hiatus," Philippine Daily Inquirer
[198] Graff, G. (Aug. 15, 2017). "Journey's Backstage Drama 'Was Not Evident at All' On Tour," Billboard.
[199] Stevens, S. (Aug. 6, 2016). "Journey's Jonathan Cain: Why He Won't Stop Believin'," Parade.
[200] Phillips, C. (Sep. 30, 2013). "'Don't Stop Believin'': The Film-maker's Journey," PBS.
[201] Amador, R. (Aug. 26, 2016). Bass Musician Magazine Interviews Ross Valory, Bass Musician.
[202] (Sep. 21, 2012). Journey Guitarist on 'Don't Stop Believin'' Origins, Fuse.
[203] (Jul. 21, 2015). Power Ballad Group Get Their Own Star on the Walk of Fame, AP.
[204] Greene, A. (Jan. 26, 2021). "Journey Frontman Arnel Pineda on the Band's New Record, Dreams of a Steve Perry Reunion," Rolling Stone.
[205] Bream, J. (Jul. 25, 2018). "Journey Bandmates Put Politics Aside for Stadium Tour," Minneapolis Star-Tribune.
[206] Weinstein , N. (2009). Carlos Santana: A Biography, p. 48, Westport, United States: Greenwood Press.
[207] Wright, J. (Jun. 1, 2003). "Gregg Rolie Interview with Classic Rock Revisited," Classic Rock Revisited.
[208] Jones, K.L. (Aug. 17, 2017). "As Journey's History Shows, Infighting is Business as Usual," KQED.
[209] Huff, D. (Sep. 1, 1979). "The Journey Has Only Begun," Jam Magazine.
[210] McDonough, J. (Jul. 12, 1980). "The Carefully Plotted Route to Rock's Summit," Billboard.
[211] Abrams, R. (Apr. 1, 2017). "Gregg Rolie: The Journey Continues," Island Zone Update.
[212] Anderson, D. (Sep. 30, 2021). "Neal Schon: The Music Journey," Guitar Connoisseur.
[213] Serba, J. (Nov. 6, 2012). "Journey's Jonathan Cain Talks Legacy of 'Don't Stop Believin'," The Grand Rapids Press.
[214] Gold, J. (Jun. 2, 2021). "Neal Schon on Finding His Voice as an Instrumentalist," Guitar Player.
[215] Greene, A. (Mar. 5, 2020). "Flashback: Journey Fire Bassist Ross Valory, Drummer Steve Smith in 1985," Rolling Stone.
[216] Spears, S. (Mar. 19, 2011). "Steve Perry, Randy Jackson Talk Journey Reunion," Tampa Bay Times.
[217] Edwards, G. (Mar. 1, 1990). "Walk on the Wild Side," Spin.
[218] Reesman, B. (Mar. 1, 2002). "Kevin Shirley: Mix Interview," Mix.
[219] Jennings, S. (Oct. 1, 2001). "Roy Halee: Mix Interview," Mix.
[220] Matera, J. (Mar. 1, 2002). "Gregg Rolie's Musical Journey," Mixdown.
[221] Bosso, J. (Dec. 1, 2010). "Producer Kevin Shirley on Joe Bonamassa, Iron Maiden, Led Zeppelin," Music Radar.
[222] Burgess, M. (May 3, 2006). "Interview with Ross Valory (Journey)," Metal Express.
[223] Ryan, M. (Apr. 19, 2012). "Journey's 'Separate Ways' Video: The Band Speaks," Huffington Post.
[224] Frost, (Oct. 24, 2016). "Superproducer Kevin Shirley: My 12 Career-Defining Records," Music Radar.
[225] Reesman, B. (Oct. 21, 2016). "The Big Journey Reunion That Kind of Happened, And What Might Have Been," The New York Observer.
[226] Lanham, T. (Sep. 1, 2016). "Guitar Great Neal Schon Journeys On," San Francisco Examiner.
[227] Dial, J. (Jun. 9, 2004). "Journey Keeps Fans Believing in Classic Rock," San Diego Union-Tribune.
[228] Lynn, C. (Nov. 3, 2015). "Castronovo: 'I've Let Everybody in the Community Down'," The Statesman-Journal.
[229] Iwasaki, S. (Jul. 11, 2008). "Don't Stop Believing in Journey; The New Lead Singer Fits Right In," The Deseret News.
[230] Karasinski, C.F. (Jul. 29, 2011). "Journey Drummer Deen Castronovo is Living the Dream," The Flint Journal.

[231] Condran, E. (Jun. 5, 2014). "Far from Over: Journey Has Come a Long Way," The Courier-Post.
[232] Sculley, A. (Sep. 27, 2012). "Some Have Stopped Believing in Journey," The Virginian-Pilot.
[233] (Jan. 1, 1982). Record Producers, BBC.
[234] Cain, J. (Nov. 2, 2018). A Better Man: The Faith Journey of Jonathan Cain, Zondervan.
[235] Journey, (Feb. 1, 1983). Frontiers & Beyond! Marvin Glass & Associates.
[236] Herbert, H. (Jul. 30, 1984). Walter 'Herbie' Herbert: Music of the Night, Music Vault.
[237] Journey, (Feb. 15, 1980). Journey: 1980 Tour Documentary, Blue Jean Network.
[238] Conniff, T. (Jun. 4, 1999). "Journey's Winding Road to Its New Tour," Tampa Bay Times.
[239] Cash Box. (Jul. 5, 1975). "Cash Box Singles Reviews."
[240] Masley, E. (May 9, 2016). "Interview: Neal Schon on Journey, Santana, Steve Perry and More," The Arizona Republic.
[241] Cain, J. (2018). Don't Stop Believin', p. 159, Grand Rapids, United States: Zondervan.
[242] Lindblad, P. (Apr. 29, 2013). "Trace the Musical 'Journey' Of Guitarist Neal Schon," Goldmine.
[243] DeRiso, N. (May 13, 2022). Power Station Frontman Michael Des Barres, Time Passages.
[244] Diaz, R., "Ross Valory is the Institutional Memory of Journey," (Film/Video)
[245] Milkowski, B. (May 1, 2003). "Steve Smith: Confessions of an Ethnic Drummer," Modern Drummer.
[246] Patterson, R. (Mar. 1, 2011). "Jonathan Cain: Interview," Boomerocity.
[247] Cain, J. (2018). Don't Stop Believin': The Man, the Band, and the Song That Inspired Generations, p. 120, Grand Rapids, United States: Zondervan.
[248] Rockline. (May 1, 1985). "Steve Perry Answers Your Questions."
[249] Coleman, D. (Aug. 24, 2018). "Jean-Luc Ponty Reunites with '70s and '80s Collaborators on Current Tour," NJArts.
[250] Selvin, J. (Oct. 31, 1977). "Journey Into the Future," San Francisco Chronicle.
[251] Selvin, J. (Oct. 3, 1977). "Journey Into the Future," San Francisco Chronicle.
[252] Lamarche, M. (Oct. 6, 1977). "Journey at the Waldorf," Stanford Daily.
[253] Pappademas, A. (Sep. 5, 2018). "Steve Perry Walked Away from Journey. A Promise Finally Ended His Silence.," New York Times.
[254] Ferrara, L. (Nov. 3, 2011). "Steve Perry Says Journey Reunion Not Likely," Associated Press.
[255] Wardlaw, M. (Sep. 29, 2012). "Journey's Neal Schon Finds 'the Calling' With New Solo Album," Ultimate Classic Rock.
[256] Parks, J. (Mar. 24, 2012). "Ex-Journey, Vinnie Vincent Invasion Singer Robert Fleischman Talks About the Journey, The Invasion and the Sky," Legendary Rock Interviews.
[257] Fleischman, R. (Aug. 1, 2017). Sheldon Snow: Robert Fleischman Interview, Sheldon Snow.
[258] Wardlaw, M. (Dec. 7, 2020). "Steve Perry Admits Van Halen 'Cleaned Our Clocks' On Journey Tour," Ultimate Classic Rock.
[259] Wardlaw, M. (May 21, 2012). "Journey's Neal Schon Recalls the Rise of Eddie Van Halen," Ultimate Classic Rock.
[260] Green, A. (Oct. 19, 2020). "Steve Perry Looks Back on Touring with Van Halen," Rolling Stone.
[261] Ivey, D. (Jul. 5, 2022). "The Most Joyous and Romantic of Journey, According to Neal Schon," Vulture.
[262] Sharp, K. (May 13, 2015). "Q&As with Steve Lukather and Gregg Rolie on Ringo Starr's All-Starr Band," Rock Cellar.
[263] Cain, J. (2018). Don't Stop Believin': The Man, the Band, and the Song That Inspired Generations, p. 136, Grand Rapids, United States: Zondervan.
[264] Rotter, J. (Jul. 30, 2004). "Evolution, Continued," The (Stockton, Calif.) Record.
[265] Mouse, S., "Stanley Mouse on Creating Journey's Beetle Image," (Film/Video)
[266] Edgars, G. (May 22, 2015). "Meet the Artist Who Invented the Grateful Dead's Skull and Roses Logo," Washington Post.
[267] Arrington, C. (May 13, 1980). "Steve Perry Evolves from Yeoman Rocker to Journey-Man," Circus.
[268] Cherry Lane (2006). Open Arms: The Steve Perry Anthology, p. 4, NewYork City, United States: Cherry Lane
[269] Stix, J. (2006). Open Arms: The Steve Perry Anthology, p. 4, New York City, United States: Cherry Lane.
[270] Stix, J. (2006). Open Arms: The Steve Perry Anthology, p. 10, New York City, United States: Cherry Lane.
[271] Stix, J. (2006). Open Arms: The Steve Perry Anthology, p. 12, New York City, United States: Cherry Lane.
[272] Stix, J. (2006). Open Arms: The Steve Perry Anthology, p. 14, New York City, United States: Cherry Lane.
[273] Stix, J. (2006). Open Arms: The Steve Perry Anthology, p. 16, New York City, United States: Cherry Lane.
[274] Stix, J. (2006). Open Arms: The Steve Perry Anthology, p. 18, New York City, United States: Cherry Lane.
[275] Stix, J. (2006). Open Arms: The Steve Perry Anthology, p. 20, New York City, United States: Cherry Lane.
[276] Stix, J. (2006). Open Arms: The Steve Perry Anthology, p. 22, New York City, United States: Cherry Lane.
[277] Shasho, R. (2020). The Rock Star Chronicles: Truths, Confessions and Wisdom From the Music Legends That Set Us Free, p. 356, Pennsauken Township, United States: BookBaby.
[278] Hagar, S. (2012). Red: My Uncensored Life in Rock, p. 141, New York City, United States: It Books.
[279] McIver, J. (Jul. 19, 2022). "Journey Man," Bass Player.
[280] Gold, J. (Mar. 6, 2021). "The Body Electric," Guitar Player.
[281] Miller, J.M. (Jul. 12, 2022). "Makin' Tracks: Neal Schon," Guitar World.
[282] Bosso, J. (Jan. 14, 2020). "My Career in Five – No, Six – Songs," Guitar Player.
[283] Flans, R. (Aug. 1, 1986). "Steve Smith: Interview," Modern Drummer.
[284] DeRiso, N. (Oct. 31, 2016). "How Journey Powered Up for 'Trial by Fire,' Then Disintegrated," Ultimate Classic Rock.
[285] Wilmington Star-News. (Jul. 29, 1979). "Rowdy Crowd Leaves 1 Dead Before Concert."
[286] Smith, T.L. (Jun. 17, 2020). "Revisiting the World Series of Rock 1979 In All Its Insanity and Greatness," Cleveland Plain Dealer.
[287] New York Times. (Jul. 29, 1979). "Youth is Killed as Crowd Gathers for Rock Concert."
[288] Diaz, R., "Ross Valory is the Institutional Memory of Journey by Ramona Diaz," (Film/Video)
[289] Singer, K. (Nov. 9, 2005). "Hold on to That Feelin': Journey Still Plays Fan Faves," The Star News.
[290] Waddell, R. (Nov. 8, 2011). "Journey's Road to Billboard Legend of Live Award: A Candid Q&A with Neal Schon," Billboard.
[291] Turner, G.K. (Sep. 1, 1986). "Duck Soup: Journey, 'Raised on Radio'," Creem.
[292] Benson, J. (Jan. 7, 2020). "Why Steve Perry Didn't Like Journey's 'Captured' Album," Ultimate Classic Rock.
[293] Benson, J. (May 27, 2019). "Steve Perry Recalls Ac/DC Opening for Journey: 'They Spanked Us Bad'," Ultimate Classic Rock.
[294] Gray, A. (Aug. 28, 2017). "The Babys Return to Ohio, The State Where it Ended," Tribune Chronicle.
[295] Langerman, K. (Jul. 31, 2009). "Of a Lifetime: An Exclusive Interview with Legendary Santana, Journey Vocalist Gregg Rolie," Nightwatcher's House of Rock.
[296] Wright, J. (Aug. 4, 2018). "Jonathan Cain: Believin' Now ... More Than Ever Before," Classic Rock Revisited.
[297] Wardlaw, M. (May 3, 2017). "Journey Drummer Steve Smith Talks Rock Hall, Steve Perry and Upcoming Vegas Run," Las Vegas Weekly.
[298] Caine, J., "I Am Second: Jonathan Cain," (Film/Video)
[299] Perry, S. (Aug. 11, 2022). Rock Classics Radio: Steve Perry, Apple Music Hits.
[300] DeRiso, N. (Mar. 18, 2022). Jan Hammer: 2022 Interview, Time Passages.
[301] Perry, S. (May 21, 1984). Bill Graham Archives: Steve Perry, Bill Graham Archives.
[302] Hunt, D. (Oct. 27, 1985). "Jan Hammer Scores a Hit," Los Angeles Times.
[303] DeRiso, N. (Jun. 21, 2022). MTV's Martha Quinn: 2022 Interview, Time Passages.
[304] Spears, S. (Apr. 12, 2007). "Loving Kenny Loggins," Tampa Bay Times.
[305] Loggins, K. (1997). Album Credits/Liner Notes: 'Yesterday, Today, Tomorrow'.
[306] Doerschuk, B. (Jun. 15, 1983). "Jan Hammer, 'Here to Stay': Review," Keyboard Magazine.

[307] Anderson, D. (Jan. 28, 1983). "The Powerhouse Partnership of Neal Schon and Jan Hammer," Buffalo Evening News.
[308] Skuce, L. (Jan. 1, 1982). "Keyboard Phenomenon Jan Hammer and His Electric Rendezvous Tour," San Diego People Magazine.
[309] Rolling Stone: Europe. (Feb. 1, 1982). "'Die Rolling Stone-Platte Des Jahres 1981 (The Rolling Stone Record of 1981)'."
[312] Baltin, S. (Jul. 6, 2022). "Q&A: Neal Schon on the 'Freedom' Of Journey, His Friendship with Carlos Santana and Much More," Forbes.
[313] Hunt, D. (Jun. 1, 1984). "Solo Album Sets Perry Free," Faces.
[314] Bowcott, N. (Oct. 3, 2008). The Setlist: Neal Schon of Journey, Guitar World.
[315] Marks, C. (2012). I Want My MTV: The Uncensored Story of the Music Video Revolution, p. 65, New York City, United States: Plume.
[316] Wardlaw, M. (May 3, 2017). "Journey Drummer Steve Smith Talks Rock Hall, Steve Perry and Upcoming Vegas Run," Las Vegas Weekly.
[317] Krueger, A. (Mar. 20, 2018). "WCSX Classic Cuts : Only the Young," WCSX.
[318] Cain, J. (2018). Don't Stop Believin': The Man, the Band, and the Song that Inspired Generations, pp. 186-187, Grand Rapids, United States: Zondervan.
[319] Journey, N. (1992). Album Credits/Liner Notes: Time³.
[320] Rosenthal, G., "Behind the Music: Journey," (Film/Video)
[321] Cain, J. (2018). Don't Stop Believin': The Man, the Band and the Song That Inspired Generations, p. 61, Grand Rapids, United States: Zondervan.
[322] Benitez-Eves, T. (Sep. 10, 2021). "Behind the Song: \"Faithfully\" By Journey," American Songwriter.
[323] MacIntosh, D. (Nov. 10, 2016). "Jonathan Cain of Journey: Interview," Songfacts.
[324] Record World. (Jul. 12, 1975). "Single Picks: Journey, \"To Play Some Music\"."
[326] Bensoua, J. (May 10, 1975). "Pop, \"Journey\"," San Pedro News-Pilot.
[327] Ragusa, L. (May 10, 1975). "Journey Jumps in with Solid Sounds," Record World.
[328] Bishop, P. (Apr. 6, 1975). "Something Good," The Pittsburgh Press.
[329] Diana, M. (Sep. 7, 1975). "Hear Say: Journey," Newport News Daily Press.
[330] The (San Mateo, Calif.) Times. (Apr. 10, 1974). "Legal Notices: Fictitious Business Name Statement, Journey."
[331] Elwood, P. (Sep. 14, 1974). "Santana, Journey Open Winterland Rock Year," The San Francisco Examiner.
[332] The San Francisco Examiner. (May 25, 1975). "George Tickner, Rhythm Guitarist for McNeice."
[333] Hosie, E. (Feb. 20, 1976). "Journey, ElO Reviewed: A Second Effort Comes Closer," The Berkeley Gazette.
[334] Andrews, C. (May 20, 1976). "Rock's Best-Known Unknown," Albuquerque Journal.
[335] Rudis, A. (Feb. 19, 1977). "Journey Scores 2nd Time Around," Chicago Sun-Times.
[336] Smith, S. (Sep. 22, 1979). "Revised Journey is Taking New Routes," Knight-Ridder News Service.
[337] Robinson, L. (Mar. 27, 1980). "Rock Talk: Musical Adventures of Journey's Neal Schon," The Durham (N.C.) Sun.
[338] Kawashima, D. (Jun. 22, 2020). "Hall of Fame Songwriter Randy Goodrum Talks About His Classic Hits," Songwriter Universe.
[339] Wiser, C. (Oct. 22, 2008). "Interview: Randy Goodrum," Songfacts.
[340] McCullaugh, J. (Oct. 29, 1977). "Soud Tracks," Billboard.
[341] Baker, R.T., "Roy Thomas Baker on Working with Queen, The Cars, Journey, Foreigner," (Film/Video)
[342] McCullaugh, J. (Oct. 29, 1977). "Studio Track," Billboard.
[343] Billboard. (Jan. 21, 1978). "Full-Page Ad: Journey, Infinity."
[344] Record World. (Jan. 22, 1978). "Journey, Infinity."
[345] Record World. (Feb. 4, 1978). "Full-Page Ad: Journey, Infinity."
[346] Billboard. (Feb. 11, 1978). "Billboard Front-Page Ad, Infinity."
[347] Record World. (Mar. 11, 1978). "Single Picks: \"Wheel in the Sky\"."
[348] Billboard. (Mar. 18, 1978). "New Singer Speeds Journey LP Sales."
[349] Billboard. (Jun. 3, 1978). "Top Singles Picks: Journey, \"Any-time\"."
[350] Billboard. (Jul. 8, 1978). "Full-Page Ad: Journey, Infinity (Radio)."
[351] Cashbox. (Jul. 15, 1978). "East Coastings/Points West."
[352] Billboard. (Jul. 15, 1978). "Full-Page Ad: Journey, Infinity (Zep-pelin)."
[353] Billboard. (Aug. 5, 1978). "Top Single Picks: Journey, \"Lights\"."
[354] Cashbox. (Dec. 16, 1978). "Full-Page Ad: Journey, Infinity (Plat-inum)."
[355] Cashbox. (Mar. 31, 1979). "Cashbox Album Reviews: Journey, Evolution."
[356] Billboard. (Mar. 31, 1979). "Billboard Top Album Reviews: Journey, Evolution."
[357] Cashbox. (Apr. 7, 1979). "Full-Page Ad: Journey, Evolution."
[358] Gardner, E. (Sep. 14, 2012). "Producer Sues Sony Music Over Revenue from Journey Songs," The Hollywood Reporter.
[359] Selvin, J. (Oct. 30, 1977). "Lively Arts: The Night the Studio Burned," The San Francisco Examiner.
[360] Bream, J. (Jan. 5, 1978). "Pop-Music Record Producer 'Puts it All Together'," Minneapolis Star.
[361] Atkinson, R. (Jan. 22, 1978). "Journey Turns Corner," The (Hackensack, N.J.) Recordq.
[362] Olivere, M. (Apr. 20, 1979). "Journey's De-Evolution," The (Urbana, Ill.) Daily Illini.
[363] Bishop, P. (May 31, 1979). "Rock: A Gratifying Journey," The Pittsburgh Press.
[364] Smith, S. (Jun. 15, 1979). "Popular Record Review: Journey, Evolution," The Shreveport (La.) Journal.
[365] Spies, M. (Jun. 22, 1979). "Journey Journies Here for Sunday Concert," Corpus Christi Times.
[366] Robinson, L. (Jun. 28, 1979). "Journey: Steve Perry Helped Push Group Into World of Gold," Field News Service.
[367] Frolick, J. (Jun. 30, 1979). "Riffs: Journey Onward," Austin (Tex.) American-Statesmen.
[368] Record World. (Jan. 31, 1976). "Record World, Album Picks: Journey, Look Into the Future."
[369] Record World. (Mar. 25, 1978). "The Singles Chart: Journey, \"Wheel in the Sky\"."
[370] Cashbox. (Mar. 11, 1978). "Cashbox Singles Feature Picks: Journey, \"Wheel in the Sky\"."
[371] Cashbox. (Jun. 3, 1978). "Cashbox Singles Feature Picks: Journey, \"Anytime\"."
[372] Teverbaugh, K. (Mar. 22, 1981). "'Captured' Is a Must for Journey Fans," The (Muncie, Ind.) Star-Press.
[373] Marymont, M. (Nov. 10, 1996). "Journey: Trial by Fire," The Springfield (Mo.) Star-Ledger.
[374] Smith, A. (Jul. 31, 1983). "More Holleder Busses for the Journey Home," Democrat and Chronicle.
[375] DeRiso, N. (Mar. 14, 2023). "Journey Reunion Stirs 50 Years of Memories for Gregg Rolie," Ultimate Classic Rock.
[376] McNeice, A. (Mar. 1, 2008). Herbie Herbert: One Man's Journey, Melodic Rock.
[377] Goldmine Staff, (Apr. 29, 2013). "Trace the Musical 'Journey' of Guitarist Neal Schon," Goldmine Magazine.
[378] Lindblad, P. (Apr. 29, 2013). "Trace the Musical 'Journey' Of Guitarist Neal Schon," Goldmine Magazine.
[379] Lindblad, P. (Apr. 30, 2013). "Santana or Slowhand? That's the Choice Neal Schon Had to Make," Goldmine Magazine.
[380] Shapiro, M. (2000). Back on Top, p. 108, New York City, United States: St. Martin's Press.
[381] Epstein, D.M. (Jul. 1, 2010). "Interview with Pete Sears," DMME.
[382] Selvin, J. (Oct. 8, 2001). "Peter Sears: Starship Veteran Back on Course," San Francisco Chronicle.
[383] Cashbox. (Jul. 5, 1975). "Picks of the Week: Journey."
[384] Waddell , R. (Nov. 8, 2011). "Journey's Road to Billboard Legend of Live Award: A Candid Q&A with Neal Schon," Billboard.
[385] Cavacini, M. (Sep. 26, 2015). "A Conversation with Neal 'Vortex' Schon," MichaelCavacini.com.
[386] Fong-Torres, B. (Jul. 12, 1980). "Journey: The Platinum Game Plan," Rolling Stone.
[387] Seigal, B. (May 30, 1995). "If Santana's Roots Can Be Found, Abraxas Says it Knows Where," Los Angeles Times.
[388] Tarquin, B. (Feb. 15, 2009). "Neal Schon Has His 'I on U'," Premier Guitar.
[389] Rising, A. (Sep. 1, 2008). "Conversation with Ross Valory," Charlotte Magazine.
[390] DeRiso, N. (Jan. 20, 2015). "Journey Began Unlikely Shift to Pop Stardom with Arrival of Steve Perry: 'I Welcomed It'," Something Else!

[391] Donevan, C. (Oct. 3, 2018). "Steve Perry's New Life: 'I've Rediscovered the Passion for Music'," NPR.
[392] Anderson, D. (Sep. 30, 2021). "Neal Schon: The Music Journey," Guitar Connoisseur
[393] Lewry, (Oct. 19, 2020). "Steve Perry Clarifies Infamous Van Halen Guacamole Incident," Classic Rock.
[394] DeRiso, N. (Apr. 17, 2023). Music Historian Ted Gioia: Time Passages Interview, Time Passages.
[395] Hill, M. (Apr. 20, 1976). "Journey Into the Future: Faith in Themselves Marks Trip Into Progressive Rock," Baltimore Evening Sun.
[396] Cashbox. (Oct. 6, 1979). "New Faces to Watch: The Scorpions."
[397] Kelp, L. (Feb. 27, 1981). "Journey's New LP Documents World Tour," Oakland Tribune.
[398] Teverbaugh, K. (Mar. 22, 1981). "'Captured' Is a Must for Journey Fans," Muncie (Ind.) Star-Press.
[399] Secher, A. (Jun. 7, 1981). "Group Finds Success Despite Changes," Asbury Park Press.
[400] Simmons, S. (Oct. 1, 1981). "Journey to the Centre of the AoRth," Kerrang!!.
[401] Van Matre, L. (Aug. 30, 1981). "Journey to the Top 10: Changes, Challenges Along the Rock Road," Chicago Tribune.
[402] Farkesh, M. (Jan. 21, 1983). "Journey Still Trekking Down Touring Road," Simi Valley (Ca.) Star.
[403] Tobler, J. (Jan. 1, 1982). "The Record Producers," BBC.
[404] Dion, M. (May 2, 1986). "Tuned in: EndTv? Journey Says No to Videos," Daily Hampshire Gazette.
[405] DeRiso, N. (Mar. 10, 2023). Gregg Rolie Bandmate Josh Ramos: Time Passages Interview, Time Passages.
[406] Parks, J. (Mar. 24, 2012). "Legendary Rock Interview with Ex-Journey, Vinnie Vincent Invasion Singer Robert Fleischman (The Sky)," Legendary Rock Interviews.
[407] DeRiso, N. (Apr. 28, 2023). "Jonathan Cain Looks Back as Journey's 50th Anniversary Dates End," Ultimate Classic Rock.
[408] DeRiso, N. (Mar. 27, 2023). "How Tragedy and Triumph Sparked Deen Castronovo's Comeback," Ultimate Classic Rock.
[409] Wolfgang's. (Apr. 10, 2021). "Journey & Friends."
[410] DeRiso, N. (Apr. 21, 2023). Radio Executive John Gorman: Time Passages Interview, Time Passages.
[411] DeRiso, N. (Apr. 20, 2023). Rolling Stone Contributing Editor David Wild: Time Passages Interview, Time Passages.
[412] DeRiso, N. (Jun. 10, 2022). Styx Singer Lawrence Gowan: Time Passages Interview, Time Passages.
[413] Cioffi, B. (Jul. 1, 1987). "Prairie Prince, Mike Baird and the Art of Drumming," Creem.
[414] Goldberg, M. (Apr. 1, 1979). "Truth About 'Evolution': Journey's Road," Crawdaddy.
[415] Spears, S. (Sep. 15, 2011). "Greg Kihn Pulled Brutal Joke on Journey's Steve Perry," Tampa Bay Times.
[416] Snow, S. (Aug. 1, 2017). Robert Fleischman Interview, Eye on Jamz Radio.
[417] NBC. "Stanley Mouse on Creating Journey's Beetle Image," (Film/Video)
[418] San Francisco Art Exchange. (Sep. 1, 1970). "Image of Unused Jimi Hendrix Album Cover."
[419] Fort Worth Business Press. (May 22, 2015). "Grateful Dead Logo Creator Looks Back on a Long, Strange Trip."
[420] Sullivan, S. (Nov. 1, 2014). "Jim Welch: Exclusive Interview," Journey WWW Page.
[421] Crespo, C. (Jul. 1, 1981). "Journey: A Small Circle of Friends," Hit Parader.
[422] Graff, G. (Apr. 27, 2023). "Deen Castronovo Explains How Journey Keeps it Together on Stage," Ultimate Classic Rock.
[423] Kielty, M. (Jan. 7, 2020). "Why Steve Perry Didn't Like Journey's 'Captured' Album," Ultimate Classic Rock.
[424] Waddell, R. (Nov. 8, 2011). "Journey's Road to Billboard Legend of Live Award: A Candid Q&A with Neal Schon," Billboard.
[425] Robinson, L., "Steve Perry of Journey 1984 Interview," (Film/Video)
[426] Flick, L. (Sep. 28, 1996). "Reviews & Previews: Journey, Trial by Fire," Billboard.
[427] Newman, M. (Oct. 5, 1996). "Columbia's Journey Gets Warm Welcome at Radio," Billboard.
[428] Newman, M. (Mar. 15, 1997). "The Beat," Billboard.
[429] Graff, G. (Apr. 26, 2016). "Why Prince Asked for Journey's Blessing Before Releasing 'Purple Rain'," Billboard.
[430] Falleti, R. (Jul. 31, 2018). "Journey is Coming to Columbus: Exclusive Interview," City Scene.

[431] Cummings, H. (Aug. 1, 1979). "The Outspoken Irreverent Roy Thomas Baker," Recording Engineer Producer Magazine.
[432] Barton , G. (Apr. 8, 2014). "Steve Perry Remembers Journey's 'Wheel in the Sky'," Classic Rock Magazine.
[433] Dreyfuss, A. (Mar. 29, 2013). "Don't Stop Believing," Richmond Magazine.
[434] Anderton, C. (Apr. 1, 1980). "A Session with Journey," Modern Recording.
[435] DeRiso, N. (May 23, 2023). Video Producer/Journalist Paul Flattery: Time Passages Interview, Time Passages.
[436] The Telegraph. (Jan. 23, 2023). "Bruce Gowers, Director Who Blazed a Trail with Music Videos from Queen's Bohemian Rhapsody to Peter Kay – Obituary."
[437] Patterson, E. (Oct. 31, 2015). "How Queen's 'Bohemian Rhapsody' Pop Video Almost Ended Up on the Cutting Room Floor," The Mirror.
[438] Cashbox. (Oct. 19, 1991). "Music Reviews: The Storm."
[439] Selvin, J. (Jun. 28, 1982). "Journey's Home Run in Oakland," San Francisco Chronicle.
[440] Selvin, J. (Dec. 24, 1978). "The Chair Went Out the Window," San Francisco Chronicle.
[441] Wardlaw, M. (Aug. 21, 2014). "Sammy Hagar and Neal Schon's Forgotten Team-Up: The History of HsAs," Ultimate Classic Rock.
[442] DeRiso, N. (Feb. 8, 2020). "How a Leftover Song Changed Journey Forever," Ultimate Classic Rock.
[443] Wardlaw, M. (May 21, 2012). "Journey's Neal Schon Recalls the Rise of Eddie Van Halen and the Birth of 'Don't Stop Believin'," Ultimate Classic Rock.
[444] Daniels, N. (2011). Don't Stop Believin': The Untold Story of Journey, p. 68, London, United Kingdom: Omnibus Press.
[445] Secher, A. (Sep. 1, 1983). "Journey: Riding High," Hit Parader.
[446, 447, 448] Secher, A. (Jun. 1, 1983). "Adventures in Frontierland," Hit Parader.
[449] Greene, A. (Oct. 17, 2018). "13 Things We Learned Hanging Out with Steve Perry," Rolling Stone.
[450] Blush, S. (2016). New York Rock, p. 122, Duxbury, United States: Griffin Publishing.
[451] Bosso, J. (May 31, 2011). "Journey's Neal Schon Talks New Album 'Eclipse,' 'the Sopranos,' Guitars and Gear," Music Radar.
[452] Winwood, I. (Oct. 5, 2018). "Don't Stop Believin': Steve Perry on Fame, Journey and That Song," Kerrang!.
[453] Wiser, C. (Oct. 12, 2008). "Randy Goodrum Interview: Oh Sherrie," Songfacts.
[454] Flans, R. (May 1, 1986). "On the Cover: Craig Krampf," Modern Drummer.
[455] Journey, "Holiday Greetings from Journey," (Film/Video)
[456] Spears, S. (Nov. 27, 2011). "S. Perry: The Voice," Tampa Bay Times.
[457] Platania, M. (Sep. 30, 2019). "Back in the Spotlight: Retired Rock Photographer Adds Some Shine to Short Pump Side Gig," Richmond Business Scene.
[458] Nobleman, M.T. (Jul. 13, 2013). "The Girl in the Video: \"Separate Ways (Worlds Apart)\" (1983) And \"Oh Sherrie\" (1984)," Noblemania.
[459] DeRiso, N. (Mar. 31, 2022). Steve Perry Guitarist Michael Landau: Time Passages Interview, Time Passages.
[460] Bosso, J. (Mar. 21, 2023). "Session Veteran Waddy Wachtel Reveals His Top Six Career-Defining Tracks," Guitar Player.
[461] Bream, J. (Jul. 25, 2018). "How Journey's Neal Schon Found Out Prince Was a Fan of His," Star-Tribune.
[462] Kielty, M. (Dec. 30, 2020). "How Neal Schon Completed a Circle with His 'Purple Rain' Cover," Ultimate Prince.
[463] Greenwald, T. (Nov. 1, 1986). "The Long and Winding Journey," Keyboard Magazine.
[464] Cain, J. (2018). Don't Stop Believin': The Man, the Band, and the Song That Inspired Generations, p. 186, Grand Rapids, United States: Zondervan.
[465] Derrough, L.M. (Apr. 17, 2017). "Newest Two-Time Rock and Roll Hall of Fame Inductee Gregg Rolie Talks Past and Present," Glide Magazine.
[466] Daniels, N. (2011). Don't Stop Believin': The Untold Story of Journey, p. 22, London, United Kingdom: Omnibus Press.
[467] D'Agostino, R. (Jun. 24, 2020). "'We Are the World': Inside Pop Music's Most Famous All-Nighter," Esquire.
[468] Cain, J. (2018). Don't Stop Believin': The Man, the Band and the Song that Inspired Generations, p. 194, Grand Rapids, United States: Zondervan.

[469] Orlando Sun-Sentinel. (Nov. 14, 1986). "New, Improved Journey Back on Stage."

[470] DeRiso, N. (Apr. 9, 2020). "How Journey Helped Bryan Adams Reach No. 1 With 'Heaven'," Ultimate Classic Rock.

[471] Vallance, J. (May 27, 2004). "Heaven by Bryan Adams and Jim Vallance," JimVallance.com.

[472] Arnold, C. (Oct. 28, 2022). "Bryan Adams Reveals Stories Behind Hits from 'Heaven' To 'Summer of '69'," New York Post.

[473] McIver, J. (Aug. 31, 2022). "Randy Jackson on His Return to Journey," Bass Player.

[474] (Oct. 1, 1984). "Street Talkin': An Exclusive Interview with Journey's Steve Perry," Song Hits.

[475] Billboard. (Sep. 24, 1983). "Frontiers and Beyond."

[476] Billboard. (Sep. 24, 1983). "Frontiers and Beyond."

[477] Billboard. (Sep. 24, 1983). "Rise of the Nightmare Family."

[478] Cee, G. (Jul. 1, 1986). "Journey and Van Halen Nix Videos," Circus.

[479] Ahrens, S. (Apr. 1, 1977). "Journey Begins Climb Up," Circus.

[480] Arthur, G. (Jan. 1, 1985). "Good Timing Greets Sammy Hagar at Last," Circus.

[481] Fuchs, A. (Feb. 2, 1980). "Journey's Manager Takes Care of Growing Business," Cash Box.

[482] Vanity Fair. (Sep. 28, 2021). "Steven Van Zandt on Making, And Ending, 'the Sopranos'."

[483] Power, E. (May 27, 2020). "The Immortal Power of Journey's 'Don't Stop Believin'," The Telegraph.

[484] Record World. (Oct. 10, 1981). "Opening for the Rolling Stones."

[485] PinkPop.org. (Jun. 8, 2003). "Pink Pop 1978."

[486] Sounds. (May 27, 1978). "Richman Rouses Dozy Dutch."

[487] Daniels, N. (2011). Don't Stop Believin': The Untold Story of Journey, p. 79, London, United Kingdom: Omnibus Press.

[488] Modern Recording. (Apr. 1, 1980). "S. Perry on Recording Vocals."

[489] Cain, J. (2018). Don't Stop Believin': The Man, the Band and the Song That Inspired Generations, p. 188, Grand Rapides, United States: Zondervan.

[490] Cain, J. (2018?). Don't Stop Believin': The Man, the Band and the Song That Inspired Generations, p. 192, Grand Rapides, United States: Zondervan.

[491] Cain, J. (2018). Don't Stop Believin': The Man, the Band and the Song That Inspired Generations, p. 193, Grand Rapids, United States: Zondervan.

[492] dutchcharts.nl. (Aug. 26, 2016). "Dutch Charts."

[493] offiziellecharts.de. (Mar. 26, 2019). "German Charts."

[494] officialcharts.com. (Feb. 23, 2015). "UK Charts."

[495] Loder, K. (Nov. 12, 1981). "The Stones' Sloppy Start," Rolling Stone.

[496] Discogs. (Nov. 1, 2000). "Journey - Raised on Radio."

[497] Gett, S. (Apr. 26, 1986). "No Video for Journey Album," Billboard.

[498] Gett, S. (Apr. 26, 1986). "No Video for Journey Album," Billboard.

[499] Billboard. (Nov. 17, 2021). "Journey Chart History."

[500] Michellini, G., "Rockline: Journey, Raised on Radio," (Film/Video)

[501] Kaufman, R. (Jul. 5, 2006). "Portuguese Radio Station Stands the Test of Time," Valley Voice Newspaper.

[502] Orlando Sun-Sentinel. (Nov. 14, 1986). "New Improved Journey Back on Stage."

[503] Gett, J. (Oct. 25, 1986). "Journey Glad to Be on Long and Winding Tour Road," Billboard.

[504] Songfacts. (Feb. 8, 2023). "Suzanne, By Journey."

[505] Melodic Rock. (May 7, 2014). "Steve Perry: The Melodic Rock Interview."

[506] Compuserve. (Jul. 1, 1995). "Neal Schon Q&A."

[507] Prince, P. (Mar. 20, 2016). "Prairie Prince Bio," PrairiePrince.com.

[508] del Barco, M. (Nov. 14, 2012). "A&M Records: Independent, With Major Appeal," NPR.

[509] Amendola, B. (May 1, 2006). "Prairie Prince: An Interview," Modern Drummer.

[510] Cioffi, B. (Jun. 1, 1987). "Prairie Prince, Mike Baird and the Art of Drumming," Creem.

[511] Popson, T. (Oct. 3, 1986). "The Long and Winding Trail to the Making of a New Video Clip," Chicago Tribune.

[512] FanAsylum.com. (Dec. 13, 2006). "Steve Perry: Fans Asylum Q&A."

[513] Pappademas, A. (Sep. 5, 2018). "Steve Perry Walked Away from Journey; A Promise Finally Ended His Silence," The New York Times.

[514] Schlanger, T. (Sep. 21, 2018). "Steve Perry Makes His Return," NPR.

[515] Orlando Sentinel. (Nov. 25, 1994). "Journey Singer Makes Return After 7-Year Break from Road."

[516] Elliott, P. (Sep. 12, 2012). "Neal Schon: Q&A," Classic Rock.

[517] Billboard. (Nov. 19, 2021). "Journey: Chart History."

[518] RIAA.com. (Jan. 10, 2016). "Journey – Gold and Platinum: RiAa."

[519] McIntyre, H. (Jan. 28, 2020). "Journey's 'Greatest Hits' Is the Third Album in History to Hit 600 Weeks on the Billboard 200," Forbes.

[520] Caulfield, K. (Mar. 1, 2018). "Journey's 'Greatest Hits' Becomes Only Third Album to Spend 500 Weeks on Billboard 200 Chart," Billboard.

[521] Graff, G. (Jan. 10, 2012). "Don't Stop Believin': Journey Frontman Works on New Album After Long Hiatus," News-Herald.

[522] Britt, B. (Sep. 4, 1991). "Will Steve Perry's Journey Continue?" Tampa Bay Times.

[523] McIntyre, H. (Feb. 23, 2022). "Journey's Fans Have Never Stopped Believing: The Band Makes History on Billboard's Albums Chart," Forbes.

[524] Graff, G. (Jan. 4, 2012). "Steve Perry Won't Stop Recording, But Touring is Another Story," Billboard.

[525] Journey Force. (Apr. 1, 1988). "Journey Force: One on One with Neal Schon."

[526] Cahoon, K. (May 5, 1988). "Mick Jagger Tour Rolls in Japan," Rolling Stone.

[527] Melodic Rock. (Sep. 10, 2018). "MelodicRock.Com Interviews: Neal Schon."

[528] James, G. (Sep. 27, 2007). "Gregg Rolie and Ross Valory Interview: The Storm," FamousInterview.ca.

[529] Wagner, D. (Mar. 1, 2006). "And the Journey Continues," Pop Entertainment.

[530] Monitor, L.A. (Jun. 15, 2011). "Still Journey-Ing On," Birmingham Post-Herald.

[531] Cavacini, M. (Jun. 29, 2014). "A Conversation with Jonathan Cain – Part 1," MichaelCavacini.com.

[532] Giles, J. (Jun. 26, 2015). "How Journey and Babys Alumni Rose and Fell in Bad English," Ultimate Classic Rock.

[533] Erlich, N. (Apr. 3, 1976). "Talent in Action: Journey," Billboard.

[534] Billboard. (Apr. 24, 1976). "DC-9 Promo Flight Plugs Columbia's Journey Group."

[535] Billboard. (Apr. 24, 1976). "DC-9 Promo Flight Plugs Columbia's Journey Group."

[536] Cashbox. (May 1, 1976). "Journey's Night Flight in Atlanta."

[537] Swenson, J. (Jun. 12, 1980). "Journey: Departure Album Review," Rolling Stone.

[538] Daniels, N. (2011). Don't Stop Believin': The Untold Story of Journey, p. 30, London, United Kingdom: Omnibus Press.

[539] Kubernik, H. (Jul. 10, 1976). "Concert Review: The Originals at the Civic," Record World.

[540] Mayer, I. (Jan. 15, 1977). "New York, N.Y.: Not Such Odd Couples," Record World.

[541] Mayer, I. (Jan. 15, 1977). "Not Such Odd Couples," Record World.

[542] Record World. (Feb. 4, 1978). "Journey, Infinity Advertisement."

[543] Zimmerman, D. (Nov. 1, 1979). "Journey's Aggression with Feelings," Hit Parader.

[544] Hit Parader. (Nov. 1, 1982). "Journey: Special Delivery."

[545] Los Angeles Times. (May 30, 1976). "Event Calendar."

[546] Sandler, A. (May 20, 1992). "Bryan Adams; The Storm: Concert Review," Variety.

[547] Sparks, R. (Apr. 1, 2006). "The Party's Over: An Interview with Journey Mastermind Herbie Herbert," Classic Rock Revisited.

[548] Star-Phoenix. (Aug. 9, 1974). "Nightlife: Privilege."

[549] Nicks, G. (May 6, 2019). "The Story of Journey Singer Steve Perry and Edmonton Rock Band Privilege," HicksBiz.

[550] Powers, N. (Aug. 10, 1974). "Privilege Ready to Invade East on Wings of New Single," Star-Phoenix.

[551] Hicks, G. (May 6, 2019). "The Story of Journey Singer Steve Perry and Edmonton Rock Band Privilege," HicksBiz.

[552] Hartlaub, P. (Aug. 30, 2016). "Journey's Schon Returns to San Francisco Roots," SFGate.

[553] Fan Asylum. (Jan. 21, 2011). "Steve Perry: Fan Asylum Q&A."

[554] Winwood, I. (Oct. 25, 2018). "Don't Stop Believin': Steve Perry on Fame, Journey and That Song," Kerrang!.

[555] KevinChalfant.com. (Feb. 28, 2006). "Kevin Chalfant: Biography."

[556] Illinois Entertainer. (Oct. 1, 2010). "Hello, My Name is Kevin."

[557] Fronters.it. (Jul. 25, 2010). "Two Fires: Burning Bright."

[558] Cavacini, M. (Jul. 5, 2014). "A Conversation with Jonathan Cain – Part 2," MichaelCavacini.com.

[559] Cain, J. (2018). Don't Stop Believin': The Man, the Band and the Song That Inspired Generations, p. 229, Grand Rapids, United States: Zondervan.
[560] AOL. (Apr. 19, 1993). "AoL Interview with Ross Valory of the Storm."
[561] McNeice, A. (May 7, 2014). "Steve Perry: A Legend Finds Peace," Melodic Rock.
[562] Rosen, C. (Jun. 11, 1994). "Retail's Open Arms Greet Steve Perry," Billboard.
[563] Selvin, J. (Mar. 28, 1980). "Journey's Steady Road to Success," San Francisco Chronicle.
[564] Ling, D. (Aug. 1, 1994). "Steve Perry: Raw Magazine Interview," Raw Magazine.
[565] Flans, R. (Aug. 1, 1995). "Moyes Lucas: The Right Man for the Job," Modern Drummer.
[566] Hartford Courant. (Feb. 8, 1995). "Steve Perry Returns to the Stage."
[567] Iwasaki, S. (Jan. 16, 1995). "Years Vanish as Perry Takes Cheering Crowd on a Journey," Deseret News.
[568] The Morning Call. (Nov. 12, 1994). "Steve Perry at Stabler: Mindless But Enjoyable."
[569] DeBoer, T. (May 14, 2009). "Lincoln Brewster's Journey of Faith Brings Him to Grandville," The Grand Rapids Press.
[570] Burke, D. (Aug. 29, 2013). "Brewster Trades Rock Star Life for Christian Success," Quad-City Times.
[571] Augusto, T.J. (Dec. 18, 1994). "Steve Perry: Concert Review," Variety.
[572] Wardlaw, M. (Sep. 25, 2012). "Journey Guitarist Neal Schon Hopes for Friendly Communication with Steve Perry," Ultimate Classic Rock.
[573] Cain, J. (2018). Don't Stop Believin': The Man, the Band and the Song That Inspired Generations, p. 189, Grand Rapids, United States: Zondervan.
[574] Whiting, S. (Oct. 29, 2021). "Herbie Herbert, Co-Creator of Journey and Manager of Santana, Dies at Home in Orinda at 73," San Francisco Chronicle.
[575] SyKlopps.com. (Aug. 16, 2000). "Who is Sy Klopps?."
[576] Carroll, J. (May 18, 1995). "The Many Lives of Herbie Herbert," San Francisco Chronicle.
[577] Freedman, R. (Apr. 14, 2006). "Ex-Santana, Journey Manager Bids Farewell to Memorabilia," Vallejo Times-Herald.
[578] MTV. (Oct. 2, 1995). "Journey: The Road Goes on Forever."
[579] Kreutzmann , B. (2016). Deal: My Three Decades of Drumming, Dreams, and Drugs with the Grateful Dead, p. 345, New York City, United States: St. Martin's Press.
[580] McCarthy , J. (2004). Voices of Latin Rock: The People and Events That Shaped the Sound , p. 191, Milwaukee, United States: Hal Leonard.
[581] Forgo, R. (Jun. 19, 2023). Columbia Records Designer Tommy Steele: Time Passages Interview, Time Passages.
[582] Forgo, R. (Jun. 16, 2023). Columbia Records SVP of Promotions Robert Sherwood: Time Passages Interview, Time Passages.
[583] Taylor, D. (Jun. 3, 2008). "Famed '60s Artist Alton Kelley Dies," The Press-Democrat.
[584] Whiting, S. (Jul. 2, 2015). "Book and Retrospective Give Grateful Dead Artist Mouse His Due," San Francisco Chronicle.
[585] Selvin, J. (Jun. 3, 2008). "Alton Kelley, Psychedelic Poster Creator, Dies," San Francisco Chronicle.
[586] Schon, N. (1995). Album Credits/Liner Notes: Beyond the Thunder.
[587] Carty, M. (Aug. 1, 2001). "Castles Burning: The Herbie Herbert Interview," ESC4P3.com.
[588] Daniels, N. (2011). Don't Stop Believin': The Untold Story of Journey, pp. 100-102, London, England: Omnibus Press.
[589] Newman, M. (Oct. 6, 1996). "Columbia's Journey Gets Warm Welcome at Radio," Billboard.
[590] Flans, R. (Apr. 1, 1997). "Steve Smith: Journey Revisited," Modern Drummer.
[591] Cain, J. (2018). Don't Stop Believin': The Man, the Band and the Song That Inspired Generation, p. 230, Grand Rapids, United States: Zondervan.
[592] Ramirez, C. (Oct. 10, 2009). "Interscope Co-Founder Discusses Label, Producing New Bands," Noisecreep.
[593] Greene, A. (May 19, 2016). "Santana on Reuniting Classic Lineup, How to Fight Trump," Rolling Stone.
[594] St. Louis Post-Dispatch. (Jan. 1, 1997). "'Trial by Fire' Brings Journey Back Together."
[595] Bosso, J. (Oct. 1, 2010). "Producer Kevin Shirley on Joe Bonamassa, Iron Maiden, Led Zeppelin," Music Radar.
[596] Bosso, J. (Dec. 1, 2010). "Producer Kevin Shirley on Joe Bonamassa, Iron Maiden, Led Zeppelin," Music Radar.
[597] McNeice, A. (Oct. 15, 2011). "Neal Schon: Doing it His Way," Melodic Rock.
[598] Watson, T. (Jun. 3, 2008). "Kevin Shirley Talks About Journey's 'Revelation'," Modern Guitars.
[599] Reesman, B. (Oct. 21, 2016). "The Big Journey Reunion That Kind of Happened, And What Might Have Been," Observer.
[600] Schon, N., "Journey's Neal Schon on New Album 'Freedom'," (Film/Video)
[601] McNeice, A. (Sep. 10, 2018). "MelodicRock.Com Interviews: Neal Schon," Melodic Rock.
[602] James, G. (Nov. 2, 2011). "Gary James Interview: Neal Schon of Journey," Classic Bands.
[603] Bosso, J. (Oct. 17, 2012). "Neal Schon Talks Guitars, Hendrix, Santana and New Album, 'the Calling'," Music Radar.
[604] UPI. (Jan. 7, 1997). "Nominees for 39th Annual Grammy Awards."
[605] Cain, J. (2018). Don't Stop Believin': The Man, the Band and the Song That Inspired Generations, p. 233, Grand Rapids, United States: Zondervan.
[606] Greene, A. (Oct. 5, 2018). "Steve Perry Still Believes," Rolling Stone.
[607] Fekadu, M. (Jan. 26, 2018). "Some Musical Icons Have Never Won a Grammy Award," Associated Press.
[608] McNeice, A. (Sep. 1, 2022). "A&R Guru John Kalodner: Melodic Rock Interview," Melodic Rock.
[609] Phull, H. (May 3, 2018). "Journey's Keyboardist Didn't Want His Song to Win a Grammy," New York Post.
[610] Swenson, J. (Jan. 12, 1998). "Santana Inducted in Rock Hall of Fame," UPI.
[611] Greene, A. (Jul. 25, 2020). "Flashback: Peter Green and Santana Perform 'Black Magic Woman' Together," Rolling Stone.
[612] Pareles, J. (Jan. 13, 1998). "It's a California Jam Session as Rock Hall of Fame Inducts New Members," New York Times.
[613] Hartford Courant. (Jan. 13, 1998). "Rock Names New Hall of Famers."
[614] Selvin, J. (Jan. 12, 1998). "Santana's Night to Shine," San Francisco Chronicle.
[615] Ryan, M. (Apr. 24, 2012). "Journey on the Chances of a Reunion with Steve Perry," Huffington Post.
[616] Cavacini, M. (Mar. 4, 2018). "Journey's Neal Schon Discusses Def Leppard Tour, New Solo Album and Steve Perry," MichaelCavacini.com.
[617] Klein, G. (Oct. 3, 2012). "Journey's Neal Schon Settles Lawsuit Filed by Playmate Ex-Flame," Marin Independent Journal.
[618] Business Wire. (Mar. 3, 2020). "Miller Barondess Files Lawsuit on Behalf of Key Members of Iconic Rock Band Journey."
[619] Box Office Mojo. (Dec. 20, 2019). "Domestic Box Office for 1998."
[620] Kaufman, G. (May 30, 2018). "How Music Supervisors for 'Armageddon', 'Can't Hardly Wait' & More Kept Soundtracks Weird & Wonderful in 1998," Billboard.
[621] Reines, D. (Feb. 9, 2005). "Still They Ride," San Francisco Weekly.
[622] Elkins, A. (Nov. 6, 1998). "New Voice, Same Sound for Journey," Daily Journal.
[623] Barron, J. (May 29, 1998). "Public Lives: Musical Rebirth," New York Times.
[624] Greene, A. (Jun. 6, 2022). "Before His First Gig with Journey, Steve Augeri Got So Nervous He Threw Up," Rolling Stone.
[625] Meyer, W. (Nov. 11, 1998). "Revitalized Journey Trying for a Comeback," Greensboro News and Record.
[626] Franco, J. (Nov. 13, 1998). "Journey on Path to Next Millennium," Spartanburg Herald-Journal.
[627] Setlist.fm. (Nov. 17, 2016). "Journey Setlist at Marin Veterans' Memorial Auditorium."
[628] Gett, S. (Apr. 26, 1986). "No Video for Journey Album," Billboard.
[629] DeRiso, N. (Feb. 4, 2023). Former Journey Frontman Steve Augeri: Time Passages Interview, Time Passages.
[630] Smith, B. (Apr. 1, 2010). "Music Review: Guitarist Neal Schon Journeys to El Rey Theatre," Santa Cruz Sentinel.
[631] MTV. (Nov. 21, 1997). "Hip News from Journey, Van Halen."
[632] Graff, G. (Apr. 6, 2001). "Napster Aids Journey's Comeback," ABC News.
[633] Carty, M. (Jan. 1, 2001). "Castles Burning: The Herbie Herbert Interview," ESC4P3.com.

[634] DeRogatis, J. (Jul. 20, 2001). "A Perry-Less Journey," Chicago Sun-Times.

[635] UPI. (Jan. 21, 2005). "Rock Band Journey Received Star on Hollywood Walk of Fame."

[636] Lash, J. (Jan. 24, 2005). "Journey Reunite in L.A.," Rolling Stone.

[637] Parks, J. (Mar. 24, 2012). "Ex-Journey, Vinnie Vincent Invasion Singer Robert Fleischman Talks About the Journey, The Invasion and the Sky," Legendary Rock Interviews.

[638] Grimes, C. (Nov. 19, 2020). "Neal Schon: Talking Gibson Guitars," Guitar International.

[639] Sparks, R. (Apr. 1, 2006). "The Party's Over: An Interview with Journey Mastermind Herbie Herbert," Classic Rock Revisited.

[640] New York Times News Service. (Dec. 28, 1992). "Journey's Glory Days Are Over; End of an Era."

[641] McNiece, A. (Dec. 12, 2005). "Steve Augeri: The 'Good Guy' Talks," Melodic Rock.

[642] Mossman, K. (Oct. 2, 2018). "Steve Perry of Journey: 'There Was Nowhere to Talk it Out, So I Sang it Out'," The New Statesman.

[643] Wright, J. (Mar. 1, 2002). "Neal Schon of Journey: Classic Rock Revisited Interview," Classic Rock Revisited.

[644] Melodic Rock. (Dec. 3, 2002). "MelodicRock.Com Interviews: Sammy Hagar."

[645] Yonke, D. (Jul. 4, 2004). "The Journey Continues," Toledo Blade.

[646] Toledo Blade. (Apr. 4, 2002). "Journey's New Path."

[647] Wardlaw, M. (May 21, 2012). "Journey's Neal Schon Recalls the Rise of Eddie Van Halen and the Birth of 'Don't Stop Believin''," Ultimate Classic Rock.

[648] Andrew, (Dec. 12, 2005). "Journey 2005 Generations Interviews: Deen Castronovo," McNeice.

[649] McNeice, A. (Dec. 12, 2005). "The 2005 Generations Interviews: Deen Castronovo," Melodic Rock.

[650] Anderson, J. (Jul. 12, 2019). "The Music of Journey at Batavia Downs Friday with Former Lead Singer Steve Augeri," The Daily News.

[651] Pettersson, S. (Jun. 11, 2006). "Journey Weirdness," Google Groups.

[652] AntiMusic. (Jun. 19, 2006). "Journey Lip Sync?."

[653] Greene, A. (Jul. 10, 2006). "Journey Vocalist Won't Stop Deceivin'," Rolling Stone.

[654] Daniels, N. (2011). Don't Stop Believin': The Untold Story of Journey, p. 150, London, United Kingdom: Omnibus Press.

[655] Wardlaw, M. (May 21, 2012). "Journey's Neal Schon Recalls the Rise of Eddie Van Halen," Ultimate Classic Rock.

[656] McNeice, A. (Oct. 1, 2006). "Journey - Live in Los Angeles," Melodic Rock.

[657] Cain, J. (2018). Don't Stop Believin': The Man, the Band and the Song That Inspired Generations, p. 252, Grand Rapids, United States: Zondervan.

[658] Soto, J.S. (Jun. 25, 2007). "JSS: The 'Journey' Forward," JeffScottSoto.com.

[659] Dickens, T. (Jan. 9, 2008). "His New Journey Leads to Old Frontiers," Roanoke Times.

[660] Nerres, V. (May 15, 2008). "A 'Revelation' From Journey: New Singer, New Album, New Tour," All Access Magazine.

[661] Anderson, D. (Sep. 30, 2021). "Neal Schon: The Music Journey," Guitar Connoisseur Magazine.

[662] Raihala, R. (Jul. 26, 2018). "Journey's Neal Schon Talks About Touring, Possible Collaboration with Steve Perry," Pioneer Press.

[663] Moser, J. (Aug. 28, 2011). "Talking with Journey: Drummer Deen Castronovo Says Group Still Believin' After 35 Years," The Morning Call.

[664] Parker, R. (Sep. 20, 2021). "David Chase Chose Journey for 'Sopranos' Finale Because Song Was Hated by Crew," The Hollywood Reporter.

[665] Greenberg, J. (Apr. 15, 2015). "This Magic Moment," Directors Guild of America.

[666] Pineda, A. (Oct. 22, 2015). "A Job Led Journey's Lead Singer from Homelessness to Fame," Mercury News.

[667] Biography.com. (Jul. 20, 2020). "Arnel Pineda."

[668] McElhiney , B. (Sep. 28, 2009). "New Music, Old Favorites Give Journey Universal Appeal Through the Decades," The Daily Gazette.

[669] Boucher, G. (Jun. 12, 2008). "Journey's 'Revelation' Takes No. 5 Via Wal-Mart," Los Angeles Times.

[670] Figueroa IV, D. (Jan. 8, 2018). "Foreigner Re-Records Classic Hit to Benefit Shriners, Films Video in Tampa Bay," Tampa Bay Times.

[671] Pierce, S. (Sep. 30, 2013). "Cinderella Tale of Journey's Filipino Lead Singer is Fascinating," Salt Lake Tribune.

[672] The Morning Call. (Jun. 6, 2014). "Interviewing Steve Miller and Journey: San Francisco Bands Talk About Connecting After All These Years."

[673] Grein, P. (Aug. 31, 2009). "Chart Watch: Week Ending Aug. 23, 2009," Yahoo.

[674] Yahoo. (Jan. 2, 2014). "Chart Watch: 'Radioactive' Sets a Rock Record."

[675] Grein, P. (Sep. 22, 2010). "Week Ending Sept. 19, 2010: 'it Goes on and on and on and On'," Yahoo.

[676] Official U.K. Charts. (Jan. 29, 2016). "Singles Chart: 7 November 2009-13 November 2009."

[677] Ackerman, N. (Feb. 26, 2021). "Journey's 'Don't Stop Believin\' Becomes Second-Ever Classic Tune to Reach 1 Billion Spotify Streams," Evening Standard.

[678] RPM Weekly. (Dec. 26, 1981). "Canadian Charts: Week of Dec. 26, 1981."

[679] Weatherford, M. (Feb. 18, 2011). "Journey Giving Preview of New Album at Planet Hollywood," Las Vegas Review-Journal.

[680] Wardlaw, M. (May 21, 2012). "Journey's Neal Schon Recalls the Rise of Eddie Van Halen and the Birth of 'Don't Stop Believin\'," Ultimate Classic Rock.

[681] Shaw, L. (Mar. 13, 2013). "The Long Journey to Making 'Don't Stop Believin': Everyman's Journey'," Yahoo.

[682] Brooks, B. (Mar. 7, 2013). "Specialty Preview: 'Don't Stop Believin': Everyman's Journey'," Deadline.

[683] Baltin, S. (Apr. 11, 2012). "Ronnie Montrose's Death Ruled a Suicide," Rolling Stone.

[684] RedRocker.com. (Mar. 30, 2012). "Events: A Concert for Ronnie Montrose - A Celebration of His Life in Music."

[685] DeRiso, N. (Jul. 19, 2014). "Ringo Starr's Current All-Starr Band Can't Stop Having Fun," Something Else!

[686] Charupakorn, J. (Dec. 17, 2012). "Interview: Neal Schon on 'the Calling'," Premier Guitar.

[687] Perry, S. (Jun. 6, 2013). "Fan Asylum Post: Kellie Nash and Martha Quinn," FanAsylum.com.

[688] Hann, M. (Oct. 10, 2018). "'I Believed Love Could Cure Cancer': How Grief Sent Steve Perry on a New Journey," The Guardian.

[689] Varga, G. (Aug. 27, 2016). "Carlos Santana Talks Music, Social Justice and Trump," San Diego Union-Tribune.

[690] Ling, D. (Oct. 4, 2018). "Steve Perry's Track-By-Track Guide to New Album 'Traces'," Classic Rock.

[691] Yahoo. (Sep. 17, 2018). "Steve Perry's Journey Back: How One Special Woman Made Him Start Believing Again."

[692] Halperin, S. (Sep. 20, 2018). "Journey's Steve Perry: 'I Became a Bit of a Recluse'," Hollywood Reporter.

[693] Stine, R. (Jan. 9, 2004). "Making 'Monster' For a Song," San Francisco Chronicle.

[694] Entertainment Weekly. (Jan. 27, 2004). "Charlize Theron Had a Memorable Golden Globes Moment."

[695] Rosen, S. (Nov. 1, 2010). "How 'Don't Stop Believin\' Became a 'Monster' Hit," American Songwriter.

[696] Hamilton, G.G. (Oct. 19, 2018). "Heartache Helps Singer Rediscover His Music," Associated Press.

[697] Newman, M. (Oct. 5, 1996). "Columbia's Journey Gets Warm Welcome at Radio," Billboard.

[698] Schwartz, M. (Jun. 22, 2007). "'Sopranos' Finale Has Perry 'Believin\' In Chase," Entertainment Weekly.

[699] Wiederhorn, J. (Feb. 22, 2002). "Sammy Hagar Makes Tracks with Van Halen Bassist, Journey-Men," MTV.

[700] Frontiers. (May 15, 2015). "Sammy's Other HsaS (Hagar/Schon/Anthony/Smith) In Studio."

[701] Wardlaw, M. (Mar. 19, 2014). "Journey's Neal Schon on His New Album, 'So U'," Ultimate Classic Rock.

[702] Covuoto, R. (Apr. 25, 2014). "Neal Schon: 'So U' Is for the Love of My Art and Playing Guitar," Guitar International.

[703] Ragogna, M. (Jul. 7, 2014). "'So U' And More: Conversations with Neal Schon, Judas Priest's Rob Halford and Edgar Winter," Huffington Post.

[704] Wright, J. (Nov. 24, 2005). "Steve Perry's Journey Continues," Classic Rock Revisited.

[705] Prokopy, S. (Mar. 5, 2013). "Capone Faithfully Submits This Interview with Journey Frontman Arnel Pineda," AintItCool.com.

[706] Cain, J. (2018). Don't Stop Believin': The Man, the Band, and the Song that Inspired Generations, p. 247, Grand Rapids, United States: Zondervan.

[707] Associated Press. (Apr. 9, 2014). "Journey's Lead Vocalist Arnel Pineda Plans to Launch Album."

[708] Wink, R. (Mar. 19, 2015). "Gregg Rolie to Rejoin Santana in Mexico," Noise11.

[709] Facebook. (Mar. 17, 2015). "Update from Team Santana."

[710] Ramirez , E. (May 2, 2014). "Carlos Santana Talks 'Corazon' & Reuniting with Original Band for 'Santana Iv'," Billboard.

[711] Gibbs, V. (Feb. 1, 1973). "Soul Man: Santana," Crawdaddy.

[712] Savage, M. (Oct. 10, 2018). "Steve Perry Interview: How Journey's Frontman Stopped Believin'," BBC.

[713] Wardlaw, M. (Dec. 19, 2020). "How Eels Helped Steve Perry Find 'Emotional Honesty' In His Music," Ultimate Classic Rock.

[714] Baltin, S. (Oct. 3, 2018). "Steve Perry on His Return to Music: It's a Different Steve Now'," Forbes.

[715] Mossman, K. (Sep. 26, 2018). "Steve Perry of Journey: 'Things Happened to Me as a Child. There Was Nowhere to Talk it Out, So I Sang it Out Instead'," The New Statesman.

[716] Wardlaw, M. (Dec. 11, 2020). "How Steve Perry Finally Accepted His Aging Voice," Ultimate Classic Rock.

[717] Smith, T. (Oct. 7, 2018). "How Steve Perry Started Believin' Again," CBS.

[718] Luppi, K. (Sep. 20, 2015). "Rocker Marco Mendoza's New Life with the Dead Daisies," Los Angeles Times.

[719] Suermondt, F. (Apr. 20, 2018). "Interview with Marco Mendoza and Deen Castronovo of the Dead Daisies," My Global Mind.

[720] Melodic Rock. (Jul. 1, 1999). "Melodic Rock Interview: John Sykes."

[721] Wisconsin Music. (Jun. 10, 2005). "Interview: David Coverdale."

[722] Milligan, L. (Mar. 18, 2010). "State Sells Out for Journey's Schon, Side Band," The Modesto Bee.

[723] Friedlander, M. (Jul. 29, 2021). "Journey Members Discuss Band's Plans as New Lineup Prepares for Its First Shows," ABC Radio.

[724] Greene, A. (Jul. 6, 2022). "Neal Schon on Journey's New LP 'Freedom,' Ambitious 50th Anniversary Plans," Rolling Stone.

[725] Facebook. (Jun. 18, 2015). "Journey Facebook Post: Omar Hakim."

[726] Wardlaw, M. (Nov. 3, 2015). "Deen Castronovo Confirms Journey Firing," Ultimate Classic Rock.

[727] Tomlinson, S. (Jun. 30, 2015). "Grand Jury Indicts Journey Drummer Deen Castronovo on Rape, Sex Abuse Allegations," The Oregonian.

[728] DeDekker , J. (Jul. 21, 2015). "Journey Meets Its Latest Challenge Head On," Leader-Post.

[729] Lynn, C. (Nov. 3, 2015). "Castronovo: 'I've Let Everybody in the Community Down'," Statesman Journal.

[730] Graff, G. (May 9, 2016). "Journey on Steve Perry, Releasing New Music and Whether They'd Even Accept a Rock Hall Invitation," Billboard.

[731] Lach, S. (Jun. 24, 2015). "Neal Schon Hails Journey Stand-In Hakim," Classic Rock.

[732] Katsilometes, J. (Mar. 23, 2016). "'Santana IV' Lineup is Forever Groovy in House of Blues Reunion," Las Vegas Sun.

[733] Wardlaw, M. (Aug. 13, 2014). "Gregg Rolie Shares Memories of Woodstock and Santana Reunion News," Ultimate Classic Rock.

[734] Alexander, B. (Mar. 22, 2016). "Santana Rocks Like It's Woodstock in Las Vegas Reunion Show," USA Today.

[735] Abrams, R. (Apr. 3, 2017). "Gregg Rolie Gets Ready to Celebrate Journey," Long Island Pulse.

[736] Graff, G. (Oct. 28, 2016). "Following Rock Hall Nomination, Journey Says 'Door is Open' For Reunion with Vocalist Steve Perry," Billboard.

[737] Lifton, D. (Dec. 17, 2016). "Journey Wins Rock and Roll Hall of Fame Fan Voting," Ultimate Classic Rock.

[738] SF Weekly. (Feb. 9, 2005). "Still They Ride."

[739] Marcus, G. (Dec. 1, 1981). "Food Fight: Real Life Rock Top 10, 1981," California Magazine.

[740] Smith, T. (Apr. 13, 2023). "Rock & Roll Hall of Fame's Fan Vote Has Been Eerily Precise," Axios.

[741] France, L.R. (Dec. 20, 2016). "Rock and Roll Hall of Fame Inductees Announced," CNN.

[742] Williams, W. (Aug. 2, 2022). "Journey Keyboardist Sells Berry Hill Recording Studio," Nashville Post.

[743] Cain, J. (2018). Don't Stop Believin': The Man, the Band and the Song That Inspired Generations, pp. 231-235, Grand Rapids, United States: Zondervan.

[744] Benitez-Eves, T. (Sep. 5, 2021). "Jonathan Cain Chooses Renewal on 'Oh Lord Lead Us'," American Songwriter.

[745] Wardlaw, M. (Sep. 20, 2016). "Jonathan Cain Schedules New Solo Album, 'What God Wants to Hear'," Ultimate Classic Rock.

[746] Graff, G. (May 9, 2016). "Journey on Steve Perry, Releasing New Music & Whether They'd Even Accept a Rock Hall Invitation," Billboard.

[747] Hall, H. (Oct. 4, 2016). "Journey Songwriter Knows 'What God Wants to Hear'," The Tennessean.

[748] Beeton, J. (Sep. 9, 2022). "Journey Legend Sells Nashville Recording Studio to Music Nonprofit," LoopNet.

[749] Smith, T. (Feb. 15, 2017). "Steve Perry's Status for Rock Hall Ceremony Remains Uncertain," Cleveland Plain Dealer.

[750] Thrasher, D. (Mar. 30, 2017). "Dayton to Welcome Journey to Nutter Center with Open Arms," Dayton Daily News.

[751] Masley, E. (Sep. 4, 2018). "Neal Schon Talks Journey, Solo Music, Hall of Fame and Steve Perry's Return," Arizona Republic.

[752] DeRiso, N. (Apr. 7, 2017). "Steve Perry at Rock & Roll Hall of Fame," Ultimate Classic Rock: Facebook.

[753] Greene, A. (Jan. 26, 2021). "Journey Frontman Arnel Pineda on the Band's New Record, Dreams of a Steve Perry Reunion," Rolling Stone.

[754] Wardlaw, M. (May 3, 2017). "Journey Drummer Steve Smith Talks Rock Hall, Steve Perry and Upcoming Vegas Run," Las Vegas Weekly.

[755] Nessif, B. (Aug. 26, 2012). "Journey Was Paid How Much to Play at Mitt Romney Campaign Event?" E! News.

[756] NBC. (Jul. 27, 2017). "Journey, The Band, Poses for Pictures in the White House Press Briefing Room."

[757] Schon, N. (Jul. 28, 2017). "Neal Schon: On Religious Beliefs and Politics in Journey," Facebook.

[758] Bailey, S.P. (Nov. 1, 2019). "Paula White, Trump's Key Spiritual Adviser, Will Join the White House," The Washington Post.

[759] Facebooik, Schon, N. (Jul. 28, 2017). Neal Schon: On Religion and Politics in Journey, Retrieved from https://www.facebook.com/schonmusic/posts/1497420596985077.

[760] Facebook, Schon, N. (Jul. 28, 2017). Neal Schon: On Religion and Politics in Journey, Retrieved from https://www.facebook.com/schonmusic/posts/1497420596985077.

[761] Twitter, Schon, N. (Aug. 3, 2017). Neal Schon: Reposts Negative Coverage About Paula White, Retrieved from https://twitter.com/NealSchonMusic/status/892981470796685312.

[762] Twitter, Schon, N. (Jun. 6, 2017). Neal Schon: Earlier Comments on Politics and Religion, Retrieved from https://twitter.com/NealSchonMusic/status/872174639086276608.

[763] Paulson, D. (Jul. 29, 2016). "Journey Will Play Nashville, But Turned Down RNC," The Tennessean.

[764] Instagram, Schon, N. (Jun. 4, 2017). Neal Schon: On Jonathan Cain and Paula White, Retrieved from https://www.instagram.com/p/BU7MvLLjHk8/.

[765] Instgram, Schon, N. (Jun. 4, 2017). Neal Schon: On Jonathan Cain and Paula White, Retrieved from https://www.instagram.com/p/BU7MvLLjHk8/.

[766] Twitter, Schon, N. (Aug. 3, 2017). Neal Schon: On the Others Touring Without Him, Retrieved from https://twitter.com/NealSchonMusic/status/893197767019032577.

[767] Twitter, Schon, N. (Jul. 29, 2017). Neal Schon: On Journey's Hall of Fame Induction, Retrieved from https://twitter.com/NealSchonMusic/status/891189111649968132.

[768] Mettler , M. (Sep. 27, 2017). "Ronnie Montrose Rocks the Nation with a Fabulous Final Studio Album," Sound and Vision.

[769] Mettler , M. (Feb. 7, 2018). "Who Was Ronnie Montrose? His Bandmates and Friends Shred Light on the Life and Career of a Mysterious Guitar Hero," Guitar World.

[770] Peacock, T. (Jul. 6, 2017). "Def Leppard, Journey Discussing Major 2018 North American Tour," uDiscoverMusic.com.

[771] Brickman, J. (Aug. 15, 2018). "Interview: Steve Perry," JimBrickman.com.

[772] Schlanger, T. (Sep. 21, 2018). "Steve Perry Makes His Return," NPR.

[773] Gawley, P. (Jan. 4, 2022). "Andy Cohen Will Host CNN'S New Year's Eve Special Again, Addresses His on-Air Rant," Entertainment Tonight.

[774] Graff, G. (Jan. 1, 2022). "'It's Not Journey!': CNN Hosts Debate Band's New Year's Eve Show," Ultimate Classic Rock.

[775] Wright, J. (Nov. 28, 2005). "Ross Valory: More Than Just a Bass Player," Classic Rock Revisited.

[776] Smith, A. (May 14, 2014). "Journey and Steve Miller Band a Summer Tour for All Ages," MetroWest Daily News.

[777] Wardlaw, M. (May 10, 2022). "How Journey's Arnel Pineda Fixed His Vocal Woes," Ultimate Classic Rock.

[778] Prince, P. (Jan. 14, 2020). "Gregg Rolie Delivers a 'Sonic' Solo Album," Goldmine.

[779] Runtagh, J. (Nov. 13, 2019). "Hear Rock Icon Gregg Rolie's New Single 'Give Me Tomorrow'," People.

[780] DeRiso, N. (Jan. 5, 2013). "Gregg Rolie Puts Down a Few Tracks Before Rejoining Ringo Starr on Tour," Something Else!

[781] Graff, G. (Oct. 26, 2019). "Santana/Journey Co-Founder Gregg Rolie Unveils Ringo-Inspired 'What About Love'," Billboard.

[782] Jewett, D. (Oct. 27, 2020). "San Rafael's Narada Michael Walden Joins Rock Band Journey," Marin Living.

[783] ABC Radio. (Apr. 14, 2017). "Narada Michael Walden Working on New Albums by Journey's Neal Schon, Santana Drummer Cindy Blackman Santana."

[784] Masley, E. (Feb. 27, 2019). "Neal Schon on Journey Through Time: 'It's Like the Dead on Steroids'," The Arizona Republic.

[785] Colothan, S. (Jan. 18, 2019). "Neal Schon Invites Steve Perry to Join His Journey Through Time Shows," Planet Radio.

[786] Greenhaus, M. (Oct. 26, 2022). "Reflections: Journey," Relix.

[787] Greene, A. (Jan. 7, 2021). "Neal Schon on Journey's 'New Strut,' Possible Arnel Pineda Biopic, And His New Solo LP," Rolling Stone.

[788] Kreps, D. (Apr. 1, 2021). "Journey Members Reach 'Amicable Settlement' In Battle Over Band Name," Rolling Stone.

[789] Business Wire. (Apr. 15, 2020). "Attorneys Fire Back with Cross-Complaint in Lawsuit Involving Journey Bass Player Ross Valory."

[790] DeRiso, N. (Apr. 16, 2020). "Ross Valory Countersues Bandmates as Journey Split Widens," Ultimate Classic Rock.

[791] Graff, G. (Sep. 14, 2021). "Journey is Back with a New Lineup and New Music," Cleveland Plain Dealer.

[792] Knopper, S. (Mar. 2, 2023). "Journey's Neal Schon V. Everyone: Will Band Members Go 'Separate Ways'?" Billboard.

[793] RonWikso.com, Wikso, R. (Jan. 17, 2022). Ron Wikso (1992-1998): The Storm, Retrieved from https://ronwikso.com/the-storm/.

[794] Cain, J. (2018). Don't Stop Believin': The Man, the Band and the Song That Inspired Generations, p. 247, Grand Rapids, United States: Zondervan.

[795] Jahner, K. (Mar. 31, 2020). "Journey's 'Messy' Feud Fueled by Trademark Fight, Contracts," Bloomberg Law.

[796] U.S. Patent and Trademark Office. (May 17, 2021). "Nightmare Productions, Inc. V. Schon Productions, Inc."

[797] Neale, M. (May 26, 2020). "Journey Announce Line-Up Changes as Former Bassist Randy Jackson Rejoins," NME.

[798] Kaye, B. (May 25, 2020). "Journey Reunite with Randy Jackson, Perform 'Don't Stop Believin'," Yahoo News.

[799] Ultimate Guitar. (Jul. 7, 2022). "Neal Schon Speaks on Journey's Latest Lineup Changes, Reveals Problems He Had with Bassist."

[800] Ruggieri, M. (Jul. 8, 2022). "Journey's Neal Schon Says He and Steve Perry Are 'in a Good Place' Before Band's 50th Anniversary," USA Today.

[801] Wardlaw, M. (May 13, 2022). "Why Narada Michael Walden Left Journey," Ultimate Classic Rock.

[802] Vaziri, A. (Jul. 28, 2021). "How Journey Survived Another Lineup Change to Make Its First New Music in More Than 10 Years," San Francisco Chronicle.

[803] Ultimate Guitar. (Aug. 18, 2018). "Steve Perry: What I Think About New Journey Singer Arnel Pineda."

[804] Rock Pasta. (Oct. 16, 2021). "Arnel Pineda's Voice Struggles with Recent Concert."

[805] Katsilometes, J. (Dec. 7, 2021). "Journey Singer Arnel Pineda on Fronting His Favorite Band," Las Vegas Review-Journal.

[806] Graff, G. (Jul. 12, 2022). "How Age Forces Rock Singers to Adjust: 'it Happens to All of Us'," Ultimate Classic Rock.

[807] Wardlaw, M. (May 10, 2022). "How Journey's Arnel Pineda Fixed His Vocal Woes," Ultimate Classic Rock.

[808] Gerson, R. (Jan. 5, 2012). "Interview with Star Vocal Coach, David Stroud," Huffington Post.

[809] Argyrakis, A. (Nov. 1, 2016). "'Don't Stop Believin': The Faith Journey of Jonathan Cain," CCM Magazine.

[810] SteveAugeri.com, Augeri, S. (Mar. 6, 2023). 'Seven Ways 'Til Sunday': Album Notes, Retrieved from https://www.steveaugeri.com/seven-ways-til-sunday.

[811] Graff, G. (Jul. 14, 2023). "Bret Michaels Kicks Off Parti-Gras Tour in Detroit," Ultimate Classic Rock.

[812] Baldassi, L. (Jul. 18, 2017). "Herbie Herbert: The Band Whisperer," Biz X Magazine.

[813] Kozack, R. (Nov. 3, 1979). "Lighting and Trucking Areas Attract Journey," Billboard.

[814] Carty, M. (Jul. 1, 2001). "Castles Burning: The Herbie Herbert Interview," ESC4P3.com.

[815] PR Newswire. (Jun. 2, 2011). "Production Resource Group Acquires Nocturne Productions."

[816] Lee, K., "Stanley Mouse on Journey's Scarab Image," (Film/Video)

[817] (Jun. 28, 2023). "Stanley Mouse, Sebastopol Psychedelic Poster Artist, Recovering from 'Debilitating' Stroke," The Press Democrat.

[818] Baldassi, L. (Sep. 5, 2017). "Making a Sound Living: The Second Set with Herbie Herbert," Biz X Magazine.

[819] McIver, J. (Aug. 31, 2022). "Randy Jackson on His Return to Journey," Guitar World.

[820] Adams, B. (Sep. 1, 2022). "Neal Schon: Driven Journey Man," Vintage Guitar.

[821] Beviglia, J. (Aug. 24, 2022). "Neal Schon Finds Artistic Freedom on New Journey Album," American Songwriter.

[822] Schon, M. (Jan. 5, 2023). "Michaele Schon on Gregg Rolie's Appearance on Journey's 50th Anniversary Tour," Facebook.

[823] Vaziri, A. (Jan. 6, 2023). "Journey Brings Original Vocalist Gregg Rolie Back Into Fold for 2023 Tour," San Francisco Chronicle.

[824] Ultimate Classic Rock. (Jan. 5, 2023). "Neal Schon Says He's 'Not Here to Take Orders' About Journey."

[825] Carty, M. (Jul. 1, 2001). "Castles Burning: The Herbie Herbert Interview," ESC4P3.com.

[826] Hartlaub, P. (Aug. 30, 2016). "Journey's Schon Returns to San Francisco Roots," San Francisco Chronicle.

[827] The Offices of GSS Law, PC. (Jul. 20, 2023). "Gary Stiffelman Letter to Guitare En Scène Festival."

[828] DeRiso, N. (Jul. 21, 2023). "Gregg Rolie Says 'Journey Through Time' Was 'Improperly Released'," Ultimate Classic Rock.

[829] Facebook: Guitare en Scene. (Jun. 24, 2023). "Guitare En Scene Announces 2023 Lineup."

[830] Guitare-en-Scene.com. (Jun. 23, 2023). "Cancellation: Neal Schon X Journey Through Time."

[831] Knolle, S. (Jul. 21, 2023). "Journey Cofounder Gregg Rolie Demands Refunds for Fans of 'Misleading' European Concert," The Wrap.

[832] Facebook: Guitare en Scene. (Jun. 14, 2023). "Guitare En Scene Announces 2023 Festival Lineup."

[833] Instagram: Q1043. (Oct. 8, 2022). "Neal Schon Responds to Q1043'S Report on Steve Perry Trademark Lawsuit."

[834] Instagram: Q1043. (Oct. 8, 2022). "Neal Schon Responds to Q1043'S Report on Steve Perry Trademark Lawsuit."

[835] Kielty, M. (Oct. 10, 2022). "Https://Ultimateclassicrock.Com/Journey-Neal-Schon-Steve-Perry/," Ultimate Classic Rock.

[836] Weiss, J. (Apr. 15, 2022). "Even Journey's Steve Perry Was Floored by That 'Separate Ways' Remix in 'Stranger Things 4' Trailer," Forbes.

[837] Epstein, D. (Jul. 27, 2022). "Separate Ways: Steve Perry on How a 40-Year-Old Journey Hit Found New Life Via Stranger Things," Flood Magazine.

[838] Shafer, E. (Jul. 1, 2022). "'Stranger Things 4' Unveils Complete Soundtrack," Variety.

[839] Knolle, S. (Jul. 2, 2022). "Listen to the Foreboding 'Stranger Things' Remix of Journey's 'Separate Ways'," Yahoo.

[840] Ducker, E. (Jan. 6, 2023). "Movie Trailers Keep Tweaking Well-Known Songs. The Tactic is Working," The New York Times.

[841] Graff, G. (Jul. 16, 2022). "Jonathan Cain Reveals How 'Escape' Influenced Journey's New Album," Ultimate Classic Rock.

[842] Kielty, M. (Oct. 22, 2022). "Neal Schon Says Steve Perry Forced Journey Into Partners Contract," Ultimate Classic Rock.

[843] Graff, G. (Apr. 27, 2023). "Deen Castronovo Explains How Journey Keeps it Together Onstage," Ultimate Classic Rock.

[844] Gray, M. (Jun. 23, 2022). "Neal Schon Bought 150 Guitars During the Pandemic: 'it Was Like Being Hooked on Something'," People.

[845] Superior Court of the State of California, County of Contra Costa. (Oct. 31, 2022). "Neal J. Schon vs. Jonathan Cain: Complaint for Declaratory Judgment and Injunction."

[846] Rolli, B. (Jan. 20, 2023). "Jonathan Cain Sues Neal Schon for Charging $1m to Journey Card," Ultimate Classic Rock.

[847] Sisario, B. (Dec. 22, 2022). "Journey Guitarist to Bandmate Who Played for Trump: No Political Gigs," The New York Times.

[848] Knopper, S. (Dec. 7, 2022). "Journey Hires Def Leppard Manager Amid Inter-Band Turmoil," Billboard.

[849] Facebook: Melodic Rock's Andrew McNeice. (Sep. 21, 2022). "Neal Schon Responds to Steve Perry's Legal Action."

[850] U.S. Patient and Trademark Office (Sep. 11, 2022). "Steve Perry's Trademark Trial and Appeal Board Filing."

[851] Keller, E. (Jan. 5, 2023). "Journey's Neal Schon Accuses Trump's Spiritual Adviser of Improperly Accessing Band's Bank Account," New York Post.

[852] Brown, E.R. (Nov. 15, 2021). "Journey Plots 2022 Arena Tour Supported by Billy Idol, Toto," Pollstar.

[853] Greene, A. (Feb. 15, 2018). "Journey's Jonathan Cain Talks Band Feud: 'Let's Hit Reset'," Rolling Stone.

[854] Ali, R. (Dec. 22, 2022). "Journey's Neal Schon Serves Jonathan Cain with Cease-And-Desist Letter After Donald Trump Performances," USA Today.

[855] Twitter: Neal Schon. (Jan. 6, 2023). "Steve Perry's Trademark Claim is Dropped."

[856] Wilkening, M. (Jan. 7, 2023). "Neal Schon Accuses Paula White-Cain of Improperly Accessing Journey Bank Accounts," Ultimate Classic Rock.

[857] Trakin, R. (Oct. 26, 2021). "Herbie Herbert, Longtime Manager of Journey, Dies at 73," Variety.

[858] DeRiso, N. (Mar. 8, 2023). Steve Perry Co-Producer Thom Flowers: Time Passages Interview, Time Passages.

[859] Greene, A. (Oct. 22, 2020). "Steve Perry: 'My Heart Bleeds Daily to Be in Front of People and to Sing for Them'," Rolling Stone.

[860] StevePerry.com. (Nov. 5, 2021). "Iconic Singer/Songwriter Steve Perry Releases His First-Ever Christmas Album, 'the Season'."

[861] Fuoco-Karasinski, C. (Dec. 19, 2021). "Steve Perry Recalls His Childhood in 'the Season'," Peoria Times.

[862] Caulfield, K. (Nov. 18, 2021). "Steve Perry Decks the Charts with 'the Season'," Billboard.

[863] Wardlaw, M. (Dec. 12, 2020). "Why Steve Perry Circled Back Around to 'Traces': Exclusive Interview," Ultimate Classic Rock.

[864] Caulfield, K. (Nov. 18, 2021). "Steve Perry Decks the Charts with 'the Season'," Billboard.

[865] Billboard. (Jul. 4, 1981). "Journey Escapes to the Mountains."

[866] Ruggieri, M. (Jul. 2, 2018). "Journey Guitarist Neal Schon Talks Rouring, 'Don't Stop Believin'," Cox Newspapers.

[867] Ruggieri, M. (Jul. 2, 2018). "Journey Guitarist Neal Schon Talks Touring, 'Don't Stop Believin'," Cox Newspapers.

[868] Coverson, L. (Feb. 10, 2009). "'Sopranos' Finale Puts Journey Back in the Spotlight," ABC.

[869] Wardlaw, M. (Jul. 2, 2014). "Journey Guitarist Neal Schon Reflects on the Classic Rock Band's Generation-Spanning Legacy," Cleveland Sceen.

[870] Roberts, J. (Jan. 7, 2012). "Interview: Glee Producer Ryan Murphy," Interview.

[871] Billboard. (Mar. 25, 2017). "Journey's True Believer: Manager John Baruck on How Synchs and Touring Helped the Band Reach the Rock Hall."

[872] Lindquist, D. (May 25, 2016). "Journey Keeps Moving," The Indianapolis Star.

[873] Wardlaw, M. (Jun. 25, 2016). "Former Journey Drummer Deen Castronovo One Year Later: 'I'm So Grateful I Woke Up' - Exclusive Interview," Ultimate Classic Rock.

[874] Simmons, G. (May 19, 2022). "Stratford Home of the Band's Keyboardist Recognized," The Beacon-Herald.

[875] Bowman, R. (Jul. 26, 1991). "Life is a Carnival," Goldmine.

[876] ABC Radio. (Oct. 21, 2021). "Steve Perry's Now Glad He Made the 'Journey' To His Rock & Roll Hall of Fame Induction."

[877] Chang, A. (Oct. 3, 2018). "Steve Perry's New Life: 'I've Rediscovered the Passion for Music'," NPR.

[878] DeRiso, N. (Jan. 19, 2018). "Neal Schon Says Journey Are Ready to Move on After 'Hard Times'," Ultimate Classic Rock.

[879] Rosenbaum, C. (Apr. 2, 2021). "Journey Band Members Agree to Settle $10 Million Lawsuit and Go 'Separate Ways'," Billboard.

[880] Journey WWW Page, Sullivan, S. (Feb. 1, 1997). Exclusive interview with Jim Welch, Retrieved from https://jrnyfan.tripod.com/welchinterview.html.

[881] Kielty, M. (May 21, 2018). "Watch Steve Perry Surprise American Idol Contestant Who Sang 'Don't Stop Believin'," UltimateClassicRock.com.

[882] Dugen Ramirez, C. (May 21, 2018). "Gabby Barrett Sang 'Don't Stop Believin'' In Front of Journey's Perry — And He Loved It," People.

[883] Hanford Sentinel. (Dec. 1, 1994). "Steve Perry is Back in the Building."

[884] Billboard. (Jul. 12, 1980). "Journey to Wax Score for Movie."

[885] Takada, K. (Oct. 23, 2017). "My Short-Lived Career as a Movie Director," Nikkei Asia.

[886] Feitelberg, R. (Jun. 29, 2017). "Kenzo Takada Talks Fashion, Film and New Collaborations," Women's Wear Daily.

[887] DeMain, B. (Dec. 13, 2022). "Borrowed Notes: The Complicated, Cross-Atlantic Evolution of Black Magic Woman," MSN.

[888] Grow, K. (Jun. 27, 2019). "Carlos Santana on New Album 'Africa Speaks': 'People Need Rejoicing'," Rolling Stone.

[889] Wright, J. (Jun. 25, 2014). "Wally Stocker of the Babys: Taking it All In," Classic Rock Revisited.

[890] U.S. District Court, North District of California. (Jun. 2, 2023). "Stanley Miller V. Nomota LLC."

[891] Daniels, N. (2011). Don't Stop Believin': The Untold Story of Journey, pp. 54-55, London, England: Omnibus Press.

[892] Carty, M. (Jan. 1, 2001). "Castles Burning: The Herbie Herbert Interview," ESC4P3.com.

[893] Mouse, S. (May 18, 2021). "Description of 'Power of Soul' Print," MouseStudios.com.

[894] Moen, D. (Nov. 1, 2021). "In Memoriam: Walter James \"Herbie\" Herbert Ii, 73," Projection Lights and Staging News.

[895] Wikso, R. (Jan. 17, 2022). "The Storm: 1992-1998," RonWikso.com.

[896] Ruggieri, M. (Sep. 25, 2023). "Journey to Celebrate 50th Anniversary with 30 Shows in 2024," USA Today.

[897] Sanders, C. (Mar. 7, 2022). "Gabby Barrett Admits She \"Went After\" Her Husband First After Meeting on 'American Idol'," People.

[898] Seacrest, R., "Gabby Barrett Sings 'Don't Stop Believing\" On American Idol 2018 Finale," (Film/Video)

[899] Chepurny, G. (May 21, 2018). "'American Idol' Recap: Katy Perry Calls Finale Part One a 'Disaster'," Variety.

[900] Wuench, K. (August 31, 2015). "Recognize This '80s Wife/Singer/Actress? We'll Keep Holdin' On While You Figure it Out," Tampa Bay Times.

[901] Wuench, K. (Aug. 31, 2015). "Recognize This '80s Wife/Singer/Actress? We'll Keep Holdin' On While You Figure it Out," Tampa Bay Times.

[902] Caps, J. (Sep. 1, 2017). "The Flashback Interview: Tane McClure," https://popgeeks.com/the-flashback-interview-tane-mcclure/.

[903] Carty, M. (Aug. 15, 2001). "Castles Burning, The Herbie Herbert Interview," ESC4P3.com.

[904] Billboard. (Sep. 4, 1982). "New Strategies Outlined at RCA Meeting."

[905] Billboard. (Aug. 21, 1982). "Face to Face."

[906] Discogs.com. (Dec. 17, 2022). "Tané Cain – Tané Cain (RCA Victor)."

[907] Caps, J. (Sep. 1, 2017). "The Flashback Interview: Tané McClure," Pop Geeks.

[908] Discogs.com. (May 25, 2022). "Various – The Terminator: Original Soundtrack (Enigma)."

[909] Cain, J. (2018). Don't Stop Believin': The Man, the Band and the Song That Inspired Generations, p. 202, Grand Rapids, United States: Zondervan.

[910] Jordan, M. (May 19, 2016). "Enduring Popularity Remains 'Blessing and an Honor' For Journey's Jonathan Cain," The Commercial Appeal.

[911] Riley, J. (Aug. 27, 2018). "Steve Perry on When Prince Noted the Similarity Between 'Purple Rain' And 'Faithfully'," The Current.

[912] Tudahl, D. (2018). Prince and the 'Purple Rain'-Era Studio Sessions, p. 113, Lanham, United States: Rowman and Littlefield.

[913] Hernandez, R. (May 17, 2016). "Journeyman Neal Schon: Definitely Progressive Fusion Rock," The Austin Chronicle.

[914] McNeice, A. (Aug. 18, 2005). "Journey: The 2005 Generations Interviews – Jonathan Cain," Melodic Rock.

[915] Szaroleta, T. (Jan. 14, 2022). "Former Lynyrd Skynyrd Producer Lending Hand to Young Jacksonville Band Fortune Child," The Florida Times-Union.

[916] Forgo, R. (Sep. 28, 2023). Time Passages Interview: Bad English/The Storm Graphic Artist Hugh Syme, Time Passages.

[917] Denver Post. (May 27, 2015). "Grateful Dead Logo Creator Looks Back on a Long, Strange Trip."

[918] Considine, J. (Sep. 1, 1989). "Bad English, 'Bad English': Musician Album Review," Musician.

[919] Moraski, L. (May 2, 2018). "Here's the Story Behind 'Don't Stop Believin', The Song That Keeps on Giving," The Huffington Post.

[920] Lafon, M. (Feb. 8, 2005). "Steve Perry: Mother, Father," MelodicRock.com.

[921] FanAsylum.com. (Nov. 15, 2015). "Steve Perry: November 15, 2005 Q&A."

[922] Newman, M. (Oct. 5, 1995). "Columbia's Journey Gets Warm Welcome at Radio," Billboard.

[923] Sullivan, J. (Aug. 19, 1980). "Journey Hardly Worth the Effort," The Boston Globe.

[924] Marino, R. (May 16, 1980). "Journey Plays Cobo Arena in Detroit," Getty Images.

[925] Detroit Free Press. (May 16, 1980). "\"Journey Performs in Four Concerts.\"."

[926] Discogs. (Sep. 6, 2023). "Journey, 'Captured': Credits."

[927] DeRiso, N. (Oct. 24, 2023). Pat Morrow: Journey Tour Manager and Nocturne Executive, Time Passages.

[928] Forgo, R. (Oct. 24, 2023). Interview with Stanley Mouse, Time Passages.

[929] Rose Art Museum, Brandeis University. (Aug. 4, 2021). "History of the Family Dog."

[930] Billboard. (Sep. 24, 1983). "Rise of the Nightmare Family."

[931] Front of House Magazine. (Oct. 10, 2014). "2014 Parnelli Lifetime Achievement Award Winner Benny Collins."

[932] Los Angeles Times. (Sep. 30, 1991). "Hugh Morrow; Nelson Rockefeller's Speech Writer, Adviser."

[933] Buckley, C. (Feb. 3, 1985). "In My Father's House: A Morrow Family Chronicle," Washington Post.

[934] Whiting, S. (Jan. 19, 2003). "A Work in Progress: Project Artaud is a Model of Artful, Cooperative Living," San Francisco Chronicle.

[935] Wingfield, N. (Mar. 5, 2002). "Being There," Wall Street Journal.

[936] Black, S. (Oct. 7, 2019). "WRLF-FM: John 5 Interview," WRIF-FM.

[937] Anti-Music. (Jul. 31, 2019). "Journey Icon Steve Perry Goes Inside Traces Collaboration."

[938] Perry, S. (Jul. 24, 2019). "Steve Perry: Twitter Q&A," 80s+: 103.7FM.

[939] Q104.3 New York. (Aug. 20, 2018). "Steve Perry Talks About New Music and Much More."

[940] Discogs. (Jan. 9, 2017). "Matthew Schon: Discography."

[941] Recording Industry Association of America. (Jan. 10, 2016). "Journey: Gold and Platinum Certifications."

[942] Freedman, R. (Jun. 6, 2008). "Cain, Journey Experience a Revelation," Marin Independent Journal.

[943] James, W. (Feb. 22, 2011). "Gregg Rolie of Santana/Journey F ame Releases Solo EP," All About Jazz.

[944] Freeman, P. (Jun. 1, 2011). "Gregg Rolie: His Musical Journey Continues," Pop Culture Classics.

[945] Gerard, G. (Oct. 19, 2018). "Heartache Helps Singer Rediscover His Music," The Associated Press.

[946] Herrera, R. (Dec. 12, 2020). "Front Row Live Entertainment: Arnel Pineda Interview," Front Row Live Entertainment.

[947] ABC. (Jul. 8, 2022). "Journey Guitarist Neal Schon Says Band Has 'a Different Strut' On New Album."

[948] Weatherford, M. (Mar. 17, 2016). "Santana Reunion 'Like Riding a Bicycle'," Las Vegas Review-Journal.

[949] Ragogna, M. (Mar. 18, 2016). "Santana Iv: Chatting with Carlos Santana and Gregg Rolie," Huffington Post.

[950] Kerr, J. (Apr. 15, 2016). "Interview: Carlos Santana Wants to Get Steve Perry Back in Journey," Q104.3-FM.

[951] Clark, R. (Apr. 1, 1999). "Roy Thomas Baker: Taking Chances and Making Hits," Mix.

[952] Scully, A. (Jun. 8, 2001). "A New Journey Dawns Despite Loss of Steve Perry," Florida Today.

PHOTO & ILLUSTRATION CREDITS

Every effort has been made to identify the copyright holders and obtain their permission for the use of copyrighted material. Images reproduced with permission appear below with page citation. Notification of any additions or corrections that should be incorporated in future reprints of this book would be greatly appreciated.

Cover illustration: Daniel Belchí Lorente
Pages 12-13: Paul Natkin, Paul Natkin Photography
Page 16: Pat Johnson, Pat Johnson Photography
Page 18: Paul Natkin, Paul Natkin Photography
Page 19: Pat Johnson, Pat Johnson Photography
Page 21: Michael Parrish
Page 24: Pat Johnson, Pat Johnson Photography
Page 26: Pat Johnson, Pat Johnson Photography
Page 34: Pat Johnson, Pat Johnson Photography
Page 36: Pat Johnson, Pat Johnson Photography
Page 40: Pat Johnson, Pat Johnson Photography
Page 42: Pat Johnson, Pat Johnson Photography
Page 52: Pat Johnson, Pat Johnson Photography
Page 59: Sam Emerson, Sam Emerson Photography
Page 60: Pat Johnson, Pat Johnson Photography
Page 68: Werden Allen, Creative Commons CC0 1.0
Page 70: Pat Johnson, Pat Johnson Photography
Page 74: Sam Emerson, Sam Emerson Photography
  —this image digitally edited with permission
Page 84: Paul Natkin, Paul Natkin Photography
Page 85: Paul Natkin, Paul Natkin Photography
Page 91: Paul Natkin, Paul Natkin Photography
Page 96: Sam Emerson, Sam Emerson Photography
  —this image digitally edited with permission
Page 102: Paul Natkin, Paul Natkin Photography
Page 105: Pat Johnson, Pat Johnson Photography
Page 108: Reprinted with Permission, Stanley Mouse
Page 114: Michael Putnam
Page 117 (top): Paul Natkin, Paul Natkin Photography
Page 117 (bottom): Paul Natkin, Paul Natkin Photography
Page 119: Pat Johnson, Pat Johnson Photography
Page 130: Pat Johnson, Pat Johnson Photography
  —this image digitally edited with permission
Page 136: Pat Johnson, Pat Johnson Photography
Page 140: Monique Larroux, Monique Larroux Photography
Page 142: Paul Natkin, Paul Natkin Photography
Page 151: Paul Natkin, Paul Natkin Photography

Page 155: Paul Natkin, Paul Natkin Photography
Page 156: Paul Natkin, Paul Natkin Photography
Page 160: Paul Natkin, Paul Natkin Photography
Page 170: Envato Elements Pty Ltd (dibrova)
Page 176 (3): Paul Natkin, Paul Natkin Photography
Page 184: John Scarpati
Page 185: Illustration, Duy Phan
Pages 192: Paul Natkin, Paul Natkin Photography
Pages 194: Paul Natkin, Paul Natkin Photography
Pages 206: Jim Steinfeldt, Jim Steinfeld Photography
Pages 209: Jim Steinfeldt, Jim Steinfeld Photography
Pages 213: Pat Johnson, Pat Johnson Photography
Pages 216: Jim Steinfeldt, Jim Steinfeld Photography
Page 220: Monique Larroux, Monique Larroux Photography
Pages 222: Paul Natkin, Paul Natkin Photography
Page 228: John Scarpati
Page 242: Monique Larroux, Monique Larroux Photography
Page 256: Monique Larroux, Monique Larroux Photography
Page 260: Monique Larroux, Monique Larroux Photography
Page 272: AP Photo/Nick Ut
Page 276: Jeffrey Mayer, Jeffrey Mayer Photography
Page 278: Monique Larroux, Monique Larroux Photography
Page 286: Monique Larroux, Monique Larroux Photography
Page 292: AP Photo/Evan Agostini
Page 300: Erik Kabik Photography/ MediaPunch/MediaPunch/IPx
Page 304: Monique Larroux, Monique Larroux Photography
Page 308: RockstarPix, Dalila Kriheli
Page 319: Monique Larroux, Monique Larroux Photography
Page 320-321: Kevin Kane, Kevin Kane Photography
Page 321 (3): Kevin Kane, Kevin Kane Photography
Page 322-323: Kevin Kane, Kevin Kane Photography
Page 338: Pat Johnson, Pat Johnson Photography
Page 340: Monique Larroux, Monique Larroux Photography
Page 352-353: Sam Emerson, Sam Emerson Photography
  —this image digitally edited with permission
Page 354: Monique Larroux, Monique Larroux Photography